Microsoft® Inside SQL Server™ 6.5

D1303481

Ron Soukup

Microsoft Press

PUBLISHED BY
Microsoft Press
A Division of Microsoft Corporation
One Microsoft Way
Redmond, Washington 98052-6399

Library of Congress Cataloging-in-Publication Data
Soukup, Ron.
    Inside Microsoft SQL Server 6.5 / Ron Soukup.
        p.   cm.
    Includes index.
    ISBN 1-57231-331-5
    1. Database management.   2. SQL Server.   I. Title.
QA76.9.D3S66   1997
005.75'85--dc21   97-37611
                                                            CIP

Printed and bound in the United States of America.

1 2 3 4 5 6 7 8 9   MLML   2 1 0 9 8 7

Distributed to the book trade in Canada by Macmillan of Canada, a division of Canada Publishing Corporation.

A CIP catalogue record for this book is available from the British Library.

Microsoft Press books are available through booksellers and distributors worldwide. For further information about international editions, contact your local Microsoft Corporation office. Or contact Microsoft Press International directly at fax (425) 936-7329. Visit our Web site at mspress.microsoft.com.

Acquisitions Editor: David Clark
Project Editor: Lisa Theobald
Technical Editor: John Conrow

To Kay, Kelly, and Jamie,
for your love and support during
the years of ship crunch.
And
To the SQL Server Development Team.
Working with you has been the greatest
privilege of my career.

CONTENTS

Foreword xi

Preface xiii

PART ONE   Overview

1   The Evolution of Microsoft SQL Server: 1989 to 1996 3
The Competitive Background That Spawned Microsoft SQL Server 3

The Early Days with the NDK 6

Microsoft SQL Server Ships 7

Development Roles Evolve 9

OS/2 and "Friendly Fire" 11

Version 4.2 12

OS/2 2.0 Release on Hold 13

SQL Server for Windows NT 14

Success Brings Fundamental Change 19

The End of Joint Development 21

The Charge to SQL95 23

The Next Version 26

2   A Tour of Microsoft SQL Server 27
Introduction 27

The SQL Server Engine 28

DBMS-Enforced Data Integrity 33

Transaction Processing 37

Symmetric Server Architecture 39

Security 42

High Availability 43

Distributed Data Processing 44

Data Replication 45

Systems Management 47

SQL Server Utilities and Extensions 53

Development Interfaces 58

SUMMARY 60

PART TWO   Architectural Overview

3   SQL Server Architecture 63

Overview 63

The SQL Server Engine 63

Large Memory Issues 93

Transaction Logging and Recovery 96

The SQL Server Kernel and Interaction with Windows NT 100

SUMMARY 110

PART THREE   Using Microsoft SQL Server

4   Planning for and Installing SQL Server 113

Setup Is Easy, but Think First 113

SQL Server vs. SQL Workstation 113

Choosing Hardware 114

Hardware Guidelines 118

The Operating System 141

The File System 142

Security and User Context 143

Licensing Choices 144

Network Protocol Choices 149

Character Set and Sort Order Issues 153

Running Setup 162

Basic Configuration After Setup 163

Unattended and Remote Setup 166

SUMMARY 171

5 Databases and Devices 173
  What Is a Database? 173
  Database Devices 174
  Creating Databases 180
  Maximum Database Size and Database Fragments 184
  Expanding and Shrinking Databases 184
  Databases "Under the Covers" 185
  Database Options 187
  Changing Database Options 189
  Other Database Considerations 191
  SUMMARY 194

6 Tables 195
  Introduction 195
  Creating Tables 196
  Internal Storage—The Details 207
  Indexes 218
  User-Defined Datatypes 224
  Identity Property 227
  Constraints 231
  Temporary Tables 265
  SUMMARY 267

7 Querying Data 269
  Introduction 269
  The SELECT Statement 269
  Joins 272
  Dealing with NULL 288
  Subqueries 298
  Views and Derived Tables 311
  Other Search Expressions 315
  SUMMARY 347

8 Modifying Data **349**

Introduction 349
Basic Modification Operations 349
Internal and Performance Considerations 376
SUMMARY 398

9 Programming with Transact-SQL **399**

Introduction 399
Transact-SQL as a Programming Language 400
Transact-SQL Programming Constructs—The Basics 403
SUMMARY 448

10 Batches, Transactions, Stored Procedures, and Triggers **449**

Introduction 449
Batches 449
Transactions 451
Stored Procedures 466
Executing Batches, or What's Stored About a Stored Procedure? 479
Triggers 500
Debugging Stored Procedures and Triggers 504
Working with Text and Image Data 508
Environmental Concerns 521
SUMMARY 527

11 Cursors **529**

Introduction 529
Cursor Basics 530
Important! Cursors and ISAMs 532
Cursor Models 537
Appropriate Use of Cursors 542
Transact-SQL Cursor Syntax and Behavior 552
SUMMARY 570

12 Transact-SQL Examples and Brainteasers **571**

Introduction 571
Using Triggers to Implement Referential Actions 571

Brainteasers 578
SUMMARY 637

13 Locking 639
Introduction 639
The Lock Manager 639
Lock Types for User Data 645
Viewing Locks 647
Lock Compatibility 647
Lock Escalation 654
Lock Hints and Application Issues 655
SUMMARY 655

PART FOUR Performance and Tuning

14 Design and Query Performance Implications 659
Introduction 659
Performance Guidelines 660
Develop Expertise on Your Development Team 660
Enforce Solid Application and Database Design 662
State Performance Requirements for Peak Usage 667
Consider Perceived Response Time for Interactive Systems 668
Prototype, Benchmark, and Test Throughout Development 670
Create Useful Indexes 674
Choose Appropriate Hardware 679
Use Cursors Judiciously 680
Use Stored Procedures Almost Always 680
Minimize Network Round-Trips 681
Understand Concurrency and Consistency Trade-Offs 682
Analyze and Resolve Locking (Blocking) Problems 683
Analyze and Resolve Deadlock Problems 685
Consider Segregating OLTP and DSS Applications 704
Monitor and Tune Queries 704
Monitor Query Performance 724
SUMMARY 738

15 Configuration and Monitoring for Performance 739

Introduction 739

Review and Adjust Windows NT Configuration Settings 740

Review and Adjust SQL Server Configuration Settings 742

Maintain the System 766

Monitor System Performance 767

SUMMARY 773

PART **FIVE** **Appendix**

Appendix: *SQL Server Built-In Global Variables* 777

Bibliography 781

Suggested Reading 783

Index 787

FOREWORD

Inside Microsoft SQL Server 6.5 is the definitive companion to Microsoft SQL Server. Written by Ron Soukup, who led the SQL Server team for the better part of a decade, this book is *his* guide to why SQL Server is the way it is and how it should be used. It complements the reference material in SQL Server Books Online. Anyone planning an implementation using SQL Server would do well to read this book first.

After recounting the inside story of how the PC database giant Ashton-Tate partnered with Microsoft and a start-up (Sybase) to bring SQL to the OS/2 marketplace, Ron traces the amazing history of the product and the partners. His firsthand account makes this a must-read—I cannot think of a more amazing story in our industry.

Ron then takes the reader on a whirlwind tour of SQL Server, outlining the key features, pointing out some highlights, and describing how SQL Server works inside. This detailed information lays the groundwork for much that follows.

In subsequent chapters, Ron tells us how to design for SQL Server—offering sage advice on application design, database design, and physical data layout. His advice is based on many years of watching customers use (and misuse) the product. SQL Server and the Microsoft Windows NT environment are unique in many ways—these chapters cover their standard design issues, but they focus primarily on the aspects of SQL Server that are unique. Incidental to this, Ron shows many of the pitfalls and common errors that designers and programmers make. He also conveys his sense of good and bad design.

Ron covers virtually all the extensions that SQL Server has made to the standard SQL language. He takes pride in describing these features, often explaining why they were introduced, how they compare to the competition, and how they work. This is not an SQL tutorial, but it does an excellent job of covering the intermediate and advanced features of SQL and SQL Server. Ron's descriptions are accompanied by detailed examples that are included on the companion CD.

Ron also explains how to install, administer, and tune SQL Server, and within these chapters is essential information that I have never seen covered anywhere else. Because it's so easy to get started with SQL Server—perhaps too easy—some customers just install it and start using it without thinking much. Ron walks the designer through capacity planning; hardware acquisition; Windows NT, Network, and RAID configuration; SQL Server installation and licensing; security policies; and operations procedures. He provides a valuable checklist for anyone planning to set up or operate a SQL Server system.

Several chapters are devoted to understanding performance, concurrency, and recovery issues, and throughout the book, Ron emphasizes designing for client/server and Internet environments. Within these environments, the server must process business rules (stored procedures) or set-oriented requests, rather than record-at-a-time requests. Ron discusses traditional Transact-SQL stored procedures as well as user-defined external procedures and Automation procedures.

To provide a clear picture of how SQL Server transactions work, Ron first presents tutorial material on the ACID properties, isolation levels, and locking. He then describes how SQL Server performs data locking, logging, checkpointing, and recovery. A good understanding of these issues is key to designing high-traffic and high-availability SQL Servers.

Ron also offers performance tips throughout the book, but two chapters are devoted exclusively to designing for good performance. Chapters 14 and 15 describe common performance pitfalls and offer many techniques for measuring and improving application performance.

In summary, Ron's book is the essential companion to Microsoft SQL Server—an invaluable reference for the administrator and the designer. It is a firsthand account of how SQL Server works, why it works that way, and how to use it. Ron has returned to leading one of the SQL Server development teams, but we are all glad he took the time to write this invaluable book. I certainly learned a lot from it, and I guess you can too.

Jim Gray
Senior Researcher
Microsoft San Francisco Research Lab

PREFACE

For me, Microsoft SQL Server has been a labor of love. I lived and breathed this product for years, and I look at it not unlike how I look at my children—with immense love and pride. I've helped nurture the product from its infancy, through some very tough years, to its current success. I've lost many nights' sleep, upset that some customer was disappointed with it. Fortunately, I've also had many more thrills and moments of rejoicing—like when a customer speaks glowingly of SQL Server or when we win another award. Yes, the analogy to a child is the closest thing I can think of to describe my feelings about SQL Server. Like people who have always thought that one day they'd write the Great American Novel, I felt a need to finally put down in words some hopefully unique knowledge and *opinions* I have regarding SQL Server.

This book is *not* an introductory treatise on SQL Server, although it does include one introductory chapter (Chapter 2). In Chapter 1, I discuss the history of the product (which I lived), from SQL Server's inception and partnership with Sybase to its current success. But beyond these early chapters, the book is very detailed and written for those who want to dig deeply into SQL Server. This book is a suitable read for those who have worked with SQL Server for years already. It will also be of interest to experienced database professionals new to SQL Server who are developing or considering new development projects.

In this book, I focus on the "back-end" capabilities of the database engine. Topics include choosing appropriate hardware for SQL Server, effective use of the SQL language, writing correct queries, common mistakes, consistency and concurrency trade-offs, data storage and structures, locking, and scrollable cursors. Performance considerations are covered throughout the book. The final chapters (Chapters 14 and 15) discuss specific performance issues, but because they assume that you've gained much knowledge from reading earlier in the book, I strongly discourage you from jumping directly to those chapters.

When I planned the book, I felt it was necessary to describe how SQL Server works before going into the product's functional capabilities. But that presents a "chicken-or-the-egg" problem: what should I introduce first? I decided to include architectural information near the beginning of the book—Chapter 3 provides an in-depth discussion of how SQL Server works. If you are already familiar with the functional aspects of SQL Server, I think you'll benefit most from this chapter. If you are new to SQL Server, I encourage you to go back and read Chapter 3 again in a couple months after you've gained more familiarity with the product. I think you'll get a lot more out of it. Initially, simply try to absorb just the basics.

I've included little discussion of client programming issues, such as which development tools to use or details about ODBC programming. If you need information about these topics, see the "Suggested Reading" section near the end of the book. And I'm sorry to say that there is little discussion of the replication capabilities of SQL Server. (This is also a little embarrassing because I recently took charge of managing the Replication Unit within the SQL Server development team.) But, like software, this thing had to eventually ship, and replication ended up on the "cut" list. I promise that we're doing so many exciting new things in replication for the next version that I knew I would have to almost completely rewrite any replication section before long anyway. (And a very good whitepaper about SQL Server replication capabilities is included on the companion CD.)

This book has a healthy smattering of my personal opinions about many issues in software and database development. Software development is still at least as much an art as a science, and there are different schools of thought and different approaches. Healthy, even if heated, debate is one of the things that make software development so much fun. I elected to be pretty candid and direct with my opinions in many places, rather than keep the book bland and neutral. Some people will no doubt disagree strongly with some of my opinions. That's fine. I respect your right to disagree. But I do hope you can read and accept the book for its overall merits, even if you disagree with a few topics. And, of course, the opinions I present here are mine alone and not necessarily those of Microsoft.

Now I have many people to thank. Without the product, there would be no book. So my thanks must first be to my fellow SQL Server "old-timers," who bootstrapped the product. Working with you was an amazing, unforgettable experience. We worked 80 hours a week far more often than not, but we loved it. No one deserves more credit for SQL Server's success than Rick Vicik. I'm sure Rick is a genius, but he has the rare trait among those with genius IQs of being perfectly pragmatic. He's a doer, and no one works harder or more passionately. He led the development team by sheer example. And what a team. Without the other old-timers like Mike Habben, Lale Divringi, Peter Hussey, Chris Cassella, Chris Moffatt, Kaushik Chodhury, Dave Fyffe, Don Reichart, Craig Henry, Jack Love, Karl Johnson, Ted Hart, Gavin Jancke, Dan Tyack, Trish Millines, Mike Ervin, Mike Byther, Glen Barker, Bryan Minugh, and Heidy Krauer, there simply would be no Microsoft SQL Server today. And the early documentation team of Lesley Link and Helen Meyers, and the original marketing team of Dwayne Walker, Gary Voth, and Dan Basica, made SQL Server a product, not just software. It took this unique and special blend of people to make this product and to make it viable.

There are, of course, many others of great talent who have joined the SQL Server team during the last few years. But if not for the extraordinary efforts of the original, very small team, there would be no SQL Server now. Be proud and always remember what we did together.

We needed and were backed up by a great customer support team anchored by Andrea Stoppani, Gary Schroeder, Rande Blackman, Joe Marler, Vaqar Pirzada, Damien Lindauer, and James McDaniel (several of whom are now on the SQL Server development team). You often went above and beyond the call of duty. Thank you.

Turning toward the book, I want to extend special thanks to Lesley Link. Lesley did the huge job of editing this book entirely in her "spare time" (which meant many late nights and early Sunday mornings). She really committed to editing this book because of the pride and ownership she, too, feels in the product. But while I wrote the bulk of the book more or less on a sabbatical leave, Lesley edited while she continued in her more than full-time job as the manager of the SQL Server documentation team. There is no better editor in the business. And thanks to her production team, especially Steven Fulgham, Christine Woodward, Pat Hunter, and Rasa Raisys, for helping prepare the book.

Thank you to those who provided invaluable technical reviews of various sections, especially to Jim Gray, Rick Vicik, Mike Habben, Peter Hussey, Don Vilen, Dave Campbell, and Lale Divringi. The mistakes that no doubt remain are mine alone.

Special thanks go to Gary Schroeder, who authored the Microsoft internal documentation for the on-disk data structures that I made use of when describing disk and table formats. And thanks to Betty O'Neil, who revamped and reorganized much of the internal design documentation that I used as a resource when writing.

Finally, thanks to the staff at Microsoft Press: David, Lisa, John, and those of you I never met but knew were there, who guided me through the publication process.

This is the first book I've written. I've shipped a lot more software than books. I've learned there are a lot of similarities. Like the last 10 percent takes 90 percent of the time. And that when it's done, you always have this nagging feeling that you'd like to do some part over and could do it much better the second time around. After all the demands and grief I gave them over the years, I know that the documentation team that formerly reported to me has taken great delight in watching me write and seeing me struggle to complete this work. And just as software is never perfect, neither is this book. I've always found that fact painful in shipping software—I always want it to be perfect. And I find it painful now. I wish this book were perfect, and I know it's not.

But, as I always remind my development team, "Shipping is a feature." So, after a long labor, I have shipped.

Overview

1

The Evolution of Microsoft SQL Server: 1989 to 1996

The Competitive Background That Spawned Microsoft SQL Server

In 1985, Microsoft and IBM jointly announced "a long-term joint development agreement for development of operating systems and other systems software products." This announcement was the beginning of OS/2, a successor to the Microsoft MS-DOS operating system. OS/2 was to be a more complete and robust operating system. It would exploit the powerful new personal computers based on the Intel 80286 processor. It would allow multitasking applications, each with its own address space and each running in the safe "ring 3" of the Intel 4-ring protection scheme of the 80286. Machines sold in 1986 would be vastly more powerful than the original IBM PC (an Intel 8088-based machine) of just a couple years earlier, and OS/2 would signal a new age in harnessing this power. That was the plan.

OS/2 was formally announced in April 1987, with shipment promised by the end of the year. (OS/2 version 1.0 was released to manufacturing on December 16, 1987.) But shortly after the joint declaration, IBM announced a special higher end version of OS/2 called OS/2 Extended Edition. This more powerful version would include the base OS/2 operating system plus an SQL database called OS/2 Database Manager. OS/2 Database Manager would be useful for small applications and was to be partially compatible (although not initially interoperable) with DB/2, IBM's flagship MVS mainframe database, and with the lesser-used SQL/DS, which ran on slightly smaller mainframe computers running the VM or

VSE operating systems. OS/2 Database Manager would also include SNA communications services, called OS/2 Communications Manager. As part of its sweeping Systems Application Architecture (SAA), IBM promised to make the products work well together in the future. (Database Manager would later evolve into today's DB2/2.)

But if IBM could offer a more complete OS/2 solution, who would buy Microsoft OS/2? Clearly, Microsoft needed to come up with an answer to this question.

In 1986, Microsoft was a mere $197-million-per-year business, with 1153 employees. (Ten years later, Microsoft had revenues of nearly $6 billion, with almost 18,000 employees.) Microsoft's products were entirely desktop focused, and the main bread-and-butter product was MS-DOS. Client/server computing was not yet in the vernacular of Microsoft or the computer industry. Data management on PCs was in its infancy. Most people who kept data on their PCs used the wildly popular Lotus 1-2-3 spreadsheet application to keep lists (although many were discovering the limitations of doing so). Ashton-Tate's dBASE products (dBASE II and the recently released dBASE III) had also become popular. Although a few other products existed, such as MicroRim's Rbase and a relatively new product from Ansa Software called Paradox, Ashton-Tate was clearly king of the PC data products. In 1986, Microsoft had no database management products. (Beginning in 1992, Microsoft would go on to tremendous success in the desktop database market with Microsoft Access and Microsoft FoxPro.)

IBM's Database Manager was not in the same category as products such as dBASE, Paradox, and Rbase. Database Manager was built to be a "full-fledged, blood-and-guts" database (with atomic transactions and a full SQL query processor), more similar to traditional minicomputer-oriented or mainframe-oriented systems such as IBM's DB/2, or Oracle, or Informix. Microsoft needed a database management system (DBMS) product of the same caliber, and it needed it soon.

Microsoft turned to Sybase, Inc., an upstart in the DBMS market. Sybase had not yet shipped the first commercial version of its DataServer product (which it would do in May 1987 for SUN Workstations running UNIX). Although certainly not a mainstream product, the prerelease version of DataServer had earned a good reputation both for delivering innovative new capabilities, such as stored procedures and triggers, and because it had been designed for a new paradigm in computing known as *client/server.*

As is true in all good business exchanges, the deal between the two companies was a "win-win" situation. Microsoft would get exclusive rights to the DataServer product for OS/2 and all other Microsoft-developed operating systems. Besides getting royalties from Microsoft, Sybase would get credibility from Microsoft's endorsement of its technology. Even more importantly, Sybase would gain a beachhead among the anticipated huge number of personal computers that would be running the new OS/2 operating system.

Because the transaction-processing throughput of these OS/2 systems was not expected to be high, Sybase could use the systems to seed the market for future sales on the more powerful UNIX system. Microsoft would market the product in higher volumes than Sybase could; it was simply not economically feasible for Sybase's direct sales force to deliver what would essentially be the first shrink-wrapped release of a "full-fledged, blood-and-guts database" to PC customers. Higher volumes would help Sybase win more business on its UNIX and VMS platforms. On March 27, 1987, Microsoft president Jon Shirley and Sybase cofounder and president Mark Hoffman signed the deal.

In the PC database world, Ashton-Tate's dBASE still had the reputation and the lion's share of the market, even if dBASE and Sybase DataServer offered very different capabilities. To gain acceptance, this new higher capability database management system from Microsoft (licensed from Sybase) would need to appeal to the large dBASE community. The most direct way to do that, of course, would be to get Ashton-Tate to endorse the product—so Microsoft worked out a deal with Ashton-Tate to do just that.

In 1988, a new product was announced with the somewhat clumsy name "Ashton-Tate/Microsoft SQL Server." Although not appearing in the product's title, Sybase was prominent in the product's accompanying information. This new product would be a port of Sybase DataServer to OS/2, marketed by both Ashton-Tate and Microsoft. Ashton-Tate had pledged that its much anticipated dBASE IV would also be available in a Server Edition that would use the dBASE IV development tools and language as a "client" to develop applications (for example, order-entry forms) that would store the data in the new SQL Server product. This new client/server capability promised to give dBASE new levels of power to support more than the handful of concurrent users that could be supported by its existing file-sharing architecture.

Ashton-Tate, Microsoft, and Sybase would work together to debut SQL Server on OS/2. (This was the first use of the name "SQL Server." Sybase later renamed its DataServer product for UNIX and VMS "Sybase SQL Server," the name by which it is known today.)

The first beta version of Ashton-Tate/Microsoft SQL Server shipped in the fall of 1988. Microsoft made available this prerelease version at nominal cost to developers who wanted to get a head start on learning, developing for, or evaluating this new product. It shipped in a bundle known as the NDK (network development kit) that included all the software components needed (provided that you were developing in C) to get a head start building networked client/server applications. It included prerelease versions of SQL Server, Microsoft LAN Manager, and OS/2 1.0.

The Early Days with the NDK

In 1988, I was working for Covia, the United Airlines subsidiary that provided the Apollo Reservation System and related systems for airport and travel agency use. I had spent the previous five years working with the new breed of relational database products that had appeared on the minicomputer and mainframe computer scene. I had worked with IBM's DB/2 running on MVS; IBM's SQL/DS running on VM; and Oracle, Informix, and Unify running on UNIX. I viewed PC databases of the day as essentially toys that were good for storing recipes and addresses but not for much else. I used a PC for word processing, but that was about it. But we were beginning to use more and more LAN-based and PC-based systems, and I had begun doing some OS/2 programming. So when I heard of the NDK, with this new SQL Server product that had been mentioned in the trade press, I ordered it immediately.

The NDK was very much a beta-level product. It didn't have a lot of "fit and finish," and it would crash a couple of times a day. But from practically the first day, I knew that this product was something special. I was amazed that I was using a true DBMS *on a PC(!)*, with such advanced features as transaction logging and automatic recovery. Even the performance seemed remarkably good. Having used mostly minicomputer and mainframe computer systems, I was most struck by the difference in PC response time. With the bigger systems, even a simple command resulted in an inevitable delay of at least a couple of seconds between pressing the Enter key and receiving a reply. PCs seemed almost instantaneous. I knew PCs were fast for local tasks such as word processing, but this was different. In this case, at one PC I entered an SQL command that was sent over the network to a server machine running this new SQL Server product. The response time was subsecond. I had never seen such responsiveness.

My initial "kick-the-tires" trial was encouraging, and I received approval to test the product more thoroughly. I wanted to get a feel for the types of applications and workloads for which this interesting new product might be used. For this, I wanted more substantial hardware than the desktop machine I originally tested on (a 10-MHz 286 computer with 6-MB memory and a 50-MB hard drive). Although SQL Server ran reasonably well on my desktop machine, I wanted to try it on one of the powerful new machines that used the Intel 80386 processor. I procured a monster machine for the day—a 20-MHz 386 system with 10 MB of memory and two 100-MB disk drives. I was the envy of my division!

In 1987, two of us at Covia had developed some multiuser database benchmark tests in C to help us choose a UNIX minicomputer system for a new application. I dusted off these tests and converted the embedded C to the call-level interface provided in SQL Server (DB-Library) and ported these benchmarks to the PC. I hoped SQL Server would be able to handle several simultaneous users, although I didn't even consider that it could come close to handling the 15 to 20 simulated users we tried in the earlier minicomputer tests. After many false starts and the typical problems that occur while running an early beta of a version 1.0 product, I persevered and got the test suite, 2000 lines of custom C code, running on a PC against the beta version of SQL Server.

The results were amazing. This beta version of SQL Server, running on a PC that cost less than $10,000, performed as well and in many cases better than the minicomputer systems that we had tested a few months earlier. Those systems cost probably 10 times as much as my PC, and they needed to be managed by a professional UNIX system administrator. I knew the industry was in for a big change.

In May 1989, Ashton-Tate/Microsoft SQL Server version 1.0 shipped. Press reviews were good, but sales lagged. OS/2 sales were far below what had been expected. Large numbers of users hadn't moved from MS-DOS to OS/2, as we anticipated. And about the only tool available to create SQL Server applications was C. The promised dBASE IV Server Edition from Ashton-Tate was delayed, and although several ISVs had promised front-end development tools for SQL Server, these had not yet materialized.

During the preceding six months, I had come to really know, respect, and admire SQL Server, and I felt the same about the people at Microsoft with whom I had worked during this period. So in late 1989, I accepted a position at Microsoft in the SQL Server group in Redmond, Washington. A few months later, I was running the small but talented and dedicated SQL Server development team.

Microsoft SQL Server Ships

By 1990, the comarketing and distribution arrangement with Ashton-Tate, which was intended to tie SQL Server to the large dBASE community, was simply not working. Even the desktop version of dBASE IV was very late, and it had a reputation of being buggy when it shipped in 1989. The Server Edition, which would ostensibly make it simple to develop higher performance SQL Server applications using dBASE, was nowhere to be seen.

As many others have painfully realized, developing a single-user record-oriented application is much different from developing applications for multiple users for which issues of concurrency, consistency, and network latency need to be considered. Initial attempts at marrying the dBASE tools with SQL Server had dBASE treating SQL Server as though it were an ISAM. A command to request a specific row would be issued for each row that was needed. Although this was the procedural model dBASE users were accustomed to, it was not an efficient way to use SQL Server, in which more power with less overhead could be gained by issuing SQL statements to work with sets of information. But at the time, SQL Server lacked the capabilities to make it easy to develop applications that would work in ways dBASE users were accustomed to (they could browse through data forward and backward, jump from record to record, and update records at any time). Scrollable cursors did not yet exist.

The Future...

The effort to get dBASE IV Server Edition working well did, however, provide many ideas for how scrollable cursors in a networked, client/server environment should behave. In many ways, it was the prime motivation for including this feature in SQL Server version 6.0 in 1995, six years later.

Only two years earlier, Ashton-Tate had been king of the PC database market. Now it was beginning to fight for its survival and needed to refocus on its core dBASE desktop product. Microsoft would launch OS/2 LAN Manager under the Microsoft name (as opposed to the initial attempts to create only OEM versions), and it needed SQL Server to help provide a foundation for the development of client/server tools that would run on Microsoft LAN Manager and Microsoft OS/2. So Microsoft and Ashton-Tate terminated their comarketing and distribution arrangements. The product would be repackaged and reintroduced as Microsoft SQL Server.

Microsoft SQL Server version 1.1 shipped in the summer of 1990 as an upgrade to the Ashton-Tate/Microsoft SQL Server version 1.0 that had shipped in 1989. For the first time, SQL Server was a Microsoft-supported shrink-wrapped product, and it was sold through the newly formed Microsoft Network Specialist channel, whose main charter was to push Microsoft LAN Manager.

NOTE   When version 1.1 shipped, Microsoft didn't see SQL Server as a lucrative product in its own right. Within Microsoft, SQL Server was generally thought of as a way to push LAN Manager and OS/2 and it was not viewed as a strong database product in and of itself. SQL Server would be one of the reasons to buy LAN Manager—that's all.

SQL Server 1.1 had the same features as version 1.0, although it included many bug fixes—the type of maintenance that is understandably necessary for a version 1.0 product of this complexity. But SQL Server 1.1 also supported a significant new client platform, Microsoft Windows 3.0. Windows 3.0 had shipped in May 1990, a watershed event in the computer industry. SQL Server 1.1 provided an interface that enabled Windows 3.0–based applications to be efficiently developed for it. This early and full support for Windows 3.0–based applications would prove to be vital to the success of Microsoft SQL Server. The success of the Windows platform would also mean fundamental changes for Microsoft and SQL Server, although these changes were not yet clear in the summer of 1990.

With almost every user I've met, a few key questions about SQL Server always come up. Every year the "Big Question" changes. In 1990, the question was "Where are the front-ends?" Like Ashton-Tate with dBASE, many other software makers had pledged that their development tools could be used to build applications to access SQL Server. But, with rare exception, these tools were not available in mid-1990. I was getting tired of my usual answer, "They'll be here soon," with the hope that this would indeed be the case.

With the advent of Windows 3.0 and SQL Server 1.1, many new Windows-based applications showed up and many were, as promised, beginning to support Microsoft SQL Server. By early 1991, suddenly dozens of third-party software products used SQL Server. SQL Server was one of the few database products that provided a Windows 3.0 DLL interface practically as soon as Windows 3.0 shipped, and this was now paying dividends in the marketplace. Quietly but unmistakably, Microsoft SQL Server was leading. Overall sales were still modest, but until tools beyond C existed to build solutions, sales could not be expected to be impressive. It was the classic "chicken and egg" situation.

The Big Question of 1990 was no longer being asked. Instead, some users or prospective buyers would complain that the number of tools supporting SQL Server was too large; they wanted help in selecting the appropriate tool for their needs. This early ISV support would be one of the primary reasons SQL Server would go on to further success.

Development Roles Evolve

Microsoft's development role for SQL Server 1.0 was quite limited. As a small porting team at Sybase moved its DataServer engine to OS/2 and moved the DB-Library client interfaces to MS-DOS and OS/2, Microsoft provided testing and project management. Microsoft also developed some add-on tools to help make the product easy to install and administer.

Although a number of sites were running OS/2 as an application server with SQL Server or as a file server with LAN Manager, few were using OS/2 for their desktop platforms. Before Windows 3.0, most desktops remained MS-DOS–based, with its well-known limit of 640 KB of addressable real memory. After loading MS-DOS, a network redirector, network card device drivers, and the DB-Library static link libraries that shipped with SQL Server version 1.0, developers trying to write a SQL Server application would be lucky to get 50 KB for their own use.

For SQL Server 1.1, rather than ship the DB-Library interface that Sybase had ported from UNIX to MS-DOS, Microsoft wrote its own, from scratch. Instead of 50 KB, developers might be able to get 250 KB to write their applications. Although small by today's standards, 250 KB was a huge improvement.

NOTE The same source code used for DB-Library for MS-DOS also produced the Windows and OS/2 DB-Library interfaces. But it was the MS-DOS "RAM cram" that motivated us to write a new implementation from scratch. The widespread adoption of Windows 3.0 would quickly make the MS-DOS memory issue moot—but this issue was a real problem in 1989 and 1990.

With SQL Server 1.1, Microsoft provided client software and utilities, programming libraries, and administration tools. But the core SQL Server engine was still produced entirely by Sybase; Microsoft did not even have access to the source code. Any requests for changes, even for bug fixes, had to be made to Sybase.

Microsoft was building a solid support team for SQL Server. We hired some talented and dedicated engineers with database backgrounds. But with no access to source code, the team found it impossible to provide the kind of mission-critical responsiveness that was necessary for customer support. And, again, getting bugs fixed was problematic because we were entirely dependent on Sybase, which had become successful in its own right and was grappling with its explosive growth. It was inevitable that some significant differences would arise in prioritizing which issues would be addressed, especially when some issues were specific to the Microsoft-labeled product and not to Sybase's product line. Bugs that Microsoft deemed of highest priority sometimes languished because Sybase's priorities were understandably directed elsewhere. The situation was unacceptable.

It was a great day in the SQL Server group at Microsoft when in early 1991 Microsoft's agreement with Sybase was amended to give Microsoft "read-only" access to the source code, for the purpose of customer support. Although we still could not fix bugs, at least we could read the source code for a definitive understanding of what might be happening when something went wrong. And we could also read the code to understand how something was expected to work. As anyone with software experience knows, even the best specification will at times be ambiguous. There is simply no substitute for the source code as the definitive explanation for how something works.

As a small group of developers at Microsoft became adept with the SQL Server source code and internal workings, Microsoft began to do "virtual" bug fixes. Although we were still not permitted to alter the source code, we could identify line-by-line the specific modules that needed to be changed to fix a bug. Obviously, when we handed the fix directly to Sybase, high-priority bugs identified by Microsoft got resolved much quicker.

After a few months of working in this way, the extra step was eliminated. By mid-1991, Microsoft could finally fix bugs directly. Because Sybase still controlled the baseline for the source code, all fixes were provided to Sybase for review and inclusion in the code. We had to make special efforts to keep the source code highly secured and the logistics of keeping the source code in sync with Sybase was sometimes a hassle, but all in all, this was *heaven* compared to a year earlier. Microsoft's team of developers was becoming expert in the SQL Server code, and we could now be much more responsive to our customers and responsible for the quality of the product.

OS/2 and "Friendly Fire"

In 1991, Microsoft released SQL Server 1.11, a maintenance release. SQL Server was slowly but steadily gaining acceptance and momentum—and a long list of ISV supporters. Client/server computing was not yet widely deployed, but new converts appeared every day. Customer satisfaction and loyalty were high, and press reviews of the product had all been favorable. Sales were generally disappointing, but this was hardly a surprise because OS/2 had continued to be a major disappointment. Windows 3.0, however, was a runaway hit. Rather than move their desktop platforms from MS-DOS to OS/2, huge numbers of PC users moved to Windows 3.0 instead. OS/2 had not become a widespread operating system as had been anticipated, and it was now abundantly clear that it never would be.

SQL Server's Limitations and the Marketplace

Microsoft SQL Server 1.11 clearly had a scalability limit. It was a 16-bit product because OS/2 could provide only a 16-bit address space for applications. OS/2 lacked some high-performance capabilities, such as asynchronous I/O. Even though an astonishing amount of work could be performed successfully with SQL Server on OS/2, there would come a point at which it would simply "run out of gas." No hard limit was established, but in general, SQL Server for OS/2 was used for workgroups of 50 users or less. For larger groups, customers could buy a version of Sybase SQL Server for higher performance UNIX-based or VMS-based systems.

This was an important selling point for both Microsoft and Sybase. Customers considering the Microsoft product wanted to be sure they wouldn't outgrow it. The large number of ISV tools developed for Microsoft SQL Server worked largely unchanged with Sybase SQL Server, and applications that outgrew OS/2 could be moved quite easily to a bigger, more powerful, more expensive UNIX system. This relationship still made sense for both Microsoft and Sybase.

The need for compatibility and interoperability made it especially important for Microsoft SQL Server to be based on the 4.2 source code as soon as possible. Furthermore, a major features version had not been released since version 1.0 in 1989. In the rapidly moving PC marketplace, the product was in danger of becoming stale. Customers had begun to do serious work with Microsoft SQL Server, and new features were in great demand. Microsoft's version 4.2 would add a long list of significant new features, including server-to-server stored procedures, UNION, online tape backup, and greatly improved international support that would make SQL Server more viable outside the United States.

At the same time, we were working on a new SQL Server version that would sync up with the newest Sybase product on UNIX, version 4.2. When Microsoft SQL Server 1.0 shipped, Sybase's product was designated version 3.0. We had added some new features deemed necessary for the PC marketplace, such as *text* and *image* data types and browse mode. Sybase subsequently shipped version 4.0 for most platforms and version 4.2 on a more limited basis.

Meanwhile, in May 1991, Microsoft and IBM announced an end to their joint development of OS/2. It was clear that most customers were voting with their dollars for Windows, not OS/2. Microsoft decided to concentrate on future versions of Windows and applications for Windows. The announcement, although not a surprise, rocked the industry nonetheless. Microsoft was well underway in the development of a new microkernel-based operating system that was internally code-named "NT" (for "new technology"). This new system was originally envisioned as a future release of OS/2 and was sometimes referred to as "OS/2 3.0." After the termination of joint OS/2 development, the NT project was altered to include the Windows user interface and API (Win32), and it became known henceforth as Microsoft Windows NT.

The first version of Windows NT wasn't expected for two years. Microsoft SQL Server would eventually be moved to Windows NT—that was a no-brainer. But in the meantime, we had to continue developing SQL Server on OS/2, even though OS/2 was now a competitive product for Microsoft. We had no alternative. For the next couple years, we in the SQL Server group got used to getting hit by "friendly fire" as Microsoft competed vigorously against OS/2.

Version 4.2

We had been developing SQL Server 4.2 for the forthcoming OS/2 2.0, the first 32-bit version of OS/2. Since SQL Server 4.2 was also planned to be 32-bit, porting the product from its UNIX lineage would be easier because we wouldn't have to be concerned with memory segmentation issues. In theory, SQL Server would also perform faster. Many articles comparing 32-bit and 16-bit performance issues appeared in the press, and everyone assumed the 32-bit environment would bring awesome performance gains (although few articles explained correctly why this might or might not be true).

The principal performance gain expected would be due to memory addressing. To address memory in the 16-bit segmented address space of OS/2 1.*x*, basically two instructions were required: one to load the correct segment and one to load the memory address within that segment. With 32-bit addressing, the instruction to load the segment was unnecessary and memory could be addressed with one instruction, not two. Because addressing memory is so common, some quick calculations showed that the 32-bit version might yield an overall performance increase of perhaps 20 percent or more, if all other operations were of equal speed.

The 32-bit Platform and Memory Gains

Many people mistakenly believed that SQL Server needed to be a fully 32-bit platform to address more than 16 MB of memory. Under OS/2 1.*x*, an application could access a maximum of 16 MB of real memory; although an application could access more than 16 MB of *virtual* memory, paging would result. In OS/2 2.0, an application could access more than 16 MB of real memory and thus avoid paging. This would allow SQL Server to have a larger cache, and getting data from memory rather than from disk always results in a huge performance gain. However, to the application, all memory in OS/2 is virtual memory—in versions 1.*x* and 2.0. So even the 16-bit version of SQL Server would be able to take advantage of the ability of OS/2 2.0 to access larger real-memory spaces. A 32-bit version was unnecessary for this.

Unfortunately, the early beta versions of OS/2 2.0 were significantly slower than OS/2 1.*x*, more than offsetting the efficiency in addressing memory. So rather than a performance gain, we saw a significant loss of performance in running Microsoft SQL Server 1.1 and preliminary builds of the 32-bit SQL Server 4.2 on OS/2 2.0.

OS/2 2.0 Release on Hold

Suddenly, the plans for the release of OS/2 2.0 were suspect. Instead of being delivered by the end of 1991, it was unclear whether IBM could deliver version 2.0 at all. At any rate, it appeared doubtful that OS/2 would ship any sooner than the end of 1992. The decision became clear—Microsoft would move SQL Server back to a 16-bit implementation and target it for OS/2 1.3.

Reworking back to 16-bit would cost us about three months, but we had little choice. In the meantime, another problem appeared. IBM shipped OS/2 1.3, but this version worked only for its brand of PCs. Theoretically, other computer manufacturers could license OS/2 from Microsoft and ship it as part of an OEM agreement. However, the demand for OS/2 had become so small that most OEMs did not ship it; as a result, buying OS/2 for other PCs was difficult for customers. For the first time, despite the seeming incongruity, Microsoft produced a shrink-wrapped version of OS/2, version 1.3, code named "Tiger." Tiger would ship in the box with Microsoft SQL Server and Microsoft LAN Manager, lessening the problem that our product was essentially targeted to a dead operating system.

Version 4.2 Released

Microsoft SQL Server version 4.2 entered beta testing in the fall of 1991, and in January 1992 Microsoft CEO Bill Gates (with Sybase's Bob Epstein sharing the stage) formally announced the product at a Microsoft SQL Server developers' conference in San Francisco. Version 4.2 truly had been a joint development between

Microsoft and Sybase. The database engine was ported from the UNIX version 4.2 source code, with both Microsoft and Sybase engineers working on the port and fixing bugs. In addition, Microsoft produced the client interface libraries for MS-DOS, Windows, and OS/2, and for the first time it included a Windows GUI tool to make administration easier. Source code for the database engine was merged back at Sybase headquarters, with files exchanged via modem and magnetic tape.

Microsoft SQL Server version 4.2 shipped in March 1992 to good reviews and positive customer feedback. As it would turn out, the source code for the database engine in this version would be the last code that Microsoft would receive from Sybase (with the exception of a few bug fixes we exchanged from time to time).

After Microsoft SQL Server 4.2 shipped, the Big Question for 1992 was "When will a 32-bit version of Microsoft SQL Server be available?" The issue of "32 bitness" became an emotional one: Many people who were the most strident in their demands for it were unclear or confused about what the benefits would be. They assumed that it would automatically have a smaller footprint, run faster, address more memory, and generally would be a much higher performing platform. But our internal work with a 32-bit version for OS/2 2.0 had shown that this wouldn't necessarily be the case.

SQL Server for Windows NT

Contrary to what I'm sure many people assume, I never got pressure from Microsoft senior management *not* to develop a full 32-bit version for OS/2. One of the joys of working for Microsoft is that senior management empowers the people in charge of projects to make the decisions, and this decision would be mine.

In early 1992, however, we faced some uncertainty and *external* pressures. On one hand, our entire customer base was by definition using OS/2. Those customers made it clear that they wanted, indeed expected, a 32-bit version of SQL Server for OS/2 2.0 as soon as IBM shipped 2.0, and they intended to remain on OS/2 for the foreseeable future. But when OS/2 2.0 might be available was unclear. IBM claimed that OS/2 2.0 would ship by the fall of 1992. Steve Ballmer, Microsoft senior vice president, made a well-known pledge that he'd eat a floppy disk if IBM shipped the product in 1992. I was not one to doubt Steve.

I was pressured to have a version of SQL Server running on Windows NT as soon as possible, with prerelease beta versions available when Windows NT was prereleased. It was clear to all of the SQL Server team members that Windows NT was our future. It would be the high-end operating system solution from Microsoft, and from a developer's perspective, Windows NT would offer many technical advantages over OS/2, including asynchronous I/O, symmetric multiprocessing, and portability to RISC architectures. We were champing at the bit to get started.

Although we had decided in 1991 to fall back to a 16-bit version of SQL Server, we had continued to work on the 32-bit version. By March 1992, just after shipping version 4.2, we saw that both the 16-bit and 32-bit versions ran slower on the beta versions of OS/2 2.0 than the 16-bit version ran on Tiger (OS/2 1.3). Perhaps by the time OS/2 2.0 actually shipped it might run faster. But then again it might not—the beta updates of OS/2 2.0 that we had received did not give us any reason to think it was getting faster. In fact, it seemed to be getting slower and more unstable.

For a product the scope of SQL Server, there is no such thing as a small release. There are big releases and bigger releases. Because resources are finite, we knew that working on a product geared toward OS/2 2.0 would slow down the progress of Windows NT development and could push back its release. Adding more developers was not a good solution. (As many in the industry have come to learn, adding more people often is the cause, and seldom the solution, to software development problems.) Furthermore, if we chose to develop simultaneously for both OS/2 2.0 and Windows NT, we'd encounter another set of problems. We'd have to add an abstraction layer to hide the differences in the operating systems, or we'd need substantial reengineering for both, or we'd simply take a lowest-common-denominator approach and not fully use services or features of either system.

So we decided to stop work on the 32-bit version of SQL Server for OS/2 2.0. We would move full-speed ahead in developing SQL Server for Windows NT, an operating system with an installed base of zero. We would not constrain the architecture in order to achieve portability back to OS/2 or to any other operating system. We would vigorously consume whatever interfaces and services Windows NT exposed. Windows NT would be our only horse, and we would ride as hard as we could. Except for bug fixing and maintenance, development ceased for SQL Server for OS/2.

From the Author...

Microsoft might seem to be an anonymous software behemoth, but it is in fact built of people who care passionately about our products and our customers. I lost countless nights of sleep when the decision to discontinue targeting OS/2 was made; I was personally and deeply hurt to hear that some of our customers felt betrayed. But I knew that the reason Microsoft had ceased development of OS/2 far transcended its support of SQL Server. Although painful for us and for some of our customers, it was clear that we had to move ahead not only for SQL Server to be successful but in order for it to have a future at all.

We began to tell customers that future versions, or a 32-bit version, for OS/2 2.0 would depend on the volume of customer demand and that our primary focus was now on Windows NT. Most customers seemed to understand and accept our position, but for customers who had committed their businesses to OS/2, this was understandably not the message they wanted to hear.

At this time, Sybase was working on a new version of its product, to be named "System 10." As was the case when we were working on version 4.2, Microsoft SQL Server needed to be compatible with and have the same version number as the Sybase release on UNIX. OS/2 versus Windows NT was foremost to us at Microsoft, but at Sybase, the success of System 10 was foremost.

Although System 10 was not yet even in beta, a schedule mismatch existed between the goal of getting a version of Microsoft SQL Server onto Windows NT as soon as possible and getting a version of System 10 onto Windows NT and/or OS/2 2.0 as soon as possible. We decided to compromise and specialize. Microsoft would port SQL Server version 4.2 for OS/2 to Windows NT, beginning immediately. Sybase would bring Windows NT into its umbrella of "core" operating systems for System 10. Windows NT would be among the first operating system platforms on which System 10 would be available. In addition, Microsoft would turn the OS/2 product back over to Sybase so those customers who wanted to stay with OS/2 could do so. Although we hoped to migrate most of our installed customer base to Windows NT, we knew that this could never be 100 percent. We were honestly pleased to be able to offer those customers a way to continue with their OS/2 plans, via Sybase. We truly didn't want them to feel abandoned.

This compromise and specialization of development made a lot of sense for both companies. We would be working from the stable and mature 4.2 source code that we had become experts in. Bringing up the product on a brand new operating system was difficult enough, even *without* having to worry about the infant System 10 code line. And Sybase could concentrate on the new System 10 code line, without worrying about the inevitable problems of a prebeta operating system. Ultimately, System 10 and SQL Server for Windows NT would both ship, and we'd again move back to joint development. That was the plan, and I think both sides expected this to be the case in 1992.

We started racing at breakneck speed to build the first version of SQL Server for Windows NT. Time to market was of course a prime consideration. Within Microsoft, we had committed to shipping within 90 days of the release of Windows NT; within the development group, we aimed for 30 days. But time to market was not our only, or even chief, goal. We wanted to build the best database server for Windows NT that we could. Because Windows NT would be SQL Server's only platform, we didn't need to be concerned about portability issues and we didn't need to create an abstraction layer that would make all operating systems look alike. All we had to worry about was doing the best job possible with Windows NT. Windows NT was designed to be a portable operating system, and it would be available for many different machine architectures. Our "portability layer" would be Windows NT itself.

We would tie SQL Server into management facilities provided by Windows NT, such as raising events to a common location, installing SQL Server as a Windows NT service, and exporting performance statistics to the Windows NT performance monitor. Because Windows NT allows applications to dynamically load code (using DLLs), we would provide an open interface and allow SQL Server to be extended by developers who wanted to write their own DLLs.

The Windows NT–Only Strategy

The Windows NT–only strategy has been questioned by many. But in 1992, the UNIX DBMS market was already overcrowded, so we would not bring anything unique to that market. We recognized that SQL Server couldn't even be in the running when UNIX was a customer's only solution. Our strategy was based on our doing the best possible job for Windows NT, being the best product on Windows NT, and helping make Windows NT compelling to customers.

The decision to concentrate only on Windows NT has had far-reaching effects. To be portable to many operating systems, the Sybase code base had to take on or duplicate many operating system services. For example, since threads either didn't exist on many UNIX operating systems or the thread packages differed substantially, Sybase had essentially written its own thread package into SQL Server code. The Windows NT scheduling services, however, were all based on a thread as the schedulable unit. If multiprocessors were available to the system and an application had multiple runnable (not blocked) threads, the application would automatically become a multiprocessor application. So we decided to use native Windows NT threads and not use the Sybase threading engine.

We made similar choices for our use of asynchronous I/O, memory management, network protocol support, user authentication, and exception handling. (Later on, I will discuss the SQL Server architecture in depth and delve into more of these specifics. For now, I want to make the point that the goals intrinsic to portability are in conflict with the goal to create the best possible implementation for a single operating system.)

This first version of Microsoft SQL Server for Windows NT was far more than a port of the OS/2 4.2 product. We essentially rewrote the "kernel" of SQL Server—the portion of the product that interacts with the operating system—directly to the Win32 API.

Another goal of SQL Server for Windows NT was to make it easy to migrate current installations on OS/2 to the new version and operating system. We wanted all applications that were written to SQL Server version 4.2 for OS/2 to work unmodified against SQL Server for Windows NT. Because Windows NT could be dual-booted with MS-DOS or OS/2, we decided that SQL Server for Windows NT would directly read from and write to a database created for the OS/2 version. During an evaluation phase, for example, a customer could work with the OS/2 version, reboot the same machine and work with the Windows NT version, and then go back to OS/2. Although it would be difficult to achieve, we wanted 100-percent compatibility.

We reworked a large portion of SQL Server's internals and added many new management, networking, and extensibility features; we did not add new external core database engine features that would compromise compatibility. For example, we would ensure that there were no differences in the SQL dialect or capabilities of the Windows NT and OS/2 versions. The plan was for the future System 10 version to implement many new features. Our release would be fundamentally a platform release. To emphasize compatibility with the OS/2-based 4.2 product and with the Sybase product line, we decided to call the first version of SQL Server for Windows NT "version 4.2." (We often referred to the product as simply "Microsoft SQL Server for Windows NT" and often internally as "SQL NT," a designation that the press and many customers also began to use.)

In July 1992, Microsoft hosted a Windows NT developers' conference and distributed a prebeta version of Windows NT to attendees. Even though we did not yet have SQL Server at a beta level, we immediately made available via CompuServe the 32-bit programming libraries that developers would need for porting their applications from OS/2 or 16-bit Windows to Windows NT. Just as we had enjoyed success back in 1990 by being among the first database products to provide the DLLs necessary for writing Windows 3.0–based applications, we sought to do the same with Windows NT.

In October 1992, we shipped the first beta version of SQL Server for Windows NT. The product was essentially feature complete, provided a full Win32 version of all components, and shipped to more than 100 beta sites. For a database server, having 100 beta sites was unprecedented, as the typical number of beta sites for such a product would be approximately 10.

From the Author...

Incidentally, at approximately the same time, we also shipped a maintenance release for SQL Server for OS/2 (and we shipped another the following year). In porting to Windows NT, we found and fixed many bugs that were generic to all platforms. Even though we would not create new SQL Server versions for OS/2, we meant it when we said that we did not want to abandon our OS/2 customers.

By March 1993, we went a step further and made a public beta release; anyone (even our competitors) could obtain a SQL Server Client/Server Development Kit (CSDK), the prerelease product, for a nominal charge that essentially covered our expenses. We set up a public support forum on CompuServe and did not demand that participants sign a nondisclosure agreement. We shipped more than 3000 CSDKs. By May 1993, the volume on the support forum for the prerelease product exceeded that for the shipping OS/2 product. The feedback was highly positive, and we knew we had a winner. It looked like our dream of eventual "client/server for the masses" was beginning to be realized.

In July 1993, Microsoft shipped Windows NT 3.1. Within 30 days, achieving our internal goal, we released the first version of Microsoft SQL Server for Windows NT to manufacturing. Customer and press reaction was terrific. SQL Server for Windows NT was listed in many publications as among the top and/or most important new products of 1993.

Success Brings Fundamental Change

Microsoft SQL Server for Windows NT was a success by nearly all measures. The strategy of integrating the product tightly with Windows NT resulted in a product that was substantially easier to use than high-end database products had ever been. Sales were above our internal projections and increased as Windows NT began to win acceptance.

By early December 1993, a large percentage of the SQL Server for the OS/2 customer base had already migrated to SQL Server for Windows NT. Our surveys showed that most of those who had not yet upgraded to Windows NT planned to do so, despite the fact that Sybase had publicly announced its intention to develop System 10 for OS/2.

The upgrade from "SQL OS/2" to "SQL NT" was virtually painless. When applications were moved from one platform to the other, not only did they still work but they worked better. "SQL NT" was much faster than "SQL OS/2," and most significantly, it was scalable far beyond the limits imposed by OS/2. Within another nine months, Microsoft's SQL Server business had more than doubled, with nearly all sales coming on the Windows NT platform. Although we continued to offer the OS/2 product, it accounted for well below 10 percent of current sales.

A Faster SQL Server

Focusing the product on Windows NT had made the product fast. Studies conducted internally at Microsoft, as well as those from private customer benchmarks, all showed similar results: SQL Server for Windows NT (running on low-cost commodity hardware) was competitive in performance with database systems running on UNIX (on much more costly hardware).

In September 1993, Compaq Computer Corporation published the first official, audited Transaction Processing Council (TPC) benchmarks. At that time, on the TPC-B benchmark, well over $1000/TPS (transactions per second) was common, and it was an impressive number that broke the $1000/TPS barrier. Running on a dual-Pentium, 66-MHz machine, SQL Server achieved 226 transactions-per-second at a cost of $440 per transaction, less than half of the cost of the lowest benchmark ever published by any other company. The raw performance number of 226 transactions-per-second was equally astonishing. At that time, most of the TPC-B numbers on file for UNIX minicomputer systems were still below 100 TPS. Certainly a handful of numbers were higher, but all occurred at a price point of much more than $440/TPS. And looking back perhaps just 18 months, the raw performance of 226 TPS was about as high as any mainframe or minicomputer system had ever achieved.

The implications were clear. Microsoft SQL Server for Windows NT was not simply a low-end or workgroup system. Its performance was competitive with more costly UNIX systems, and the trend toward faster systems running Windows NT was unmistakable. The 66-MHz Pentium processors were the first generation of Pentiums from Intel. Much higher clock speeds could be expected within a few months; hardware with additional processors was anticipated. Furthermore, Microsoft SQL Server for Windows NT would soon also be available on RISC processors such as the DEC Alpha-AXP at 250 MHz and the MIPS R4400. The so-called *Moore's Law* (named after Gordon Moore, cofounder of Intel Corporation), which postulates that computing power doubles every 18 months, was clearly being proven true for the type of commodity hardware for which Windows NT, and Microsoft SQL Server, were designed. We took a serious look at what would be required to achieve 1000 TPS, definitely putting our raw performance in the same league as even the largest systems of the day.

The End of Joint Development

Microsoft's success strained its relationship with Sybase. The competitive landscape of late 1993 was very different from that of 1987 when Microsoft and Sybase had inked their deal. By 1993, Sybase was a successful software company, by most accounts second only to Oracle in the DBMS market. The credibility and visibility Microsoft brought Sybase was far less important in 1993 than it had been to the upstart company of 1987. Similarly, Microsoft had grown a great deal since 1987. The growth had been not just in revenues (although that had been one of the great success stories of the industry) but in an emphasis on "enterprise applications," such as Microsoft SQL Server, that Fortune 1000 companies could use as a platform upon which to run their businesses.

The SQL Server development team had grown as well, from a handful of people in 1990 to more than 50 professionals (not including marketing, support, or field operations), with significant, additional growth planned. Our first-rate team of engineers knew database and transaction processing and the inner workings of SQL Server, and they were experts in developing for Windows NT. We now had the talent, size, motivation, and mandate, yet we were still constrained in what we could do with the product and where we could take it: the 1987 agreement with Sybase had merely licensed to Microsoft the rights to the Sybase product. Because of this restricted agreement, Microsoft could not unilaterally implement new features or changes without Sybase's approval. Contrary to what many people thought, Microsoft had no ownership stake in Sybase and by no means could Microsoft simply call the shots.

Obviously, Sybase had different business needs and therefore different priorities than Microsoft. We at Microsoft might, for example, want to integrate SQL Server with messaging by using MAPI (messaging API), but because this was a feature specific to the Microsoft operating system, Sybase would not be excited about it. As is always the case in development, many features *could* be done for every feature that *will* actually be done: features specific to Windows NT didn't tend to interest Sybase as much as those that would benefit its UNIX products.

Sybase engineers had to wrestle with the issue of portability to multiple operating systems. In fact, the implementation by Microsoft of version 4.2 for Windows NT was already causing friction since Sybase was progressing with System 10 for Windows NT. Sybase was understandably implementing System 10 in a more portable manner than we had done. This was entirely rational for Sybase's objectives, but from our perspective, it meant a less tight bond with Windows NT. System 10 would not, *could not,* perform as well on Windows NT as the product that had been designed and written exclusively for Windows NT.

The economics involved, as well as the changing competitive landscape, made it clear that the Microsoft/Sybase agreement of 1987 no longer worked. Microsoft SQL Server was now a viable competitive alternative to Sybase SQL Server running on UNIX, Novell NetWare, and VMS. Far from seeding the market for Sybase, Microsoft SQL Server was now taking sales away from Sybase. Instead of choosing a UNIX solution, customers could buy Microsoft SQL Server at a fraction of the cost of a UNIX solution, run it on less expensive PC hardware, and install and administer it more easily. Although Sybase earned royalties on sales of Microsoft SQL Server, these amounted to a small fraction of the revenue Sybase would have received if the customer bought Sybase for UNIX in the first place. Microsoft and Sybase were now often vigorously competing for the same customers. Both sides recognized that a fundamental change in the relationship was needed.

On April 12, 1994, Microsoft and Sybase announced an end to joint development. Each company would separately develop its own SQL Server products. Microsoft would be free to evolve and change Microsoft SQL Server. Sybase would bring its System 10 products (and subsequent versions) to Windows NT—the first time that the Sybase-labeled SQL Server would be available for a Microsoft operating system. (The original agreement gave Microsoft exclusive rights on Microsoft operating systems.) Both companies' products would be backward-compatible for applications that had been developed for the shipping version of Microsoft SQL Server. However, the products would diverge in the future and would have different feature sets and design points. Sybase's product would be fully compatible with its UNIX versions. Microsoft's product would continue to be integrated with Windows NT as much possible. In short, the products would directly compete.

SQL Server Performance: No Secret Formulas

Although Microsoft SQL Server is designed for and optimized for Windows NT, it uses only publicly documented interfaces. From time to time I see articles or hear a speaker suggest that Microsoft SQL Server uses private, undocumented APIs in Windows NT to achieve its performance. But this assumption is false, without exception. SQL Server's performance results from using the available and published Windows NT services without any compromise. This is something that other products could also do if developers were willing to dedicate themselves to doing the best possible job for Windows NT, without making compromises for portability to other operating systems.

> **NOTE** Although the Sybase product would compete with Microsoft SQL Server, Microsoft encouraged and provided support to get Sybase System 10 shipping on Windows NT as soon as possible, because it was important to the acceptance and success of Windows NT. This is typical of many other relationships that are competitive on one level and cooperative on another.

The Charge to SQL95

As late as the beginning of 1994, we had planned that the next version of the product would pick up the Sybase System 10 source code and new features. But the termination of joint development changed that plan. Sybase would contribute no more code, and Microsoft would release no System 10 product. Except for a couple of bug fixes, the last code drop we received from Sybase was in early 1992, as we were shipping version 4.2 for OS/2.

Time was at a premium. Besides growing sales with new customers, Microsoft had to fight for its significant installed base. Sybase would deliver System 10 on Windows NT later that year. That would be potentially an easy upgrade for Microsoft's installed customer base; so if we lost customers to System 10, we'd likely lose them forever.

From the Author...

When we announced the end of joint development with Sybase, many analysts publicly questioned Microsoft's ability to deliver SQL Server without help from Sybase. Internally, we were confident. We knew we had rewritten the product to bring it to Windows NT in the first place, and we hadn't done any true joint development with Sybase for two years.

The first version of SQL Server for Windows NT had been well received; it was both solid and fast from the day it shipped. It had become commonplace in the database industry to take at least a year to work out the bugs in new releases. We had shipped a stable version from day one, and this had been instrumental in winning acceptance of SQL Server for Windows NT much quicker than most had predicted. Our team was proud of the product we had delivered. But we knew that the industry at large, which thought the core expertise resided at Sybase, didn't give us credibility yet. We were eager to show what we could do.

We quickly planned for an ambitious release that was loaded with new features and performance improvements. We tagged it "SQL95," borrowing the working moniker from the well-known upcoming Windows 95 release. Because the Big Question of 1994 was "What are your plans for replication?" replication would become a keystone of the release. So would scrollable cursors, a feature that we had learned (from the ill-fated dBASE IV interface) was necessary to bridge the "impedance mismatch" between many record-oriented applications and a relational database. No mainstream DBMS product had yet provided a fully functional implementation of scrollable cursors in a client/server environment, and we believed this was imperative to add to the database engine. We had also been working on a dramatic new set of management tools, code named "Starfighter" (today's SQL Enterprise Manager), which would also be included in the next release. The new feature list went on and on.

From the Author...

Some skeptics were concerned that the release might be too ambitious—that it could get bogged down and be significantly delayed. But within the group we were confident. We understood the problems well and had made the right trade-offs to deliver an impressive new release within 18 months. Given that a beta test of such a product would need to be at least 6 months long, this left at most a year for core development.

Our customers were clamoring to hear about our plans for SQL Server post-Sybase. So on June 14, 1994, we put together a briefing event in San Francisco for key customers, analysts, and the press. Jim Allchin, Microsoft senior vice president, walked the attendees through our plans for the future and for the "SQL95" release. Attendees were impressed with the plans and direction, but many were openly skeptical of our ability to deliver such an impressive product by the end of 1995.

RANT! Some industry press began to sarcastically refer to our planned release as "SQL97" and even "SQL2000." Internally, we were still targeting the first half of 1995. Outside the company we were more cautious—this is software development, which is still more art than science. Stuff happens, so we said nothing more ambitious than "1995." (Everyone assumed that the planned date was December 31, 1995, and that we'd miss that date, too.) The rampant skepticism only served to motivate the SQL Server team even more to show that we could deliver. After all, the team rightly felt that it had *already* delivered an impressive release independent of Sybase. But no one gave us credit for that, so we'd just have to show them.

The team worked incredibly hard, even by Microsoft standards, to make this deadline and still deliver a full-featured, high-quality product. We released our first beta at the end of October 1994. Although Starfighter was not yet feature complete, the database server was complete, and since the server takes the longest lead time for beta sites to really stress it, we went ahead with the beta release. We followed up with a series of beta updates for the next several months, and gradually expanded the number of beta sites, eventually surpassing 2000 sites.

For nine months, dinner was delivered each night for late-night workers on the development team—usually a majority. On June 14, 1995, we released the product to manufacturing. Microsoft SQL Server 6.0, our "SQL95," had shipped within our original internal target date, much sooner than nearly everyone outside our team expected.

Microsoft SQL Server 6.0 was an immediate hit. Positive reviews appeared in nearly all the trade publications; even more significantly, none were negative or even neutral. Even more important than the press reviews, customer reaction was terrific. Feedback was extremely positive, and sales easily surpassed what I had feared was an overly optimistic plan.

InfoWorld, in its second annual survey of the 100 companies with the most innovative client/server applications in the previous year, showed Microsoft SQL Server as the number two database. SQL Server jumped from 15 percent to 18 percent of those surveyed as the database server of choice—for a virtual tie with Oracle, which dropped from 24 percent to 19 percent. Sybase rose from 12 to 14 percent. Three of the top 10 applications highlighted by *InfoWorld* were built with Microsoft SQL Server.

Team Building with Top Talent

Besides working hard on the development of version 6.0, we were also working to increase the size and strength of the team. We had built a small, crackerjack team that had delivered SQL Server for Windows NT, and this team was the core that delivered "SQL95." But we needed more people, more expertise, and exposure to broader ideas. So we went after top talent in the industry.

We attracted some industry luminaries—Jim Gray, Dave Lomet, and Phil Bernstein—to Microsoft. We also attracted many lesser known but top development talent from throughout the industry. For example, DEC shopped Rdb around, looking to generate cash, and Oracle eventually spent a few hundred million dollars for it. But Microsoft wasn't interested in buying Rdb. Instead, we hired many of the project's best developers. We augmented this by hiring several of the best recent masters' graduates who had specialized in databases.

Of course, we were happy to see this data, but we took it with a grain of salt. Other data could be interpreted to suggest our presence was substantially less than this. And we recognized that we were still relative newcomers. From a sales perspective, Oracle was clearly king of the hill for now, and Sybase, Informix, and IBM were also formidable competitors in the DBMS market. We had not previously been a significant competitive threat. But now we were, and all companies were arming their sales forces with bundles of information for tactics to use to sell against Microsoft SQL Server. Sybase, Informix, and Oracle all promised hot new releases. Although the SQL Server team had been sprinting for nearly four years, now was certainly not the time to get complacent.

The Next Version

After shipping version 6.0, many team members took well-deserved vacations after months of working in "crunch mode." But within a month, we were actively beginning work on SQL Server version 6.5. With any huge release like version 6.0, some features get deferred due to schedule constraints. And during this ambitious 18-month project, new demands came up that weren't even conceived of as requirements when the project began. For example, the Internet and data warehousing both exploded in importance and demand in 1995. Version 6.5 would add capabilities for both. It would also include further ease-of-use improvements, gain certification as conforming to the ANSI SQL standard, and provide much richer distributed transactions.

Although version 6.0 had been released to manufacturing in June 1995, on December 15, 1995, we shipped a feature-complete beta version of 6.5 to 150 beta sites. The production version of 6.5 released to manufacturing in April 1996, a scant 10 months after 6.0 was released. We were not about to slow down.

2

A Tour of Microsoft SQL Server

Introduction

Microsoft SQL Server is a high-performance, client/server relational database management system (RDBMS). It was designed to support high-volume transaction processing (such as that for online order entry, inventory, accounting, or manufacturing) as well as data warehousing and decision-support applications (such as sales analysis applications) on Microsoft Windows NT Server–based networks. SQL Server is fully operational on all hardware architectures supported by Windows NT, including Intel, DEC Alpha AXP, MIPS R4000, and Motorola PowerPC-based systems. For all these hardware platforms, SQL Server versions are built simultaneously from the same source code baseline, and all versions ship together on the same CD-ROM. SQL Server also provides many client tools and networking interfaces for the Microsoft Windows 95, Windows 3.1, and MS-DOS operating systems. And because of SQL Server's open architecture, other systems (for example, UNIX-based systems) can interoperate with it as well.

SQL Server is part of the core of a family of integrated products, including development tools, systems management tools, distributed system components, and open development interfaces, as shown in Figure 2-1 on the following page. It is also a key part of Microsoft BackOffice.

This book focuses on the capabilities and uses of the SQL Server engine; this chapter provides an overview of the entire SQL Server family of components and describes the features and benefits of each component. Understanding these features and benefits will prove helpful to you as you develop applications.

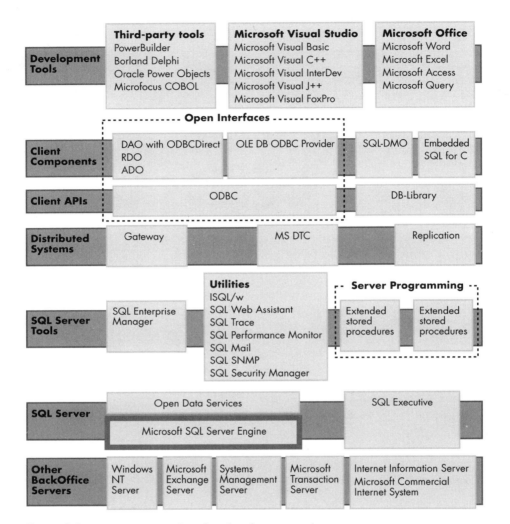

Figure 2-1. *SQL Server and its family of integrated components.*

The SQL Server Engine

The Microsoft SQL Server engine is designed to support a variety of demanding applications, such as online transaction processing (OLTP) and decision-support applications. At the core of its decision-support capabilities is Transact-SQL, Microsoft's version of Structured Query Language. Beneath this query language are the components that support transaction processing and recoverability.

Transact-SQL

Industrywide, SQL is a well-known and widely used data access tool. Every mainstream database management system (DBMS) product implements SQL in some way. Transact-SQL (often referred to as "T-SQL") is a powerful and unique superset of the SQL standard.

The SQL SELECT statement provides tremendous power and flexibility for retrieving information. Data from multiple tables can be easily projected and the results returned in tabular format with information chosen and correctly combined from the multiple tables. Check out the following two tables from the *pubs* sample database. (The *pubs* database, used for many examples in this book, is installed when Microsoft SQL Server is installed. For brevity, an abbreviated amount of the data will sometimes be used, as is true in this example.)

publishers Table

pub_id	pub_name	city	state
0736	New Moon Books	Boston	MA
0877	Binnet & Hardley	Washington	DC
1389	Algodata Infosystems	Berkeley	CA

titles Table

title_id	title	pub_id
BU1032	The Busy Executive's Database Guide	1389
BU1111	Cooking with Computers: Surreptitious Balance Sheets	1389
BU2075	You Can Combat Computer Stress!	0736
BU7832	Straight Talk About Computers	1389
MC2222	Silicon Valley Gastronomic Treats	0877
MC3021	The Gourmet Microwave	0877
MC3026	The Psychology of Computer Cooking	0877

The following simple SELECT statement logically joins the *titles* and *publishers* tables to project the names of the book titles with the names of the companies publishing each title.

```
SELECT title, pub_name, city, state
FROM titles, publishers
WHERE titles.pub_id = publishers.pub_id
```

Here's the result:

title	pub_name	city	state
The Busy Executive's Database Guide	Algodata Infosystems	Berkeley	CA
Cooking with Computers: Surreptitious Balance Sheets	Algodata Infosystems	Berkeley	CA
You Can Combat Computer Stess!	New Moon Books	Boston	MA
Straight Talk About Computers	Algodata Infosystems	Berkeley	CA
Silicon Valley Gastronomic Treats	Binnet & Hardley	Washington	DC
The Gourmet Microwave	Binnet & Hardley	Washington	DC
The Psychology of Computer Cooking	Binnet & Hardley	Washington	DC

This query, a simple SQL statement, shows that standard SQL provides a powerful way to query and manipulate data. (In Chapters 7 and 10, we'll explore SQL queries in much greater depth.)

The National Institute of Standards and Technology (NIST) has certified Microsoft SQL Server version 6.5 as compliant with the American National Standards Institute (ANSI) SQL-92 standard. However, considerably more power is available in Transact-SQL because of its unique extensions to the standard.

Standards and Testing

Although the ANSI standard is commonly referred to as "SQL-92," the official standard is ANSI X3.135-1992 and is entitled "American National Standards Institute Database Language-SQL." "X3H2" is the designator for the ANSI SQL committee. NIST, a division of the United States Department of Commerce, conducts a suite of tests (which vendors pay the costs of running) to certify compliance with the standard. You can find a summary of products currently certified as compliant at ftp://speckle.ncsl.nist.gov/sql-testing/VPLs.

Transact-SQL extensions

Transact-SQL provides a number of capabilities that extend beyond typical implementations of SQL. Queries that are difficult to write in standard SQL can be easily and efficiently written using these capabilities. Some of my favorites include the ability to embed additional SELECT statements in the SELECT list and the ability to drill into a result set by further selecting data directly from a SELECT statement, a feature known as a *derived table*. Transact-SQL provides many system functions for dealing with strings (for finding substrings and so on), for converting datatypes, and for manipulating and formatting date information. Transact-SQL also provides mathematical operations such as square root. In addition, special operators, such as CUBE and ROLLUP, allow multidimensional analysis to be efficiently projected at the database server, where the analysis can be optimized as part of the execution plan of a query. The CASE operator allows for complex conditional substitutions to be made easily in the SELECT statement. Multidimensional (sometimes referred to as OLAP, or online analytic processing) operators, such as CUBE, and conditional operators, such as CASE, are especially useful in implementing data warehousing solutions with SQL Server.

The query optimizer

In Transact-SQL, a cost-based query optimizer determines the likely best way to access data. This allows you to concentrate on defining your query criteria rather than defining how the query should be executed. For example, this nonprocedural approach eliminates the need for you to know which indexes exist and which, if any, should be used. Would it be more efficient to incur additional I/Os to read index pages in addition to data pages, or would it be better just to scan the data and then sort it? The optimizer automatically, invisibly, and efficiently resolves these types of important questions for you.

The SQL Server optimizer maintains statistics about the volume and dispersion of data, which it then uses to estimate the plan most likely to work best for the operation requested. Because a cost-based optimizer is by definition probability-based, an application might want to override the optimizer in some specialized cases. In your application, you can specify *optimizer hints* that will direct the execution plan chosen. In addition, you can use SQL Server's SHOWPLAN feature, which explains the execution plan chosen, provides insight into why it was chosen, and even allows for tuning of the application and database design.

The programmable server

Transact-SQL provides programming constructs—such as variables, conditional operations (IF-THEN-ELSE), and looping—that can dramatically simplify application development by allowing you to use a simple SQL script rather than a third-generation programming language (3GL). These branching and looping constructs can dramatically improve performance in a client/server environment by eliminating the need for network conversations. Minimizing network latency is a key aspect of maximizing client/server application performance. For example, instead of returning a value to the calling application, which requires that the application evaluate and subsequently issue another request, you can build conditional logic directly into the SQL batch file so that the routine is completely evaluated and executed at the server.

You can use Transact-SQL to write complex batches of SQL statements. (A batch of SQL statements in a complex application can be up to several hundred lines long.) An important new capability of SQL Server 6.5 is the SQL Debugging Interface (SDI), which allows debuggers such as those available with Microsoft Visual Studio 97 to fully debug Transact-SQL routines, including stepping through the statements, setting breakpoints, and setting watchpoints on Transact-SQL variables.

Stored procedures

Simply put, *stored procedures* are collections of SQL statements stored within a SQL Server database. You can code complex queries and transactions into stored procedures and then invoke them directly from the front-end application. Whenever a dynamic SQL command is sent to a database server for processing, the server must parse the command, check its syntax for sense, determine whether the requester has the permissions necessary to execute the command, and formulate an optimal execution plan to process the request. Stored procedures execute faster than dynamic SQL batches, sometimes dramatically faster, because they eliminate the need for reparsing and reoptimizing the requests each time they are executed. SQL Server supports stored procedures that let developers store *groups* of compiled SQL statements on the server for later recall, to limit the overhead when the procedures are subsequently executed.

Stored procedures differ from ordinary SQL statements and from batches of SQL statements in that they're checked for syntax and compiled the *first time* they are executed. SQL Server stores this compiled version and then uses it to process subsequent calls, resulting in faster execution times. Stored procedures can also accept parameters, so a single procedure can be used by multiple applications using different input data.

Even if stored procedures provided no performance advantage (which, of course, they do), there would still be a compelling reason to use them: they provide an important layer of insulation from changes in business practices. Suppose, for example, that an application is used to maintain a mailing list for a retailer's catalog distribution. Subsequent to the application being deployed, a change in criteria and logic (that is, the business rules) occurs, thus affecting which customers should automatically receive new catalogs. If the business rules had been programmed directly into the company's applications, every application would need to be modified, likely an expensive and time-consuming operation. Furthermore, if multiple developers worked on the applications, the rules might not have been programmed with the exact same semantics by every programmer. A stored procedure, on the other hand, could be modified *once,* in seconds, at the server. The applications would not need to be changed or even restarted. The next time each application executed the stored procedure, the new rules would be in place automatically.

In addition to providing a performance advantage, stored procedures can provide an important security function. By granting users access to a stored procedure but not to the underlying tables, you can allow them to access or manipulate data only in the way prescribed by the stored procedure.

Extended stored procedures

A unique capability of Microsoft SQL Server, *extended stored procedures* allow developers to extend the programming capabilities provided by Transact-SQL and to access resources outside of SQL Server. Messaging integration, security integration, the ability to write HTML (Hypertext Markup Language) files (files formatted for use on the Internet), and much of the power of SQL Enterprise Manager are all implemented using extended stored procedures. You can create extended stored procedures as external dynamic link libraries (DLLs). (DLLs are typically written in C and C++, although implementation in other languages is also possible.)

For example, you could write a DLL to establish a modem connection, dial the ACME Credit Service, and return a status indicating credit approval or rejection. (The C language more readily lends itself to particular tasks because of such language constructs as arrays, structures, and pointers.) For example, writing a financial function that uses recursion in C (for example, the internal rate of return, or IRR) might be more efficient that writing it as a Transact-SQL stored procedure. *Open Data Services (ODS)* is an application programming interface that lets you build extended stored procedures that can return self-describing result sets to the calling client applications, just as a "normal" procedure would.

Extended stored procedures allow even Microsoft to extend SQL Server. Good engineering practices dictate that where code does not benefit from being shared or is not in common, it should be segregated and isolated. With this principle in mind, Microsoft added integration with messaging via MAPI as a set of extended stored procedures (**xp_sendmail, xp_readmail,** and so on) instead of directly modifying the SQL Server engine. Extended stored procedures allow us to add powerful features without any chance of disrupting the core server engine so that more features can be added quickly, with less risk of destabilizing the server. And because the code is loaded dynamically, the DLL is loaded only if a routine is implemented as an extended stored procedure, so the memory footprint of SQL Server does not grow for services that aren't being used.

DBMS-Enforced Data Integrity

A database is only as useful as the user's confidence in it. That's why the server must enforce data integrity rules and business policies. SQL Server enforces data integrity within the database itself, guaranteeing that complex business policies will be followed and that mandatory relationships between data elements are complied with.

Because SQL Server's client/server architecture allows you to use a variety of front-end applications to manipulate and present the same data from the server, it would be cumbersome to encode all the necessary integrity constraints, security permissions, and business rules into each application. If business policies were all coded in the front-end applications, *every* application would need to be modified *every time* a business policy changed. Even if you attempted to encode business rules into every client application, the danger of an application misbehaving still exists. Most applications cannot be fully trusted. Only the server can act as the final arbiter, and the server must not provide a back door for a poorly written or malicious application to subvert its integrity.

SQL Server uses advanced data integrity features, such as declarative referential integrity (DRI), datatypes, defaults, constraints, rules, stored procedures, and triggers, to enforce data integrity. Each of these features has its own use within a database; combining these integrity features can make your database flexible and easy to manage, yet secure.

Declarative Referential Integrity

A central tenet of relational database theory is that every *tuple* of every *relation* (more colloquially, every *row* of every *table*) can be uniquely identified. The attribute or combination of attributes (the column or combination of columns) that ensures uniqueness is known as the *primary key*. A table can have only one primary key. SQL Server allows you, when defining a table, to designate the column(s) that make up the primary key. This is known as a *PRIMARY KEY constraint*. SQL Server uses this PRIMARY KEY constraint to guarantee that the uniqueness of the designated column(s) is never violated.

Sometimes multiple columns of a table can uniquely identify a row—for example, an employee table might have an employee ID (*emp_id*) and a social security number (*soc_sec_num*) column, and both are considered unique. Such columns are often referred to as *alternate* or *candidate keys*. These keys must also be unique. Although a table can have only one primary key, it can have multiple alternate keys. SQL Server supports the multiple alternate key concept via *UNIQUE constraints*. When a column or combination of columns is declared unique, SQL Server prevents any record being added or updated that would violate this uniqueness.

Assigning an arbitrary unique number as the primary key when no natural or convenient key exists is often most efficient. For example, businesses commonly use customer numbers or account numbers as unique identifiers or primary keys. SQL Server makes it easy to efficiently generate unique numbers by allowing one column in a table to have the *Identity property*. You use the Identity property to make sure that each value in the column is unique and that the values will increment (or decrement) by the amount you specify from a starting point that you specify. (A column having the Identity property will typically also have a PRIMARY KEY or UNIQUE constraint, but this is not required.)

SQL Server enforces logical relationships between tables with *FOREIGN KEY constraints*. A *foreign key* in a table is a column or combination of columns that match the primary key (or possibly an alternate key) of another table. The logical relationship between those two tables is the basis of the relational model.

For example, the simple SELECT example shown earlier in this chapter includes a *titles* table and a *publishers* table. The *titles* table column *title_id* (title ID) is its primary key. The *publishers* table column *pub_id* (publisher ID) is its primary key. The *titles* table also includes a *pub_id* column, which is not the primary key because a publisher can publish multiple titles. Instead, *pub_id* is a *foreign key,* and it references the primary key of the *publishers* table. After this relationship is declared when the table is defined, SQL Server ensures that a title cannot be entered unless a valid publisher for it is in the database and that a publisher cannot be deleted if any titles in the database reference that publisher.

To further enforce data integrity, SQL Server makes sure that any data entered matches the type and range of the specified data type and, for example, allows a NULL value to be entered only if the column has been declared as allowing NULLs. SQL Server supports a wide range of datatypes, allowing for great flexibility with efficient storage.

Datatypes

SQL Server datatypes provide the simplest form of data integrity by restricting the types of information (for example, characters, numbers, or dates) that can be stored in the columns of the database tables. You can also design your own datatypes (*user-defined* datatypes) to supplement those supplied by the system. For example, you could define a *state_code* datatype as two characters (CHAR(2)); SQL Server would then accept only two-character state codes. A user-defined datatype can be used to define columns in *any* table. An advantage of user-defined datatypes is that rules and defaults, which are discussed in the next two sections, can be bound to them for use in multiple tables, eliminating the need to include these types of checks in the front-end application.

CHECK Constraints and Rules

CHECK constraints and *rules* are integrity constraints that go beyond those implied by a column's datatype. Whenever a user enters a value, SQL Server checks that value against any CHECK constraint or rule created for the specified column to ensure that only values that adhere to the definition of the constraint or rule are accepted. Although CHECK constraints and rules are essentially equivalent in functionality, CHECK constraints are easier to use and provide more flexibility. A CHECK constraint can be conveniently defined when a column is defined, and constraints can be defined on multiple columns. Rules, however, must be defined and then bound to a column or user-defined datatype separately. While a column or user-defined datatype can have only one rule associated with it, a CHECK constraint can reference multiple columns in the same table or it can reference one of the built-in functions that SQL Server provides.

Both CHECK constraints and rules can require that a value fall within a particular range, match a particular pattern, or match one of the entries in a specified list. An advantage of CHECK constraints is that they can depend on either the value of another field or fields in the row or on the value returned by one of the system-supplied functions. A rule cannot reference other fields. As an example of applying a CHECK constraint or rule, a database containing information on senior citizens could have the CHECK constraint or rule *"age field must contain a value between 65 and 120 years."* A birth certificate database could require that the date in the *birth_date* field be the current date—checking the value returned by SQL Server's built-in GETDATE()function—or that it be some date prior to the current date.

Defaults

Defaults allow you to specify a value that SQL Server inserts if no explicit value is entered in a particular field. For example, you could set the current date as the default value for an *order_date* field in a customer order record. Then, if a user or front-end application doesn't make an entry in the *order_date* field, SQL Server automatically inserts the current date. You can also use the keyword DEFAULT as a placeholder in an INSERT or UPDATE statement, instructing SQL Server to set the value to the declared default value.

Triggers

Triggers are a special type of stored procedure. Stored procedures can be executed only when explicitly called; triggers are automatically invoked, or "triggered," by SQL Server, and this is their main advantage. Triggers are associated with particular pieces of data and are called automatically whenever an attempt to modify that data is made, no matter what causes the modification (a user's entry or an application action).

Conceptually, triggers are similar to a CHECK constraint or rule. SQL Server automatically activates triggers, constraints, and rules whenever an attempt is made to modify the data they protect. CHECK constraints and rules then perform fairly simple types of checks on the data—for example, *"make sure the age field has a value between 0 and 120."* Triggers, on the other hand, can perform extremely elaborate restrictions on the data, which helps to ensure that the rules by which your business operates cannot be subverted. Because triggers are a form of stored procedure, they have the full power of the Transact-SQL language at their disposal and they can invoke other stored and extended stored procedures. You can write a trigger that enforces complex business rules, such as this:

> Don't accept an order
> If the customer has any past due accounts with us
> > OR
> If the customer has a bad credit rating by ACME Credit Service (with the trigger calling an extended procedure that automatically dials up ACME to get the credit rating)
> > OR
> If the order is for more than $50,000 and the customer has had an account with us for less than six months

This is a powerful integrity check. Yet the trigger to enforce it is simple to write.

Triggers can also enforce *referential integrity*, ensuring that relationships between tables are maintained. For example, a trigger can prohibit a customer record from being deleted if open orders exist for the customer or it can prohibit any new order for a customer for which no record exists. Triggers can go beyond simply insisting that relationships exist: they can perform *referential actions*. This means that triggers can cause changes to ripple through to other tables. For example, if you want to drop a delinquent customer from your system and delete all of that customer's active orders, a trigger on the *customer* table could automatically delete all entries in the *orders* table.

Triggers automatically execute whenever a specified change to a data object is attempted. A trigger executes once per statement, even if multiple rows are affected. It has access to the before and after images of the data. (These before and after images are reconstructed from the transaction log into pseudo tables that can be accessed from within the trigger.) The trigger can then take further action, including rolling back the transaction. Although you can use triggers to enforce referential integrity, it is usually more convenient to establish these relationships when you create the tables by using declarative referential integrity.

Transaction Processing

Transaction processing guarantees the consistency and recoverability of SQL Server databases. A *transaction* is the basic unit of work under SQL Server. Typically, it consists of several SQL commands that read and update the database, but the update is executed only when a COMMIT command is issued. (Note that the example below is pseudocode and that error handling is required to achieve the behavior described.)

Transaction processing in SQL Server assures that all transactions are performed as a single unit of work—even in the presence of a hardware or general system failure. Such transactions are referred to as having the *ACID properties*: atomicity, consistency, isolation, and durability. In addition to the explicit multistatement transactions such as those provided in the *DEBIT_CREDIT* example below, SQL Server guarantees that a single command that affects multiple rows maintains the ACID properties.

Here is an example in pseudocode of an ACID transaction, followed by an explanation of each of the ACID properties.

```
BEGIN TRANSACTION DEBIT_CREDIT
Debit Savings account $1000
Credit Checking account $1000
COMMIT TRANSACTION DEBIT_CREDIT
```

Atomicity

SQL Server guarantees the *atomicity* of its transactions. With atomicity, each transaction is treated as all-or-nothing—it either commits or aborts. If a transaction commits, all of its effects remain. If it aborts, all of its effects are undone. In the *DEBIT_CREDIT* example above, if the savings account debit is reflected in the database but the checking account credit is not, funds will essentially disappear from the database; that is, funds will be debited from the savings account but never credited to the checking account. If the reverse occurred (if the checking account were credited and the savings account were *not* debited), the customer's account would mysteriously increase in value without a corresponding customer cash deposit or account transfer. Because of SQL Server's atomicity feature, both the debit and credit must be completed or neither event is completed.

Consistency

The *consistency* property ensures that a transaction will not allow the system to enter an incorrect logical state—the data must always be logically correct. Constraints and rules are honored, even in the event of a system failure. For the *DEBIT_CREDIT* example, the logical rule is that money cannot be created or destroyed—a corresponding, counter-balancing entry must be made for each entry. (Consistency is implied by, and for most situations is redundant to, atomicity, isolation, and durability.)

Isolation

Isolation separates concurrent transactions from the updates of other incomplete transactions. In the *DEBIT_CREDIT* example, another transaction cannot see the "work in progress" while the transaction is being carried out. For example, if another transaction read the balance of the savings account after the debit occurred, and then the *DEBIT_CREDIT* transaction was aborted, the other transaction would be working from a balance that never logically existed.

Isolation among transactions is accomplished automatically by SQL Server. It locks data to allow multiple concurrent users to work with data, but it prevents side effects that could distort the results and make them different than would be expected if users serialized their requests (that is, if requests were queued and ran one at a time). This *serializability* feature is one of the isolation levels that SQL Server supports. SQL Server supports multiple degrees of isolation levels that allow you to make the appropriate trade-off between how much data to lock and how long locks must be held. This trade-off is known as *concurrency* versus *consistency*. Locking reduces concurrency (because locked data is unavailable to other users), but it provides the benefit of higher consistency. (I'll discuss locking in greater detail in Chapter 13.)

Durability

After a transaction commits, SQL Server's *durability* property ensures that its effects will persist even if a system failure occurs. Conversely, if a system failure occurs while a transaction is in progress, the transaction will be completely undone, leaving no partial effects on the data. For example, if a power outage occurs in the midst of a transaction before the transaction is committed, the entire transaction will be automatically rolled back when the system is restarted. If the power fails immediately after the acknowledgment of the commit is sent to the calling application, the transaction is guaranteed to exist in the database. Write-ahead logging and automatic rollback and rollforward of transactions during the recovery phase of starting SQL Server assure durability.

Symmetric Server Architecture

SQL Server uses a single-process, multithreaded architecture known as *Symmetric Server Architecture* that provides scalable high performance with efficient use of system resources. With Symmetric Server Architecture, only one memory address space is provided for the DBMS, eliminating the overhead of having to manage shared memory.

Traditional Process/Thread Model

To understand and contrast the architecture of Microsoft SQL Server, it is useful for you to first understand the traditional architectures that have been used by UNIX-based DBMS products. UNIX-based DBMS products are usually structured in one of two ways. In the first way, multiple processes (or *shadow processes*) are used, with one process per user, which makes the system quite resource intensive. The second type of architecture employs a single process that tries to simulate an operating system threading facility by moving in a round-robin way among multiple requests, maintaining a stack for each request and switching to that specific stack for whatever unit is being executed.

> **NOTE** A *stack* is a LIFO (last-in, first-out) data structure kept in memory that basically serves as the control block for the executable unit to the operating system (a *thread* on Microsoft Windows NT, often called a *lightweight process* on other operating systems). A stack stores status data such as function call addresses, passed parameters, and some local variables.

In the first approach, because each process has its own address space, processes must resort to shared memory to communicate with one another. Unfortunately, shared memory is less efficient to use than the private memory of a process's own address space because of the weight of synchronization mechanisms (semaphores, mutexes, and so on) that are needed to avoid collisions while accessing shared memory. In addition, the implementation of stack switching and efficient access to shared memory adds overhead and complexity. Adding complexity to a system is never good. The best way to avoid bugs in software and maximize performance is to keep code simple and, better yet, to write no new code when an existing tried-and-true service exists.

In the second approach—simulated multithreading—the DBMS performs duties that should be performed by the operating system: at best, the DBMS can only simulate operating system behavior and give the illusion of providing threads. Typically, using such an architecture requires that the executing task be trusted to "yield" back to the system so another task can be run. If the task does not yield (because of software or hardware failure), *all* other tasks will be severely, perhaps fatally, affected. Trust is not a good basis upon which to build a multiuser system. Furthermore, if the schedulable unit in an operating system is the process, an instance of even a process that round-robins multiple requests can at most run only one request, no matter how many CPUs are available to service requests. Hence, multiple processes must be executed so that multiple CPUs can be used, with all the aforementioned drawbacks associated with multiple processes.

Microsoft SQL Server Process/Thread Model

A *thread* (more formally called a *thread of execution* and sometimes referred to as a *lightweight process*) is the executable unit on the Windows NT operating system. Threads, not processes, are scheduled for execution by Windows NT.

Rather than move a single thread among all user tasks, SQL Server employs a *pool* of threads. On a single CPU machine, a process using multiple threads is more efficient because even if one thread is not currently runnable (for example, it is waiting for an I/O to complete), another thread may well be runnable and will be executed. In a symmetric multiprocessor system, a process that has multiple threads (such as SQL Server) can use all the processors.

Windows NT provides *symmetric multiprocessor support* that allows execution of threads in parallel on multiple CPUs. Thus, SQL Server's process/thread model allows multiple SQL Server user connections to execute in parallel on multiprocessor hardware. In addition, certain discrete tasks, such as scanning data, can use multiple threads. For some tasks, a request by one user will run simultaneously across multiple CPUs. But more typically, a single user's task will run on one available CPU, another user's task will run on some other CPU, and so forth. (A more complete description of the Windows NT process and thread model is beyond the scope of this book. For more information, I suggest you read *Inside Windows NT* by Helen Custer [Microsoft Press, 1995].)

Because SQL Server uses native Windows NT threads, it automatically scales well to multiprocessor hardware with no special configuration or programming required. In addition, a relatively small amount of memory (about 55 KB) is required for each user connection. A large number of simultaneous users can be connected without consuming a lot of memory on the server.

Each user thread is maintained separately, so if one thread causes an access violation, only that thread will be affected; other threads will continue to operate unaffected. SQL Server's process/thread model greatly exceeds the reliability of typical UNIX-based database servers.

Multiuser Performance

The efficiency of the SQL Server threading model is borne out by its multiuser performance. SQL Server is able to efficiently handle hundreds, even thousands, of simultaneous active users. Built-in thread pooling allows workloads of this magnitude to be performed without the need for an external Transaction (TP) Monitor, which adds cost and complexity to a system.

> **NOTE** There can, of course, never be a simple answer to questions such as "How many users can SQL Server handle?" or "How big a database can it handle?" The answers to these questions depend on the application and its design, required response times and throughput, and the hardware on which the system is running.

A majority of the systems that just a couple of years ago had required a mainframe or large minicomputer-based solution can now be efficiently built, deployed, and managed with SQL Server. Such industry-standard benchmarks as TPC-C can be illuminating. Today's SQL Server can perform workloads that surpass those submitted by the largest mainframe systems of a few years ago. As computer resources continue to grow, SQL Server will extend its reach into systems that traditionally would have required a mainframe solution.

Security

SQL Server provides numerous levels of security. At the outermost layer, SQL Server logon security is integrated directly with Windows NT security. With this *integrated security* in place, SQL Server can take advantage of the security features of Windows NT, such as password encryption, password aging, and maximum length restrictions on passwords.

Without integrated security, the administrator creates user accounts in the network/operating system and in SQL Server. A user logs on to the network and then must log on again to SQL Server. With integrated security, SQL Security Manager automatically copies Windows NT user accounts to SQL Server, providing an easy one-step process to implement integrated security. The user accounts created in Windows NT are automatically used to log a user on to SQL Server.

Integrated security relies on *trusted connections,* which makes use of the impersonation feature of Windows NT. Through impersonation, SQL Server can take on the security context of the Windows NT user account initiating the connection and test whether the Security Identifier (SID) has a valid privilege level. Windows NT impersonation and trusted connections are available with both the Named Pipes and Multi-Protocol network interfaces (Net-Libraries). Integrated security can be used with all the most popular network protocols, including TCP/IP, IPX/SPX, and NetBEUI.

For installations with a mix of named pipes and other clients (such as IPX/SPX or TPC/IC sockets), SQL Server can be installed in a *mixed security* model: named pipe clients will use integrated security and other clients will use standard SQL Server logon security. In addition, an application can request a trusted connection even if SQL Server has not been configured for integrated or mixed security. (You can also choose to disallow trusted connections.)

The Multi-Protocol Net-Library also allows all communications and data between the client application and the server to be optionally encrypted, which prevents even someone using a hardware "sniffer" from eavesdropping on the data. This is accomplished by using the Windows NT remote procedure call (RPC) services to encrypt the network traffic. This encryption uses a 40-bit key for versions of Windows NT Server sold outside of the United States and has an "RC4" designation by the U.S. National Bureau of Standards. The U.S. version of Windows NT Server uses a 128-bit key for much stronger security; however, it is not exportable due to U.S. government restrictions. Since SQL Server uses only the underlying services, the key length is transparent.

Monitoring and Managing Security

SQL Server makes it easy to monitor logon successes and failures. Administrators can simply check the appropriate box in the SQL Server Setup program. When logon monitoring is enabled in this way, each time a user successfully or unsuccessfully attempts to log on to SQL Server, a message is written to the Windows NT event log indicating the time, date, and user who tried to log on.

SQL Server has a number of facilities for managing data security. Access privileges (select, insert, update, and delete) can be granted and revoked to users or groups of users on objects such as tables and views. Execute privilege can be granted on local and extended stored procedures. For example, to prevent a user from directly updating a specific table, you can write a stored procedure that updates the table and then cascades those updates to other tables as necessary. You can grant the user access to execute the stored procedure, thereby ensuring that all updates will take place through the stored procedure, eliminating the possibility of integrity problems arising from ad hoc updates to the base table.

High Availability

In many mission-critical environments, it is imperative that the application be available at all times—24 hours a day, seven days a week. SQL Server helps availability by providing online backup, online maintenance, automatic recovery, disk mirroring, and the ability to configure a fallback (or failover) server.

SQL Server's dynamic online backup allows databases to be backed up while users are actively querying and updating in the database. The SQL Executive service provides a built-in scheduling engine that enables backups to be scheduled to occur automatically, without involving the administrator. Other maintenance tasks, such as diagnostics, design changes (for example, adding a column to a table), and integrity changes can be accomplished without having to shut down SQL Server or restrict user access.

Only a few system-wide configuration changes, such as changing the amount of memory configured for use, require that SQL Server be restarted. Although these activities do not commonly occur in a well-planned and well-deployed production system, they can typically be completed with less than a minute of system downtime if and when they are necessary.

In the event of a system failure, such as a power outage, SQL Server ensures rapid database recovery when services are restored. By using the transaction logs associated with each database, SQL Server quickly recovers each database upon startup, rolling back transactions that had not yet completed and rolling forward transactions that had committed but were not yet written to disk. In addition, the SQL Executive service can be set to continually monitor the state of SQL Server. If an error occurs that causes SQL Server to stop unexpectedly, SQL Executive will detect this and can automatically restart SQL Server with minimal interruption.

In cooperation with shared-disk cluster hardware (such as the Compaq Online Recovery Server), SQL Server 6.5 provides fallback (also known as failover) capability. You can designate a SQL Server *standby server* to back up the *primary server*. Should the primary server fail, the hardware support will signal the standby machine. SQL Server on the standby server will then mount and recover the databases of the primary server and take over its workload. The standby server does not need to be inactive while the primary server is working—it can also be functioning as a primary server. In fact, two primary servers can be configured as standbys for each other as well as for other servers.

Support is built into DB-Library and the SQL Server ODBC driver so that the primary-standby relationship is silently made known to the application when it initially connects. Should the primary server unexpectedly become unavailable, the application can automatically reconnect to the "hot backup" standby server and resume work with no user intervention and minimal disruption.

Distributed Data Processing

SQL Server provides features such as transactional remote stored procedure calls and two-phase commit for easily managing and using data in distributed environments. Although even Microsoft SQL Server version 1.1 supported a two-phase commit protocol, the new Microsoft Distributed Transaction Coordinator (MS DTC) that ships as part of SQL Server 6.5 has made those capabilities obsolete.

MS DTC was designed to be the "vote collector" and coordinator of transactions, and it allows many different types of systems to participate, laying the foundation for ACID transactions among heterogeneous systems. A system participating in a transaction coordinated by MS DTC manages its own work and is called a *resource manager*. This resource manager system communicates with MS DTC, which coordinates all the resource managers participating in the transaction to implement the two-phase commit protocol. Distributed transactions honoring the ACID properties are supported as a whole: the entire distributed transaction at all sites either commits or aborts.

SQL Server 6.5 is the first resource manager coordinated by MS DTC. However, by providing an X/Open DTP XA–compliant interface, MS DTC, and hence SQL Server, also interoperate with several transaction processing monitors, including Encina, Topend, and Tuxedo. MS DTC implements the OLE (Object Linking and Embedding) Transaction interfaces. Because all OLE Transaction interfaces are public, any database system can become an OLE Transaction resource manager and consequently participate in distributed transactions with SQL Server. In the future, Microsoft and other software companies will add other transactional resource managers, such as transactional behaviors, to the file system and workflow management systems. Transactional resource managers would, for example, allow a transaction with ACID properties to span Microsoft SQL Server, the Informix RDBMS, and the NTFS file system. (I can even imagine smart hardware devices participating in such transactions—such as a check-writing transaction in which the transaction is complete only when and if the check is printed correctly.) So far, both Informix and Sybase have also pledged support for MS DTC.

In the first phase of the two-phase commit protocol, all participating resource managers (that is, those that have "enlisted" in the transaction) *prepare to commit*. This means that they have acquired all the locks and resources they need to complete the transaction. MS DTC then acts as a vote collector. If it gets confirmation that all participants are prepared to commit, it signals "go ahead and commit."

The actual *COMMIT* is the second phase of the protocol. If one or more participants notify the system that it cannot successfully prepare the transaction, MS DTC will automatically send a message to all participants indicating that they must abort the transaction. (In this case, an *abort,* rather than a commit, is the second phase of the protocol.) If one or more participants do not report back to MS DTC in phase one, the resource managers that have indicated that they are prepared to commit (but have not yet committed, since they have not received the instruction to do so yet), are said to be *in doubt*. Resource managers that have transactions in doubt will indefinitely hold the locks and resources necessary to ultimately commit or roll back the transaction, preserving the ACID properties. (SQL Server provides a way to force in doubt transactions to abort.)

Another important distributed capability is the ability for a SQL Server to issue remote procedure calls (RPCs) to other SQL Servers. *Remote procedure calls* are stored procedures that can be invoked from a remote server, allowing server-to-server communication. This communication can be accomplished transparently to the client application, since the client can execute a procedure on one server, and that procedure can then invoke a procedure located on a different server. Using RPCs can easily extend the capacity of an application without the added cost of reengineering the client application. And these RPCs can be coordinated by the MS DTC service to ensure that the transactions maintain their ACID properties.

Data Replication

Replication allows you to automatically distribute copies of data from one server to one or more destination servers at one or more remote locations. A key design point of the replication capabilities of Microsoft SQL Server is data integrity. The data at subscribing sites may be slightly out of date, but it will accurately reflect the state of the master copy of the data at some recent point in time. Because of this emphasis on the correctness of data, the replication metaphor used is *publish and subscribe*. For each piece of data participating in replication in the entire system, one site is the designated owner of that data, and that site *publishes* it to the other sites, which *subscribe* to that data. (A given site can publish some data and subscribe to other data.)

Distributed transactions using the two-phase commit protocol guarantee ACID properties, but replication does not. Replication is not strongly consistent (the *C* in ACID). Instead, replication provides *loosely consistent* data. Recall that with the two-phase commit protocol, a transaction is an all-or-nothing proposition and the data is assured to be *strongly consistent.* But inherent in the two-phase commit algorithm is the fact that a failure at any one site makes the entire transaction fail or can keep the transaction in doubt for long periods of time, during which all participants need to hold locks, crippling concurrency.

At first look, you may think a system should require that updates be made at all sites in *real time.* In fact, when the costs of two-phase commit are realized (chiefly, the vulnerability that can result due to a failure at just one node), the most pragmatic solution might be to make changes in *real enough time.*

For example, suppose you run a car rental agency, with 500 rental counters worldwide, and you maintain a customer profile table containing 500,000 renters who belong to your Gold Card program. You want to store this customer profile locally at all 500 rental counters so that even if a communication failure occurs, the profile will be available wherever a Gold Card member might walk up to do business. Although all sites should have up-to-date records of all customers, it would be disastrous to insist that an update of the Gold Card profile must occur as part of a two-phase transaction for all 500 sites or not at all. With this scenario, because of the realities of worldwide communications, or because at one site a storm might have knocked out the power, it is likely that you would seldom be able to perform a simple update to the customer profile.

Replication is a much better solution in such a case. The master customer profile table would be maintained at your corporate headquarters. Replication publishes this data, and the rental counters then subscribe to this information. When customer data is changed, or when a customer is added or removed, these changes (and *only* the changes) are propagated to all the subscribing sites. In a well-connected network, the time delay might be just a few seconds. If a particular site is unavailable, no other sites are affected—they still get their changes. When the unavailable site is back online, the changes are automatically propagated and the subscriber is brought up to date. At any time, a given rental counter may not have exactly the same information as the corporate site—it might be slightly out of date. The data at the rental counter is consistent with the state of the data at the corporate headquarters at some earlier time; it is not necessarily currently consistent with the corporate site data. This is what is meant by *loosely consistent,* as opposed to the *strongly consistent* model of two-phase commit in which all sites (or none) immediately reflect the change.

Although a time delay can occur in loosely consistent systems, maintaining transactional consistency is one of the chief design points of SQL Server replication. If multiple updates occur as a single atomic transaction to data being replicated, the entire transaction will also be replicated. At the subscribing site, the transaction will either entirely commit or it will again be replicated until it commits.

With SQL Server, data can be replicated continuously or at specified intervals. It can be replicated in its entirety or as filtered subsets (known as *horizontal* and *vertical partitions*). In addition to replication to other SQL Servers, version 6.5 can replicate to Microsoft Access databases, ORACLE databases, or other ODBC subscribers (so long as they provide an appropriate ODBC driver).

Unlike SQL Server, some products on the market promote replication as an "Update Anywhere-Anytime-Anyway" model. However, this model has inherently unstable behavior if many nodes participate and update activity is moderate to heavy.[1] Updates made at multiple sites will conflict with one another and must be reconciled. A small system with few changes might appear to use the "Update Anywhere-Anytime-Anyway" model effectively, but a large system with a tenfold increase in nodes and traffic gives a thousandfold increase in deadlocks or reconciliations. Before long, even accurate reconciliation will be impossible because updates will have been made based on data that has not been accurately reconciled. The system will degrade into an inconsistent state, with no clear way to fix it or even to know what is the "correct" state.

Systems Management

The difficulty of systems management is probably the single biggest obstacle that has inhibited mass deployment of client/server solutions. Far from being a "downsized" version of the mainframe, today's distributed client/server system may be deployed on dozens or even hundreds of distributed servers, all of which must be controlled to the same exacting standards as mainframe production software systems. The issues here reside both inside and outside of the database environment. SQL Server provides a comprehensive architecture and tools for managing the database and related activities.

SQL Enterprise Manager

SQL Server's SQL Enterprise Manager is a major advancement in making client/server deployments manageable. Easy to use, SQL Enterprise Manager supports centralized management of all aspects of multiple SQL Servers, including managing security, events, alerts, scheduling, backup, server configuration, tuning, and replication. SQL Enterprise Manager allows SQL Server database schemas and objects such as tables, views, and triggers to be created, modified,

---

1. Gray, Helland, O'Neil, and Shasha, "The Dangers of Replication and a Solution," SIGMOD (1996). SIGMOD (Special Interest Group Management of Data) is a yearly database-oriented conference for developers. For more information, see http://bunny.cs.uiuc.edu.

and copied. Because groups of servers can be associated, SQL Enterprise Manager can manage hundreds of servers simultaneously.

Although it can run on the same computer as the SQL Server engine, SQL Enterprise Manager offers the same management capabilities while running on any Windows NT workstation or Windows NT server in the environment. SQL Enterprise Manager also runs on Windows 95, although a few capabilities are not available in this environment (most notably the ability to use Service Control Manager, a feature of Windows NT, to remotely start and stop SQL Server). In addition, the efficient client/server architecture of SQL Server makes it practical to use the remote access (dial-up networking) capabilities of Windows NT and Windows 95 for administration and management.

SQL Enterprise Manager provides an easy-to-use interface, as shown in the illustration below. You can perform even complex tasks with just a few mouse clicks.

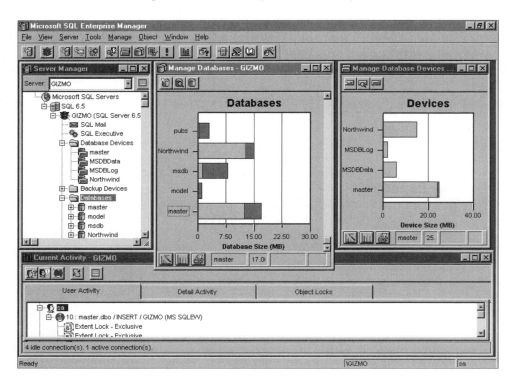

SQL Enterprise Manager relieves you from having to know the specific steps and syntax to complete a job. You can use the Database Maintenance Plan Wizard, shown below, to set up and schedule key maintenance tasks to help keep your system running properly.

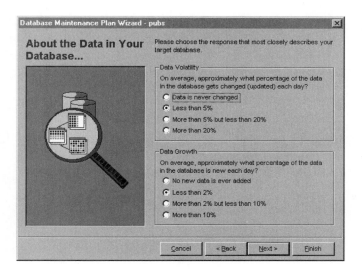

Distributed Management Objects

In the Microsoft Windows 95 and Microsoft Windows NT operating systems, *Microsoft SQL Server Distributed Management Objects (SQL-DMO)* provides 32-bit Automation (formerly known as OLE Automation). These objects, properties, methods, and collections are used to write scripts and programs that can administer multiple SQL Servers distributed across a network. SQL Enterprise Manager is built entirely with SQL-DMO. You can customize your own specific management needs using SQL-DMO, or you can integrate management of SQL Server into other tools you use or provide.

All SQL Server functions are exposed in the form of objects, methods, and properties. The SQL-DMO model simplifies the management "surface" of SQL Server by organizing management functions in terms of the SQL Server object model. The primary object is SQLServer, which contains a collection of Database objects. The Database object contains a collection of Table, View, and StoredProcedure objects. Objects contain properties (SQLServer.Name = "MARKETING_SVR") and methods (SQLServer.Start or SQLServer.Shutdown).

Here are some examples of SQL-DMO objects and methods:

Object.Method	Action
SQLServer.Shutdown	Stops a SQL Server
SQLServer.Start	Starts a SQL Server
Database.Dump	Performs a database dump
Index.UpdateStatistics	Updates optimizer information for indexes
Database.Table.Add	Adds a table to a database

The SQL-DMO object model is comprehensive, consisting of more than 70 distinct objects and more than 1500 COM interfaces. The organization of these objects greatly reduces the task of learning and fully using SQL Server management components, as shown in Figure 2-2.

Any 32-bit Automation controlling application can harness the power and services of SQL-DMO. Probably the most common such Automation controller is Microsoft Visual Basic.

Automation and Visual Basic Scripting

The power of using an ActiveX interface (Automation) for SQL Server management becomes clear when you consider the potential of using a robust language such as Visual Basic as a scripting environment for administrative tasks. The following sample code lists the name and space available on all databases on a server. This code is simple, compact, easy to write and read, and yet very powerful. (Traditionally, programming such a task would have required several pages of much more complex C code.)

```
Dim MyServer as New SQLServer    'Declare the SQL Server Object
MyServer.Name = "MARKETING_SVR"
MyServer.Login = "sa"
MyServer.Connect         ' Connect to the SQL Server
' list the name, space available for all databases
For each MyDB in MyServer.Databases
    Print MyDB.Name, MyDB.SpaceAvailable
Next MyDB
MyServer.Disconnect        ' Disconnect
```

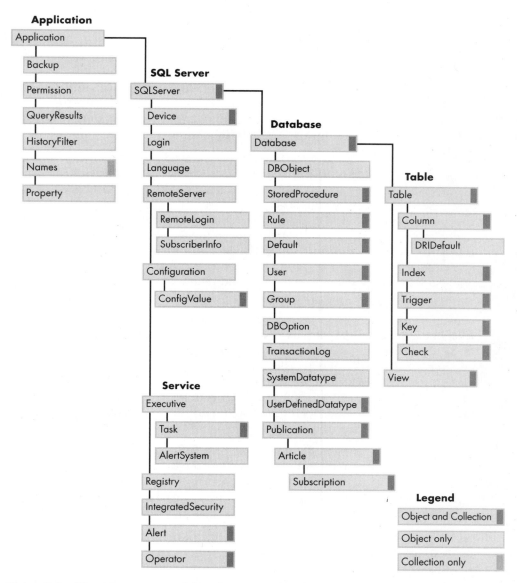

Application

- Application
  - Backup
  - Permission
  - QueryResults
  - HistoryFilter
  - Names
  - Property

SQL Server

- SQLServer
  - Device
  - Login
  - Language
  - RemoteServer
    - RemoteLogin
    - SubscriberInfo
  - Configuration
    - ConfigValue

Service

- Executive
  - Task
  - AlertSystem
- Registry
- IntegratedSecurity
- Alert
- Operator

Database

- Database
  - DBObject
  - StoredProcedure
  - Rule
  - Default
  - User
  - Group
  - DBOption
  - TransactionLog
  - SystemDatatype
  - UserDefinedDatatype
  - Publication
    - Article
      - Subscription

Table

- Table
  - Column
    - DRIDefault
  - Index
  - Trigger
  - Key
  - Check
- View

Legend

- Object and Collection
- Object only
- Collection only

Figure 2-2. *The SQL-DMO model makes using the objects easy.*

SQL Executive

SQL Executive is an active, intelligent agent that plays an integral role in the management of the SQL Server environment. It provides a full-function scheduling engine designed to support regular tasks for the management and administration of SQL Server, and it allows you to schedule your own tasks and programs. SQL Executive plays a fundamental role in replication, acting as the mechanism that runs the distribution tasks that propagate data changes to subscribing sites. It is also the foundation for the SQL Server alerting system.

SQL Executive is a Windows NT–based service that can be started when Windows NT starts. It can also be controlled and configured from within SQL Enterprise Manager or SQL Service Manager. SQL Executive is entirely driven by entries in a SQL Server table that act as its control block. Clients never directly communicate with or connect to SQL Executive to add or modify scheduled tasks. Instead, they simply make the appropriate entries in the SQL Server table (although this typically occurs through SQL Enterprise Manager via a simple dialog box that's similar to a typical calendar program). At startup, SQL Executive connects to the SQL Server that contains its task table and then loads the list of tasks.

SQL Executive, like the SQL Server engine, is a single multithreaded process. It runs in its own process space and manages the creation of Windows NT threads to execute scheduled tasks. Its discrete managed subsystems (for replication, task management, and event alerting) are responsible for all aspects of processing specific tasks. When tasks are completed (successfully or not), the subsystem returns a result status (with optional messages) to SQL Executive. SQL Executive then records the completion status in the Windows NT event log and task history table in SQL Server and optionally sends e-mail to the designated administrator reporting the task status.

The event/alert subsystem gives SQL Server its ability to support proactive management. The primary role of the event/alert subsystem is to respond to events by raising alerts and invoking responses. As triggering activities (or user-defined activities) occur in the system, an event is posted to the Windows NT event log. The event log then notifies SQL Executive that an event has occurred.

SQL Executive determines whether any alerts have been defined for this event by examining the event's error number, severity, database of origin, and message text. If an alert has been defined (in the alert table), the administrator(s) can be alerted via e-mail, pager, or by raising a Simple Network Management Protocol (SNMP) trap (discussed later in this chapter). Or a SQL Executive on-demand task can be invoked and can take corrective action. (For example, SQL Executive might automatically expand a database that is almost full.)

If no alerts are defined locally, the event can be forwarded to another server for processing. This feature allows groups of servers to be monitored centrally so that alerts and administrators can be defined once and then applied to multiple servers. Beyond the database environment, Microsoft Systems Management Server (SMS)—a BackOffice component—is available to provide key services to manage the overall software configuration of all the desktops and servers in the environment.

SQL Server Utilities and Extensions

SQL Server also includes utilities and extensions that provide increased functionality, such as Internet enabling, monitoring capability, easy setup, and easy data importing.

SQL Server Web Assistant and Internet Enabling

SQL Server provides dynamic ways in which to work with the Internet: SQL Server Web Assistant and interoperability with Microsoft Internet Information Server (IIS). Although both the SQL Server Web Assistant and IIS enable SQL Server data to be used with Web pages, they satisfy different needs.

SQL Server Web Assistant generates HTML files from the result sets of SQL Server queries, making it simple to publish SQL Server data on the Internet. Let's say, for example, that a parts supplier keeps its inventory list in SQL Server. The supplier could publish its current parts inventory as a Web page (an HTML file) using SQL Server Web Assistant. SQL Server Web Assistant allows an ad hoc query or stored procedure to be submitted, provides some simple formatting capabilities, allows for the inclusion of links to other Web pages, and allows a template to be used for more advanced formatting. The output of the query is written as an HTML 2.0 table, and a Web page is created. The process to create or update the Web page can be automated by SQL Server Web Assistant to occur at a regular interval or whenever the data changes (via a trigger).

SQL Server Web Assistant is distinct from but complementary to the IIS in Microsoft BackOffice. With SQL Server Web Assistant, users browsing the Web page work separately from SQL Server, because the data on the Web page has been extracted. SQL Server Web Assistant does not use or require IIS, and a SQL Server Web Assistant page can be viewed using any Internet browser.

IIS uses SQL Server's high performance native ODBC interface to allow SQL queries to be fired from a Web page when a user accesses a particular region on the page. The results are then dynamically retrieved and combined with the HTML file for up-to-date viewing. In addition to SQL Server Web Assistant and the dynamic query capabilities enabled with IIS, SQL Server is Internet-enabled in several other important ways. By minimizing network traffic and handshaking, SQL Server is inherently designed for efficient client/server computing. Extremely rich requests can be packaged via stored procedures or Transact-SQL batches for resolution entirely at the server with only the results sent back to the initiating client application. This capability has been a hallmark of SQL Server's client/server architecture from the outset, but nowhere is it more important than on the Internet, where network speed and bandwidth are often quite limited. In addition, SQL Server's networking architecture allows for ease of use and security on the Internet, including network name resolution. For example, Internet users can connect via a friendly name such as "sql.microsoft.com" instead of via an arcane IP address such as 200.154.54.678:1433. Secure encryption of data over the Internet is also possible.

SQL Trace

SQL Trace is a Win32-based graphical utility that allows database administrators and application developers to monitor and record database activity. SQL Trace can display all server activity in real time, or it can create filters that focus on the actions of particular users, applications, or types of commands. SQL Trace can display any SQL statement or stored procedure sent to any SQL Server (assuming your security privileges allow it) as well as the output or response sent back to the initiating client. The capabilities of SQL Trace provide an important tool for tuning and debugging applications and for auditing and profiling the use of the SQL Server.

SQL Service Manager

SQL Service Manager, shown below, manages the SQL Server, SQL Executive, and MS DTC services. It provides a simple way to start, stop, or check the state of any of these services. Many applications have "borrowed" its original intuitive traffic-light graphic as a way to provide a simple visual representation of a process's state.

Windows NT Performance Monitor Integration

SQL Server provides an extension DLL (SQLCTR60.DLL) that integrates with the Windows NT Performance Monitor and graphically displays important performance statistics, such as memory usage, number of users, transactions per second, and CPU use as well as many others (there are more than 75 such counters). Integrating with the Windows NT Performance Monitor is advantageous because it allows you to use a single tool to measure all aspects of a system's performance. If SQL Server simply provided its own performance-monitoring tool, it would still be necessary to check the performance of the operating system and network. Integration with the system performance monitor provides "one-stop shopping." A Performance Monitor graph is shown in the illustration below.

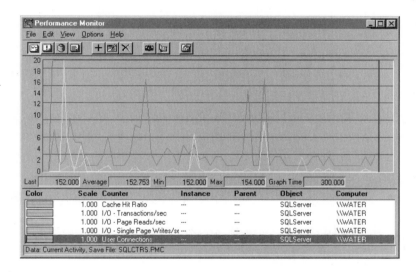

Using Performance Monitor, you can set an "alert" on any statistic that is being monitored; when a predefined threshold is reached, Windows NT will automatically execute a predefined command. For example, you can set an alert that is generated when a SQL Server database's transaction log becomes 90 percent full. The alert will execute a batch program to back up the log and purge it, freeing up space for new transactions.

SQL Security Manager

SQL Security Manager simplifies the management of user logons with SQL Server. It provides an interface to integrate Windows NT user accounts directly into SQL Server without having to redefine each user logon. SQL Server uses the Windows NT user accounts to validate database users and administrators.

SQL Client Configuration Utility

The SQL Client Configuration Utility is used with applications written with the DB-Library API. You use it to set up specific networking options for the application. In most cases, network name resolution is now automatic and the SQL Client Configuration Utility is usually not required.

SQL Server Setup

SQL Server's graphical Setup program allows SQL Server installation to be performed with a degree of ease and speed unprecedented for a full-feature DBMS. If the defaults are chosen, SQL Server can be installed in 5 to 10 minutes, depending on the speed of the computer. A custom installation typically takes well under 30 minutes. Traditional DBMS products usually require several days for installation and often require that you enroll in training classes before installing the product. SQL Server Setup can even install the product on a remote computer, a particularly useful feature if you manage a large number of servers. Setup initialization is easily specified so that it can be fully automated for numerous installations, or you can encapsulate the installation of SQL Server in the rest of an application's installation process.

After you've installed SQL Server, you use the Setup program to configure networking choices and server environment options (such as the security mode desired). The program also provides a simple uninstall process.

ISQL/w & ISQL

Having a simple interactive window in which to submit basic SQL commands and get results is essential to a database developer—as a hammer is to a carpenter. Even though other, more sophisticated, power tools are useful, there is always need for the basics. SQL Server provides the basics in two styles: ISQL/w and ISQL.

For interactive use, ISQL/w (ISQLW.EXE) provides a clean and simple Windows-based interface. It provides a graphical representation of SHOWPLAN, the steps chosen by the optimizer for query execution. ISQL/w allows for multiple windows so that simultaneous database connections (to one or more servers) can exist and be separately sized, tiled, or minimized.

ISQL (ISQL.EXE) is a character-based command-line utility. Every parameter, including the SQL statement or the name of the file containing the statement, can be passed to this character-based utility. Upon exit, it can return status values to Windows NT that can be checked within a command file (.CMD or .BAT). Consequently, programs commonly launch scripts of SQL commands by spawning the character-based ISQL utility and passing the appropriate parameters and filenames. SQL Server Setup itself spawns ISQL.EXE numerous times with scripts that install various database objects and permissions.

Bulk Copy Utility

SQL Server provides a character-based utility called **bcp**, or "bulk copy" (BCP.EXE), for flexible importing and exporting of SQL Server data. Similar to ISQL, **bcp** allows all parameters to be passed to it and is often called from command files. A special set of functions exists in DB-Library that lets you easily create a custom loader or unloader for your application; the **bcp** utility is a generalized wrapper application that calls these functions. SQL Enterprise Manager and SQL-DMO also provide facilities to simplify the transfer of data into or out of SQL Server, but their emphasis is on data migration between SQL Servers. The **bcp** utility provides an important capability by allowing you to specify the exact data format to be read or written, thus giving you the ability to exchange data with other data sources.

SNMP Integration

Support for Simple Network Management Protocol (SNMP, a standard protocol within TCP/IP environments) is provided via the SQL Server Management Information Block (MIB, another standard of the SNMP and TCP/IP environment). A group of database vendors, including Microsoft, cooperated in defining a standard MIB that would report certain status data about a database environment for monitoring purposes.

> **NOTE** This group was a subcommittee of the IETF, the Internet Engineering Task Force, and the draft specification is known as "IETF SNMP RDBMS-MIB (RFC 1697)." The SQL Server MIB is generally based on this proposal but provides additional data beyond that called for in the specification.

For example, status information (such as whether SQL Server is currently running, when it was last started, and how many users are connected) is reported to SNMP via this MIB. A variety of SNMP management and monitoring tools exist and can access this data. If, for example, you use Hewlett-Packard's OpenView or Computer Associate's CA-Unicenter in managing your network, the SQL Server MIB enables those tools to also monitor multiple statistics regarding SQL Server.

SQL Server also supports the ability to raise *SNMP traps*. An SNMP trap sends notification to the *SNMP agent* that some type of change in status or condition has occurred. The SNMP agent can then forward that notification to prespecified workstations that are running SNMP monitoring application(s). This means that it is simple to configure alerts within SQL Enterprise Manager that will notify your network management application, such as OpenView or CA-Unicenter, of some situation that warrants attention (that the database should be expanded in size, for example).

SQL Server Books Online

In addition to being available in printed form, all SQL Server documentation is available online. A powerful viewer makes it simple to find and search for topics within seconds. (The viewer is the same one used by MSDN, the Microsoft Developer Network Library, which provides technical information to developers by subscription.)

Even if you favor printed books, you'll appreciate the speed and convenience of the search capabilities of SQL Server Books Online. In addition, because of the lead time required in the production of the printed manuals that ship with SQL Server, SQL Server Books Online is more complete and accurate than those manuals. Because this book cannot hope to and does not try to replace the complete documentation set, the CD-ROM included with this book also contains the complete SQL Server Books Online documentation.

Development Interfaces

SQL Server provides several development interfaces, supporting client *and* server application development. These interfaces—the DB-Library, ODBC, the Embedded SQL precompiler, and Microsoft Open Data Services—are described below.

DB-Library

DB-Library is a SQL Server–specific API that provides all the necessary macros and functions for an application to open connections, format queries, send them to the server, and process the results. It also includes the special purpose bulk copy interface used by the **bcp** utility. You can write custom DB-Library applications using either C/C++ or Microsoft Visual Basic (or any programming language that is capable of calling a C function).

DB-Library is the original programming interface to SQL Server. Libraries are provided for MS-DOS, Windows 3.1, Windows 95, and Windows NT. (The Windows NT library for Intel computers is the same library used for Windows 95, so you can write a single application that targets both environments.) Developers are granted licensed rights to redistribute the DB-Library runtimes royalty-free.

ODBC

ODBC (Open Database Connectivity) is an API for database access that is both a formal and de facto industry standard. Besides being the most popular database interface used by applications today, ODBC has gained status as the formal call-level interface standard by ANSI and ISO. Microsoft SQL Server provides a high-performance, *native* ODBC interface for all Windows-based programming environments, and like DB-Library, it can be distributed royalty-free with any application. The SQL Server ODBC driver implements every function in the

ODBC 2.0 specification. In "ODBC-speak," this makes it fully "Level 2" (the highest level) conformant.

ODBC drivers for other operating systems (Macintosh System 7, many flavors of UNIX, and OS/2) are available from Visigenic. (You can check out Visigenic's Web site at http://www.visigenic.com.) Microsoft licenses the source code for the SQL Server ODBC driver to Visigenic so that high-performance interfaces are available for those operating systems as well.

Most new application development is probably best targeted toward ODBC, rather than DB-Library. If you are already using DB-Library or have a lot invested in DB-Library in terms of knowledge and applications, then don't think you must abandon it. DB-Library will remain supported indefinitely, and that's why it was significantly enhanced for SQL Server version 6.5. In the future, though, you should expect fewer enhancements for DB-Library. It will likely continue to be maintained simply for backward compatibility. (You may also be steered to DB-Library if your application must include an MS-DOS version or if you will be directly using the **bcp** library, for which there is no current ODBC equivalent.)

If you are starting new development, however, most applications would be better served using ODBC. Having had the benefit of learning from DB-Library and going through a long design and specification phase, I've found that ODBC is a simpler, more elegant API than DB-Library. Despite some myths to the contrary, ODBC is as fast or faster than DB-Library. We call the ODBC driver for SQL Server a *native interface* to make it clear that it is not mapped onto DB-Library and does not incur more overhead than DB-Library. It directly reads and writes the SQL Server data stream protocol, Tabular Data Stream (TDS), just as DB-Library does. Perhaps the best proof of Microsoft's confidence in its performance is the fact that ODBC is used in SQL Server's published performance benchmarks. Since the name of the game in benchmarking is to eke out every last ounce of performance, if using the ODBC driver caused even a tiny slowdown, you can bet we'd use DB-Library instead.

ESQL for C

SQL Server provides an Embedded SQL precompiler (ESQL for C) that allows developers to write SQL Server applications by "embedding" the SQL queries directly in their C source code. Many minicomputer and mainframe developers are already accustomed to this style of programming, and ESQL might be a natural choice for that reason. In addition, Microsoft has licensed some of the Embedded SQL run-time environment to Microfocus, the leading provider of Cobol compilers and tools. Microfocus offers an embedded SQL interface for SQL Server directly in its Cobol development environment.

Open Data Services

SQL Server offers an open API for developing server-based gateway and connectivity applications that work in conjunction with SQL Server. Microsoft Open Data Services (ODS) is an event-driven API that provides a programmable gateway platform for server applications that can access any data source. ODS can be used to develop custom database gateways, data-driven event alerters, external program triggers, request auditing, extended stored procedure DLLs, and more. ODS is actually a core part of the SQL Server architecture and benefits from the high-performance architecture. It provides all the network, connection, and thread management that SQL Server uses.

ODS-based applications can function as stand-alone gateways, or as data-access servers, supporting connections from the same client platforms as SQL Server. They can also integrate with SQL Server directly through remote stored procedure calls.

Microsoft TransAccess uses ODS to provide data connectivity from SQL Server to the MVS CICS environment, including access to DB/2, VSAM, and IMS data. In addition, ODS is used by many other software vendors to provide SQL Server–compatible gateways to popular host computing platforms, including IBM DB2, IBM SQL/DS, CICS, IBM AS/400, and others.

SUMMARY

The Microsoft SQL Server component and product family, including the SQL Server RDBMS, visual systems management tools, distributed systems components, open client/server interfaces, and visual development tools, provides a complete and robust platform for developing and deploying large-scale applications.

The remainder of this book concentrates on the capabilities and uses of the SQL Server engine, which is the foundation of the product.

Architectural
Overview

3

SQL Server Architecture

Overview

Throughout this book, I'll describe functional characteristics and features of the SQL Server engine. But first I'll present an overview of what makes up that engine and some basic concepts about how it works. I'll try to provide a general conceptual understanding that's specific enough to allow some insight. If you are interested only in the functional operations of SQL Server and you want to simply consider everything as a "black box operation," you can safely skip this chapter. Or if you are new to databases and don't have a clear picture of what makes up an RDBMS, you might want to come back to this chapter after you're a bit more familiar with SQL Server's external capabilities. The heart of this chapter will discuss much of what happens inside the engine. If you are a serious SQL Server developer, you'll benefit by understanding what's happening inside the box, or at least in a few compartments of it. I'll also try to point out system behavior that might affect your application development and what action you might consider because of it.

The SQL Server Engine

Figure 3-1 on the following page shows the general architecture of SQL Server. In order to be both understandable and accurate, I've made some simplifying omissions and I've ignored certain "helper" modules.

> **NOTE** Much of the information in this chapter is based on internal Microsoft design documentation. As such, the information is a composite that was built up over several years, and the contributors to this information were numerous.[1]

---

1. Special thanks go to Betty O'Neil, who reworked, updated, and improved much of the internal documentation in 1995.

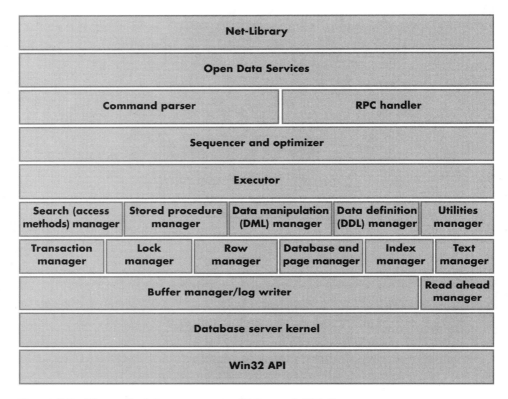

Figure 3-1. *The underlying structure of Microsoft SQL Server.*

Now let's look in detail at these major modules.

The Net-Library

The Net-Library (often called Net-Lib, but in this book, we'll use Net-Library) abstraction layer enables SQL Server to read from and write to many different network protocols, and each such protocol (such as TCP/IP sockets) can have a specific driver. The Net-Library layer makes it relatively easy to support many different network protocols without having to change the core server code to do so.

A specific Net-Library is basically a driver that is specific to a particular network interprocess communication (IPC) mechanism. (Be careful not to confuse my use of "driver" with a device driver. All code in SQL Server, including Net-Library, makes calls only to the Win32 subsystem of Windows NT, never directly into privileged mode.) SQL Server uses a common internal interface between Open Data Services (ODS), which manages its use of the network, and each Net-Library. All network-specific considerations that would go into development to support a new and different network protocol are confined to simply writing a new Net-Library. In addition, multiple Net-Libraries, one for each network IPC mechanism in use, can be loaded simultaneously.

SQL Server uses the Net-Library abstraction layer at both the server and the client machines, making it possible to support several clients simultaneously on different networks. Windows NT allows multiple protocol stacks to be in use simultaneously on one system. (You can easily configure multiple Net-Libraries via the SQL Server Setup program.)

It is important to distinguish between the IPC mechanisms and the underlying network protocols. *IPC mechanisms* used by SQL Server include named pipes, remote procedure call (RPC), SPX, and Windows Sockets. *Network protocols* used include TCP/IP, NetBEUI, NWLink (IPX/SPX), VINES IP, Appletalk, and DecNet. Two Net-Libraries, Multi-Protocol and Named Pipes, can be used simultaneously over multiple network protocols (NetBEUI, NWLink IPX/SPX, and TCP/IP). You can have multiple network protocols in your environment and still use only one Net-Library.

The Multi-Protocol Net-Library uses the RPC services of Windows NT. It could just as well have been called the "RPC Net-Library," but "Multi-Protocol" better conveys its key benefit. Because this Net-Library uses the RPC services of Windows NT, it is optionally able to encrypt all traffic (including requests, data, and passwords) between the client application and the SQL Server engine.

Both named pipes and RPC services in Windows NT support impersonation of security contexts to provide an *integrated login capability* (also known as "integrated security" and "trusted connections"). Instead of requiring a separate user ID/password login each time a connection to SQL Server is requested, SQL Server can impersonate the security context of the user running the application that requests the connection. If that user has sufficient privilege (or is part of a Windows NT domain group that does), the connection is established.

Some History...

Had RPCs been available years ago, we might never have invented Net-Library. When SQL Server ran only on OS/2, it supported only named pipes. We wanted to broaden this support to SPX and TCP/IP and maybe other protocols, too, so we developed Net-Library as an abstraction layer. Now RPC services are available with so many network protocols that we might well have decided that RPC alone met the need.

You can configure the size of the network packet sent by SQL Server. The client application can request a specific packet size of 512 bytes or greater using an option provided in DB-Library and ODBC. (Theoretically, the limit is 32 KB, but based on our internal performance testing, that's higher than you'd want to use.) If the client application does not request a specific network packet size, the default packet size (4096 bytes), which is configurable for the SQL Server installation (by **sp_configure**), is used. Empirical testing has shown that this default is a good choice for general use. However, for large result sets or to move large amounts of text data, you might want to increase the packet size. It's usually not optimal to use a packet size of more than 8192 bytes (8 KB).

Which Net-Library Is Fastest?

Strictly speaking, the TCP/IP Sockets Net-Library has been shown to be the fastest based on internal network testing. In a pure network test that does nothing except throw packets back and forth between Net-Library pairs, the TCP/IP Sockets Net-Library is perhaps 30 percent faster than the slowest Net-Library. But for LAN environments and applications, I doubt that the speed of the Net-Library makes much of a difference. The network interface is generally not a limiting factor in a well-designed application's performance.

On a LAN, a Net-Library's speed is probably not an important consideration. Turning on encryption with the Multi-Protocol Net-Library does cause a performance hit—it's the slowest Net-Library option, although only when encryption is turned on. Again, however, most applications probably wouldn't notice the difference. Your best bet is to choose the Net-Library that matches your network protocols and provides the services you need in terms of unified login, encryption, and dynamic name resolution. (I'll explain these choices further in Chapter 4.)

Open Data Services

Open Data Services functions as the client manager for SQL Server. ODS manages the network: it listens for new connections, cleans up failed connections, acknowledges "attentions" (cancellations of commands), coordinates threading services to SQL Server, and returns result sets, messages, and status back to the client. SQL Server clients and the server speak a private protocol known as *tabular data stream* (TDS). TDS is a self-describing data stream. In other words, TDS contains *tokens* that describe column names, datatypes, events (such as cancellations), and return statuses in the "conversation" between client and server. Encoded in TDS, the server notifies the client that it is sending a result set, indicates the number of columns and datatypes of the result set, and so on. Neither clients nor servers write directly to TDS. Instead, the open interfaces of DB-Library and ODBC at the client emit TDS. Both use a client implementation of the Net-Library.

Net-Libraries are paired. So, for example, if the client application is using a Named Pipes Net-Library, the SQL Server must also be listening on a Named Pipes Net-Library. ODS accepts new connections, and if a client unexpectedly disconnects (for example, a user reboots the client computer instead of cleanly terminating the application), resources such as locks held by that client are automatically freed.

You can use the ODS open interface to help you write a server application, such as a gateway. (MicroDecisionware, subsequently purchased by Sybase, developed its successful database gateway using Microsoft Open Data Services.) Such applications are called *ODS server applications*. SQL Server is an ODS application, and it uses the same DLL (OPENDS60.DLL) used by all other ODS applications.

After SQL Server puts result sets into a network output buffer that's equal in size to the configured packet size, the Net-Library dispatches the buffer to the client. The first packet is sent as soon as the network output buffer (the *write buffer*) is full or, if an entire result set fits in one packet, when the batch is completed. In some exceptional operations (such as providing progress information for database dumping or providing DBCC messages), the output buffer will be flushed and sent even before it is full or before the batch completes.

SQL Server has two input buffers (or *read buffers*) and one output buffer per client. Double-buffering is needed for the reads because while SQL Server is reading a stream of data from the client connection, it must also be looking for a possible *attention,* a cancellation request from the client. (This allows that "Query That Ate Cleveland" to be canceled directly from the issuer. Although the ability to cancel a request is extremely important, it's relatively unusual among client/server products.) Attentions can be thought of as "out-of-band" data, although they can be sent with network protocols that do not explicitly have an out-of-band channel. This module's developer has experimented with double-buffering and asynchronous techniques for the write buffers. But because these didn't provide any substantial performance improvement, the single network output buffer works nicely. Even though the writes are not posted asynchronously, we do not need to write through the Windows NT caching for these as we do for writes to disk.

Of course, these issues are not the same types of transaction recoverability issues that necessitate write-ahead logging for disk writes. (Write-ahead logging is discussed in more detail later in this chapter.) Because Microsoft Windows provides caching of network writes, write operations appear to complete immediately with no significant latency. But if several writes are issued to the same client and the client is not currently reading data from the network, eventually the network cache will become full and the write will block. This essentially acts as a throttle. As long as the client application is processing results, SQL Server will have a few buffers queued up and ready for the client connection to process. But if the client's queue is already stacked up with results and is not processing them, SQL Server will stall sending them, and the network write operation to that connection will have to wait. Since the server has only one output buffer per client, data cannot be sent to that client connection until it reads information off the network to free up room for the write to complete. (Writes to other client connections are not held up, however; only those for the laggard client are affected.)

SQL Server adds rows to the output buffer as it retrieves them. Often, SQL Server can still be gathering additional rows that meet the query's criteria while rows already retrieved are being sent to the client.

Stalled network writes can also affect page locks. For example, if READ COMMITTED isolation is in effect (the default), a share lock can normally be released after SQL Server has completed its scan of that page of data. (Exclusive locks used for changing data must always be held until the end of the transaction to ensure that the changes can be rolled back.) However, if the scan finds more qualifying data and the output buffer is not free, the scan stalls. When the previous network write completes, the output buffer will be available and the scan will resume. But, as stated above, that write won't complete until the client connection "drains" (reads) some data to free up some room in the *pipe* (the virtual circuit between the SQL Server and client connection).

In summary, if a client connection delays processing results that are sent to it, concurrency issues can result because locks are being held longer than they otherwise would be. A sort of chain reaction occurs: If the client connection has not read several outstanding network packets, further writing of the output buffer at the SQL Server side must wait. The pipe is full. Since the output buffer is not available, the scan for data can also be suspended because no space is available to add qualifying rows. Since the scan is held up, any lock on the data cannot be released. In short, if a client application does not process results in a timely manner, database concurrency can suffer.

The size of the network buffer can also affect the speed at which the client receives the first result set. As you read earlier, the output buffer is sent when the batch, not simply the command, is done, even if the buffer is not full. (A *batch* is one or more commands sent together for execution. For example, if you are using ISQL.EXE, a batch is the collection of all the commands that appear before a specific GO statement.) If two queries exist in the same batch, and the first query has only a small amount of data, its results won't get sent back to the client until the second query is either done or has supplied enough data to fill the output buffer. If both queries are fast, this is not a problem. But suppose the first query is fast and the second is slow. And suppose the first query returns 1000 bytes of data. If the network packet size is 4096 bytes, the first result set will wait in the output buffer for the second query to fill it. The obvious solution here is either to make the first command its own batch or to make the network packet size smaller. The first solution is probably the best one in this case, since it would typically be difficult to fine-tune your application to determine the best buffer size for each command. But this should not be inferred to mean that each command should be its own batch. Quite the contrary is true. In fact, under normal circumstances, grouping multiple commands into a single batch is efficient and recommended since it reduces the amount of handshaking that must occur between client and server, thus saving time.

By default, SQL Server always listens on named pipes. You can add other Net-Library interfaces. You can also remove the Named Pipes Net-Library, but I wouldn't recommend it. All the other Net-Libraries require a network. Because named pipe services exist in Windows NT even when no network is present, using named pipes leaves you a back door into SQL Server, even if your network becomes totally nonfunctional.

Figure 3-2, on the following page, shows the path from the SQL Server client application to the SQL Server engine and shows the Net-Library interfaces. At the server side, ODS provides functionality that mirrors that of ODBC or DB-Library at the client. Calls exist for an ODS server application to describe and send result sets, to convert values between datatypes, to assume the security context associated with the specific connection being managed, and to raise errors and messages to the client application.

ODS uses an event-driven programming model. Requests from servers and clients trigger events that your server application must respond to. Using the ODS API, you create a custom routine, called an *event handler,* for each possible type of event. Essentially, the ODS library drives a server application by calling its custom event handlers in response to incoming requests.

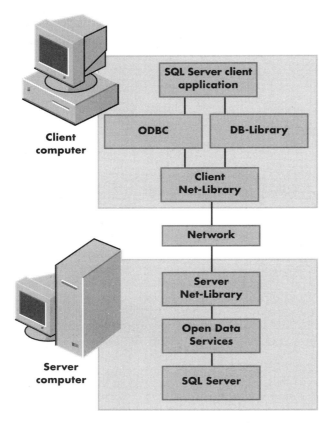

Figure 3-2. *The path from the SQL Server client application to the SQL Server engine.*

ODS server applications respond to the following events:

■ Connect events. When a connect event occurs, SQL Server initiates a security check to determine whether a connection is allowed. Other ODS applications, such as a gateway to DB/2, have their own login handlers that determine whether connections can be allowed. Events that close a connection also exist to allow the proper connection cleanup to occur.

■ Language events. When a client sends a command string, such as an SQL statement, SQL Server passes this command along to the command parser. A different ODS application, such as a gateway, would install its own handler that would accept and be responsible for execution of the command.

■ Remote stored procedure events. These events occur each time a client or a SQL Server directs a remote stored procedure request to ODS for processing.

ODS also generates events based on certain client activities and application activities. These events allow an ODS server application to respond to changes to the status of the client connection or to changes to the status of the ODS server application.

In addition to handling connections, ODS manages threads for SQL Server. It takes care of thread creation and termination and thread pooling. Since ODS is an open interface with a full programming API and toolkit, other ISVs writing server applications with ODS get the same benefits that SQL Server derives from this component, including SMP-capable thread management and pooling as well as network handling for multiple simultaneous networks. This multithreaded operation enables ODS server applications to maintain a high level of performance and availability and allows these applications to transparently use multiple processors under Windows NT since the operating system can schedule any thread on any available processor.

The Command Parser

The *Command Parser* handles language events raised by ODS. It checks for proper syntax and translates Transact-SQL commands into an internal format that can be operated on. This internal format is known as a *sequence tree,* or *query tree*. If the parser does not recognize the syntax, a syntax error is immediately raised. Starting with SQL Server version 6.0, syntax error messages try to explicitly identify where the error occurred. However, non–syntax error messages cannot be explicit as to the exact source line that caused an error. Because only the parser can access the source of the statement, the statement is no longer available in source format when the command is actually executed. Exceptions to the calling sequence for the Command Parser are EXECUTE(*"string"*) and cursor operations. Both of these operations can recursively call the parser.

The Remote Stored Procedure Call Handler

Because the sequence tree is stored and can be retrieved, stored procedures can be sent directly to a handler instead of being parsed. Sending procedures as remote stored procedure events basically bypasses the need for parsing. This *RPC Handler* simply retrieves and sets up the sequence tree to be acted on. In version 6.5, many remote procedures can be batched together to provide optimized performance; batching significantly reduces network round-trips.

The Sequencer and the Optimizer

The *Sequencer* takes the sequence tree from the Command Parser or RPC Handler and prepares it for execution. In this module, an entire command batch is compiled, queries are optimized, and security is checked. The query optimization and compilation results in an execution plan.

The first step in producing such a plan is to *normalize* the query, which potentially breaks down a single query into multiple, fine-grained queries. After the query is normalized, it will be *optimized,* which means that a plan for executing it will be determined. Query optimization is cost-based; the optimizer chooses the plan that it determines would cost the least based on the estimated number of I/Os that will be required. The optimizer considers the type of statement requested, checks the amount of data in the various tables affected, looks at the indexes available for each table, and then looks at a sampling of the data values kept for each index (known as the *distribution page*). Based on these parameters, SQL Server considers the various access methods and steps it could use to resolve a query and chooses the most cost-effective plan. It decides the order in which the tables should be accessed (in the case of a join) and which indexes, if any, should be used for each table.

The SQL Server optimizer also uses pruning heuristics to ensure that more time isn't spent optimizing a query than it would take to simply choose a plan and execute it. The optimizer does not necessarily do exhaustive optimization. Some products designed for exhaustive optimization consider every possible plan and then choose the one determined to cost least. The advantage of this exhaustive strategy is that the syntax chosen for a query would theoretically never cause a performance difference, no matter what syntax the user used. Theoretically, that's quite nice, but if you deal with an involved query, it could take much longer to estimate the cost of every conceivable plan than it would to accept a good plan, even if not the best, and execute it. For example, in one product review, SQL Server (and some other products) consistently executed one complex eight-table join faster than a product whose optimizer produced the same "ideal" execution plan each time, even though SQL Server's execution plan varied somewhat. This was a case in which a pruning technique produced faster results than pure exhaustive optimization. When joining many tables, rather than choose from every possible sequence in which the tables could be accessed, SQL Server considers the order in groups of four and produces an intermediate result that is then joined with the remaining tables. So while there are instances like this one in which the syntax or table order do make a difference, by and large that will not be the case. You will typically get the same execution plan no matter what equivalent syntax you use to specify the query. Some products have no cost-based optimizer and rely purely on rules to determine the query execution plan. In such cases, the syntax of the query is vitally important (for example, the execution would start with the first table in the FROM clause). Such products sometimes claim to have a "rule-based optimizer." Personally, I've always felt this is simply a euphemism for "no optimizer." Any optimization that occurred was done by the person who wrote the query, not by an "optimizer."

The SQL Server optimizer is cost-based, and with every release it is made "smarter" to consider more possibilities, to handle more special cases, and to add more access method choices. However, by definition, the optimizer relies on probability in choosing its query plan; this means that sometimes the optimizer will be wrong. (Even an 80 percent chance of choosing correctly means that something will be wrong one in five times.) Recognizing that the optimizer will never be perfect, you can use SQL Server's *optimizer hints* to direct the optimizer to use a certain index, for example, or to force the optimizer to follow a specific sequence while working with the tables involved.

After normalization and optimization are completed, the normalized tree produced by those processes is compiled into the execution plan, which is actually a data structure. Each command included in it specifies exactly which table will be affected, which index will be used (if any), which security checks must be made, and which criteria (such as equality to a specified value) must evaluate to TRUE for selection. This execution plan might be considerably more complex than is immediately apparent. In addition to the actual commands, the execution plan includes all the steps necessary to ensure that constraints are checked. If a trigger is included for the action being taken, a call to the procedure that comprises the trigger is appended. In this case, the execution plan includes specific steps for constraints, but a trigger has its own plan that is branched to just before the commit. The specific steps for the trigger are not compiled into the execution plan.

A simple request to insert one row into a table with multiple constraints can result in an execution plan that requires many other tables to also be accessed or expressions to be evaluated. The existence of a trigger can also cause many additional steps to be executed. The step that carries out the actual INSERT statement might be just a small part of the total execution plan necessary to ensure that all actions and constraints associated with adding a row are carried out.

The Executor

The *Executor* (also called the *Execution Engine*) runs the execution plan that was produced by the Sequencer and the optimizer. The Executor acts as a dispatcher for all the commands in the execution plan. This module loops through each command step of the execution plan until the batch is complete. Each command is dispatched to a module that performs its function. For example, Data Definition

Language (DDL) statements, such as CREATE TABLE, will be dispatched to the *DDL Manager*. Data Manipulation Language (DML) statements, such as SELECT, UPDATE, INSERT, and DELETE, go to the *DML Manager* and then typically move on to the *Search Manager*. Miscellaneous commands, such as DBCC and WAIT-FOR, go to the *Utility Manager*. Stored procedures (for example, *EXEC sp_who*) are dispatched to the *Stored Procedure Manager*. A statement with an explicit BEGIN TRAN first interacts directly with the *Transaction Manager*. From then on, execution proceeds much like any other SQL batch. A manager must exist to handle every command in Transact-SQL. Many managers, of course, handle several different but related commands. (SQL Server has more managers than those shown earlier in Figure 3-1. If every manager and possible interaction were included, the diagram would be overly complex and unreadable.)

Managers interact directly with other managers. For example, an UPDATE statement that affects multiple rows is implicitly an atomic transaction; in this case, the interaction with the Transaction Manager is from the DML Manager, which processes the UPDATE statement, not directly from the Executor.

The Search Manager

When data is to be located, the *Search Manager* (or the *Access Methods Manager*) is called. The Search Manager provides a row-level, table-scanning interface to the Executor (and other managers). The Search Manager sets up and requests scans of data pages and index pages. It contains services to open a table, retrieve qualified data, and update data. Generally speaking, it is similar to an indexed sequential access method (ISAM), but the Search Manager doesn't actually retrieve the pages. Instead, it makes the request of the *Buffer Manager*. The Buffer Manager then ultimately either serves up the page already in its cache or reads it to cache from disk. When the scan is started, a look-ahead mechanism qualifies the rows or index entries on a page. A routine called *qualpage* is called during the scan initialization to fill an array of offsets based on the search argument (SARG) information. This offset array is then used by ISAM-like operations such as (*getnext*) and (*getprev*) to quickly retrieve the qualifying rows or index entries.

A SARG has this form: *column OPERATION constant* (for example, *age > 30*). Retrieving rows that meet specified criteria is known as a *qualified retrieval*. The Search Manager is employed not only for queries (selects) but also for qualified updates and deletes (for example, UPDATE with a WHERE clause).

A session begins by opening a table, proceeds to request and evaluate a range of rows against the search arguments, and ends by closing the table. A session descriptor data structure (SDES) keeps track of the current row and the SARGs to be met for the object being operated on (identified by the object descriptor data structure, or DES).

The Database and Page Managers

The *Database Manager* and *Page Manager* cooperate to manage a collection of pages as named databases. Each database is a sequence of 2-KB disk pages, numbered by logical page numbers (0, 1, 2, and so on). These page numbers are mapped into SQL Server virtual devices that are Windows NT files. (In Chapter 5, "Databases and Devices," I'll offer more details about the physical organization of databases.)

SQL Server uses four types of disk pages: data, text, index, and allocation. (In addition, a distribution page maintains a histogram of values for an index. Although you might legitimately argue that's a fifth type of page, I think of it as an index page.) All user data, except for *text* and *image* datatypes, are stored on *data pages*. The *text* and *image* datatypes, used for storing binary large objects (or BLOBS, large elements—up to 2 GB each—of text or binary data), use a separate page chain for each column. A pointer on the regular data page identifies the starting page in the text/image chain. *Index pages* store the B-Trees that allow fast access to data. (See "The Index Manager" section for information about B-Trees.) As I just mentioned, *distribution pages,* which can be considered a part of an index, keep a histogram of data values for the index keys. Each index has one distribution page, which the optimizer uses to decide if the index is likely to be useful. *Allocation pages* keep track of the other pages. They contain no database rows and are used only internally.

The Page Manager allocates and deallocates all types of disk pages, organizing extents of eight pages each. This optimization prevents the overhead of allocation from being incurred every time a new page is required; rather, it is incurred only every eighth time. Perhaps most importantly, this optimization forces data of the same table to be contiguous for the most part.

To determine how contiguous a table's data is, use the DBCC SHOWCONTIG command. A table with a lot of allocation and deallocation can get fairly fragmented, and rebuilding the clustered index (which rebuilds the table and all nonclustered indexes, too) can improve performance, especially when the Read Ahead Manager is busy doing table scans. Every table and index requires at least one extent, no matter how little data is included in the table. Even an empty table will effectively use 16 KB of disk space because one extent comprises eight pages of 2 KB each. An empty table with a nonclustered index declared will use 32 KB (an extent each for the table and the index).

The Transaction Manager

A core feature of SQL Server is its ability to ensure that transactions follow the ACID properties (discussed in Chapter 2). Transactions must be *atomic*—that is *all* or *nothing*. If acknowledgment indicates that a transaction has committed, that transaction must be recoverable by SQL Server no matter what—even if a total system failure occurs 1 millisecond after the commit was acknowledged. In SQL Server, if work was in progress and a system failure occurred before the transaction was committed, all the work in progress will be rolled back to the state that existed before the transaction began. *Write-ahead logging* makes it always possible to roll back (undo) work in progress or roll forward committed work not yet applied to the data pages. Write-ahead logging assures that a transaction's changes, the "before and after" images of data, are captured on disk in the transaction log before a transaction is acknowledged as committed. Writes to the transaction log are always synchronous—that is, SQL Server must wait for them to complete. Writes to the data pages can be asynchronous, because all the effects can be reconstructed from the log if necessary. The Transaction Manager coordinates logging, recovery, and buffer management, but it does not directly perform these functions.

The Transaction Manager delineates the boundaries of those statements that must be grouped together to form an operation. The Transaction Manager handles transactions that cross databases within the same SQL Server, and it allows nested transaction sequences. (However, nested transactions simply execute in the context of the first-level transaction; no special action occurs when they are committed. And a rollback specified in a lower level of a nested transaction undoes the entire transaction.) For a distributed transaction to another SQL Server (or to any other resource manager), the Transaction Manager coordinates with the Microsoft Distributed Transaction Coordinator (MS DTC) service using Windows NT remote procedure calls. The Transaction Manager marks *savepoints,* which allow you to designate points within a transaction at which work can be partially rolled back, or undone.

The Transaction Manager also coordinates with the Lock Manager regarding when locks can be released, based on the isolation level that is in effect. The *isolation level* in which your transaction runs determines how sensitive your application is to changes made by others and consequently how long your transaction will need to hold locks to protect against changes made by others. Three isolation-level semantics can be chosen in SQL Server 6.5, although syntactically four options are available. The three actual behaviors are *Uncommitted Read* (also called "dirty read"), *Committed Read*, and *Serializable*.

The fourth syntactical option, REPEATABLE READ, corresponds to a fourth isolation level—Repeatable Read—but in SQL Server it behaves exactly the same as Serializable, which is a higher level of isolation than Repeatable Read. (That's fine per ANSI and ISO, which specify that a given isolation level must provide *at least* certain characteristics, not *at most*. According to the standard, Serializable is a superset of Repeatable Read.)

Your transactions will behave differently, depending on which isolation level is chosen. I'll describe these levels now, but this is impossible to do without also discussing locking because the topics are closely related. The next section gives an overview of locking, but more detailed information can be found in Chapter 13, "Locking."

Uncommitted Read

Uncommitted Read is also commonly known as dirty read. (Be careful—do not confuse the term "dirty read" with "dirty page," which I discuss later related to the Buffer Manager.) An Uncommitted Read allows your transaction to read any data that is currently on a data page, whether that data has been committed or not. Another user, for example, might have a transaction in progress that has updated data, and even though it is holding exclusive locks on the data, your transaction can read it anyway. Subsequently, the other user may decide to roll back his or her transaction, so logically those changes were never made. If the system is a single-user system, and everyone queued up to access it, the changes would never have been visible to other users. In a multiuser system, however, you read the changes and possibly took action on them. Although this scenario isn't desirable, the Uncommitted Read advantages are that you won't get stuck waiting for a lock, nor will *your* reads issue share locks (described below) that might affect others.

When using Uncommitted Read, you give up assurances of having strongly consistent data for the benefit of having high concurrency in the system, without having users lock each other out. So when should you choose Uncommitted Read? Clearly, you don't want to choose Uncommitted Read for financial transactions in which every number must balance. But it might be fine for certain decision-support analyses—for example, when looking at sales trends, for which complete precision is simply not necessary and the trade-off in higher concurrency makes it worthwhile.

Committed Read

Committed Read is the default isolation level of SQL Server. Using it assures that an operation will never read data that another application has changed but not yet committed (that is, it will never read data that logically never existed). With Committed Read, if a transaction is updating data and consequently has exclusive locks on data pages, your transaction must wait for those locks to be released before you can use that data (whether reading or modifying). Also, your transaction must put *share locks* (at a minimum) on the data that will be visited, meaning that data is potentially unavailable to others to use. A share lock doesn't prevent others from reading the data, but it makes them wait to update the data. Share locks can be released after the data has been sent to the calling client—they do not have to be held for the duration of the transaction.

> **NOTE** Although you will never read uncommitted data, if a transaction running with Committed Read isolation subsequently revisits the same data, that data might have changed or new rows might suddenly appear that now meet the criteria of the original query. Rows that appear in this way are called *phantoms*.

Serializable

The Serializable isolation level adds to the properties of Committed Read by ensuring that if a transaction revisits data or if a query is reissued, the data will not have changed and rows will not have been added in the interim. In other words, when you choose Serializable, issuing the same query twice within a transaction will not pick up any changes made by some other user's transaction and phantoms will not appear.[2]

Preventing phantoms from appearing is a desirable safeguard. But there's no free lunch. The cost of this extra safeguard is that all the share locks in a transaction must be held until the completion (COMMIT or ROLLBACK) of the transaction. (Exclusive locks must always be held until the end of a transaction, no matter what the isolation level, so that a transaction can be rolled back if necessary. If the locks were released sooner, it might be impossible to undo the work.) No other user will be able to modify the data visited by your transaction as long as your transaction is outstanding. Obviously, this can seriously reduce concurrency and degrade performance. If transactions are not kept short and/or if applications are not written to be aware of such potential lock contention issues, SQL Server can appear to "hang" when it is simply waiting for locks to be released.

The Serializable level gets its name from the fact that running multiple serializable transactions at the same time is the equivalent of running them one at a time— that is, *serially*—without regard to sequence. For example, transactions A, B, and C are serializable only if the result obtained by running all three simultaneously is the same as if they were run one at a time, though in any order. Serializable does not imply a known order in which the transactions would be run. The order is considered a chance event. Even on a single-user system, the order of transactions hitting the queue would be essentially random. If the batch order is important to your application, you should implement it as a pure batch system.

---

2. More precisely, choosing Serializable affects sensitivity to some other connection's changes, regardless of whether the user ID of the other connection is the same or not. Every connection within SQL Server has its own transaction and lock space. I use the term "user" above loosely so as to not obscure the central concept.

Repeatable Read

The ANSI SQL standard also prescribes another important isolation level, Repeatable Read. The Repeatable Read isolation level is midway between Committed Read and Serializable. Per ANSI, Repeatable Read would never allow data changes that others have made to appear in a transaction that rereads the data. However, it can allow phantoms. You can specify Repeatable Read with SQL Server, but this option is currently simply a synonym for Serializable and, as such, it ensures that phantoms will *not* occur.

> **NOTE** A future version of SQL Server might distinguish between REPEATABLE READ and SERIALIZABLE, so you should specify the one that you require.

The tough part of transaction management, of course, is not dealing with the situation in which everything goes well and the transaction simply commits but rather in dealing with rollback/rollforward and recovery operations. I'll return to the topic of transaction management and recovery in a moment. But first it's necessary to further discuss locking and logging.

The Lock Manager

Locking is a crucial function of a multiuser database system like SQL Server. Recall from Chapter 2 that SQL Server enables you to manage multiple users simultaneously and ensures that the transactions observe the properties of the chosen isolation level. At the highest level, Serializable, SQL Server must make the multiuser system perform like a single-user system, as though every user is queued up to use the system alone with no other user activity. Locking guards data and the internal resources that make this possible, and it strives to do so in a way that allows many users to simultaneously access the database and not be severely affected by others' use.

The Lock Manager acquires and releases various types of locks, such as shared read locks, exclusive locks for writing, intent locks to signal a "plan" to perform some operation, extent locks for space allocation, and so on. It manages the compatibility between the lock types, resolves deadlocks, and escalates locks if needed. The Lock Manager controls table and page locks as well as system data locks. (System data, such as page headers and indexes, is private to the database system.)

The Lock Manager provides two separate locking systems. The first enables page locks and table locks for all fully shared data tables, data pages, text pages, and leaf-level index pages. The second locking system is used internally only for restricted system data; it protects root and intermediate index pages while indexes are being traversed. This internal mechanism uses *resource locks,* or *rlocks,* which are used for performance optimization—full-blown locks could be used throughout, but this would slow the system down. If you examine locks by using the **sp_lock** stored procedure or a similar mechanism that gets its information from the *syslocks* table, you won't see or be aware of rlocks; you'll see only the locks for fully shared data.

Locking is an important aspect of SQL Server. Many developers are keenly interested in locking because of its possible effects on their applications' performance. Chapter 13 is devoted to the subject, so I won't go further into locking here.

The Row Operations, Index, and Text Managers

The *Row Operations Manager, Index Manager,* and *Text Manager* are distinct managers, each of which has responsibility for manipulating and maintaining its respective on-disk data structures, namely rows of data, B-Tree indexes, and text/image pages. (Remember that *text* and *image* datatypes are maintained in a separate chain of pages from the rest of the data.) The Row Operations and Index Managers, discussed in detail below, understand and manipulate information on data and index pages. The Text Manager handles the data in text pages.

The Row Operations Manager

The Row Operations Manager retrieves, modifies, and performs operations on individual rows. (For more information on the Row Manager and on-disk structures, see Chapter 5, "Databases and Devices"; for more on data page and row format, see Chapter 6, "Tables.") The manager performs an operation within a row, such as "retrieve column 2" or "write this value to column 3." As a result of the work performed by the Search Manager, Lock Manager, and Transaction Manager, the row will already have been found and will be appropriately locked and part of a transaction. Having formatted or modified a row in memory, the Row Operations Manager has routines that insert or delete a row.

The Row Operations Manager also handles updates, and the update strategy can include such information as *when* the update can be made and *how* it will be made. As for *when,* updates can be either *deferred* ("in a moment") or *direct* (immediately). A deferred operation would be appropriate when an update could modify the primary key of multiple rows. In that case, the update could not occur immediately because some rows might be changed to duplicate values and would need to be rolled back. Deferred updates are also used when updating a column that is part of a FOREIGN KEY constraint (either on the referencing or referenced by side of the constraint). In addition, *interim violations* could occur to create values that would be duplicates only until a statement has finished executing.

For example, suppose you want to increase all primary keys by one. As rows begin sequential processing, number 1 becomes number 2. The original number 2 exists until it increments to number 3, and so on, until all numbers are incremented at the end of the process. The deferred mode can deal with these interim violations, when duplicate primary keys exist temporarily but are "fixed up" by the end of the operation. Deferred updates are necessary any time there is potential for the "Halloween problem" to occur.

The Halloween Problem

The *Halloween problem* is a commonly used database term that refers to a row that is repeatedly and erroneously updated. The deferred update mode is necessary if there appears to be a chance that a Halloween problem can occur.

The Halloween problem occurs when performing an operation of the type *Update T set x=x+1*. If an index on *x* were used to locate qualifying rows, the same rows could be repeatedly updated. After an update to the value of *x*, the affected row might be relocated further down in the scan, so it is updated again and again since it keeps moving each time it is updated.

Supposedly, the Halloween problem is so named because the bug was originally discovered on Halloween night. But the name also is appropriate because a row can exhibit behavior best described by the phrase, *"It's b-a-a-ck!"*

Every deferred update is performed with a two-step logging mechanism and a deletion of the original row image followed by an insertion of the new image. Initially in a deferred update, only the row IDs (RIDs) of each qualifying row are logged. (The full image of the original row is not logged here.) The log identifies the rows to be deleted in a deferred update. Next, the after-image for the same row is logged. When all qualifying rows have been identified and the new after-images have been recorded, the RIDs from the first step are used to delete the appropriate rows. Finally, the new images are inserted for the same RIDs. (In Chapter 8, "Modifying Data," I'll show the specific log records that must be written for actual update examples.)

If an update is not deferred, it is direct. The log records are written (without the first step of identifying only the RIDs and without the subsequent relogging) and then the data pages are modified. A direct update is most common when it can be determined during compile time (when the execution plan is created) that only a single row could qualify for the update (when, for example, the WHERE clause is an exact match on a unique index). In SQL Server versions prior to 6.5, any update that could affect multiple rows was always deferred; additional optimizations were made in 6.5 so that direct update mode often can be used even if multiple rows are affected. Direct update mode can now be used in multiple-row updates if the updates do not affect any columns that are part of the clustered index key, if columns in the index used to find the qualifying rows are not updated, and if variable-length fields are not updated. (If no variable-length columns are affected the row cannot change in size, which could force it to move to another page.) Another requirement for using multiple-row direct update is that no row can be updated more than once—avoiding the Halloween problem. Searched updates using joins and subqueries with IN revert to a deferred update.

Now let's discuss *how* the update is made. You can use three strategies for how updates are carried out, depending on the columns being updated: *update-in-place*, *on-page delete/insert*, and *full delete/insert*. (In Chapter 8, I'll outline the specific conditions that drive the update mode—direct or deferred—and the type of strategy that will be picked for the direct case. The cases I'll discuss here are slightly simplified.)

Update-in-place   Update-in-place is the most efficient form of update because it requires only a simple MODIFY log record and because the changed values for the row overwrite the previous values in the same slot on the same data page. Update-in-place is used only when the update mode is direct and the row length of the new row is exactly the same as the previous one (the update fits perfectly in the old slot).

On-page delete/insert   An on-page delete/insert is used when an old row value is deleted and the new copy of the row is inserted in the same page as the old. In terms of efficiency, this strategy isn't quite as good as update-in-place, but it is better than a full delete/insert, which requires retrieving two pages and modifying all indexes. This strategy is used when the update mode is direct and the new row isn't exactly the same size as the old but can still fit on the same page.

Full delete/insert   As its name implies, full delete/insert involves the deletion of the original copy and insertion of a new row. The insert goes wherever the clustered index takes it—not necessarily to the same page. All deferred updates are full delete/insert. A direct update can also be full delete/insert if the new row image cannot fit on the same page. All indexes must be modified whenever this update mode is employed, even if the index keys are not affected, because the row will (likely) move to a different page.

A new insert will occur on a specific page as indicated by a clustered index. This is true whether the new row is the direct result of an INSERT statement or the result of an UPDATE statement that executed via the full delete/insert strategy.

If there is no clustered index, a new row is always inserted at the end of the table, even if free slots (from rows that have been deleted) are available elsewhere in the table. For this reason alone, nearly every table should have a clustered index. (From a performance perspective, I could recount many other reasons why clustered indexes are good.) In reality, almost every table has a clustered index that does a good job of managing space in a table. New rows are inserted into their clustered positions, splicing in a page via a *page split* if no room is available on the original page. Because of these updating features, regular database "re-orgs" that are commonplace in many systems are rarely needed in SQL Server.

If you want to reorganize a table, say to reestablish a FILLFACTOR value or to make data more contiguous after a lot of data modification has occurred, using a clustered index makes the reorganization a simple operation. You simply rebuild the clustered index, which rebuilds the table and all nonclustered indexes as well. In the case of a delete, if the row deleted is the last row on a data page, that page is deallocated. (The only exception occurs if that page is the only one remaining in the table. A table always contains at least one page, even if it is empty.) Occasionally, some competitor's marketing propaganda will claim that SQL Server does not reuse space in tables after deletes. That's baloney as long as a clustered index exists, and—practically speaking—all tables of any serious size will have one.

The Index Manager

The Index Manager maintains and supports searches on B-Trees, which are used for SQL Server indexes. An *index* is structured as a *tree,* with a root page and intermediate and lower level pages (or branches). A *B-Tree* groups records that have similar index keys, thereby allowing fast access to data by searching on a key value. The B-Tree's core feature is its ability to balance the index tree. (*B* stands for "balanced.") Branches of the index tree are spliced together or split apart as necessary so that finding any given record always traverses the same number of levels and thus requires the same number of page accesses.

The traverse begins at the root page, progresses to intermediate index levels, and finally moves to bottom-level pages called *leaf pages.* The index is used to find the correct leaf page. On a qualified retrieval or delete, the correct leaf page will be the lowest page of the tree at which one or more rows with the specified key(s) reside. SQL Server supports both clustered and nonclustered indexes. In a nonclustered index, shown in Figure 3-3 on the following page, the lowest level of the tree (the leaf page of the index) will point to the data page that includes a row of data containing the value of the index key.

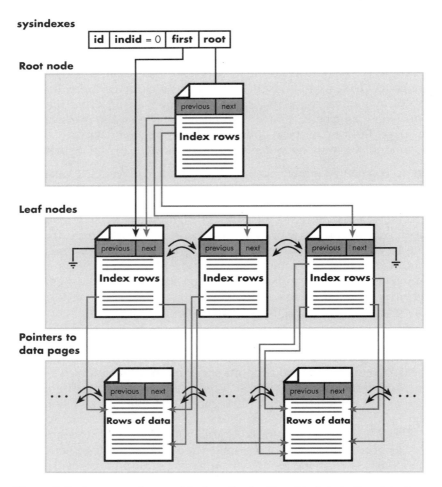

Figure 3-3. *In a nonclustered index, the leaf level points to the data page.*

After reaching the leaf level in a nonclustered index, you have the exact page number at which the data resides, although that data page must still be subsequently and separately retrieved. By knowing the data's exact page number, you eliminate the need to scan all the data pages looking for a qualifying row. Better yet, in a clustered index, shown in Figure 3-4, the leaf level actually contains the data row, not simply the index key. A clustered index keeps the data in a table physically ordered around the key of the clustered index, and the leaf page of a clustered index is in fact the data page itself.

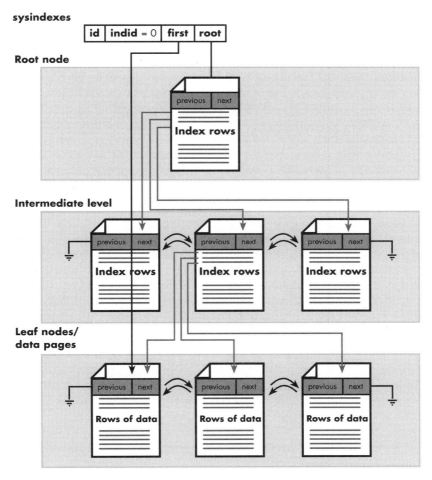

Figure 3-4. *In a clustered index, the data is located at the leaf level.*

Because data can be physically ordered in only one way, only one clustered index can exist per table. This makes the selection of the appropriate key value on which to cluster data an important performance consideration.

You can also use indexes to ensure the uniqueness of a particular key value. In fact, the PRIMARY KEY and UNIQUE constraints on a column work by making a unique index on the column's values. The optimizer can use the knowledge that an index is unique in formulating an effective query plan.

Because an index doesn't need to be unique, and the leaf of a clustered index is in fact the data page, you can have a case in which there are more rows than will fit on the page where the clustered index decides they are "supposed" to go.

Overflow pages For any given key value, there must, of course, be a leaf page as you traverse down the index. But what happens with a clustered index if there are too many rows with the same key value and they won't all fit on one leaf (data) page? The SQL Server answer to this is to create an overflow page. *Overflow pages* handle the data when the keys are equivalent and all the rows can't fit on one page. Inserting a new row that duplicates an existing key value is made easier by the overflow pages: the new row is simply appended to the overflow list, or, if it's the first row that won't fit on the leaf page, an overflow list is started.

Since SQL Server maintains clustering, you do not need to unload and reload data to maintain clustering properties. The correct leaf page will be the data page in which a row will be inserted (for a clustered index), or the leaf page will contain a pointer to the data page in which the row will be inserted (for a nonclustered index). If data is updated and the key values of an index change, or if the row is moved to a different page, SQL Server's transaction control ensures that all affected indexes are modified to reflect these changes. Under transaction control, index operations are done as atomic operations. The operations are logged and fully recovered in the event of a system failure.

By now, you know that whereas an index can greatly speed data retrieval, it can slow data modification because the index records must be changed along with the data. Indexes must, of course, always be updated for insert and delete activities. For update activity, they must be maintained if the index key is updated or if the update causes the row to move to a different data page.

Locking and Index Pages

Regular (nonleaf) pages of an index are not subject to the same physical locking mechanisms as data or leaf pages (as discussed in "The Lock Manager" section). A resource lock (rlock) is used to lock a single regular page of the index. To increase concurrency, the Index Manager can search and update on an index without holding more than two locked pages at any time. Usually, only one page is held, but at times, two pages can be held simultaneously as the tree is being traversed. This process is known as *crabbing*; the rlock on the page pointing to another page is not released until the rlock on the page being pointed to has been safely acquired.

Splitting pages   When a row needs to be added to a data page that does not have enough room to accommodate the row, the page splits into two or three pages, one of which will hold the new row. After the split, one or two rows are promoted to the parent page. An index tree is always searched from the root down, so during an insert operation it is "split on the way down." This means that while the index is being searched on an insert, the index is being protected in anticipation of possibly being updated. A parent node (not a leaf node) is resource locked (rlocked) until the child node is known to be available for its own rlock. Then the parent rlock can be released safely. Before the rlock on a parent node is released, SQL Server determines whether the page will accommodate another two rows and splits it if not. This occurs only if the page is being searched with the objective of adding a row to the index. The goal is to ensure that the parent page always has room for the row or rows that result from a child page splitting. (Occasionally this results in pages being split that do not need to be—at least not yet. In the long run it's a performance optimization.) Three types of splits can occur, depending on the type of page being split: root page of an index, intermediate index page, and data page.

Splitting the root page of an index: If the root page of an index needs to split, a new root is created by allocating a new page, placing a single row in it that points to the old root page, and then treating the old root page as an intermediate index page split. A root page split creates a new level in the index. Because indexes are usually only a few levels deep, this type of split does not often occur.

Splitting the intermediate index page: An intermediate index page split is accomplished simply by locating the midpoint of the index keys on the page, allocating a new page, and then copying the lower half of the old index page into the new page. Again, this does not occur often, although it is more common than splitting the root page.

Splitting the data page: A data page split is the most interesting and potentially common case, and it's probably the only split that you, as a developer, should be concerned with. Data pages split only under insert activity and only when a clustered index exists on the table. If no clustered index exists, the insert goes to the end of the table, where it might require allocation of a new page rather than a page split. Although splits are caused only by insert activity, that activity can be a result of an UPDATE statement, not just an INSERT statement. As I mentioned earlier (and as I will discuss in Chapter 8), if the row cannot be updated in place or at least on the same page, the update is performed as a delete of the original row followed by an insert of the new image. The insertion of the new image can, of course, cause a page split.

Splitting a data page is a complicated operation. It requires that the Index Manager determine the page on which to locate the new row; create overflow pages, perhaps turning them into "real" pages; and then handle large rows that don't fit on either the old page or the new page. When a data page is split, the nonclustered indexes that point to the new page must also be updated. This in turn can cause nonclustered indexes to also split.

Although the typical page split is not too expensive, you'll want to minimize the frequency of page splits in your production system, at least during peak usage times. To give you an idea of the cost, a page split of a table with a row length of 150 bytes and two nonclustered indexes in addition to the clustered index, might require about 20 to 30 I/O operations to split the data and fix up the two indexes. That's not too bad if the splits are relatively infrequent, but this could be a problem for you if splits are rampant or if they occur during a period in which your system is heavily taxed. You can avoid system disruption during busy times by reserving some space on pages using the FILLFACTOR parameter when you're creating the clustered index on existing data. You can use this parameter to your advantage during your least busy operational hours by periodically re-creating the clustered index with the desired FILLFACTOR. That way the extra space is available during your peak usage times, and you will save the overhead of splitting then. (Using SQL Executive, you can easily schedule the rebuilding of indexes to occur at times when activity is lowest.)

> **NOTE** Using the FILLFACTOR setting is helpful only when you're creating the index on existing data. Trying to maintain extra space on the page would actually defeat the purpose because you'd need to split pages anyway to keep that amount of space available.

Reclaiming pages   When the last row is deleted from a data page, the entire page is deallocated. This also results in the deletion of the row in the index page that pointed to the old data page. If the deletion results in an empty index page, the Index Manager will also deallocate the index page.

The Buffer Manager and the Log Writer

The *Buffer Manager* manages all data caching, retrieving, and writing and records all writes in the transaction logs. It also attempts to maintain a supply of free buffers that can be used immediately without having to flush pages to make some available. Through techniques like the ones described in this section, the Buffer Manager "tunes" itself. It doesn't require the operational and administration issues of having to carefully lay out separate and designated caches, that is, *named caches,* which some products have managed to declare as a "feature."

Only the Buffer Manager directly requests a data read or write, including writes to the transaction log. Because of this, the Buffer Manager is sometimes referred to as the Log Writer. All other managers get data via requests to the Buffer Manager. (A couple of exceptions do exist: The Read Ahead Manager will attempt to preload the data cache with pages that it detects the Buffer Manager might want soon. And the Lazywriter and Checkpoint Manager processes flush buffers out to data pages. But for the purpose of this discussion, I consider all of these Buffer Manager functions; I will discuss the other two processes later.)

All changes are "written ahead" by the Buffer Manager to the transaction log. *Write-ahead logging* ensures that all databases can be recovered to a consistent state even in the event of a complete server failure, as long as the physical media (hard disk) survives. A process will never be given acknowledgment that a transaction has been committed unless it is assured to be on disk in the transaction log. For this reason, all writes to the transaction log are synchronous—SQL Server must wait for acknowledgment of completion. Writes to data pages can be made asynchronously, without waiting for acknowledgment, because if a failure occurs, the transactions can be "undone" or "redone" from the information logged.

Protection against media failure is achieved using whatever level of RAID (redundant array of independent disks) technology you choose. (I'll discuss RAID technology, provide guidelines for choosing the appropriate RAID level, and discuss why backups are still essential in Chapter 4, "Planning for and Installing SQL Server.") Write-ahead logging in conjunction with RAID protection assures that you will never lose a transaction. (However, a good backup strategy is still essential to provide safety from some situations, such as when an administrator accidentally clobbers a table.) SQL Server always opens its files by instructing Windows NT to write through any other caching that the operating system might be doing. Hence, SQL Server ensures that transactions are atomic—even a sudden interruption of power will result in no partial transactions existing in the database, and all completed transactions are guaranteed to be reflected. (It is crucial, however, that a hardware disk-caching controller not "lie" and claim that a write has been completed unless it really *has* or it is guaranteed that it *will be*. I'll discuss the use of a hardware caching controller in Chapter 4.)

Getting into a bit more detail, the Buffer Manager is responsible for these functions:

- Coherent disk cache. Makes sure each page has one and only one consistent image that is obtainable in memory.

- Initiating buffer I/O using read ahead, lazy writing, and checkpointing as appropriate. For example, when you look at activity on SQL Server using the **sp_who** stored procedure, you will see these three processes: RA (Read Ahead) Manager, Lazywriter, and Checkpoint.

■ Least recently used (LRU) caching of pages, so that the "hottest" data can be read from memory, not disk.

■ Page "pinning" and other consistency needs. Ensures that a "dirty" buffer cannot be written out to the data page until its change is known to have been logged (that is, the page is temporarily "pinned" to the cache).

■ Mapping of database-logical addresses to various virtual disks.

■ Flushing writes of the data pages (not the log) to disk. Occurs when a checkpoint occurs, when requested by the Lazywriter process (explained a bit later), or when a buffer is "stolen."

A *checkpoint* flushes the changes reflected in memory out to the data pages and then makes a record in the log indicating that, as of that time, the data pages reflect all committed changes. This speeds up recovery because only transactions that were still in progress when the checkpoint occurred and those that occurred after the checkpoint completed need to be considered. If heavy activity occurred between checkpoints, recovery will have more work to do (redoing and undoing transactions), and it will take longer for the system to restart.

Checkpoints and Performance Issues

A checkpoint will be issued as part of an *orderly shutdown,* so a typical recovery upon restart takes only seconds to complete. (An orderly shutdown occurs any time you explicitly shut down SQL Server, unless you do so via the SHUTDOWN WITH NOWAIT command.) Although a checkpoint speeds up recovery, it does slightly degrade run-time performance when the checkpoint process occurs.

Unless your system is being pushed with high transactional activity, the run-time impact of checkpoint will probably not be noticeable. It is minimized via the *fuzzy checkpoint* technique, which reflects the changes to the data pages incrementally. You can also use the **recovery interval** option of **sp_configure** to influence checkpointing frequency, balancing the time to recover versus any impact on run-time performance.

Writes to the data pages are asynchronous and sorted for added efficiency. If your system has been heavily updated, you will see bursts of write I/O operations during checkpoints. The benefits of RAID technology will be most significant for write activities during checkpoints, and you might see many hundred writes posted simultaneously to Windows NT for servicing.

Buffer steals and "favored" pages

A *buffer steal* occurs when no page in memory is free to use, so a page must be flushed out to disk to make room for a current operation. Buffer steals occur based on a queue in which all pages start at the top and are considered for replacement when they've reached the bottom. You can loosely consider this an *LRU algorithm*, but that's not exactly the case: notice that I said buffer steals "are considered" for replacement at the bottom of the queue. A page marked "favored" will not be stolen even if it is at the bottom of the queue. A favored page will be exempted—it gets a free trip back through the queue. During that trip, it might be marked "favored" again; as long as it's favored, it will never be stolen. (Certain "internal use" and frequently needed pages are marked "favored." For example, pages from the *sysindexes* table are doubly favored and will get two extra trips through the queue. All allocation pages are singly favored.)

If the server is operating with trace flag 1081, index pages (root, intermediate, and leaf pages for nonclustered indexes) get one free trip through the queue. That is, when index pages are accessed, they are marked "favored" and will get at least two trips in the queue. (A nonfavored page gets only one trip unless accessed again.) If the page is accessed again, it is again granted favored status and gets at least two more trips, and so on.

Your specific usage profile will help you to decide whether this trace flag should be enabled. For example, it might make sense to enable the trace flag if data access is random and cache-hit ratios for data pages are not very high, and if pages are mostly located via indexes. Enabling the trace flag keeps the index pages around longer because they are closer to the top of the pyramid and might result in a better cache-hit ratio, but this is hard to predict. If you think this option might work for you, my best advice is to test both: monitor your cache-hit ratio with and without the trace flag enabled. If the cache-hit ratio is increased significantly after enabling the trace flag, it's a win. The *cache-hit ratio* is the percentage of time that a page already exists in memory and does not have to be read in from disk. The ratio applies to all pages, not just data pages.

The queue of pages being considered for replacement is still loosely referred to as the *LRU list,* although, as I pointed out earlier, it is not quite correct to call it *least recently used.*

Keeping pages permanently in the cache

Some pages can be permanently removed from the LRU list and therefore kept in the data cache indefinitely. Any page (data, index, or text) belonging to a table pinned via DBCC PINTABLE is removed from the queue and will never be stolen unless it is freed using the DBCC UNPINTABLE command. The DBCC PINTABLE command doesn't cause the table to be brought into cache, nor does it mark pages of the table as "favored"; instead, it avoids the unnecessary overhead and simply doesn't put that table's pages on the LRU list for possible replacement.

Because mechanisms such as write-ahead logging and checkpointing are completely unaffected, such an operation in no way impairs recovery. Still, pinning too many tables could result in few or even no pages being available for buffer steals. In general, you should use DBCC PINTABLE only if you have carefully tuned your system, plenty of memory is available, and you have a good feel for which tables constitute hot spots.

Pages that are "very hot" (accessed repeatably) do not get placed on the LRU list. A page in the buffer pool that has a nonzero use count, such as one that is newly read or newly created, should not be added to the LRU list until its use count falls to zero. Prior to that point, the page is clearly hot and wouldn't be a good candidate for a buffer steal. Very hot pages may never even get on the LRU list—which is as it should be.

A buffer will also be temporarily marked exempt from being stolen while it is still being used, which is known as a *buffer keep*. Some database textbooks refer to this process as *pinning the page*. In SQL Server, however, "pinning" means something slightly different. Pinning a page ensures that a dirty page cannot be written to disk until its changes have been logged. (As mentioned earlier, a dirty page is a page that has been changed and therefore differs from the page that was read into memory from disk.)

Accessing pages via the Buffer Manager

The Buffer Manager handles the in-memory version of each physical disk page and provides all other modules access to it (with appropriate safety measures). The memory image in the data cache, if one exists, takes precedence over the disk image. That is, the copy of the data page in memory might include updates that have not yet been written to disk. (It may be dirty.) When a page is needed for a process, the page must exist in memory (that is, in the data cache). If the page is not there, a physical I/O is performed to get it. Obviously, because physical I/Os are expensive, the fewer the better. Clearly, the more memory (the bigger the data cache) that exists, the more pages can reside there and the more likely a page can be found there.

> **NOTE** Adding memory, as long as your cache-hit ratio keeps improving, is a good strategy. You should stop when the increases in your cache-hit ratio become marginal or when you exceed your hardware budget and your cost accountant begins to scream, whichever comes first.

A database appears as a simple sequence of numbered pages. The database ID (dbid) and page number (pageno) uniquely specify a page for the entire SQL Server environment. When another module (such as the Search Manager, Row

Manager, Index Manager, or Text Manager) needs to access a page, it requests access from the Buffer Manager by specifying the dbid and pageno.

The Buffer Manager responds to the calling module with a pointer to the memory buffer holding that page. The response could be immediate if the page is already in the cache, or it could take an instant for a disk I/O to complete and bring the page into memory. Typically, the calling manager will also request that the Lock Manager perform the appropriate level of locking on the page. The calling manager notifies the Buffer Manager if and when it is finished dirtying, or making updates to, the page. After that, the Buffer Manager is responsible for writing these updates to disk in a way that coordinates with logging and transaction management.

Large Memory Issues

Systems with hundreds of megabytes of RAM are not uncommon these days. In fact, for benchmark activities, we at Microsoft run with a memory configuration of as much as 2 GB of physical RAM. In the future, Windows NT will support a 64-bit address space and memory prices probably will continue to decline, so huge data caches of many gigabytes will not be so unusual.

The reason you'd want to run with more memory is, of course, to reduce the need for physical I/O by increasing your cache-hit ratio. But if the issues caused by working with huge amounts of memory are not dealt with intelligently by the RDBMS, you can see performance decrease, not increase, as more memory is added. In fact, some well-known competitive products have experienced performance degradation as more memory was added to a system. This was likely due either to inefficient access to pages in memory or to too much time spent looking for a free memory page to work with.

Memory: How Much Is Too Much?

Most systems would not benefit from huge amounts of memory. For example, if you have 2 GB of RAM and your entire database is 1 GB, clearly you won't even be able to fill the cache, let alone benefit from its size. A pretty small portion of most databases is "hot," so a cache that is only a small percentage of the entire database size can often yield a high cache-hit ratio. Adding additional memory beyond this might bring only marginal improvement at best and is not cost effective.

Considerable effort has gone into SQL Server to make sure both of these issues are dealt with wisely. Adding memory will either improve performance or result in no difference if the additional memory isn't needed. But additional memory will certainly not degrade performance. In dealing with large memory, SQL Server considers access to in-memory pages and the time spent looking for a free page.

Fast Access to In-Memory Pages

It is imperative that access to pages in memory be fast. Even with real memory, it would be ridiculously inefficient to have to scan the whole cache for a page when you're talking about hundreds of megabytes, or even gigabytes, of data. To avoid this inefficiency, buffer pages are hashed for fast access. *Hashing* is a technique that uniformly maps a key (in this case a dbid-pageno identifier) via a *hash function* across a set of *hash buckets*. A hash bucket is a page in memory that contains an array of pointers (implemented as a linked list) to the buffer pages. If all the pointers to buffer pages will not fit on a single hash page, a *linked list* will chain to additional hash pages.

Given a dbid-pageno value, the hash function converts that key to the hash bucket that should be checked; the hash bucket, then, serves as an index to the specific page needed. Using hashing, even when large amounts of memory are present, a specific data page can be found in cache with only a few memory reads (typically two or less).

Finding a data page might require that multiple hash bucket pages be accessed via the chain (linked list). The hash function attempts to uniformly distribute the dbid-pageno values throughout the available hash buckets. It follows that the more hash buckets are available, the less likely a given bucket will require long chains, so fewer pages will need to be accessed to determine the exact buffer holding a given page. You can use **sp_configure hash buckets** to increase the number of pages to be used for hash buckets and use DBCC BUFCOUNT to determine the length of the longest chains of hash buckets.

NOTE Beginning with Service Pack 2 for version 6.5, SQL Server provides a better way to monitor hash buckets: DBCC SQLPERF(HASHSTATS).

Fast Access to Free Pages (Lazywriter)

Whenever a data page or an index page is to be used, it must exist in memory. For this to occur, an open page in the data cache must be available for the page to be read into. Keeping a supply of free pages available for immediate use is an important performance optimization. If a free page weren't readily available, many memory pages might need to be searched simply to locate a buffer to use as a workspace.

The Lazywriter process ensures that a supply of free pages is available, and in this way it minimizes buffer steals, which are a relatively expensive operation. Lazywriter is idle until the number of free buffers falls below a certain threshold (which can be configured via ***sp_configure*** *free buffers*). At that point, Lazywriter automatically starts flushing buffers until the threshold is met. The Lazywriter process eliminates the need to do frequent checkpoints to ensure that "clean" buffers are available, and, as a result, buffer steals are greatly reduced.

Read Ahead

Read Ahead, also called *parallel data scan,* is a performance optimization. Read Ahead works on separate Windows NT threads to process a data scan in parallel with any other work that the server process is performing. Read Ahead "guesses" which data pages will be needed and places those pages into the buffer. If and when the Buffer Manager needs a particular page, chances are that page will be waiting in the buffer; a physical I/O operation is not necessary to make the page available. The page is ultimately served up to the calling module via the normal Buffer Manager.

If Read Ahead were disabled, the system would work fine, but more slowly. When the Buffer Manager detects that a horizontal scan is underway, it can automatically request that the Read Ahead process be initiated. A *horizontal scan* occurs when consecutive pages of the same type and level are being retrieved. This is the case when data pages are scanned (either from a full table scan or from a range search when a clustered index is used), when leaf pages of an index are scanned, or when a chain of text/image pages are retrieved. Although Read Ahead is obviously useful for queries, it's also important to operations such as creating indexes, updating statistics for indexes, DBCC operations, and backups.

By "guessing" that a page will be requested, Read Ahead makes it more likely that the page will already be in memory. That the page will be requested is not guaranteed, however, in which case Read Ahead will have done unnecessary work. By automatically tracking how many cache hits and cache misses have been encountered, Read Ahead can stop prefetching additional buffers if those already gathered are not, in fact, being requested.

Normally, the Buffer Manager retrieves one page from disk at a time, so the I/O size is 2 KB. However, because Read Ahead is used for situations in which many pages are probably needed, it fetches a full extent (eight pages) at a time. So the effective I/O size for Read Ahead is 16 KB for a single read (eight pages of 2 KB each)—far more efficient than eight separate reads of 2 KB each.

Read Ahead uses threads separate from the normal worker pool of Windows NT threads. Multiple *RA threads* can be active at one time, each posting asynchronous read I/O requests. Consequently, on a system with multiple processors and a strong I/O hardware subsystem, you will probably want to configure Read Ahead such that more RA threads are available than you would use for a single processor system with only a few disks. You can configure such settings via **sp_configure**.

Transaction Logging and Recovery

The transaction log records all changes made to the database and stores enough information to allow any change to be undone (rolled back) or redone (rolled forward) in the event of a system failure or if directed to do so by the application (in the case of a rollback). Physically, the transaction log is a normal system table, *syslogs,* that exists separately for each database. Because the log is implemented as a normal table, it can be read internally using the same methods used for other pages in the database. Modules that perform database updates write log entries that exactly describe the changes made. (More accurately, they request that the Buffer Manager perform the write for them. Recall that the Buffer Manager performs all I/O operations, including writing to the log.)

The data (including index) pages are pinned to the log—that is, the Buffer Manager guarantees that the log is written before the database changes (write-ahead logging). The Buffer Manager also guarantees that log pages are written in a specific order, making it clear which log pages must be processed after a system failure, regardless of when the failure occurred. The log records for a transaction are written to disk before the commit acknowledgement is sent to the client process, but the actual changed data may not have been physically written out to the data pages. So although the writes to the log must be synchronous (SQL Server must wait for them to complete so it knows that they are safely on disk), writes to data pages can be asynchronous. That is, writes to the data pages need only to be posted to Windows NT, and SQL Server can check later to see that they completed. It is not necessary that they complete immediately because the log contains all the information needed to redo the work, even in the event of a power failure or system crash before the write completed. The system would be much slower if it had to wait for every I/O request to complete before proceeding.

The use of asynchronous I/O is an important performance optimization, especially when bursts of I/O activity occur, such as during a checkpoint. Another performance optimization that occurs during this I/O blast is that the pages that need to be written are first sorted so they can be written out in order. This increases the system's overall speed, as the I/O can sweep across the disks rather than incur a lot of random back-and-forth seek activity.

Logging involves demarcation of the beginning and ending of each transaction (and also savepoints, if a transaction uses them). Between the beginning and ending demarcations, information exists about the changes made to the data. This information can take the form of the actual "before and after" data values, or it can refer to the operation that was performed so that those values can be derived. The end of a typical transaction is marked with a Commit record, which indicates that the transaction must be reflected in the database or redone if necessary. A transaction can also be marked with a Rollback record, which indicates that the transaction cannot be allowed to reflect partial changes in the database. If any such changes were written out to the data pages, they must be undone. A transaction aborted during normal runtime (not system restart), due to an explicit rollback or to something like a resource error (for example, out of memory), needs to be concerned only with an undo operation. Redo operations come into play only when recovery must be run.

If the system crashes after a transaction commits but before the data is written out to the data pages, the transaction must be recovered. The recovery process runs automatically at system startup. I'll continue to refer to recovery as a system startup function, which is its most common role by far. However, recovery is also run when a dismountable database (a database on removable media, such as a floptical drive) is opened as well as during the final step of restoring a database from backup.

Recovery performs both redo (rollforward) and undo (rollback) operations. In a redo operation, the log is examined and each change is verified as being already reflected in the database. (After a redo, every change of the transaction is guaranteed to have been applied.) If the change does not appear in the database, it is again performed from the information in the log. Undo requires the removal of partial changes of a transaction when the transaction had not entirely completed.

During recovery, only changes that occurred or were still open (in progress) since the last checkpoint must be redone or undone. The two main phases of recovery reference the last checkpoint record in the transaction log:

- Phase 1 scans from the then oldest active transaction to the last checkpoint log record.
- Phase 2 scans from the last checkpoint log record to the end of the log.

During Phase 1, recovery looks for transactions that started before the last checkpoint occurred. If the transaction committed before the checkpoint, nothing happens because the checkpoint indicates that all the changes have reached disk. If the transaction aborted subsequent to the checkpoint or simply does not have a commit record (it had still not committed at the time the system terminated), any partial changes that might have been written during the checkpoint must be undone (rolled back).

In Phase 2, all transactions that committed after the checkpoint must be redone (rolled forward). Any transactions that were aborted or that are still in progress must be undone (rolled back). The transactions must be terminated or redone in exactly the same order in which they occurred to achieve the same final results. The database is not accessible to any other processes until recovery is complete.

Locking and Recovery

Locking, transaction management (rollback and rollforward), and recovery are all closely related. A transaction can be rolled back only if all affected data pages were locked exclusively so that no other process could have either seen changes in progress (which might still be rolled back) or made changes to resources used by the transaction that would prevent its being rolled back. Only one active transaction can modify a page at a time. This is why exclusive locks must be held until a transaction is either committed or aborted. Until the moment it is committed, the transaction logically does not exist. A transaction operating with Read Uncommitted isolation (dirty read) can sometimes read data that logically never existed because it does not honor the existence of exclusive locks. But any other transaction operating with a higher level of isolation (which occurs by default—operating with Read Uncommitted isolation must be requested) would never allow such a phenomenon.

Timestamps and Recovery

Every database page has a timestamp that uniquely identifies it, by version, as it is changed over time. (As is true for the *timestamp* datatype, this is not a system time that would make sense outside of the context of SQL Server. Rather, it is simply an ever-increasing value known to be unique within the database.) Log records of each database change include old timestamps and new timestamps that respectively correspond to the page timestamps before and after the change they describe. In some cases, more than one page needs to be changed in the logged action, so more than one before/after timestamp pair is recorded.

During a redo operation of transactions, the old timestamp in the log record must match the data page timestamp to indicate that the log entry should be processed, as shown in Figure 3-5.

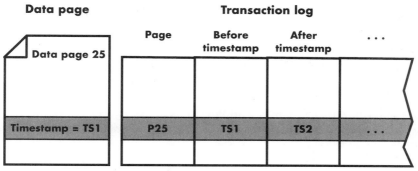

Data page timestamp (TS1) = **Before** timestamp in log (TS1)
Thus, the change recorded in the transaction log has not been applied to the database.
If the transaction was committed, this change must be rolled forward.

Data page   **Transaction log**

Page	Before timestamp	After timestamp	. . .
P42	TS71	TS77	. . .

Data page timestamp (TS77) = **After** timestamp in log (TS77)
Thus, the change recorded in the transaction log has already been applied to the database.
If the transaction was committed, no action is necessary. If the transaction was not
committed, this change must be rolled back.

Figure 3-5. *SQL Server compares timestamps to decide whether to process the
log entry.*

Conversely, during an undo operation, the new timestamp value in the log must
match the disk page timestamp. Two changes to the same page will result in two
log entries with (*old, new*) timestamps, such as (A, B) and (B, C). This assures
that the changes can be redone in the same order and undone in the opposite
order, as necessary. If recovery itself must be restarted, some changes will be
recognized as already completed and will be skipped over. The use of timestamp
values during recovery necessitates that a newly created database have all of its
pages initialized to nothing. If, by some stroke of bad luck, an old timestamp value

from previous use was still lying around on disk, the recovery process might make a bad decision based on that value. By cleanly initializing the pages, this possibility, remote though it is, is eliminated.

The initialization can be safely skipped as a performance optimization when it can be determined that a new device (file) is being used. A new file is known not to have old values visible because Windows NT always provides a completely clean image of a newly created file. So creating a database on a new device can be considerably faster than doing so on an existing device. For details, see Chapter 5, "Databases and Devices."

Because recovery finds the last checkpoint record in the log (plus transactions that were still active at the time of checkpoint) and proceeds from there, recovery time is short and the transaction log can be purged or archived for all changes committed before the checkpoint. Otherwise, recovery could take a long time and transaction logs would become unreasonably large. A transaction log cannot be purged beyond the point of the earliest transaction that is still open, no matter how many checkpoints might have occurred subsequently. If a transaction remains open, the log must be preserved because it is still not clear whether the transaction is done or ever will be done. The transaction may ultimately need to be rolled back or rolled forward.

Some SQL Server administrators have noted that the transaction log seems unable to be purged to free up space, even after the log has been archived. This problem often results from some process having opened a transaction, which it then forgot about. For this reason, from an application development standpoint, you'll want to ensure that transactions are kept short. Another possible reason for this problem relates to a table being replicated, when the replication log reader hasn't processed it yet. This situation is less common, though, because typically only a latency of a few seconds occurs while the log reader does its work. You can use DBCC OPENTRAN to look for the earliest open transaction, or oldest replicated transaction not yet processed, and then take corrective measures (such as killing the offending process or running the **sp_repldone** stored procedure to allow the replicated transactions to be purged).

The SQL Server Kernel and Interaction with Windows NT

The SQL Server kernel is responsible for interacting with Windows NT operating system services. It's a bit of a simplification to suggest that SQL Server has one module for all operating system calls, but for ease of understanding, you can think of it in this way. All requests to operating system services are made via the Win32 API and C run-time libraries. SQL Server runs entirely in the Win32 protected subsystem of Windows NT. Absolutely no calls are made in Windows NT Privileged Mode. Instead, all calls are made in User Mode. This means that SQL Server cannot crash the entire system, it cannot crash another process running in User Mode, and other such processes cannot crash SQL Server. SQL Server has no device driver–level calls, nor does SQL Server use any undocumented calls to Windows NT. If the entire system crashes (giving you the so-called "Blue Screen of Death") and SQL Server happens to have been running there, one thing is absolutely certain: SQL Server *did not* crash the system. Instead, such a crash must be the result of faulty or incompatible hardware, a buggy device driver operating in Privileged Mode, or a critical bug in the Windows NT operating system code (which is doubtful).

NOTE The "Blue Screen of Death," a blue "bug check" screen with some diagnostic information, appears if a crash of Windows NT occurs. The blue screen looks similar to the screen that appears when Windows NT initially boots up.

From the Author...

I've worked with Windows NT every day on multiple systems since 1992, and I've experienced less than a handful of system crashes with a publicly released version of the product. Although I'm not certain that none of these crashes occurred because of an issue in the operating system itself, I cannot recall such an incident. The system crashes I can recall occurred when I was working with a prebeta build, when I had suffered a legitimate hardware failure, or when I had used a faulty third-party device driver with some specialized hardware.

Windows NT is quite remarkable in its resiliency and is truly the epitome of a protected operating system. I have used many other operating systems, including various flavors of UNIX and assorted mainframe operating systems. No other system has exhibited the stability I experience with Windows NT. If I see a blue screen, I first suspect a hardware issue and then suspect some device driver issue. Even though "conventional wisdom" sometimes says that Windows NT is less mature, this does not match my experience.

Exploiting the Windows NT Platform

Competitors have occasionally, and completely falsely, claimed that SQL Server must have special, secret hooks into the operating system. Such claims are likely the result of SQL Server's astonishing levels of performance. Yes, it is tightly integrated with the Windows NT operating system. But this tight integration of the two products is accomplished via completely public interfaces—there are no secret "hooks" into the operating system. Yes, our product is optimized for Windows NT. That's our only platform. But other products could also achieve this level of optimization and integration if they made it a chief design goal to do so. Instead, most other products tend to try to abstract away the differences between different operating systems. Of course, there's nothing wrong with that. If I had to make my product run on 44 different operating systems, I'd also try to take a lowest-common-denominator approach to engineering—to do anything else would be almost impossible. So although such an approach is quite rational, it is in direct conflict with the goal of fully exploiting all services of a given operating system. Since SQL Server runs exclusively on the Windows NT operating system, it intentionally uses every service in the smartest way possible.

A key design goal of both SQL Server and Windows NT is *scalability*. The same binary executable files that run on notebook computer systems run on symmetric multiprocessor super servers with loads of processors. SQL Server includes versions for Intel and RISC hardware architectures on the same CD-ROM. Except for less than 20 lines of assembly language code for the spinlock macro specific to the processor type, SQL Server is built simultaneously using the same source code for both Intel and RISC processors.

Windows NT is an ideal platform for a database server because it provides a fully protected, secure 32-bit environment. Preemptive scheduling, virtual paged memory management, symmetric multiprocessing, and asynchronous I/O are the foundations needed for a great database server platform. Windows NT provides these foundations, and SQL Server uses them fully. The SQL Server engine runs as a single process on Windows NT. Within that process are multiple threads of execution. Windows NT schedules each thread to the next processor available to run one.

Threading and Symmetric Multiprocessing

SQL Server approaches multiprocessor scalability in a different way than most other symmetric multiprocessing (SMP) database systems. Two characteristics separate this approach from other implementations: single-process architecture and native thread-level multiprocessing.

■ Single-process architecture. SQL Server maintains a single-process, multithreaded architecture that reduces system overhead and memory use. This is called the *Symmetric Server Architecture*.

■ Native thread-level multiprocessing. SQL Server supports multiprocessing at the thread rather than at the process level, which allows for preemptive operation and dynamic load balancing across multiple CPUs. Using multiple threads is significantly more efficient than using multiple processes.

In explaining how SQL Server works, it is useful to compare SQL Server's strategies to strategies generally used by other products. On a nonthreaded operating system such as some UNIX variants, a typical SMP database server has multiple DBMS processes, each bound to a specific CPU. Some implementations even have one process per user, which results in a high memory cost. These processes intercommunicate using shared memory, which maintains the cache, locks, task queues, and user context information. The DBMS must include complex logic that takes on the role of an operating system: it schedules user tasks, simulates threads, coordinates multiple processes, and so on. Because processes are bound to specific CPUs, dynamic load balancing can be difficult or impossible. Seeking to be portable, products often take this approach even when they are running on an operating system that offers native threading services, such as Windows NT.

SQL Server, on the other hand, uses a clean design of a single process and multiple operating system threads, as shown in Figure 3-6 on the following page. SQL Server makes extensive use of the native thread services of Windows NT.

As I mentioned in Chapter 2, single-threaded processes do not efficiently exploit multiple CPUs. In a symmetric multiprocessor system, a process that uses multiple threads (such as SQL Server) can use all processors simultaneously. For specialized use patterns, SQL Server is "affinitized" so that threads can be limited from running on certain processors, and the threads will be "sticky." That is, they can signal Windows NT to schedule them only to the same processor on which they ran previously.

In SQL Server, because all threads belong to the same process, they use a single address space and there is no need to coordinate processes through shared memory. By using native operating system threads, task scheduling within SQL Server is preemptive, providing smoother operation and greater fault isolation. Windows NT schedules threads dynamically on the most available CPU, automatically load balancing across multiple CPUs. The same SQL Server binary supports both single-processor and multiprocessor systems: no special configuration is necessary.

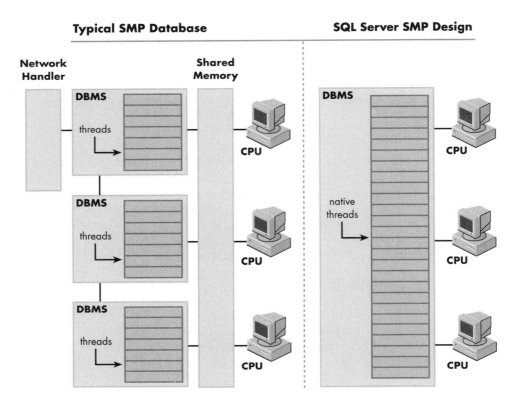

Figure 3-6. *SQL Server uses a single-process multiple thread design.*

SQL Server always uses multiple threads, even on a single-processor system. Threads are created and destroyed depending on system activity, so thread count is not constant. Typically, the number of active threads in SQL Server will range from 16 to 100, depending on system activity and configuration. A pool of threads handles each of the networks that SQL Server simultaneously supports, another thread handles database checkpoints, and another handles the Lazywriter process. Read Ahead is performed with separate threads, and a pool of threads handles all user commands.

Worker Thread Pool

Although it may seem that SQL Server offers each user a separate operating system thread, the system is actually a bit more sophisticated than that. Because it is inefficient to use hundreds of separate operating system threads to support hundreds of users, SQL Server establishes a *pool* of *worker threads*.

When a client issues a command, the SQL Server network handler places the command in a "queue" and the next available thread from the worker thread pool takes the request and services it. Technically, this "queue" is a Windows NT facility called an *IOCompletion port*. The SQL Server worker thread waits in the completion queue for incoming network requests to be posted to the IOCompletion port. If no idle worker thread is available to wait for the next incoming request, SQL Server dynamically creates a new thread, until the maximum configured worker thread limit is reached. The client's command must wait for a worker thread to be freed.

Even in a system with thousands of connected users, most are typically idle at any given time. As the workload decreases, SQL Server gradually eliminates idle threads to improve resource and memory utilization.

Active vs. Idle

In the above context, a user is considered *idle* from the database perspective. The human end user might be quite active, filling in the data entry screen, getting information from customers, and so forth. But those activities don't require any server interaction until a command is actually sent. So from the SQL Server engine perspective, the connection is idle.

When you think of an *active* versus an *idle* user, be sure to consider the user in the context of the back-end database server. In practically all types of applications that have many end users, at any given time the number of users who have an active request with the database tends to be relatively small. A system with 1000 active connections might reasonably be configured with 150 or so worker threads. But this doesn't mean that all 150 worker threads will be created at the start—they'll be created only as needed, and the 150 is only a high-water mark. In fact, fewer than 100 worker threads might be active at a time, even if end users all think they are actively using the system all the time.

The worker thread pool design is efficient for handling large numbers of active connections—literally thousands—without the need for a transaction monitor. Most competing products, including those found on the largest mainframe systems, need to use a transaction monitor to achieve the level of active users that SQL Server can handle without such an extra component. If you support a large number of connections, this is an important capability.

You should allow users to stay connected—even if they will be idle for periods of, say, an hour—rather than have them continually connect and disconnect. Repeatedly incurring the overhead of the login process will be more expensive than simply allowing the connection to remain live but idle.

A thread from the worker thread pool services each command to allow multiple processors to be fully utilized as long as multiple user commands are outstanding. However, generally speaking, a single user command with no other activity on the system will not benefit greatly from multiple processors. Because the command is serviced by one thread, it executes on only one processor. Offloading other services, such as Windows NT operations and various other SQL Server threads, to the other processors can result in some benefit. And if the Read Ahead Manager prefetches data in response to a query, that will indeed result in a nice win on a multiprocessor system. But a specific user command is not decomposed into multiple steps for parallel execution. Such intraquery parallelism is definitely planned for future versions of SQL Server, but for now the benefits of multiple processors will be far more evident and substantial when multiple user requests are made simultaneously, which is by far the most common use.

Under this pooling scheme, a worker thread runs each user request to completion. Because each thread has its own stack, stack switching is unnecessary. If a given thread performs an operation that causes a page fault, only that thread, and hence only that one client, is blocked. (A page fault occurs if the thread makes a request for memory and the virtual memory manager of the operating system must swap that page in from disk since it had been paged out. Such a request for memory must wait a long time relative to the normal memory access time, as a physical I/O is thousands of times more expensive than reading real memory.)

Now consider something more serious than a page fault. Suppose in carrying out some user request, a bug is exposed in SQL Server that results in an illegal operation that would cause an access violation (for example, the thread tries to read some memory outside the SQL Server address space). Windows NT will immediately terminate the offending thread—an important feature of a truly protected operating system. Because SQL Server makes use of structured exception handling in Windows NT, only the specific SQL Server user who made the request will be affected. All other users of SQL Server or other applications on the system will be unaffected and the system at large will not crash. Of course, such a bug should never occur and in reality is indeed rare. But this is software, and software is never perfect. Having this important reliability feature is like wearing your seat belt—you hope you never need to use it, but you're glad it's there, just in case of a crash.

Memory use per SQL Server user is extremely efficient. A configured user connection requires about 28 KB for private context. This context area per user is an all important data structure known as the Process Status Structure (PSS). The PSS stores the current state of activity for each connection so that the connection can be worked on for a while, scheduled out, worked on again, and so on. Each active worker thread has about 27 KB available, 20 KB of which is a private stack for the thread. The 27 KB is allocated when (and if) the thread is actually created.

Memory Use: A Real-World Example

A large user environment supports 900 active users on a two-processor Pentium Pro, and 900 user connections are configured. The maximum number of worker threads is set to 100 and is generally not reached, so the amount of memory used for user context is under 28 MB—(900 × 28 KB) + (100 × 27 KB). In reality, the amount of memory used is usually even less, as typically not all 100 worker threads will exist at any one time. This environment runs with total physical memory of 128 MB. Of this, more than 70 MB is still available for the data cache even after accounting for the needs of Windows NT itself, the 28-MB user connection needs, memory for the SQL Server code, and other static structures. Contrast this with a process-per-user architecture, typically requiring perhaps 350 KB per user: supporting 900 concurrent users at a cost of 350 KB per user would mean user context memory requirements of more than 300 MB even before any memory was used for a data cache!

Scalability, Performance, and Benchmarks

When I speak to customers about SQL Server and discuss its architecture, I often get a response such as, "Architecture? Who cares? How does it perform? How does it scale? Show me the numbers."

Here's the short answer. It performs wonderfully well.

Here's the long answer. SQL Server makes efficient use of the CPU, memory, and disk I/O in such a way that overall performance continues to increase to a point that is specific to the application as more processors are added. However, as with any real-world application, the performance gained by each additional processor will be less than the percentage that was gained by the previous processor. SQL Server exhibits SMP scalability that is extremely competitive given equal hardware with any other product, anywhere, *period*. In most real-world application use, SMP systems generally will not continue to benefit significantly with more than six to eight processors, and this is often the case with considerably fewer. I realize that there are exceptions to this, and it is difficult to make a blanket statement because everything is so much in the "It depends" category.

More Information...

A good source of information regarding scalability limits of SMP systems, like Amdahl's Law, the Von Neumann bottleneck, and other considerations SMP systems must face, is Gregory F. Pfister's *In Search of Clusters*.[3] I especially recommend Chapters 6 and 11.

I would not categorically state that SMP systems don't scale beyond eight processors. However, I don't know of any real-world applications using any combination of SMP hardware and software that benefits nearly as much from their eighth processor as they benefit from their second processor. The incremental gain in going from a single processor to a second processor will be much greater than that in going from the seventh processor to the eighth. Depending on the application, you might get little or no increased benefit from that eighth processor.

> **NOTE** I am talking here about the limits of symmetric multiprocessing (SMP) systems. Certainly other architectures, such as "shared nothing" clusters, can scale much higher. A future direction for SQL Server, in conjunction with the Microsoft Transaction Server, is to participate in such shared nothing implementations.

From the Author...

We have generally tried to be clear on the limits of scalability in our marketing materials (at least whenever I had anything to do with them), but competitors often make claims of much higher scale-up on SMP. Claims of "linear" scaling are common. The term "linear" is actually meaningless here—I guess it's used because it sounds technical. But if going from one to two processors yields only a 10 percent improvement, and going from two to three also yields only 10 percent, that's certainly "linear" but not at all impressive. The marketing claims of "linear" scaling are supposed to mean that going from the $N-1$ to the Nth processor yields as much improvement as going from the first to the second. Common sense alone says that this can nearly never be the case. So take such claims with a grain of salt.

---

3. Gregory F. Pfister, *In Search of Clusters* (Prentice Hall, 1995). ISBN 0-13-437625-0.

Simply put, when a task is broken down into multiple parts that run in parallel, the system will only run in aggregate (in the best case) as fast as the slowest part runs. This is the basic tenet of Amdahl's Law. And coordinating between multiple processors and threads running simultaneously takes increasingly high overhead and resources as you add more and more processors, so the benefits diminish as the number increases.

Benchmarks sometimes get a lot of bad press, but I know of no better way to compare performance. Industry standard benchmarks that are jointly defined by representatives from all product manufacturers, that are independently audited and reproducible, and with all implementation details completely disclosed are far preferable to simply accepting a vendor's claims at face value. Relying on such benchmarks is also far better than relying on word of mouth or conventional wisdom. It's also usually better than press reviews. Since a reviewer can test spreadsheets one week, word processors the next, and RDBMs the week after, the reviewer can never really be expert enough to do the job right.

I have a lot of respect for TPC-C benchmarks, having been personally involved with Microsoft initially joining the Transaction Processing Council (TPC) and subsequently with the work to get benchmarks audited and published. The benchmarks are conceived by experts working in the database field; they are tough and fair, and every detail is scrupulously reviewed by all competitors. And the benchmarks actually test more than performance. Before a benchmark number can be published, the system must prove its ability to maintain without exception the ACID properties. A system fully running the benchmark at thousands of transactions per minute will literally have the power suddenly pulled (without backup power), and then a complete audit is taken. Not only must the system restart and recover to a consistent state, but every transaction on which a client got a Commit acknowledgment must be accurately reflected. Not even a single transaction can have been lost.

TPC benchmarks are not perfect, and they should not be the only data you consider when making buying decisions, but they are extremely valuable. Every major product participates in TPC benchmarking, and if a product or an environment does not have a current benchmark published, it's a good bet that's because it cannot produce a compelling number. (The first rule of the benchmarking game is "Don't play unless you can win." It's better not to have a number at all than to have a bad number.) Benchmark results change rapidly, and any number that appears in this book will be obsolete long before the book goes to print. But a constant factor is that SQL Server continually performs extremely well in these comparisons across all dimensions—raw performance, SMP scalability, and price-performance ratios. And nearly all the SQL Server benchmarks were set without the use of a transaction monitor, which is needed by nearly every other product to handle the high numbers of active users that these benchmarks represent.

> ## More Information...
>
> For information about TPC, the benchmark tests, and current results, see
> http://www.tpc.org. It's useful to look at a history of results. Tomorrow some
> competitor might publish a benchmark that invalidates any one or all of the
> statements I've made here. But if that happens, it's a good bet that the SQL Server
> performance team will do yet another benchmark to reclaim SQL Server's usual
> top spot. It's a matter of pride.

As of this writing, SQL Server holds top honors in the following categories:

- The number one total performance (that is, the highest transactions per minute) for any Windows NT system.[4]

- The best performance of any product on any operating system for which multiple identical Pentium Pro SMP systems have numbers published.[5]

- The top seven spots in price performance (lowest price/transaction total costs).[6]

I have confidence that SQL Server will continue to outshine other products.

SUMMARY

In this chapter, I've tried to describe the general workings of the SQL Server
engine, including the key modules and functional areas that make up the engine.
I've also discussed integration with Windows NT, threading, and scaling issues.
By necessity, I've made some simplifications throughout. But the information
should provide you with some insight into the roles and responsibilities of the
major subsystems in SQL Server, the general flow of the system, and the inter-
relationships among subsystems. Hopefully, if you, as a developer, have some
insight into how the product performs its magic, you can work with it that much
more effectively.

---

4. As of December 19, 1996. Number referenced is 7521.13 tpmC, $77.59/tpmC achieved on Compaq ProLiant 5000 6/200, 4-proc P6, 200 MHz.

5. Comparison as of December 19, 1996. Number referenced is 7128.20 tpmC, $79.78/tpmC achieved on Compaq ProLiant 5000 6/166, 4-proc P6, 166 MHz.

6. As of December 19, 1996, per all results posted on http://www.tpc.org.

THREE

Using Microsoft
SQL Server

4

Planning for and Installing SQL Server

Setup Is Easy, but Think First

If you already have the appropriate hardware running Microsoft Windows NT, installing Microsoft SQL Server is a snap. It requires little more than double-clicking SETUP.EXE and answering a few questions. I'm proud to say that even a novice can comfortably install SQL Server in less than 10 minutes. I won't spend much time discussing the mechanics of the Setup program. You can consult the online Help and the documentation's step-by-step guide if you need to.

Setup is so easy that you might be tempted to dive in a bit too soon. That's OK if you're in "learning mode," but an installation that will be part of a production system deserves some thoughtful planning. A basic design goal, what I refer to as the *prime directive* of the Setup program, is to get users up and running quickly, 100 percent reliably. Setup does not ask a lot of questions about how to best configure your system, nor does it try to do a lot of autoconfiguration. This means that you (or whoever runs the Setup program) will need to do some basic configuration directly after Setup or you can configure your system by using a script that can automate the setup process for you.

SQL Server vs. SQL Workstation

Most SQL Server applications are deployed on the SQL Server product (as opposed to SQL Workstation), which allows multiple users. SQL Server is supported only on Microsoft Windows NT Server. SQL Workstation, on the other hand, is intended primarily as a development platform and is licensed for use by a single user. SQL Workstation is supported on both Windows NT Server and Windows NT Workstation. SQL Workstation has all the same components and binary files included in SQL Server, but Workstation is limited to 15 connections (which can be made via the network or from the same machine). Although this 15-connection limit is sufficient for most development and initial testing, it is not suitable for the deployment of most applications. (Even if an application needs no more than 15 connections, SQL Workstation's licensing restricts it to a single user. A single developer testing his or her application from multiple workstations is in compliance with this licensing restriction.)

> **NOTE** Because SQL Server and SQL Workstation are identical except for their licensing and connection limits, I refer only to SQL Server throughout this book.

Choosing Hardware

Because SQL Server runs on any hardware that runs Windows NT, you can choose from among thousands of hardware options. Although SQL Server is sometimes labeled (correctly) as running "only" on Windows NT, the number of hardware possibilities is actually so vast that it can be confusing. Following are some practical guidelines to keep in mind when you're choosing hardware.

Use Hardware on the Windows Hardware Compatibility List

Although you can cobble together a system from spare parts and Windows NT will run just fine, the reliability of such a system can be questionable. Sufficient if you're a hobbyist and you like to tinker, this method isn't what I'd recommend for a production system. Reliability isn't the only issue. I know people who have bought motherboards, chassis, processors, hard drives, memory, video cards, and assorted other peripherals all separately and have put together terrific systems— but the support options are limited. The best approach is to use a system that is not only reliable but also supported by a reputable supplier.

Keep in mind that even name-brand systems will occasionally fail. If you're using hardware that's included on the Windows Hardware Compatibility List (HCL) and you get a "blue screen" (Windows NT system crash), you're more likely to be able to isolate the issue to a hardware failure or to find out, for example, that some known device driver problem occurs with that platform (and you can get an update for the driver). With a homegrown system, such a problem can be nearly impossible to isolate. If you plan to use SQL Server, data integrity is probably a key concern for you. The majority of cases of corrupt data in SQL Server can be traced to hardware or device driver failure. (These device drivers are often supplied by the hardware vendor.)

NOTE   Over the life of a system, hardware costs will be a relatively small portion of your overall cost. In my opinion, using no-name or homegrown hardware is being penny-wise and pound-foolish. You can definitely get a good and cost-effective HCL-approved system without cutting corners.

Although many good choices are available, from personal experience, I think Compaq servers are great systems. Compaq systems are reliable, well supported, great on the basis of price/performance, and used extensively within the labs at Microsoft. I also am impressed with servers based on the Intel Xxpress motherboards provided by many major hardware vendors such as AT&T, DEC, Dell, Intergraph, and Hewlett-Packard. If you are considering a non–Intel-based solution, I suggest DEC's Alpha processor-based servers. Obviously, I do not have direct experience with all or even most of the many excellent systems available. Choose carefully.

Choose a Good Processor

SQL Server 6.5 runs on the four major processor architectures supported by Windows NT: Intel *x*86, MIPS R4000, DEC Alpha-AXP, and Motorola PowerPC. Note that future versions of SQL Server will likely drop support for the MIPS and PowerPC platforms because few hardware vendors are still building machines using these processors. So if you are deciding on your platform, I'd suggest that you choose either an Intel or a DEC Alpha solution.

Today the majority of SQL Server customers use machines with the Intel architecture. Although the SQL Server product versions for all processor architectures ship on the same CD-ROM, many other vendors' software components for SQL Server might ship first, or only, for the Intel platform. For example, you might use an accounting software package that is first released or available only for Intel-based machines. You could run the accounting application on an Intel-based server and use it to communicate via the network to a SQL Server running on a DEC Alpha-AXP–based system, as long as the application isn't required to run on the same machine as SQL Server (and you have multiple machines in your environment). In addition, if you ever need to dual-boot your system to MS-DOS or Microsoft Windows 95, you will want to go with Intel. An Intel-based solution is likely to provide all the horsepower your application needs. But the processor is only part of the equation, as I will discuss later.

If you're part of a large organization, you probably have a set of standard hardware requirements. SQL Server 6.5 will run well if you've settled on a RISC platform with Windows NT. SQL Server provides a small amount of processor-specific assembly language (less than 20 lines) for the spinlock macro for each environment, but otherwise the code is all-common. We in the SQL Server group have no "porting" team. Versions for all supported processor architectures are built and tested at the same time, and, as I said earlier, they ship on the same CD-ROM. If this is the first time you've used a RISC platform with Windows NT (that is MIPS, Alpha-AXP, or PowerPC), you'll be surprised at how "normal" it seems compared to the Intel-based systems you probably already use. In my office, I have two Intel-based machines, an Alpha-based workstation, and a PowerPC. All four systems are configured with a switch box that allows them to use the same keyboard, monitor, and mouse. All run Windows NT and SQL Server virtually identically. In fact, I cannot tell one system from another unless I make an effort to find out which is currently running.

Performance = Fn(Processor Cycles, Memory, I/O Throughput)

The system throughput is only as fast as the slowest component. A bottleneck in one area brings the rest of the system to the speed of the slowest part. So it is important to remember that the performance of your hardware is a function of the processing power available, the amount of physical memory (RAM) in the system, and the number of I/Os per second that the system can support.

Of course, the most important aspect of performance is the application's design and implementation. You want to carefully choose your hardware, but there is no substitute for efficient applications. Although SQL Server can be a brilliantly fast system, it's still easy to write an application that performs poorly, one that's impossible to "fix" simply by "tuning" the server or by "killing it with hardware." You might be able to double performance by upgrading your hardware or fine-tuning your system, but application changes can often yield *hundredfold* increases.

Unfortunately, no simple formula allows you to plug in a few variables and come up with the appropriately sized system. Many people ask for this, and it is common for minicomputer and mainframe vendors to provide "configuration programs" that purport to do just this. But the goal of those systems often seems to be to sell more hardware.

Once again, your application is the key here. In reality, sizing the hardware to your needs is dependent on your application. How CPU-intensive is it? How much data will you store? How random are the requests for data? Can you expect to often get "cache hits" with the most frequently requested data often being found in memory, without having to perform physical I/Os? How many users will simultaneously and actively use the system?

Problem: Mismatching Systems

I see many people today overbuying hardware or buying mismatched systems. For example, it is not unusual to hear of someone who has purchased a dual 166-MHz Pentium with 256 MB of memory and 4 GB of disk space. Usually such a system has a single 4-GB disk drive rather than multiple drives. This is a badly mismatched system. With sufficient I/O capacity, I'd expect this system to perform more than 500 transactions per second (TPS) on a standard test such as the Debit-Credit benchmark. But such a test uses about 2.1 I/Os per transaction, and a single typical 8 ms disk drive can perform only about 80 to 90 random I/Os of 2 KB per second (the size SQL Server most often uses). Hence, this system could do only about 35 TPS. A single processor 486-66 with about 32 MB of memory could probably do 70 TPS. So the power (and expense) of dual fast processors and loads of memory is mostly wasted. To get the most out of that system, you'd want to add additional disk drives or a drive array. If your budget is fixed, you would do well to reduce the memory, make it a single CPU system, and spend the savings on a fast disk array of multiple disk drives.

Invest in Benchmarking

If you are planning a large system, it's worthwhile to invest up front in some benchmarking. Microsoft SQL Server has numerous published benchmarks. Most are Transaction Processing Council (TPC) benchmarks. Although benchmarks such as these are useful in comparing systems and hardware, they can give you only broad guidelines and it is unlikely that the benchmark workload will compare directly to yours. It's probably best to do some custom benchmarking for your own system. Benchmarking can be a difficult, never-ending job, so you'll need to keep the process in perspective. Remember that, ultimately, the only thing that counts is how fast your application runs, not how fast your benchmark performs. And sometimes it is unnecessary to undertake a significant benchmarking effort—the system might perform clearly within parameters or similar enough to other systems. Your experience will be the best guide. But if you are testing a new application that will be widely deployed, the up-front cost of a

More Information...

For information on TPC benchmarks and a summary of results, see the TPC home page at http://www.tpc.org. For an overview of benchmarking, see Chapter 3, "SQL Server Architecture."

benchmark can pay big dividends in terms of a successful system rollout. Benchmarking is the developer's equivalent of the carpenter's adage, "Measure twice, cut once."

Nothing beats a real-world system test, but that is not always practical. You might need to make hardware decisions before or at the same time the application is being developed. In that case, you will want to develop a proxy test. Much of the work in benchmarking comes from developing the appropriate *test harness*—the mechanisms used to simultaneously dispatch multiple clients running the test program, to run for exactly an allotted time, and to gather the results.

Microsoft provides, free of charge, a benchmark kit. (See the companion CD-ROM.) This benchmark kit allows you to "add water and stir" to produce a benchmark environment within a few hours and simply substitute your own transactions in place of the kit's transactions. The kit includes the source code and executables used in previous TPC-B benchmarks. Although TPC-B might not be directly relevant to your system, the real value is in the kit's test harness—the framework that drives "virtual clients" and synchronizes start and stop times, records results, and so on. If you decide to use the kit, I'd advise you to first try to run the TPC-B test without modification. Try to achieve results roughly comparable with those listed in the kit. (Allow for hardware differences—you're just looking for a "reasonableness quotient.") This ensures that your system is generally properly configured. Then you can easily modify the tests with your own custom transaction to better simulate your actual system. Some products, such as Dynameasure by Bluecurve, Inc. (http://www.bluecurve.com), are also available to aid in benchmarking for SQL Server performance.

Hardware Guidelines

As I've said, no magic formula can help you produce an optimal hardware configuration. Even though the following general guidelines will be helpful, they might be dead wrong because of the many variables that could exist. Your mileage *will* vary.

If you've already deployed SQL Server, your experience with your application will certainly be more relevant than these general guidelines. Also, I have assumed that the server is basically dedicated to running SQL Server, with little else going on. (You can certainly combine SQL Server with other applications on the same machine, and you can choose to administer SQL Server on the same machine and run SQL Enterprise Manager there as well. Or you can support multiple databases from one SQL Server machine. All of these scenarios are typical, but you'll need to adjust the guidelines in a corresponding manner.) Keeping all this in mind, consider these "in-the-ballpark" guidelines.

The Processor

SQL Server is CPU intensive, more so than those who assume it is mostly I/O constrained might think. Plenty of processing capacity is a good investment. Managing many connections, managing its data cache effectively, optimizing and executing queries, checking constraints, executing stored procedures, locking tables and indexes, and enforcing security all use a lot of processing cycles. Because SQL Server typically performs few floating-point operations, a processor that is fabulous with such operations but mediocre with integer operations is not the ideal choice. Before choosing a processor, you should check benchmarks such as SPECInt (integer)—not SPECfp (floating-point) or any benchmark that is a combination of floating-point and integer performance. Performance on SPECInt correlates to the relative performance of SQL Server among different processor architectures, given sufficient memory and I/O capacity. The correlation is a bit loose, of course, as other factors (the size of the processor cache, the system bus efficiency, the efficiency of the optimizing compiler used to build the system when comparing processor architectures, and many other variables) all also play an important role. But holding those things equal, integer-processing performance is a key metric for SQL Server.

Figure 4-1 on the following page shows SPECInt92 ratings for various processors running Windows NT. These figures are based on each processor vendor's data as stated in February 1996 on their respective Internet Web pages. To highlight the tremendous increases in performance over mainstream hardware of just a couple years ago, I have included some old figures for i386 and i486 processors, even though you clearly would not go out and buy these today.

> **NOTE** I use SPECInt92 because it is easier to do comparisons showing the historical pattern. SPECInt95 is a newer, improved benchmark of integer performance, but results for it are harder to come by, especially for the processors from a few years ago.

SQL Server is built for symmetric multiprocessing (SMP), but if your system is dedicated to SQL Server and supports less than 100 simultaneous users, a single CPU system will likely meet your needs. This is one of those cases in which you'll see definite exceptions to the general guidelines, depending on your system's specific application and performance characteristics. If you are uncertain about your needs or you expect them to grow, get a single-processor system that can be upgraded to a dual (or even quad) system later.

Since Moore's Law (processing power doubles every 18 months) has proven true year after year, it's a good idea to buy the fastest single-processor system in its class. Buy tomorrow's technology, not yesterday's. With many other applications, the extra processing power doesn't make much difference, but SQL Server is CPU intensive. The 46 percent difference in SPECInt92 performance between a 166 MHz Pentium and a 180 MHz Pentium Pro can yield a similar difference in SQL Server performance.

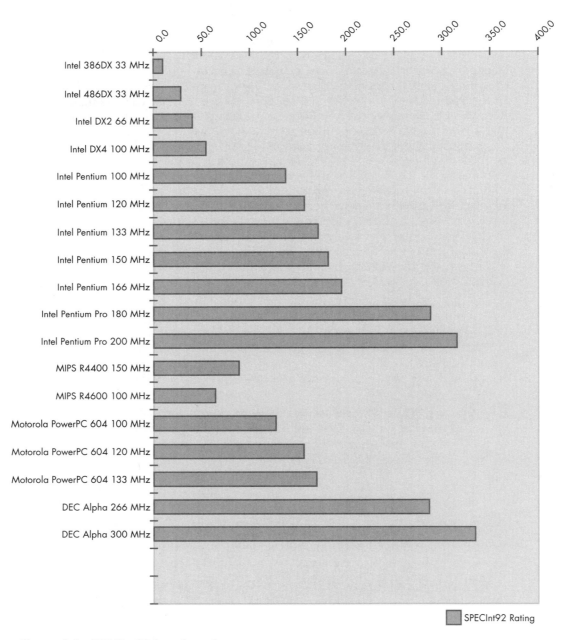

Figure 4-1. *SPECInt92 benchmarks.*

From the Author...

Remember that the processor's cache is important to its performance. A big "L2" (level 2, or secondary) cache (512 KB or more) is a good investment. Using the same system, I have seen a difference of 20 percent or better simply by using a 512-KB L2 cache instead of a 256-KB L2 cache. The cost difference is perhaps $100, so this is money well spent.

Final Comments About SMP Systems

I've seen some sites try to re-create the mainframe model of computing by procuring a single "monster" machine with the intention of supporting many totally separate SQL Server applications. Or they combine SQL Server with many other services. Obviously, it makes sense to employ underused resources: if you have a SQL Server machine that is half-idle, you should use it for your file server, too, or use it to run Microsoft Systems Management Server. But it makes less sense to buy a quad-processor system, for example, so that you can run everything on one machine. First, you pay a premium for SMP systems. They are terrific for supporting large SQL Server applications that cannot be easily separated into smaller units, but you can probably buy four single-CPU systems for the price of one loaded quad system. Using four systems better protects you from a single catastrophic failure, and it better insulates the applications from each other. While it might be true that using only one machine reduces the maintenance burden, the administration tools of SQL Server, Windows NT, and products such as Systems Management Server make it easier to administer many systems from one site.

The isolation of the four services offers other benefits, too. If, for example, you upgrade your SQL Server, you won't affect your file server. Also, the "per-user" licensing option of SQL Server makes it cost effective to deploy many SQL Server installations, so there is no major financial incentive to keep you from doing the right thing.

Finally, the performance of the different SMP systems can vary greatly. Vendor A's four-processor system might scale poorly, but vendor C's system scales great, running the same application. SMP systems are complex and most definitely are not all created equal. From personal experience, I know that the Compaq Proliant 4500, DEC AlphaServer, and various other systems (AT&T, DEC, DELL, Intergraph, Hewlett-Packard) that use the Intel Xxpress motherboards scale nicely.

If your application is available or you can conduct a fairly realistic system test, you can be much more exacting in evaluating your hardware needs. Using the Windows NT Performance Monitor, simply profile the CPU usage of your system during a specified period of time. (Use the *Processor* object and the *% Processor Time* counter.) Watch all processors if you're using an SMP system. If your system is consistently above 70 percent usage or can be expected to grow to that level relatively soon, or if it frequently spikes to greater than 90 percent for durations of 10 seconds or more, you should consider getting a faster or an additional processor. You can use the SPECInt92 guidelines to determine the relative additional processing power that would be available to you by upgrading to a different or an additional processor.

> **NOTE** Remember that adding an additional processor does not double your processing power. For a system of up to four processors, adding another processor on an efficient SMP hardware platform usually yields at most an additional 80 to 90 percent of the processing power of the first CPU. Gains above 70 percent can be achieved in the four-to-eight CPU range if your system is really CPU hungry. But, by far, most systems today would be bottlenecked somewhere else before they'd demand the amount of processing power that a modern four-way CPU system could deliver. If your system already has plenty of CPU cycles to spare, adding a processor contributes little.

Memory

SQL Server uses memory for two broad purposes: for its own code and internal data structures and for its data cache. SQL Server uses only about 3 MB of real memory for its code and internal structures. (People are often surprised that the value is this small.) User connections consume about 55 KB of memory for each connection configured. Other configurations affect memory (and will be discussed later), but user connections are typically the most important. Additional memory configured for SQL Server is mostly available for SQL Server's data cache.

If data can be found in the cache (memory), physical I/Os can be avoided. As discussed earlier, retrieving data from memory is tens of thousands of times faster than the mechanical operation of performing a physical I/O. (And performing physical I/O operations also consumes thousands more CPU clock cycles than simply addressing real memory.) As a rule, you should add physical memory to the system until you stop getting significant increases in cache hits—or until you run out of money. You can easily monitor cache hits with Performance Monitor. (For more information, see Chapters 14 and 15.) Using the *SQLServer* object, watch *Cache Hit Ratio*. If adding additional physical memory (and configuring SQL Server to use it) makes *Cache Hit Ratio* increase significantly, the memory is a good investment.

Configuring memory appropriately is crucial to good performance. Be sure that the system's memory is not overcommitted. (This occurs when the aggregate working sets of the operating system and all applications exceed real memory, requiring memory to be paged to and from disk.) You can monitor paging in Performance Monitor using statistics such as the *Memory* object's counter for *Page Faults/Sec*.

Fortunately, adding physical memory to systems today is usually quite simple (pop in some SIMMs) and economical. I recommend starting conservatively and adding memory based on empirical evidence as you test your application. SQL Server needs no single correct amount of memory, so it's pointless to try to establish a uniform memory configuration for all SQL Server applications you might ever deploy.

SQL Server can run effectively with a minimum 16-MB system, but as is typically the case with a minimum requirement, this is not an ideal environment. If your budget isn't constrained, I'd recommend starting with enough memory to give SQL Server at least a 10-MB cache. Because of the way memory SIMMs are sold, this often means a system with 32 MB of RAM. (If your budget is flexible or you have good reason to believe that your application will be more demanding, you might want to bump up memory to 64 MB. But I wouldn't start with more than 64 MB without some evidence that your SQL Server application will use it.) About 16 MB of a 32-MB system will be configured for SQL Server, and the other 16 MB will be used for Windows NT, the network, SQL Executive, and so on. Of the 16 MB for SQL Server, you are left with a cache of slightly less than 12 MB if you have configured SQL Server for 50 users (and not changed other configurations yet). That's a reasonable place to start.

NOTE The code sizes of both SQL Server and Windows NT system executables are larger for RISC architectures than for Intel architectures. SQL Server data structures are essentially the same size for both Intel and RISC, but the starting "tax" is higher for RISC. If you are running on a RISC platform, I'd recommend starting with an additional 16 MB of memory.

When you buy your initial system, give some consideration to the configuration of the memory SIMMs, not only to the total number of megabytes, so that you can later expand in the most effective way. If you're not careful, you can get a memory configuration that makes it difficult to upgrade. For example, suppose that your machine allows four memory banks for SIMMs and you want 64 MB of memory that you might upgrade in the future. If your initial configuration of 64 MB was done with four 16-MB SIMMs, you're in trouble. If you want to upgrade, you'll have to remove the 16-MB SIMMs and buy all new memory. But if you configure your 64 MB as two 32-MB SIMMs, you can add another one or two such SIMMs to get to 96 MB or 128 MB without replacing any of the initial memory.

In deciding on the initial amount of memory, you should also consider whether your system will be more *query-intensive* or *transaction-intensive*. Although more memory can help both, it will typically benefit query-intensive systems the most, especially if part of the data is "hot" and often queried. That data will tend to remain cached, and more memory will allow more of the data to be accessed from the cache instead of necessitating physical I/Os. If you have a query-intensive system, you might want to start with more memory than 32 MB. In contrast, a system that will be transaction-intensive might get relatively few cache hits, especially if the transactions are randomly dispersed or don't rely much on preexisting data. In a transaction-intensive system, the amount of memory needed might be low, and adding a faster I/O subsystem would make more sense than adding more memory.

Disk Drives, Controllers, and Disk Arrays

Obviously, you need to acquire enough disk space to store all your data, plus more for working space and system files. But you should not simply buy storage capacity—you should buy I/O throughput and fault tolerance as well. A single 4-GB drive will store as much as eight 0.5-GB drives, but its maximum I/O throughput is likely to be only about one-eighth as much as the combined power of eight smaller drives (assuming the speed of each drive is the same). Even relatively small SQL Server installations should have at least two or three physical disk drives, rather than a single large drive. Systems we have benchmarked that could do, say, 1000 TPS (in a Debit-Credit scenario) used more than 40 physical disk drives and multiple controllers to achieve the I/O rates necessary to sustain that level of throughput.

If you know your transaction level or you can perform a system test to determine it, you might be able to produce a good estimate of the number of I/Os per second you need to support during peak use. Then you need to procure a combination of drives and controllers that are capable of delivering that number.

Typically, you will want to buy a system with SCSI drives, not IDE or EIDE drives. An IDE channel supports only two devices. An EIDE setup consists of two IDE channels and can support four (2×2) devices. But more importantly, an IDE channel can work with only a single device at a time—and even relatively small SQL Server installations usually have at least two or three disk drives. If multiple disks are connected on an IDE channel, only one disk at a time can do I/O. (This would be especially problematic if the channel also supported a slow device such as a CD-ROM. With an average access time of 250 ms, your disk I/O would be held up for 0.25 second, on average, while the CD-ROM is accessed. A hard drive today usually has access times of 8 to 10 ms, which is 25 times faster.)

SCSI is a lot smarter than IDE or EIDE. A SCSI controller will hand off commands to a SCSI drive and will then logically disconnect and issue commands to other drives. If multiple commands are outstanding, the SCSI controller will queue the commands inside the associated device (provided that the device supports command queuing) so that the device can immediately start on the next request as soon as the current request finishes. When a request finishes, the device notifies the controller. A SCSI channel can support multiple fast drives and allow them to work at full speed. Slow devices such as CD-ROMs or tape drives do not hog the SCSI channel since the controller logically disconnects. A single SCSI channel can support many drives, but from a practical standpoint, I recommend about a 5:1 ratio if you need to push the drives close to capacity. (That is, add an additional channel for every 5 drives or so.) If you are not pushing the drives to capacity, you might be able to use as many as 8 to 10 drives per channel—even more with some high-end controllers or random I/O patterns.

In our TPC benchmarks (which are I/O-intensive, and the I/O is deliberately random), we generally follow a 6:1 ratio of drives per SCSI channel. (Since TPC-C measures both performance and cost, we must balance the cost and benefits, just as we would for a real application.) Most real applications don't have such perfectly random I/O characteristics, though. When the I/O is perfectly random, a significant amount of the I/O time is spent with the disk drives seeking (that is, with the disk arm positioning itself to the right spot) rather than transferring data, which would consume the SCSI channel. Seeking is taxing only on the drive itself, not on the SCSI channel, so the ratio of drives per channel can be higher in the benchmark.

Note that I speak in terms of *channels,* not *controllers.* Most controllers have a single SCSI channel, so you can think of the two terms as synonymous. Some high-end cards (typically RAID controllers, not just standard SCSI) are dual-channel cards. For example, the Compaq Smart-2 Array controller is a dual-channel controller that can efficiently push 12 to 14 drives (6 to 7 per channel).

Some History...

The original acronym *RAID* apparently stood for redundant array of *inexpensive* disks, as per the Patterson, et al., paper presented to the 1988 ACM SIGMOD.[1] However, the current *RAIDbook,* published by the industrywide RAID Advisory Board, uses *independent,* which does seem a better description because the key function of RAID is to make separate, physically independent drives logically function as one drive.

---

1. Patterson, Gibson, and Katz, "A Case for Redundant Arrays of Inexpensive Disks (RAID)," SIGMOD (1988).

RAID Solutions

Simply put, RAID solutions are usually the best choice for SQL Server:

- RAID makes multiple physical disk drives appear logically as one drive.

- Different levels of RAID provide different performance and redundancy features.

- RAID provides different ways of distributing physical data across multiple disk drives.

- RAID can be provided as a hardware solution (with a special RAID disk controller card), but it does not necessarily imply special hardware. RAID can also be implemented via software.

- Windows NT Server provides in software RAID levels 0 (striping), 1 (mirroring), and 5 (striping with parity).

The different RAID levels provide different solutions—some provide increased I/O bandwidth (striping), and others provide fault-tolerant storage (mirroring or parity). With a hardware RAID controller, you can employ a combination of striping and mirroring, often referred to as RAID-0&1 (and sometimes also RAID-10 or RAID-0+1). RAID solutions vary in how much additional disk space is required to protect the data and how long it takes to recover from a system outage. The type and level of RAID you choose will depend on your I/O throughput and fault tolerance needs.

RAID-0

RAID-0, or striping, offers pure performance but no fault tolerance. I/O is done in "stripes" and is distributed among all drives in the array. Instead of the I/O capacity of one drive, you get the benefit of all the drives. A table's hot spots are

---

Choose an Appropriate Backup Strategy

Although you can use RAID for fault tolerance, remember that it is no substitute for doing regular backups. If your data is critical, it is still imperative to have an appropriate backup strategy that is rigorously followed. RAID solutions can protect against a pure disk-drive failure, such as a head crash, but that's far from the only case in which you'll need a backup. If the controller fails, garbage data could appear on both your primary and redundant disks. Even more likely, an administrator could accidentally clobber a table; a disaster at the site, such as a fire, flood, or earthquake, could occur; or a simple software failure (in a device driver, the operating system, or SQL Server) could threaten your data. RAID does not protect your data against any of those problems, but backups do.

dissipated, and the data transfer rates go up cumulatively with the number of drives in the array. So although a 4-GB disk might do 80 to 90 random I/Os per second, an array of eight 0.5-GB disks striped with Windows NT Server's RAID-0 might in aggregate perform more than 400 I/Os per second, which is a lot. With a price of under $200 each for such drives, getting I/O rates of 400 per second for a total cost of under $1,600 is simply phenomenal.

> **NOTE** You could argue that RAID-0 shouldn't be considered RAID at all because there is no redundancy. I guess that's why it's classified as Level 0.

Windows NT Server provides RAID-0, or a hardware RAID controller can provide it. RAID-0 requires little processing overhead, so a hardware implementation of RAID-0 offers at best a marginal performance advantage over the built-in Windows NT capability. One possible advantage is that RAID-0 in hardware often lets you adjust the stripe size, while the size is fixed at 64 KB in Windows NT and cannot be changed.

RAID-1

RAID-1, or mirroring, is conceptually simple: a mirror copy exists for every disk drive. Writes are made to the primary disk drive and to the mirrored copy. Because writes can be made concurrently, the elapsed time for a write is usually not much greater than it would be for a single, unmirrored device. The write I/O performance to a given logical drive is only as fast as a single physical drive can go.

From the Author...

The hardware implementation of RAID-0 might provide a small advantage, although I am not familiar with any sites that could quantify a measurable performance difference. Because most SQL Server write operations occur in 2-KB page sizes, you'd have to define a tiny stripe size to have a single write I/O be processed by multiple drives. I'd question the benefit of this because multiple drives would be incurring the seek-time cost for a very small amount of data transfer. Given the 2-KB writes, reads will usually be spread evenly automatically.

I don't want to be misinterpreted on this topic, so let me be very clear. I like hardware RAID and know of some great products (for example, the Compaq Smart-2 Array controller). But the software RAID capabilities of Windows NT are ideally suited for many environments. If you have a fixed budget, the money you save on hardware RAID controllers could be better spent elsewhere, such as on a faster processor, more disks, more memory, or an uninterruptible power supply.

Therefore, you can at best get I/O rates of perhaps 80 to 90 I/Os per second to a given logical RAID-1 drive, as opposed to the much higher I/O rates to a logical drive that can be achieved with RAID-0. You can, of course, use multiple RAID-1 drives. But if a single table is the hot spot in your database, even multiple RAID-1 drives will not be of much help from a performance perspective. (SQL Server offers a capability, known as *segments,* that allows you to place a table on a specific drive or drives. But currently no range partitioning capability is available, so this option doesn't really give you the control you'd need to eliminate hot spots.) If you require fault tolerance, RAID-1 is normally the best choice for the transaction log. Because transaction log writes are synchronous and sequential, unlike writes to the data pages, they are ideally suited to RAID-1.

Read performance with RAID-1 can be significantly increased in aggregate because a read can be obtained from either the primary device or the mirror device. (A single read is not performed faster, but multiple reads are faster in aggregate because they can be performed simultaneously.) If one of the drives fails, the other continues and SQL Server uses the surviving drive. Until the failed drive is replaced, fault tolerance is unavailable unless multiple mirror copies were used.

> **NOTE** The ability to keep multiple mirror copies is not provided by the Windows NT RAID software, which allows only one copy, but some RAID hardware controllers do offer it. You could keep one or more mirror copies of a drive to ensure that even if a drive failed, a mirror would exist. If a crucial system is difficult to access in a timely way to replace a failed drive, this option might make sense.

Windows NT Server provides RAID-1, and some hardware RAID controllers also provide it. RAID-1 requires little processing overhead, so a hardware implementation of RAID-1 offers at best a marginal performance advantage over the built-in Windows NT capability (although the hardware solution might provide the ability to mirror more than one copy of the drive).

RAID-5

RAID-5, or striping with parity, is a common choice for SQL Server use. RAID-5 not only logically combines multiple disks to act like one, but it also records extra parity information on every drive in the array (requiring only one extra drive). If any one drive fails, the others will be able to reconstruct the data and continue without any data loss or immediate down time. By doing an Exclusive OR (XOR) between the surviving drives and the parity information, the bit patterns for a failed drive can be derived on the fly.

RAID-5 is less costly to implement than mirroring all the drives, since only one additional drive is needed rather than the double drives that mirroring requires.

Although RAID-5 is commonly used, it is often not the best choice for SQL Server because it imposes a significant I/O hit on write performance, as both the data and the parity information must be written. RAID-5 can turn one write into two reads and two writes to keep the parity information updated. This doesn't mean that a single write will take four or five times as long, because the operations are done in parallel. It does mean, however, that many more I/Os will occur in the system, so many more drives and controllers will be required to reach the I/O levels that RAID-0 can achieve. So, although RAID-5 certainly is less costly than mirroring all the drives, the performance overhead for writes is significant. Read performance, on the other hand, is excellent, essentially equivalent to that of RAID-0.

RAID-5 makes good sense, then, for the data portion of a database that needs fault tolerance, that is heavily read, and that does not demand high write performance. Typically, you should not place the transaction log on a RAID-5 device unless the system has a low rate of changes to the data. (As I mentioned, RAID-1 is a better choice for the transaction log because of the sequential nature of I/O to the log.) Windows NT Server provides RAID-5 or, like RAID-0 and RAID-1, a hardware RAID controller can provide it.

RAID-5 requires more overhead for writes than RAID-0 or RAID-1, so the incremental advantage provided by a hardware RAID-5 solution instead of the Windows NT software solution can be somewhat higher because more work needs to be offloaded to the hardware. However, such a difference would be noticeable only if the system were nearly at I/O capacity. If this is the case in your system, you'd probably not want to use RAID-5 in the first place because of the write performance penalty. You would probably be better served to look at the combination of RAID-0 and RAID-1, known as RAID-0&1.

RAID-0&1

RAID-0&1, or striping and mirroring, is the ultimate choice for performance and recoverability. (This capability is sometimes also referred to as RAID 0+1 or RAID10.) A set of disks is striped to provide the performance advantages of RAID-0, and the stripe is mirrored to provide the fault-tolerance features and increased read performance of RAID-1. Performance for both writes and reads is excellent.

The most serious drawback to RAID 0&1 is cost. Like RAID-1, it demands duplicate drives. In addition, the built-in RAID software of Windows NT does not provide this solution, so RAID-0&1 requires a hardware RAID controller. Some hardware RAID controllers explicitly support RAID-0&1. But you can achieve this support using virtually any RAID controller by combining its capabilities with those of Windows NT. For example, you can set up two stripe sets of the same size and number of disks using hardware RAID. Then you can use Windows NT mirroring on the two stripe sets, which Windows NT sees as two drives of equal size. If you need high read and write performance and fault tolerance, and you cannot afford an outage or decreased performance if a drive fails, RAID-0&1 is your best choice.

A separate RAID-0&1 array usually is not an appropriate choice for the transaction log. Because the write activity tends to be sequential and is synchronous, the benefits of multiple spindles are not realized. A simple RAID-1 mirroring of the transaction log is preferable and cheaper. With internal Debit-Credit benchmarks, we have demonstrated that the transaction log on a simple RAID-1 device is sufficient to sustain literally thousands of transactions per second—likely many more than you will need. Log records are packed, and a single log write can commit multiple transactions (known as *group commit*). In the Debit-Credit benchmarks, 40 transactions can be packed into a log record. At a rate of 100 writes per second (writes/second), the log on a RAID-1 mirror would not become a bottleneck until around 4000 TPS.

| NOTE | Practically speaking, this threshold is probably even higher than 4000 TPS—for pure sequential I/O, 100 writes/second is a conservative estimate. Although a typical disk drive is capable of doing 80 to 90 random I/Os per second, the rate for pure sequential I/O—largely eliminating the seek time of the I/Os—is probably better than 100 writes/second. |

In a few cases, a physically separate RAID-0&1 array for the log might make sense—for example, if your system required high OLTP (online transaction processing—write) performance but you also used replication of transactions. Besides performing sequential writes to the log, the system would also be doing many simultaneous reads of the log for replication and might benefit from having the multiple spindles available. (In most cases, however, the log pages would be in cache, so it is unlikely that RAID-0&1 would provide a significant benefit. However, if replication was in a "catch-up" mode because the distribution database was not available or for some other reason, some significant benefit might exist.)

Choosing the best RAID solution

Table 4-1 summarizes the characteristics of certain RAID configurations on SQL Server. Obviously, innumerable additional configurations are possible, but understanding this basic chart will help you predict the characteristics for additional configurations as well as typical ones.

In Table 4-1, I would discard the suitability of Option 1 for all but the smallest environments. In Option 1, the entire system is running with one disk drive. This is not an efficient proposition even for a low-end system, unless you have little

Option	Description	Relative read performance	Relative write performance	Eases I/O hotspots and does not require handcrafting physical layout	Relative cost	Up-to-the minute data protection (for failure of one drive)	Any single drive failure does not cause immediate outage of SQL Server	Can sustain multiple drive failures without an outage of SQL Server	Supported with Windows NT Server software, without need for special hardware controller
1	1 physical drive	Very low	Very low	No	Very low	No	No	No	Yes
2	2 physical drives: DATA: Separate LOG: Separate No RAID	Low	Low	No	Low	No	No	No	Yes
3	Multiple drives: (3+) DATA: RAID-0 LOG: Separate, physical non-RAID drive	High[1]	High	Yes	Low-Moderate	No	No	No	Yes
4	Multiple drives: DATA: RAID-0 LOG: Separate, physical mirrored, RAID-1 devices	High	High	Yes	Moderate	Yes	No[2]	No	Yes
5	Multiple drives: DATA: RAID-1 LOG: Separate, physical RAID-1 devices	Varies widely[3]	Varies widely[3]	No	High	Yes	Yes	Partial[4]	Yes
6	Multiple drives: DATA: RAID-5 LOG: Separate, physical RAID-1 devices	High	Low-Moderate	Yes	Moderate	Yes	Yes	No	Yes
7	Multiple drives: DATA: RAID-0&1 LOG: Separate, physical RAID-1 devices	Very high	High	Yes	High	Yes	Yes	Partial[4]	No
8	Multiple drives: DATA: RAID-0&1 with multiple, mirrored copies LOG: Separate, physical RAID-1 devices with multiple, mirrored copies	Very high	High	Yes	Very high	Yes	Yes	Yes	No

[1] For all "high" read/write performance classifications noted here, understand that the performance will increase as more drives are added. For example, with a RAID-0 array of two drives, you might not yet classify read/write performance as high, but you can add more drives until you reach the I/O rates you require.

[2] Except that a failure to the log drive, which is mirrored, can be sustained without an immediate outage.

[3] This is case-by-case dependent. The degree to which I/Os can be balanced by carefully laying out the database will determine if this is a good performing option. This is a difficult proposition to get right and one I'd typically try to avoid.

[4] If a primary is lost, and then its mirror is also lost, drive failures cannot be sustained. With the loss of two different primaries (or mirrors), drive failures can be sustained.

Table 4-1. *Characteristics of RAID configurations for SQL Server.*

write performance and enough memory to get a high cache-hit. Disk drives are cheap. Unless you're running on a laptop, there's little excuse for using only one drive if you're running SQL Server.

Option 2, two physical drives and no use of RAID, represents an entry-level or development system. It is far from ideal for performance and offers no fault tolerance. But it is significantly better than having only a single drive. RAID is unnecessary with just two drives, and separating your log from your data on the drives is the best you can do.

If you don't need fault tolerance and limited recovery ability is sufficient, Option 3, using RAID-0 for the data and placing the transaction log on a separate physical device (without mirroring), is an excellent configuration. It offers peak performance and low cost. One significant downside, however, is that if a drive fails, you can recover the data only to the point of your last transaction log or database backup. Because of this, Option 3 is not appropriate for many environments.

Option 4 is the entry level for environments which must ensure that no data is lost should a drive fail. This option uses RAID-0 (striping, without parity) for the devices holding the data and RAID-1 (mirroring) for the transaction log, so data can always be recovered from the log. However, any failed drive in the RAID-0 array will cause SQL Server to be unable to continue operation on that database until the drive is replaced. You can recover all the data from the transaction logs, but you will experience an outage while you replace the drive and load your transaction logs. Should a drive fail on either a transaction log or its mirrored

Data Placement Using Segments

You might wonder whether you are better off simply putting all your data on one big RAID-0 striped set or whether you should use segments to carefully place your data on specific disk drives. Unless you are expert at performance tuning and really understand your data access patterns, I don't recommend using segments as an alternative to RAID. To use segments to handcraft your physical layout, you must understand and identify the hot spots in the database. And although segments do allow you to place tables on certain drives, doing so is tricky to get right. Because it's currently not possible to partition certain ranges of a table to different disks, hot spots will often occur no matter how clever you have been while designing your data distribution.

If you have three or more physical disk drives, you probably should use some level of RAID, not segments. Segments are a vestige of days when RAID was not yet in widespread use. Although segments can be useful for expert users in specific cases, I consider them essentially an obsolete feature for most users and recommend that you use RAID instead.

copy, the system continues, unaffected, using the surviving drive for the log. However, until the failed log drive is replaced, fault-tolerance is disabled and you are back to the equivalent of Option 3. Should that surviving drive then also fail, you must revert to your last backup, losing changes that occurred since the last transaction log or database backup.

Option 4's performance aspects are excellent and approach those of Option 3, which may come as a surprise to those concerned with the mirroring of the log. RAID-1, of course, turns a single write into two. However, since the writes are done in parallel, the elapsed time for the I/O is approximately the same as it would be for a single drive, assuming that both the primary and mirrored drives are physically separate and used only for log operations. If you need to protect all data, but recovery time is not a major concern and an outage while you recover is acceptable (that is, if loading transaction logs or database backups is acceptable), Option 4 is ideal.

When you cannot tolerate an interruption of operations because of a failed drive, you need to consider some form of RAID-1 or RAID-5 for your database (as well as for the *master* database and *tempdb,* the internal workspace area), as described in Options 5 through 8. Note that SQL Server provides disk mirroring capabilities (DISK MIRROR, DISK UNMIRROR, and DISK REMIRROR) independent of Windows NT or hardware RAID. These capabilities are also a vestige of the days before RAID solutions were commonplace and economical. Fault tolerance for storage is better left to a lower level—to the operating system or hardware. Instead of counting on these SQL Server mirroring capabilities, which will probably be discontinued in some future releases, you should use Windows NT or hardware solutions for data redundancy.

> **NOTE** When I refer to mirroring in this book, I refer to RAID capabilities and not to SQL Server specific mirroring.

I don't like Option 5, which uses basic RAID-1, a one-for-one mirroring of drives for the data as well as the log. RAID-1 does not provide the performance characteristics of RAID-0. If you recall, RAID-0 enables multiple drive spindles to operate logically as one, with additive I/O performance capabilities. Although RAID-1 could theoretically work well if you handcrafted your data layout, in practice this shares the same drawbacks I discussed for using segments instead of RAID-0. (See the sidebar on the facing page.) This high-cost option usually will not be a high-performing option, at least if the database has significant hot spots. Option 5 is appropriate only for very specialized purposes, where I/O patterns can be carefully balanced.

Option 6, using RAID-5 for the data and RAID-1 for the log, is appropriate if the write activity for the data is moderate at most and the update activity can be sustained. Remember that RAID-5 imposes a significant penalty on writes because of its need to maintain parity information so that the data of a reconstructed drive can be regenerated on the fly. Although the system does remain usable, while operating with a failed drive, I/O performance is terrible: each read of the failed disk becomes four reads of the other disks, and each write becomes four reads plus a write, so throughput drops precipitously on RAID-5 when a drive fails. With RAID-5, should you lose another drive in the system before you replace the first failed drive, you can't recover because the parity information can't continue to be maintained after the first drive is lost. Until the failed drive is replaced and regenerated, continued fault-tolerance capability is lost. RAID-5 uses less bytes for storage overhead than are used by mirroring all drives, but with the low price of disk drives and since disks are rarely full, the performance tradeoff often is simply not worth it.

Finally, RAID-5 has more exposure to operational error than mirroring. If the person replacing the failed drive in a RAID-5 set makes a mistake and pulls a good drive instead of the failed drive, recovering the failed drive can be impossible.

If you need high read and write performance, cannot lose any data, and cannot suffer an unplanned system outage when a drive fails, RAID-0&1 and a simple RAID-1 mirror for your log (Option 7) is the way to go. As I mentioned earlier, RAID-0&1 offers the ultimate combination of performance and fault-tolerance characteristics. Its obvious disadvantage is cost. Option 7 requires not only a doubling of disk drives but also requires special hardware array controllers, which command a premium price. Options 7 and 8 differ in whether additional mirrored

From the Author...

The case I mentioned above is by no means far-fetched—I can recall a painful personal experience. When a drive failed in our RAID-5 system, we promptly called the help desk to replace the failed drive. An error by the technician who was sent to replace the bad drive resulted in the RAID-5 set being broken. We had to go back to our tape backups, as though we had not used RAID-5 at all. Had we actually mirrored the drives, a human error like this wouldn't have mattered.

The error was quite understandable and didn't mean the technician was inept—it's easy to yank the wrong drive or board. With drive mirroring, if the wrong drive were pulled, you'd simply have to put it back and pull the correct one. There would be no irreparable problem. (I know we aren't the only ones who have suffered from this: I subsequently noticed the prominent, bold print on the instruction card for the array controller that warned of exactly this problem!)

additional mirrored copies are kept. Option 7 presents the typical case, with one-for-one mirroring of every physical drive in the system. If the primary drive fails, the mirror continues seamlessly. If the mirror fails, the primary drive, of course, continues. Other drives in a different primary-mirror pair could also conceivably fail and the system could still continue. However, if one drive in a pair fails, the system cannot continue should its mirror also fail. (This is really bad luck, but it happens.) Option 7, using the combined capabilities of striping and mirroring (RAID-0&1), would probably be a better choice for many sites that are today using RAID-5. The performance and fault-tolerance capabilities are significantly better, and today's low-priced hardware does not make the cost prohibitive.

If you need the utmost in fault tolerance to drive failures and your application is extremely mission critical, you can consider more than a single mirrored copy of the data and log. Option 8 is overkill for most environments, but today's cost of hard drives doesn't necessarily make this option prohibitive. You might have a server in a remote, offsite location. Because it can be difficult to get a technician to the site in a timely manner, building in significant fault-tolerance capabilities, although expensive, can make sense.

The bottom line: buy the right system

By now, you should know that there is no one correct answer to the RAID-level question. The appropriate decision depends on your performance characteristics and fault-tolerance needs. A complete discussion of RAID and storage systems is beyond the scope of this book. But the most important point is that you do not want to simply buy storage space—you need to buy the right performing system and the one that gives you the appropriate level of redundancy and fault tolerance for your data.

More Information...

You can find a good general discussion of RAID in the SQL Server documentation (in the appendix of the *Administrator's Companion*) available on the CD-ROM included with this book. If you want to see a detailed, authoritative discussion, consult the *RAIDbook* produced by the RAID Advisory Board, an industrywide group of vendors that supply storage-management solutions. For more information about the RAID Advisory Board, consult its home page at http://www.raid-advisory.com.

Hardware or software RAID?

Having chosen the RAID level to use, you must decide whether to use the RAID capabilities of Windows NT Server or those of a hardware controller. If you choose to use RAID-0&1 (to keep more than one mirror copy of a drive), the choice is simple. Windows NT Server RAID does not currently offer these capabilities, so you need to use hardware array controllers. Regarding solutions using RAID-0 and RAID-1, I have seldom seen much performance advantage of a hardware array controller over the capabilities of Windows NT Server. I'd use standard fast-wide SCSI controllers, and I'd use the money I'd saved to buy more drives or more memory. Several of the formal TPC benchmarks submitted using SQL Server used only the Windows NT versions of RAID-0 and RAID-1 solutions (Option 4) and standard SCSI controllers and drives, with no special hardware RAID support. Hardware RAID solutions provide the largest relative performance difference over the equivalent Windows NT software solution if you use RAID-5, but even in this case, the difference is usually marginal at best. Each hardware RAID controller can cost thousands of dollars, and a big system will still need multiple controllers. Using hardware controllers makes the most sense when they provide additional capabilities, most notably RAID-0&1 support, rather than using them as an alternative mechanism to duplicate capabilities already provided by Windows NT Server with standard hardware.

More About Drives and Controllers

No matter what RAID level you use, you will want to replace a failed drive as soon as possible. For this reason, consider a system offering *hot pluggable drives*. These drives allow the faulty drive to be quickly replaced without shutting down the system. If the drive is part of a RAID-1 or RAID-5 set, SQL Server can continue to run without error or interruption when the drive fails and even when it is physically replaced. If you use the Windows NT version of RAID-1 or RAID-5, SQL Server will need to be shut down only briefly to regenerate the drive, as that process requires an exclusive lock on the disk drive by the operating system. Once completed, SQL Server can be restarted and the server computer does not even need to be rebooted. (Some hardware RAID solutions might also be able to regenerate or remirror the drive "below" the level of the operating system and hence not require SQL Server to be shut down to regenerate the drive.) Some systems also offer *hot standby drives,* which are simply extra drives that are already installed, waiting to take over. Either of these approaches will help you get back in business as quickly as possible.

Your disk controller must guarantee that any write operation reported to the operating system as successful will actually be completed. Write-back caching controllers that "lie" (that report a write as completed but do not guarantee to actually perform the write) can result in corrupt databases and must never be used. In a write-back cache scheme, performance is increased because the bits are simply written to the cache (memory) and the I/O completion is immediately acknowledged. The controller writes the bits to the actual media a moment later. This introduces a timing window that makes the system vulnerable unless the controller designer has protected the cache (with a battery backup and so on) and has provided correct recovery logic. Let's say, for example, that a power failure occurs immediately after the controller reports that a write operation has completed but before the cache is actually written to disk. With *write-ahead logging,* SQL Server assumes that any change is physically written to its transaction log before acknowledging the commit to the client. If the controller has just cached the write and then fails and never completes it, the system's integrity is broken. If a controller provides write-back caching as a feature, it must also guarantee that the writes will be completed and that they are properly sequenced should they be reported to the operating system as successful. To be reliable, the caching controller also must guarantee that once it reports that an I/O has completed, the I/O actually gets carried out, no matter what. As an example, a good solution is the Compaq SMART-2 Array Controller, which uses write-back caching. It employs a built-in battery backup and has thoughtfully provided solutions that guarantee that any write reported as completed will in fact be complete. If the system fails before a write operation has completed, the operation is maintained in the controller's memory and will be performed immediately when the system restarts, before any other I/O operations occur.

If a controller cannot guarantee that the write will ultimately complete, you should disable the write-back caching feature of the controller or use a different controller. In my experience, disabling write-back caching in an I/O-intensive test (more than 250 I/Os per second) resulted in a SQL Server performance penalty of less than five percent. (After all, those writes have to get performed eventually. The caching reduces the latency, but ultimately just as much I/O must be carried out.) In a less I/O-intensive test, the effect would likely have been negligible. Realistically, the amount of the penalty doesn't matter much if the write isn't guaranteed to complete. Write-back caching must be disabled or you will eventually get corrupt data.

This point warrants repeating: To be reliable, the caching controller must assure that *no matter what,* once an I/O has been reported to be complete, the I/O gets carried out. It must intercept the IOCHCK (I/O Channel Check) and RESET bus signal and not reset the controller logic, discarding any cached writes. If a motherboard glitch causes an abrupt system halt (such as a single-bit parity error), the controller must preserve the cached data and must know how to flush it upon startup. And a UPS can itself fail: its batteries can run down, or perhaps it wasn't properly configured and doesn't engage on power failure. The cost of any of these problems is a potentially corrupted database. Either don't use a write-caching controller, or buy one (like the Compaq SMART-2) that can handle these issues.

Using Uninterruptible Power Supply

As long as you are not using a write-back caching controller, you do not need UPS hardware to protect the integrity of your data from a power outage. SQL Server will recover your system to a consistent state every time following a sudden loss of power. However, I strongly recommend using a UPS, and support for UPS hardware is built into Windows NT Server. Most hardware failures, such as memory failures and hardware crashes, result from power spikes that a UPS would prevent. Adding a UPS (a $200 to $500 proposition) is probably the single most important thing you can do from a hardware perspective to maximize the availability and reliability of your system.

Without a UPS, after a power flicker or power spike the machine will reboot and perhaps do a CHKDSK of the file system, which can take several minutes. During this time, your SQL Server will not be available. A UPS can prevent these interruptions. Even if a power outage lasts longer than the life of your UPS, you'll have time to do an orderly shutdown of SQL Server, checkpointing all the databases and hence making the subsequent restart much faster since no transactions need to be rolled back or rolled forward.

Battery Backup, UPS, and Caching

A UPS is not the same as the battery backup of the on-board controller RAM. The job of a UPS is to bridge power failures and to give you time to do an orderly shutdown of the system. The computer continues to run for a while from the power supplied by the UPS, and it can be shut down in an orderly way (which the UPS software will do) if power doesn't get restored within the expected battery life.

The battery backup on a caching controller card ensures that the contents of the controller's volatile memory survive—the memory is not lost, so when the system restarts the write will complete. But it doesn't provide the power to actually make sure that a write succeeds. Some cards even allow the battery backed-up RAM to be moved to a different controller, should the initial controller fail. Some provide two sets of batteries so that one can be replaced while the other maintains the RAM's contents, theoretically allowing you to keep adding new batteries indefinitely.

You might expect that using a caching controller that doesn't have a battery backup in combination with a UPS would generally be OK provided that you did an orderly shutdown of SQL Server during the life of the UPS's power. Even I assumed this was the case until I talked with a top SQL Server support engineer who deals with getting customers' servers back up and running. He recounted his experiences with customers who used write-caching controllers that were not designed around transactional integrity. The caching controller needs to take into account other issues besides power. For example, how does the controller respond to the user pressing the Reset button on the computer? A well-known caching controller of a couple years ago used to dump its cache if you hit the Reset button—those writes never got carried out even though the calling application (SQL Server) was notified that they had been carried out. This situation could (and often did) lead to corrupt databases.

Testing Your Disk Subsystem

The reliability of the disk subsystem (including device drivers) is vitally important to the integrity of your SQL Server data. To help you uncover faulty disk systems, the Microsoft SQL Server support team has created a stand-alone, I/O-intensive, multithreaded file system stress test application. It exercises the Win32 overlapped (asynchronous) I/O services, opens its files with the same write-through cache flags used by SQL Server, and does similar types of I/O patterns. But the test is totally distinct from SQL Server. If this non–SQL Server I/O test cannot run without I/O errors, you do not have a reliable platform on which to run SQL Server, period. Of course, like any diagnostic program, the test could miss some subtle errors. But your confidence should certainly be higher than it would be without testing. You can download the test program for free from the Microsoft Web site at http://www.microsoft.com/KB/SoftLib; search for file *SQLHDTST.EXE*. SQLHDTST.EXE is also included on this book's accompanying CD-ROM.

Fallback Server Capability

With cooperating hardware, SQL Server 6.5 can have a *fallback* (*failover* or *hot-standby*) server in place, ready to take over the workload of a failed server. Should the SQL Server become disabled (for example, if the motherboard shorts out) but its disk drives remain intact, a secondary server can automatically take its place by picking up the failed server's disks and adding them to its disk set. That fallback server also runs SQL Server and then automatically recovers and runs the databases that had been run on the failed server.

Fallback capability requires specialized hardware. By using various RAID options, you can protect your data without a fallback server; but without a fallback server, you are not protected against an application outage should the machine fail. This specialized hardware, such as Compaq's On-Line Recovery Server option, can automatically shift the control of a "switchable" hard-drive array from a damaged primary server to a fallback server. For example, hardware can be configured with one separately housed hard-drive array that's connected to two computers. Only one of the connections to the hard-drive array is active at any time. The other hard-drive connection becomes active only if the system detects that the computer currently in control of the hard drive has shut down because of a hardware failure. Detection of such failures is made possible by a direct connection between a serial port on both computers, over which "heartbeat" signals are continuously transmitted. The automatic process can also invoke a user-written program when the hard-drive array is switched to the fallback server.

The secondary server can itself perform useful work while the primary server operates normally. The secondary server can run SQL Server (using different databases than those used by the primary server), or it can act as a file and print server, or it can run some other application. If the secondary server needs to take over the work of the primary server, the secondary server needs to have enough resources to add the primary server's workload to its existing workload. (As an alternative, you could decide that the primary server's existing workload should take a back seat and that the secondary server's previous applications should be shut down when it takes over.)

| NOTE | Keep in mind that even with a fallback server, you need RAID to protect against media failure. The log, at least, needs to be mirrored to protect against a disk failure. The secondary server can run the disk drives of the failed primary server, but those drives also need to be protected against media failure. |

Most applications probably do not need a fallback server because today's hardware is highly reliable. The most common hardware failure occurs in a disk drive, which can be protected without the need for a fallback server by using RAID. As with RAID, a fallback server does not mitigate the need for comprehensive and rigorous backup procedures. You'll likely need your backups to recover from an occasional administrator mistake (human error), a catastrophe such as a fire or flood at the site, or a software anomaly. But some applications are so critical that the redundancy of the fallback server is necessary.

Other Hardware Considerations

If the server is mostly a "lights-out" operation and you will not be administering it locally or running other applications from the actual server machine, it doesn't make much sense to buy a first-class monitor or video card. Consider using an electronic switch box and sharing a monitor, keyboard, and mouse among multiple servers. If you do not use multiple servers, use a basic VGA monitor and video card.

From a performance perspective, a single high-quality network card is sufficient to handle virtually every SQL Server installation I've seen. Windows NT Server can support multiple network cards simultaneously, and sometimes your network topology will compel you to use this configuration with SQL Server as well (perhaps you are supporting both Ethernet and Token Ring clients on the same server). The largest SQL Server installation I know of supports more than 4000 concurrent physical workstations, and it does so using a single 100-megabit FDDI card. I'm also aware of sites that support from hundreds to thousands of users with a single 10-megabit Ethernet card. I do not know of any sites that require, from a performance perspective, multiple network cards.

When you plan your hardware configuration, be sure to plan for your backup needs. You can back up to either tape or disk devices. As you do with regular I/O, you will frequently want multiple backup devices to sustain the I/O rates required for backup. SQL Server is able to stripe its backup to multiple devices, including tape devices, for higher performance. For the same reasons I mentioned earlier when discussing disk devices, a SCSI tape device is typically preferable to an IDE/EIDE device.

From the Author...

Not long ago, backup automatically meant tape. Today, with disk costs at less than $0.30 per MB, I see many sites configuring their hardware with additional disk devices purely for backup use because they prefer the extra speed and ease that backup to disk offers over tape backup. I even see sites use "hot pluggable drives" for their backup; these sites rotate between a few sets of such drives, keeping a set in an off-site location in case of disaster.

The Operating System

The Microsoft SQL Server engine runs best and is officially supported only on Windows NT Server. Technically, SQL Server will install and run fine on Windows NT Workstation (although Windows NT Workstation networking restricts more than 10 client workstations from simultaneously accessing it). But memory management and the process-scheduling behavior on Windows NT Server are better tailored to services such as SQL Server than is Windows NT Workstation, which focuses on desktop applications. The simple fact is that SQL Server runs better with medium to large workloads on Windows NT Server than on Windows NT Workstation. At low workloads, the difference is negligible, so SQL Workstation is supported on both Windows NT Workstation and Windows NT Server.

SQL Server's being supported on a particular platform or version of Windows NT does not necessarily mean that it will not work with other configurations. But you should stick with the supported platforms for several reasons. Only supported platforms get significant test coverage. An unsupported platform might seem to work, but a subtle problem could occur later. An authorized SQL Server support provider or Microsoft SQL Server Enterprise Technical Services (ETS) will also focus on the supported platforms; if your problem is specific to the unsupported platform, you might be unable to get help to your satisfaction. Typically, a new release of SQL Server will be targeted to the most recent (or sometimes an impending) release of Windows NT Server and will also support the prior major release. For example, SQL Server 6.5 is targeted to and supported on Windows NT Server 4.0 and 3.51. It is not supported on Windows NT Server 3.50 or earlier. SQL Server will not fully work on Windows NT Server 3.50 because it uses new operating services that first appeared in version 3.51. If you try to run Setup on a Windows NT version earlier than 3.51, you will receive an error and be prevented from continuing.

You can install SQL Server on any Windows NT Server in your domain, but for highest performance it's usually best not to install it on your primary or backup domain controllers (PDC or BDC). Although SQL Server will run fine on a PDC or BDC, the controller's tasks of maintaining and replicating the Windows NT user database take up processing cycles and memory. In less resource-intensive environments, this usually doesn't make much of a difference, but if your system is part of a large domain, it is better to separate SQL Server processing from those activities.

The File System

The performance difference in running SQL Server on the two major file systems of Windows NT—NTFS and FAT—is minimal. This isn't surprising, because SQL Server typically creates a few large files and then manages the structures within those files without much use of the operating system.

I recommend NTFS as the file system of choice for SQL Server. It's a more robust file system than FAT, and it's better able to recover fully and quickly from an ungraceful system shutdown. The integrity of the file system is vital to the integrity of your data, so this fact alone should drive most SQL Server users to NTFS. And the security features of NTFS are vital if security is important to you. Unlike FAT, NTFS allows security and auditing on all files; these are important ways to protect your data when SQL Server is not running. (SQL Server provides its own robust security.) When SQL Server is not running, the operating system is your prime protection. If you have a legitimate need to dual-boot your system to MS-DOS or Microsoft Windows 95 or if you need to use some disk utilities that work only with FAT, you might choose FAT. (You could, of course, make the boot partition FAT and format the other partitions with NTFS.)

You can safely use NTFS file compression, but you will see a substantial decrease in performance—perhaps as much as 50 percent if your system is I/O-intensive. So, typically, file compression is not an appropriate choice for SQL Server.

NOTE HPFS, a legacy file system supported by Windows NT, allows for backward compatibility with Microsoft LAN Manager for OS/2. It provides neither the functionality nor the performance necessary to be a consideration here.

It is possible to run SQL Server on a new partition that is not formatted with any file system. Such a partition is commonly referred to as a *raw partition*. Running on raw partitions is common for UNIX database products, and users who have UNIX DBMS backgrounds sometimes want to do this with SQL Server as well. Under heavy workloads, raw partitions can provide a small (couple of percent) performance benefit. If the I/O system is not at capacity, you will probably notice no performance difference at all. For the majority of installations, using raw partitions is not an appropriate choice. Even if you gain some performance benefits by foregoing a file system, you forego benefits such as basic file operations and utilities (copy, delete, rename, dir) and important operations such as detecting and resolving bad disk sectors that a file system provides. If there's no file system to perform bad sector operations, you must be sure your hardware will take care of this. (This type of hardware is available but costly.) Running on raw partitions was common in UNIX environments because the UNIX file system could not always be counted on to write through its cache and hence could not be trusted (for the same reasons I discussed earlier with write-back caching controllers). The UNIX file system was also sometimes avoided because it caused a significant performance penalty in SQL Server. Neither of these cases is true with Windows NT. SQL Server opens its files with the FILE_FLAG_WRITE-_THROUGH flag, which instructs Windows NT to acknowledge the operation as completed only when hardware reports that the bits are actually on disk.

Security and User Context

To install SQL Server on a machine, you need not be an administrator of the domain, but you must have administrator privileges on the machine. Users can install the SQL Server client utilities without administrator privileges.

Before you set up your system, give some thought to the user context in which SQL Server and SQL Executive will run. A new SQL Server environment sets up the SQL Server engine to run in the context of the special system (LocalSystem) account. This account is typically used to run services, but it has no privileges on other machines nor can it be granted such privileges. Because LocalSystem is always present, Setup can reliably use it. This follows the prime directive of the Setup program because the inability to validate a domain account during setup (for example, because the domain controller is unavailable) could compromise Setup's ability to complete the installation successfully. Often, however, you will want to set up SQL Server later to run with a domain account. This allows SQL Server to more easily perform tasks that require an external security context, such as backing up to another machine or using replication.

Changing the account in which SQL Server runs is easy: you use the Services applet within the Windows NT Control Panel. In choosing or creating a user account for running SQL Server, it's a good idea to choose the Password Never Expires option for that account in Windows NT User Manager; if the password expires, SQL Server will fail to start until the information in the Services applet is updated. If you will use the mail integration features (SQLMail), you should be aware of a couple situations that could arise. If you will be using the Microsoft Mail 3.*x* client on the same machine as SQL Server, you should use the System Account option and the Allow Service To Interact With Desktop option in the Services applet. If you are using Microsoft Exchange on the same machine, you should run SQL Server in the user account for which your Exchange client is configured. SQL Server can then pick up the Exchange configuration for that user automatically.

The Setup program asks for a domain user account within which to run SQL Executive. This might seem inconsistent because Setup used the LocalSystem account, not a domain account, for the SQL Server engine. However, SQL Executive needs a security context to connect to other computers in more typical situations than does SQL Server. For example, if you will publish data for replication, SQL Executive needs a security context to connect to the subscribing machines. Since SQL Executive is not run during the installation process as the SQL Server engine is, an inability to validate the user account chosen for SQL Executive during setup does not compromise the prime directive of the Setup program.

If you will not be publishing data for replication or scheduling tasks on SQL Server requiring access to other computers, you can choose to have SQL Executive run in the LocalSystem account. If you specify a domain account but the domain controller cannot validate the account (perhaps the domain controller is temporarily unavailable), go ahead and install using the LocalSystem account and change it later via the Services applet or from SQL Enterprise Manager.

Licensing Choices

When installing SQL Server, you'll see a dialog box asking which licensing choice you want to use. It's worthwhile to understand the two general licensing options for which you can support multiple users with SQL Server: Per-Server and Per-Seat. A special licensing option, the Internet Connector, is important to know about if you will be using SQL Server on the Internet.

> **NOTE**   The license agreement in the SQL Server product box is a legal document that you should read and understand. This section explains the intent of the licensing schemes but should not be inferred to be the official licensing policy of the product. Packaging and licensing periodically changes. Consult the licensing agreement to be sure you are in compliance and have chosen the best options for your needs.

Per-Server licensing lets you support a stated maximum number of simultaneous users for a specific installation of SQL Server. This is probably the simplest option, although it may not be the best choice for you. Choose Per-Server if you have only one or two SQL Servers in your environment or if you use SQL Server with a large number of occasional users, with a minority of them being connected to the specific SQL Server at any time. Per-Server licensing is considered unlimited for more than 250 users.

Per-Seat (or Per-User) licensing allows you to economically deploy multiple SQL Servers to serve a given population of users. Once a user has a Per-Seat license, he or she is licensed to access any SQL Server in the environment. You can then deploy additional SQL Servers with minimal expense and with no need to buy additional client licenses. You simply acquire as many additional server licenses as you need, and your users are already licensed to use them. User licenses (also referred to as CALs, or client access licenses) must be acquired with either of the above options. But you (the administrator) need to decide whether to aggregate the count of user licenses and use the Per-Server option to support a maximum number of simultaneous users or to designate each license to a specific user, who can then access any number of SQL Servers in the environment. If need be, you can start with Per-Server licensing and later convert to Per-Seat licensing. The conversion is done on the honor system; it's not necessary to notify Microsoft. It is, however, intended to be a one-time, one-way conversion.

Estimated Retail Pricing (Non-upgrade) as of February 1996

License Type	ERP U.S.
Server license	$999
User license	$149
User license when bought in 20 quantity	$119
Internet Connector licensing option	$2,995

These two licensing options can be easily understood by considering a couple of scenarios. First, the setup: The ACME Company is deploying its first SQL Server. All 100 employees in the company will access the application from time to time, but ACME is confident that no more than 20 users will do so simultaneously. ACME chooses Per-Server licensing and buys 20 user licenses and 1 SQL Server license. This choice is most economical for ACME. Each of its 100 users does not need to have a license to access any SQL Server (especially since ACME will initially have only one SQL Server).

Scenario #1

After three months, the popularity of the application grows and periodically someone trying to connect to SQL Server gets error message 18458, which states that all licensed connections are in use. ACME calculates that it now needs to support 35 simultaneous users. The company purchases 15 new user licenses in addition to the 20 originally purchased (ACME might well choose another "20 pack" of user licenses because of the cost savings, rather than 15 individual user licenses, especially if more growth is anticipated). Using the Licensing applet in the Windows NT Control Panel, the company updates the Per-Server licensing option for SQL Server to indicate its new status of supporting 35 simultaneous connections.

Scenario #2

ACME decides to expand its use of SQL Server. It initially plans to deploy eight new SQL Server machines and might add more later. All 100 employees will never access any single SQL Server simultaneously, but they all will use one or more applications that use SQL Server as a regular part of their jobs. ACME decides to move to Per-Seat licensing. It converts its 35 user licenses to specific users and buys 65 additional user licenses. The company buys seven more SQL Server packages, installs each of them with the Per-Seat option, and then converts the existing SQL Server from the Per-Server to the Per-Seat option. Later in the year, ACME grows even more and decides to roll out two more SQL Server installations, for a total of 10. But because its user base remains at 100, ACME needs to procure only two new SQL Server packages. All of its 100 employees are already licensed to use any and all SQL Servers deployed, and the cost of each new SQL Server, even if accessed by every employee in the company, is only $999.

Internet Licensing

Neither of the licensing options makes good sense when using SQL Server on the Internet. The Per-Seat choice makes no sense because potentially millions of "users" can access your Web site and behind the scenes cause a query to get executed that extracts data from SQL Server. It is impossible, not to mention cost-prohibitive, to know if the users are licensed for SQL Server use. Similarly, the Per-Server option isn't practical because Internet access is usually stateless. Unlike in a typical client/server environment, a client on the Internet rarely stays connected to SQL Server. Using a product such as Microsoft Internet Information Server (IIS) with the Internet Database Connector (IDC) feature, users on the Internet cause commands and queries to be dynamically dispatched to SQL Server. For example, a user might click on a region of a Web page that shows current seat availability for a concert, resulting in a query to SQL Server. A connection is established on behalf of the user, the query is processed, the user disconnects, and the results set of the query is dynamically merged into the Web page that the user is viewing. All this happens in perhaps a second or two. When the user makes another request a moment later, the same process occurs.

In a normal LAN-based client/server application, a client remains connected at least for several minutes, even while the client has no active query processing. On the Internet, it is impractical to count distinct SQL Server users—at least in the same way that the Per-Server license option was intended to support. For this reason, Microsoft offers the SQL Server Internet Connector licensing option, which you can use instead of or in addition to user licenses, depending on your situation. SQL Server can be accessed through your Web server software (such as, but not limited to, IIS) on an unlimited basis in a cost-effective way. If you use SQL Server only for publishing data on your Web server, the Internet Connector license is essentially all you need. But remember that if you are also supporting a number of more traditional client/server users, you must have the appropriate user licenses.

Note that you do not need the Internet Connector option if users are simply accessing an HTML file that was statically built with SQL Web Assistant. Unlike the dynamic situation in which Internet users are causing queries to be dispatched dynamically to SQL Server, in this case users are not causing statements to be issued to SQL Server; they are simply reading an HTML file created and periodically updated with SQL Server data. Therefore, the file is essentially static. Reading the file does not cause work to be performed at the SQL Server. (The user running the SQL Web Assistant, of course, must be a licensed user.)

Licensing Limits

Strict enforcement is not the goal of the SQL Server license option implementation. Its goals are to let honest users be honest and to make it easier for users to manage their environment and remain in compliance with their license. The standard Windows NT Server licensing dialog box appears during setup. The user chooses the appropriate licensing option and, in the case of the Per-Server option, enters the number of user licenses purchased specifically for that server.

For Per-Server licensing, SQL Server keeps a list of all workstations currently connected. Each workstation represents one user. In this respect, a *user* is different from a SQL Server *connection,* since an application often has several connections open to the same SQL Server. In addition, it's common for a given workstation to use multiple applications that could access the same SQL Server. The user count for Per-Server licensing is based on a unique value for each workstation. Typically, this value reflects the identifier for the first Network Interface Card (NIC) found in the system. (Network software relies on a unique signature that is included on each NIC upon its manufacture.) The SQL Server client interfaces, DB-Library and the ODBC driver, grab the NIC's identifier and pass it as part of the login handshake between client and server. The count is incremented if the NIC signature is not included in SQL Server's list of connected workstations. If the signature does exist in the list, SQL Server recognizes that the connection is from a workstation that is already connected and the count does not change. When all connections having a given NIC ID disconnect, the count decreases. Even if multiple application types from a given workstation connect to the server, they will all contain the same NIC ID and will be recognized as one user. For example, a Windows NT Workstation might be simultaneously running an old MS-DOS–based application, a Windows 3.11 DB-Library application, a Windows 3.11 ODBC application, a 32-bit Windows DB-Library application, and a 32-bit ODBC application. Although all of these are accessing SQL Server, and perhaps some are using multiple connections each, the SQL Server Per-Server counting mechanism recognizes all of them as the same user and the count for all is one.

It is possible for a client without a network card to access SQL Server using Remote Access Services (RAS). When no NIC ID is available, DB-Library and ODBC create a random number and use it for all connections from that workstation. (If a machine has a NIC, the NIC ID is used even when the connection is via RAS rather than the network card.) Although it is theoretically possible that this random number could collide with another random number, the chances of this happening are less than those for winning the lottery. Even if it did happen, the collision would reduce the count and would never cause the count to inaccurately exceed the stated limit.

To change the Per-Server count, you simply use the Licensing applet and adjust the count accordingly. The next time SQL Server is started, the new value takes effect. Obviously, this does not enforce license compliance—it is completely up to you to enter and keep the correct value. But the applet provides a way for you to monitor your compliance and meets the goal of letting honest people stay honest. You should also be aware that a small overhead in static memory structures exists at the server to keep the count for each user licensed. If a reasonable value is entered, overhead should never be an issue.

In Per-Seat licensing, SQL Server simply calls the Windows NT "honesty" API and reports each user who logged on. SQL Server cannot know or enforce that a workstation that just connected actually has a user license to access the server. But by providing the information to the Windows NT services, you can use the Windows NT Server License Manager (in the Network Administrative Tools program group) to monitor compliance. Both Per-Server and Per-Seat licensing options call the Windows NT "honesty" services. In the future, licensing services will likely manage licensing compliance for all products, including SQL Server.

Even if you are licensed for 1000 simultaneous users, the total memory overhead is trivial (about 32 KB). However, I've had a few client sites ask me why their memory usage for SQL Server had gone up considerably. I discovered that they had indiscriminately (and disregarding their license) entered a ridiculously high value of 999,999 for their concurrent users. Hence, they were seeing an increase of almost 32 MB in their static memory structure use.

One final point about licensing. In a three-tier architecture, sometimes clients connect to an application server, which in turn connects to SQL Server. In effect, the application server is multiplexing the client connections to SQL Server. The application as a whole may be servicing a large number of clients, but only the single, middle-tier application server directly connects to SQL Server. However, the licensing policies of SQL Server are based on the clients who access SQL Server services, albeit by a proxy in this case. So even though the physical connection in this case is from the single application server machine, if 50 users make use of SQL Server by proxy, SQL Server must be licensed for all 50 users.

Network Protocol Choices

If you accept the default installation option during setup, SQL Server uses named pipes as its interprocess communication (IPC) mechanism for communication with its clients. SQL Server is able to simultaneously use many IPC mechanisms and networking protocols (but any specific client connection uses only one for its connection). Each SQL Server networking interface is known as a Net-Library and represents a specific IPC mechanism. In addition to Named Pipes, you can install one or more of the following Net-Libraries shown in Figure 4-2 on the following page.

- Multi-Protocol
- TCP/IP Sockets
- NWLink IPX/SPX
- Appletalk ADSP
- DECNet Sockets
- Banyan VINES

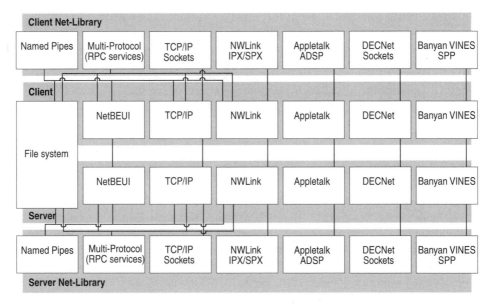

Figure 4-2. *SQL Server Net-Library interface options.*

The Named Pipes and Multi-Protocol Net-Libraries use protocol-independent IPC mechanisms (named pipes and RPC services). This means that either of these interfaces can be used with multiple underlying network protocols, including TCP/IP, NetBEUI, and NWLink IPX/SPX. All of the other choices imply not only the IPC mechanism but the specific network protocol that both the client and the server must use.

Although the Named Pipes Net-Library remains a good choice, its use as the default occurs mostly for historical reasons. Named pipes was the first, and for a while the only, IPC mechanism used by the early versions of Microsoft SQL Server. Later, even when TCP/IP sockets and IPX/SPX were supported, those protocols were more difficult to configure than named pipes, requiring configuration at each client. For example, using TCP/IP required that the administrator configure an arcane IP address at every client workstation for every SQL Server it might access. Now, with the sophisticated network naming services provided by Windows NT (for example, WINS, DHCP, and DNS), other Net-Libraries such as Multi-Protocol and TCP/IP Sockets are practically as easy to use as Named Pipes.

Unless you have a compelling reason to choose a different network interface (the most compelling, of course, is if your existing network or network standards dictate some other network choice), you should choose Named Pipes and/or Multi-Protocol. They provide the most functionality. Both are protocol-independent and allow the use of SQL Server's *integrated security* features, which lets you provide a single logon name to your users rather than their having to log on to both the

Windows NT domain and the SQL Server. SQL Server integrated security uses the Windows NT impersonation features, which are available only with these two networking choices. Integrated security is an important feature for convenience and ease of administration as well as for making your system more secure. Integrated security is also assumed with SQL Server replication services. The Multi-Protocol interface is built using Windows NT RPC services. It offers one important feature that none of the other networks offer—encryption. All conversation between the client and server can be encrypted using the encryption services provided by Windows NT. (A 40-bit key is the maximum currently allowed by the U.S. government to be exported, so this is the key size used for Windows NT versions sold outside the United States. Windows NT 4.0, sold in the United States, uses a 128-bit key for tighter security.) Your data is secure even from someone using a hardware device such as a "network sniffer" to intercept network packets right off the wire. The encryption services work across the Internet as well.

More Information...

Performance data indicates that encryption services impose about a 25 percent performance overhead for network traffic. However, in use on a LAN, the network is rarely the performance bottleneck in a well-designed application and the actual performance difference is usually much less noticeable. But network performance is a bigger concern with a slow WAN (wide area network) or Internet application. In those cases, it can become a bottleneck. Even with slow networks, however, the performance issues usually relate to how often you are making requests to the server (that is, how many network "round trips" you make), rather than the speed of the Net-Library.

When you use the Multi-Protocol interface and provide multiple underlying network protocols from which it can choose, the default binding can be chosen explicitly. For example, by default the Multi-Protocol network interface might, under the covers, use named pipes over NWLink. However, you can configure the interface explicitly to choose TCP/IP sockets instead if this is important in your network. (For details, see the name resolution information in the Multi-Protocol Clients section of the *Microsoft SQL Server Administrator's Companion*.) The ability to dynamically enumerate on a network computers that are running SQL Server is not available with the Multi-Protocol network interface.

For those many sites that use TCP/IP as their network protocol, you can choose Named Pipes, Multi-Protocol, or direct use of TCP/IP Sockets. I recommend using Named Pipes or Multi-Protocol as your networking choice. Neither integrated security nor dynamic enumeration of SQL Servers on the network is available with TCP/IP Sockets. If your system will support client environments that are not provided by the Microsoft networking software (for which neither compatible named pipes nor RPC services exist), such as UNIX, Macintosh, OS/2, or VMS, the TCP/IP Sockets Net-Library is a good choice—and often the only choice.

> **NOTE** Support for these client environments is provided by the ODBC drivers that Visigenic provides. These drivers are built from source code for the Microsoft SQL Server drivers for Windows-based environments. The source code is licensed to Visigenic, which provides drivers for any environment for which there is sufficient customer demand.

In Microsoft internal testing, we have found the TCP/IP Sockets Net-Library to be the fastest networking choice. (As I stated earlier, in typical LAN use you will rarely see the network as a performance bottleneck. In a low-speed WAN, however, this can be an important issue.) Some network administrators have also been concerned about potentially routing NetBIOS traffic across their LANs and WANs. However, if SQL Server is not using the Named Pipes Net-Library and the Multi-Protocol Net-Library is not using named pipes under the covers for IPC, SQL Server is not using NetBIOS at all, and this is not a concern.

The NWLink IPX/SPX Net-Library will be of most interest to those running Novell networking software on their clients accessing SQL Server. If you are using a Novell NetWare–based network and file server but your SQL Server clients use Windows 95, Windows NT, or Windows for Workgroups 3.11 running with the built-in Microsoft networking software, using the NWLink IPX/SPX Net-Library is unnecessary. Either Named Pipes or Multi-Protocol over the underlying NWLink network protocol is probably a better choice because integrated security is not available with the IPX/SPX Net-Library. If your clients are using networking software provided by Novell, NWLink IPX/SPX is probably your best choice. Server enumeration is available with NWLink IPX/SPX using the NetWare Bindery services.

Choose Banyan VINES and DECNet Sockets if you interoperate with those environments. The Banyan VINES Net-Library uses StreetTalk naming services for server enumeration and name resolution. There is no support for dynamic SQL Server enumeration on DECNet. Integrated security is not an option with either of these Net-Libraries.

Use Appletalk ADSP Net-Library if you will be supporting Apple Macintosh clients (using the Visigenic ODBC driver for Macintosh) running only Appletalk, not TCP/IP.

During setup, you must click the Networks button for Additional Network Support or only Named Pipes will be installed. If you choose Additional Network Support, you can choose any other networks that you want. With most choices, a dialog box will appear, asking for the port number or network name on which the SQL Server will "listen" for new connections or broadcast its existence to a network naming service. In most cases, you should accept the default unless you have a compelling reason not to. In the case of TCP/IP Sockets, it's recommended that you accept the default port number of 1433. This port number is reserved for use with SQL Server by the Internet Assigned Numbers Authority (IANA), and as such it should not conflict with a port used by any other server application on your computer. (This assumes that the developers of other applications also followed the proper protocol of getting assigned numbers.)

Even if you will primarily use another Net-Library for SQL Server use, I recommend that you do not remove Named Pipes. If your network should fail entirely, you can still access your SQL Server machine locally using named pipes as the IPC mechanism, because it is an intrinsic service of Windows NT even when the computer is not part of a network. Named pipes can provide a convenient "last chance" way to access the SQL Server if, for example, your network card has failed and network access is currently unavailable. If you decide not to install the Named Pipes Net-Library, remove it *after* setup is complete. Setup assumes the existence of named pipes services so that it can operate if the computer is not in a network environment.

TIP If you are new to networking and don't know your IP from your DHCP, don't fret. Accept the defaults and configure your networking later as your understanding improves (or get your network administrator to help you). Although it's a good idea to understand your networking choices before running Setup, you can later change the networking options easily without disturbing your SQL Server environment.

Character Set and Sort Order Issues

During installation, you must decide which character set and sort order to use. A SQL Server installation has a single character set and sort order defined. *If you decide later that you want a different character set or sort order, all databases, including SQL Server's master database, must be rebuilt.*

Character Sets

A single character is stored in SQL Server as 1 byte (8 bits), which means that 256 (2^8) different possible characters can be represented in 1 byte. But all the world's languages in aggregate have many more than 256 characters. Hence, you must choose a character set that contains all the characters (referred to as the "repertoire") with which you will need to work. For installations in the Western Hemisphere and Western Europe, the ISO character set (also often referred to as Windows Characters, ISO 8859-1, Latin-1, or ANSI) is the default character set and is compatible with the character set used by all versions of Windows in those regions. (Technically, there is a slight difference between the Windows character set and ISO 8859-1.) If you choose ISO, you might want to skip the rest of this section regarding character sets, but you should still familiarize yourself with sort order issues.

You'll also want to ensure that all your client workstations use a character set that is consistent with the characters used by your SQL Server. SQL Server stores a byte value for a character. If, for example, the character ¥, the symbol for the Japanese Yen, is entered by a client application using the standard Windows character set, its byte value (known as the *code point*) of 165 (0xA5) is stored in SQL Server. If an MS-DOS–based application using code page 437 retrieves that value, that application would display the character Ñ. (MS-DOS used the term "code pages" to represent different character sets. Think of "code pages" and "character sets" as interchangeable terms.) In both cases, the byte value of 165 is stored, but the Windows character set and the MS-DOS code page 437 render it differently. You must consider whether the ordering of characters is what is semantically expected (discussed later in the "Sort Orders" section) and whether the character is rendered on the application monitor (or other output device) as expected. SQL Server provides services in DB-Library and the ODBC driver that use Windows services to perform character set conversions. Conversions cannot always be exact, however, because by definition each character set has a somewhat different repertoire of characters. For example, there is no exact match in code page 437 for the Windows character Ô, so the conversion must give a close, but different, character.

The ASCII Character Set

It is worth pointing out that the first 128 characters are the same for the character sets ISO, code page 437, and code page 850. These 128 characters make up the *ASCII character set*. (Standard ASCII is only a 7-bit character set. This made ASCII simple and efficient to use in telecommunications, because the character and a "stop bit" used for synchronization could all be expressed in a single byte.) If your application uses ASCII characters, but not the so-called *extended characters* (typically characters with diacritical marks, such as à, Ä, ä) that differentiate the upper 128 characters between these three character sets, it probably doesn't matter what character set you choose. In this situation (only), whether you choose any of these three character sets or use different character sets on your client and server machines doesn't matter because the rendering and sorting of every important character will have the same byte value in all cases.

Windows NT supports 2-byte characters that allow representation of virtually every character used in any language. This is known as *Unicode,* and it provides many benefits—with some costs. The principal cost is that 2 bytes instead of 1 are needed to store a character. SQL Server 6.5 does not support the Unicode character set, but future versions of SQL Server will support it. Storage overhead, data page size, use by applications not supporting Unicode (applications for 16-bit Windows, Windows 95, and MS-DOS), and backward compatibility issues will all need to be addressed in future versions. Most likely, SQL Server will support Unicode with an optional new character datatype. (Think of it as *unichar* and *univarchar* that will require 2 bytes of storage if used instead of the traditional *char* and *varchar* types that would, of course, remain.)

Although SQL Server 6.5 does not support Unicode, it does support *double-byte character sets* (DBCS). DBCS is a hybrid approach and is the most common way industrywide for applications to support Asian languages such as Japanese and Chinese. With DBCS encoding, some characters are 1 byte and others are 2 bytes. The first bit in the character indicates whether the character is a 1-byte or a 2-byte character. (In Unicode, every character is 2 bytes.) However, to SQL Server each character is considered 1 byte for storage. To store two DBCS characters, a field would need to be declared as *char(4)* instead of *char(2)*. But SQL Server will correctly parse and understand DBCS characters in its string functions.

Table 4-2 lists the character sets available in SQL Server and notes DBCS's. As I mentioned earlier, most sites in countries of the Western Hemisphere and in Western Europe will be best served by accepting the default ISO character set. The choices for code page 437 and code page 850 might be of interest if you are supporting many previous MS-DOS–based applications that use those code pages or for other backward compatibility reasons. The other character sets are mostly locale-specific.

ISO	Character Set
850	Multilingual
437	U.S. English
932	Japanese (DBCS)
936	Chinese—simplified (DBCS)
949	Korean (DBCS)
950	Chinese—traditional (DBCS)
1250	Central European
1251	Cyrillic

Table 4-2. *SQL Server character sets.* *(continued)*

Table 4-2. *continued*

ISO	Character Set
1253	Greek
1254	Turkish
1255	Arabic
1257	Baltic

Sort Orders

Character sets will not be important at many sites, but at nearly every site, whether you realize it or not, the basics of *sort orders* (more properly called *collating sequences*) is important. Sort order determines how characters compare and assign their values. Sort order determines whether your SQL Server installation is case-sensitive. (For example, is an uppercase *A* considered identical to a lowercase *a*?) If you use only ASCII characters and no extended characters, you should simply decide your case-sensitivity preference and choose accordingly. By default, SQL Server installs a case-insensitive sort order. (That is, *A* and *a* are considered equivalent.) To change the default, you simply choose an option during setup that provides case sensitivity, such as Binary Order or Dictionary Order, Case-Sensitive.

It's important to realize that sort order affects not only the ordering of a result set but also more fundamentally which rows of data qualify for that result set. If a query's criterion is

```
where name='Smith'
```

the case sensitivity installed will determine whether a row having the name "Smith" qualifies.

Character matching, string functions, and aggregate functions MIN(), MAX(), COUNT (DISTINCT), GROUP BY, UNION, CUBE, LIKE, and ORDER BY all behave differently with character data depending on which sort order is chosen.

Sort order semantics

More subtle semantic differences are also defined by the sort order. The following lengthy discussion principally applies to those using extended characters. If you will be working with only 7-bit ASCII characters, you might want to skip the information in this section.

A given sort order option is specific to a character set. Not every sorting option is available in every character set. For example, you will find the option for Croatian Dictionary Order, Case-Sensitive, only with the 1250, Central European character set. The DBCS character sets (Japanese, Chinese, and Korean) each provide two sort options. The first is Binary, which means that characters are sorted on the basis of their internal byte values, without regard to cultural correctness. The other choice makes use of Windows NT NLS (National Language Support) capabilities and provides a Case-Insensitive, Dictionary option consistent with the Windows NT character sorting in the respective localized version of the operating system. Hence, the English version of SQL Server can be used on the Chinese version of Windows NT, and it can work properly with double-byte Chinese characters and can sort them in a culturally correct manner.

For non-DBCS character sets, SQL Server provides more sorting options (which I'll explain in a moment), and each sort order is defined in a special file format. If during setup (or subsequently, while rebuilding the *master* database), you choose a character set/sort order combination other than the default, the Setup program silently spawns the CHARSET.EXE program to load and configure the SQL Server *master* database with this option. Setup always copies all the sort order files to your hard disk in the CHARSETS subdirectory.

> **NOTE** You can delete these files after setup, because SQL Server never uses them again. However, should you ever want to rebuild the *master* database, you'll have to copy these files back or install them from the CD-ROM. These are small files with a total size of only about 0.5 MB, so unless you're tight on disk space, it's probably best to save them. They are also useful for examining exactly why a certain query might behave the way it does, if you understand how to read the file.

Figure 4-3 on the following page shows a fragment of one sort-order definition file, NOCASEPR.437, which specifies the semantics for Dictionary Order, Case-Insensitive, Uppercase Preference for the 437 U.S. English character set. This fragment shows the file's general structure. The file is fairly self-explanatory once you understand the basics.

The actual code points are typically expressed by their hexadecimal byte values. (It is possible to specify the character directly rather than by its hexadecimal value. However, you would need to ensure that the editor being used to specify the file is also using the specific character set to which the sort order applies. It is safer to specify the values in hexadecimal notation, and this is done by convention.) For example, the letter *A* has a byte value of 0x41 (or decimal 65) in code page 437 and is defined by this sort order definition file as having this collating sequence:

;A=a, à, á, â, Ä=ä, Å=å

```
; semi-colon is the comment character
[sortorder]
;=======================================================
; @(#)nocasepr.srt    28.1
;
; Sort Order Overview:
; --------------------
; Based on the Code Page 437 character set, this sort order is a
; case-insensitive ordering. Upper case letters are equal to and
; always sort before their lower case counterparts.
;
; It is useful for use in the United States.
;
; Ligatures, Sort-Doubles, etc.:
; ------------------------------
; AE, ae ligatures
;
; The ordering:
; -------------
; first all non-alphanumeric characters in binary order
; followed by all numeric digits
; then followed by all alphabetic characters used in English, French and German
; and ended by all alphabetic characters not used in English, French or German
;
; Note:
; -----
; Some applications require that diacritic marks be ignored as well as
; the case for alpha letters. This can easily be accomplished by setting
; all variants of each letter to be equivalent.
;
; For instance, the letter 'E', for a case-insensitive scenario where
; diacritics are to be ignored would look like this:
;
; char = 0x45=0x65=0xC8=0xE8=0xC9=0xE9=0xCA=0xEA=0xCB=0xEB
;   ; E, e, E-grave, e-grave, E-acute, e-acute,
;     ; E-circumflex, e-circumflex, E-diaeresis, e-diaeresis
;=======================================================
class = 0x01                    ; Class `1' sort order
id = 0x21                       ; Unique ID # (33) for the sort order
name = nocasepref               ; US, case-insensitive with preference
menuname = " Dictionary Order, Case Insensitive, Uppercase Preference"
charset = cp437
preference = true               ; Use case-insensitivity with preference
description = "Case-insensitive dictionary sort order, with case preference
for collating purposes, for use in the US. Uses the Code Page 437 character set."
; Ligatures
lig = 0x92=0x91, after AE       ; AE ligature

; Latin Alphabet
char = 0x41=0x61, 0x85, 0xA0, 0x83, 0x8E=0x84, 0x8F=0x86
  ;A, a, a-grave, a-acute, a-circumflex,
  ;A-diaeresis, a-diaeresis, A-ring, a-ring
  ;A=a, à, á, â, Ä=ä, Å=å
```

Figure 4-3. *The sort order definition file NOCASEPR.437.*

These hexadecimal values are the actual directive to SQL Server:

```
char = 0x41=0x61, 0x85, 0xA0, 0x83, 0x8E=0x84, 0x8F=0x86
```

This definition states that *A* (0x41) should be treated identically to *a* (0x61). Both *A* and *a* have a value before *à* (*a*-grave, 0x85) followed by *á* (*a*-acute, 0xA0) and then *â* (*a*-circumflex, 0x83). Next is *Ä* and *ä*, which are considered equal. These are then followed by *Å* and *å*, which are also considered equal.

But there is another entry that is essential to understand:

```
preference = true; Use case insensitivity with preference
```

Although *A* has been defined as equal to *a* for the purposes of string comparison (affecting character searches, including the constructs DISTINCT, UNION, LIKE, and so on), the *preference = true* directive causes all collating (order by) to present the *A* before the *a*. In general terms, the semantics are "For the search process, treat *A* and *a* as identical, but show it to me with the *A* results preceding *a*." You might prefer this behavior, for example, when you want to print a list of both uppercase and lowercase entries, without regard to case but with names in uppercase printing before those in lowercase rather than their being randomly intermixed.

To be more precise, the above *char* = entry defines all *A-like* values as having the same primary sort value. *A* and *a* not only have the same primary sort value, they also have the same secondary sort value, because within the *char* = entry they are defined as equal. The character *à* has the same primary value as *A* and *a* but is not declared equal to them, so *à* has a different secondary value. And although *A* and *a* have the same primary and secondary sort values, each automatically retains a different tertiary sort value, which allows it to compare identically but sort differently.

A character's primary sort value is used to distinguish it from other characters, without regard to case and diacritical marks. It is essentially an optimization: if two characters do not have the same primary sort value, they cannot be considered identical for either comparison or sorting and there is no reason to look further. The secondary sort value distinguishes two characters that share the same primary value. If the characters share the same primary and secondary values (for example *A = a*), they are treated as identical for comparisons. The tertiary value allows the characters to compare identically, but sort differently. Hence, based on *A = a*, *apple* and *Apple* are considered equal. However, *Apple* will sort before *apple* when *preference = true*. If there is no *preference = true* entry, whether *Apple* or *apple* sorts first will simply be a random event based on the order in which the data is encountered when retrieved. If instead of *A = a*, the points were defined as *a = A*, *apple* would sort before *Apple* when *preference = true*.

Some sort order choices allow for Accent Insensitivity. This means that extended characters with diacritics have been defined with primary and secondary values equivalent to those without. If you want a search of *name = 'Jose'* to find both *Jose* and *José*, you should choose Accent Insensitivity. Such a sort order would have all *E*-like characters defined as equal. Consider the following, for example:

```
char = 0x45=0x65=0x8A=0x90=0x82=0x88=0x89
;E  =e  =e-grave  =E-acute  =e-acute  =e-circumflex  =e-diaeresis
;E  =e  =è        =É        =é        =ê             =ë
```

All the Accent Insensitive sort orders provided by SQL Server also have Upper-case Preference enabled (*preference = true*), which means that in an ORDER BY, the *E*-like characters above, although considered equivalent for character matching, would sort as *E, e, è, É, é, ê, ë*, with each uppercase letter paired with its lower-case equivalent and distinguished from the other *E*-like characters. Technically, there is no reason you couldn't have a sort order of Accent Insensitive Without Preference. But because the large number of existing sort orders are confusing to most people, not every conceivable variation of this is offered. It is possible to define your own sort order definition file (although it must use one of the supplied character sets) and change it to suit your needs. The Setup program allows you to load a custom sort order. However, for most users, I do not rec-ommend this. Setup provides many choices, which will meet almost every need. If you define your own and subsequently realize you make a mistake, you must rebuild the *master* database and all user databases, and reload your data.

Used by some languages, *ligatures* are two characters joined as one. For example, in the German language, *Æ* is a single character that should be defined as sort-ing immediately after the two-character combination *AE*. Instead of a *char* entry, this code point is defined as a *lig*, as shown below. Every code point from 1 through 255 must be defined exactly once, with either a *char* or a *lig* entry.

```
lig = 0x92=0x91, after AE    ; AE ligature
```

Binary sorting

Each character set offers a Binary sorting option. With Binary sorting, there is no need to specify each character's sort position. Characters are sorted based on their internal byte representation. If you look at a chart for the character set, you will see the characters ordered by this numeric value. In a Binary sort, the char-acters will sort according to their position by value, just as they are in the chart. Hence, by definition, a Binary sort is always case- and accent-sensitive and ev-ery character has a unique byte value.

Binary sorting is the fastest sorting option because all that is required internally is a simple byte-by-byte comparison of the values. But if you use extended char-acters, Binary sorting is not semantically desirable. Characters that are *A*-like, such as *Ä, ä, Å*, and *å,* would all sort after *Z*, because those extended character *A*'s are in the top 128 characters and *Z* is a standard ASCII character in the lower 128. If you deal with only ASCII characters (or otherwise don't care about the sort order of extended characters), you want case sensitivity, and you don't care about "dictionary" sorting, Binary sorting is an ideal choice. (In case-sensitive dictionary sorting, the letters *ABCXYZabcxyz* sort as AaBbCcXxYyZz. In Binary sorting, all uppercase letters appear before any lowercase letters: for example, *ABCXYZabcxyz.*)

Performance considerations

Binary sorting uses significantly fewer CPU instructions than sort orders with defined sort values. So Binary sorting is the ideal choice if it fulfills your semantic needs.

However, you won't pay a noticeable penalty for using either a simple case-insensitive sort order (for example, Dictionary Order, Case-Insensitive) or a case-sensitive choice that offers better support than Binary for extended characters (for example, Dictionary Order, Case-Sensitive). Most large sorts in SQL Server tend to be I/O bound, not CPU bound, so the fact that there are fewer CPU instructions used by Binary sorting doesn't typically translate to a significant performance difference. When you sort a small amount of data that is not I/O bound, even though Binary sorting is faster, the difference is minimal; the sort will be fast in both cases.

A more significant performance difference results if you choose a sort order that is Case-Insensitive, Uppercase Preference. Recall that this choice considers all values as equal from the comparison standpoint, which also includes indexing. Characters retain a unique tertiary sort order, so they might be treated differently by an ORDER BY clause. Choosing Uppercase Preference can often require an additional sort operation in queries, more than with simple case insensitivity. Consider a query specifying *WHERE LAST_NAME >= 'Jackson' ORDER BY LAST_NAME*. If an index exists on the *last_name* field, the query optimizer likely will use it to find rows whose *last_name* value is greater than or equal to Jackson. If there is no need to use Uppercase Preference, the optimizer knows that because it is retrieving records based on the order of *last_name*, there is also no need to physically sort the rows, because they were extracted in that order already. *Jackson, jackson,* and *JACKSON* are all qualifying rows. All are indexed and treated identically, and they will simply appear in the results set in the order in which they were encountered. If Uppercase Preference is required for sorting, a subsequent sort of the qualifying rows will be required to differentiate the rows, even though the index can still be used for selecting qualifying rows. If many qualifying rows are present, the performance difference between the two cases (one needs an additional sort operation) can be dramatic. All this doesn't mean you shouldn't choose Uppercase Preference. If you require those semantics, the performance aspect might well be a secondary concern. But you should be aware of the trade-off and decide which is most important to you. Determine whether your application can simply be made to input character data in all lowercase or uppercase consistently.

Running Setup

Now that you understand all the preliminary considerations of installing and using SQL Server, you're ready to install the software. You should be able to make the best choices for licensing, networking requirements, character set, and sort order. The actual mechanics of running the Setup program are simple—you execute the Setup program and answer a few easy questions.

The most lengthy operation of Setup, along with the mechanics of copying the files, is building and configuring SQL Server's *master* database, in which SQL Server stores configuration information and information about all other databases, in addition to many system stored procedures. If you accept the default character set and sort order, Setup simply expands a mostly prebuilt *master* database copied from the file MASTER.DA@ and then does a small amount of additional configuration. A new install using the default character set can typically be performed in less than 10 minutes from start to finish (sometimes in as little as 5 minutes, depending on the speed of your hardware and how much "think time" you need for the questions). If you do not accept the default character set or sort order, the Setup program builds the *master* database. Setup expands a copy of MASTER.AL@ and then runs several large sets of scripts that build system stored procedures and other objects. This is a totally automatic operation, but it typically adds 15 to 20 minutes to setup time. The total setup time is still usually well under 30 minutes.

Both MASTER.DA@ and MASTER.AL@ are copied to the \MSSQL\INSTALL subdirectory. Although these files are not used by subsequent SQL Server operations and you can delete them, they can help you subsequently rebuild the *master* database if you need to without you having to locate the SQL Server CD-ROM. The two database files use about 9.5 MB of disk space. If you have limited space, you can safely delete these.

NOTE Setup does not actually visit or modify the data pages of user databases. Although the upgrading process will likely be smooth, it is always a good idea to have a backup copy of your installation before upgrading. Also be sure that you have run the CHKUPG65.EXE utility (discussed in the SQL Server documentation). This utility looks for keyword conflicts, which you should resolve before performing the upgrade if possible. Generally speaking, if you are upgrading from a 6.0 version and were cautious about not using documented reserved words, upgrading to version 6.5 should be quite simple. Upgrading from version 4.21 is often more complex because of the large number of new keywords and reserved words contained in version 6.0.

When the Setup program is run and upgrades a previous installation, it rebuilds all the system stored procedures to ensure that the most recent versions are installed. Setup also checks all user databases for possible conflicts with keywords that the new version might use. This can be a time-consuming operation.

Basic Configuration After Setup

After completing Setup, you will want to verify the basic operation of SQL Server and perform some basic reconfiguration. The initial configuration provided by Setup is typically not optimal. Theoretically, Setup could try to do a lot of auto-configuration, but this would require that it ask a lot of questions about intended use, which could be confusing to a new user. Setup could also try to make assumptions based on the hardware profile of the machine (how much memory, how many processors, and so on), but without knowing what other applications will be run on the machine, these assumptions could be wrong.

Following the prime directive to get your system up quickly and with 100-percent reliability, Setup instead installs a conservative initial configuration. In a future SQL Server version, after SQL Server is initially set up, a Configuration Wizard will be available to help you further configure your machine.

After rebooting at the end of a successful installation, start SQL Server. The most common way to do this is by using SQL Service Manager, better known as the "stop light" applet. You can also use the Services applet of the Windows NT Control Panel, use SQL Enterprise Manager, issue a *NET START MSSQLSERVER* command from a Windows NT console (DOS Prompt), or use SQL Server Setup to have SQL Server start automatically whenever the machine is started. After SQL Server is running (the stop light will be green), use one of the most basic applications, ISQL/w, to ensure that you can connect. Initially, the SA password is null, so leave the password field blank or simply choose the Use Trusted Connection option. Then change your database to the *pubs* sample database and run a couple of simple queries (for example, *SELECT * FROM authors ORDER BY au_lname*) to be sure that SQL Server is running correctly. After you have verified this, you can change some basic configuration settings. You should change the following settings immediately:

- Password for the System Administrator
- Configuration for User Connections
- Memory Configuration

The easiest way to change these settings is to use SQL Enterprise Manager. You can also change the settings using the supplied system stored procedures in any program that lets you issue ad hoc commands, such as ISQL/w. SQL Enterprise Manager ultimately issues these same stored procedures to the user invisibly.

From ISQL/w, use **sp_password** to change the SA password. As mentioned earlier, initially the password is null (no password). If you run Integrated Security, a null password for SA might be fine. Standard security is the default at installation, so you should change the password. Be sure to pick a password you'll remember, because, by design, there is no way to read a password (it is stored encrypted)—it can only be changed to something else. Using ISQL/w from the *master* database to change the password to *Banks_14*, you'd issue the following command:

```
sp_password NULL, 'Banks_14', SA
```

Using SQL Enterprise Manager, you can change the password from the Manage Logins dialog box.

Note that the actual password is stored in a table as SQL Server data. So if you've chosen a case-sensitive sort order, passwords also will be case-sensitive and must be entered exactly as defined.

Setup initially configures SQL Server to allow a maximum of 20 user connections. Note that the number of user connections is different from the number of licensed users you chose during the setup process. A single instance of an application can have multiple connections open to the same SQL Server. For example, if an application has 3 connections open in a 20-connection configuration, 17 connections would still be available. If all configured connections are being used, a subsequent attempt to connect will result in error 17809 being returned to the client. ("Unable to connect. The maximum number of '20' user connections are already connected. System Administrator can configure to a higher value with **sp_configure**.") Every configured user connection uses about 55 KB of SQL Server's memory allocation. It's no shortcut to set the User Connection value higher, because you will waste memory that could be put to much better use in SQL Server's data cache. Use a value that you believe will be sufficient to handle your peak usage, without being excessive.

The initial memory setting done by the Setup program is conservative for many machines, especially if a lot of physical RAM is available. If your machine has less than 32 MB of memory, SQL Server is configured to use no more than 8 MB. If your machine has 32 MB of memory, SQL Server is configured to use 16 MB. Regardless of the amount of available memory, Setup does not automatically configure a machine to use more than 16 MB of memory. As a beginning guideline, assuming the machine will be mostly dedicated to SQL Server, you can use the data shown in Table 4-3 to determine the amount of memory to allocate to SQL Server. Adjust these numbers down if you are running other applications on the machine. It is better to have too little memory allocated to SQL Server than to be overcommitted on memory so that Windows NT has to page virtual memory in and out of RAM. (I'll discuss how to fine-tune memory allocations later in this book.)

Physical RAM (MB)	Approximate SQL Server Memory Allocation (MB)	Approximate SQL Server Memory Allocation (2-KB Pages)
16	4	2048
24	8	4096
32	16	8192
48	28	14,336
64	40	20,480
128	100	51,200
256	216	110,592
512	464	237,568

Table 4-3. *SQL Server can continue to use up to 2 GB of RAM effectively.*

From SQL Enterprise Manager, you can easily change both the User Connections and Memory options on the Configuration tab of the Server Configuration-/Options dialog box, accessible through the SQL Server Configuration command on the Server menu. Memory values are entered as the number of 2-KB pages.

From ISQL/w, you can use **sp_configure** to change user connections and memory settings. To set user connections to 50, and memory to 28 MB (14336 2-KB pages), you'd issue the following:

```
sp_configure 'user connections',50
GO
sp_configure 'memory',14336
GO
RECONFIGURE
GO
```

The new configuration values take effect the next time SQL Server is started.

SQL Enterprise Manager vs. SQL Statements

There are ways to do nearly any configuration task with SQL Server. At the lowest level, you can issue an SQL statement or a stored procedure. However, it's usually simpler to use SQL Enterprise Manager, which provides a front-end for these commands and frees you from needing to know exact steps and syntax. Administrators who are proficient with Visual Basic for Applications (VBA) might choose to use simple VBA scripts that use the SQL Server database administration object model, SQL-DMO (SQL Distributed Management Objects).

This book is geared toward database developers and administrators. I typically show the SQL statements and stored procedures that are used to accomplish a task and simply reference the easier methods, assuming that this will provide the best explanation of what's going on—even though in many cases, you'll use the higher level tools. I also focus more on what to do, rather than provide a step-by-step cookbook of how to complete every step. You might want to consult the SQL Server documentation for exact syntax of all options and so on. This book is meant to complement, but not replace, the product's documentation. It is not meant to be a reference for syntax, for example.

Unattended and Remote Setup

SQL Server Setup can be installed on a remote computer, and it can be totally scripted, requiring no user intervention. The remote setup option can be useful when you are responsible for many SQL Server installations. In fact, the feature was added (in the days predating Microsoft Systems Management Server) at the behest of Microsoft's own MIS organization, which manages more than 150 SQL Server machines (and thousands of databases). Installing and upgrading on any of those 150 servers from one computer greatly simplified MIS's work.

Other sites choose to script their installations by using the unattended setup feature to deploy many servers instead of using the remote setup option, which is still an interactive process. Microsoft Systems Management Server uses this capability and can be used to install SQL Server at multiple sites. (In fact, unattended setup scripts and a .PDF file, used by Systems Management Server, are provided on the root directory of the SQL Server CD-ROM.)

The unattended setup option is also useful if you are embedding SQL Server into a turnkey solution and want to provide a single, unified setup. As should be apparent by now, SQL Server Setup makes multiple entries to the Windows NT Registry, changes system paths and various system settings, creates program groups and user accounts, and performs basic initial configuration for its operation. The Setup program is far from a glorified file-copy program. It would not be realistic for solution providers to create their own Setup programs to install SQL Server as part of their services or products. But they can easily achieve the same results by simply creating a script that can drive the SQL Server Setup program without any user intervention. An unattended setup is not a completely hidden setup: although it requires no user intervention, the SQL Server Setup background is visible on the monitor while Setup is running.

Remote Setup

Remote setup is similar to a normal, local setup. After you choose the remote setup option (by clicking Remote in the Options dialog box of the Setup program), you are prompted to answer a few questions in addition to those a local setup needs. Along with providing the machine name of the anticipated SQL Server, you will need to do the following:

- Run Setup from an account with Administrator privileges on the remote (target) server.

- Be aware that drive paths should be relative to the remote server. For this reason, it is best to use the automatic administrative shares, such as C$, D$, and so on.

- Realize that a program group cannot be created on the Windows NT desktop at the remote machine. Typically, if you are installing remotely you will also be administrating remotely, so this should not be an issue.

Unattended Setup

Unattended setup involves creating a text file with your choices (when they deviate from the default choices) for the questions posed by the Setup program. It is easy to create an unattended install script. You can also append SQL commands that will be run automatically at the end of Setup. This is a useful way to automate the basic configuration process. Solution providers who want to launch SQL Server Setup from within their own setup programs can write a script file or generate some or all of it on the fly in response to prompts from the front-end program.

It's easiest to illustrate unattended setup by discussing a working example. Figure 4-4 on the following page provides a template you can use and modify for your own needs. To run Setup with this file (assuming that it is located in the C:\SQLSTUFF directory), type:

```
setup /t IniFilePath = C:\sqlstuff\custom_sqlsetup1.ini
```

The case and spacing of the **/t** parameter are important. It must be lowercase and a space must appear on both sides of the equal sign.

```
' An apostrophe at beginning of line is a COMMENT.
' FILE: custom_sqlsetup1.ini
[License]
FullName=Ronald Soukup
OrgName=Microsoft Corporation
' Get the Real Product ID from the CD-ROM jewel case or sleeve
ProductID=1234-56789ABCDEF
' Mode=0 means Per Server. Mode=1 means Per Seat.
Mode=0
PerServerUsers=27
[SQLPath]
LogicalSQLDrive=D:
SQLPath=\SQL65
[MasterPath]
MasterSize=40
LogicalDBDrive=D:
MasterDBPath=\SQL65\DATA
MasterDBFileName=MASTER.DAT
[NewOptions]
AutoServerService=NOTCHECKED
AutoExecutiveService=NOTCHECKED
BooksOnline=1
[CharSet]
CharSet=cpISO
[SortOrder]
' Sort order is ISO, Case Sensitive, Dictionary Sorting, which has sort order ID of 51
SortFileName=diction.iso
SortConfigValue=51
[Network]
' Named Pipes Netlib is SSNMPN60. Multiprotocol is SSMSRP60.
NetLibList={"SSNMPN60","SSMSRP60"}
ServerNMPipe=\\.\pipe\sql\query
MultiProtEncrypt=CHECKED
[LogonAccount]
LocalSystem=NOTCHECKED
Username=REDMOND\ronsou
UserPassword=Williams_26
[Scripts]
'When done with setup, run the simple configuration file to change password, and
set initial memory and user connections
CustScPath= C:\sqlstuff
CustomScriptList=Óconfig1.sqlÓ
ForceReboot=FALSE
-- FILE: config1.sql
sp_password null,'Santo_10',sa
go
sp_configure 'user connections',50
go
sp_configure 'memory',12288
go
reconfigure
go
```

Figure 4-4. *Sample install script (*custom_sqlsetup1.ini*).*

(The script in Figure 4-4 is available on the accompanying CD-ROM.)

The following installation results:

- SQL Server installed to the D drive, in the \SQL65 directory

- 40-MB MASTER device

- ISO character set with case-sensitive dictionary sorting

- Per Server licensing for 27 users

- Named Pipes and Multi-Protocol network support

- Multi-Protocol network encryption turned on

- Memory initially configured to 24 MB (12,288 pages)

- User connections configured to 50

- The SA password changed to *Santo_10*

Using Setup after Initial Installation

The Setup program is often useful after the first installation, so do not delete it. You can later use Setup to perform the following functions:

- Change network interface choices.

- Specify global security choices; for example, have SQL Server entrust user authentication to Windows NT (Integrated Security) instead of doing its own.

- Rebuild the *master* database, optionally with a different character set and sort order. This is almost a new setup, except that the program files are not recopied and you do not have to use the distribution CD-ROM. Using this option will require that you re-create all your databases and reload your data.

- Change certain global configuration options; for example, have SQL Server or SQL Executive automatically started each time Windows NT is started. You can also specify settings for SQLMail integration and specify parameters that are passed to the SQL Server program at startup.

- Install Client Utilities. The Setup program is used to install the client and administration utilities of SQL Server. In Windows 95, use the Setup program from the i386 subdirectory; Setup detects on loading that it is running on Windows 95, not Windows NT, and allows only the Client Utilities portion of Setup to proceed. (The same binary programs for client access are used on both Windows NT for Intel architecture and Windows NT for other platforms.)

■ Add locale support for another language.

■ Remove SQL Server. When removing SQL Server, you can choose to remove all SQL Server files. If you do not remove the files, this option simply removes all SQL Server–related entries in the Windows NT Registry.

An important option, but one that does not appear on the Setup screen, enables you to rebuild the SQL Server entries in the Windows NT Registry without reinstalling or otherwise disturbing your existing SQL Server environment or data. To rebuild SQL Server Registry entries, enter the following:

```
setup /t RegistryRebuild = ON
```

Rebuilding the Registry is useful in the following circumstances:

■ The Windows NT Registry was partially corrupted (for example, inadvertently deleted using the REGEDT32.EXE program).

■ Windows NT was reinstalled (not upgraded) on a machine and consequently an entirely new Registry was written and is not aware of the previous SQL Server installation.

■ To configure one of multiple SQL Server installations as the active one. Although the MSSQLServer service can have only one instance (you cannot run multiple, simultaneous instances of MS SQL Server 6.*x* as a service on the same machine), you can install multiple copies on one machine. You do this by using the Remove option without deleting the files between installations, and by choosing different paths for installation. You then use the Registry rebuild option to specify which installation you want to run.

NOTE Although only one instance of SQL Server can be run as a service, you can simultaneously run multiple instances if the subsequent instances are run from the command line. This is less optimal than having multiple databases in a single SQL Server installation, so it is not generally recommended. If you choose to do this, each instance of SQL Server requires its own license.

■ You want to change the registered owner of SQL Server. You can first "remove" SQL Server without removing the files; then use this option to rebuild the Registry settings and specify a new registered owner.

SUMMARY

Microsoft SQL Server offers unprecedented ease of installation for a database server of its caliber. But it pays to understand your choices in hardware, licensing, and sort orders before proceeding too far down the path of a major application rollout. SQL Server Setup is also fast and reliable. It does little custom configuration, so be aware that the initial installation is likely not optimal.

Setup offers options for unattended and remote installation, for client-tools–only installation, and for various configuration settings. The Setup program is useful and sometimes necessary beyond the initial installation, so you should not delete it after the initial installation.

5

Databases and Devices

What Is a Database?

Simply put, a *SQL Server database* is a collection of objects that hold and manipulate data. A typical SQL Server installation has only a handful of databases, but it's not unusual for a single installation to contain several dozen databases. (Theoretically, one SQL Server can have as many as 32,767 databases. But practically speaking, this limit would never be reached.)

A SQL Server database:

- Is a collection of many *objects*, such as tables, views, stored procedures, and constraints. The theoretic limit is 2^{31} (or more than 2 billion) objects. Typically, the number of objects ranges from hundreds to tens of thousands.

- Is owned by a single user account but can contain objects owned by other users.

- Has its own set of system tables that catalog the definition of the database.

- Maintains its own set of user accounts and security.

- Is the primary unit of recovery and maintains logical consistency among objects in the database. (For example, primary and foreign key relationships always refer to other tables within the same database, not to other databases.)

- Has its own transaction log and manages the transactions within the database.

- Can participate in two-phase commit transactions with other SQL Server databases on the same or different servers.

- Can span multiple disk drives and operating system files.

- Can be from 1 MB through 1 TB (theoretic limit) in size.

- Can be enlarged fairly easily after it is created and can also be shrunk, with some restrictions.

- Can have objects joined in queries with objects from other databases in the same SQL Server installation.

- Can have specific options set or disabled. (For example, a database can be set to be read-only or can be published in replication, and a column can be set by default to allow nulls.)

- Is conceptually similar to but richer than the ANSI SQL-schema concept (discussed later in this chapter).

A SQL Server database is *not*:

- Synonymous with an entire SQL Server installation.

- A single SQL Server table.

- A specific operating system file (although a database could reside entirely in one such file).

Because a database is not an operating system file or structure, you must first create such a file. This file is known as a SQL Server *database device,* and it is created before a database is created.

Database Devices

A database device is usually a logical mapping to a Microsoft Windows NT system file. (In addition to database devices, SQL Server also has *dump devices,* which are logical devices that map to operating system files, to physical devices such as tape drives, or even to named pipes.) A database resides on at least one, and typically several, logical database devices, and these devices are specified when a database is created or enlarged. You could ask, "Why use database devices at all? Why not simply specify the operating system files directly?" The concept of logical database devices exists for two chief reasons: SQL Server's UNIX legacy and the continued occasional use (although rare) of raw devices. If a database device always mapped to an operating system file, there would be few compelling reasons not to simply specify the filename and perhaps a size, instead of specifying the logical device name. (This is true if you consider it the job of the file system or hardware to provide disk mirroring.) But it is too simplistic to *always* deem a SQL Server database device an operating system file. More correctly, a SQL Server database device is a logical mapping to *physical disk storage,* which is usually further abstracted by specifying an operating system file. A database device *can* be an unformatted raw-disk partition, although this is unusual and not typically recommended.

SQL Server provides device *mirroring,* independent of the RAID capabilities of Windows NT and/or the hardware. Mirroring also exists largely for historical reasons, a legacy of some UNIX platforms in which fault-tolerant features did not exist. Low-level I/O capabilities, such as mirroring and striping, are better performed "below" SQL Server, at the operating system or hardware level. Rather than use mirroring in SQL Server, I recommend using Windows NT RAID features (stripe sets, volume sets, mirroring, and striping with parity) or hardware RAID controllers (as discussed in Chapter 4).

SQL Server database devices are preallocated in size. There is minimal file overhead, and because the file grabs all its disk space at once, the file is likely to be as contiguous as possible and less susceptible to being part of a fragmented operating system file. The device also defines an upper limit for how much of the file the database can use. (You can expand the size of database devices, but you must do so manually.) A device does not automatically grow when a database uses all the space allocated to it. This throttle on size can be an advantage or a disadvantage: from an administrative control standpoint it can be advantageous to define the upper bounds of the database in advance, but it can be a nuisance to have the device fill up and have to manually expand it. Only the system administrator (SA) can create or expand a device; permission to do so cannot be granted to other users.

The Future...

It is likely that in some future release of SQL Server, you'll be able to directly specify a filename rather than have to create a logical database device first. It is also likely that files will be able to grow dynamically. And it is quite possible that SQL Server mirroring will be removed, in favor of exclusively using Windows NT or hardware capabilities.

Creating Database Devices

You create a database device by using the DISK INIT command, specifying as parameters a logical name, a physical name, a unique virtual device number (*VDEVNO*) by which the device will be internally identified, and its size in 2-KB pages. Although you can use long filenames for physical filenames, you should use only 8.3-character names for directories and should not use spaces in filenames because Setup and some older SQL Server utilities assume that directory structures use 8.3-character names.

Here is an example of using the DISK INIT command (from any interactive SQL utility, such as ISQL/w) to create a 40-MB (20,480 2-KB pages) device:

```
DISK INIT
    NAME='MORESPACE',
    PHYSNAME='D:\SQL65\MORESPACE.DAT',
    VDEVNO=10,
    SIZE=20480
```

Microsoft SQL Enterprise Manager, shown below, makes this operation much easier. It graphically displays all the disk space on the computer and the current database devices, and it automatically assigns the next available value for *VDEVNO*.

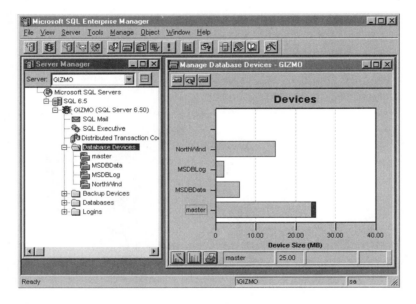

When the device is created, an operating system file composed entirely of nulls (0x0 byte values) is created. If the NTFS file system is used, as a security feature the creating application (in this case, SQL Server) is always presented with an all-zero image of the file. The file is mapped from memory as all zeros, but it is not physically initialized. If the file allocation table (FAT) file system is used, Windows NT physically zeros-out the file so that every bit is initialized to 0. Because this can be time-consuming, initializing a disk device file on NTFS can be dramatically faster than doing so on FAT.

As discussed in Chapter 4, the underlying operating system disk partition should often be a RAID device. For example, partition "E:" might be a striped set, which might also be mirrored or have parity for recoverability.

The MASTER device (typically, the MASTER.DAT file) is a special device created at the time SQL Server is installed. MASTER.DAT contains the *master* database and a special set of system tables for the entire installation. (The MASTER device cannot be created with DISK INIT.) The *master* database and its system tables are vital—they maintain the definition for all subsequent databases you will create, as well as all information for physical disk storage (in a table called *sysdevices*). The first four 2-KB pages of the MASTER device are not used by any database; instead, that area is known as the *configuration block* and contains basic configuration information, such as the settings for memory and user connections. It is read each time SQL Server is started.

The Device Number

As each device is created, it is given a unique virtual device number (corresponding to the *VDEVNO* parameter of DISK INIT) and a new row is inserted in the *master..sysdevices* system table for that device. Only the *master* database contains a *sysdevices* table. Figure 5-1 shows a list of devices in the *sysdevices* system table.

Low	High	Status	Cntrltype	Name	Phyname
0	20479	3	0	MASTER	C:\MSSQL\DATA\MASTER.DAT
16777216	16797695	3	0	MORESPACE	D:\SQL65\MORESPACE.DAT
2130706432	2130709503	2	0	MSDBDATA	C:\MSSQL\DATA\MSDB.DAT
2113929216	2113930239	2	0	MSDBLOG	C:\MSSQL\DATA\MSDBLOG.DAT

Figure 5-1. *Partial listing of devices from the* sysdevices *table.*

Microsoft SQL Server supports up to 256 devices (not including dump devices, which are used for backups and not for storing online data). Virtual device number 0 is reserved for the MASTER database device, and device numbers 126 and 127 are reserved for the MSDBLOG and MSDBDATA devices. The remaining device numbers through 255 are available for user-created devices.

It is not at all obvious what a device's VDEVNO is. The device number is the high byte of the 4-byte low and high fields in *sysdevices*. For example, the low field for MSDBDATA is 2130706432, or 0x7F000000. The high byte, 0x7F, or decimal 127, is the VDEVNO. An easier way to see the value, rather than masking off this value yourself, is to execute the system stored procedure **sp_helpdevice**, which returns detailed information about devices. Better still, use SQL Enterprise Manager: it handles the device number invisibly.

Each device is composed of a contiguous group of 2-KB pages. The low and high values in *sysdevices* indicate the starting and ending page numbers, respectively, within each device. The virtual device number is contained in the high byte of the 4-byte values for low and high. The remaining 3 bytes specify the page number relative to the beginning of the device. For example, 0x01000000 is page 0 on device 1, and 0x0F000057 is page 87 (0x57) on device 15 (0x0F).

In the *sysdevices* table shown in Figure 5-1, the MORESPACE device has a low value of 16777216 (0x01000000) and a high value of 16797695 (0x01004FFF), indicating that the device number is 1 and that it contains 20,480 pages, numbered 0x0 through 0x4FFF (20,479). You can figure out the size of the device by multiplying the page size by the number of pages in the device: the MORESPACE device is 40 MB (2 KB × 20480).

Any one device can have a maximum of 16,777,216 (0 through 0xFFFFFF) 2-KB pages, or 32 GB of storage. Each SQL Server installation can have up to 256 devices defined.

If you create a device with a VDEVNO greater than 127, you will see negative values for low and high (when they are displayed as decimal values). This is because those columns are signed 4-byte integers and thus overflow when the device number is greater than 127. This is not a problem—the high byte still maintains the device number (through 255) and the lower 3 bytes maintain the proper page offset in the device. Because of the way these columns are used, you'll want to look at these values in hex rather than in decimal. The real reason that the MSDBLOG and MSDBDATA devices use the values 126 and 127 respectively, instead of the top entries of 254 and 255, is so that new users would not see the negative values and think there was a problem.

Because the device number is a part of the virtual page numbers assigned to devices and because device numbers must be unique within a SQL Server, it follows that virtual page numbers are unique across all devices within a SQL Server. Given a virtual page number, you can easily find the device containing that page by looking in *sysdevices* for the range of low/high values in which that number falls. For example, you can determine that virtual page 5125 is located on the MASTER device because the value 5125 falls between the low (0) and high (20479) values for the MASTER device in *sysdevices*.

Expanding Devices

You can expand a device by using the DISK RESIZE command. (Currently, you can only enlarge a device, not make it smaller. Hence, you might want to err on the side of creating a device somewhat smaller rather than larger.) The DISK RESIZE command simply moves out the operating system file pointer to enlarge the file and fixes up the corresponding entries in the *sysdevices* table. For example, to increase the MORESPACE device we created earlier from 40 MB to 75 MB (38,400 2-KB pages), you'd use this command:

```
DISK RESIZE
NAME='MORESPACE',
SIZE=38400
```

Notice that the SIZE parameter specifies the final, total size of the device in 2-KB pages, not the amount of incremental growth.

Default Devices

The relationship between databases and devices is not one-to-one. When you create a database, you define whether it will reside on one or more devices. A database can span multiple devices, and a device can contain multiple databases. If you do not specify that a database will exist on a specific device, SQL Server will try to create the database on a device marked as default. Multiple devices can be marked as default, forming the *default device pool*. A device is added to the default pool either by the **sp_diskdefault** system stored procedure or by SQL Enterprise Manager.

Initially, the MASTER device is the only default device. But because MASTER is a special purpose device, you should remove it from the default pool. I do not recommend creating new databases on the MASTER device. Instead, you should create one or more new devices for "user" databases. You can add other devices to the default pool, or you can choose to have no default pool, in which case all databases must be defined as residing on specific devices. Specifying devices is good practice; practically speaking, you lose little and perhaps gain a control safeguard by not having a default pool.

Mounting and Dismounting Devices

Devices can be *mounted* and *dismounted* by using a simple statement (**sp_devoption**) that instructs SQL Server to consider the device ready for use. A typical device that resides on permanent hard-disk storage is almost always permanently mounted. SQL Server's ability to mount and dismount enables it to support databases that reside on removable media such as CD-ROMs. This ability is also used by the fallback server capabilities that allow a backup server to pick up and use the databases of a failed primary server.

Errors Related to Device Creation and Initialization

Most problems that occur during DISK INIT result in the following generic error message being returned to the client:

```
Msg 5123, Level 16, State 1
DISK INIT encountered an error while attempting to open/create
the physical file. Please consult the SQL Server error log (in
the SQL Server boot directory) for more details.
```

These are the most common reasons for this error:

- Incorrect or nonexistent path for the *PHYSNAME* parameter. Note that although the file is created by the DISK INIT command, the directories specified in the path must already exist.

- The physical file already exists in the specified path. By design, DISK INIT will not overwrite a file.

■ Insufficient disk space for the given *size* parameter.

■ Insufficient file-system permissions to create the file. Remember that the account in which SQL Server is running (not the account of the person issuing the command to SQL Server) must have permission to create the file.

You can avoid most DISK INIT errors by using SQL Enterprise Manager, which lets you browse for the paths, checks disk space, and performs other tasks. If you issue the command and get an error, the SQL Server error log and the Windows NT event log will typically contain the operating system error and a message indicating the reason for the failure. Following is a portion of the SQL Server error log indicating the reason for a failed DISK INIT command. In this case, the DISK INIT command specified a physical filename that already existed:

```
kernel udcreate: Operating system error 80(The file exists.)
encountered
```

Mirroring

SQL Server provides DISK MIRROR and related commands to mirror SQL Server devices. However, these capabilities are redundant to the RAID capabilities of Windows NT (and possibly your hardware). It is better to leave such low-level I/O operations as mirroring writes to the operating system or hardware. Use the fault tolerance features of Windows NT (or the hardware) instead of SQL Server mirroring.

The Future...

The DISK MIRROR, DISK UNMIRROR, and DISK REMIRROR commands will likely be dropped in a future SQL Server release in favor of RAID. More accurately, these commands would be accepted but would do nothing except issue a warning message that they are now a NOOP (no operation) and that RAID should be used instead.

Creating Databases

After you have created your devices, you create the database. Several special databases are already in the system before you create any new databases. These are *master, model, tempdb, pubs,* and *msdb.* I'll describe these databases near the end of this chapter. First let's discuss the databases that you create for your work, referred to as *user databases*.

The easiest way to create or expand a database is to use SQL Enterprise Manager, which provides a graphical front-end to Transact-SQL commands and stored procedures that accomplish those tasks. Figure 5-2 shows SQL Enterprise Manager's New Database dialog box, which represents the CREATE DATABASE Transact-SQL command. I'll discuss the underlying commands here.

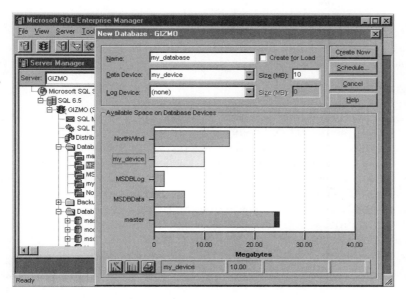

Figure 5-2. *The New Database dialog box.*

Only the SA or a user who has been granted CREATE DATABASE permission by the SA can issue the CREATE DATABASE command. The command is used to create, or build, a new user database. (This differs from the special *master* database that is created during setup and is used to keep information about all user databases, user login accounts, and systemwide settings.)

When you create a new user database, SQL Server copies the *model* database. The *model* database is simply a template database. For example, if you have an object you'd like created in every subsequent user database, create that object in *model* first. (You can also use *model* to set default database configuration options in all subsequent databases.) In addition to objects you may create in *model,* 18 system tables are included in *model,* which means that every new database also includes these 18 system tables. These tables are used by SQL Server for the definition and maintenance of each database. (The *syskeys* system table is considered obsolete and is no longer documented. It is still built purely for backward compatibility but has no current functionality.) If you have not added any other objects to *model,* these 18 system tables will be the entire contents of a newly created database. Every Transact-SQL command or system stored procedure that creates, alters, or drops a SQL Server object will result in entries being made to system tables.

Do not directly modify the system tables. You can render your database unusable by doing so. Direct modification is prevented by default. It takes deliberate action via the **sp_configure** stored procedure on the part of the SA to allow system tables to be modified directly.

A new user database must be 1 MB or greater in size or at least the size of the *model* database if *model* is larger than 1 MB. It is possible to create a database using a simple form of CREATE DATABASE, such as this:

```
CREATE DATABASE testdb
```

This would create the *testdb* database, with a default size, on the first available device that is part of the default device pool. The SQL Server login account that created the database is known as the *database owner,* or DBO. The database might be created on multiple devices if the first device in the default pool does not have enough space for it, in which case the next device is also used, and so on. The default size is defined by the *database size* configuration option (set by **sp_configure**). Whether the database name, *testdb,* is case-sensitive or not depends on the sort order you choose during setup. If you accepted the default, the name is case-insensitive. (Note that the actual command CREATE DATABASE is case-insensitive, regardless of the case sensitivity chosen for data.)

When CREATE DATABASE is run, it detects whether the database is being created on a new device. If the database is being created on a previously used device, CREATE DATABASE initializes all the pages. This can be a time-consuming operation when working with a large database. Pages are initialized to wipe clean any SQL Server data pages that might still be lying around on disk from a previous use. If you want to reuse a SQL Server device and you are using the NTFS file system (which presents a zero-image file to SQL Server without physically initializing) it can be much faster to drop and re-create the device and then create the database. This can result in only 1/256 as much initialization. When SQL Server determines that a device is new and has no prior contents, it safely eliminates the initialization except for *allocation pages.* An allocation page occurs as the first of every 256 pages. It keeps track of the usage of the other 255 pages, sometimes referred to as *data pages* (although they are also used for indexes, the transaction log, and so on), in the *allocation unit,* which is a block of 256 contiguous pages (or 0.5 MB—databases are always created or altered in multiples of allocation units, and hence their sizes are always in multiples of 0.5 MB).

Separating the Transaction Log

The example above shows the simplest form of CREATE DATABASE, but you will usually need to be more specific. CREATE DATABASE allows you to control the exact database size and devices used and, probably most important, to separate the database's transaction log from its data space. Here is a better example:

```
CREATE DATABASE testdb
ON MORESPACE=50
LOG ON LOGSPACE=10
```

This command creates a 60-MB database—50 MB for data and 10 MB for the transaction log. The data will reside on the MORESPACE device, and the transaction log will reside on a device called LOGSPACE. (The names can be almost anything, and the spacing of the command on multiple lines here is only for readability—it's not required.) If you specify ON DEFAULT (instead of ON MORESPACE, as in this example), SQL Server will use the default pool of devices. You can specifically name a device even if it is part of the default pool.

Why separate the transaction log from the data in the database? It is important to back up your data. But having to back up an entire database each time you want to do a backup can be cumbersome and problematic. Separating the transaction log from the data allows you to perform dumps (backups) of only the transaction log. Dumping the transaction log creates an *incremental backup,* a record of the changes made only since the last full database dump. Always using full database backups is appropriate for some sites, but the ability to back up only the transaction log is an important feature used by most production applications.

You can specify up to 32 multiple devices simply by tagging them, one after the other, like this:

```
CREATE DATABASE testdb
ON MORESPACE=50, MORESPACE2=30, MORESPACE3=20
LOG ON LOGSPACE=10, LOGSPACE2=10
```

However, it is usually easier to specify (and more importantly, later maintain) a small number of database devices and transaction log devices. If your database is like the large majority of databases in which the data and log are each under 32 GB, you can have just one data device and one log device. By using RAID devices, you still get the performance benefits of multiple disks. The data device for an I/O-intensive database should usually be a RAID device (0, 1, 0 + 1, or 5 depending on your I/O needs, budget, and fault tolerance needs). Write operations to the log are sequential, and writes appear at the end of the file. It is best to keep the log on a physically separate hard drive/RAID set so that the disk head(s) stay in place for the next operation, because the writes simply keep extending. Typically, most sites will want to protect at least the transaction log from media failure, and because the transaction log is I/O intensive, RAID-1 mirroring (rather than RAID-5) is usually the best choice for the log. (See Chapter 4 for more on RAID.) Making sure the transaction log is physically separated from SQL Server data space is also an important performance concern.

Maximum Database Size and Database Fragments

A single SQL Server device is limited to 32 GB. Databases needing more data space will, by definition, have more than one data device. As stated earlier, up to 32 devices can be included in a CREATE DATABASE statement. More specifically, each database can have up to 32 device *fragments*. For example, if I create a database on a device and subsequently alter the database to have additional space on the same device, I have used 2 device fragments. The limit of 32 device fragments, each of which can be a maximum of 32 GB, is the basis for the database limit of 1 terabyte (32 × 32 GB = 1 TB).

If you have used the ALTER DATABASE command and as a result multiple fragments are stored on the same device, you can use the **sp_coalesce_fragments** stored procedure to "massage" the fragments back into one if the pages are contiguous and of the same type (data or log).

Expanding and Shrinking Databases

You can easily expand a database by using the ALTER DATABASE command. ALTER DATABASE is similar to CREATE DATABASE, except that it does not allow you to designate additional space specifically for the log. Instead, the command simply gives the database as a whole the additional space. If the space is needed for the log, you can use the **sp_logdevice** stored procedure to designate that space for the log. For example:

```
ALTER DATABASE testdb ON MORELOGSPACE=10
GO
sp_logdevice testdb, MORELOGSPACE
GO
```

You would also use **sp_logdevice** to create log space if the database was not initially created with the log separate from the data.

Although it is easy to increase the size of a database, it is more difficult to shrink a database. The DBCC SHRINKDB command has limitations, and understanding these limitations may make you change your database creation strategy. DBCC SHRINKDB is not a compaction utility. It starts at the tail of the database and works back toward the top of the database through unused pages until it finds space being used by an object; then it stops. It truncates everything after that point. The last object is often the transaction log (the *syslogs* system table) for the database. This is the case when the entire database and log space were created in the initial CREATE DATABASE command and the database was never subsequently expanded with ALTER DATABASE. For example, suppose I create a 525-MB database as follows:

```
CREATE DATABASE sales_data ON DATADEV1=500 LOG ON LOGDEV1=25
```

Subsequently I realize that I grossly overestimated the size needs of the database. It really needs to have only 75 MB for data and a 25-MB log, so it has 425 MB of wasted space. In this example, the DBCC SHRINKDB command would be almost useless, because working from the tail, it encounters *syslogs* and stops. Although I might shrink the transaction log, I'd gain nothing; I still can't get to the data space, where the real free space is. My only alternative would be to create a new, smaller database and reload the database. If I had instead created the database with a smaller data space, as shown in the following example, and subsequently altered it to 525 MB, I would be able to shrink it to 100 MB (51,200 pages) with the command· *DBCC SHRINKDB(sales_data, 51200)*.

```
CREATE DATABASE sales_data ON DATADEV1=25 LOG ON LOGDEV1=25
GO
ALTER DATABASE sales_data ON DATADEV1=475
GO
```

I now have the same 525-MB database as before, but I can shrink it to 100 MB, or 51,200 pages.

More Information...

For even more gory details about DBCC SHRINKDB, see article Q141163, "INF: Issues with Shrinking SQL Server Databases" in the Microsoft KnowledgeBase, (available at http://www.microsoft.com) or check out the Microsoft Developer Network Library (MSDN).

Databases "Under the Covers"

A database consists of user-defined space for the permanent storage of user objects such as tables and indexes. This space is allocated within one or more devices. A single database can span multiple devices, and a single device can contain multiple databases.

Databases are divided into logical pages (of 2 KB each), numbered contiguously from 0 to x, with the upper value x being defined by the size of the database. When you use the ALTER DATABASE command to enlarge a database, the new space is added to the end of the database. That is, the first page of the newly allocated space is page $x + 1$. When you shrink a database by using the DBCC SHRINKDB command, pages are removed starting at the highest page in the database (at the end) and moving toward lower-numbered pages. This ensures that page numbers within a database are always contiguous.

Pages within a database are numbered the same way for every database. That is, two databases, each 50 MB in size, will have logical pages numbered 0 through 25,599. Associated with each database is an in-memory controlling structure known as the DBTABLE, which is not accessible to users. One of the functions of the DBTABLE is to provide a mapping from the logical pages in the database to the virtual pages on the device(s) on which the database is created. For example, if a user updates a row on page 17,735 of the *sales* database, the DBTABLE structure for that database maps that logical page to its virtual page on the disk, so that SQL Server knows where on disk to write the page.

The *master* database contains 31 system tables: the same 18 tables found in user databases plus 13 tables that keep track of serverwide information. Three of these tables, *syslocks, syscurconfigs,* and *sysprocesses,* do not physically exist in the *master* database; rather, they are built dynamically each time a user queries them. The *master* database also contains 10 tables that I refer to as "pseudo–system tables." These table names begin with "*spt_*" and are used as storage areas for various system procedures, but they are not true system tables. You should never modify them directly because that could break some of the system procedures, but deleting them would not invalidate the basic integrity of the database, which is the case if true system tables are altered.

When a new database is created with the CREATE DATABASE statement, it is given a unique database ID, or *dbid,* and a new row is inserted in the *master..sysdatabases* table for that database. Only the *master* database contains a *sysdatabases* table. Figure 5-3 shows a snapshot of a sample *sysdatabases* table.

name	dbid	suid	mode	status	logptr	crdate	dumptrdate
master	1	1	0	8	5123	Feb 24 1997 10:26AM	Mar 5 1997 8:54PM
model	3	1	0	0	378	Feb 24 1997 10:26AM	Feb 24 1997 10:26AM
msdb	5	1	0	8	1369	Feb 25 1997 10:37AM	Mar 4 1997 10:23PM
pubs	4	1	0	8	909	Feb 24 1997 10:31AM	Mar 4 1997 10:23PM
Sales	6	1	0	0	51207	Mar 5 1997 8:54PM	Mar 5 1997 8:54PM
tempdb	2	1	0	4	259	Mar 5 1997 8:03PM	Mar 5 1997 8:26PM

Figure 5-3. *Partial listing of a* sysdatabases *table.*

The *sysdatabases* table contains these columns:

Column	Information
name	Name of the database.
dbid	Unique database ID; can be reused when the database is dropped.
suid	Server user ID of the database creator.
mode	Locking mode, used internally while a database is being created or loaded.
status	Bit mask that shows if a database is read-only, offline, designated for single-user use only, and so on. Some of the settings can be selected by the user with the **sp_dboption** stored procedure; others are internally set. (The SQL Server product documentation shows all the bit-mask values.)
version	Internal version of SQL Server with which the database was created. (Not shown in Figure 5-3.)
logptr	Pointer to the first page of the transaction log for this database.
crdate	Date on which the database was created.
dumptrdate	Date of the last DUMP TRANSACTION command for this database.
category	Another bit-mask–like status, added when *status* bits were used up. (Not shown in Figure 5-3.)

The rows in *sysdatabases* are updated when a database's ownership or name is changed or when options (see the next section) are changed. In addition, rows will be updated each time the transaction log for a database is dumped or when the status of a database changes (such as when it is being loaded or recovered).

Database Options

Several options exist at the database level. By default, all options are FALSE unless they were set to TRUE in the *model* database, in which case all subsequent databases will have the same values. You can easily set these options by using SQL Enterprise Manager or directly by using the **sp_dboption** system stored procedure. All options correspond to the *status* and *category* bits of *sysdatabases,* although those bits can also show states that cannot be set directly by the database owner (such as when the database is in the process of being recovered).

Executing **sp_dboption** with no parameters shows all options that can be set:

```
> EXEC sp_dboption

Settable database options:
------------------
ANSI null default
dbo use only
no chkpt on recovery
offline
published
read only
select into/bulkcopy
single user
subscribed
trunc. log on chkpt.
```

ANSI null default   If either NULL or NOT NULL is not explicitly specified when defining a column in a table, SQL Server defaults to NOT NULL. However, the ANSI SQL-92 standard is NULL. Changing this option to TRUE makes the default NULL.

dbo use only   This option prevents all users except the DBO from subsequently using the database. Usually, this option is used only temporarily, during times when you want the database to be inaccessible to other users—for example, when you want to change table structures and need to keep users out until that activity is completed. (If you *never* want some other user to access the database, you'd simply not add that user to the *sysusers* table of that database. You would not use **dbo use only**.)

no chkpt on recovery   This option is typically used only if you are regularly applying transaction log dumps to a backup server as a way to keep a completely replicated database (distinct from the replication features of SQL Server). It defines whether a checkpoint record is added to the database after it is recovered during SQL Server startup. If this option is TRUE in the secondary database, no checkpoint record is added to a database after it is recovered, so subsequent transaction log dumps from the primary database can be loaded into it.

offline   This option is typically used for databases on removable media such as CD-ROMs. Placing databases online and offline allows them to be mounted and dismounted while SQL Server is running.

published   This permits the tables of a database to be published for replication.

read only   Use this option to prevent any operation in the database that would modify, insert, or delete data; create or drop database objects; or change database configuration settings. The data can be read but cannot be changed in any way.

select into/bulkcopy   This option allows certain nonlogged operations—such as using the UPDATETEXT or WRITETEXT commands without logging—using SELECT INTO with a permanent table, using fast bulk copy (**bcp**), or performing a table load. Using nonlogged operations obviously prevents subsequent recovery from only a transaction log backup. After a nonlogged operation is performed (that is, not simply when the option is set to TRUE), further DUMP TRANSACTION commands are prohibited. Instead, you can use DUMP DATABASE to back up the entire database.

single user   This option restricts the database's use to one active SQL Server connection.

subscribed   This option permits a database to subscribe to a published (replicated) database.

trunc. log on chkpt.   When this option is set, every time an automatic checkpoint occurs (when data pages in the cache that were modified since the last checkpoint are written to disk), transactions that have already been checkpointed—flushed to disk—are purged from the log. This makes it possible to do DUMP/LOAD operations only at the database level, not at the transaction log level. But it does relieve you of having to worry about dumping the transaction log in order to keep it from filling up. There is no way to disable logging, because if an operation were not logged, it could not be recovered or rolled back. Most of the time, when someone wants to disable logging, the real question is "How can I make logging invisible and not demand any administration?" The **trunc. log on chkpt.** option usually accomplishes this; the log simply wraps and never requires intervention. Note that the log must be large enough to accommodate the single largest transaction so that it can be recovered or rolled back. This option is often used during application development; it can also be used if your backup strategy can rely solely on database dumps, not transaction log dumps.

Changing Database Options

Only the DBO or SA can change an option. To change an option, the DBO/SA specifies the database name, option, and TRUE or FALSE. It is necessary to specify only enough of the option name to ensure its recognition (even just a single letter in the case of, say, **published**). For example, to turn on **published**, **select into/bulkcopy**, and **ANSI null default**, you would type

```
> EXEC sp_dboption 'testdb', 'pub', TRUE
> EXEC sp_dboption 'testdb', 'select into', TRUE
> EXEC sp_dboption 'testdb', 'ANSI null', TRUE
```

To check that the options are set, you would type

```
> EXEC sp_dboption 'testdb'
```

and this would appear:

```
The following options are set:
-----------------------------------
select into/bulkcopy
ANSI null default
published
```

Executing the **sp_helpdb** stored procedure for a database shows which options have been enabled and provides other useful information, such as devices used, database size, creation date, and database owner. Executing **sp_helpdb** with no parameters shows information about all the databases in the installation. On a new installation, the following databases exist and **sp_helpdb** renders this output (the created dates will vary):

```
> EXEC sp_helpdb
name    db_size owner dbid created      status
------------------------------------------------------------
master 17.00MB sa    1    Mar 11 1996 trunc. log on chkpt.
model   1.00 MB sa    3    Mar 11 1996 no options set
msdb    8.00 MB sa    5    Mar 11 1996 trunc. log on chkpt.
pubs    3.00 MB sa    4    Mar 11 1996 trunc. log on chkpt.
tempdb 2.00 MB sa    2    Mar 13 1996 select into/bulkcopy
```

The *msdb* database is used as the repository for scheduling services and alerts provided by the SQL Executive and SQL-DMO components. The *pubs* database is a sample database that is installed by default. It is used for many of the examples in the SQL Server documentation and in this book.

The *tempdb* database is a special work area for SQL Server. Worktables are created in this database for SQL Server to use during processing of certain queries (such as certain GROUP BY, ORDER BY, and UNION queries). Temporary tables are also created there as well. Cursors also use *tempdb* as work space. Although *tempdb* starts at 2 MB in size, except when working with very small installations you will usually need to enlarge it relatively soon (by using the ALTER command or SQL Enterprise Manager). You will know that *tempdb* is out of space when certain queries return error message 1105 saying that *tempdb* is full. You can proactively decide on the amount of space for *tempdb* by using Performance Monitor and watching how full it becomes. The *tempdb* database differs from all other databases in that it is not recovered. Instead, it is re-created (with the size to which it was last altered, not back to its original 2 MB) every time SQL Server starts. Any contents in *tempdb* are cleared out permanently when SQL Server exits.

Other Database Considerations

Here are a few additional points to keep in mind about databases on SQL Server.

The FOR LOAD Option

The FOR LOAD option in the CREATE DATABASE command is used when the database is being created to immediately load a database dump (backup). FOR LOAD prevents the database from being used until the load operation completes and the DBO or SA makes it available to other users. Because a load operation will always initialize unused pages, specifying FOR LOAD makes the CREATE DATABASE command bypass page initialization even if the device(s) are not new and previously unused, since it would be redundant.

Database Does Not Equal Schema

The ANSI SQL-92 standard includes the notion of a *schema,* or more precisely an *SQL-schema,* which in many ways is similar to SQL Server's database concept. Per the ANSI standard, an SQL-schema is a collection of *descriptors,* each of which is "a coded description of an SQL object." Basically, a schema is a collection of SQL objects, such as tables, views, and constraints. ANSI SQL-schemas are similar to SQL Server databases.

SQL Server version 6.5 introduced support for the ANSI SQL-schema. However, the notion of a database within SQL Server is long-standing and much richer than its concept of a schema. SQL Server provides more extensive facilities for working with a database than for working with a schema. SQL Server includes commands, stored procedures, and powerful tools such as SQL Enterprise Manager that are designed around the fundamental SQL Server concept of a database. These tools control backup, loading, security, enumeration of objects, and configuration; counterparts do not exist for schemas. The SQL Server implementation of schema is essentially a "checkbox" feature providing conformance with the ANSI standard; it is not the preferred choice. Generally speaking, you will want to use databases, not schemas.

Removable Media

After a database is created, you can package it so that it can be distributed via removable media such as CD-ROM. This can be useful for distributing large data sets. For example, perhaps you want to put detailed sales history on a CD-ROM database and send a copy to each of your branch offices. Typically, such a database would be read-only (since CD-ROMs are read-only), although that is not absolutely required.

To create a removable media database, you create the database as usual—with a few restrictions. You must use new and unique devices that are not being used for any other database. At least three devices must be used, because when the removable media database is ultimately distributed and installed, the system tables will be installed to a writable device (so that users can be added, and so on), even though the database itself is likely to remain on a read-only device. You can use the **sp_create_removable** stored procedure to manage these restrictions, although you can also directly use the underlying DISK INIT and CREATE DATABASE commands. Because removable media devices such as CD-ROMs are typically slower than hard drives, it is also possible to distribute on removable media a database that will then be moved to a hard disk. If you are using a writable removable device, such as an optical drive, you should be sure that the device and controller are both on the Windows NT hardware compatibility list. I also recommend that you run the hard-disk test discussed in Chapter 4 on any such device. In my experience, the failure rates of removable media devices are typically higher than those for standard hard disks.

A database can use multiple CD-ROMs or removable media devices. However, all media must be available simultaneously. For example, if a database uses three CD-ROMs, the system needs to have three CD-ROM drives so that all discs can be available when the database is used.

You can use the **sp_certify_removable** stored procedure to ensure that a database created with the intention of being "burned" onto CD-ROM or other removable media meets the restrictions noted above. Use the **sp_dbinstall** stored procedure the first time a site wants to use a database sent to it on removable media. Subsequently, to use a removable media database, use the **sp_dboption** stored procedure **offline** option to toggle its availability. The CD-ROM included with this book contains an example script that creates a database, ensures that it is appropriate for removable media use, and then installs it on your system. However, a database with no tables or data is pretty useless, so in the next chapter I'll discuss how to create tables.

Special System Databases

A new SQL Server installation will automatically include several databases: *master, model, tempdb, pubs,* and *msdb.*

master
The *master* database is composed of system tables that keep track of the server installation as a whole and all other databases that are subsequently created. Although every database has a set of system catalogs that maintain information about objects it contains, the *master* database has system catalogs that keep information about disk space and device allocations and usage, systemwide configuration settings, login accounts, the existence of other databases, and the existence of other SQL Servers (for distributed operations). The *master* database is absolutely critical to your system, so be sure that you always keep a current

backup copy of it. Operations such as creating another database, changing configuration values, or modifying login accounts all make modifications to *master,* so after doing such activities, make sure you back up *master.*

model

The *model* database is simply a template database. Every time a new database is created, it makes a copy of *model.* If you would like every new database to start out with certain objects or permissions, you can put them in *model* and the new databases will inherit them.

tempdb

The temporary database, *tempdb,* is a workspace. SQL Server's *tempdb* database is unique among all other databases because it is re-created, not recovered, every time SQL Server is restarted. It is used for temporary tables explicitly created by users, for worktables to hold intermediate results created internally by SQL Server during query processing and sorting, and for the materialization of static cursors and the keys of keyset cursors. Operations within *tempdb* are logged so that transactions on temporary tables can be rolled back. But there is no recovery aspect of transactions in *tempdb,* because every time SQL Server is started, *tempdb* is completely re-created; any previous user-created objects (that is, all your tables and data) will be gone.

Because no recovery issues are associated with *tempdb,* it alone has the option to be placed entirely in RAM (volatile random access memory), although most of the time this probably isn't your best use of RAM.

All users have the privileges to create and use private and global temporary tables that reside in *tempdb.* (Private and global table names have # and ## prefixes, respectively, which I'll discuss in more detail in Chapter 6.) However, by default, users do not have the privileges to use or select *tempdb* and then create a table there (not prefaced with # or ##). But such privileges can be easily added to *model,* from which *tempdb* is copied every time the server is restarted, or the privileges can be granted in an autostart procedure that runs each time SQL Server is restarted. I prefer adding them to *model;* if you choose to do likewise, you must remember to revoke those privileges on some other new database you subsequently create if you don't want them to appear there as well.

pubs

The *pubs* database is a sample database used extensively by much of the SQL Server documentation and in this book. It can safely be deleted if you like, although it consumes only 3 MB of space. So if you're not scrounging for a few more megabytes of disk space, I'd recommend leaving *pubs* there. This database is admittedly fairly simple, but that's a feature not a bug. As I hope will become clear, *pubs* allows good examples to be used and illustrated, without a lot of peripheral issues obscuring the examples' central points. Another nice thing about *pubs* is that it is pretty ubiquitous in the SQL Server community. That makes it easy to use it to illustrate examples without the audience needing to spend a lot of time trying to understand the underlying tables. As you become more expert with SQL Server, chances are you will find yourself using it also to illustrate examples with your developer and/or user community.

msdb

The *msdb* database is used by the SQL Executive service, which performs scheduled activities such as backups and replication tasks. In general, other than doing backups and maintenance on it, you should ignore *msdb*. (But you might take a peek at the backup history and other such information kept there.) All the information in *msdb* is accessible from the SQL Enterprise Manager tools, so there is usually no need to access these tables directly. Think of the *msdb* tables as another form of system tables: just as you should generally never directly modify system tables, you should not directly add data to or delete data from tables in *msdb* unless you really know what you're doing or are instructed to do so by a Microsoft SQL Server technical support engineer.

SUMMARY

A database is a collection of objects, such as tables, views, and stored procedures. Every database has its own transaction log, and a database is kept logically consistent in terms of integrity constraints among objects in the database. A typical SQL Server installation will have many databases but will always have at least three: *master, model,* and *tempdb* (and usually also *pubs* and *msdb*).

A database device is a logical mapping to physical disk storage, which is nearly always a Windows NT file. (In unusual cases, it could be mapped to a raw-disk partition.) There is a possible many-to-many relationship among databases and database devices. A database always resides on one or more database devices. A database device can contain all or part of multiple databases. Both databases and devices can be expanded easily. Databases can be made smaller with limits, but database devices cannot be shrunk. Both devices and databases have a fixed size and do not automatically expand if full.

Now that you understand the basics of devices and databases, it is time to move on to tables, the fundamental data structures you work with.

6

Tables

Introduction

In this chapter, I'll show you some in-depth implementation examples. But let's start with a basic introduction to tables. Simply put, a *table* is a collection of data about a specific *entity* (person, place, thing) that has a discrete number of named *attributes* (for example, quantity or type). Tables are at the heart of SQL Server and of the relational model in general. Tables are easy to understand—they're just like the everyday lists you make for yourself. In SQL Server, a table is often referred to as a *base table* to emphasize where data is stored. Using "base table" also distinguishes the table from a *view,* a virtual table that is an internal query of a base table.

Attributes of a table's data (such as color, size, quantity, order date, and supplier's name) take the form of named *columns* in the table. Each instance of data in a table is represented as a single entry, or *row* (formally called a *tuple*). Every row in a table is unique, and each row has a unique identifier called the *primary key*. (SQL Server, in accordance with the ANSI SQL standard, does not require that you make a row unique or declare a primary key. However, since both of these concepts are central to the relational model, they should always be implemented.)

Tables are usually related to other tables. For example, in an order-entry system the *orders* table likely has a *customer_number* column where it keeps track of the customer number for an order; *customer_number* also appears in the *customer* table. Assuming that *customer_number* is a unique identifier, or the primary key, of the *customer* table, a *foreign key* relationship is established by which the *orders* and *customer* tables can subsequently be joined.

So much for the 30-second database primer. You can find plenty of books that discuss logical database and table design, but this is not one of them. I assume that you understand basic database theory and design and that you know basically what your tables will look like. The rest of this chapter discusses the internals of tables and implementation considerations.

Creating Tables

SQL Server uses the ANSI SQL standard CREATE TABLE syntax. SQL Enterprise Manager provides a front-end, "fill-in-the-blanks" table editor, which makes your job easier. Ultimately, the SQL syntax is always sent to SQL Server to create a table. You can do this directly using a tool such as ISQL or ISQL/w, from SQL Enterprise Manager, or using a third-party data modeling tool (such as ER*win* or InfoModeler) that emits the SQL syntax under the covers of a friendly interface.

In this chapter, I emphasize direct use of the data definition language (DDL) rather than discussing the interface tools. You should keep all DDL commands in a script so that they can be run easily at a later time to re-create the table. (Even if you use one of the friendly front-end tools, it is critical that you can later re-create the table.) SQL Enterprise Manager and other front-end tools can create files with the SQL DDL commands necessary to create the object. This DDL is essentially source code, and you should treat it as such. Keep a backup copy. I also suggest that you keep these files under version control using a source control product such as Microsoft Visual SourceSafe or INTERSOLV's PVCS.

At the basic level, creating a table requires little more than knowing what you want to name the table, what columns it will contain, and what range of values (domain) each column will be able to store. Here's the basic syntax for creating the *customer* table, with three fixed-length character (*char*) columns. (Note that this is not necessarily an efficient way to store data since it always requires 48 bytes per entry regardless of the actual length of the data.)

```
CREATE TABLE customer
(
name        char(30),
phone       char(12),
emp_id      char(4)
)
```

This example shows each column on a separate line for readability. As far as the SQL Server parser is concerned, whitespaces created by tabs, carriage returns, and pressing the Spacebar are identical. From the system's standpoint, the following CREATE TABLE example is identical to the one above; but it is harder to read from a user's standpoint:

```
CREATE TABLE customer (name char(30), phone char(12), emp_id char(4))
```

This simple example shows just the basics of creating a table. I'll give you many more detailed examples later in this chapter.

Naming Tables and Columns

A table is always created within a database and is owned by its creator. A database can contain multiple tables with the same name, because the full name of a table has three parts, in this form:

database.owner.tablename

For example, say that I (username Ron) created my example *customer* table in the *pubs* sample database. My table would have the *pubs.ron.customer* three-part name. (If I am also the database owner, *pubs.dbo.customer* would be my table's name because *dbo* is the special username for the database owner in every database.)

NOTE If no ambiguities exist, you do not need to use all three parts of a table's name when referring to it. For example, if you are working in the *pubs* database and it includes only one *customer* table, you can refer to that table simply as *customer*.

Column names should be descriptive, and since you will use them repeatedly, it is best to avoid unnecessary wordiness. The name of the column (or any object in SQL Server, such as a table or a view) can be whatever you choose, as long as the name conforms to the SQL Server rules for *identifiers*. Identifiers must consist of from 1 through 30 letters, digits, or the symbol #, $, or _. (For more specific rules for identifiers, see the *Microsoft SQL Server Transact-SQL Reference*. The discussions here and in the *Transact-SQL Reference* are true for all SQL Server object names, not only for column names.)

Keywords and Reserved Words

Certain *keywords,* such as *table, create, select,* and *update,* have special meaning to the SQL Server parser, and collectively they make up the SQL language implementation. You cannot use keywords in your object names. If you inadvertently use a keyword in a name, a syntax error will occur, the statement will fail, and you will have to choose another name.

You should be even more careful to watch out for *reserved words*. Reserved words are not keywords, but they could become keywords in a future SQL Server version. Using a reserved word might require that you alter your application before upgrading if the reserved word has become a keyword. Using the SQL Server CHKUPG65 utility, you can check for keyword problems before upgrading to version 6.5. The utility issues warnings when SQL Server encounters reserved words. Before deploying a newly created version 6.5 database, it's a good idea to run CHKUPG65.EXE against it to see if you might have inadvertently used a keyword or a reserved word. (Note that CHKUP65.EXE warns you about keyword and reserved word problems, but it does not correct the problems for you.)

If you use a reserved word, no syntax error or warning occurs at runtime. For example, in SQL Server 6.0, the words *inner* and *outer* are reserved words. In version 6.5, both *inner* and *outer* are keywords used in the version's improved outer-join capabilities. If you were careful to not use reserved words in databases created for version 6.0, you probably had (or will have) an easy upgrade to version 6.5.

Some History...

Here's the rationale behind reserved words. For version 6.0, we needed to add a large number of new keywords to support all the new functionality. In general, these words had not been reserved in version 4.21. Adding so many new keywords made it tough for many sites, because they had to modify their applications by changing these keywords in order to upgrade. Although it might seem capricious and unwarranted to add keywords that simply *might* be used in the future, we know we'll add functionality in future versions, so we continue to designate reserved words for future use.

If you want to use a keyword or a reserved word in your table as a column or object name, you can use *quoted identifiers*. By using *SET QUOTED_IDENTIFIER ON*, you can use keywords or reserved words as object or column names by enclosing them in double quotation marks. Theoretically, you could use quotation marks with all object and column names all the time, and then you'd never have to worry about keywords or reserved words. However, I don't recommend this. I have seen many third-party tools for SQL Server that don't handle quoted identifiers very well. Using quoted identifiers also makes it more difficult to upgrade to future versions of SQL Server. During the upgrade process between SQL Server versions, objects such as views and stored procedures are automatically dropped and re-created so that they include the structures of the latest version. When you use quoted identifiers, upgrading cannot be fully automated, and you must run the Setup program with a special flag (*setup /t SetQuotedID = ON*), which causes Setup to bypass dropping and re-creating objects. You must subsequently rebuild these objects manually. (Other application issues get complicated with the use of quoted identifiers as well, but I won't get into these here.)

Rather than use quoted identifiers to protect against keyword/reserved word problems, it is best to simply adopt some simple naming conventions. For example, you can precede column names with the first few letters of the table name and an underscore (_). Not only does this naming style make the column or object name more readable, it also makes it highly unlikely that you will encounter a keyword or reserved word conflict.

Because future needs cannot be anticipated perfectly, there is no guarantee that a word not previously identified as a reserved word won't be added as a keyword in the future. Nevertheless, your chances of avoiding future keyword conflicts are good if you don't use reserved words. If you've deployed an application that uses a reserved word, don't panic. Simply change it the next time you upgrade the application.

On the flip-side, just because a word is reserved, you should not necessarily assume that it will be used as a keyword in the next version—or ever, for that matter. Reserved words are chosen based on general notions of what features subsequent releases will include, but this occurs well before specifications or schedules are firm.

NOTE You can find the current list of keywords and reserved words in the SQL Server documentation under "Keywords."

From the Author...

Between versions 6.0 and 6.5, many new keywords were added. All but one, *distributed,* were previously identified as reserved words in version 6.0. This one was an oversight with 6.0. We should have realized it at the time, and its necessity for inclusion in version 6.5 caused significant "displeasure" on the development team when we did realize it.

Having both caused and experienced pain during upgrades from version 4.21 to 6.0, the SQL Server development team takes seriously the significance of keywords and reserved words. The team makes every attempt not to introduce new keywords unless they were previously reserved. We try hard to anticipate the needs of the next version and make the reserved word list known in advance. Sometimes the desire to do this causes some odd syntax. For example, version 6.5 allows you to temporarily disable, or pause, constraint checking. A word such as *pause* or *disable* might seem the natural syntax. But instead, the somewhat odd syntax of *nocheck* was implemented. Unfortunately, *pause* had not been previously declared a reserved word, and *nocheck* was already designated as a keyword. To avoid introducing a new keyword that had not previously been reserved that would make it difficult for sites to upgrade, we adopted the less intuitive *nocheck* syntax.

Naming Conventions

Many organizations and multiuser development projects adopt standard naming conventions, which are a good thing, in general. For example, assigning a standard moniker of *cust_id* to represent a customer number in every table makes it obvious that all the tables have data in common. If, instead, several monikers were used in the tables to represent a customer number, such as *cust_id, cust_num, customer_number,* and *customer_#,* it would not be so obvious that these monikers represented common data. One convention I see occasionally and recommend *against* using is Hungarian-style notation for column names. (Hungarian notation is a widely used practice in C programming, whereby variable names include information about their datatypes. Its name is attributed to its use by legendary Microsoft programmer Charles Simonyi, who is of Hungarian ancestry.) Hungarian-style notation uses names such as *sint_nn_custnum* to represent that the *custnum* column is a small integer (*smallint* of 2 bytes) and is NOT NULL (does not allow nulls). Although this practice makes good sense in C programming, it defeats the datatype independence that SQL Server provides.

Suppose it is discovered, for example, that the *custnum* column requires a 4-byte integer (*int*) instead of a 2-byte small integer. It is relatively simple to re-create the table with the column as an *int* instead of a *smallint*. In SQL Server, stored procedures will deal with the different datatype automatically. Applications using DB-Library or ODBC that bind the retrieved column to a character or integer datatype will be unaffected. The applications would need to change if they bound the column to a small integer variable, as the variable's type would need to be larger. For this reason, it is best to try not to be overly conservative with variable datatypes, especially in your client applications. You should be most concerned with the type on the server side; the type in the application can be larger and will automatically accommodate smaller values. By overloading the column name with datatype information, which is readily available from the system catalogs, the insulation from the underlying datatype is compromised. (You could, of course, change the datatype from a *smallint* to an *int,* but then the Hungarian-style name would no longer accurately reflect the column definition. Changing the column name would then result in the need to change application code or stored procedures or both.)

Datatypes

SQL Server provides a large number of datatypes, as shown in Table 6-1 on pages 202–03. Choosing the appropriate datatype is simply a matter of mapping the domain of values you need to store to the corresponding datatype. In choosing datatypes, you want to avoid wasting storage space while allowing enough space for a sufficient range of possible values over the life of your application.

Datatype synonyms

SQL Server syntactically accepts as datatypes both the words listed as synonyms and the base datatypes shown in Table 6-1, but it uses only the type listed as the datatype. For example, a column can be defined as *character(1)*, *character*, or *char(1)*, and SQL Server will accept all these as valid syntax. Internally, however, the expression is considered *char(1)*, and subsequent querying of the SQL Server system catalogs for the datatype will show it as *char(1)*, regardless of the syntax that was used when it was created.

Nullable columns are variable-length

Before deciding to use an ostensibly fixed-length datatype such as *char* instead of a variable-length one such as *varchar*, it is important that you understand *nullability*: all datatypes, with the exception of *bit*, can be declared either NULL or NOT NULL (that is, they can allow or disallow a null entry). Internally, declaring a column to allow a null entry makes that column a variable-length column. For example, a column declared as *char(5) NULL* is internally identical to one declared *varchar(5) NULL*. In both cases, if a null value is entered, no storage is consumed. If only 3 bytes are entered, then only 3 bytes of storage are used, even for the fixed-length type.

> **NOTE** There is an exception to this. The command *SET ANSI_PADDING ON* instructs SQL Server to physically store spaces in the remaining 2 bytes of the *char(5)* type, in which case 5 bytes of storage would be used. This setting conforms to the ANSI SQL-92 standard.

Variable-length vs. fixed-length datatypes

Deciding to use a variable-length or a fixed-length datatype is not always straightforward or obvious. As a general rule, variable-length datatypes are most appropriate when you expect significant variance in the size of the data for a column and the data in the column will not be frequently changed.

Using variable-length datatypes can yield important storage savings. Choosing them can sometimes result in performance loss (as I will explain in a moment) and at other times can result in improved performance. A row with variable-length columns (including supposed fixed-length columns that allow NULLs) requires special offset and adjust entries to be internally maintained. These entries keep track of the actual length of the column. Calculating and maintaining the offsets requires slightly more overhead than a pure fixed-length row, which needs no such offsets at all. This is a CPU task of a few addition and subtraction operations to maintain the offset value. However, the extra overhead of maintaining these offsets is generally inconsequential, and I have not seen a system in which this alone made a significant difference. A more significant performance difference might arise from the method by which updates are processed.

Type of Data	Base Datatype	Synonyms	Range/Domain	Storage Size
Integer	int	integer	Whole numbers from $-2{,}147{,}483{,}648$ to $2{,}147{,}483{,}647$	4 bytes
	smallint		Whole numbers from $-32{,}768$ to $32{,}767$	2 bytes
	tinyint		Whole numbers from 0 to 255	1 byte
Packed decimal (exact numeric)	numeric (p,s) decimal (p,s)	dec	Whole or fractional numbers from -10^{38} to 10^{38}	2–17 bytes, depending on specified precision, p, which can range to 38 digits. On average, 1 byte of storage is required per every 2 digits of precision.
Floating point (approx numeric)	float (15-digit precision)	float(n), where n is between 8 and 15 Double precision	Approximations of numbers from $-1.79E^{308}$ to $1.79E^{308}$ Positive range: $2.23E^{-308}$ to $1.79E^{308}$ Negative range: $-2.23E^{-308}$ to $-1.79E^{308}$	8 bytes
	real (7-digit precision)	float(n), where n is between 1 and 7	Approximations of numbers from $-3.40E^{38}$ to $3.40E^{38}$ Positive range: $1.18E^{-38}$ to $3.40E^{38}$ Negative range: $-1.18E^{-38}$ to $-3.40E^{38}$	4 bytes
Character (fixed length)	char(n)	character (n) character (character without a specific size is synonymous to a 1-character field, char(1))	Up to 255 characters, as designated by n, of the installed character set	1 byte per character n declared, even if partially unused.
Character (variable length)	varchar(n)	character varying (n), char varying (n)	Up to 255 characters, as designated by n, of the installed character set	1 byte per character stored. Declared but unused characters do not consume storage.
Monetary	money		Numbers with accuracy to one ten-thousandth of a unit (four decimal places), typically used to store currency values. From $-922{,}337{,}203{,}685{,}477.5808$ to $922{,}337{,}203{,}685{,}477.5807$	8 bytes
	smallmoney		Numbers with accuracy to one ten-thousandth of a unit (four decimal places), typically used to store currency values. From $-214{,}748.3648$ to $214{,}748.3647$	4 bytes

Table 6-1. *SQL Server supplies many datatypes.*

Type of Data	Base Datatype	Synonyms	Range/Domain	Storage Size
Date and Time	datetime		Combined date and time representation. (SQL Server does not have separate DATE and TIME datatypes.) Date part: 01-JAN-1753 to 31-DEC-9999 Time part: Number of milliseconds since midnight of the given date	8 bytes
	smalldatetime		Combined date and time representation. Date part: 01-JAN-1900 to 06-JUN-2079 Time part: Number of minutes since midnight of the given date	4 bytes
Binary (fixed length)	binary[n]		Any binary representation (bit patterns) up to 255 bytes	n bytes, even if n is partially unused.
Binary (variable length)	varbinary[n]	binary varying	Any binary representation (bit patterns) up to 255 bytes	The number of bytes actually stored. No storage for space declared but not used.
Long text/BLOB	text and image		Text: Character data up to 2 GB. Image: Binary data up to 2 GB. The text and image datatypes are always variable length.	If not null, a 16-byte pointer is used on the data page, plus however many 2-KB pages are required to store the actual length. Text and image pages cannot be shared. A single byte entered in a text or image column requires its own 2-KB page (most being unused).
Boolean	bit		0 or 1	Bit datatypes share a byte with other bit columns of the same table. Hence, 8-bit columns of the same table use 1 byte of storage. If the table has only 1-bit columns, it still uses 1 byte, although 7 more such columns could be added "for free."

Row updating is done internally (and invisibly to the user) either by deleting the old image followed by inserting the new image or as an update-in-place. (There are actually multiple different levels of update strategies that correspond to certain optimizations that can be made at runtime. I'll discuss these in detail in Chapter 8, "Modifying Data.") The fastest direct-mode update can be done if the updated row is exactly the same size as the original row. In that case, the update can be performed exactly in place. (That is, the new values are simply written over the old—in the same location.) Obviously, the most likely way to ensure that an updated row is exactly the same size as the original row is for the datatypes to be completely fixed-length. (This alone might drive you to use only fixed-length datatypes.) If you update a row with variable-length columns and the row grows and no longer fits on the page, the update strategy must be a delete followed by an insert. (In SQL Server versions prior to 6.0, updating variable-length columns always made the update mode become a delete/insert, regardless of the net effect in row length. With version 6.5, this is no longer true.) If a row with variable-length data is updated such that its size is exactly the same, it

NULL or NOT NULL

If possible, avoid allowing NULL on columns. The issue of allowing or disallowing NULL has become an almost religious one for many in the industry, and no doubt my statement will outrage a few people. I don't intend to enter the philosophical debate here. Pragmatically, dealing with NULL brings issues and added complexity. As I mentioned on page 201, a column allowing NULL is internally variable-length and can potentially degrade update performance. But more significantly, allowing NULL adds complexity and often leads to bugs in application code. Special logic must always be added to account for the case of NULL. You, as the database designer, might understand the nuances of NULL and three-valued logic when used in aggregate functions, when doing joins, and when searching by values, but does your development staff understand as well? I recommend, if possible, that you use all NOT NULL columns and define *default* values (which I'll discuss later in this chapter) for missing or unknown entries (and possibly make such character columns *varchar* if the default value is significantly different in size from the typical entered value).

In any case, it is good practice to explicitly declare NOT NULL or NULL. If no such declaration exists, SQL Server assumes NOT NULL. However, the default can be set to NULL via *SET ANSI_NULL_DFLT_ON*. The ANSI SQL standard says that if neither is specified, NULL should be assumed. If you have scripted your DDL and then run it against another server that has a different default setting, you will get different results if you did not explicitly declare NULL or NOT NULL. Declaring NULL or NOT NULL explicitly removes all ambiguity and ensures that the same table will be built regardless of the default nullability setting.

can use some (but not all) of the same update-in-place optimizations as fixed-length. Of course, it's probably uncommon for variable-length rows to be updated to exactly the same length. This is the primary reason why variable-length columns can result in reduced performance.

Other forms of "direct" updates also exist; they are not quite as optimal, but they allow a row to be updated on the same page as the original and are preferable over a two-step "deferred" update (delete/insert). However, if the table has an update trigger or is being replicated (using continuous transaction-based replication), the updates must always be delete/insert because both the trigger and replication require the materialization of both the before-image and the after-image in the transaction log, regardless of whether the rows are fixed-length or variable-length. In this case, you might as well simply use variable-length data-types if the storage difference is significant; making the columns fixed-length in hopes of preserving update-in-place will be fruitless.

On the other hand, using variable-length columns can sometimes improve performance because they can allow more rows to fit on a page. But the efficiency results from more than simply requiring less disk space. A data page for SQL Server is 2 KB (2048 bytes), of which 2016 bytes are available to store data. (The rest is for internal use to manage the page chains.) One I/O brings back the entire page. If you can fit 20 rows on a page, a single I/O brings back 20 rows. But if you can fit 40 rows on a page, one I/O is essentially twice as efficient. In operations that scan for data and return lots of adjacent rows, this can amount to a significant performance improvement. The more rows you can fit per page, the better your I/O and cache-hit efficiency will be.

For example, consider a simple customer table. Suppose that you could define it in two ways, fixed-length and variable-length, as shown in Figure 6-1 and in Figure 6-2 on the following page.

```
CREATE TABLE customer
(
cust_id       smallint   NOT NULL,
cust_name     char(50)   NOT NULL,
cust_addr1    char(50)   NOT NULL,
cust_addr2    char(50)   NOT NULL,
cust_city     char(50)   NOT NULL,
cust_state    char(2)    NOT NULL,
cust_zip      char(10)   NOT NULL,
cust_phone    char(20)   NOT NULL,
cust_fax      char(20)   NOT NULL,
cust_email    char(30)   NOT NULL,
cust_web_url  char(20)   NOT NULL
)
```

Figure 6-1. *A customer table with fixed-length columns.*

```
CREATE TABLE customer
(
cust_id        smallint      NOT NULL,
cust_name      varchar(50)   NOT NULL,
cust_addr1     varchar(50)   NOT NULL,
cust_addr2     varchar(50)   NOT NULL,
cust_city      varchar(50)   NOT NULL,
cust_state     varchar(2)    NOT NULL,
cust_zip       varchar(10)   NOT NULL,
cust_phone     varchar(20)   NOT NULL,
cust_fax       varchar(20)   NOT NULL,
cust_email     varchar(30)   NOT NULL,
cust_web_url   varchar(20)   NOT NULL
)
```

Figure 6-2. *A customer table with variable-length columns.*

Columns that contain addresses, names, or Internet URLs all have data that varies significantly in length. Let's look at the differences between these two choices. In Figure 6-1, using all fixed-length columns, every row uses 304 bytes, regardless of the size of the actual data. But assume that even though the table must accommodate addresses and names up to the specified size, on average the actual entries are only half the maximum size. In Figure 6-2, assume that for all the variable-length (*varchar*) columns, the average actual entry is only about half the maximum. Instead of a row length of 304 bytes, the average length is 164 bytes. The *smallint* and *char(2)* columns total 4 bytes. The *varchar* columns' maximum total length is 300, half of which is 150 bytes. And there is a 1-byte overhead for each of nine *varchar* columns, for 9 bytes. Add 1 more byte for any row that has one or more variable-length columns. So the total is 4 + 150 + 9 + 1, or 164. In the fixed-length example in Figure 6-1, you always fit 6 rows on a data page (2016/304, truncating the remainder). In the variable-length example in Figure 6-2, you can fit an average of 12 rows per page (2016/164, truncating the remainder). The table using variable-length columns will consume only half as many pages in storage, a single I/O will retrieve twice as many rows, and a page cached in memory is twice as likely to contain the row you are looking for.

In deciding on lengths for columns, don't be wasteful—but don't be cheap, either. Allow for future needs, and realize that if the additional length doesn't change how many rows will fit on a page, the additional size is free anyway. Consider again the examples in Figures 6-1 and 6-2. The *cust_id* was declared as a *smallint,* meaning that its maximum positive value is 32,767 (unfortunately, there are no unsigned *int* or unsigned *smallint* datatypes), and it consumes 2 bytes of storage. Although 32,767 customers may seem like a lot to a new company, the company might be surprised by its own success and in a couple of years find out that 32,767 is too limited. The database designers might regret that they tried to save 2 bytes and didn't simply make the datatype an *int,* using 4 bytes but with a maximum positive value of 2,147,483,647. They will be especially disappointed if they realize they didn't really save a thing. If you go through the rows-per-page calculations shown on the previous page, increasing the row size by 2 bytes, you will see that the same number of rows still fit on a page. The additional 2 bytes are free—they were simply wasted space previously. They never cause fewer rows per page in the fixed-length example, and they will rarely cause fewer rows per page even in the variable-length case.

So which strategy wins? Potentially better update performance or more rows per page? Like most such questions, there is no one correct answer—it depends on your application. If you understand the trade-offs, you will be able to make the best choice. Now that the issues have been explained, this general rule bears repeating: variable-length datatypes are most appropriate when you expect significant variance in the size of the data for that column and when the column will not be frequently updated.

Internal Storage—The Details

In this section, I'll discuss the effects of system catalogs and the internal data storage of tables. Although you can effectively use SQL Server without understanding the internals, understanding the details of how SQL Server stores data will help you develop efficient applications.[1] (If you don't care to read about this in-depth information, you can skip this discussion and proceed to the section entitled "User-Defined Datatypes.")

When you create a table, one or more rows are inserted into a number of system catalogs to manage that table. At a minimum, rows are added to the *sysobjects, sysindexes,* and *syscolumns* system catalogs (tables). When the new table is defined with one or more constraints, rows are added to the *sysreferences* and *sysconstraints* system tables.

For every table created, a single row that contains, among other things, the name, object ID, and owner of the new table is added to the *sysobjects* table. The *sysindexes* table will gain a single row that contains pointers to the first and last data pages used by the new table and information regarding the size of the table, including the number of extents, pages, and rows currently being used. The *syscolumns* table will gain one row for each column in the new table, and each row will contain information such as the column name, datatype, and length. Each column is given a column ID, which directly corresponds to the order in which

---

1. Special thanks to Gary Schroeder, who documented most of the page format examples for internal use. The information here is largely an abstract of his work.

the columns were specified when the table was created. That is, the first column listed in the CREATE TABLE statement will have a column ID of 1, the second column listed will have a column ID of 2, and so on. Figure 6-3 shows the rows added to the *sysobjects, sysindexes,* and *syscolumns* system tables when a table is created. (Not all columns are shown for each table.)

```
CREATE TABLE Employee   ( Emp_ID int,
                          Emp_LName varchar(15),
                          Emp_FName varchar(10),
                          Address char(30),
                          Phone char(12) NULL,
                          Job_level smallint )
GO

sysobjects    id           name         uid   type
              ----------   ----------   -----  -------
              480004741    Employee      1      U

sysindexes    id           indid dpages reserved rows first root
              ----------   ----- ------ -------- ---- ----- -----
              480004741    0     1      8          0  1392  1392

syscolumns    id           colid name          type  length offset
              ----------   ----- ------------  ----- ------ ------
              480004741    1     Emp_ID         56     4      2
              480004741    2     Emp_LName      39     15    -1
              480004741    3     Emp_FName      39     10    -2
              480004741    4     Address        47     30     6
              480004741    5     Phone          39     12    -3
              480004741    6     Job_level      52      2     36
```

Figure 6-3. *Catalog information stored after creating a table.*

Notice in the *syscolumns* output in the figure that the offset column contains negative numbers in some rows. Any column that contains variable-length data will have a negative offset value in *syscolumns*. The negative numbers are assigned to the variable-length columns in decreasing order (−1, −2, −3, and so on) in the order in which the column is specified in the CREATE TABLE statement. You can see in Figure 6-3 that the employee last name (*Emp_LName*) is the first variable-length column in the table. Note that any column that allows NULL values will be considered variable-length, as is the case with the *Phone* column in this example.

Data Pages

Data pages are the structures that contain all the non–text/image data of a table. As with all other types of pages in SQL Server, data pages have a fixed size of 2 KB. Data pages consist of three major components: the page header, data rows, and the row offset table, as shown in Figure 6-4.

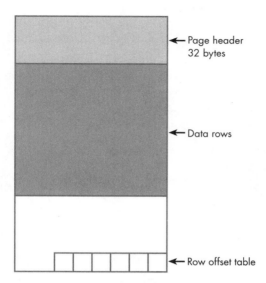

Figure 6-4. *The structure of a data page.*

Page header

As you can see in Figure 6-4, the page header occupies the first 32 bytes of each data page (leaving 2016 bytes for data and row offsets). The page header contains the following fields:

Field	Contains
pageno	4-byte logical page number of this page in the database
nextpg	4-byte logical page number of the next page in the page chain
prevpg	4-byte logical page number of the previous page in the page chain
objid	4-byte ID of the object to which this page belongs
timestamp	6-byte value used for changes/updates to this page
nextrno	2-byte value indicating the next available row number on this page
level	1-byte value for the index level of this page (always 0 for data pages)
indid	1-byte value for the index ID of this page (always 0 for data pages)
freeoff	2-byte value indicating the byte offset of the first free space on this page
minlen	2-byte value indicating the minimum length of rows on this page

(continued)

continued

Field	Contains
status	2-byte value that contains additional information about the page

The *status* field can have these 2-byte values:

0x0001	A data page
0x0002	The leaf page of a nonclustered index
0x0004	An overflow page
0x0008	This page has an overflow page
0x0010	This page has a free row number in the row offset table
0x0020	A text/image page
0x0040	A distribution page
0x0080	This page has no variable-length columns
0x0100	The last row inserted was at *freeoff* (end of the page)
0x0200	This page has a disconnected overflow page
0x1000	This page has an offset table for binary searching
0x4000	The first page of text/image page chain

Data rows

Following the page header is the area in which the table's actual data rows are stored. The maximum size of a single data row is 1962 bytes. A data row cannot span multiple pages (except for text/image columns, which are stored in a separate chain of pages). The number of rows stored on a given page will vary depending on the structure of the table and on the data being stored. A table that has all fixed-length columns will always store the same number of rows per page; variable-length rows will store as many rows as will fit based on the actual length of the data entered. A data page can hold a maximum of 256 rows, although in most cases the actual number of rows per page is considerably less than this. Keeping row length compact allows more rows to fit on a page, thus reducing I/O and improving the cache-hit ratio.

Row offset table

The row offset table is a block of 2-byte entries, each of which indicates the offset on the page where the corresponding data row begins.

Examining Data Pages

You can view the contents of a data page by using the DBCC PAGE statement, which allows you to view the page header, data rows, and row offset table for any given data page in a database. (Only the system administrator can use DBCC PAGE.) But because you typically won't need to view the content of a data page, you won't find much about DBCC PAGE in the SQL Server documentation. Nevertheless, in case you want to use it, here's the syntax:

```
DBCC PAGE ( {dbid | dbname}, pagenum [, printopt] [, cache][, log_virt] )
```

The DBCC PAGE command includes these parameters:

Parameter	Description
dbid	ID of the database containing the page
dbname	Name of the database containing the page
pagenum	Logical or virtual page number
printopt	Optional; print option; takes one of these values:
	0 Default; print the buffer header and page header
	1 Print the buffer header, page header, each row separately, and the row offset table
	2 Print the buffer and page headers, page as a whole, and the offset table
cache	Optional; location of page; takes one of these values:
	0 Print the page as found on disk
	1 Default; print the page as found in cache (if it resides in cache); otherwise, retrieve and print the page from disk
log_virt	Optional; type of page to print; takes one of these values:
	0 Specified pagenum is a virtual page
	1 Default; specified pagenum is a logical page

Figure 6-5 on the following page shows sample output from DBCC PAGE. Note that DBCC TRACEON (3604) instructs SQL Server to return the results to the calling client instead of only to the error log, as is the default for many of the DBCC commands that deal with internals issues.

As you can see, the output from DBCC PAGE is divided into four main sections: Buffer, Page Header, Data, and Offset Table. The Buffer section shows information about the buffer for the given page. (A *buffer* in this context is an in-memory structure that manages a page.)

```
DBCC TRACEON (3604)
GO
DBCC PAGE (6, 1392, 2)
GO


PAGE:
Page found in cache.

BUFFER:
Buffer header for buffer 0xafc4a0
page=0x11d7800 bdnew=0xafc4a0 bdold=0xafc4a0 bhash=0x0
bnew=0xaca4f0 bold=0xafc540 bvirtpg=83887472 bdbid=6
bpinproc=0 bkeep=0 bspid=0 bstat=0x1000 bpageno=1392

PAGE HEADER:
Page header for page 0x11d7800
pageno=1392 nextpg=0 prevpg=0 objid=160003601
timestamp=0001 000028c6
nextrno=5 level=0 indid=0  freeoff=321 minlen=46
page status bits: 0x100,0x1

DATA:
011d7820:    01007b00 0000416e 6e652020 20202020   ..{...Anne
011d7830:    20202020 20202020 20204101 00000000           A.....
011d7840:    0000602d 2d1dbf7d 00000000 00003900   ..`--..}......9.
011d7850:    52696e67 65722036 300101ea 00000044   Ringer.60......D
011d7860:    69726b20 20202020 20202020 20202020   irk
011d7870:    202020b0 01000000 00000080 62581af2           .........bX..
011d7880:    83000000 0000003b 00446546 72616e63   .......;.DeFranc
011d7890:    65023830 0102c801 00005379 6c766961   e.80......Sylvia
011d78a0:    20202020 20202020 20202020 20208e02                   ..
011d78b0:    00000000 00000085 6e25397a 00000000   ........n%9z....
011d78c0:    00003900 48756e74 65722036 30010337   ..9.Hunter.60..7
011d78d0:    02000044 65616e20 20202020 20202020   ...Dean
011d78e0:    20202020 202020fd 02000000 000000a0           ........
011d78f0:    a60c20c6 82000000 0000003b 00537472   .. .......;.Str
011d7900:    61696768 74023830 0104a602 00005265   aight.80......Re
011d7910:    67696e61 6c642020 20202020 20202020   ginald
011d7920:    20206c03 00000000 000050b0 c322817f    l.......P..".
011d7930:    00000000 00003900 47726565 6e650236   ......9.Greene.6
011d7940:    30                                     0

OFFSET TABLE:
Row - Offset
4 (0x4) - 264 (0x108),    3 (0x3) - 205 (0xcd),
2 (0x2) - 148 (0x94),    1 (0x1) - 89 (0x59),
0 (0x0) - 32 (0x20),
```

Figure 6-5. *Sample output from DBCC PAGE.*

The Page Header section displays the data for all the header fields on the page. Looking at the page status bits in Figure 6-5 (the segments of the bit mask have been separated for readability), you can see that this is a data page (status 0x1) and that the last row was inserted at the end of the page (status 0x100).

The Data section has three parts. The left column indicates the physical byte address on the page. Note that the first byte address will always end in 0x20 (32), because the first 32 bytes of the page are used by the page header. The next four columns contain the actual data stored on the page, displayed in hexadecimal. The right column contains a character representation of the data. Only character data will be readable in this column.

The Offset Table section shows the contents of the row offset table at the end of the page. In the figure, you can see that this page contains five rows, with the first row (row 0) beginning at offset 32 (0x20).

Computers that run Windows NT, whether they are based on Intel, DEC Alpha, PowerPC, or MIPS architectures, store integer data in *little endian* format. That is, within each memory word (16 bits), the least-significant byte contains the two high-order digits and the most-significant byte contains the two low-order digits. This is how DBCC PAGE presents the data. For example, the number 1,234,567,890 (0x499602D2) would be stored and displayed by DBCC PAGE in the form D2029649.

Data Rows

A table's data rows have the general structure shown in Figure 6-6. The data for all fixed-length columns is stored first, followed by the data for all variable-length columns.

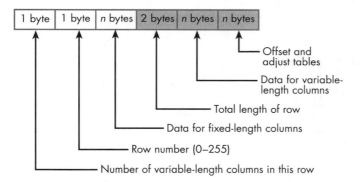

Figure 6-6. *The structure of data rows.*

Within each block of fixed-length or variable-length data, the data is stored in the column order in which the table was created. For example, suppose a table is created with the following statement:

```
CREATE TABLE Test1    (Col1 int NOT NULL,
                       Col2 char(25) NOT NULL,
                       Col3 varchar(60) NULL,
                       Col4 money NOT NULL,
                       Col5 char(20) NULL)
```

The fixed-length data portion of this row would contain the data for *Col1,* followed by the data for *Col2,* followed by the data for *Col4.* The variable-length data portion would contain the data for *Col3,* followed by the data for *Col5.*

Remember, a column that allows NULL (such as *Col5* in this example) is considered to be variable-length, so the data for that column will be stored after the data for fixed-length columns.

The 1-byte row number associated with each data row refers to the row number *on that data page*. There is no internal global row number for every row in a table. The combination of page number and row number on the page can be used to uniquely identify each row in a table.

For rows that contain only fixed-length data, the following is true:

- The first byte of the data row will be zero, indicating that there are no variable-length columns.

- The data row ends after the fixed-length data. (That is, the shaded portion shown in Figure 6-6 will not exist in rows with only fixed-length data.)

- The total length of every data row will be the same as the *sysindexes-.minlen* value for the table, as well as the *minlen* field in the page header.

Offset and Adjust Tables

A data row that has all fixed-length columns has no *offset table* or *adjust table*. A data row that has variable-length columns has an offset table in a data row with a 1-byte entry for each variable-length column, indicating the offset within the row where each column begins. The offset table has a 1-byte entry that indicates the offset from the beginning of the row to the end of the variable-length data. The adjust table contains at least one 1-byte entry as well as an additional 1-byte entry for each 256-byte boundary crossed by variable-length columns.

How Fixed-Length and Variable-Length Rows Are Stored

Following are two examples that illustrate how fixed-length and variable-length data rows are stored.

Fixed-length row

Here is the more simple case of an all–fixed-length row:

```
CREATE TABLE Fixed
    (Col1 char(5)     NOT NULL,
     Col2 int         NOT NULL,
     Col3 char(3)     NOT NULL,
     Col4 char(6)     NOT NULL,
     Col5 float       NOT NULL)
```

When this table is created, this row is inserted into the *sysindexes* system table:

```
id          name    indid  first  root  minlen  maxlen
---------   -----   -----  -----  ----  ------  ------
288004057   Fixed   0      1432   1432  28      28
```

And these rows are inserted into the *syscolumns* system table:

```
name    colid   type    length   offset
----    -----   ----    ------   ------
Col1    1       47      5        2
Col2    2       56      4        7
Col3    3       47      3        11
Col4    4       47      6        14
Col5    5       62      8        20
```

For tables containing only fixed-length columns, the minimum and maximum column lengths (as indicated by *sysindexes.minlen* and *sysindexes.maxlen*) are the same. The *minlen* and *maxlen* values will be equal to the sum of the column lengths (from *syscolumns.length*), plus 2 bytes.

To look at a specific data row in this table, first insert a new row:

```
INSERT Fixed VALUES ('ABCDE', 123, 'BBB', 'CCCC', 4567.8)
```

Figure 6-7 on the following page shows the row offsets of this example. The first byte indicates that the row has no variable-length columns. You can identify the data in the row for each column simply by using the offset value in the *syscolumns* table: the data for column *Col1* begins at offset 2, the data for column *Col2* begins at offset 7, and so on. Because the row has no variable-length columns, the row ends after the data for column *Col5*.

Variable-length row

Here is the somewhat more complex case of a row with variable-length data. The row uses *varchar* columns and allows NULL on otherwise fixed-length datatypes.

```
CREATE TABLE Variable
    (Col1 char(3)        NOT NULL,
     Col2 varchar(250)   NOT NULL,
     Col3 char(5)        NULL,
     Col4 varchar(20)    NOT NULL,
     Col5 smallint       NOT NULL)
```

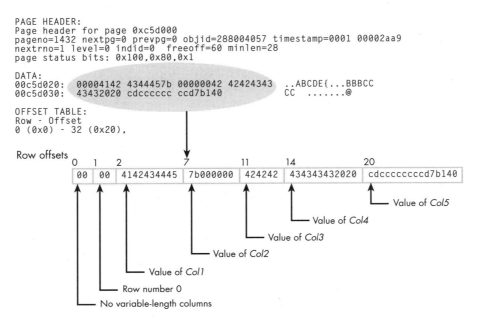

```
PAGE HEADER:
Page header for page 0xc5d000
pageno=1432 nextpg=0 prevpg=0 objid=288004057 timestamp=0001 00002aa9
nextrno=1 level=0 indid=0  freeoff=60 minlen=28
page status bits: 0x100,0x80,0x1

DATA:
00c5d020:  00004142 4344457b 00000042 42424343    ..ABCDE{...BBBCC
00c5d030:  43432020 cdcccccc ccd7b140             CC .......@

OFFSET TABLE:
Row - Offset
0 (0x0) - 32 (0x20),
```

Row offsets

| 0 | 1 | 2 | 7 | 11 | 14 | 20 |

| 00 | 00 | 4142434445 | 7b000000 | 424242 | 434343432020 | cdcccccccccd7b140 |

Value of *Col5*

Value of *Col4*

Value of *Col3*

Value of *Col2*

Value of *Col1*

Row number 0

No variable-length columns

Figure 6-7. *This data row has all fixed-length columns.*

When this table is created, the following row is inserted into the *sysindexes* system table:

id	name	indid	first	root	minlen	maxlen
416004513	Variable	0	1440	1440	7	290

And these rows are inserted into the *syscolumns* system table:

name	colid	type	length	offset
Col1	1	47	3	2
Col2	2	39	250	-1
Col3	3	39	5	-2
Col4	4	39	20	-3
Col5	5	52	2	5

For tables containing variable-length columns, the *minlen* and *maxlen* values are not the same. The *minlen* will be equal to the sum of all fixed-length columns in the table, plus 2 bytes overhead. The *maxlen* will be equal to the sum of both fixed-length and variable-length column lengths (from *syscolumns.length*), plus some amount of overhead that varies depending on the number of columns in the table.

Now insert a row into the table:

```
INSERT Variable VALUES
    ('AAA', REPLICATE('X',250), NULL, 'ABC', 123)
```

The REPLICATE function is used here to simplify populating a column; this function builds a string of 250 *X*s to be inserted into *Col2*.

As shown in Figure 6-8, the data for the fixed-length columns is located using the offset value in *syscolumns*. In this case, *Col1* begins at offset 2, and *Col5* begins at offset 5.

```
PAGE HEADER:
Page header for page 0xc2b000
pageno=1440 nextpg=0 prevpg=0 objid=416004513 timestamp=0001 00002b5e
nextrno=1 level=0 indid=0  freeoff=300 minlen=7
page status bits: 0x100,0x1

DATA:
00c2b020:   03004141 417b000c 01585858 58585858   ..AAA{...XXXXXXX
00c2b030:   58585858 58585858 58585858 58585858   XXXXXXXXXXXXXXXX
  :
00c2b100:   58585858 58585858 58585858 58585858   XXXXXXXXXXXXXXXX
00c2b110:   58585858 58585858 58585858 58585858   XXXXXXXXXXXXXXXX
00c2b120:   58585841 42430403 06030309            XXXABC......

OFFSET TABLE:
Row - Offset
0 (0x0) - 32 (0x20),
```

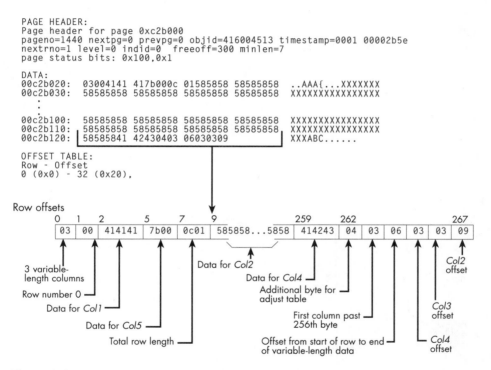

Figure 6-8. *This data row has variable-length columns.*

To find the variable-length columns, first locate the offset and adjust tables in the row. The total row length is the 2-byte value appended to the fixed-length data. Figure 6-8 shows a length of 268 bytes (0x010C, byte swapped from the 0C01 displayed by DBCC PAGE). This means that the offset table begins at byte 267 (the numbering starts with 0, so 267 is the 268th byte), and that byte contains the offset for the first variable-length column, *Col2*. Moving to the left, the next 2 bytes contain the offsets for *Col3* and *Col4*, respectively. Notice that they both contain the same offset value, indicating that *Col3* contains a NULL, so no data will be stored in the row for this column. Finally, notice that the adjust table shows that the third variable-length column, *Col4*, begins after the 256th byte boundary. By adding 256 to the offset value of 3, you can compute that *Col4* begins at offset 259 in the row.

Indexes

Indexes are the other significant user-defined on-disk data structure (in addition to tables). An index provides fast access to data when the data can be searched by the value that is the index key. I've discussed indexes in Chapter 3, but some of that information bears repeating and elaboration here in our discussion of tables. Think of indexes in your everyday life. You're reading a SQL Server book and you want to find entries for the word *SELECT*. You have two basic choices for doing this: you can open the book and scan through the whole thing page by page; or you can look in the index in the back, find the word *SELECT*, and then turn to the page numbers listed. That is conceptually exactly how an index works in SQL Server. SQL Server supports clustered and nonclustered indexes. Both types use standard B-Trees, as shown in Figure 6-9.

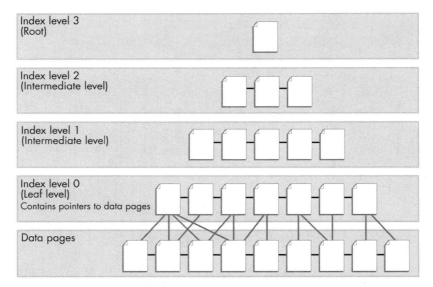

Figure 6-9. *A standard B-Tree for a SQL Server index.*

A B-Tree provides fast access to data by searching on a key value of the index. B-Trees cluster records with similar keys. The *B* stands for *balanced,* and balancing the tree is a core feature of a B-tree's usefulness. The trees are managed and branches are grafted as necessary so that navigating down the tree to find a value and locate a specific record always takes only a few page accesses. Because the trees are balanced, finding any record requires about the same amount of resources, and retrieval speed will be consistent because the index has the same depth throughout.

An index consists of a tree with a root from where navigation begins, possible intermediate index levels, and bottom-level leaf pages. The index is used to find the correct leaf page. The number of levels in an index will vary depending on the number of rows in the table and the size of the key column(s) for the index. If an index is created with a large key, there is room for fewer entries on a page, so more pages (and possibly more levels) will be needed for the index. On a qualified retrieval or delete, the correct leaf page will be the lowest page of the tree where one or more rows with the specified key(s) reside. In a nonclustered index, the lowest level of the tree (the leaf page) points to the page that has a row of data containing the value of the index key. In a clustered index, the leaf page *is* the data page. (Detailed information about how SQL Server manages indexes is found in Chapter 3. If indexing is a topic of interest to you, make sure you read through "The Index Manager" section of that chapter.)

Clustered Indexes

The leaf level of a clustered index *contains* the data pages, not just the index keys. A clustered index keeps the data in a table physically ordered around the key. Deciding what key to cluster on is an important performance consideration. When the index is traversed to the leaf level, the data itself has been *retrieved,* not simply *pointed to*. Figure 6-10 shows the structure of a clustered index.

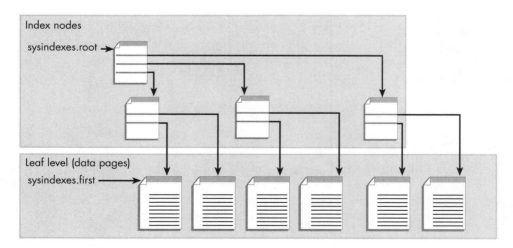

Figure 6-10. *In a clustered index, the leaf level* contains *the data pages.*

Because data can be physically ordered in only one way, a table can have only one clustered index. The query optimizer strongly favors a clustered index because it allows the data to be found directly at the leaf level. Because it defines the actual order of the data, a clustered index allows especially fast access for queries looking for a range of values. The query optimizer knows that only a certain range of data pages must be scanned.

Most tables should have a clustered index. If your table will have only one index, it generally should be clustered. Using clustered indexes is important for space management issues, such as where new rows will appear in the table. Recall that if a table has no clustered index, all new rows are appended to the table, even if open slots are available for rows due to previous deletions.

Nonclustered Indexes

The leaf level of the tree in a nonclustered index *points to* the page that has a row of data containing the value of the index key, as shown in Figure 6-11.

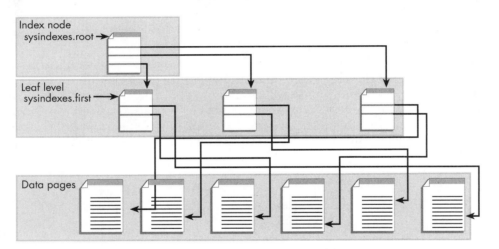

Figure 6-11. *In a nonclustered index, the leaf level* points to *the data pages.*

The presence or absence of a nonclustered index does not affect how the data pages are organized, so you are not restricted to having only one nonclustered index per table, as is the case with clustered indexes. Each table can include as many as 254 nonclustered indexes, but you'll usually want to be more judicious and have just a few per table (unless you have a true read-only situation, in which case the more indexes the merrier—except for storage space issues).

Indexing can speed up queries (if the index is found useful to the query), but it can slow down updates as well as use up storage space. In general, you'll declare additional nonclustered indexes when you expect to query on fields or to use fields in joins, or when you want to ensure the uniqueness of fields other than (or in addition to) those used in your clustered index.

> **NOTE** If you are using an index to enforce uniqueness, there's a better way. PRIMARY KEY and UNIQUE constraints make use of indexing for enforcement. I'll discuss these in a moment.

Searching for data using a nonclustered index requires first that the index is traversed and then that the data page pointed to is retrieved. For example, to get to a data page using an index with a depth of three—a root page, one intermediate page, and the leaf page—all three index pages must be traversed. The data page still must be retrieved, although it has been exactly identified so there's no need to scan. Still, it took four logical I/Os to get one data page. You can see that a nonclustered index is a "win" only if it is highly selective.

It might be helpful to recall the idea of searching for a topic in a book. If the index cites many pages for the topic you're looking for, you might decide to leaf through the book from the first page cited, rather than flip back and forth between the index and the cited pages. If the book is short, you might start from the beginning and scan all the way through it. In either case, the index wasn't very useful to you. This type of information is the same as that considered by the SQL Server optimizer when it decides whether to use a nonclustered index. Nonclustered indexes are most useful for exact match-type queries when the predicate in the WHERE clause can be expected to eliminate the majority (typically, 80 to 85 percent) of pages from consideration. When this is not the case, SQL Server usually decides to use some other, more useful, index or simply scan the entire table because then it incurs the cost of doing I/O only for the data pages rather than incurring the I/O cost of both the data pages and the index pages.

SQL Server looks at the *distribution page* for the index to decide how selective an index likely is and to decide which index to use. The distribution page is a single page devoted to serve as a histogram—a sampling of the key values in the index. Distribution pages provide a ratio comparing the number of rows for which the selection clause will qualify to the number of rows in a table. A distribution page is created when you run UPDATE STATISTICS on a table containing one or more indexes or when you create an index on already existing data. If the table contains no data when you initially create the index, there can be no data to sample so the distribution page is empty. Note that this is *always* the case when an index is created for use by a PRIMARY KEY or UNIQUE constraint declared in the CREATE TABLE statement. So be sure to run UPDATE STATIS-TICS after those tables are loaded so that the indexes can be used intelligently. Run UPDATE STATISTICS periodically when the data changes significantly. (Index selection is an important performance consideration, and I'll discuss it further in Part Four, "Performance and Tuning.")

Creating Indexes

The typical syntax for creating an index is straightforward:

```
CREATE [UNIQUE] [CLUSTERED | NONCLUSTERED] INDEX index_name
    ON [[database.]owner.]table_name (column_name [,
    column_name]...)
```

CREATE INDEX has some additional options available for specialized purposes:

```
[WITH
    [FILLFACTOR = x]
    [[,] PAD_INDEX]
    [[,] IGNORE_DUP_KEY]
    [[,] {SORTED_DATA | SORTED_DATA_REORG}]
    [[,] {IGNORE_DUP_ROW | ALLOW_DUP_ROW}]]
```

From what I've observed, none of these options is used extensively, although FILLFACTOR is probably the most commonly used. FILLFACTOR lets you reserve some space on each leaf page of an index (in a clustered index, this equals the data page). By reserving some free space with FILLFACTOR, you can later avoid the need to split pages to make room for an entry. (Refer to the discussion of index management and page splitting in Chapter 3.) But remember that FILL-FACTOR is not maintained; it indicates only how much space is reserved with the existing data. If you need to, you can use the DBCC DBREINDEX command to rebuild the index and to reestablish the original FILLFACTOR specified.

> **TIP** If you will be rebuilding all of a table's indexes, simply specify the clustered index with DBCC DBREINDEX. Doing so internally rebuilds the entire table and all nonclustered indexes.

FILLFACTOR is not usually specified on an index-by-index basis, but you can specify it this way for fine-tuning. If FILLFACTOR is not specified, the serverwide default is used. The value is set for the server via **sp_configure, fillfactor**. This value is by default 0, which means that leaf pages of indexes are made as full as possible. FILLFACTOR generally applies only to the index's leaf page (the data page for a clustered index). In specialized and high-use situations, you might want to reserve space in the intermediate index pages to avoid page splits there, too. You can do this by using the PAD_INDEX option, which uses the same value as FILLFACTOR.

The SORTED_DATA and SORTED_DATA_REORG options tell SQL Server that the data is already sorted so that it can skip that step as a performance optimization when creating the index. Although the two options are similar to each other, SORTED_DATA_REORG can be especially useful if you are rebuilding a clustered index for the purpose of reorganizing the table (to make pages more contiguous, for example). In that case, SORTED_DATA_REORG instructs SQL Server to rebuild the table but skip the sort step.

You can ensure uniqueness of a key by using the PRIMARY KEY and UNIQUE constraints, which I'll discuss beginning on page 231. These constraints work by making a unique index on the key value(s). (Of course, indexes do not need to be unique.) If an UPDATE or INSERT statement would affect multiple rows, and if even one row is found that would not be unique, the entire statement is aborted and no rows are affected. With a unique index, you can use IGNORE_DUP_KEY so that a nonunique error on a multirow UPDATE or INSERT will not cause the entire statement to be rolled back. The nonunique row will be discarded, and all other rows will be affected. IGNORE_DUP_KEY does not allow the uniqueness of the index to be violated; instead, it makes a violation in a multirow data modification nonfatal to all the nonviolating rows.

You need to be careful when using IGNORE_DUP_KEY because it can cause you to "lose" some rows. With this option, if you try to update a row in a way that creates a duplicate key, that row will be discarded; it will not be rolled back to its prior value. Neither the new value nor the original value of the row that would produce the duplicate exists in the updated table. For example, if you try to update "Smith" to "Jones" and "Jones" already exists, you end up with one "Jones" and no "Smith." Frankly, I think it is better to first "scrub" your data. You can do a SELECT statement with a COUNT(*) grouped by the index key on the table with a similar WHERE clause that your multirow update would perform to make sure that the key value will not have any rows with a count greater than 1. If any rows are found to have a count greater than 1, you can fix the data or your WHERE clause.

The IGNORE_DUP_ROW and ALLOW_DUP_ROW options are rarely used. They determine how rows should be dealt with for nonunique clustered indexes when an entire row might duplicate another. I'm not going to further discuss these situations, because I strongly advise that you always have a unique identifier (a primary key) on *every table*—then you will never have an entirely duplicate row. IGNORE_DUP_ROW and ALLOW_DUP_ROW can be valuable if you are creating a new table based on preexisting data from some other source. You may need to scrub the data to get rid of duplicates before you take the proper step of identifying or fabricating a primary key. In this specialized case, IGNORE-_DUP_ROW can help you clean up your data.

User-Defined Datatypes

User-defined datatypes (UDDTs) provide a convenient way for you to guarantee consistent use of underlying native datatypes for columns known to have the same domain of possible values. For example, perhaps your database will store various phone numbers in many tables. Although there is no single definitive way to store phone numbers, in this database consistency is important. You can create a *phone_number* UDDT and use it consistently for any column in any table that keeps track of phone numbers to ensure that all use the same datatype. Here's how to create this UDDT:

```
EXEC sp_addtype phone_number, 'varchar(20)', 'not null'
```

And here's how to use the new UDDT when creating a table:

```
CREATE TABLE customer
(
cust_id        smallint       NOT NULL,
cust_name      varchar(50)    NOT NULL,
cust_addr1     varchar(50)    NOT NULL,
cust_addr2     varchar(50)    NOT NULL,
cust_city      varchar(50)    NOT NULL,
cust_state     char(2)        NOT NULL,
cust_zip       varchar(10)    NOT NULL,
cust_phone     phone_number,
cust_fax       varchar(20)    NOT NULL,
cust_email     varchar(30)    NOT NULL,
cust_web_url   varchar(20)    NOT NULL)
```

When the table is created, internally the datatype of *cust_phone* is known to be *varchar(20)*. Notice that both *cust_phone* and *cust_fax* are *varchar(20)*, although *cust_phone* has that declaration through its definition as a UDDT.

Here's how the *customer* table appears in the entries in the *syscolumns* table for this table:

```
SELECT colid, name, type, length, usertype, offset
FROM syscolumns WHERE id=object_id('customer')
```

colid	name	type	length	usertype	offset
1	cust_id	52	2	6	2
2	cust_name	39	50	2	-1
3	cust_addr1	39	50	2	-2
4	cust_addr2	39	50	2	-3
5	cust_city	39	50	2	-4

6	cust_state	47	2	1	4
7	cust_zip	39	10	2	-5
8	cust_phone	39	20	104	-6
9	cust_fax	39	20	2	-7
10	cust_email	39	30	2	-8
11	cust_web_url	39	20	2	-9

You can see that both the *cust_phone* and *cust_fax* columns have the same *type* (datatype), although the *cust_phone* column shows that the datatype is a UDDT (*usertype* = 104). The *type* is resolved when the table is created, and the UDDT cannot be dropped or changed as long as one or more tables are currently using it. Once declared, a UDDT is static and immutable, so no inherent performance penalty occurs in using a UDDT instead of the native datatype.

The use of UDDTs can make your database more consistent and clear. One potential drawback, however, is that at times UDDTs can make joining columns a bit more difficult. Typically, SQL Server allows any two columns to be joined if they are compatible and not necessarily identical. For example, columns of type *smallint* and *int* are compatible and can be joined. SQL Server automatically and implicitly converts the *smallint* to an *int*. Under some circumstances, an error occurs when you try to join two UDDTs that seem to be compatible. You can still join the columns, but you'll need to explicitly use the CONVERT( ) function to do so.

For example, suppose that I create another table, *fax_list,* that maintains a list of numbers to use for mass fax broadcasts. Rather than reuse the existing *phone-_number* UDDT, I create another one that is identical except for the name:

```
sp_addtype fax_number, 'varchar(20)', 'not null'

CREATE TABLE fax_list
(
fax_number      fax_number,
fax_name        varchar(30)
)
```

Now let's say that when I created the table, I didn't plan to join a column of UDDT *fax_number* with one of *phone_number*. Later, I realized that in some cases I have a customer's phone number but no fax number. So I want to join the two tables to see all the cases for which this is so. Issuing the following SELECT statement yields an error:

```
SELECT cust_name, cust_phone, cust_fax, fax_name
    FROM customer, fax_list
WHERE customer.cust_phone=fax_list.fax_number
```

```
>>> Msg 305, Level 16, State 1
The column 'cust_phone' (user type:phone_number) is joined with 'fax_number'
(user type:fax_number). The user types are not compatible: user types must be
identical in order to join.
```

Changing the query to include an explicit conversion allows the columns to be joined:

```
SELECT cust_name, cust_phone, cust_fax, fax_name
    FROM customer, fax_list
WHERE customer.cust_phone=
    CONVERT(varchar(20),fax_list.fax_number)
```

Of course, simply reusing the existing *phone_number* UDDT instead of defining a new *fax_number* UDDT would have eliminated the need to do an explicit conversion.

Even though you might need to occasionally explicitly convert UDDTs to join them, in most cases SQL Server handles conversions transparently. For example, if the *fax_number* UDDT had been declared as *char(20)* instead of *varchar(20)*, the SQL Server optimizer would have already implicitly converted between *varchar(20)* and *char(20)* and a join would have worked without an explicit conversion. It is counter-intuitive that two UDDTs can be joined if one is declared *varchar(20)* and the other is declared *char(20)*, yet they cannot be joined (without an explicit conversion) if both are declared *varchar(20)*. Here's why. The SQL Server optimizer produces error message 305 (noted above) if the following conditions are met:

- There is a predicate (a search condition) of the form *table1.col* **relop** *table2.col* where **relop** (relational operation) is the term used internally and is =, >=, >, and so on.

- *table1* and *table2* are in the same database.

- The datatypes of *table1.col* and *table2.col* are UDDTs.

- The datatypes of *table1.col* and *table2.col* are not the same UDDT.

The error doesn't occur when you're joining a *varchar* UDDT column with a *char* UDDT column because the query processor's tree normalization step inserts an implicit conversion operator, making the statement of the form *table1.col1* relop *CONVERT(table2.col)*. This conversion operator causes the first condition to no longer be true at optimization time, so no error is reported. However, in the case of two UDDTs that are both declared as *varchar(20) NOT NULL,* all of the above conditions are met and the error occurs.

SQL Server automatically implicitly converts between compatible columns of different types (either native types or UDDTs of different types). Error message 305 occurs only when you are operating on two different UDDTs with the same underlying type. This error message can help nudge you away from inadvertently assigning multiple UDDTs to represent the same domain of values. Yet, as I said earlier, if there is some odd case in which this makes sense, you can still handle it quite easily by using CONVERT().

Currently, UDDTs do not support the notions of subtyping or inheritance, nor do they allow a DEFAULT value or CHECK constraint to be declared as part of the UDDT itself. These are powerful object-oriented concepts that will likely make their way into future versions of SQL Server. These limitations not withstanding, UDDT functionality is a powerful and often underused feature of SQL Server.

Identity Property

It is common to provide simple counter-type values for tables that don't have a natural or efficient primary key. Columns such as *customer_number* are usually simple counter fields. SQL Server provides the Identity property that makes it easy to generate unique numeric values. Identity is not a datatype; it is a *column property* that you can declare on a whole-number datatype such as *tinyint, smallint, int,* and *numeric/decimal* (having a scale of zero). Each table can have only one column with the Identity property. The table's creator can specify the starting number (seed) and the amount that values increment or decrement. If not otherwise specified, the seed value starts at 1 and increments by 1, as shown in this example:

```
CREATE TABLE customer
(
cust_id      smallint       IDENTITY  NOT NULL,
cust_name    varchar(50)    NOT NULL,
)
```

To find out what seed and increment values were defined for a table, you can use the functions IDENT_SEED(*tablename*) and IDENT_INCR(*tablename*). The statement

```
SELECT IDENT_SEED('CUSTOMER'), IDENT_INCR('CUSTOMER')
```

produces

```
1    1
```

for the *customer* table because values were not explicitly declared and the default values were used.

This example explicitly starts the numbering at 100 (seed) and increments the value by 20:

```
CREATE TABLE customer
(
cust_id      smallint      IDENTITY(100,20)  NULL,
cust_name    varchar(50)   NOT NULL,
)
```

The value produced with the Identity property is unique, but it is not guaranteed to be consecutive. For efficiency, a value is considered used as soon as it is presented to a client doing an INSERT operation. If that client doesn't ultimately commit the INSERT, the value will never appear, so a break will occur in the consecutive numbers. There would be an unacceptable level of serialization if the next number couldn't be parceled out until the previous one was actually committed or rolled back. (And even then, as soon as a row was deleted, the values would no longer be consecutive. Gaps are inevitable.) If you need exactly sequential values without gaps, Identity is not the appropriate feature to use. Instead, you should implement a *next_number* type table in which you can make the operation of bumping the number contained there part of the larger transaction (and incur the serialization of queuing for this value).

To temporarily disable the automatic generation of values in an IDENTITY column, use the *SET IDENTITY_INSERT tablename ON* option. This option is useful for tasks such as bulk loading data in which the previous values already exist. For example, perhaps you are loading a new database with customer data from your previous system. You might want to preserve the previous customer numbers but have new ones automatically assigned using Identity. The SET option was created exactly for cases like this.

Because of the SET option's ability to override values, it is important to know that the Identity property alone does not enforce uniqueness of a value within the table. Although Identity will generate a unique number, it can be overridden with the SET option. To enforce uniqueness (which you'll almost always want to do when using Identity), you should also declare a UNIQUE or PRIMARY KEY constraint on the column. If you insert your own values for an Identity column (using SET IDENTITY_INSERT), when automatic generation resumes, the next value will be the next incremented value (or decremented value) of the highest value that exists in the table, whether it was generated previously or explicitly inserted.

TIP If you're using the **bcp** utility for bulk loading data, you should also be aware of the /E parameter if your data already has assigned values that you want to keep for a column having the Identity property. For more information, see the SQL Server documentation for **bcp**.

The keyword IDENTITYCOL automatically refers to the specific column in a table, whatever its name, that has the Identity property. If *cust_id* is that column, you can refer to the column as IDENTITYCOL without knowing or using the column name or you can refer to it explicitly as *cust_id*. For example, the following two statements work identically and return the same data:

```
SELECT IDENTITYCOL FROM customer
SELECT cust_id FROM customer
```

The column name returned to the caller is *cust_id,* not IDENTITYCOL, in both cases.

When inserting rows, you can omit an Identity column from the column list and VALUES section. If you do supply a column list, you must omit the column for which the value will be automatically supplied. Here are two valid INSERT statements for the *customer* table shown earlier:

```
INSERT customer VALUES ('ACME Widgets')
INSERT customer (cust_name) VALUES ('AAA Gadgets')
```

Selecting these two rows produces this output:

```
cust_id    cust_name
-------    ---------
1          ACME Widgets
2          AAA Gadgets

(2 row(s) affected)
```

Sometimes in applications it is desirable to immediately know the value produced by Identity for subsequent use. For example, a transaction might first add a new customer and then add an order for that customer. To add the order, you probably need to use the *cust_id*. Rather than select the value from the *customer* table, you can simply select the special global variable @@IDENTITY, which contains the last Identity value used by that connection. It does not necessarily provide the last value inserted into the table, however, because another user might have subsequently inserted data. If multiple INSERT statements are carried out in a batch to the same or different tables, the variable has the value for the last statement only.

You cannot define the Identity property as part of a UDDT, but you can declare the Identity property on a column that uses a UDDT. A column having the Identity property must always be declared NOT NULL (either explicitly or implicitly) or error message number 8147 will result from the CREATE TABLE statement and CREATE will not succeed. Likewise, you cannot declare the Identity property and a DEFAULT on the same column. To check that the current Identity value is valid based on the current maximum values in the table, and to reset it if an invalid value is found (which should never be the case), use the DBCC CHECKIDENT (*tablename*) statement.

Identity values are fully recoverable. If a system outage occurs while insert activity is taking place with tables that have Identity columns, the correct value will be recovered when SQL Server is restarted. This is accomplished during the SQL Server checkpoint processing by flushing the current Identity value for all tables. For activity beyond the last checkpoint, subsequent values are reconstructed from the transaction log during the standard database recovery process. Any inserts into a table having the Identity property are known to have changed the value, and the current value is retrieved from the last INSERT statement (post checkpoint) for each table in the transaction log. The net result is that when the database is recovered, the correct current Identity value is also recovered.

SQL Server, unlike some other products, does not require that you maintain a large "safety buffer" or "burning set." After a system failure, products that do not recover their autosequencing values sometimes add a large number to the last known value on recovery to ensure that a number is not reused. This can result in odd and probably undesirable values. For example, values might be progressing nicely as 101, 102, 103, 104, 105, and so on. Then a system outage occurs. Because the next value is not recovered, these products don't know for sure exactly where to resume (104? 105? 106? 107?). To avoid reusing a number, these products simply add a safety buffer; the number after 105 might be 1106 with a safety buffer of 1000. This can result in some odd patterns for what are loosely thought of as sequential numbers (for example, 102, 103, 104, 105, 1106, 1107, 2108, 2109, 3110). Because SQL Server recovers the exact value, large gaps like this never occur.

Constraints

Constraints provide a powerful yet easy way for you to enforce relationships between tables (*referential integrity*) by declaring primary, foreign, and alternate keys. CHECK constraints enforce *domain integrity*. Domain integrity enforces valid entries for a given column by restricting the type (through datatypes), the format (through CHECK constraints and rules), or the range of possible values (through REFERENCES to foreign keys, CHECK constraints, and rules). The declaration of a column as either NULL or NOT NULL can be thought of as a type of constraint. And you can declare DEFAULT values for use when a value is not known at insert or update time.

PRIMARY KEY and UNIQUE Constraints

A central tenet of the relational model is that every tuple (row) in a relation (table) is in some way unique and can be distinguished in some way from every other row in the table. The combination of all columns in a table could be used as this unique identifier, but in practice the identifier is usually at most the combination of a handful of columns and often it's just one column: the *primary key*. Although some tables might have multiple unique identifiers, each table can have only one primary key. For example, perhaps the *employee* table maintains both an *Emp_ID* column and an *SSN* (social security number) column, both of which can be considered unique. Such column pairs are often referred to as *alternate keys* or *candidate keys,* although both terms are design terms and are not used by the ANSI SQL standard or by SQL Server. In practice, one of the two columns is logically promoted to primary key with the PRIMARY KEY constraint and the other will usually be declared by a UNIQUE constraint. Although neither the ANSI SQL standard nor SQL Server require it, it is good practice to always declare a PRIMARY KEY constraint on every table. Furthermore, you must designate a primary key for a table that will be published for transaction-based replication.

Internally, PRIMARY KEY and UNIQUE constraints are handled almost identically, so I will discuss them together here. Declaring a PRIMARY KEY or UNIQUE constraint simply results in a unique index being created on the column(s), and this index enforces the column's uniqueness, in the same way that a unique index created manually on a column would. The query optimizer makes decisions based on the presence of the unique index rather than on the fact that a column was declared as a primary key. How the index got there in the first place is irrelevant to the optimizer.

Nullability

All columns that are part of a primary key must be declared (either explicitly or implicitly) as NOT NULL. Columns that are part of a UNIQUE constraint can be declared to allow NULL. However, only one NULL value can be stored (another good reason to try to avoid NULL whenever possible).

Index attributes

The index attributes of CLUSTERED or NONCLUSTERED can be explicitly specified when declaring the constraint. If not specified, the index for a UNIQUE constraint will be nonclustered and the index for a PRIMARY KEY constraint will be clustered (unless CLUSTERED has already been explicitly stated for a unique index, because only one clustered index can exist per table). However, you're often better off making the PRIMARY KEY constraint nonclustered and saving the clustered index for another column or columns in which it might be better used.

The index FILLFACTOR attribute can be specified if a PRIMARY KEY or UNIQUE constraint is added to an existing table using the ALTER TABLE command. FILLFACTOR doesn't make sense in a CREATE TABLE statement because the table has no existing data and FILLFACTOR on an index affects how full pages are only when the index is initially created. FILLFACTOR is not maintained when data is added.

Choosing keys

Try to keep the key lengths as compact as possible. Columns that are the primary key or that are unique are most likely to be joined and frequently queried. Compact key lengths allow more index entries to fit on a given 2-KB page, reducing I/O, increasing cache hits, and speeding character matching. When there is no naturally efficient compact key, it is often useful to manufacture a surrogate key using the Identity property on an *int* column. (If *int* doesn't provide enough range, a good second choice is a *numeric* column with the required precision and with scale 0.) You might use this surrogate as the primary key, use it for most join and retrieval operations, and declare a UNIQUE constraint on the natural but inefficient columns that provide the logical unique identifier in your data. (Or you might dispense with creating the UNIQUE constraint altogether if there is no need to have SQL Server enforce the uniqueness. Indexes slow performance of data modification statements because the index, as well as the data, must be maintained.)

Although it is permissible to do so, do not create a PRIMARY KEY constraint on a column of type *float* or *real*. Because these are approximate datatypes, the uniqueness of such columns is also approximate and the results can sometimes be unexpected.

Removing constraints

A unique index created as a result of a PRIMARY KEY or UNIQUE constraint cannot be directly dropped using the DROP INDEX statement. Instead, you must drop the constraint by using *ALTER TABLE DROP CONSTRAINT* (or you have to drop the table itself). This feature was designed so that a constraint cannot accidentally be compromised by someone who does not realize that the index is being used to enforce the constraint. There is no way to temporarily suspend enforcement of a PRIMARY KEY or UNIQUE constraint. If this is required, use *ALTER TABLE DROP CONSTRAINT* and then later restore the constraint by using *ALTER TABLE ADD CONSTRAINT*. If the index used to enforce uniqueness is clustered, when the constraint is added to an existing table the entire table and all nonclustered indexes are internally rebuilt to establish the cluster order. This can be a time-consuming task, and it requires about 1.2 times the existing table space as a temporary work area in the database would require (2.2 times in total, counting the permanent space needed) so that the operation can be rolled back if necessary.

Creating constraints

Typically, you declare PRIMARY KEY and UNIQUE constraints when you create the table (CREATE TABLE). However, you can add or drop both by subsequently using the ALTER TABLE command. To simplify things, you can declare a PRIMARY KEY or UNIQUE constraint that includes only a single column on the same line where you define that column in the CREATE TABLE statement. Such a constraint is known as a *column-level constraint*. Or you can declare the constraint after all columns have been defined; this constraint is known as a *table-level constraint*. Which approach you use is largely a matter of personal preference. I find the column-level syntax more readable and clear. You can use abbreviated syntax with a column-level constraint, in which case SQL Server will generate the name for the constraint, or you can use a slightly more verbose syntax that uses the clause CONSTRAINT *name*. A table-level constraint must always be named by its creator. If you will be creating the same database structure across multiple servers, it is probably wise to explicitly name column-level constraints so that the same name will be used on all servers.

Following are examples of three different ways to declare a PRIMARY KEY constraint on a single column. All cause a unique, clustered index to be created. Note the (abridged) output of the **sp_helpconstraint** procedure for each—especially the constraint name.

EXAMPLE 1

```
CREATE TABLE customer
(
cust_id       int           IDENTITY  NOT NULL  PRIMARY KEY,
cust_name     varchar(30)   NOT NULL
)
GO

EXEC sp_helpconstraint customer
GO

>>>>

Object Name
-----------
customer

constraint_type            constraint_name
----------------------     -------------------------------
PRIMARY KEY (clustered)    PK__customer__cust_i__68E79C55
```

EXAMPLE 2

```
CREATE TABLE customer
(
cust_id       int           IDENTITY  NOT NULL
                            CONSTRAINT cust_pk PRIMARY KEY,
cust_name     varchar(30)   NOT NULL
)
GO

EXEC sp_helpconstraint customer
GO

>>>>

Object Name
-----------
customer

constraint_type            constraint_name
----------------------     ---------------
PRIMARY KEY (clustered)    cust_pk

No foreign keys reference this table.
```

EXAMPLE 3

```
CREATE TABLE customer
(
cust_id        int         IDENTITY  NOT NULL,
cust_name      varchar(30)  NOT NULL,
CONSTRAINT customer_PK PRIMARY KEY (cust_id)
)
GO

EXEC sp_helpconstraint customer
GO

>>>>

Object Name
-----------
customer

constraint_type             constraint_name
---------------             ---------------
PRIMARY KEY (clustered)     customer_PK

No foreign keys reference this table.
```

In Example 1, the constraint name bears the seemingly cryptic name of *PK-
__customer__cust_i__68E79C55*. There is some method to the apparent madness—all types of column-level constraints use this naming scheme (which I'll
discuss later in this chapter). Whether you choose a more intuitive name of your
own, such as *customer_PK* in Example 3, or the less intuitive (but information-
packed) system-generated name produced with the abbreviated column-level
syntax is up to you. However, when a constraint involves multiple columns, such
as is often the case for PRIMARY KEY, UNIQUE, and FOREIGN KEY constraints,
the only way to syntactically declare them is with a table-level declaration. The
syntax for creating constraints is quite broad and has many variations. A given
column could have the Identity property, be part of a primary key, be a foreign
key, and be declared NOT NULL. The order of these specifications is not mandated and can be interchanged. Here's an example of creating a table-level,
UNIQUE constraint on the combination of multiple columns. (The primary key
case is essentially identical.)

```
CREATE TABLE customer_location
(
cust_id                int   NOT NULL,
cust_location_number   int   NOT NULL,
CONSTRAINT customer_location_unique UNIQUE
    (cust_id, cust_location_number)
)
```

```
GO

EXEC sp_helpconstraint customer_location
GO

>>>
Object Name
----------------
customer_location

constraint_type   constraint_name          constraint_keys
---------------   ----------------------   ---------------
UNIQUE            customer_location_unique cust_id,
(non-clustered)                            cust_location_number

No foreign keys reference this table.
```

As noted earlier, a unique index is created to enforce either a PRIMARY KEY or a UNIQUE constraint. The name of the index is based on the constraint name, whether it was explicitly named or system-generated. The index used to enforce the CUSTOMER_LOCATION_UNIQUE constraint in the above example is also named *customer_location_unique*. The index used to enforce the column-level, PRIMARY KEY constraint of the *customer* table in Example 1 is named *PK__customer__cust_i__68E79C55*, which is the system-generated name of the constraint. You can use the **sp_helpindex** stored procedure to see information for all indexes of a given table. For example:

```
EXEC sp_helpindex customer

>>>
index_name                      index_description     index_keys
----------------------------    ------------------    ----------
PK__customer__cust_i__68E79C55  clustered, unique,    cust_id
                                primary key
                                located on default
```

You cannot directly drop an index created to enforce a PRIMARY KEY or UNIQUE constraint. However, you can rebuild the index by using DBCC DBRE-INDEX, which is useful when you want to reestablish a given FILLFACTOR for the index or to reorganize the table in the case of a clustered index.

FOREIGN KEY Constraints

As the term implies, logical relationships between tables is a fundamental concept of the relational model. In most databases, certain relationships must exist (that is, the data must have *referential integrity*) or the data will be logically corrupt.

SQL Server automatically enforces referential integrity through the use of FOR-EIGN KEY constraints. (This feature is sometimes referred to as declarative referential integrity, or DRI, to distinguish it from other features, such as triggers, that can also be used to enforce the existence of the relationships.)

A foreign key is one or more columns of a table whose values must be equal to a PRIMARY KEY or UNIQUE constraint in another table (or the same table when it references itself). After the foreign key is declared in a CREATE TABLE or ALTER TABLE statement, SQL Server restricts a row from being inserted or updated in a table that *references* another table if the relationship would not be established. SQL Server also restricts row updates or inserts in the table being referenced from being deleted or changed in a way that would destroy the relationship.

Here's a simple way to declare a primary key/foreign key relationship:

```
CREATE TABLE customer
(
cust_id      int          NOT NULL  IDENTITY  PRIMARY KEY,
cust_name    varchar(50)  NOT NULL
)

CREATE TABLE orders
(
order_id     int          NOT NULL  IDENTITY  PRIMARY KEY,
cust_id      int          NOT NULL  REFERENCES customer(cust_id)
)
```

The *orders* table contains the column *cust_id,* which references the primary key of the *customer* table. An order (*order_id*) must not exist unless it relates to an existing customer (*cust_id*). No row can be deleted from the *customer* table if a row that references it currently exists in the *orders* table, and the *cust_id* column cannot be modified in a way that would destroy the relationship.

This example shows the syntax for a column-level constraint, which can be declared only if the foreign key is a single column. This syntax uses the keyword REFERENCES, and the term foreign key is implied but not explicitly stated. The name of the FOREIGN KEY constraint is generated internally, following the same general form described earlier for PRIMARY KEY and UNIQUE constraints. Here is a portion of the output of **sp_helpconstraint** for both the *customer* and *orders* tables. (The tables were created in the *pubs* sample database.)

```
EXEC sp_helpconstraint customer
>>>

Object Name
-----------
customer

constraint_type     constraint_name                    constraint_keys
---------------     ------------------------------     ---------------
PRIMARY KEY         PK__customer__cust_i__0677FF3C     cust_id
(clustered)

Table is referenced by
----------------------
pubs.dbo.orders: FK__orders__cust_id__09546BE7

EXEC sp_helpconstraint orders
>>>

Object Name
-----------
orders

constraint_type     constraint_name                    constraint_keys
---------------     ------------------------------     ---------------------
FOREIGN KEY         FK__orders__cust_id__09546BE7      cust_id REFERENCES
                                                       pubs.dbo.customer
                                                       (cust_id)

PRIMARY KEY         PK__orders__order_id_086047AE      order_id
(clustered)

No foreign keys reference this table.
```

Like PRIMARY KEY and UNIQUE constraints, FOREIGN KEY constraints can be declared at the column and table levels. If the foreign key is a combination of multiple columns, you must declare FOREIGN KEY constraints at the table level. This example shows a table-level, multicolumn FOREIGN KEY constraint:

```
CREATE TABLE customer
(
cust_id         int           NOT NULL,
location_num    smallint      NULL,
cust_name       varchar(50)   NOT NULL,
CONSTRAINT CUSTOMER_UNQ UNIQUE CLUSTERED (location_num, cust_id)
)
```

```
CREATE TABLE orders
(
order_id     int        NOT NULL  IDENTITY CONSTRAINT ORDER_PK
                                  PRIMARY KEY NONCLUSTERED,
cust_num     int        NOT NULL,
cust_loc     smallint   NULL,
CONSTRAINT FK_ORDER_CUSTOMER FOREIGN KEY (cust_loc, cust_num)
REFERENCES customer (location_num, cust_id)
)

GO

EXEC sp_helpconstraint customer
EXEC sp_helpconstraint orders
GO

>>>

Object Name
-----------
customer
```

constraint_type	constraint_name	constraint_keys
UNIQUE (clustered)	CUSTOMER_UNQ	location_num, cust_id

```
Table is referenced by
----------------------
pubs.dbo.orders: FK_ORDER_CUSTOMER

Object Name
-----------
orders
```

constraint_type	constraint_name	constraint_keys
FOREIGN KEY	FK_ORDER_CUSTOMER	cust_num, cust_loc REFERENCES pubs.dbo.customer (cust_id,location_num)
PRIMARY KEY (non-clustered)	ORDER_PK	order_id

```
No foreign keys reference this table.
```

The above example also shows the following variations in how constraints can be created.

FOREIGN KEY constraint   A FOREIGN KEY constraint can reference a UNIQUE constraint (an alternate key) instead of a PRIMARY KEY constraint. (Note, however, that referencing a PRIMARY KEY is much more typical and is generally better practice.)

Matching column names and datatypes   Using identical column names in tables involved in a foreign key reference is not necessary, but it is often good practice. The *cust_id* and *location_num* column names are defined in the *customer* table. The *orders* table, which references the *customer* table, uses the names *cust_num* and *cust_loc*. Although the column names of related columns can differ, the datatypes of the related columns must be identical, except for nullability and variable-length attributes. (For example, a column of *char(10) NOT NULL* can reference one of *varchar(10) NULL*, but it cannot reference a column of *char(12) NOT NULL*. A column of type *smallint* cannot reference a column of type *int*.) Notice in the example that *cust_id* and *cust_num* are both *int NOT NULL* and that *location_num* and *cust_loc* are both *smallint NULL*.

UNIQUE columns and NULL values   You can declare a UNIQUE constraint on a column that allows NULL, but only one all-NULL UNIQUE column is allowed when multiple columns make up the constraint. More precisely, the UNIQUE constraint would allow one entry for each combination of values that includes a NULL, as though NULL were a value in itself. For example, if the constraint contained two *int* columns, exactly one row of each of these combinations (and so on) would be allowed:

<NULL,NULL>

<0,NULL>

<NULL,0>

<1,NULL>

<NULL,1>

In my opinion, this is a case of questionable semantics; NULL represents an unknown, yet using it in this way clearly implies that NULL is equal to NULL. (As stated previously, I recommend that you avoid using NULLs, especially in key columns.)

Index attributes   You can specify the CLUSTERED and NONCLUSTERED index attributes for a PRIMARY KEY or UNIQUE constraint. (You can also specify FILLFACTOR when using ALTER TABLE to add a constraint.) The index keys will be created in the order in which columns are declared. In this example, I specify *location_num* as the first column of the UNIQUE constraint, even though it follows *cust_id* in the table declaration, because I want the clustered index to be created with *location_num* as the lead column of the B-Tree and consequently to keep my data clustered around the location values.

CONSTRAINT syntax   You can explicitly name a column-level constraint by declaring it with the more verbose CONSTRAINT syntax on the same line or section as a column definition. You can see this syntax for the PRIMARY KEY constraint on the *orders* table. There is no difference in the semantics or run-time performance of a column-level or table-level constraint, and it doesn't matter whether the constraint name is user-specified or system-generated. (There is a slight added efficiency in initially creating a column-level constraint rather than a table-level constraint on only one column, but I view that as irrelevant since typically only run-time performance matters.) However, as mentioned earlier, the real advantage of explicitly naming your constraint rather than using the system-generated name is improved understandability. The constraint name is used in the error message for any constraint violation, so creating a name such as CUSTOMER_PK will probably make more sense to users than a name such as *PK__customer__cust_i__0677FF3C*. You should choose your own constraint names if such error messages are visible to your users.

Unlike a PRIMARY KEY or UNIQUE constraint, no index is automatically built for the column(s) declared as a foreign key. However, in many cases, you will want to build indexes on these columns because they are often used for joining to other tables. To enforce foreign key relationships, SQL Server must add additional steps to the execution plan of every insert, delete, and update (if the update affects columns that are part of the relationship) that affects *either* the table referencing another table or being referenced itself. The execution plan, determined by the SQL Server optimizer, is simply the collection of steps that will be performed to carry out the operation. (As I will discuss in Chapter 14, "Design and Query Performance Implications," you can see the actual execution plan by using the SET SHOWPLAN ON statement.)

If no FOREIGN KEY constraints exist, a statement specifying the update of a single row of the *orders* table might have an execution plan that looks like this:

Execution Plan Steps with No FOREIGN KEY Constraint

1. Find a qualifying *order* record using clustered index.

2. Update the *order* record.

When a FOREIGN KEY constraint exists on the *orders* table, the same operation would have additional steps in the execution plan:

Execution Plan Steps with FOREIGN KEY Constraint

1. Check for the existence of a related record in the *customer* table (based on the updated *order* record) using a clustered index.

2. If no related record is found, raise an exception and terminate the operation.

3. Find a qualifying *order* record using a clustered index.

4. Update the *order* record.

The execution plan would be more complex if the *orders* table had many FOREIGN KEY constraints declared. Internally, a simple update or insert operation might no longer be possible. Any such operation would require checking a large number of other tables for matching entries. Because a seemingly simple operation could require checking as many as 31 other tables (see below) and possibly creating multiple worktables, the operation might be much more complicated than it looks and much slower than expected.

A table can have a maximum of 31 FOREIGN KEY references. This limit is derived from the internal limit of 32 tables in a single query. A user can specify up to 16 tables, leaving the balance of (32 − *number_specified_by_user*) available for worktables for internal processing. Querying a table with 31 FOREIGN KEY constraints would require at least 32 tables internally—the base table plus the 31 tables it references. In practice, an operation on a table with 31 or fewer FOREIGN KEY constraints might still fail with an error due to the 32-table query limit if work-tables are required for the operation. (Worktables might be needed for a variety of reasons. The most common would be if the data modification statement were based on a query doing join operations and worktables were needed for the join operation. *SET SHOWPLAN ON* shows the specific execution plan and reveals where worktables were needed.)

A database designed for excellent performance would not be expected to reach this limit. Performance concerns should drive you toward judicious use of FOR-EIGN KEY constraints. I have seen some cases in which sites have reached the limit because the constraints they had declared were logically redundant. Take the case in the following example. The *orders* table declares a FOREIGN KEY constraint to both the *master_customer* and *customer_location* tables.

```
CREATE TABLE master_customer
(
cust_id      int            NOT NULL  IDENTITY  PRIMARY KEY,
cust_name    varchar(50)    NOT NULL
)

CREATE TABLE customer_location
(
cust_id     int           NOT NULL,
cust_loc    smallint      NOT NULL,
CONSTRAINT PK_CUSTOMER_LOCATION PRIMARY KEY (cust_id,cust_loc),
CONSTRAINT FK_CUSTOMER_LOCATION FOREIGN KEY (cust_id)
    REFERENCES master_customer (cust_id)
)

CREATE TABLE orders
(
order_id    int           NOT NULL  IDENTITY  PRIMARY KEY,
cust_id     int           NOT NULL,
cust_loc    smallint      NOT NULL,
CONSTRAINT FK_ORDER_MASTER_CUST FOREIGN KEY (cust_id)
    REFERENCES master_customer (cust_id),
CONSTRAINT FK_ORDER_CUST_LOC FOREIGN KEY (cust_id, cust_loc)
    REFERENCES customer_location (cust_id, cust_loc)
)
```

Although logically the relationship between the *orders* and *master_customer* tables exists, the relationship is redundant to and subsumed by the fact that *orders* is related to *customer_location,* which has its own FOREIGN KEY constraint to *master_customer.* Declaring a foreign key for *master_customer* adds unnecessary overhead without adding any further integrity protection.

NOTE	In the case just described, declaring a foreign key does perhaps add readability to the table definition, but you can achieve this by simply adding comments to the CREATE TABLE command. It is perfectly legal to add a comment practically anywhere—even in the middle of a CREATE TABLE statement. A more subtle way to achieve this would be to declare the constraint so that it would appear in **sp_help-constraint** and in the system catalogs, but to then disable the constraint by using the ALTER TABLE NOCHECK option. Because the constraint would then be unenforced, an additional table would not be added to the execution plan.

The CREATE TABLE statement shown in the following example for the *orders* table omits the redundant foreign key and, for illustration purposes, includes a comment. Despite the lack of a FOREIGN KEY constraint in the *master_customer* table, you still could not insert a *cust_id* that did not exist in the table, because the reference to the *customer_location* table would prevent it.

```
CREATE TABLE orders
(
order_id     int        NOT NULL  IDENTITY  PRIMARY KEY,
cust_id      int        NOT NULL,
cust_loc     smallint   NOT NULL,
-- Implied Foreign Key Reference of:
-- (cust_id) REFERENCES master_customer (cust_id)
CONSTRAINT FK_ORDER_CUST_LOC FOREIGN KEY (cust_id, cust_loc)
    REFERENCES customer_location (cust_id, cust_loc)
)
```

Note that additional execution steps are required not only by the table on which the foreign key is declared (the referencing table, which in this example is *orders*). In addition, when being updated, the table being referenced (in this case *customer_location*) must have additional steps in its execution plan to ensure that an update of the columns being referenced would not break a relationship and create an orphan entry in the *orders* table. Without making any changes directly to the *customer_location* table, you could see a significant decrease in update or delete performance on it because of foreign key references added to other tables.

Practical considerations for FOREIGN KEY constraints
When using constraints, you should consider triggers, performance, and indexing.

Constraints and triggers   I won't discuss triggers in detail until Chapter 10, but for now you should simply note that constraints are enforced before a triggered action is performed. If the constraint is violated, the statement will be aborted before the trigger fires.

NOTE The owner of a table is not allowed to declare a foreign key reference to another table unless the owner of the other table has granted REFERENCES permission to the first table owner. Even if the owner of the first table is allowed to select from the table to be referenced, that owner must have REFERENCES permission. This prevents another user from changing the performance of operations on your table without your knowledge or consent. You can grant any user REFERENCES permission even if you do not also grant SELECT permission, and vice versa.

Performance considerations   In deciding on the use of foreign key relationships, you must balance the protection provided with the corresponding performance overhead. Be careful not to add constraints that form logically redundant relationships. Excessive use of FOREIGN KEY constraints can severely degrade the performance of seemingly simple operations.

Constraints and indexing   The columns specified in FOREIGN KEY constraints often will be strong candidates for index creation. You should build the index with the same key order used in the PRIMARY KEY or UNIQUE constraint of the table it references so that joins can be performed efficiently. Also be aware that a foreign key is often a subset of the primary key of the table. In the *customer_location* table used in the preceding two examples, *cust_id* is part of the primary key as well as a foreign key in its own right. Given that *cust_id* is part of a primary key, it is already part of an index. In this example, *cust_id* is the lead column of the index and it is doubtful that building a separate index on it alone would be warranted. However, if *cust_id* were *not* the lead column of the B-Tree, it might make sense to build an index on it.

Constraint Checking Solutions

Sometimes two tables reference one another, creating a "bootstrap" problem. Suppose *Table1* has a foreign key reference to *Table2*. But *Table2* has a foreign key reference to *Table1*. Even before either table contains any data, you will be prevented from inserting a row into *Table1* because the reference to *Table2* will fail. Similarly, you cannot insert a row into *Table2* because the reference to *Table1* would fail.

ANSI SQL has a solution: *deferred constraints,* in which you can instruct the system to postpone constraint checking until the entire transaction is committed. This elegant remedy would put both INSERT statements into a single transaction that would result in the two tables having correct references by the time COMMIT occurs. Unfortunately, I know of no mainstream product that provides the deferred option for constraints. The deferred option is part of the complete SQL-92 specification, which no product has yet fully implemented. It is not required for NIST certification as ANSI SQL-92 compliant, a certification that Microsoft SQL Server has achieved.

SQL Server 6.5 provides *immediate* constraint checking; it has no *deferred* option. SQL Server offers three options for dealing with constraint checking: it allows you to add constraints after adding data, it lets you temporarily disable checking of foreign key references, and it allows you to use the **bcp** (bulk copy) program to initially load data and avoid checking FOREIGN KEY constraints. To add constraints after adding data, do not create constraints during the CREATE TABLE command. After adding the initial data, you can add constraints by using the ALTER TABLE command. With the second option, the table owner can temporarily disable checking of foreign key references by using the ALTER TABLE *table* NOCHECK CONSTRAINT statement. Once data exists, the FOREIGN KEY constraint can be reestablished by using ALTER TABLE *table* CHECK CONSTRAINT. Note that when an existing constraint is reenabled using this method, SQL Server does not automatically check to see that all rows still satisfy the constraint. To do this, you can simply issue a "dummy update" by setting a column to itself for all rows, determining if any constraint violations are raised, and then fixing them. (For example, you could issue UPDATE ORDERS SET *cust_id = cust_id*.) Finally, you can use the **bcp** program or a custom program that uses the special-purpose bulk copy libraries (that the **bcp** utility uses) to initially load data. The **bcp** program does not check FOREIGN KEY constraints. These libraries are special-purpose tools used by the calling application that format SQL Server data pages, which SQL Server then accepts. The libraries are faster than regular INSERT commands because they bypass normal integrity checks and (usually) most logging.

When adding (not reenabling) a new FOREIGN KEY constraint using ALTER TABLE where data already exists, the existing data is checked by default. If constraint violations occur, the constraint will not be added. With large tables, such a check can be quite time-consuming. You do have an alternative—you can add a FOREIGN KEY constraint and omit the check. To do this, specify the WITH NOCHECK option with ALTER TABLE. All subsequent operations will be checked, but existing data will not be checked. As in the case for reenabling a constraint, you could then carry out a dummy update to flag any violations in the existing data. If you use this option, it is a good idea to do the dummy update as soon as possible to ensure that all the data is clean. Otherwise, your users might see constraint error messages when they do update operations on the preexisting data, even if they haven't changed any values.

Restrictions on Dropping Tables

If you are dropping tables, you must drop all *referencing* tables before dropping the *referenced* table. For example, in the preceding example's *orders, customer_location,* and *master_customer* tables, the following sequence of DROP statements fails because a table being dropped is referenced by a table that still exists—that is, *customer_location* cannot be dropped because the *orders* table references it, and *orders* is not dropped until later.

```
DROP TABLE customer_location
DROP TABLE master_customer
DROP TABLE orders
```

Changing the sequence to the following works fine because *orders* is dropped first:

```
DROP TABLE orders
DROP TABLE customer_location
DROP TABLE master_customer
```

When two tables reference each other, the constraints must first be dropped or must be set to NOCHECK (both operations use ALTER TABLE) before the tables can be dropped. Similarly, a table that is being referenced cannot be part of a TRUNCATE TABLE command. You must drop or disable the constraint, or you must simply drop and rebuild the table.

Self-Referencing Tables

A table can be *self-referencing*—that is, the foreign key can reference one or more columns in the same table. The following example shows an employee table, in which a column for manager references another *employee* entry:

```
CREATE TABLE employee
(
emp_id      int             NOT NULL PRIMARY KEY,
emp_name    varchar(30)     NOT NULL,
mgr_id      int             NOT NULL REFERENCES employee(emp_id)
)
```

The *employee* table is a perfectly reasonable table. It illustrates most of the issues we've discussed. However, in this case, a single INSERT command that satisfies the reference is legal. For example, if the CEO of the company has an *emp_id* of 1 and it is reasonable to think of that person as also being his or her own manager, the following INSERT will be allowed and can be a useful way to insert the first row in a self-referencing table:

```
INSERT employee VALUES (1,'John Smith',1)
```

Although, as I mentioned earlier, SQL Server does not currently provide a deferred option for constraints, self-referencing tables add a twist that sometimes makes SQL Server use deferred operations internally. Consider the case of a nonqualified DELETE statement that would delete many rows in the table. After all rows are ultimately deleted, you can assume that no constraint violation would occur. However, during the delete operation while internally some rows are deleted and others remain, violations would occur since some of the referencing rows would be orphaned before they were actually deleted. SQL Server handles such *interim violations* automatically and without any user intervention. As long as the self-referencing constraints are valid at the *end* of the data modification statement, no errors are raised during processing.

To gracefully handle these interim violations, however, additional processing and worktables are required to hold the work in progress. This adds substantial overhead and can also limit the actual number of foreign keys that can be used. An UPDATE statement can also cause an interim violation. For example, if all employee numbers are to be changed by multiplying each by 1000, the following UPDATE statement would require worktables to avoid the possibility of raising an error on an interim violation that would be fine at the end of the statement:

```
UPDATE employee SET emp_id=emp_id * 1000, mgr_id=mgr_id * 1000
```

The additional worktables and the processing needed to handle the worktables are made part of the execution plan. This means that if the optimizer sees that a data modification statement *could* cause an interim violation, the additional temporary worktables will be created, even if no such interim violations ever actually occur. These additional steps are needed only in the following situations:

- A table is self-referencing (it has a FOREIGN KEY constraint that refers back to itself).

- A single data modification statement (UPDATE, DELETE, or INSERT based on a SELECT) is performed and can affect more than one row. (The optimizer can't determine *a priori,* based on the WHERE clause and unique indexes, whether more than one row could be affected.) Multiple data modification statements within the transaction do not apply—this condition must be a single statement that affects multiple rows.

- Both the referencing and referenced columns are affected (which is always the case for DELETE and INSERT operations, but might or might not be the case for UPDATE).

If the above criteria are met by a data modification statement in your application, you can be sure that SQL Server is automatically using a limited and special-purpose form of deferred constraints to protect against interim violations. But this costs substantial overhead. If you know that interim violations would not occur with your data, you can instruct SQL Server not to handle them. To do this, use *SET DISABLE_DEF_CNST_CHK ON* (disable deferred constraint checking). Note that disabling the handling of interim violations will never allow you to violate a constraint. Rather, it could result in a false error message that says that a constraint violation occurred when, in fact, a violation would not exist by the end of the processing of the statement. If you find that interim violations occur, although rarely, you might still choose to turn off these checks and reenable them only when a premature violation message is actually encountered.

Referential Actions

The full ANSI SQL-92 standard contains the notion of the *referential action,* sometimes (incompletely) referred to as a *cascading delete.* SQL Server 6.5 does not provide this feature as part of FOREIGN KEY constraints, but this notion warrants some discussion here because the capability exists via triggers.

The idea behind referential actions is this: sometimes, instead of just preventing an update of data that would violate a foreign key reference, you might be able to perform an additional, compensating action that would enable the constraint to still be honored. For example, if you were to delete a *customer* table, which had references to *orders,* it would be possible to have SQL Server automatically delete all those related *order* records (that is, cascade the delete to *orders*), in which case the constraint would not be violated and the *customer* table could be deleted. This feature is intended for both UPDATE and DELETE statements, and four possible actions are defined: NO ACTION, CASCADE, SET DEFAULT, and SET NULL.

- **NO ACTION** The update is prevented. This default mode, per the ANSI standard, occurs if no other action is specified. SQL Server 6.5 constraints provide this action (without the NO ACTION syntax). NO ACTION is often referred to as RESTRICT, but this usage is slightly incorrect in terms of how ANSI defines RESTRICT and NO ACTION. ANSI uses RESTRICT in DDL statements such as DROP TABLE and it uses NO ACTION for FOREIGN KEY constraints. (In my opinion, it's a subtle and unimportant difference. It's common to refer to the FOR-EIGN KEY constraint as having an action of RESTRICT.)

- **CASCADE** A delete of all matching rows in the referenced table will occur.

- **SET DEFAULT** The delete will be performed, and all foreign key values in the referencing table will be set to a default value.

- **SET NULL** The delete will be performed, and all foreign key values in the referencing table will be set to NULL.

Implementation of referential actions is not required for NIST certification as ANSI SQL-92 conformant. SQL Server will provide referential actions in a future release. Until then, it performs these actions via triggers, as I will discuss in Chapter 10. Creating triggers for such actions or for constraint enforcement is easy. Performance is usually equivalent, practically speaking, to that of a FOREIGN KEY constraint, as both need to do the same type of operations to check the constraint.

NOTE There are a couple of subtle differences between update triggers and a FOREIGN KEY constraint. For example, the execution plan for a trigger remains cached, while a constraint is compiled into the execution plan of the statement. (Although if the statement is part of a stored procedure, it will also be cached and will not need to be recompiled.) There are also differences between them in regard to update strategies that I'll mention in Chapter 8, "Modifying Data."

Because a constraint is checked before a trigger fires, you cannot have both a constraint to enforce the relationship and a trigger that does an operation such as cascade delete. The trigger will need to do *both* the enforcement and referential action. Otherwise, the constraint will fail and the statement will be aborted before the trigger to cascade the delete fires.

TIP You might still want to declare the foreign key relationship largely for readability so that the relationship between the tables is clear. Simply use the NOCHECK option of ALTER TABLE to ensure that the constraint will not be enforced, and then the trigger will fire. (The trigger will also need to take on the enforcement of the constraint.)

Support for referential actions is often requested, and I'm sure it will be implemented in a future version. However, I think using application logic for such actions and SQL Server constraints (without referential actions other than NO ACTION) to safeguard the relationship is more often applicable. Although referential actions are intuitive, I question how many applications really could avail themselves of this feature. I cannot think of many real-world examples in which the application is so simplistic that you would unconditionally go ahead and delete (or set to default or to NULL) all matching rows in a related table. Most applications would perform some additional processing, such as asking a user if he or she *really* intends to delete a customer who has open orders. The declarative nature of referential actions does not provide a way to hook in application logic to handle cases like these. I think the most useful course, then, is to use SQL Server's constraints to restrict breaking relationships and have the application deal with updates that would produce constraint violations. This will probably continue to be the case even after referential actions are added.

CHECK Constraints

Enforcing *domain integrity* (that is, ensuring that only entries of expected types, values, or ranges can exist for a given column) is also important. SQL Server provides two ways to enforce domain integrity: CHECK constraints and rules. CHECK constraints allow you to define an expression for a table that must not evaluate to false for a data modification statement to succeed. (Note that I do not say the constraint must evaluate to true. The constraint will allow the row if it evaluates to true or to unknown. The constraint evaluates to unknown when NULL values are present, and this introduces three-value logic. I'll discuss the issues of NULLs and three-value logic in depth in Chapter 7, "Querying Data.") Rules perform almost the same function as CHECK constraints, but they use different syntax and a couple of fewer capabilities. Rules have existed in Microsoft SQL Server since its initial release in 1989, well before CHECK constraints, which are part of the ANS ISQL-92 standard and were added in version 6.0 in 1995.

CHECK constraints make a table's definition more readable by including the domain checks in the DDL. Rules have a potential advantage in that they can be defined once and then bound to multiple different columns and tables (using **sp_bindrule** each time), while a CHECK constraint must be respecified for each column and table. But the extra binding step can also be a hassle, so this capability for rules is beneficial only if a rule will be used in many places. Although performance between the two approaches is identical, CHECK constraints are generally preferred over rules because they are directly part of the table's DDL, they are ANSI-standard SQL, they provide a few more capabilities than rules (such as the ability to reference other columns in the same row or to call a system function), and perhaps most importantly, they are more likely than rules to be further enhanced in future releases of SQL Server. Because of these reasons, I'm going to concentrate on CHECK constraints.

CHECK constraints (and rules) add additional steps to the execution plan to ensure that the expression does not evaluate to false (which would result in the operation being aborted). Although steps are added to the execution plan for data modifications, these are typically much less expensive than the extra steps discussed earlier for FOREIGN KEY constraints. For foreign key checking, another table must be searched, requiring additional I/O. CHECK constraints deal only with some logical expression for the specific row already being operated on, so no additional I/O is required. Because additional processing cycles are used to evaluate the expressions, the system will require more CPU use. But if there is plenty of CPU to spare, the effect might well be negligible. (You can watch this by using Performance Monitor.)

Like other types of constraints, CHECK constraints can be declared at the column or table level. There is no run-time performance difference between the two methods for a constraint on one column. You must declare a CHECK constraint that refers to more than one column as a table-level constraint. Only a single column-level CHECK constraint is allowed for a specific column, although the constraint may have multiple logical expressions that can be AND'ed or OR'ed together. And a specific column can have or be part of many table-level expressions.

Some CHECK constraint features have often been overlooked, including the ability to reference other columns in the same row, use system and niladic functions (which are evaluated at runtime), and use AND/OR expressions. The following example shows a table with multiple CHECK constraints (as well as a PRIMARY KEY constraint and a FOREIGN KEY constraint) and showcases some of these features:

```
CREATE TABLE employee
(
emp_id          int          NOT NULL PRIMARY KEY
                             CHECK (emp_id BETWEEN 0 AND 1000),

emp_name        varchar(30)  NOT NULL CONSTRAINT no_nums
                             CHECK (emp_name NOT LIKE '%[0-9]%'),

mgr_id          int          NOT NULL REFERENCES employee(emp_id),

entered_date    datetime     NULL CHECK (entered_date >=
                             CURRENT_TIMESTAMP),

entered_by      int          CHECK (entered_by IS NOT NULL),
                             CONSTRAINT valid_entered_by CHECK
                             (entered_by = SUSER_ID(NULL) AND
                             entered_by <> emp_id),

CONSTRAINT valid_mgr CHECK (mgr_id <> emp_id OR emp_id=1),

CONSTRAINT end_of_month CHECK (DATEPART(DAY, GETDATE()) < 28)
)
GO

EXEC sp_helpconstraint employee
GO
```

```
>>>>

Object Name
-----------
employee

constraint_type        constraint_name                  constraint_keys
---------------        ------------------------------   ------------------
CHECK on column        CK__employee__emp_id__7F95F783   (emp_id >= 0 and
emp_id                                                  (emp_id <= 1000))

CHECK on column        CK__employee__entere__0272642E   (entered_date >=
entered_date                                            getdate())

CHECK on column        CK__employee__entere__03668867   (entered_by is
entered_by                                              not null)

CHECK Table Level      end_of_month                     (datepart(day,
                                                        getdate()) < 28)

FOREIGN KEY            FK__employee__mgr_id__017E3FF5   mgr_id REFERENCES
                                                        pubs.dbo.employee
                                                        (emp_id)

CHECK on column        no_nums                          (emp_name not
emp_name                                                like '%[0-9]%')

PRIMARY KEY           PK__employee__emp_id__7EA1D34A   emp_id

CHECK Table Level     valid_entered_by                 (entered_by =
                                                        suser_id(null)
                                                        and (entered_by
                                                        <> emp_id))

CHECK Table Level     valid_mgr                        (mgr_id <> emp_id
                                                        or (emp_id = 1))


Table is referenced by
----------------------
pubs.dbo.employee: FK__employee__mgr_id__017E3FF5
```

In this example, the following points are evident:

Constraint syntax CHECK constraints can be expressed at the column level with abbreviated syntax (leaving naming to SQL Server), such as the check on *entered_date*; or at the column-level with an explicit name, such as the NO_NUMS constraint on *emp_name*; or as a table-level constraint, such as the VALID_MGR constraint.

Regular expressions CHECK constraints can use *regular expressions*: for example, NO_NUMS ensures that a digit can never be entered as a character in a person's name.

AND/OR Expressions can be AND'ed and OR'ed together to represent more complex situations: for example, VALID_MGR.

Constraint reference Table-level CHECK constraints can refer to more than one column in the same row. For example, VALID_MGR insists that no employee can be his or her own boss, with the exception of employee number 1, who is assumed to be the CEO. SQL Server currently has no provision that allows you to check a value from another row or from a different table.

NULL prevention It is possible to make a CHECK constraint prevent NULL values: for example, *CHECK (entered_by IS NOT NULL)*. Generally, you would simply declare the column NOT NULL.

Unknown expressions A NULL column might make the expression logically "unknown." For example, a NULL value for *entered_date* makes the CHECK *entered-_date >= CURRENT_TIMESTAMP* have an unknown value. This does not reject the row, however. The constraint rejects the row only when the expression is clearly false, even if it is not necessarily true.

System functions System functions, such as GETDATE( ), APP_NAME( ), DATA-LENGTH( ), and SUSER_ID( ), as well as niladic functions, such as SYSTEM_USER, CURRENT_TIMESTAMP, and USER, can be used in CHECK constraints. This subtle feature is powerful and can be useful, for example, for assuring that a user can change only records that he or she has entered by comparing *entered_by* to the user's system ID, as generated by SUSER_ID( ) (or by comparing *emp_name* to SYSTEM_USER). Note that niladic functions such as CURRENT_TIMESTAMP are provided for ANSI SQL conformance and simply map to an underlying SQL Server function, in this case GETDATE( ). So while the DDL to create the constraint on *entered_date* uses CURRENT_TIMESTAMP, **sp_helpconstraint** shows it as GETDATE( ), which is the underlying function. Either expression is valid and equivalent in the CHECK constraint. The VALID_ENTERED_BY constraint ensures that the *entered_by* column can be set only to the currently connected user's ID, and it ensures that users cannot update their own records.

System functions and column references A table-level constraint can call a system function without referencing a column in the table. In this example, the END_OF_MONTH CHECK constraint calls two date functions, DATEPART( ) and GETDATE( ), to ensure that updates cannot be made after day 28 of the month (when the business's payroll is assumed to be processed). The constraint never references a column in the table. Similarly, a CHECK constraint might call the APP_NAME( ) function to ensure that updates can be made only from an application of a certain name, instead of from an ad hoc tool such as ISQL/w. Note, however, that a CHECK constraint cannot use a global variable, such as @@spid.

As with FOREIGN KEY constraints, you can add or drop CHECK constraints by using ALTER TABLE. When adding a constraint, by default the existing data is checked for compliance; you can override this with the NOCHECK syntax. You can later do a dummy update to check for any violations. The table or database owner can also temporarily disable CHECK constraints by using WITH NOCHECK in the ALTER TABLE statement.

Default Constraints

A *default* allows you to specify a constant value, NULL, or the run-time value of a system function if no known value exits or if the column is missing in an INSERT statement. Although you might argue that a default is not truly a constraint (because a default doesn't enforce anything), you can create defaults in a CREATE TABLE statement using the CONSTRAINT keyword; therefore I will refer to them here as constraints. Defaults add little overhead, and you can use them liberally without too much concern about performance degradation.

SQL Server provides two ways of creating defaults. Since the original SQL Server release in 1989, you can create a default (CREATE DEFAULT) and then bind the default to a column (**sp_bindefault**). Default constraints as part of the CREATE TABLE and ALTER TABLE statements were introduced in 1995 with version 6.0 and are based on the ANSI SQL standard (which includes such niceties as being able to use system functions). Using defaults is pretty intuitive. The type of default you use is a matter of preference; both do the same thing internally. Future enhancements are likely to be made to the ANSI-style implementation. In my opinion, having the default within the table DDL is a cleaner approach. I recommend using defaults within CREATE TABLE and ALTER TABLE rather than within CREATE DEFAULT, and so I will focus on that style here.

Here is the example from the previous CHECK constraint discussion now modified to include several defaults:

```
CREATE TABLE employee
(
emp_id        int          NOT NULL  PRIMARY KEY  DEFAULT 1000
                           CHECK (emp_id BETWEEN 0 AND 1000),

emp_name      varchar(30)  NULL  DEFAULT NULL  CONSTRAINT no_nums
                           CHECK (emp_name NOT LIKE '%[0-9]%'),

mgr_id        int          NOT NULL  DEFAULT (1)  REFERENCES
                           employee(emp_id),

entered_date  datetime     NOT NULL  CHECK (entered_date >=
                           CONVERT(char(10), CURRENT_TIMESTAMP, 102))
                           CONSTRAINT def_today DEFAULT
                           (CONVERT(char(10), GETDATE(), 102)),

entered_by    int          NOT NULL  DEFAULT SUSER_ID()  CHECK
                           (entered_by IS NOT NULL),

CONSTRAINT valid_entered_by CHECK (entered_by=SUSER_ID() AND
entered_by <> emp_id),

CONSTRAINT valid_mgr CHECK (mgr_id <> emp_id OR emp_id=1),
```

```
CONSTRAINT end_of_month CHECK (DATEPART(DAY, GETDATE()) < 28)
)
GO


EXEC sp_helpconstraint employee
GO

>>>

Object Name
-----------
employee
```

constraint_type	constraint_name	constraint_keys
CHECK on column emp_id	CK__employee__emp_id__52593CB8	(emp_id >= 0 and (emp_id <= 1000))
CHECK on column entered_date	CK__employee__entere__571DF1D5	(entered_date >= convert(char(10), getdate(),102))
CHECK on column entered_by	CK__employee__entere__59FA5E80	(entered_by is not null)
DEFAULT on column entered_date	def_today	(convert(char(10), getdate(),102))
DEFAULT on column emp_id	DF__employee__emp_id__5165187F	(1000)
DEFAULT on column emp_name	DF__employee__emp_na__534D60F1	(null)
DEFAULT on column entered_by	DF__employee__entere__59063A47	(suser_id(null))
DEFAULT on column mgr_id	DF__employee__mgr_id__5535A963	(1)
CHECK Table Level	end_of_month	(datepart(day, getdate())< 28)
FOREIGN KEY	FK__employee__mgr_id__5629CD9C	mgr_id REFERENCES pubs.dbo.employee (emp_id)

CHECK on column emp_name	no_nums	(emp_name not like '%[0-9]%')
PRIMARY KEY (clustered)	PK__employee__emp_id__5070F446	emp_id
CHECK Table Level	valid_entered_by	(entered_by = suser_id(null) and (entered_by <> emp_id))
CHECK Table Level	valid_mgr	(mgr_id <> emp_id or (emp_id = 1))

```
Table is referenced by
----------------------
pubs.dbo.employee: FK__employee__mgr_id__5629CD9C
```

The code above demonstrates the following about defaults:

Column-level A default constraint is always a column-level constraint because it pertains to only one column. You can use the abbreviated syntax that omits the keyword CONSTRAINT and the specified name, letting SQL Server generate the name, or you can specify the name by using the more verbose CONSTRAINT *name* DEFAULT syntax.

Clashes with CHECK constraint A default value can clash with a CHECK constraint and will not be allowed. This problem appears only at runtime, not when the table is created or when the default is added via ALTER TABLE. For example, a column with a default of 0 and a CHECK constraint that states that the value must be greater than 0 would never be able to insert or update the default value.

PRIMARY KEY or UNIQUE constraint You can assign a default to a column having a PRIMARY KEY or a UNIQUE constraint. Such columns must have unique values, so only one row could exist with the default value in that column. The example above sets a DEFAULT on a primary key column for illustration, but in general this practice would be unwise.

Parentheses and quotation marks A constant value can be written within parentheses, as in DEFAULT (1), or without them, as in DEFAULT 1. A character or date constant must be enclosed in either single or double quotation marks.

NULL vs. default value When NULL is inserted into a column versus when a default value is entered is often a misunderstood concept. A column declared NOT NULL with a default defined will use the default only under one of the following conditions:

- The INSERT statement specifies its column list and omits the column with the default.

- The INSERT statement specifies the keyword DEFAULT in the values list (whether the column is explicitly specified as part of the column list or implicitly specified in the values list and the column list is omitted, meaning "All columns in the order in which they were created"). If the values list explicitly specifies NULL, an error is raised and the statement fails; the default value is not used. If the INSERT statement omits the column entirely, the default is used and no error occurs. (This behavior is in accordance with ANSI SQL.) The keyword DEFAULT can be used in the values list, and this is the only way the default value will be used if a NOT NULL column is specified in the column list of an INSERT statement (either, as in the following example, by omitting the column list—which means all columns—or by explicitly including the NOT NULL column in the columns list).

```
INSERT EMPLOYEE VALUES (1, 'The Big Guy', 1, DEFAULT, DEFAULT)
```

Table 6-2 below summarizes the behavior of INSERT statements based on whether a column is declared NULL or NOT NULL and whether it has a default specified. It shows the result for the column for three cases:

- Omitting the column entirely (no entry)

- Having the INSERT statement use NULL in the values list

- Specifying the column and using DEFAULT in the values list

	No Entry		Enter NULL		Enter DEFAULT	
	No Default	Default	No Default	Default	No Default	Default
NULL	NULL	default	NULL	NULL	NULL	default
NOT NULL	error	default	error	error	error	default

Table 6-2. *INSERT behavior with defaults.*

NOTE Although you can declare DEFAULT NULL on a column allowing NULL, SQL Server does this without declaring a default at all, even when using the DEFAULT keyword in an INSERT or UPDATE statement.

Declaring a default on a column that has the Identity property would not make sense, and an error will be raised if you try this. The Identity property acts as a default for the column. But the DEFAULT keyword may not be used as a placeholder for an Identity column in the values list of an INSERT statement. A special form of INSERT statement can be used if a table has a default value for every column (if an Identity column does meet this criteria) or allows NULL. The following statement uses the DEFAULT VALUES clause instead of a column list and values list:

```
INSERT EMPLOYEE DEFAULT VALUES
```

> TIP   You can generate some test data by putting the Identity property on a primary key column and declaring default values for all other columns, and then repeatedly issuing an INSERT statement of this form within a Transact-SQL loop.

More About Constraints

This section covers some tips and considerations that you should know about when working with constraints.

Constraint names and system catalog entries

Earlier in this chapter, I stated that there was some method to the apparent madness of the cryptic-looking constraint names generated by SQL Server. Here I will attempt to explain the naming. Consider again the following simple CREATE TABLE statement as an example:

```
CREATE TABLE customer
(
cust_id      int         IDENTITY  NOT NULL  PRIMARY KEY,
cust_name    varchar(30) NOT NULL
)
```

The constraint produced from this simple statement bears the nonintuitive name *PK__customer__cust_i__68E79C55*. All types of column-level constraints use this naming scheme. (Note that although the NULL/NOT NULL designation is often thought of as a constraint, it is not quite the same. It is instead treated as an attribute of the column and has no name or representation in the *sysobjects* system table.)

The first two characters (*PK*) show the constraint type—PK for PRIMARY KEY, UN for UNIQUE, FK for FOREIGN KEY, and DF for Default. Next are two underscore characters (__) as a separator. (It might seem better to use one underscore as a separator, to conserve characters and to avoid having to truncate as much. However, it is common to use an underscore in a table name or a column name, both of which appear in the constraint name. Using two underscore characters makes it clear what kind of a name this is and where the separation occurs.) Next comes the table name (*customer*), limited to nine characters. After two more underscore characters for separation, the next sequence of characters is the column name (*cust_i*), again truncating if necessary so that the total number of characters for table name and column name doesn't exceed 14. And finally, after another separator, is the hexadecimal representation of the object ID for the constraint (68E79C55). (This value is used as the *id* column of the *sysobjects* system table and the *constid* column of the *sysconstraints* system table.)

Note the following queries and output using this value, shown in Figure 6-12.

```
SELECT  OBJECT_NAME(0x68E79C55),  OBJECT_ID('customer')

>>>
PK__customer__cust_i__68E79C55      1744009244

SELECT * FROM sysconstraints WHERE constid=0x68E79C55

>>>
constid       id          colid  sparel  status   actions   error
----------    ----------  -----  ------  ------   --------  -----
1760009301    1744009244  0      0       133633   4096      0

SELECT name, id, type FROM sysobjects WHERE id=0x68E79C55

>>>
name                                       id          type
-------------------------------    ----------  ----
PK__customer__cust_i__68E79C55     1760009301  K
```

Figure 6-12. *Queries and output using 68E79C55.*

TIP   The hexadecimal value 0x68E79C55 is equal to the decimal value 1760009301, which is the value of *constid* in *sysconstraints* and of *id* in *sysobjects*.

These example queries of system tables show the following:

A constraint is an object A constraint is an object, with an entry in the *sysobjects* table of type C, D, F, or K for CHECK, Default, FOREIGN KEY, and PRIMARY KEY/UNIQUE, respectively. Note that the type K in *sysobjects* does not differentiate a PRIMARY KEY constraint from a UNIQUE constraint.

sysconstraints* relates to *sysobjects Every constraint results in a row in the *sysconstraints* system table. The *constid* column of this table is the object ID of the constraint, and it is related to the *id* column in *sysobjects* for the row representing the constraint. The *id* column of *sysconstraints* is the object ID of the base table on which the constraint is declared. It is related to the row in *sysobjects* for the base table. (Hence, *constid* and *id* are essentially foreign key references to *sysobjects,* although such constraints are not formally declared.)

***colid* values** If the constraint is a column-level CHECK, FOREIGN KEY, or Default, the *colid* has the *colid* of the column. This *colid* is related to the *colid* of *syscolumns* for the base table represented by *id*. A table-level constraint, or any PRIMARY KEY/UNIQUE constraint (even if column-level), always has 0 in this column.

NOTE
To see the names and order of the columns in a PRIMARY KEY or UNIQUE constraint, you can query the *sysindexes* and *syscolumns* tables for the index being used to enforce the constraint. The name of the constraint and that of the index enforcing the constraint are the same, whether the name was user-specified or system-generated. The columns in the index key are somewhat cryptically encoded in the *keys1* and *keys2* fields of *sysindexes*. The easiest way to decode these values is to simply use the **sp_helpindex** system stored procedure, or you can use the code of that procedure as a template if you need to decode them in your own procedure.

Decoding the *status* field

The *status* field of *sysconstraints* is a pseudo–bit-mask field packed with information. If you know how to crack this column, you can essentially write your own **sp_helpconstraint**–like procedure. Note that the version 6.0 documentation is somewhat erroneous regarding the values of this column.

The lowest 4 bits, obtained by AND'ing *status* with $0 \times F$ (*status & $0 \times F$*), contain the constraint type. A value of 1 is PRIMARY KEY, 2 is UNIQUE, 3 is FOREIGN KEY, 4 is CHECK, and 5 is Default. The fifth bit is on (*status & 0×10 <> 0*) when the constraint was created at the column level. The sixth bit is on (*status & 0×20 <> 0*) when the constraint was created at the table level. But both bits 5 and 6 will be off for PRIMARY KEY and UNIQUE constraints.

Some of the higher bits are used for internal status purposes, such as noting whether a nonclustered index is being rebuilt, and for other internal states. I doubt that there is much need for anyone to know these values, but for completeness, here are the bit-mask values of the higher bits:

Bit-Mask Value	Description
64	Allow duplicate rows
128	Toggle bit for status
512	Create index with sorted data
2048	Index used to enforce primary keys
4096	Index used to enforce UNIQUE constraint
16384	Need to rebuild nonclustered index

Using this information, and not worrying about the higher bits used for internal status, you could use the following query to show constraint information for the *employee* table:

```
SELECT
    OBJECT_NAME(constid) 'Constraint Name',
    constid 'Constraint ID',
    CASE (status & 0xF)
        WHEN 1 THEN 'Primary Key'
        WHEN 2 THEN 'Unique'
        WHEN 3 THEN 'Foreign Key'
        WHEN 4 THEN 'Check'
        WHEN 5 THEN 'Default'
        ELSE 'Undefined'
    END 'Constraint Type',
    CASE (status & 0x30)
        WHEN 0x10 THEN 'Column'
        WHEN 0x20 THEN 'Table'
        ELSE 'NA'
    END 'Level'
FROM sysconstraints
WHERE id=OBJECT_ID('employee')

>>>
```

Constraint Name	Constraint ID	Constraint Type	Level
PK__employee__emp_id__0C85DE4D	210099789	Primary Key	NA
VALID_ENTERED_BY	386100416	Check	Table
VALID_MGR	402100473	Check	Table
END_OF_MONTH	418100530	Check	Table
DF__employee__emp_id__0D7A0286	226099846	Default	Column
CK__employee__emp_id__0E6E26BF	242099903	Check	Column
FK__employee__mgr_id__123EB7A3	306100131	Foreign Key	Column
DF__employee__emp_na__0F624AF8	258099960	Default	Column
NO_NUMS	274100017	Check	Column
DF__employee__mgr_id__114A936A	290100074	Default	Column
CK__employee__entere__1332DBDC	322100188	Check	Column
DEF_TODAY	338100245	Default	Column
DF__employee__entere__151B244E	354100302	Default	Column
CK__employee__entere__160F4887	370100359	Check	Column

Constraint failures in transactions and multirow data modifications

I have seen many bugs in application code that occur because the developers did not understand how a failure of a constraint affects a multiple-statement transaction declared by the user. It is not true that any error, such as a constraint failure, automatically aborts and rolls back the entire transaction. Rather, after an error is raised, it is up to the transaction to either proceed and ultimately commit or to roll back. This is a feature in that it provides the developer with the flexibility to decide how to handle errors. (The semantics are also in accordance with the ANSI SQL-92 standard for COMMIT behavior.)

Following is an example of a simple transaction that tries to insert three rows of data. The second row contains a duplicate KEY and violates the PRIMARY KEY constraint. Some developers believe that this example would not insert *any* rows because of the error that occurred in one of the statements; they believe that this causes the *entire* transaction to be aborted. However, these are incorrect beliefs— instead, the statement inserts two rows and then commits that change. Although the second INSERT fails, the third INSERT is processed because no error checking was done between the statements, and then the transaction does a COMMIT. Because no instructions were provided to take some other action after the error other than to proceed, this is exactly what SQL Server does. The first and third INSERT statements are added to the table, and the second statement is ignored.

```
IF EXISTS (SELECT * FROM sysobjects WHERE name='show_error' AND
    type='U')
    DROP TABLE show_error
GO

CREATE TABLE show_error
(
col1    smallint NOT NULL PRIMARY KEY,
col2    smallint NOT NULL
)
GO

BEGIN TRANSACTION

INSERT show_error VALUES (1, 1)
INSERT show_error VALUES (1, 2)
INSERT show_error VALUES (2, 2)

COMMIT TRANSACTION
GO

SELECT * FROM show_error
GO

Msg 2627, Level 14, State 1
Violation of PRIMARY KEY constraint 'PK__show_error__col1__236943A5':
Attempt to insert duplicate key in object 'show_error'.
Command has been aborted.
col1      col2
----      ----
1         1
2         2
```

Here's a modified version of the transaction. This example does some simple error checking using the built-in global variable @@ERROR and rolls back the transaction if any statement results in an error. In this example, no rows are inserted because the transaction is rolled back.

```
IF EXISTS (SELECT * FROM sysobjects WHERE name='show_error'
    AND type='U')
    DROP TABLE show_error
GO

CREATE TABLE show_error
(
col1    smallint NOT NULL PRIMARY KEY,
col2    smallint NOT NULL
)
GO

BEGIN TRANSACTION
INSERT show_error VALUES (1, 1)
IF @@ERROR <> 0 GOTO TRAN_ABORT
INSERT show_error VALUES (1, 2)
if @@ERROR <> 0 GOTO TRAN_ABORT
INSERT show_error VALUES (2, 2)
if @@ERROR <> 0 GOTO TRAN_ABORT
COMMIT TRANSACTION
GOTO FINISH

TRAN_ABORT:
ROLLBACK TRANSACTION

FINISH:
GO

SELECT * FROM show_error
GO

Msg 2627, Level 14, State 1
Violation of PRIMARY KEY constraint
'PK__show_error__col1__2645B050': Attempt to insert duplicate key
in object 'show_error'.
Command has been aborted.
col1    col2
----    ----
```

Because quite a few developers have handled transaction errors in the wrong way, and because it can be tedious to add an error check after every command, SQL Server version 6.5 includes a SET statement that will abort a transaction if any error is encountered during the transaction. (Transact-SQL has no WHENEVER statement, although such a feature would be useful for situations like this one.) Using *SET XACT_ABORT ON* causes the entire transaction to be aborted and rolled back if any error is encountered. The default setting of this is OFF, which is consistent with semantics prior to version 6.5 as well as with ANSI-standard behavior. By setting the option *XACT_ABORT ON,* I can now rerun the example that does no error checking and no rows will be inserted.

```
IF EXISTS (SELECT * FROM sysobjects WHERE name='show_error'
    AND type='U')
    DROP TABLE show_error
GO

CREATE TABLE show_error
(
col1    smallint NOT NULL PRIMARY KEY,
col2    smallint NOT NULL
)
GO

SET XACT_ABORT ON
BEGIN TRANSACTION

INSERT show_error VALUES (1, 1)
INSERT show_error VALUES (1, 2)
INSERT show_error VALUES (2, 2)

COMMIT TRANSACTION
GO

SELECT * FROM show_error
GO

Msg 2627, Level 14, State 1
Violation of PRIMARY KEY constraint
'PK__show_error__col1__29221CFB': Attempt to insert duplicate key
in object 'show_error'.

col1    col2
----    ----
```

A final comment about constraint errors and transactions: A single data modification statement (such as an UPDATE statement) that affects multiple rows is automatically an atomic operation, even if it is not part of an explicit transaction. If such an UPDATE statement finds 100 rows that meet the criteria of the WHERE clause but 1 row fails because of a constraint violation, 0 rows will be updated.

The order of integrity checks

The modification of a given row will fail if any constraint is violated or if a trigger aborts the operation. As soon as a failure in a constraint occurs, the operation is aborted and subsequent checks for that row are not performed, and no trigger fires for the row. Hence, the order of these checks can be important:

1. Defaults are applied as appropriate.

2. NOT NULL violations are raised.

3. CHECK constraints are evaluated.

4. FOREIGN KEY: Checks of *referencing to* other tables are applied.

5. FOREIGN KEY: Checks of *referenced by* are applied.

6. UNIQUE/PRIMARY KEY is checked for correctness.

7. Triggers fire.

Temporary Tables

Temporary tables are useful work spaces, like scratch pads, that you can use to "try out" intermediate data processing or to share work in progress with other connections. Temporary tables can be created from within any database, but they exist only in the *tempdb* database, which is created every time the server is restarted. (This means that a table or any object created in *tempdb* can never exist beyond the instance of SQL Server that is currently running.)

It is incorrect to assume that temporary tables are not logged: temporary tables are logged in *tempdb*. Transactions on temporary tables exist so that actions can be rolled back as necessary. However, the log is not used for recovery of the database at system restart since the database is entirely re-created.

Temporary tables can be used in three ways in SQL Server: privately, globally, and directly.

Private Temporary Tables (#)

By prefixing a table name with a single # (for example, *CREATE TABLE #my_table* ...), the table can be created from within any database as a private temporary table. Only the connection that created the table can access the table, making it truly private. Privileges cannot be granted to another connection. As a temporary table, it exists for the life of that connection only; that connection can drop the table via DROP TABLE. Because the scoping of a private temporary table is specific to the connection that created it, you will not encounter a name collision should you choose a table name that is used in another connection. Private temporary tables are analogous to local variables—each connection has its own private version and private temporary tables held by other connections are irrelevant.

Global Temporary Tables (##)

By prefixing the table name with a double ## (for example, *CREATE TABLE ##our_table ...*), a global temporary table can be created from within any database and any connection. Any connection can subsequently execute the table, even without EXECUTE permission being specifically granted. Unlike private temporary tables, the single copy of a global temporary table can be used by all connections. Because of this, you can encounter a name collision if another connection has created a global temporary table of the same name and the CREATE TABLE statement will fail.

A global temporary table exists until the creating connection terminates and all current use of the table completes. After the creating connection terminates, however, only those connections already accessing it are allowed to finish and no further use of the table is allowed. If you want a global temporary table to exist permanently, you can create the table in a stored procedure that is marked to autostart whenever SQL Server is started. That procedure can be put to sleep using WAITFOR and it will never terminate, so the table will never be dropped. Or you can choose to use *tempdb* directly, which is discussed next.

Direct Use of *tempdb*

Realizing that *tempdb* is re-created every time SQL Server is started, you can use *tempdb* to create a table or you can fully qualify the table as part of *tempdb* in the CREATE TABLE statement from another database. To do this, you will need to establish create table privileges in *tempdb*. Privileges in *tempdb* can be set up in one of two ways every time SQL Server starts: you can set the privileges in *model* (the template database) so that they are copied to *tempdb* when it is created at system restart, or you can have an *autostart* procedure set the *tempdb* privileges every time SQL Server is started.

Tables created in *tempdb* can exist even after the creating connection is terminated, and the creator can specifically grant and revoke execute permissions to specific users.

```
-- Creating a table in tempdb from pubs. Another method would be
-- to first do a 'use tempdb' instead of fully qualifying
-- the name.
CREATE TABLE tempdb..testtemp
(coll int)
```

Constraints on Temporary Tables

I have read a few articles about SQL Server that erroneously state that constraints do not work on temporary tables. All constraints will work on temporary tables explicitly built in *tempdb* (not using the # or ## prefixes). All constraints except FOREIGN KEY constraints will work with tables using the # (private) and ## (global) prefixes. FOREIGN KEY references on private and global temporary tables are designed not to be enforced, because such a reference could prevent the temporary table from being dropped at close-connection time for private temporary tables or when a table goes out of scope (for global temporary tables) if the referencing table wasn't first dropped.

SUMMARY

Tables are the heart of relational databases in general and of SQL Server in particular. In this chapter, I've discussed datatype issues, including size and performance trade-offs. SQL Server provides a datatype for almost every use. Declaring a column as allowing NULL internally makes that column variable-length, even if it was declared with a fixed-length datatype. Here I've discussed variable-length datatype issues and pointed out that it is simplistic to think that variable-length datatypes are either always good or always bad to use. I also showed how data is physically stored in data pages and discussed system table entries that are made to support tables.

SQL Server provides user-defined datatypes for support of domains and the Identity property to make a column produce autosequencing numeric values. SQL Server also provides constraints that give you a powerful way to ensure the logical integrity of your data. In addition to the NULL/NOT NULL designation, SQL Server provides PRIMARY KEY, UNIQUE, FOREIGN KEY, CHECK, and Default constraints. I hope the discussion of these features has made you aware of a number of pragmatic issues, such as performance implications, conflicts between different constraints and triggers, and transaction semantics when a constraint fails.

Understanding tables, datatypes, and constraints is crucial to the optimal use of SQL Server. I hope that this chapter has provided some insight into subtleties that you might not have gleaned from the reference documentation of these features.

7

Querying Data

Introduction

There would be no reason to store data if you didn't want to retrieve it. Relational databases gained wide acceptance principally because they enabled users to query, or access, data easily, without using predefined, rigid navigational paths. Indeed, the acronym *SQL* stands for Structured *Query* Language. Microsoft SQL Server provides rich and powerful query capabilities.

In this chapter, I'll discuss the SELECT statement and emphasize features beyond the basics, including NULL, OUTER JOIN, correlated subqueries, aggregates, UNION, and the special CUBE operator. In Chapter 8, I'll discuss modifying data. Then, in Chapters 9 and 10, I'll build on these topics and show you the constructs and techniques that make Transact-SQL more than simply a query language.

The SELECT Statement

The SELECT statement is the most frequently used SQL command and is the fundamental way to query data. The syntax is intuitive—at least in its simplest forms—and resembles how you might state a request in English. As its name implies, however, SQL is not only intuitive but also *structured* and precise. But even though a SELECT statement can be intuitive, it can also be obscure or even tricky. Brainteasers showing how to write a SELECT statement to perform some tricky task often appear in database publications, and as long as the query represented is syntactically correct, you will get a result. However, it might *not* be the result you really want—you might get the answer to a different question from the one you thought you posed! Incorrectly stated queries (queries with incorrect semantics) commonly cause bugs in applications, so it is important that you understand proper query formulation.

Here is the basic form of SELECT using [] to identify optional items:

```
SELECT [DISTINCT] <columns to be chosen, optionally eliminating
                    duplicate rows from result set>
[FROM] <table names>
[JOIN] <if multiple tables, declare how they relate to each other>
[WHERE] <criteria that must be true for a row to be chosen>
[GROUP BY] <columns for grouping aggregate functions>
[HAVING] <criteria that must be met for aggregate functions>
[ORDER BY] <optional specification of how the results should be
            sorted>
```

Note that the only section that must always be present is the verb SELECT itself; the other clauses are optional. For example, a query that retrieves data from only one table has no need to perform a JOIN operation. Or, if the entire table is needed, there is no need to restrict data to certain criteria, so there is no need for the WHERE clause.

Here's a simple query that retrieves all columns of all rows from the *authors* table in the *pubs* sample database:

```
select * from authors
```

Here's the output:

```
au_id        au_lname      au_fname    phone        address               city           state zip    contract
172-32-1176  White         Johnson     408 496-7223 10932 Bigge Rd.       Menlo Park     CA    94025 1
213-46-8915  Green         Marjorie    415 986-7020 309 63rd St. #411     Oakland        CA    94618 1
238-95-7766  Carson        Cheryl      415 548-7723 589 Darwin Ln.        Berkeley       CA    94705 1
267-41-2394  O'Leary       Michael     408 286-2428 22 Cleveland Av. #14  San Jose       CA    95128 1
274-80-9391  Straight      Dean        415 834-2919 5420 College Av.      Oakland        CA    94609 1
341-22-1782  Smith         Meander     913 843-0462 10 Mississippi Dr.    Lawrence       KS    66044 0
409-56-7008  Bennet        Abraham     415 658-9932 6223 Bateman St.      Berkeley       CA    94705 1
427-17-2319  Dull          Ann         415 836-7128 3410 Blonde St.       Palo Alto      CA    94301 1
472-27-2349  Gringlesby    Burt        707 938-6445 PO Box 792            Covelo         CA    95428 1
486-29-1786  Locksley      Charlene    415 585-4620 18 Broadway Av.       San Francisco  CA    94130 1
527-72-3246  Greene        Morningstar 615 297-2723 22 Graybar House Rd.  Nashville      TN    37215 0
648-92-1872  Blotchet-Halls Reginald   503 745-6402 55 Hillsdale Bl.      Corvallis      OR    97330 1
672-71-3249  Yokomoto      Akiko       415 935-4228 3 Silver Ct.          Walnut Creek   CA    94595 1
712-45-1867  del Castillo  Innes       615 996-8275 2286 Cram Pl. #86     Ann Arbor      MI    48105 1
722-51-5454  DeFrance      Michel      219 547-9982 3 Balding Pl.         Gary           IN    46403 1
724-08-9931  Stringer      Dirk        415 843-2991 5420 Telegraph Av.    Oakland        CA    94609 0
724-80-9391  MacFeather    Stearns     415 354-7128 44 Upland Hts.        Oakland        CA    94612 1
756-30-7391  Karsen        Livia       415 534-9219 5720 McAuley St.      Oakland        CA    94609 1
807-91-6654  Panteley      Sylvia      301 946-8853 1956 Arlington Pl.    Rockville      MD    20853 1
846-92-7186  Hunter        Sheryl      415 836-7128 3410 Blonde St.       Palo Alto      CA    94301 1
893-72-1158  McBadden      Heather     707 448-4982 301 Putnam            Vacaville      CA    95688 0
899-46-2035  Ringer        Anne        801 826-0752 67 Seventh Av.        Salt Lake City UT    84152 1
998-72-3567  Ringer        Albert      801 826-0752 67 Seventh Av.        Salt Lake City UT    84152 1
```

Using tools such as ISQL, ISQL/w, and SQL Enterprise Manager's Query window, you can issue queries interactively. You can also, of course, build queries into applications. The calling application determines the formatting of the data output. SQL Server returns the data back to the calling application, which then works with the data. In the case of an ad hoc query tool, it displays the output on a monitor.

The power of the SQL language begins to reveal itself when you limit the information to be returned to specified ranges of information. For example, you could specify that a query from one table return only certain columns or rows that meet your stated criteria. In the select list, you would specify the exact columns you

More Information...

In general, this book concentrates on topics specific to Microsoft SQL Server, but it would not be complete without some discussion of the SQL language. Because my treatment of SQL is, by design, far from complete, and the SQL language warrants extensive coverage in its own right, here's a list of my favorite books about SQL. (For complete publication details and more references, see "Suggested Readings" near the end of this book.)

Using SQL, by James Groff and Paul Weinberg, is excellent for users new to the SQL language who are looking for a good primer. Experienced users will probably want to use one of the other books mentioned here instead.

Understanding the New SQL: A Complete Guide, by Jim Melton and Alan R. Simon, is an excellent reference that I consult frequently for issues regarding ANSI SQL-92 semantics and conformance issues. (Jim Melton is an active participant in the SQL standards work and was the editor of the ANSI SQL-92 standard.) Although you can get the ANSI SQL-92 specification directly from ANSI, this book translates the standard into understandable English.

A Guide to the SQL Standard, by C. J. Date with Hugh Darwin. Similar in purpose and focus to the Melton and Simon book, this book's coverage is more compact, gives some additional insight into why something is the way it is, and provides more discussion of semantics. It's an especially good reference for issues about the use of NULL. I use this book hand-in-hand with the Melton and Simon book, and I find that their differences complement each other well.

SQL for Smarties, by Joe Celko, is the book to consult for insight into subtle but powerful ways to write queries that are nonintuitive. In places, this one is truly the SQL book for the Mensa crowd—it has many mind-bending puzzles about how to write an SQL query to perform some nonobvious task. It's loaded with examples, and you can often find a solution to a problem similar in scope to one you might face. (Note that the answers to the problems are nearly all formulated using only ANSI-standard SQL. In some cases, a SQL Server–specific extension would provide a more intuitive or more efficient solution. Throughout this chapter, I will try to point out the SQL Server–unique extensions.) Although it focuses on advanced topics, Celko's book also provides a comprehensive treatment of many query topics in an easy-to-read, conversational style. This is an underrated book that is well worth a spot on the shelf of any SQL database developer.

want, and then in the WHERE clause, you would specify the criteria that determine whether a row should be included in the answer set. Still using the *pubs* sample database, suppose that I want to find the first name and city/state/zip residence for authors whose last name is *Ringer*:

```
SELECT au_lname, au_fname, city, state, zip
FROM authors
WHERE au_lname='Ringer'
```

Here's the output:

```
au_lname     au_fname     city              state     zip
--------     --------     --------------    -----     -----
Ringer       Albert       Salt Lake City    UT        84152
Ringer       Anne         Salt Lake City    UT        84152
```

The results of this query tell me that two authors are named Ringer. But I am interested only in Anne. Retrieving only Anne Ringer's data requires an additional expression that is combined (AND'ed) with the original. In addition, I'd like the output to have more intuitive names for some columns, so I respecify the query:

```
SELECT 'Last Name'=au_lname, 'First'=au_fname, city, state, zip
FROM authors
WHERE au_lname='Ringer' and au_fname='Anne'
```

Here's the output, just as I wanted it:

```
Last Name    First     city              state     zip
---------    -----     --------------    -----     -----
Ringer       Anne      Salt Lake City    UT        84152
```

Joins

You gain much more power when you *join* tables, which typically results in combining columns of matching rows to project and return a *virtual table*. Usually, joins are based on the primary and foreign keys of the tables involved, although it is not required that the tables have keys explicitly declared. The *pubs* sample database contains a table of authors (*authors*) and a table of book titles (*titles*). An obvious query would be "Show me the titles that each author has written, and sort the results alphabetically by author. I'm interested only in authors who live outside of California." Neither the *authors* table nor the *titles* table alone has all this information. Furthermore, there is a many-to-many relationship between authors and titles; an author might have written several books, and books of the same title might have been written by multiple authors. So an intermediate table, *titleauthor,* exists expressly to associate authors and titles, and this table is necessary to correctly join the information from *authors* and *titles*. To join these tables, you must include all three tables in the FROM clause of the SELECT statement, specifying that the columns that make up the keys have the same values. Figure 7-1 shows you how:

```
SELECT
'Author'=RTRIM(au_lname) + ', ' + au_fname,
'Title'=title
FROM authors A, titles T, titleauthor TA
WHERE
A.au_id=TA.au_id AND T.title_id=TA.title_id    -- JOIN CONDITIONS
AND A.state <> 'CA'
ORDER BY 1
```

Figure 7-1. *Joining two tables via a third, virtual table.*

Here's the output:

```
Author                      Title
-----------------------     -----------------------------------
Blotchet-Halls, Reginald    Fifty Years in Buckingham Palace
                            Kitchens
DeFrance, Michel            The Gourmet Microwave
del Castillo, Innes         Silicon Valley Gastronomic Treats
Panteley, Sylvia            Onions, Leeks, and Garlic: Cooking
                            Secrets of the Mediterranean
Ringer, Albert             Is Anger the Enemy?
Ringer, Albert             Life Without Fear
Ringer, Anne               The Gourmet Microwave
Ringer, Anne               Is Anger the Enemy?
```

Before discussing join operations further, I want to point out a few things about the example in Figure 7-1. I've chosen to concatenate the author's last and first names into one field. I use the RTRIM (right trim) function to strip off any trailing white space from the *au_lname* column, add a comma and a space, and then concatenate on the *au_fname* column. This column is then *aliased* as simply *Author* and is returned to the calling application as a single column.

NOTE   The RTRIM function is not needed for this example, because since the column is of type *varchar*, trailing blanks would not be present. I show RTRIM for illustration purposes only.

Another important point is that the ORDER BY 1 clause indicates that the results should be sorted by the first column. It is more typical to use the column name rather than its number, but using the column number provides a convenient shorthand when the column is derived and hence is not present in the base table or view (virtual table) being queried. I could have specified the same expression of the column using *ORDER BY RTRIM(au_lname) + ', ' + au_fname* instead. SQL Server provides an extension to the ANSI standard that allows sorting by columns that are not included in the select list. So even though I do not individually select the columns *au_lname, au_fname,* or *state,* I could nonetheless choose to order the query based on these by specifying columns *ORDER BY au_lname, au_fname, state.* I will do this in the next example (Figure 7-2 on the following page). Notice also that the query contains a comment (- - *JOIN CONDITIONS*). A double hyphen (- -) signifies that the rest of the line is a comment (similar to // in C++), or you can use the C-style */* comment block */,* which allows blocks of lines of comments.

> **TIP** Comments can be nested, but generally it is a good idea to avoid this. You can easily introduce a bug by not realizing that a comment was nested within another comment and misreading the code.

Now let's examine the join in Figure 7-1: The WHERE clause specifies how the tables relate and sets the join criteria, stating that *au_id* in *authors* must equal *au_id* in *titleauthor,* and *title_id* in *titles* must equal *title_id* in *titleauthor.* This type of join is referred to as an *equijoin,* and it is the most common join operation. To remove ambiguity, you must qualify the columns. You can do this by specifying the columns in the form *table.column,* such as *authors.au_id = title_author.au_id.* The more compact and common way to do this, however, is by specifying a *table alias* in the FROM clause, as I have done here. By following the *titles* table with the letter *T,* the *titles* table will be referred to as *T* from that point. Typically, such an alias consists of one or two letters, although it can be much longer (following the same rules as identifiers).

After a table is aliased, it must be referred to by the alias, so now I cannot refer to *authors.au_id* because I've aliased *authors* as *A.* I must use *A.au_id.* Note also that I refer to the *state* column of *authors* as *A.state.* There is no *state* column in the other two tables, so qualifying it with the *A.* prefix is unnecessary, but doing so makes the query more readable—and less prone to subsequent bugs.

One of the most common errors new SQL users make is that of not specifying the join condition. Omitting the WHERE clause is still a valid SQL request and will cause an answer set to be returned. However, that answer set is likely not what the user wanted. In this example, omitting the WHERE clause would return the *Cartesian product* of the three tables: it would generate every possible combination of rows between them. Although a few unusual cases might want all permutations (and such an operation even has an operator, CROSS JOIN, in ANSI SQL-92 and SQL Server 6.5 to do explicitly this), usually this is just a user error. The number of rows returned is huge and typically doesn't represent anything meaningful. For example, a CROSS JOIN (Cartesian product) of the three small tables here (with no one table having more than 25 rows) generates 10,350 rows of (probably) meaningless output.

The join in Figure 7-1 is accomplished using the *old style JOIN* SQL syntax and is the most commonly used formulation. (The term "old style JOIN" is actually used by the SQL-92 specification.) However, ANSI SQL-92 and SQL Server 6.5 also support an *explicit JOIN* syntax, which segregates join conditions from search conditions such as *state <> 'CA'*. Although slightly more verbose, the explicit JOIN syntax is more readable. There is no difference in performance; behind the scenes, the operations are the same. Figure 7-2 shows how the query in Figure 7-1 can be equivalently respecified using the explicit JOIN syntax:

```
SELECT
'Author'=RTRIM(au_lname) + ', ' + au_fname,
'Title'=title
FROM
    authors AS A
    JOIN titleauthor AS TA ON (A.au_id=TA.au_id)
    JOIN titles AS T ON (T.title_id=TA.title_id)
WHERE
A.state <> 'CA'
ORDER BY au_lname, au_fname
```

Figure 7-2. *The explicit JOIN syntax produces the same result produced in Figure 7-1.*

The query in Figure 7-2 produces the same output and the same execution plan produced by the query in Figure 7-1. The query in Figure 7-2 is referred to as a *named columns join* per the ANSI syntax, for reasons that should be apparent. Instead of specifying the column equality conditions in the WHERE clause, as did the old style JOIN example in Figure 7-1, this syntax specifies the conditions in the ON clauses, such as *ON (A.au_id = TA.au_id)*.

> **NOTE** In other examples throughout this book, I will use old style joins and SQL-92 named columns joins interchangeably, without comment. It will help you to be familiar with both.

The most common form of joins is an *equijoin,* sometimes also referred to as an *inner join* to differentiate it from an *outer join,* which I'll discuss shortly. Strictly speaking, an inner join is not quite the same as an equijoin, which by definition means that the condition is based on equality; an inner join can use an operator such as > or <, although this is relatively unusual and esoteric. To make this distinction clear, you can use the INNER JOIN syntax in place of JOIN, as in this example:

```
INNER JOIN titleauthor AS TA ON (A.au_id=TA.au_id)
```

Other than making the syntax more explicit, there is no difference in the semantics or the execution. By convention, the modifier INNER generally is not used.

ANSI SQL-92 also specifies the natural join operation, in which you do not have to specify the column names of the tables. By specifying syntax such as *FROM authors NATURAL JOIN titleauthor*, the system automatically knows how to join the tables without your specifying the column names to match. SQL Server does not yet support this feature.[1]

The AS clause in Figure 7-2 shows an alternative way to specify a table alias that conforms to ANSI SQL-92. From SQL Server's standpoint, it is equivalent to the alias specification in Figure 7-1 (stating *FROM authors A* is identical to stating *FROM authors AS A*). Commonly, the AS formulation is used when doing ANSI SQL-92 join operations, and the formulation that omits AS is used with the old style join formulation. However, you can use either alias formulation in either case—it is strictly a matter of preference.

Outer Joins

Equijoins choose only rows from the respective tables that match the equality condition. In contrast, outer joins preserve some or all of the unmatched rows. To illustrate how easily subtle semantic errors can be introduced, let's refer back to the queries in Figures 7-1 and 7-2 where I wanted to see the titles written by all authors not living in California. The result omitted two writers who do not in fact live in California. *Was the query wrong?* No! The query performed exactly as written—I did not specify that authors who currently have no titles in the database should be included. The results of the query were as I requested. In fact, the *authors* table has four rows that have no related row in the *titleauthor* table, two of which do not contain the value CA in the *state* column:

au_id	Author	state
341-22-1782	Smith, Meander	KS
527-72-3246	Greene, Morningstar	TN
724-08-9931	Stringer, Dirk	CA
893-72-1158	McBadden, Heather	CA

The *titles* table has one row for which there is no author in our database, as shown on the facing page. (Later in this chapter, I'll show the types of queries used to produce these two result sets).

---

1. The ANSI specification calls for the natural join to be resolved based on identical column names between the tables. I think a better way to do this would be based on a declared primary key–foreign key relationship, *if it exists*. Admittedly, declared key relationships have issues, too, because there is no restriction that only one such foreign key relationship is set up. Also, if the natural join were limited only to such relationships, all joins would have to be known in advance—sort of like the old CODASYL days.

```
title_id    title
--------    -----------------------------------
MC3026      The Psychology of Computer Cooking
```

If the queries in Figure 7-1 and 7-2 were meant to be "Show me the titles that each author has written; include authors even if there is no title by that author currently in our database; if there is a title for which there is no author, show me that as well; sort the results alphabetically by the author; I'm interested only in authors who live outside of California," the query would use an outer join so that authors with no matching titles would be selected. Figure 7-3 shows this outer-join query:

```
SELECT
'Author'=RTRIM(au_lname) + ', ' + au_fname,
'Title'=title
FROM
    (                    -- JOIN CONDITIONS
    -- FIRST join authors and titleauthor
        (authors as A
        FULL OUTER JOIN titleauthor AS TA ON (A.au_id=TA.au_id)
        )
    -- The result of the previous join is then Joined to titles
        FULL OUTER JOIN titles AS T ON (TA.title_id=T.title_id)
    )
WHERE
state <> 'CA' OR state IS NULL
ORDER BY 1
```

Figure 7-3. *An outer-join query preserves rows that have no match.*

Here's the output:

```
Author                       Title
-----------------------      -----------------------------------
,                            The Psychology of Computer Cooking
Blotchet-Halls, Reginald     Fifty Years in Buckingham Palace
                             Kitchens
DeFrance, Michel             The Gourmet Microwave
del Castillo, Innes          Silicon Valley Gastronomic Treats
Greene, Morningstar          (null)
Panteley, Sylvia             Onions, Leeks, and Garlic: Cooking
                             Secrets of the Mediterranean
Ringer, Albert               Is Anger the Enemy?
Ringer, Albert               Life Without Fear
Ringer, Anne                 The Gourmet Microwave
Ringer, Anne                 Is Anger the Enemy?
Smith, Meander               (null)
```

From the Author...

At the beginning of this chapter, I promised not to go into much detail about generic SQL operations. The OUTER JOIN formulations here are standard ANSI SQL-92. However, I find that I need to say more because this is one area where I have not seen enough good examples; using OUTER JOIN with more than two tables introduces some obscure issues. Very few products provide support for full outer joins and frankly, the current SQL Server documentation is thin in its discussion of outer joins. Because you need a thorough understanding of outer joins if you are to use OUTER JOIN, I am going to deviate from my promise in this section.

The query in Figure 7-3 demonstrates a *full outer join*. Rows in the *authors* and *titles* tables that do not have a corresponding entry in *titleauthor* are still presented, but with a NULL entry for the *title* or *author* column. A full outer join preserves nonmatching rows from both the left-hand and right-hand tables. In Figure 7-3, the *authors* table is presented first, so it is the left-hand table when joining to *titleauthor*. The result of that join is the left-hand table when joining to *titles*.

You can generate missing rows from one or more of the tables by using either a *left outer join* or a *right outer join*. So if I want to preserve all authors and generate a row for all authors who have a missing title, but I do not want to preserve titles that have no author, I can reformulate the query using LEFT OUTER JOIN, as shown in Figure 7-4. This join preserves entries only on the left-hand side of the join. Note that the left outer join of the *authors* and *titleauthor* columns generates two such rows (for Greene and Smith). The result of the join in Figure 7-4 is the left-hand side of the join to *titles*; therefore, the LEFT OUTER JOIN must be specified again to preserve these rows with no matching *titles* rows.

```
    ⋮
FROM
    (
        (authors as A
        LEFT OUTER JOIN titleauthor AS TA ON (A.au_id=TA.au_id)
        )
        LEFT OUTER JOIN titles AS T ON (TA.title_id=T.title_id)
    )
    ⋮
```

Figure 7-4. *LEFT OUTER JOIN preserves rows on only the left-hand side of the joins.*

Here's the output:

```
Author                      Title
------------------------    -----------------------------------
Blotchet-Halls, Reginald    Fifty Years in Buckingham Palace
                            Kitchens
DeFrance, Michel            The Gourmet Microwave
del Castillo, Innes         Silicon Valley Gastronomic Treats
Greene, Morningstar         (null)
Panteley, Sylvia            Onions, Leeks, and Garlic: Cooking
                            Secrets of the Mediterranean
Ringer, Albert              Is Anger the Enemy?
Ringer, Albert              Life Without Fear
Ringer, Anne               The Gourmet Microwave
Ringer, Anne               Is Anger the Enemy?
Smith, Meander             (null)
```

The query in Figure 7-4 produces the same rows as the full outer join, with the exception of the row for *The Psychology of Computer Cooking*. Because only LEFT OUTER JOIN was specified, there was no request to preserve *titles* (right-hand) rows that have no matching rows in the result of the join of *authors* and *titleauthor*.

You must use care with OUTER JOIN operations, because the order in which tables are joined affects which rows are preserved and which are not. In an equijoin, the associative property holds (if A equals B, then B equals A) and no difference results, whether something is on the left or the right side of the equation, and no difference results in the order in which joins are specified. This is definitely *not* the case for OUTER JOIN operations. For example, consider the following two queries and their results:

QUERY 1

```
SELECT
'Author'=RTRIM(au_lname) + ', ' + au_fname,
'Title'=title
FROM (titleauthor AS TA
RIGHT OUTER JOIN authors AS A ON (A.au_id=TA.au_id))
FULL OUTER JOIN titles AS T ON (TA.title_id=T.title_id)
WHERE
A.state <> 'CA' or A.state is NULL
ORDER BY 1
```

```
Author                          Title
----------------------          ------------------------------------
,                               The Psychology of Computer Cooking
Blotchet-Halls, Reginald        Fifty Years in Buckingham Palace
                                Kitchens
DeFrance, Michel                The Gourmet Microwave
del Castillo, Innes             Silicon Valley Gastronomic Treats
Greene, Morningstar             (null)
Panteley, Sylvia                Onions, Leeks, and Garlic: Cooking
                                Secrets of the Mediterranean
Ringer, Albert                  Is Anger the Enemy?
Ringer, Albert                  Life Without Fear
Ringer, Anne                    The Gourmet Microwave
Ringer, Anne                    Is Anger the Enemy?
Smith, Meander                  (null)
```

This query produces results semantically equivalent to the previous FULL OUTER JOIN formulation in Figure 7-3, preserving both authors with no matching titles and titles with no matching authors. It might not be readily apparent that this is true, because obviously RIGHT OUTER JOIN is different from FULL OUTER JOIN. However, in this case I know it is true because FOREIGN KEY and NOT NULL constraints exist on the *titleauthor* table to ensure that there can never be a row in the *titleauthor* table that does not match a row in the *authors* table. So I can be confident that the *titleauthor* RIGHT OUTER JOIN to *authors* cannot produce any fewer rows than would a FULL OUTER JOIN.

But if I modify the query ever so slightly by changing the join order, see what happens:

QUERY 2

```
SELECT
'Author'=RTRIM(au_lname) + ', ' + au_fname,
'Title'=title
FROM (titleauthor AS TA
FULL OUTER JOIN titles AS T ON (TA.title_id=T.title_id))
RIGHT OUTER JOIN authors AS A ON (A.au_id=TA.au_id)
WHERE
A.state <> 'CA' or A.state is NULL
ORDER BY 1

Author                          Title
----------------------          ------------------------------------
Blotchet-Halls, Reginald        Fifty Years in Buckingham Palace
                                Kitchens
```

```
DeFrance, Michel          The Gourmet Microwave
del Castillo, Innes       Silicon Valley Gastronomic Treats
Greene, Morningstar       (null)
Panteley, Sylvia          Onions, Leeks, and Garlic: Cooking
                          Secrets of the Mediterranean
Ringer, Albert            Is Anger the Enemy?
Ringer, Albert            Life Without Fear
Ringer, Anne              The Gourmet Microwave
Ringer, Anne              Is Anger the Enemy?
Smith, Meander            (null)
```

At a glance, this second query looks equivalent to the first, although the join order is slightly different. But notice how the results differ. This query did not achieve the goal of preserving the *titles* rows without corresponding *authors,* and the row for *The Psychology of Computer Cooking* is again excluded. This row would have been preserved in the first join operation:

```
FULL OUTER JOIN titles AS T ON (TA.title_id=T.title_id))
```

But then this row is discarded, because the second join operation,

```
RIGHT OUTER JOIN authors AS A ON (A.au_id=TA.au_id)
```

preserves only authors without matching titles. Because the title row for *The Psychology of Computer Cooking* is on the left-hand side of this join operation and only a RIGHT OUTER JOIN operation is specified, this title is discarded.

> **NOTE** Just as INNER is an optional modifier, so is OUTER. Hence, LEFT OUTER JOIN can be equivalently specified as LEFT JOIN and FULL OUTER JOIN can be equivalently expressed as FULL JOIN. However, although INNER is seldom used by convention and is usually only implied, OUTER is almost always used by convention when specifying any type of outer join.

Because join order matters, I urge you to use parentheses and indentation carefully when specifying OUTER JOIN operations. Indentation, of course, is always optional, and use of parentheses is often optional. But as this example shows, it is easy to make mistakes that result in your queries returning the wrong answers. As is true with almost all programming, simply getting into the habit of using comments, parentheses, and indentation will often result in such bugs being noticed and fixed by a developer or database administrator before they make their way into your applications.

> ## From the Author...
>
> Notice that I say "developer" or "database administrator" on the preceding page, not "end user." SQL is often regarded as a language suitable for end users as well as database professionals. To an extent, such as with straightforward single table queries, this is true. But I would argue that if you expect end users to understand the semantics of outer joins or to deal correctly with NULL, you might as well just give them a random data generator. These are tricky concepts, and it is your job to insulate your users from these concepts. Later in this chapter, I will discuss how you can use views to help accomplish this.

The Obsolete *= OUTER JOIN Operator

Prior to version 6.5, SQL Server had limited outer-join support in the form of special operators *= and =*. Many people have assumed that the LEFT OUTER JOIN syntax of SQL Server 6.5 is simply a synonym for *=, but this is not the case. LEFT OUTER JOIN is semantically different from and superior to *=.

For equijoins, the associative property holds and so the issues with old style syntax don't exist. You can use either new or old style syntax with equijoins. For outer joins, you should consider the *= operator obsolete and move to the OUTER JOIN syntax as quickly as possible—the *= operator might be dropped entirely in future releases of SQL Server.

Because I've been a tad critical of ANSI SQL in the past, this time I'll pay it a compliment. ANSI's OUTER JOIN syntax, which was adopted in SQL Server version 6.5, recognizes that for outer joins, the conditions of the join must be evaluated separately from the criteria applied to the rows that are joined. ANSI gets it right by separating the JOIN criteria from the WHERE criteria. The old SQL Server *= and =* operators are prone to ambiguities, especially when there are three or more tables, views, or subqueries. Often the results are not what you'd expect, even though you might be able to explain them. But sometimes there is no way to get the result you want. These are not implementation bugs; more accurately, these are inherent limitations in trying to apply the outer-join criteria in the WHERE clause.

When *= was introduced, there was no ANSI specification for OUTER JOIN, or even for INNER JOIN. There was just the old style join with operators like =* in the WHERE clause. So the designers quite reasonably tried to fit an outer-join operator into the WHERE clause, which was the only place that joins were ever stated. Other products, notably Oracle with its (+) syntax, also followed this approach, and consequently they suffer from similar ambiguities and limitations.

However, efforts to resolve this situation helped spur the specification for proper OUTER JOIN syntax and semantics within the ANSI SQL committee. Using outer joins correctly is difficult, and SQL Server 6.5 is one of the few mainstream products that has done so.

To illustrate the semantic differences and problems with the old *= syntax, I'll quickly walk through a series of examples using both new and old outer-join syntax. Here is essentially the outer-join query shown in Figure 7-3, but this one returns only a count. It correctly finds the 11 rows, preserving both authors with no titles and titles with no authors.

```
-- New style OUTER JOIN correctly finds 11 rows
SELECT COUNT(*)
FROM
    (
    -- FIRST join authors and titleauthor
        (authors AS A
        LEFT OUTER JOIN titleauthor AS TA ON (A.au_id=TA.au_id)
        )

    -- The result of the previous join is then joined to titles
        FULL OUTER JOIN titles AS T ON (TA.title_id=T.title_id)
    )
WHERE
state <> 'CA' OR state IS NULL
ORDER BY 1
```

There really is no way to write this query, which does a full outer join, with the old syntax because the old syntax is simply not expressive enough. Here's what looks to be a reasonable try—but it generates a bunch of rows that you would not expect.

```
-- Attempt with Old Style Join. Really no way to do FULL OUTER
-- JOIN. This query finds 144 rows. - WRONG !!
SELECT COUNT(*)
FROM
    authors A, titleauthor TA, titles T
WHERE
A.au_id *= TA.au_id
AND
TA.title_id =* T.title_id
AND
(state <> 'CA' OR state IS NULL)
ORDER BY 1
```

Now I want to step back and show you some issues with the old style outer join using a simple example of only two tables, *customers* and *orders*:

```
CREATE TABLE Customers
(
Cust_ID        int  PRIMARY KEY,
Cust_Name      char(20)
)

CREATE TABLE Orders
(
OrderID    int    PRIMARY KEY,
Cust_ID    int    REFERENCES Customers(Cust_ID)
)
GO

INSERT Customers VALUES (1, 'Cust 1')
INSERT Customers VALUES (2, 'Cust 2')
INSERT Customers VALUES (3, 'Cust 3')
INSERT Orders VALUES (10001, 1)
INSERT Orders VALUES (20001, 2)
GO
```

At a glance, in the simplest case, the new and old style syntax appear to work the same. Here's the new syntax:

```
SELECT
'Customers.Cust_ID'=Customers.Cust_ID, Customers.Cust_Name,
    'Orders.Cust_ID'=Orders.Cust_ID
FROM Customers LEFT JOIN Orders
    ON Customers.Cust_ID=Orders.Cust_ID
```

Here's the output:

```
Customers.Cust_ID        Cust_Name        Orders.Cust_ID
-----------------        ---------        --------------
1                        Cust 1           1
2                        Cust 2           2
3                        Cust 3           (null)
```

And here's the old style syntax:

```
SELECT 'Customers.Cust_ID'=Customers.Cust_ID, Customers.Cust_Name,
    'Orders.Cust_ID'=Orders.Cust_ID
FROM Customers, Orders WHERE Customers.Cust_ID *= Orders.Cust_ID
```

Here's the output:

```
Customers.Cust_ID        Cust_Name        Orders.Cust_ID
-----------------        ---------        --------------
1                        Cust 1           1
2                        Cust 2           2
3                        Cust 3           (null)
```

But as soon as you begin to add restrictions, things get tricky. What if you want to filter out Cust 2? With the new syntax, it is easy, but remember not to filter out the row with NULL that the outer join just preserved!

```
SELECT 'Customers.Cust_ID'=Customers.Cust_ID, Customers.Cust_Name,
'Orders.Cust_ID'=Orders.Cust_ID
FROM Customers LEFT JOIN Orders
    ON Customers.Cust_ID=Orders.Cust_ID
WHERE Orders.Cust_ID <> 2 OR Orders.Cust_ID IS NULL
```

Here's the output:

```
Customers.Cust_ID        Cust_Name        Orders.Cust_ID
-----------------        ---------        --------------
1                        Cust 1           1
3                        Cust 3           (null)
```

Now try to do this query using the old style syntax and filter out Cust 2:

```
SELECT 'Customers.Cust_ID'=Customers.Cust_ID, Customers.Cust_Name,
'Orders.Cust_ID'=Orders.Cust_ID
FROM Customers, Orders
WHERE Customers.Cust_ID *= Orders.Cust_ID
AND (Orders.Cust_ID <> 2 OR Orders.Cust_ID IS NULL)
```

Here's the output:

```
Customers.Cust_ID        Cust_Name        Orders.Cust_ID
-----------------        ---------        --------------
1                        Cust 1           1
2                        Cust 2           (null)
3                        Cust 3           (null)
```

Notice that, this time, I don't get rid of Cust 2. The check for NULL is done before the JOIN, so the outer-join operation puts Cust 2 back. This result might be less than intuitive, but at least I can explain and defend it. That's not always the case, as I'll show you in a moment.

If you look at the preceding query, you might point out that I should have fil-tered out *Customers.Cust_ID* rather than *Orders.Cust_ID*. Oh yeah, how did I miss that? Surely this will fix the problem:

```
SELECT 'Customers.Cust_ID'=Customers.Cust_ID, Customers.Cust_Name,
'Orders.Cust_ID'=Orders.Cust_ID
FROM Customers, Orders
WHERE Customers.Cust_ID *= Orders.Cust_ID
AND (Customers.Cust_ID <> 2 OR Orders.Cust_ID IS NULL)
```

Here's the output:

Customers.Cust_ID	Cust_Name	Orders.Cust_ID
1	Cust 1	1
2	Cust 2	(null)
3	Cust 3	(null)

Oops! Same thing. The problem here is that *Orders.Cust_ID IS NULL* is now being applied *after* the outer join so the row is presented again. If I'm very careful and understand exactly how the old outer join is processed, I can get the results I want with the old style syntax for this query. I need to understand that the *OR Orders.Cust_ID IS NULL* puts back *Cust_ID 2*, so I'll take that out:

```
SELECT 'Customers.Cust_ID'=Customers.Cust_ID, Customers.Cust_Name,
    'Orders.Cust_ID'=Orders.Cust_ID
FROM Customers, Orders
WHERE Customers.Cust_ID *= Orders.Cust_ID
AND Customers.Cust_ID <> 2
```

Here's the output:

Customers.Cust_ID	Cust_Name	Orders.Cust_ID
1	Cust 1	1
3	Cust 3	(null)

Finally…this is what I want. And if I really think about it, it has understandable semantics (although different from the new style). So I guess this is much ado about nothing; all I have to do is understand how it works, right?

Wrong. Besides the issues of joins with more than two tables and lack of full outer join, there are also issues with views (virtual tables) and subqueries that I can't deal with. For example, let's try creating a view with the old style outer join:

```
CREATE VIEW Cust_old_OJ AS
(SELECT Orders.Cust_ID, Customers.Cust_Name
FROM Customers, Orders
WHERE Customers.Cust_ID *= Orders.Cust_ID)
```

A simple select from the view looks fine:

```
SELECT * FROM Cust_old_OJ
```

And it gives this output:

```
Cust_ID         Cust_Name
-------         ---------
1               Cust 1
2               Cust 2
(null)          Cust 3
```

But restricting from this view doesn't seem to make sense:

```
SELECT * FROM Cust_old_OJ WHERE Cust_ID <> 2
    AND Cust_ID IS NOT NULL
```

The output shows NULLs in the *Cust_ID* column, even though we tried to filter them out:

```
Cust_ID         Cust_Name
-------         ---------
1               Cust 1
(null)          Cust 2
(null)          Cust 3
```

If I expand the view to the full select, and I realize that *Cust_ID* is *Orders.Cust_ID*, not *Customers.Cust_ID*, perhaps I can understand why this happened. But I still can't restrict out those rows!

In contrast, if I create the view with the new syntax and correct semantics, it works exactly as I expect:

```
CREATE VIEW Cust_new_OJ AS
(SELECT Orders.Cust_ID, Customers.Cust_Name
FROM Customers LEFT JOIN Orders
    ON Customers.Cust_ID=Orders.Cust_ID )
GO

SELECT * FROM Cust_new_OJ WHERE Cust_ID <> 2 AND Cust_ID IS NOT NULL
```

Here's what I expected:

```
Cust_ID         Cust_Name
-------         ---------
1               Cust 1
```

In these examples, the behavior of the new syntax is to perform the outer join and then to apply the restrictions in the WHERE clause to the result. In contrast, the old style applied the WHERE clause to the tables being joined and then performed the outer join, which can reintroduce NULL rows. This is why the results often seemed bizarre. However, if that is the behavior you want, you could apply the criteria in the JOIN clause instead of in the WHERE clause.

Here is an example using the new syntax to mimic the old behavior. The WHERE clause is shown here simply as a placeholder to make it clear that the statement *Cust_ID <> 2* is in the JOIN section, not in the WHERE section.

```
SELECT 'Customers.Cust_ID'=Customers.Cust_ID, Customers.Cust_Name,
    'Orders.Cust_ID'=Orders.Cust_ID
FROM Customers LEFT JOIN Orders
    ON Customers.Cust_ID=Orders.Cust_ID
    AND Orders.Cust_ID <> 2
WHERE 1=1
```

Here's the output:

```
Customers.Cust_ID       Cust_Name       Orders.Cust_ID
-----------------       ---------       --------------
1                       Cust 1          1
2                       Cust 2          (null)
3                       Cust 3          (null)
```

As you can see, the row for Cust 2 was filtered out from the *Orders* table before the join, but then, because it was NULL, it was reintroduced because of the OUTER JOIN operation.

With the improvements in outer-join support, you can now use outer joins in places where previously you couldn't. A bit later, I will show you how an outer join can be used instead of a correlated subquery in a common type of query.

Dealing with NULL

The FULL OUTER JOIN example shown in Figure 7-3 has a twist that is necessary because of the NULL value that is generated for the missing author *state* column. Note the WHERE clause:

```
WHERE state <> 'CA' OR state IS NULL.
```

Without

```
OR state IS NULL
```

our favorite row, containing the title *The Psychology of Computer Cooking,* would not have been selected. Because this title is missing its corresponding author, the *state* column for the query is NULL. The expression

```
state <> 'CA'
```

does not evaluate to TRUE for a NULL value. NULL is considered unknown. If you were to omit the expression

```
OR state IS NULL
```

and execute the query once with the predicate

```
state = 'CA'
```

and once with the predicate

```
state <> 'CA'
```

it might seem intuitive that, between the two queries, all rows must have been selected. But this is not the case. A NULL *state* satisfies neither condition, and the row with the title *The Psychology of Computer Cooking* would not be part of either result. This example illustrates the essence of *three-valued logic,* so named because a comparison can evaluate to one of three conditions: TRUE, FALSE, or Unknown. Dealing with NULL entries requires three-valued logic. If you allow NULL entries or have cases in which outer joins are necessary, correctly applying three-valued logic is necessary to avoid introducing bugs into your application.

Assume that my table *Truth_Table* has columns *X* and *Y.* I have only one row in the table, as follows, with *X* being *NULL* and *Y* being *1*:

```
X        Y
------   -
(null)   1
```

Without looking ahead, test yourself to see which of the following queries will return *1*:

```
SELECT 1 FROM Truth_Table WHERE X <> Y  -- NOT EQUAL
SELECT 1 FROM Truth_Table WHERE X = Y   -- EQUAL
SELECT 1 FROM Truth_Table WHERE X != Y  -- NOT EQUAL
                                        -- (alternative formulation)
SELECT 1 FROM Truth_Table WHERE X < Y   -- LESS THAN
SELECT 1 FROM Truth_Table WHERE X !< Y  -- NOT LESS THAN
SELECT 1 FROM Truth_Table WHERE X > Y   -- GREATER THAN
SELECT 1 FROM Truth_Table WHERE X !> Y  -- NOT GREATER THAN
```

In fact, none of the previous SELECT statements returns *1*, because none of the comparison operations against *X,* which is NULL, evaluate as TRUE. All evaluate as Unknown. Did you get 100 percent? If so, are you confident that all your developers would also score 100? If you allow NULL, your answer had better be "yes."

Further complexity arises when expressions that can be Unknown are used with the logical operations of AND, OR, and NOT. Given that an expression can be TRUE, FALSE, or Unknown, the following truth tables summarize the result of logically combining expressions:

AND with Value	*True*	*Unknown*	*False*
TRUE	TRUE	Unknown	FALSE
Unknown	Unknown	Unknown	FALSE
FALSE	FALSE	FALSE	FALSE

OR with Value	*True*	*Unknown*	*False*
TRUE	TRUE	TRUE	TRUE
Unknown	TRUE	Unknown	Unknown
FALSE	TRUE	Unknown	FALSE

NOT	*Evaluates to*
TRUE	FALSE
Unknown	Unknown
FALSE	TRUE

The truth tables can reveal some situations that otherwise might not be obvious. For example, you might assume that the condition (X >= 0 OR X <= 0) must be TRUE, because *X* for any number will always evaluate as TRUE; it must be either zero or greater, or zero or less. However, if *X* is NULL, then X >= 0 is Unknown, and X <= 0 is also Unknown. Therefore, the expression evaluates as Unknown OR Unknown. As the OR truth table shows, this evaluates as Unknown. To illustrate all this, the following SELECT statement does not return a *1*:

```
SELECT 1 FROM Truth_Table WHERE (X >= 0 OR X <= 0)
```

And because *(X >= 0 OR X <= 0)* is Unknown, the condition:

```
WHERE NOT(X >= 0 OR X <= 0)
```

is equivalent (in pseudocode) to:

```
WHERE NOT (Unknown)
```

The NOT truth table shows that *NOT (Unknown)* is Unknown, so the following negation of the previous SELECT statement also returns nothing:

```
SELECT 1 FROM Truth_Table WHERE NOT(X >= 0 OR X <= 0)
```

And, at the possible risk of belaboring this point, since neither expression evaluates as TRUE, OR'ing them makes no difference either, and consequently this SELECT also returns nothing:

```
SELECT 1 FROM TRUTH_TABLE WHERE (X >= 0 OR X <= 0) OR NOT(X >= 0 OR X <= 0)
```

The fact that none of these SELECT statements evaluates as TRUE, even when negating the expression, illustrates that *not* evaluating as TRUE does not imply evaluating as FALSE. Rather, it means either evaluating to FALSE or evaluating to Unknown.

Two special operators, IS NULL and IS NOT NULL, exist to deal with NULL. Checking an expression with one of these operators always evaluates as either TRUE or FALSE. No Unknown condition is produced when using IS NULL or IS NOT NULL, as shown in the following truth tables:

IS NULL	*Evaluates to*	*IS NOT NULL*	*Evaluates to*
TRUE	FALSE	TRUE	TRUE
NULL	TRUE	NULL	FALSE
FALSE	FALSE	FALSE	TRUE

In the full outer-join query example, the search criteria was

```
WHERE state <> 'CA' OR state IS NULL
```

For the row with the title *The Psychology of Computer Cooking* (which was produced from the outer-join operation preserving the *titles* row with an unmatched *authors* entry), the *authors.state* column is NULL. Hence the expression

```
state <> 'CA'
```

is Unknown for that row, but the expression

```
state IS NULL
```

is TRUE for that row. The full expression evaluates as (Unknown OR TRUE), which is TRUE, and the row qualifies. Without

```
OR state IS NULL
```

the expression is only (Unknown), so the row does not qualify.

NULL in the Real World

Although many might argue eloquently about the virtue and beauty of NULL, it is the source of many application errors. I urge you to minimize the use of NULL and, in outer-join operations, to carefully account for NULL values that are generated to preserve rows that do not have a match in the table being joined. And even if you are comfortable with three-valued logic, make sure that your developers and anyone querying the data using the SQL language are comfortable also. If they are not, which is typical, introducing NULL will be a source of bugs just waiting to happen. You can, of course, make all column definitions NOT NULL and declare default values if no value is specified. Problems of no matching rows can often be avoided—without the need for outer-join operations—by providing *placeholder,* or *dummy,* rows. For example, you could easily create a dummy *titles* row and a dummy *authors* row. By using constraints or triggers, you could insist that every row in *authors* must have a matching entry in *titleauthor,* even if the ultimate matching row in *titles* is simply the dummy row. Likewise, every row in *titles* could be made to reference *titleauthor,* even if the matching row in *authors* is just the dummy row. Having done this, a standard equijoin will return all rows because there are no unmatched rows. There is no outer join or NULL complication.

Here's an example: After adding a dummy row for *authors,* one for *titles,* and one for each unmatched row into the *titleauthor* table, a standard inner join (with INNER specified purely to emphasize the point) is used to produce essentially the same results as the FULL OUTER JOIN. The only difference in the results is that the placeholder values ****No Current Author**** and ****No Current Title**** are returned instead of NULL.

```
BEGIN TRAN -- Transaction will be rolled back so as to not make
             -- permanent changes

-- Dummy Authors row
INSERT authors
(au_id, au_lname, au_fname, phone, address, city, state, zip, contract)
VALUES
('000-00-0000', '***No Current Author***',
'', 'NONE', 'NONE', 'NONE', 'XX', '99999', 0)


-- Dummy Titles Row
INSERT titles
(title_id, title, type, pub_id, price, advance, royalty, ytd_sales,
notes, pubdate)
VALUES
('ZZ9999', '***No Current Title***',
'NONE', '9999', 0.00, 0, 0, 0, '', '1900.01.01')


-- Associate Authors with no current titles to Dummy Title
INSERT titleauthor VALUES ('341-22-1782', 'ZZ9999', 0, 0)
INSERT titleauthor VALUES ('527-72-3246', 'ZZ9999', 0, 0)
INSERT titleauthor VALUES ('724-08-9931', 'ZZ9999', 0, 0)
INSERT titleauthor VALUES ('893-72-1158', 'ZZ9999', 0, 0)

-- Associate Titles with no current author to Dummy Author
INSERT titleauthor VALUES ('000-00-0000', 'MC3026', 0, 0)

-- Now do a standard INNER JOIN
SELECT
'Author'=RTRIM(au_lname) + ', ' + au_fname,
'Title'=title
FROM
        authors AS A              -- JOIN CONDITIONS
        INNER JOIN titleauthor AS TA ON (A.au_id=TA.au_id)
        INNER JOIN titles AS T ON (t.title_id=TA.title_id)
WHERE
A.state <> 'CA'
ORDER BY 1

ROLLBACK TRAN     -- Undo changes
```

This is the result:

```
Author                    Title
-------------             -----------------
***No Current Author***,  The Psychology of Computer Cooking
Blotchet-Halls, Reginald  Fifty Years in Buckingham Palace
                          Kitchens
DeFrance, Michel          The Gourmet Microwave
del Castillo, Innes       Silicon Valley Gastronomic Treats
Greene, Morningstar       ***No Current Title***
Panteley, Sylvia          Onions, Leeks, and Garlic: Cooking
                          Secrets of the Mediterranean
Ringer, Albert            Is Anger the Enemy?
Ringer, Albert            Life Without Fear
Ringer, Anne              The Gourmet Microwave
Ringer, Anne              Is Anger the Enemy?
Smith, Meander            ***No Current Title***
```

Earlier, you saw how OUTER JOIN got tricky and was prone to mistakes. It is comforting to know that no matter in what order I specify the tables for the join operation using dummy rows, the semantics and results are the same (which I'll leave to you to verify) because now this is simply an equijoin.

It would be misleading, however, to suggest that dummy values will solve all the woes introduced by using NULL. First, using dummy values demands more work in your application to ensure that relationships to the placeholder values are maintained. Even more important, many queries will still need to be aware of the placeholder values as special values, or the results of the query could be suspect. For example, if you used the placeholder value of 0 (zero) instead of NULL for a *salary* field in an *employee* table, you'd have to be careful not to use such a value in a query looking for average values or minimum salaries because a salary of 0 would alter your average or minimum calculations inappropriately. If the placeholder is simply another designation for "unknown," you must write your queries with that in mind. Placeholder values usually will solve the issues that arise in joining tables, and they can be an effective alternative to using OUTER JOIN. With placeholder values, it is less likely that incorrect queries will be written, especially by those with only basic SQL knowledge.

In the example above, the naïve query returns the same result set as the query with an OUTER JOIN and the criteria *OR state IS NULL*. It took careful work to construct the placeholder data and maintain the relationships for this to be the case. But that work can be done by the group database expert (probably you!), and once done, individuals without as much SQL or database knowledge will be less likely to introduce bugs in their queries simply because they are less familiar with the issues of OUTER JOINS and three-valued logic. I recognize that you will need to use NULL in many cases; my point is that if you can avoid these cases, you are wise to do so.

If dummy entries are not practical, here are a few other tricks. A handy and underused function is ISNULL. Using ISNULL(*expression, value*) substitutes the specified value for the expression when the expression evaluates to NULL. In the earlier outer-join example, the WHERE clause was specified as

```
WHERE state <> 'CA' OR state IS NULL
```

By using the ISNULL function, a special value (in this case, XX) can be assigned to any NULL *state* values. Then the expression <> '*CA*' will always evaluate as TRUE or FALSE rather than as Unknown. The clause *OR state IS NULL* is not needed.

The following query produces the full outer-join result, without using IS NULL:

```
SELECT
'Author'=RTRIM(au_lname) + ', ' + au_fname,
'Title'=title
FROM
    authors AS A              -- JOIN CONDITIONS
    FULL OUTER JOIN titleauthor AS TA ON (A.au_id=TA.au_id)
    FULL OUTER JOIN titles AS T ON (t.title_id=TA.title_id)
WHERE
ISNULL(state, 'XX') <> 'CA'
ORDER BY 1
```

IS NULL and = NULL

I've shown you how the IS NULL operator exists to handle the special case of looking for NULL. Because NULL is considered Unknown, ANSI-standard SQL does not provide for an equality expression of NULL—that is, there is no *WHERE name = NULL*. Instead, you must use the IS NULL operator *WHERE name IS NULL*. This can make queries more awkward to write and less intuitive to non-SQL experts. My colleague and friend Rick Vicik says tongue-in-cheek that this is because "NULLs are evil and you should experience extra pain every time you use one." And it is somewhat curious, or at least nonorthogonal, that ANSI SQL doesn't force an UPDATE statement to set a value TO NULL but instead uses the = NULL formulation.

ANSI SQL Does Not Provide for This	And Provides Only for This
SELECT... WHERE salary = NULL	SELECT... WHERE salary IS NULL

Yet ANSI SQL Uses Only This	And Not Something Like This
UPDATE employee SET salary = NULL	UPDATE employee SET salary TO NULL

> **NOTE** *Orthogonal* is an adjective, somewhat jargonish, that is often applied to programming languages and APIs. It is a mathematical term meaning that the sum of the products of corresponding elements in a system equals zero. This implies that a system is orthogonal if all of its primitive operations fully describe the base capabilities of the system and those primitives are independent and mutually exclusive of one another. In broader usage, the term also denotes a certain symmetry and consistency in use. For example, an API that has a *GetData* call would also have a *PutData* call, each taking arguments that are as consistent as possible between the two. The two APIs make up a mutually exclusive domain of operations you can perform on data, and the two are named and invoked in a consistent manner. Such a pair of APIs would be considered orthogonal. So if SQL had a LOAD TABLE command but no DUMP TABLE command, this situation would be *nonorthogonal*.

Microsoft SQL Server provides an extension to ANSI SQL that allows queries to use = NULL as an alternative to IS NULL. (There is an oblique reference to this extension under the SET ANSI_NULLS option, but it's never been thoroughly explained.)

Be sure to note that the formulation is not "NULL"—the quotation marks would have the effect of searching for a character string containing the word *NULL*, as opposed to searching for the special meaning of NULL. This way of specifying = NULL is simply a shorthand for IS NULL and provides a more convenient formulation of queries, especially by allowing NULL within an IN clause. The IN clause is a standard SQL shorthand notation for an expression that checks multiple values.

Multiple OR Conditions	Equivalent Shorthand Formulation
WHERE state = 'CA' OR state = 'WA' OR state ='IL'	WHERE state IN ('CA', 'WA', 'IL')

Some History...

Rick Vicik was the brains behind the redesign and port of Microsoft SQL Server to Windows NT, and he led the database engine group through all its releases, including the watershed version 6.0. No one deserves more credit for Microsoft SQL Server's success than Rick.

If you wanted to find states that are either one of those three values or NULL, ANSI SQL prescribes that the condition be stated using both an IN clause and an *OR state IS NULL* expression; SQL Server also allows all the conditions to be specified with the IN clause.

ANSI SQL Prescribes	*SQL Server Also Allows*
WHERE state IN ('CA', 'WA', 'IL') OR state IS NULL	WHERE state IN ('CA', 'WA', 'IL', NULL)

The = NULL shorthand can be particularly handy to use when you're dealing with parameters passed to a stored procedure, and this is the main reason it exists. Here's an example:

```
CREATE PROCEDURE get_employees (@dept char(8), @class char(5))
AS
    SELECT * FROM employee WHERE employee.dept=@dept
        AND employee.class=@class
```

By default, I can pass NULL to this procedure for either parameter; no special treatment is necessary. But without the = NULL shorthand, I need to put in extensive special handling even for this simple procedure:

```
CREATE PROCEDURE get_employees (@dept char(8), @class char(5))
AS
    IF (@dept IS NULL AND @class IS NOT NULL)
        SELECT * FROM employee WHERE employee.dept IS NULL
        AND employee.class=@class
    ELSE IF (@dept IS NULL AND @class IS NULL)
        SELECT * FROM employee WHERE employee.dept IS NULL
        AND employee.class IS NULL
    ELSE IF (@dept IS NOT NULL AND @class IS NULL)
        SELECT * FROM employee WHERE employee.dept=@dept
        AND employee.class IS NULL
    ELSE
        SELECT * FROM employee WHERE employee.dept=@dept
        AND employee.class=@class
```

This example is pretty trivial, and the situation becomes much more complex if you have multiple parameters and any one of them might be NULL. You then need a SELECT statement for every combination of parameters that might be NULL or NOT NULL. It can get ugly quickly.

As I mentioned earlier, dealing with NULL becomes an issue of nearly religious fervor to some in the database industry. No doubt, a few people will find the

SQL Server extension that allows an expression to be checked for = NULL to be a grave and serious deviation from three-valued logic (which is the primary reason this extension has not been well-documented, although I know many users have discovered it). As long as you realize that = NULL is purely a convenient shorthand for IS NULL, it should be clear that there is no violation of three-value logic. I favor practical solutions that make writing applications easier and less prone to bugs. I think more developers will correctly specify queries by using the SQL Server extensions that allow the equality and IN expressions to evaluate as TRUE. For those of you who are vehemently opposed to such formulations, there is, of course, nothing that forces you use these extensions, as SQL Server provides support for the pure ANSI-style IS NULL operator. You can also prevent this extension from working by enabling the SET ANSI_NULLS option.

Subqueries

SQL Server has an extremely powerful capability to nest queries, which provides a natural and efficient way to express WHERE clause criteria in terms of the results of other queries. Most joins can be alternatively expressed as *subqueries,* although this is often less efficient than doing the join operation. For example, using the *pubs* database to find all employees of the New Moon Books publishing company, I can write the query as either a join (using SQL-92–style join syntax) or as a subquery.

Here's the query as a join (equijoin, or inner join):

```
SELECT emp_id, lname
FROM employee JOIN publishers ON employee.pub_id=publishers.pub_id
WHERE pub_name='New Moon Books'
```

This is the query as a subquery:

```
SELECT emp_id, lname
FROM employee
WHERE employee.pub_id IN
(SELECT publishers.pub_id
FROM publishers WHERE pub_name='New Moon Books')
```

A join (equijoin) can be alternatively written as a subquery (subselect), but the converse is not necessarily true. The equijoin has the advantage in that the two sides of the equation equal each other and the order does not matter. Clearly, in a subquery, it does matter which query is the nested query. This difference is why a join can often be evaluated more quickly than an apparently equivalent subquery (subselect). A join gives the optimizer more options to choose from.

Subqueries make it simple to do relatively complex operations. For example, I showed that the *pubs* sample database has four rows in the *authors* table that have no related row in the *titleauthor* table (which prompted our outer-join discussion). The following simple subquery returns those four *author* rows:

```
SELECT 'Author ID'=A.au_id,
    'Author'=CONVERT(varchar(20), RTRIM(au_lname) +', '
    + RTRIM(au_fname)), state
FROM authors A WHERE A.au_id NOT IN
(SELECT B.au_id FROM titleauthor B)
```

Here's the output:

```
Author ID            Author                  state
---------            -------------------     -----
341-22-1782          Smith, Meander          KS
527-72-3246          Greene, Morningstar     TN
724-08-9931          Stringer, Dirk          CA
893-72-1158          McBadden, Heather        CA
```

It is common to use the IN operation for subqueries, either to find matching values (similar to a join) or to find nonmatching values by negating it (NOT IN), as shown above. Using the IN predicate is actually equivalent to saying = ANY. If I changed my query to find every row in *authors* that had at least one entry in the *titleauthor* table, I could use either of these queries.

Here's the query using IN:

```
SELECT 'Author ID'=A.au_id,
    'Author'=CONVERT(varchar(20), RTRIM(au_lname) + ', '
    + RTRIM(au_fname)), state
FROM authors A WHERE A.au_id IN
(SELECT B.au_id FROM titleauthor B)
```

This is the query using equivalent formulation with = ANY:

```
SELECT 'Author ID'=A.au_id,
    'Author'=CONVERT(varchar(20), RTRIM(au_lname) + ', '
    + RTRIM(au_fname)), state
FROM authors A WHERE A.au_id=ANY
(SELECT B.au_id FROM titleauthor B)
```

Here's the output:

```
Author ID            Author                  state
---------            -------------------     -----
172-32-1176          White, Johnson          CA
213-46-8915          Green, Marjorie         CA
238-95-7766          Carson, Cheryl          CA
```

```
267-41-2394      O'Leary, Michael          CA
274-80-9391      Straight, Dean            CA
409-56-7008      Bennet, Abraham           CA
427-17-2319      Dull, Ann                 CA
472-27-2349      Gringlesby, Burt          CA
486-29-1786      Locksley, Charlene        CA
648-92-1872      Blotchet-Halls, Regi      OR
672-71-3249      Yokomoto, Akiko           CA
712-45-1867      del Castillo, Innes       MI
722-51-5454      DeFrance, Michel          IN
724-80-9391      MacFeather, Stearns       CA
756-30-7391      Karsen, Livia             CA
807-91-6654      Panteley, Sylvia          MD
846-92-7186      Hunter, Sheryl            CA
899-46-2035      Ringer, Anne              UT
998-72-3567      Ringer, Albert            UT
```

Each of these formulations is equivalent to testing the value of *au_id* in the *titles* table to the *au_id* value in the first row in the *titleauthor* table, and then OR'ing it to a test of the *au_id* value of the second row, and then OR'ing it to a test of the value of the third row, and so on. As soon as one row evaluates as TRUE, the expression is TRUE and further checking can stop because the row in *titles* qualifies. However, it is an easy mistake to conclude that NOT IN must be equivalent to <> ANY, and some otherwise good discussions of the SQL language have made this exact mistake. And, more significantly, some products have also erroneously implemented it as such. Although IN is equivalent to = ANY, NOT IN is instead equivalent to <> ALL, not to <> ANY.

> **NOTE** Careful reading of the ANSI SQL-92 specifications also makes it clear that NOT IN is equivalent to <> ALL but is not equivalent to <> ANY. Section 8.4 of the document shows that R NOT IN T is equivalent to NOT (R = ANY T). With this in hand, further careful study of section 8.7 <quantified comparison predicate> reveals that NOT (R = ANY T) is TRUE if and only if R <> ALL T is TRUE. In other words, NOT IN is equivalent to <> ALL.

By using NOT IN, you are stating that *none* of the corresponding values can match. In other words, *all* of the values must not match (<> ALL), and if even one does match, it is FALSE. With <> ANY, as soon as one value is found to be not equivalent, the expression is TRUE. This, of course, would be the case for every row of *authors*—there will always be rows in *titleauthor* for other *au_id* values, and hence all *authors* rows would have at least one nonmatching row in *titleauthor*. That is, every row in *authors* would evaluate to TRUE for a test of <> ANY row in *titleauthor*.

The following query using <> ALL returns the same four rows as the earlier one that used NOT IN:

```
SELECT 'Author ID'=A.au_id,
    'Author'=CONVERT(varchar(20), RTRIM(au_lname) + ', '
    + RTRIM(au_fname)), state
FROM authors A WHERE A.au_id <> ALL
(SELECT B.au_id FROM titleauthor B)
```

The output:

Author ID	Author	state
341-22-1782	Smith, Meander	KS
527-72-3246	Greene, Morningstar	TN
724-08-9931	Stringer, Dirk	CA
893-72-1158	McBadden, Heather	CA

If I make the mistake of thinking that because IN is equivalent to = ANY, then NOT IN is equivalent to <> ANY and I write the query as follows. I return all 23 rows in the *authors* table:

```
SELECT 'Author ID'=A.au_id,
    'Author'=CONVERT(varchar(20), RTRIM(au_lname) + ', '
    + RTRIM(au_fname)), state
FROM authors A WHERE A.au_id <> ANY
(SELECT B.au_id FROM titleauthor B)
```

Here's the output:

Author ID	Author	state
172-32-1176	White, Johnson	CA
213-46-8915	Green, Marjorie	CA
238-95-7766	Carson, Cheryl	CA
267-41-2394	O'Leary, Michael	CA
274-80-9391	Straight, Dean	CA
341-22-1782	Smith, Meander	KS
409-56-7008	Bennet, Abraham	CA
427-17-2319	Dull, Ann	CA
472-27-2349	Gringlesby, Burt	CA
486-29-1786	Locksley, Charlene	CA
527-72-3246	Greene, Morningstar	TN
648-92-1872	Blotchet-Halls, Regi	OR
672-71-3249	Yokomoto, Akiko	CA
712-45-1867	del Castillo, Innes	MI
722-51-5454	DeFrance, Michel	IN

```
724-08-9931        Stringer, Dirk          CA
724-80-9391        MacFeather, Stearns     CA
756-30-7391        Karsen, Livia           CA
807-91-6654        Panteley, Sylvia        MD
846-92-7186        Hunter, Sheryl          CA
893-72-1158        McBadden, Heather       CA
899-46-2035        Ringer, Anne            UT
998-72-3567        Ringer, Albert          UT
```

The examples I've just shown use IN, NOT IN, ANY, and ALL to compare values to a set of values from a subquery. This is common. However, it is also common to use expressions and compare a set of values to a single, scalar value. For example, to find *titles* whose royalties exceed the average of all royalty values in the *roysched* table by 25 percent or more, you could use this simple query:

```
SELECT titles.title_id, title, royalty
FROM titles WHERE titles.royalty
    >= (SELECT 1.25 * AVG(roysched.royalty) FROM roysched)
```

This is a perfectly good query, and what makes it so is that the aggregate function AVG (*expression*) stipulates that the subquery must return exactly one value and no more. Without using IN, ANY, or ALL (or their negations), a subquery that returned more than one row would result in an error. If I incorrectly rewrite the query as follows, without the AVG function, I get run-time error 512:

```
SELECT titles.title_id, title, royalty
FROM titles WHERE titles.royalty
    >= (SELECT 1.25 * roysched.royalty FROM roysched)
```

This returns:

```
Msg 512, Level 16, State 1
Subquery returned more than 1 value.This is illegal when the subquery
follows =, !=, <, <= , >, >=, or when the subquery is used as an
expression.
```

It is significant that this is a run-time error, not a syntax error, meaning that in the SQL Server implementation, if that subquery did not produce more than one row, the query would be considered valid and would execute. For example, with the knowledge that the subquery here would return only one row, this query is valid and returns six rows:

```
SELECT titles.title_id, title, royalty
FROM titles WHERE titles.royalty
    >= (SELECT 1.25*roysched.royalty FROM roysched
WHERE roysched.title_id='MC3021' AND lorange=0)
```

The output:

```
title_id    title
--------    -------------------------------------------
BU2075      You Can Combat Computer Stress!
MC2222      Silicon Valley Gastronomic Treats
MC3021      The Gourmet Microwave
PC1035      But Is It User Friendly?
PS2091      Is Anger the Enemy?
TC4203      Fifty Years in Buckingham Palace Kitchens
```

However, this sort of query can be dangerous, and you should avoid it or use it only when you know there is a PRIMARY KEY or UNIQUE constraint that would ensure that the subquery returns only one value. The query here appears to work, but it is a bug waiting to happen. As soon as another row is added to the *roysched* table, say with *title_id* of MC3021 and a *lorange* of 0, the query would return an error—and no constraint exists to prevent such a row from being added. You might argue that SQL Server should determine whether a query formation could conceivably return more than one row regardless of the data at the time and then disallow such a subquery formulation. The decision to allow this was a result of the philosophy that such a query might be quite valid when the database relationships are properly understood, so the power should not be limited to try to protect naïve users. Whether you agree with this philosophy or not, it is consistent with SQL in general—and it should be clear by now that it is easy to write a perfectly legal, syntactically correct query that answers a question entirely different from the one you thought you were asking!

Correlated Subqueries

Powerful *correlated subqueries* can be used to compare specific rows of one table to a condition in a matching table. For each row otherwise qualifying in the main (or top) query, the subquery is evaluated. Conceptually, a correlated subquery is similar to a loop in programming, although it's entirely without procedural constructs such as *do-while* or *for*. The results of each execution of the subquery must be correlated to a row of the main query. In the following example, for every row in the *titles* table that has a price of $19.99 or less, the row is compared with sales in stores in California, for which the revenue (price × qty) is greater than $250. In other words, "Show me titles with prices of under $20 that have sales of more than $250 in California."

```
SELECT T.title_id,title
FROM titles T
WHERE price <= 19.99
AND T.title_id IN (
    SELECT S.title_id FROM sales S, stores ST
    WHERE S.stor_id=ST.stor_id
    AND ST.state='CA' AND S.qty*T.price > 250
    AND T.title_id=S.title_id)
```

Here's the result:

```
title_id        title
--------        -----------------------------
BU7832          Straight Talk About Computers
PS2091          Is Anger the Enemy?
TC7777          Sushi, Anyone?
```

Notice that this correlated subquery, like many subqueries, could have been written as a join (here using the old-style JOIN syntax):

```
SELECT T.title_id, T.title
FROM sales S, stores ST, titles T
WHERE S.stor_id=ST.stor_id
AND T.title_id=S.title_id
AND ST.state='CA'
AND T.price <= 19.99
AND S.qty*T.price > 250
```

It gets more difficult, if not impossible, to create alternative joins when the subquery is not doing a simple IN or when it uses aggregate functions. For example, suppose that I want to find titles that lag in sales for each store. I'll define this as "Find any title for every store in which the title's sales in that store are below 80 percent of the average of sales for all stores that carry that title, and ignore titles that have no price established (that is, the price is NULL)." An intuitive way to do this is to first think of the main query that will give me the gross sales for each title and store, and then for each such result, do a subquery that finds the average gross sales for the title for all stores. Then I correlate the subquery and the main query, and keep only rows that fall below the 80 percent standard.

Such an example follows. For clarity, notice the two distinct queries, each of which answers a separate question. Then notice how they can be combined into a single correlated query to answer the specific question posed here. All three queries use the old-style JOIN syntax.

```
-- This query computes gross revenues by
-- title for every title and store
SELECT T.title_id, S.stor_id, ST.stor_name, city, state,
    T.price*S.qty
FROM titles AS T , sales AS S , stores AS ST
WHERE T.title_id=S.title_id AND S.stor_id=ST.stor_id

-- This query computes 80% of the average gross revenue for each
-- title for all stores carrying that title:
SELECT T2.title_id, .80*AVG(price*qty)
FROM titles AS T2, sales AS S2
WHERE T2.title_id=S2.title_id
GROUP BY T2.title_id
```

```
-- Correlated subquery that finds store-title combinations whose
-- revenues are less than 80% of the average of revenues for that
-- title for all stores selling that title
SELECT T.title_id, S.stor_id, ST.stor_name, city, state,
    Revenue=T.price*S.qty
FROM titles AS T, sales AS S, stores AS ST
WHERE T.title_id=S.title_id AND S.stor_id=ST.stor_id
AND T.price*S.qty <
    (SELECT 0.80*AVG(price*qty)
    FROM titles T2, sales S2
    WHERE T2.title_id=S2.title_id
    AND T.title_id=T2.title_id )
```

And my answer is (from the third query):

title_id	stor_id	stor_name	city	state	Revenue
BU1032	6380	Eric the Read Books	Seattle	WA	99.95
MC3021	8042	Bookbeat	Portland	OR	44.85
PS2091	6380	Eric the Read Books	Seattle	WA	32.85
PS2091	7067	News & Brews	Los Gatos	CA	109.50
PS2091	7131	Doc-U-Mat: Quality Laundry and Books	Remulade	WA	219.00

When I first started using the newer SQL-92 explicit JOIN syntax, it wasn't obvious to me how to use it to write a correlated subquery. And I suspect that the creators of the syntax forgot about the correlated subquery case, because using the syntax seems like a hybrid of the old and the new: the correlation is still done in the WHERE clause, rather than in the JOIN clause. For illustration, here are two equivalent formulations of the above query using the SQL-92 JOIN syntax:

```
SELECT T.title_id, S.stor_id, ST.stor_name, city, state,
    Revenue=T.price*S.qty
FROM titles AS T JOIN sales AS S ON T.title_id=S.title_id
    JOIN stores AS ST ON S.stor_id=ST.stor_id
WHERE T.price*S.qty <
    (SELECT 0.80*AVG(price*qty)
    FROM titles T2 JOIN sales S2 ON T2.title_id=S2.title_id
    WHERE T.title_id=T2.title_id )

SELECT T.title_id, S.stor_id, ST.stor_name, city, state,
    Revenue=T.price*S.qty
FROM titles AS T JOIN sales AS S
    ON T.title_id=S.title_id
    AND T.price*S.qty <
```

```
     (SELECT 0.80*AVG(T2.price*S2.qty)
     FROM sales AS S2 JOIN titles AS T2
         ON T2.title_id=S2.title_id
     WHERE T.title_id=T2.title_id)
  JOIN stores AS ST ON S.stor_id=ST.stor_id
```

Often, correlated subqueries use the EXISTS statement, which is the most convenient syntax to use when multiple fields of the main query are to be correlated to the subquery. (In practice, EXISTS is seldom used other than with correlated subqueries.) EXISTS simply checks for a nonempty set. It returns (internally) either TRUE or NOT TRUE, which I won't refer to as FALSE, given the issues of three-valued logic and NULL. Because no column value is returned, TRUE or NOT TRUE, convention dictates that a column list is not specified and also dictates that the * character is used instead.

A common use for EXISTS is to answer a query such as "Show me the titles for which no stores have sales."

```
SELECT T1.title_id, title FROM titles T1
WHERE NOT EXISTS
(SELECT *
FROM titles T2 JOIN sales S ON (T2.title_id=S.title_id)
WHERE T2.title_id=T1.title_id )
```

```
title_id    title
--------    ----------------------------------
MC3026      The Psychology of Computer Cooking
PC9999      Net Etiquette
```

Conceptually, this query is pretty straightforward. The subquery, a simple equijoin, finds all matches of *titles* and *sales*. Then NOT EXISTS correlates *titles* to those matches, looking for *titles* that do not have even a single row returned in the subquery.

Another common use of EXISTS determines whether or not a table is empty. The optimizer knows that as soon as it gets a single hit using EXISTS, the operation is TRUE and further processing is unnecessary. For example, here's how you determine whether the *authors* table is empty:

```
SELECT 'Not Empty' WHERE EXISTS (SELECT * FROM authors)
```

Earlier, when discussing outer join, I mentioned that it is now possible to use an outer-join formulation to address what traditionally has been a problem in need of a correlated subquery solution. Here is an outer join formulation for the problem described above, "Show me the titles for which no stores have sales."

```
SELECT T1.title_id, title FROM titles T1
    LEFT OUTER JOIN sales S ON T1.title_id=S.title_id
WHERE S.title_id IS NULL
```

> **HINT** Depending on your data and indexes, the outer-join formulation might sometimes be considerably faster than the correlated subquery. Correlated subqueries can be expensive, as they are more or less a FOR EACH ROW–type loop. Often, they are the only tool for the job. But before automatically deciding on a correlated subquery, you might want to see if the query can be rewritten as a join of some type and, if so, whether it runs more quickly. It often will.
>
> In this example, for which there is little data, both solutions run in subsecond elapsed time. But the outer-join query requires fewer than half the number of logical I/Os than does the correlated subquery. With more data, that difference would be significant.

This query works by joining the *stores* and *title* tables and by preserving the titles for which no store exists. Then, in the WHERE clause, it specifically chooses *only* the rows that it preserved in the outer join. Those are the rows for which a title had no matching store.

Other times, a correlated subquery might be preferable to a join, especially if it is a self-join back to the same table or some other exotic join. Here is an example. Given the following table (and assuming that the *row_num* column is guaranteed unique), suppose that I want to identify the rows for which *col2* and *col3* are duplicates of another row:

row_num	col2	col3
1	C	D
2	A	A
3	A	D
4	C	B
5	C	C
6	B	C
7	C	A
8	C	B
9	C	D
10	D	D

I can do this in two standard ways. The first uses a self-join. In a self-join, the table (or view) is used multiple times in the FROM clause and aliased at least once. Then it can be treated as an entirely different table, comparing columns, and so on. A self-join to find the rows having duplicate values for *col2* and *col3* is easy to understand:

```
SELECT DISTINCT A.row_num, A.col2, A.col3
FROM match_cols AS A, match_cols AS B
WHERE A.col2=B.col2 AND A.col3=B.col3 AND A.row_num <> B.row_num
ORDER BY A.col2, A.col3
```

row_num	col2	col3
4	C	B
8	C	B
1	C	D
9	C	D

But in this case, a correlated subquery using aggregate functions will provide a considerably more efficient solution, especially if there are a lot of duplicates:

```
SELECT A.row_num, A.col2, A.col3 FROM match_cols AS A
WHERE EXISTS (SELECT B.col2, B.col3 FROM match_cols AS B
                WHERE B.col2=A.col2
                AND B.col3=A.col3
                GROUP BY B.col2, B.col3 HAVING COUNT(*) > 1)
ORDER BY A.col2, A.col3
```

This correlated subquery has another advantage over the self-join example—it is not necessary for the *row_num* column to be unique in order for it to solve the problem at hand.

You can take a correlated subquery a step further to ask a seemingly simple question that is surprisingly tricky to answer in SQL: "Show me the stores that have sold every title." I use a variation of this question when interviewing testing candidates who profess strong SQL knowledge. Even though it would seem a reasonable request, relatively few candidates can answer this, especially if I throw in the restrictions that they are not allowed to use an aggregate function like COUNT(*) and that the solution must be a single SELECT statement (that is, creating temporary tables or the like is not allowed).

The query above already revealed two titles that no store has sold, so we know that with the existing data set, no stores can have sales for all titles. So for illustration purposes, let me fabricate a store and sales records so that this new store does in fact have sales for every title. Following that, I'll show you the query that will find all stores that have sold every title (which we know ahead of time is only the phony one I'm entering here):

```
-- The phony store
INSERT stores (stor_id, stor_name, stor_address, city, state, zip)
VALUES ('9999', 'WE SUPPLY IT ALL', 'One Main St', 'Itasca',
    'IL','60143')

-- By using a combination of hard-coded values, and selecting every
-- title , generate a sales row for every title.
INSERT sales (stor_id, title_id, ord_num, ord_date, qty, payterms)
SELECT '9999', title_id, 'PHONY1', GETDATE(), 10, 'Net 60'
FROM titles

-- Find stores that supply every title.
SELECT ST.stor_id, ST.stor_name, ST.city, ST.state
FROM stores ST
WHERE NOT EXISTS
    (SELECT * FROM titles T1
    WHERE NOT EXISTS
        (SELECT *
        FROM titles T2 JOIN sales S ON (T2.title_id=S.title_id)
        WHERE T2.title_id=T1.title_id AND ST.stor_id=S.stor_id)
    )
```

Here's the result:

```
stor_id         stor_name               city        state
-------         ---------               ----        -----
9999            WE SUPPLY IT ALL        Itasca      IL
```

Although this query might be difficult to think of immediately, it is pretty easy to understand why it works. In English, it says "Show me the store(s) such that there does not exist a title that the store does not sell." This query consists of the two subqueries that are applied to each store. The bottommost subquery produces all the titles that have been sold by the store. The upper subquery is then correlated to that bottom one to look for any titles that are *not* in the list of those that have been sold by the store. The top query returns any stores that are not in this list. This type of query is known as a *relational-divide,* and unfortunately it is not as easy to express as one would like. Although the query above is quite understandable, once you have a solid foundation in SQL, it is hardly intuitive. As is almost always the case, you could probably use other formulations to write this query.

I've already alluded to doing this query without using an aggregate function like COUNT. There is nothing wrong with using an aggregate function—I imposed the restriction only to make it more of a brainteaser. If you think of the query in English as alternatively but equivalently stated as "Find the stores that have sold as many unique titles as there are total unique titles," you will find the following formulation somewhat more intuitive. Of those who get this brainteaser right, this formulation (or a slight variation) is probably the most popular (if I don't impose the restriction of not using the COUNT function). It runs slightly less efficiently than the NOT EXISTS formulation mentioned earlier.

```
SELECT ST.stor_id, ST.stor_name
FROM stores ST, sales SA, titles T
WHERE SA.stor_id=ST.stor_id AND SA.title_id=T.title_id
GROUP BY ST.stor_id,ST.stor_name
HAVING COUNT(DISTINCT SA.title_id)=(SELECT COUNT(*) FROM titles T1)
```

The following formulation also runs efficiently (on par with the NOT EXISTS formulation). It is similar to the one above but still novel in its approach because it is just a standard subquery, not a join or a correlated subquery. At first I looked at it and thought it was an illegal query, since it does a GROUP BY and a HAVING without an aggregate in the select list of the first subquery. But that's OK, both in terms of what SQL Server allows and in terms of the ANSI specification. What is not allowed is having an item in the select list that is not an aggregate function but then omitting it from the GROUP BY clause if there is a GROUP BY clause.

```
-- Find stores that have sold every title.
SELECT stor_id, stor_name FROM stores WHERE stores.stor_id IN
(SELECT stor_id FROM sales GROUP BY stor_id
    HAVING COUNT(DISTINCT title_id)=(SELECT COUNT(*) FROM titles)
)
```

And as a lead-in to the next topic, here's a formulation that uses a derived table, a feature new to SQL Server 6.5. This capability takes a SELECT statement and aliases it as though it is a table, and then it allows you to select from the select list. This query also runs very efficiently.

```
SELECT ST.stor_id, ST.stor_name
FROM stores ST,
    (SELECT stor_id, COUNT(DISTINCT title_id) AS title_count
        FROM sales
```

```
        GROUP BY stor_id
    ) as SA
WHERE ST.stor_id=SA.stor_id AND SA.title_count=
    (SELECT COUNT(*) FROM titles)
```

Views and Derived Tables

Think of a *view* as a virtual table. Simply put, a view is a named SELECT statement that will dynamically produce a result set that can be further operated on. A view has no rows stored. It acts as a filter to underlying tables. The SELECT statement that defines the view can be from one or more underlying tables, or from other views. To relieve users of the complexity of having to know how to properly write an outer join, I can turn my prior outer-join query into a view:

```
CREATE VIEW outer_view AS
(
SELECT
    'Author'=RTRIM(au_lname) + ', ' + au_fname, 'Title'=title
FROM (titleauthor AS TA
FULL OUTER JOIN titles AS T ON (TA.title_id=T.title_id))
RIGHT OUTER JOIN authors AS A ON (A.au_id=TA.au_id)
WHERE
A.state <> 'CA' OR A.state IS NULL
)
```

Now, instead of formulating the outer join, I can simply query the outer-join view, *outer_view*. Then I can do an inexact search for author names starting with *Ri*.

```
SELECT * FROM outer_view WHERE Author LIKE 'Ri%' ORDER BY Author
```

Here's the output:

```
Author          Title
-------------   ---------------------
Ringer, Albert  Is Anger the Enemy?
Ringer, Albert  Life Without Fear
Ringer, Anne    The Gourmet Microwave
Ringer, Anne    Is Anger the Enemy?
```

Notice that the view defines the set of rows that will be included, but it does not define the rows' ordering. If I want a specific order, I must specify the ORDER BY clause in the SELECT statement on the view rather than on the SELECT statement that defines the view.

A *derived table* is a fancy name for the result of using another SELECT statement in the FROM clause of a SELECT statement. This fits the relational model nicely, because the result of a SELECT statement is a table—so it is nicely orthogonal that I can subsequently select from that table. You can think of a view as a named derived table. A view is named, and its definition is persistent and reusable; a derived table is a completely dynamic, temporal concept. To show the difference, here is an equivalent *LIKE 'Ri%'* query using a derived table instead of a view:

```
SELECT * FROM
(SELECT
'Author'=RTRIM(au_lname) + ', ' + au_fname, 'Title'=title
FROM (titleauthor AS TA
FULL OUTER JOIN titles AS T ON (TA.title_id=T.title_id))
RIGHT OUTER JOIN authors AS A ON (A.au_id=TA.au_id)
WHERE A.state <> 'CA' OR A.state IS NULL
) AS T
WHERE T.Author LIKE 'Ri%'
```

You can insert, update, and delete rows in a view but not in a derived table. However, there are some limitations, which are explained in the SQL Server documentation, but they bear repeating here with a bit more comment.

Modifications restricted to one base table Data modification statements (INSERT, UPDATE, and DELETE) are allowed on multiple-table views if the data modification statement affects only one base table. You cannot use data modification statements on more than one underlying table in a single statement.

INSERT statements and NOT NULL columns INSERT statements are not accepted unless all the NOT NULL columns without defaults in the underlying table or view are included in the view through which you are inserting new rows, and values for those columns are included in the INSERT statement. (SQL Server has no way to supply values for NOT NULL columns in the underlying table or view.)

Data restrictions must apply All columns being modified must adhere to all restrictions for the data modification statement as if they were executed directly against the base table. This applies to column nullability, constraints, identity columns, and columns with rules and/or defaults and base table triggers.

Limitations on INSERT and UPDATE statements INSERT and UPDATE statements cannot add or change any column in a view that is a computation, nor can they change a view that includes aggregate functions, built-in functions, UNION, a GROUP BY clause, or DISTINCT.

READTEXT or WRITETEXT You cannot use READTEXT or WRITETEXT on text or image columns in views.

Modifications and view criteria By default, data modification statements on views are not checked to determine whether the rows affected will be within the scope of the view. For example, you can issue an INSERT statement on a view that adds a row to the underlying base table, but that does not add the row to the view. This occurs because the column values are all valid to the table, so they can be added, but if the column values don't meet the view's criteria, they are not represented in the selection for the view. Similarly, you can issue an UPDATE statement that changes a row in a way that the row no longer meets the criteria for the view. If you want all modifications to be checked, use the WITH CHECK OPTION option when creating the view.

If you are a longtime user of SQL Server, you might also believe that a view cannot contain a DISTINCT clause or a UNION. However, neither of these restrictions exists now. The restriction on DISTINCT was lifted in version 6.0, and the restriction on UNION was removed in version 6.5. (Version 6.5 also, for the first time, allows UNION in subqueries.)

These restrictions are, for the most part, logical and understandable, with the exception of WITH CHECK OPTION. For example, if you use a view that defines some select criteria and allows the rows produced by the view to be modified, you must use WITH CHECK OPTION or you might experience the bizarre results of inserting a row that you can never see or updating rows in such a way that they disappear from the view.

Here's just such a case:

```
CREATE VIEW CA_authors AS
(
SELECT * FROM authors
WHERE state='CA'
)
GO

BEGIN TRAN -- So I can roll this nonsense back
SELECT * FROM CA_authors

-- (returns 15 rows)

UPDATE CA_authors SET state='IL'
SELECT * FROM CA_authors

-- (returns 0 rows)

ROLLBACK TRAN
```

Should I be able to update rows in a way that causes them to disappear from the view or add rows and never see them again? I say no; WITH CHECK OPTION should be automatic behavior for a view being updated. But because the SQL Server behavior is as ANSI SQL specifies, and such disappearing rows are as specified, I recommend that you *always* use WITH CHECK OPTION if a view is to be updated and the criteria are such that WITH CHECK OPTION might be violated.

If I rewrite the view, as follows

```
CREATE VIEW CA_authors AS
(
SELECT * FROM authors
WHERE state='CA'
)
WITH CHECK OPTION
```

when I attempt to update the state column to *'IL'*, the command fails and I get this error message:

```
Msg 550, Level 16, State 2
The attempted insert or update failed because the target view either
specifies WITH CHECK OPTION or spans a view which specifies WITH
CHECK OPTION and one or more rows resulting from the operation did
not qualify under the CHECK OPTION constraint. Command has been
aborted.
```

Views also have an often overlooked ability to use a system function in the view definition, making it dynamic for the connection. For example, suppose that I keep a personnel table that has a column called *sqldb_name,* which is the person's login name to SQL Server. The function SUSER_NAME(*server_user_id*) returns the login name for the current connection. I can create a view using the SUSER_NAME system function to limit that user to only his or her specific row in the table:

```
CREATE VIEW My_personnel AS
(
SELECT * FROM personnel WHERE sqldb_name = SUSER_NAME()
)
WITH CHECK OPTION
```

SQL Server provides system functions that return the application name, database user name (which may be different from the server login name), and workstation name, and these functions can be used in similar ways. You can see from the example above that a view can also be important in dealing with security. For details on the system functions, see the SQL Server documentation.

Other Search Expressions

In addition to the SELECT statement and joins, SQL Server provides other useful search expressions that enable you to tailor your queries.

LIKE

In an earlier example, I used LIKE to find authors whose names started with *Ri*. LIKE allows you to search using the simple pattern matching that is standard with ANSI SQL, but SQL Server adds capability by introducing wildcard characters that allow the use of regular expressions. The following table shows how wildcard characters are used in searches:

Wildcard	Searches for
%	Any string of zero or more characters
-	Any single character
[ ]	Any single character within the specified range (for example, [a-f]) or the specified set (for example, [abcdef])
[^]	Any single character not within the specified range (for example, [^a-f]) or the specified set (for example, [^abcdef])

The following examples from the SQL Server documentation show how LIKE can be used:

Form	Searches for
LIKE 'Mc%'	All names that begin with the letters *Mc* (McBadden)
LIKE '%inger'	All names that end with *inger* (Ringer, Stringer)
LIKE '%en%'	All names that include the letters *en* (Bennet, Green, McBadden)
LIKE '-heryl'	All six-letter names ending with *heryl* (Cheryl, Sheryl)
LIKE '[CK]ars[eo]n'	All names that begin with *C* or *K*, then *ars*, then *e* or *o*, and then end with *n* (Carsen, Karsen, Carson, and Karson)
LIKE '[M-Z]inger'	All names ending with *inger* that begin with any single letter from *M* through *Z* (Ringer)
LIKE 'M[^c]%'	All names beginning with the letter *M* that do not have the letter *c* as the second letter (MacFeather)

Trailing blanks

Trailing blanks (blank spaces) can cause considerable confusion and errors. In SQL Server, using trailing blanks requires that you be aware of differences in how *varchar* and *char* data is stored and of how the *SET ANSI_PADDING* option is used.

Suppose that I create a table with five columns and insert data as follows:

```
SET ANSI_PADDING OFF    -- OFF is the default if nothing is set

DROP TABLE checkpad
GO

CREATE TABLE checkpad
(
rowid       smallint      NOT NULL PRIMARY KEY,
c10not      char(10)      NOT NULL,
c10nul      char(10)      NULL,
v10not      varchar(10)   NOT NULL,
v10nul      varchar(10)   NULL
)

-- Row 1 has names with no trailing blanks
INSERT checkpad VALUES (1, 'John', 'John', 'John', 'John')

-- Row 2 has each name inserted with three trailing blanks
INSERT checkpad VALUES
    (2, 'John   ', 'John   ', 'John   ', 'John   ')

-- Row 3 has each name inserted with a full six trailing blanks
INSERT checkpad VALUES
    (3, 'John      ', 'John      ', 'John      ', 'John      ')

-- Row 4 has each name inserted with seven trailing blanks too many
INSERT checkpad VALUES
    (4, 'John       ', 'John       ', 'John       ', 'John       ')
```

I can then use the following query to analyze the contents of the table. I use the DATALENGTH(*expression*) function to determine the actual length of the data, and I convert to VARBINARY() to display the hex values of the characters stored. (For those who don't have the ASCII chart memorized, a blank space is 0x20.) I then use a LIKE to try to match each column, once with one trailing blank and once with six trailing blanks.

```
SELECT ROWID,
"0xC10NOT"=CONVERT(VARBINARY(10), c10not), L1=DATALENGTH(c10not),
"LIKE 'John %'"=CASE WHEN (c10not LIKE 'John %') THEN 1 ELSE 0 END,
```

```
"LIKE 'John      %'"=CASE WHEN (c10not LIKE 'John      %')
    THEN 1 ELSE 0 END,
"0xC10NUL"=CONVERT(VARBINARY(10), c10nul), L2=DATALENGTH(c10nul),
"LIKE 'John %'"=CASE WHEN (c10nul LIKE 'John %') THEN 1 ELSE 0 END,
"LIKE 'John      %'"=CASE WHEN (c10nul LIKE 'John      %')
    THEN 1 ELSE 0 END,
"0xV10NOT"=CONVERT(VARBINARY(10), v10not), L3=DATALENGTH(v10not),
"LIKE 'John %'"=CASE WHEN (v10not LIKE 'John %') THEN 1 ELSE 0 END,
"LIKE 'John      %'"=CASE WHEN (v10not LIKE 'John      %')
    THEN 1 ELSE 0 END,
"0xV10NUL"=CONVERT(VARBINARY(10), v10nul), L4=DATALENGTH(v10nul),
"LIKE 'John %'"=CASE WHEN (v10nul LIKE 'John %') THEN 1 ELSE 0 END,
"LIKE 'John      %'"=CASE WHEN (v10nul LIKE 'John      %')
    THEN 1 ELSE 0 END
FROM checkpad
```

Figure 7-5 shows the results of this query from the *checkpad* table:

ROWID	0xC10NOT	L1	LIKE 'John %'	LIKE 'John %'	0xC10NUL	L2	LIKE 'John %'	LIKE 'John %'	0xV10NOT	L3	LIKE 'John %'	LIKE 'John %'	0xV10NUL	L4	LIKE 'John %'	LIKE 'John %'
1	0x4a6f686e2020 20202020	10	1	1	0x4a6f686e	4	0	0	0x4a6f686e	4	0	0	0x4a6f686e	4	0	0
2	0x4a6f686e2020 20202020	10	1	1	0x4a6f686e	4	0	0	0x4a6f686e	4	0	0	0x4a6f686e	4	0	0
3	0x4a6f686e2020 20202020	10	1	1	0x4a6f686e	4	0	0	0x4a6f686e	4	0	0	0x4a6f686e	4	0	0
4	0x4a6f686e2020 20202020	10	1	1	0x4a6f686e	4	0	0	0x4a6f686e	4	0	0	0x4a6f686e	4	0	0

Figure 7-5. *Results with* SET ANSI_PADDING OFF.

By default (that is, without enabling *SET ANSI_PADDING ON*), SQL Server trims trailing blanks for variable-length columns. Recall that a *char* column that allows NULL is internally a variable-length column, so *c10nul* is a variable-length column even though it is declared as *char(10)*, not *varchar(10)*. Notice that only column *c10not* has a length of 10. The other three columns are internally identical, with a length of 4 and no padding. For the variable-length columns, even trailing blanks explicitly entered within the quotation marks are trimmed. All the variable-length columns have only the 4 bytes J-O-H-N (4a-6f-68-6e) stored. The true fixed-length column, *c10not,* is automatically padded with six blank spaces (0x20) to fill the entire 10 bytes.

All four columns would match *LIKE 'John%'* (no trailing blanks), but only the fixed-length column *c10not* matches *LIKE 'John %'* (one trailing blank) and *LIKE 'JOHN   %'* (six trailing blanks). The reason for this should be apparent when you realize that those trailing blanks are truncated and are not part of the stored values for the other columns. A column query will get a hit with LIKE and trailing blanks only when the trailing blanks are stored. In this example, only the *c10not* column stores trailing blanks, so that's where the hit occurs.

SQL Server has dealt with trailing blanks in this way for a long time. However, when we began work to pass the NIST (National Institute of Standards and Technology) test suite for ANSI SQL conformance, we realized that this behavior was not consistent with the ANSI specification. The specification requires that you always pad *char* datatypes and do not truncate trailing blanks entered by the user, even for *varchar*. I can argue for either side—both the long-standing SQL Server behavior and the ANSI specification behavior can be desirable, depending on the circumstances. However, if we changed this behavior to conform to ANSI, it would break many deployed SQL Server applications. So, to satisfy both sides, we added the ANSI_PADDING option in version 6.5. If I enable *SET ANSI_PADDING ON* and re-create the table, reinsert the rows, and then issue the same query, I get very different results from those shown in Figure 7-5. Figure 7-6 shows these results.

ROWID	0xC10NOT	L1	LIKE 'John %'	LIKE 'John %'	0xC10NUL	L2	LIKE 'John %'	LIKE 'John %'	0xV10NOT	L3	LIKE 'John %'	LIKE 'John %'	0xV10NUL	L4	LIKE 'John %'	LIKE 'John %'
1	0x4a6f686e202020202020	10	1	1	0x4a6f686e202020202020	10	0	0	0x4a6f686e	4	0	0	0x4a6f686e	4	0	0
2	0x4a6f686e202020202020	10	1	1	0x4a6f686e202020202020	10	0	0	0x4a6f686e202020	7	0	0	0x4a6f686e202020	7	0	0
3	0x4a6f686e202020202020	10	1	1	0x4a6f686e202020202020	10	0	0	0x4a6f686e2020202020	10	0	0	0x4a6f686e2020202020	10	0	0
4	0x4a6f686e202020202020	10	1	1	0x4a6f686e202020202020	10	0	0	0x4a6f686e2020202020	10	0	0	0x4a6f686e2020202020	10	0	0

Figure 7-6. *Results with* SET ANSI_PADDING ON.

By setting *ANSI_PADDING ON,* the *char(10)* columns *c10not* and *c10nul,* whether declared NOT NULL or NULL, are always padded out to 10 characters, regardless of how many trailing blanks were entered. In addition, the variable-length columns *v10not* and *v10nul* contain the number of trailing blanks that were inserted. Trailing blanks are not truncated. Because the variable-length columns now store any trailing blanks that were part of the INSERT (or UPDATE) statement, the columns now get hits in queries with LIKE and trailing blanks if the query finds that number of trailing blanks (or more) in the columns' contents. Notice that no error occurs by inserting a column with seven (instead of six) trailing blanks. The final trailing blank is simply truncated. If you want a warning message to appear in such cases, you can use *SET ANSI_WARNING ON*.

It's important to note that the *SET ANSI_PADDING ON* option applies to a table only if the option was enabled at the time the table was created (or to the column if it was added via ALTER TABLE). Enabling this option for an existing table does nothing. To determine whether a column has ANSI_PADDING set to ON, examine the status field of the *syscolumns* table and do a bitwise AND 20 (decimal). If the bit is ON, you know the column was created with the option enabled. For example:

```
SELECT name, 'Padding On'=CASE WHEN status & 20 <> 0
    THEN 'YES' ELSE 'NO' END
FROM syscolumns WHERE id=OBJECT_ID('checkpad') AND name='v10not'
GO
```

Regardless of how the column was created, SQL Server provides functions that can help you deal effectively with trailing blanks. The RTRIM(*char_expression*) function removes trailing blanks if they exist. You can add trailing blanks to your output by concatenating with the SPACE(*integer_expression*) function. An easier way is to use the CONVERT function to convert to a fixed-length *char( )* of whatever length you want. Then variable-length columns will be returned as fully padded, regardless of the ANSI_PADDING setting and regardless of the columns' actual storage, by converting them to *char(10)* or whatever size you want. The following SELECT statement against the *checkpad* table illustrates this:

```
SELECT CONVERT(VARBINARY(10), CONVERT(char(10), v10nul))
    FROM checkpad
```

Here's the result:

```
0x4a6f686e202020202020
0x4a6f686e202020202020
0x4a6f686e202020202020
0x4a6f686e202020202020
```

BETWEEN

BETWEEN is shorthand for greater-than-or-equal-to AND less-than-or-equal-to. The clause *WHERE C BETWEEN B AND D* is equivalent to writing *WHERE C >= B AND C <= D*. This one's not too tricky, but you should be aware of the importance of the order of the values to be checked when you use BETWEEN.

By thinking of *B, C,* and *D* as increasing values, you can see that *WHERE C BETWEEN D AND B* would not be true because it would evaluate as *WHERE C >= D AND C <= B*. Some early versions of SQL Server let you reverse the order, such that the meaning would be equivalent to *WHERE (C >= B AND C <= D) OR (C >= D AND C <= B)*. However, that behavior was considered to be a bug and it was corrected in 1993.

Aggregate Functions

Aggregate functions (sometimes referred to as *set functions*) allow you to summarize a column of output. SQL Server provides six general aggregate functions that are standard ANSI SQL-92 fare. (Therefore, I won't go into much depth about their general use; instead, I'll focus on some aspects specific to SQL Server.) The table below summarizes SQL Server's aggregate functions.

Aggregate Function	Description
AVG(*expression*)	Returns the average (mean) of all the values, or only the DISTINCT values, in the expression. AVG can be used with numeric[†] columns only. Null values are ignored.
COUNT(*expression*)	Returns the number of non-null values in the expression. When DISTINCT is specified, COUNT finds the number of unique non-null values. COUNT can be used with both numeric and character columns. Null values are ignored.
COUNT(*)	Returns the number of rows. COUNT(*) takes no parameters and cannot be used with DISTINCT. All rows are counted, even those with null values.
MAX(*expression*)	Returns the maximum value in the expression. MAX can be used with numeric, character, and datetime columns but not with *bit* columns. With character columns, MAX finds the highest value in the collating sequence. MAX ignores any null values. DISTINCT is available for ANSI compatibility, but it is not meaningful with MAX.
MIN(*expression*)	Returns the minimum value in the expression. MIN can be used with numeric, character, and datetime columns, but not with *bit* columns. With character columns, MIN finds the value that is lowest in the sort sequence. MIN ignores any null values. DISTINCT is available for ANSI compatibility, but it is not meaningful with MIN.
SUM(*expression*)	Returns the sum of all the values, or only the DISTINCT values, in the expression. SUM can be used with numeric columns only. Null values are ignored.

[†] Numeric columns as used here refer to *decimal, float, int, money, numeric, real, smallint, smallmoney,* and *tinyint* datatypes.

Consider the table *automobile_sales_detail* below. I'll use this table to demonstrate how aggregate functions make it simple to find the answers to complex questions.

rowid	model	year	color	units_sold
1	Chevy	1990	Red	5
2	Chevy	1990	White	87
3	Chevy	1990	Blue	62
4	Chevy	1991	Red	54
5	Chevy	1991	White	95
6	Chevy	1991	Blue	49
7	Chevy	1992	Red	31
8	Chevy	1992	White	54
9	Chevy	1992	Blue	71
10	Ford	1990	Red	64
11	Ford	1990	White	62
12	Ford	1990	Blue	63
13	Ford	1991	Red	52
14	Ford	1991	White	9
15	Ford	1991	Blue	55
16	Ford	1992	Red	27
17	Ford	1992	White	62
18	Ford	1992	Blue	39

You can increase the power of aggregate functions by allowing them to be grouped and by allowing the groups to have criteria established for inclusion via the HAVING clause. The following queries provide some examples:

EXAMPLE 1

Show me the oldest and newest model years for sale, and show me the average sales of all the entries in the table.

```
SELECT 'Oldest'=MIN(year), 'Newest'=MAX(year),
    'Avg Sales'=AVG(units_sold)
FROM automobile_sales_detail
```

Here's the output:

Oldest	Newest	Avg Sales
1990	1992	52

EXAMPLE 2

Do the Example 1 query, but show me the values for autos that are Chevys only.

```
SELECT 'Oldest'=MIN(year), 'Newest'=MAX(year),
    'Avg Sales'=AVG(units_sold)
FROM automobile_sales_detail
WHERE model='Chevy'
```

And the result:

```
Oldest    Newest    Avg Sales
------    ------    ---------
1990      1992      56
```

EXAMPLE 3

Show me the same values shown in Example 1, but group them based on the model and color of the cars.

```
SELECT model, color, 'Oldest'=MIN(year), 'Newest'=MAX(year),
    'Avg Sales'=AVG(units_sold)
FROM automobile_sales_detail
GROUP BY model, color
ORDER BY model, color
```

Here's the output:

```
model    color    Oldest    Newest    Avg Sales
-----    -----    ------    ------    ---------
Chevy    Blue     1990      1992      60
Chevy    Red      1990      1992      30
Chevy    White    1990      1992      78
Ford     Blue     1990      1992      52
Ford     Red      1990      1992      47
Ford     White    1990      1992      44
```

EXAMPLE 4

Show me the same values for only those model-year rows with average sales of 65 or less. Also, although I'd like the output in the same column order, I would like it instead ordered and grouped first by color and then by model.

```
SELECT model, color, 'Oldest'=MIN(year), 'Newest'=MAX(year),
    'Avg Sales'=AVG(units_sold)
FROM automobile_sales_detail
GROUP BY color, model HAVING AVG(units_sold) <= 65
ORDER BY color, model
```

Here's the output:

```
model    color   Oldest   Newest   Avg Sales
-----    -----   ------   ------   ---------
Chevy    Blue    1990     1992     60
Ford     Blue    1990     1992     52
Chevy    Red     1990     1992     30
Ford     Red     1990     1992     47
Ford     White   1990     1992     44
```

More Information...

It's important to note that I include an ORDER BY clause in these queries, even though I specify the criteria of the ORDER BY to be the same criteria that is used in the GROUP BY clause. With SQL Server 6.5 and earlier releases, doing this does not change the order of the results. A sort strategy is used to execute the GROUP BY, so even if I omit the ORDER BY, I would get the same results. If a future release were to add a new and better strategy for dealing with GROUP BY, the results could be correctly returned in the exact opposite order (the same as if I had specified ORDER BY DESCENDING). If the order truly doesn't matter, you can omit the ORDER BY clause.

I recommend that you *never* depend on the default ordering that a query might produce if you do not have an ORDER BY clause. Even though you might be able to predict the order today, without an ORDER BY, ordering is simply a "side effect" of the access methods and query execution strategies currently used; those will inevitably change in future releases. *If order is important to you, use ORDER BY.* Even if the order you choose would have been guaranteed anyway, the SQL Server optimizer recognizes that and does not perform a redundant sort.

An alternative to using COUNT(∗)

You can use COUNT(∗) to find the count of all the rows in the table, but there is a considerably faster way. The *rows* column in the *sysindexes* table keeps the current rowcount dynamically for the clustered index (if one exists, indid = 1). If no clustered index exits, *sysindexes* keeps the count for the table (indid = 0). A quicker query than using COUNT(∗) to find the count of all rows in the table looks something like this:

```
SELECT rows
    FROM sysindexes
    WHERE id=OBJECT_ID ("authors")
    AND indid < 2
```

This works only for base tables, not views, and it works only if you apply no selection criteria via a WHERE clause. If you want to respond to a query such as "Show me the count of all rows for which the author lives in California," you'd still need to use COUNT(∗).

Aggregate functions and NULLs

As usual, you must understand the effect of using NULLs to use them appropriately with aggregate functions. Unfortunately, these effects are not necessarily intuitive or even consistent. Because NULL is considered Unknown, I could certainly argue that using SUM(), MAX(), MIN(), or AVG() on a table containing one or more NULL values should also produce NULL. Obviously, if I have three employees and I don't know the salaries of two of them, it is totally inaccurate to state that the SUM() of the salaries for the three employees is equal to the one known salary. Yet this is exactly how SUM(), MIN(), MAX(), AVG(), and COUNT() work (but not COUNT(*)). Implicitly, these functions seem to tack on the criterion of "for only those values that are not null." This is likely how you'll want these operations to work most of the time, and pragmatically, it's good that they work this way because they're simpler to use for common cases. But if you don't understand exactly how these functions will affect your code, you might introduce some bugs. For example, if you were to divide SUM() by the result of COUNT(*) as a way to compute the mean value, the result would probably not be what you intended—SUM() disregards the NULL values, but COUNT(*) counts those rows.

I've suggested a few times that the use of default or dummy values can be a good alternative to using NULL. But I've also tried to make clear that although these alternatives solve some issues, they introduce other problems. You must account for aggregates, and you might want to get back to exactly the semantics that aggregates such as SUM() use with defaults, ignoring the default or dummy values. Aggregating on only one column is pretty straightforward, and your WHERE clause could simply exclude those values you want to disregard. But if you are aggregating on multiple columns, eliminating rows in the WHERE clause might be a poor solution.

For example, suppose that in my *employee* table I have both an *emp_age* column and a *emp_salary* column. To avoid using NULL, I use 0.00 when I don't know the actual value. I want one query to do aggregations of each column. Yet I don't want to disregard a row's value for *emp_age* if I don't have an actual value for *emp_salary,* or vice versa.

Here's my *employee* table:

```
emp_id    emp_name    emp_age    emp_salary
------    --------    -------    ----------
1         Smith       34         26000.00
2         Doe         30         35000.00
3         Jones       45         0.00
4         Clark       0          65000.00
5         Kent        63         0.00
```

Now suppose that I want to write a simple query to get the count of all employees, the average and lowest salaries, and the average and lowest ages. Here's my first simplistic query:

```
SELECT
'Num Employees'=COUNT(*),
'Avg Salary'=AVG(emp_salary),
'Low Salary'=MIN(emp_salary),
'Avg Age'=AVG(emp_age),
'Youngest'=MIN(emp_age)
FROM employee
```

Here's the result:

Num Employees	Avg Salary	Low Salary	Avg Age	Youngest
5	25,200.00	0.00	34	0

Obviously, this query does not correctly answer my question, because the dummy values of 0 have distorted the results for the AVG() and MIN() columns. So I decide to exclude those rows by stating in the WHERE clause that the salary not be the default value:

```
SELECT
'Num Employees'=COUNT(*),
'Avg Salary'=AVG(emp_salary),
'Low Salary'=MIN(emp_salary),
'Avg Age'=AVG(emp_age),
'Youngest'=MIN(emp_age)
FROM employee
WHERE emp_salary > 0 AND emp_age > 0
```

Here's what I get:

Num Employees	Avg Salary	Low Salary	Avg Age	Youngest
2	30,500.00	26,000.00	32	30

This query is marginally better because at least the average salary is no longer lower than any actually known salary. The values are based on only the first two employees, Smith and Doe—I have *five* employees, not just *two* as this result claims. Two other employees, Jones and Kent, are significantly older than the two who were used to compute the average age. And had Clark's salary been considered, the average salary would be much higher. I am seemingly stuck and cannot write a single query to answer my question; I might have to write separate queries to get the count, the salary info, and the age information. Fortunately, the NULLIF() function comes to the rescue. It is one of many handy functions in

Transact-SQL. NULLIF() takes two expressions, NULLIF(*expression1, expression2*), and returns NULL if the two expressions are equivalent and *expression1* if they are not equivalent. The NULLIF() function is roughly the mirror image of another function, ISNULL(), which produces a value if a NULL is encountered (discussed earlier in this chapter). The NULLIF() function is actually a special-purpose shorthand of the ANSI SQL-92 CASE expression (which I'll discuss later in this chapter). Using NULLIF() is equivalent to the following:

```
CASE
    WHEN expression1=expression2 THEN NULL
    ELSE expression1
END
```

Hence, NULLIF(*emp_salary, 0)* produces NULL for those rows in which the salary equals 0. By converting the 0 values to NULL, I can use the aggregate functions just as I'd use them with NULL so that SUM() and MIN() will disregard the NULL entries.

```
SELECT
'Num Employees'=COUNT(*),
'Avg Salary'=AVG(NULLIF(emp_salary, 0)),
'Low Salary'=MIN(NULLIF(emp_salary, 0)),
'Avg Age'=AVG(NULLIF(emp_age, 0)),
'Youngest'=MIN(NULLIF(emp_age, 0))
FROM employee
```

Here is the more accurate result:

```
Num Employees    Avg Salary    Low Salary    Avg Age    Youngest
-------------    ----------    ----------    -------    --------
5                42,000.00     26,000.00     43         30
```

Finally! This is exactly what I wanted, and all five employees are represented. Of the three whose salaries I know, the average salary is $42,000.00 and the low salary is $26,000.00. Of the four whose ages I know, the average age is 43 and the youngest is 30.

Datacube—Using Aggregate Results for Many Looks at Data

The previous aggregate examples in this chapter, all using standard SQL-92 syntax, show that by formulating a specific query on the sample table with one of the aggregate functions, I can answer almost any question regarding aggregate sales for some combination of model, year, and color of car. However, answering any of these questions requires a separate, specific query. It is, of course, common to look at data and keep formulating and posing new and different questions. Such questions are the hallmark of data mining, decision-support systems (DSS), online analytic processing (OLAP), or whatever name is being used these days for this age-old need to examine data. To address this inherent weakness in standard SQL, several front-end tools have been created that maintain a set of data that allows changes in aggregation to be easily queried, avoiding the need to sweep through data for every new aggregation request. But such operations are better performed by the database engine, which can better optimize the queries. DSS tools can still add a lot of value, and they make it easy to "slice and dice" the values pertaining to any "cut" of the data groupings. But even these tools can perform better with help from the database engine.

SQL Server 6.5 introduced two new extensions to GROUP BY—CUBE and ROLLUP—that allow SQL Server to optionally generate all the aggregate groupings in a single query.

Some History...

The motivation for inventing CUBE came from a paper written by Jim Gray, and others, soon after Jim joined Microsoft as a researcher. After reading his paper, a few of us got excited about adding the feature to our 6.5 release, and Don Reichart did a masterful job of implementing this important feature in record time. Subsequently, this feature has been submitted to the ANSI SQL committee as a proposed addition to the standard. For more details about CUBE, you can read the paper that Jim Gray submitted to the ACM on the accompanying CD-ROM.

CUBE

CUBE explodes data to produce a result set containing a superset of groups, with a cross tabulation of every column to the value of every other column, as well as a special super-aggregate value that can be thought of as meaning ALL VALUES. Here's the CUBE for the 18 rows of my *automobile_sales_detail* table. Notice that these 18 rows generate 48 rows in the datacube.

units	model	year	color
62	Chevy	1990	Blue
5	Chevy	1990	Red
87	Chevy	1990	White
154	Chevy	1990	ALL
49	Chevy	1991	Blue
54	Chevy	1991	Red
95	Chevy	1991	White
198	Chevy	1991	ALL
71	Chevy	1992	Blue
31	Chevy	1992	Red

54	Chevy	1992	White
156	Chevy	1992	ALL
508	Chevy	ALL	ALL
63	Ford	1990	Blue
64	Ford	1990	Red
62	Ford	1990	White
189	Ford	1990	ALL
55	Ford	1991	Blue
52	Ford	1991	Red
9	Ford	1991	White
116	Ford	1991	ALL
39	Ford	1992	Blue
27	Ford	1992	Red
62	Ford	1992	White
128	Ford	1992	ALL
433	Ford	ALL	ALL
941	ALL	ALL	ALL
125	ALL	1990	Blue
69	ALL	1990	Red
149	ALL	1990	White
343	ALL	1990	ALL
104	ALL	1991	Blue
106	ALL	1991	Red
104	ALL	1991	White
314	ALL	1991	ALL
110	ALL	1992	Blue
58	ALL	1992	Red
116	ALL	1992	White
284	ALL	1992	ALL
182	Chevy	ALL	Blue
157	Ford	ALL	Blue
339	ALL	ALL	Blue
90	Chevy	ALL	Red
143	Ford	ALL	Red
233	ALL	ALL	Red
236	Chevy	ALL	White
133	Ford	ALL	White
369	ALL	ALL	White

The results of the CUBE make it simple to answer just about any sales aggregation question that I can think of. If I want to get sales information for all 1992 automobiles, regardless of model or color, I can find the corresponding row and see that 284 cars were sold. To find all Chevy sales for all years and colors, it is equally easy to find 508. Such a result set might be used "as is" for a reference chart or in coordination with an OLAP tool.

The number of rows exploded by a CUBE operation can be surprisingly large. In the example above, 18 rows generated 48 rows of output. However, the result of a CUBE operation will not necessarily produce more rows of output than what appears in the underlying data. The number of rows generated will depend on the number of attributes being grouped and on the actual combinations in your data. Without detailed knowledge of your data, the number of rows produced by a CUBE operation cannot be predicted. However, the upper bound can be easily predicted. The upper bound will be equal to the cross product of the *(number of distinct values + 1)* value for each attribute. The addition of 1 is for the case of "ALL." The *automobile_sales_detail* example has three attributes: model, year, and color.

```
Upper Bound of number of rows
= (Number of models+1) * (Number of Years+1) * (Number of Colors+1)
= (2+1) * (3+1) * (3+1)
= 48
```

This example should make it clear that the upper bound of the number of rows depends not on the number of data rows but rather on the number of attributes being grouped and the number of distinct values for each attribute. For example, if my table had 18 million instead of 18 data rows but still had no more than two models, three years, and three colors (there is no stated UNIQUE or PRIMARY KEY constraint on the model, year, or color fields), the CUBE operation will again return only 48 rows.

The actual number of rows may be considerably less than the upper bound, however. This is because CUBE does not try to force a 0 or a NULL aggregate for combinations for which there are no values. In the carefully constructed example above, there is complete coverage across every attribute. Each of the two models has an entry for each of the three years and for each of the three colors. But suppose that no sales data appears for the 1990 Chevy and that no red Fords exist for any year. The raw data would look like this:

```
rowid   model   year   color   units_sold
-----   -----   ----   -----   ----------
1       Chevy   1991   Red     54
2       Chevy   1991   White   95
3       Chevy   1991   Blue    49
4       Chevy   1992   Red     31
5       Chevy   1992   White   54
6       Chevy   1992   Blue    71
7       Ford    1990   White   62
8       Ford    1990   Blue    63
9       Ford    1991   White   9
10      Ford    1991   Blue    55
11      Ford    1992   White   62
12      Ford    1992   Blue    39
```

Here's the new cube:

```
units    model    year    color
-----    -----    ----    -----
49       Chevy    1991    Blue
54       Chevy    1991    Red
95       Chevy    1991    White
198      Chevy    1991    ALL
71       Chevy    1992    Blue
31       Chevy    1992    Red
54       Chevy    1992    White
156      Chevy    1992    ALL
354      Chevy    ALL     ALL
63       Ford     1990    Blue
62       Ford     1990    White
125      Ford     1990    ALL
55       Ford     1991    Blue
9        Ford     1991    White
64       Ford     1991    ALL
39       Ford     1992    Blue
62       Ford     1992    White
101      Ford     1992    ALL
290      Ford     ALL     ALL
644      ALL      ALL     ALL
63       ALL      1990    Blue
62       ALL      1990    White
125      ALL      1990    ALL
104      ALL      1991    Blue
54       ALL      1991    Red
104      ALL      1991    White
262      ALL      1991    ALL
110      ALL      1992    Blue
31       ALL      1992    Red
116      ALL      1992    White
257      ALL      1992    ALL
120      Chevy    ALL     Blue
157      Ford     ALL     Blue
277      ALL      ALL     Blue
85       Chevy    ALL     Red
85       ALL      ALL     Red
149      Chevy    ALL     White
133      Ford     ALL     White
282      ALL      ALL     White
```

We now have 12 data rows but still three attributes and the same number of distinct values for each attribute. But instead of 48 rows for the result of the CUBE, the result contains only 39 rows because some combinations of attributes have no data. For example, there is no row for all models of red cars for 1990 because no data met that specific criterion.

If your use of CUBE would benefit from always having the full cube populated, you might want to add a placeholder row with dummy values for the columns being aggregated so that every combination will be represented. Or you could run a query that produces the cross product of all combinations not existing, and then UNION the result with the cube. (I'll show an example of this later when I discuss UNION.) Be careful: as the number of attributes and the cardinality between the values increases, the cube can quickly get very large. The full cube based on five attributes, each having 50 distinct values, with at least one matching entry for each combination, generates $(50 + 1)^5$, or 345,025,251, rows in the cube! If there is nowhere near full coverage of all these combinations, the cube might otherwise have generated "only" a few thousand rows instead of more than 345 million!

So far, I've been careful not to show the actual query used to produce the cube because I wanted to make the basic concepts clear before yet again dealing with issues of NULL. A simple GROUP BY *column* WITH CUBE will not by default produce super-aggregate rows having a value that outputs as "ALL." The ALL value is really a nonvalue, like NULL (gasp!). In fact, the ALL column is represented by (gulp!) a special kind of NULL, referred to as a *grouping NULL*.

While implementing this new feature, we wrestled with whether to use NULL or whether to invent a new marker value similar in some ways to NULL but clearly still separate from data. It wasn't an easy decision. A new data value would be more theoretically pure. The meaning of "ALL" is really different from "unknown" or "missing"—that is, it is different from NULL. However, had we introduced another special-meaning marker, it would require the same level of complexity required to work with as NULL—with special operators like "IS ALL"—and the truth tables would become all the more difficult to work with in expressions such as =, <, IN, and so on. And we did have some precedents that we wanted to avoid. In many ways, the longtime SQL Server feature COMPUTE BY is quite similar to CUBE. (Actually, it is more similar to the derivative of CUBE, ROLLUP, which I will discuss shortly.) COMPUTE BY, although useful, is a rarely used feature, largely because COMPUTE BY does not generate a standard row format for the result set but rather returns a special "alternate result set." Applications must go to significant lengths to deal with this special purpose result. Most didn't go the distance; hence most applications don't support COMPUTE BY. Because of this, we chose to overload NULL, which applications must already deal with to some extent. (This presents a few wrinkles of its own, which I'll come back to.)

Following is the basic query and a discussion of how I produced "ALL" in the results:

```
SELECT SUM(units_sold), model, year, color
FROM automobile_sales_detail
GROUP BY model, year, color WITH CUBE
```

Here's the output:

```
            model         year          color
- - - - - - - - - -   - - - - - - - - -   - - - - - - - - -   - - - - - - - - - -
62          Chevy         1990          Blue
5           Chevy         1990          Red
87          Chevy         1990          White
154         Chevy         1990          (null)
49          Chevy         1991          Blue
54          Chevy         1991          Red
95          Chevy         1991          White
198         Chevy         1991          (null)
71          Chevy         1992          Blue
31          Chevy         1992          Red
54          Chevy         1992          White
156         Chevy         1992          (null)
508         Chevy         (null)        (null)
63          Ford          1990          Blue
64          Ford          1990          Red
62          Ford          1990          White
189         Ford          1990          (null)
55          Ford          1991          Blue
52          Ford          1991          Red
9           Ford          1991          White
116         Ford          1991          (null)
39          Ford          1992          Blue
27          Ford          1992          Red
62          Ford          1992          White
128         Ford          1992          (null)
433         Ford          (null)        (null)
941         (null)        (null)        (null)
125         (null)        1990          Blue
69          (null)        1990          Red
149         (null)        1990          White
343         (null)        1990          (null)
104         (null)        1991          Blue
106         (null)        1991          Red
104         (null)        1991          White
314         (null)        1991          (null)
110         (null)        1992          Blue
58          (null)        1992          Red
116         (null)        1992          White
284         (null)        1992          (null)
182         Chevy         (null)        Blue
157         Ford          (null)        Blue
339         (null)        (null)        Blue
90          Chevy         (null)        Red
143         Ford          (null)        Red
```

```
233        (null)     (null)     Red
236        Chevy      (null)     White
133        Ford       (null)     White
369        (null)     (null)     White
```

Notice that rather than ALL, which I had constructed earlier to be a placeholder, the super-aggregate values are represented by NULL—here formatted as *(null)* as in ISQL/w, although this is application-specific. The data in this case had no NULL values, so there was no problem in sorting out NULL meaning "unknown" from NULL meaning "ALL."

If your data uses some NULL values, however, you will not be so lucky. Suppose that I add one row of data that has NULL for both model and year (assuming these columns allow NULL):

```
INSERT automobile_sales_detail values (NULL,NULL,'White',10)
```

The last row in the CUBE above (having 369 as total sales for all white cars) would be seemingly indistinguishable from this actual data row. Fortunately, the GROUPING() function comes to the rescue to differentiate the two. It returns 1 (TRUE) if the element is an ALL value and 0 (FALSE) otherwise. Here is a modified query to show the CUBE with the inclusion of the row having NULL values and with the addition of the GROUPING() function to designate ALL values:

```
SELECT 'Units Sold'=SUM(units_sold),
model, 'ALL Models'=GROUPING(model),
year, 'ALL Years'=GROUPING(year),
color, 'ALL Colors'=GROUPING(color)
FROM automobile_sales_detail
GROUP BY model, year, color WITH CUBE
```

Here is the result set:

Units Sold	model	ALL Models	year	ALL Years	color	ALL Colors
10	(null)	0	(null)	0	White	0
10	(null)	0	(null)	0	(null)	1
10	(null)	0	(null)	1	(null)	1
62	Chevy	0	1990	0	Blue	0
5	Chevy	0	1990	0	Red	0
87	Chevy	0	1990	0	White	0
154	Chevy	0	1990	0	(null)	1
49	Chevy	0	1991	0	Blue	0
54	Chevy	0	1991	0	Red	0
95	Chevy	0	1991	0	White	0

198	Chevy	0	1991	0	(null)	1
71	Chevy	0	1992	0	Blue	0
31	Chevy	0	1992	0	Red	0
54	Chevy	0	1992	0	White	0
156	Chevy	0	1992	0	(null)	1
508	Chevy	0	(null)	1	(null)	1
63	Ford	0	1990	0	Blue	0
64	Ford	0	1990	0	Red	0
62	Ford	0	1990	0	White	0
189	Ford	0	1990	0	(null)	1
55	Ford	0	1991	0	Blue	0
52	Ford	0	1991	0	Red	0
9	Ford	0	1991	0	White	0
116	Ford	0	1991	0	(null)	1
39	Ford	0	1992	0	Blue	0
27	Ford	0	1992	0	Red	0
62	Ford	0	1992	0	White	0
128	Ford	0	1992	0	(null)	1
433	Ford	0	(null)	1	(null)	1
951	(null)	1	(null)	1	(null)	1
10	(null)	1	(null)	0	White	0
10	(null)	1	(null)	0	(null)	1
125	(null)	1	1990	0	Blue	0
69	(null)	1	1990	0	Red	0
149	(null)	1	1990	0	White	0
343	(null)	1	1990	0	(null)	1
104	(null)	1	1991	0	Blue	0
106	(null)	1	1991	0	Red	0
104	(null)	1	1991	0	White	0
314	(null)	1	1991	0	(null)	1
110	(null)	1	1992	0	Blue	0
58	(null)	1	1992	0	Red	0
116	(null)	1	1992	0	White	0
284	(null)	1	1992	0	(null)	1
182	Chevy	0	(null)	1	Blue	0
157	Ford	0	(null)	1	Blue	0
339	(null)	1	(null)	1	Blue	0
90	Chevy	0	(null)	1	Red	0
143	Ford	0	(null)	1	Red	0
233	(null)	1	(null)	1	Red	0
10	(null)	0	(null)	1	White	0
236	Chevy	0	(null)	1	White	0
133	Ford	0	(null)	1	White	0
379	(null)	1	(null)	1	White	0

The GROUPING() function makes it possible to differentiate between a GROUPING NULL value and a NULL value, but it hardly makes it as intuitive to read and analyze as using ALL. I prefer to write a view that outputs a grouping value as ALL for me, and I'd be more comfortable turning loose my programmers and power users on such a view rather than relying on them to understand GROUPING NULL versus NULL value:

```
CREATE VIEW auto_cube (units, model, year, color) AS
SELECT SUM(units_sold),
CASE    WHEN (GROUPING(model)=1) THEN 'ALL'
    ELSE ISNULL(model, '????')
    END,
CASE    WHEN (GROUPING(year)=1) THEN 'ALL'
    ELSE ISNULL(CONVERT(char(6), year), '????')
    END,
CASE    WHEN (GROUPING(color)=1) THEN 'ALL'
    ELSE ISNULL(color, '????')
    END
FROM automobile_sales_detail
GROUP BY model,year,color WITH CUBE
```

Having constructed this view, it is then simple for someone to work with, to understand the difference between grouping values (represented by *'ALL'*) and NULL data values (represented by *'????'*), and to easily further refine the query if necessary to look for certain data only. This example shows a simple query:

```
SELECT * FROM auto_cube
```

And the results:

```
units   model   year   color
-----   -----   ----   -----
10      ????    ????   White
10      ????    ????   ALL
10      ????    ALL    ALL
62      Chevy   1990   Blue
5       Chevy   1990   Red
87      Chevy   1990   White
154     Chevy   1990   ALL
49      Chevy   1991   Blue
54      Chevy   1991   Red
95      Chevy   1991   White
198     Chevy   1991   ALL
71      Chevy   1992   Blue
31      Chevy   1992   Red
54      Chevy   1992   White
```

156	Chevy	1992	ALL
508	Chevy	ALL	ALL
63	Ford	1990	Blue
64	Ford	1990	Red
62	Ford	1990	White
189	Ford	1990	ALL
55	Ford	1991	Blue
52	Ford	1991	Red
9	Ford	1991	White
116	Ford	1991	ALL
39	Ford	1992	Blue
27	Ford	1992	Red
62	Ford	1992	White
128	Ford	1992	ALL
433	Ford	ALL	ALL
951	ALL	ALL	ALL
10	ALL	????	White
10	ALL	????	ALL
125	ALL	1990	Blue
69	ALL	1990	Red
149	ALL	1990	White
343	ALL	1990	ALL
104	ALL	1991	Blue
106	ALL	1991	Red
104	ALL	1991	White
314	ALL	1991	ALL
110	ALL	1992	Blue
58	ALL	1992	Red
116	ALL	1992	White
284	ALL	1992	ALL
182	Chevy	ALL	Blue
157	Ford	ALL	Blue
339	ALL	ALL	Blue
90	Chevy	ALL	Red
143	Ford	ALL	Red
233	ALL	ALL	Red
10	????	ALL	White
236	Chevy	ALL	White
133	Ford	ALL	White
379	ALL	ALL	White

Working with this view is easy. Grouping values appear as *ALL*. Actual NULL values are represented by question marks, appropriate since they are unknown.

I can easily further select from the view to drill into any dimension of the cube that I like. For example, to find all Chevy sales, regardless of the year and color:

```
SELECT * FROM auto_cube
WHERE model='Chevy' AND year='ALL' AND color='ALL'
```

Here are my results:

```
units   model   year   color
-----   -----   ----   -----
508     Chevy   ALL    ALL
```

In this view, I elected to output everything as character data, and thus ALL was a reasonable choice. If it had been important to keep the data numeric, I would have chosen some special value, such as −999999.

ROLLUP

If you are looking for a hierarchy or a "drill-down" report (what we called a "control-break" report when I programmed in COBOL long ago), CUBE can be overkill. It generates many more result rows than you want, and it obscures the information you're looking for with more data. (Never be confused by thinking that data and information are equivalent.) Using CUBE, you will get all permutations, including super-aggregates, for all attributes for which corresponding data exists. SQL Server 6.5 provides the ROLLUP operator to extract statistics and summary information from result sets. ROLLUP returns only the values for a hierarchy of the attributes you specify.

This is best explained with an example. If I change the CUBE query to use ROLLUP instead, the results are more compact and easier to interpret when I drill into progressive levels of details for sales by model. However, with ROLLUP, I do not get one-stop shopping to answer a question like "How many white cars of any model were sold?"

```
SELECT 'units sold'=SUM(units_sold),
'model'=CASE WHEN (GROUPING(model)=1) THEN 'ALL'
    ELSE ISNULL(model, '????')
    END,
'year'=CASE WHEN (GROUPING(year)=1) THEN 'ALL'
    ELSE ISNULL(CONVERT(char(6), year), '????')
    END,
'color'=CASE WHEN (GROUPING(color)=1) THEN 'ALL'
    ELSE ISNULL(color, '????')
    END
FROM automobile_sales_detail
GROUP BY model, year, color WITH ROLLUP
```

My results:

```
units sold    model    year    color
----------    -----    ----    -----
10            ????     ????    White
10            ????     ????    ALL
10            ????     ALL     ALL
62            Chevy    1990    Blue
5             Chevy    1990    Red
87            Chevy    1990    White
154           Chevy    1990    ALL
49            Chevy    1991    Blue
54            Chevy    1991    Red
95            Chevy    1991    White
198           Chevy    1991    ALL
71            Chevy    1992    Blue
31            Chevy    1992    Red
54            Chevy    1992    White
156           Chevy    1992    ALL
508           Chevy    ALL     ALL
63            Ford     1990    Blue
64            Ford     1990    Red
62            Ford     1990    White
189           Ford     1990    ALL
55            Ford     1991    Blue
52            Ford     1991    Red
9             Ford     1991    White
116           Ford     1991    ALL
39            Ford     1992    Blue
27            Ford     1992    Red
62            Ford     1992    White
128           Ford     1992    ALL
433           Ford     ALL     ALL
951           ALL      ALL     ALL
```

ROLLUP is similar to COMPUTE BY, which has nice functionality. However, COMPUTE BY is not as "relational" as ROLLUP—it does not simply produce results as an ordinary table of values. COMPUTE BY always requires special application programming to deal with its "alternate" result sets, which are essentially equivalent to super-aggregates. Recall that CUBE and ROLLUP simply use ordinary result sets and that the super-aggregates are represented as a grouping NULL. Generally speaking, you should consider CUBE and ROLLUP more preferable than COMPUTE BY because they are easier to fit into applications; they can be used with views, CASE, subselects, and column aliases; and they are internally better optimized. But for completeness, here is an example using COMPUTE BY as functionally equivalent to ROLLUP:

```
SELECT units_sold, model, year, color
FROM automobile_sales_detail
ORDER BY model, year, color
COMPUTE SUM(units_sold) BY model, year
COMPUTE SUM(units_sold) BY model
COMPUTE SUM(units_sold)
```

And the results:

```
units_sold      model      year      color
----------      -----      ----      -----
10              NULL       NULL      White

Sum
==========
10
Sum
==========
10

units_sold      model      year      color
----------      -----      ----      -----
62              Chevy      1990      Blue
5               Chevy      1990      Red
87              Chevy      1990      White

Sum
==========
154

units_sold      model      year      color
----------      -----      ----      -----
49              Chevy      1991      Blue
54              Chevy      1991      Red
95              Chevy      1991      White

Sum
==========
198

units_sold      model      year      color
----------      -----      ----      -----
71              Chevy      1992      Blue
31              Chevy      1992      Red
54              Chevy      1992      White
```

```
sum
===========
156
sum
===========
508
```

units_sold	model	year	color
63	Ford	1990	Blue
64	Ford	1990	Red
62	Ford	1990	White

```
sum
===========
189
```

units_sold	model	year	color
55	Ford	1991	Blue
52	Ford	1991	Red
9	Ford	1991	White

```
sum
===========
116
```

units_sold	model	year	color
39	Ford	1992	Blue
27	Ford	1992	Red
62	Ford	1992	White

```
sum
===========
128
sum
===========
433
sum
===========
951
```

UNION

UNION is a conceptually easy topic. Given the same number of columns and compatible datatypes, UNION combines two or more result sets into a single result set. By default, duplicate rows are eliminated, although you can include them by specifying UNION ALL. The datatypes of the result sets to be combined with UNION do not need to be identical, but they must be able to be *implicitly* converted. If this is not the case, you can *explicitly* convert them to identical or compatible types using the handy CONVERT( ) function.

Here is an example that shows UNION at its most basic level. It also demonstrates that a SELECT statement in SQL Server doesn't need to be from a table or a view but can be a constant or a variable:

```
SELECT col1=2, col2=1
UNION
SELECT xxx=1, yyy=2
UNION
SELECT CONVERT(int, '3'), CONVERT(tinyint, '0')
UNION
SELECT TAN(0), 3*1000/10/100  -- Tangent of 0 is 0.
                              -- So this row produces 0.0, 3
UNION
SELECT 1, 2
```

The output:

```
col1    col2
----    ----
0.0     3
1.0     2
2.0     1
3.0     0
```

Note that by default, in version 6.5 the rows are ordered based on the first and, if necessary, subsequent columns. This order occurs because UNION eliminates duplicate rows using a sorting strategy. The ordering exhibited is simply a by-product of the sorting to eliminate duplicates. However, if order is important to you, you should explicitly use ORDER BY, even if it seems redundant.

In the example above, the datatypes are compatible but not identical. Because TAN(0) returns a numeric datatype, *col1* is cast to numeric (since using an integer would lose precision) and the other values are implicitly converted. The character *3* could not be implicitly converted to decimal, so the CONVERT( ) function was used. In addition, the one duplicate row (1.0, 2) is eliminated, and the columns take their monikers from the first result set.

NOTE For illustration, I explicitly converted the character to an *int*, which is then implicitly converted to *numeric*. In reality, if I had to explicitly convert, I would directly convert the character to *numeric* and avoid the second conversion.

If UNION ALL were used instead of UNION, the duplicate row would not be eliminated and no automatic sorting of the results would occur. If there is no need to eliminate duplicates, there is no need for the query processor to sort them. The following query illustrates the use of UNION ALL and uses ORDER BY to present the results in approximately the inverse of the preceding example. It also converts the result of the tangent operation to a *tinyint* so that *col1* is then implicitly converted to an *int*.

```
SELECT col1=2, col2=1
UNION ALL
SELECT xxx=1, yyy=2
UNION ALL
SELECT CONVERT(int, '3'), CONVERT(tinyint, '0')
UNION ALL
SELECT CONVERT(smallint, TAN(0)), 3*1000/10/100
-- Tangent of 0 is 0. So this row produces 0.0, 3
UNION ALL
SELECT 1, 2
ORDER BY col2
```

Here's the output:

```
col1    col2
----    ----
3       0
2       1
1       2
1       2
0       3
```

Earlier in the CUBE section, I pointed out that the operation would not generate missing rows with the value 0. However, you might occasionally want the full cube, with 0 as the SUM() value for missing combinations. I promised then that I would show you an example of how this could be accomplished using UNION. Being a man of my word, here is the example. And here's the key—the table can be cross-joined to itself to produce a 0 row for every combination possible given the non-null data.

```
SELECT DISTINCT units_sold=0, A.model, B.color, C.year
FROM
automobile_sales_detail A
CROSS JOIN
automobile_sales_detail B
CROSS JOIN
automobile_sales_detail C
```

Here's the output:

```
units_sold      model     color     Year
----------      -----     -----     ----
0               Chevy     Blue      1990
0               Chevy     Blue      1991
0               Chevy     Blue      1992
0               Chevy     Red       1990
0               Chevy     Red       1991
0               Chevy     Red       1992
0               Chevy     White     1990
0               Chevy     White     1991
0               Chevy     White     1992
0               Ford      Blue      1990
0               Ford      Blue      1991
0               Ford      Blue      1992
0               Ford      Red       1990
0               Ford      Red       1991
0               Ford      Red       1992
0               Ford      White     1990
0               Ford      White     1991
0               Ford      White     1992
```

The real underlying data is the set of 12 rows shown earlier and shown again here. Recall that six combinations have no value—that is, there are no Chevys for 1990 and no red Fords:

```
model     year     color     units_sold
-----     ----     -----     ----------
Chevy     1991     Red       54
Chevy     1991     White     95
Chevy     1991     Blue      49
Chevy     1992     Red       31
Chevy     1992     White     54
Chevy     1992     Blue      71
Ford      1990     White     62
Ford      1990     Blue      63
```

```
Ford     1991     White     9
Ford     1991     Blue      55
Ford     1992     White     62
Ford     1992     Blue      39
```

Having generated all the dummy rows as such, I can then easily UNION the cross-joined dummy results with the output of the CUBE. But that still would not do because I would get both a real row and a dummy row whenever a real combination exists. SQL Server gives you several good ways to solve this dilemma. You can use NOT EXISTS to produce the dummy rows only for combinations that do not exist. Another approach, and perhaps the most intuitive one, is to make a view of the cross-joined dummy rows and the actual data and then do the CUBE on the view. The 0 values, of course, don't affect the SUM, so this works nicely:

```
CREATE VIEW fullcube
    (
    units_sold,
    model,
    year,
    color
    )
    AS
    (
    SELECT D.units_sold, D.model, D.year, D.color
    FROM automobile_sales_detail D
    UNION ALL
    SELECT DISTINCT 0,
    A.model, C.year, B.color
    FROM
    automobile_sales_detail A
    CROSS JOIN
    automobile_sales_detail B
    CROSS JOIN
    automobile_sales_detail C
    )
```

> **NOTE** You must have installed SQL Server 6.5 Service Pack 2 or later for this code to work.

Having constructed the view, I can then issue my CUBE query against it, just as I did previously against the base table:

```
SELECT units_sold=SUM(units_sold), model, year, color
FROM fullcube
GROUP BY model, year, color WITH CUBE
```

Here's the output:

```
units_sold    model    year    color
----------    -----    ----    -----
0             Chevy    1990    Blue
0             Chevy    1990    Red
0             Chevy    1990    White
0             Chevy    1990    (null)
49            Chevy    1991    Blue
54            Chevy    1991    Red
95            Chevy    1991    White
198           Chevy    1991    (null)
71            Chevy    1992    Blue
31            Chevy    1992    Red
54            Chevy    1992    White
156           Chevy    1992    (null)
354           Chevy    (null)  (null)
63            Ford     1990    Blue
0             Ford     1990    Red
62            Ford     1990    White
125           Ford     1990    (null)
55            Ford     1991    Blue
0             Ford     1991    Red
9             Ford     1991    White
64            Ford     1991    (null)
39            Ford     1992    Blue
0             Ford     1992    Red
62            Ford     1992    White
101           Ford     1992    (null)
290           Ford     (null)  (null)
644           (null)   (null)  (null)
63            (null)   1990    Blue
0             (null)   1990    Red
62            (null)   1990    White
125           (null)   1990    (null)
104           (null)   1991    Blue
54            (null)   1991    Red
104           (null)   1991    White
262           (null)   1991    (null)
110           (null)   1992    Blue
31            (null)   1992    Red
116           (null)   1992    White
257           (null)   1992    (null)
120           Chevy    (null)  Blue
157           Ford     (null)  Blue
277           (null)   (null)  Blue
```

```
85          Chevy      (null)    Red
0           Ford       (null)    Red
85          (null)     (null)    Red
149         Chevy      (null)    White
133         Ford       (null)    White
282         (null)     (null)    White
```

Then I can define yet another view on top to generate the *'ALL'* and *'????'* place-holders. No NULL data exists in this example, so I'll show only the *'ALL'* case:

```
CREATE VIEW auto_cube (units, model, year, color) AS
SELECT SUM(units_sold),
ISNULL(model, 'ALL'), ISNULL(CONVERT(char(4), year), 'ALL'),
ISNULL(color, 'ALL')
FROM fullcube
GROUP BY model, year, color WITH CUBE
```

One advantage of filling out the cube with placeholder rows is that no matter what combination I formulate, I will get an answer. There are no unknowns. Had I not constructed the cube, this query would return no rows found instead of 0:

```
SELECT * FROM auto_cube WHERE model='Chevy' AND color='ALL'
AND year='1990'
```

```
units     model     year         color
-----     -----     ----         -----
0         Chevy     1990         ALL
```

Just for fun, here's the equivalent of the *fullcube* view as a derived table:

```
SELECT units_sold=SUM(T1.units_sold), T1.model, T1.year, T1.color
FROM (
      SELECT D.units_sold, D.model, D.year, D.color
      FROM automobile_sales_detail D
      UNION ALL
      SELECT DISTINCT 0,
      A.model, C.year, B.color
      FROM
      automobile_sales_detail A
      CROSS JOIN
      automobile_sales_detail B
      CROSS JOIN
      automobile_sales_detail C
      )
          AS T1
GROUP BY T1.model, T1.year, T1.color WITH CUBE
GO
```

Having shown you all these somewhat exotic uses of CROSS JOIN and views to fill out the cube, I will admit that if I had wanted the whole cube to be generated, I might have inserted some placeholder rows with a value of 0 in the base table itself (assuming I had access to do so) so that every combination was accounted for in the base table.

SUMMARY

This chapter examined the SELECT statement, the hallmark of the SQL language. Although I attempted to present a fairly well-rounded treatment of SELECT, I focused not on basic queries but rather on more subtle issues and SQL Server–specific capabilities.

I discussed the issues of NULL and three-value logic, since they must always be considered while you are properly formulating queries. In three-value logic, an answer is TRUE, FALSE, or Unknown. If you must work with NULL values but you do not understand three-value logic, you will introduce bugs, so it is imperative to fully understand three-value logic or to structure the database to avoid the use of NULL. You must understand NULL when doing JOIN operations, and I presented issues concerning OUTER JOIN with several examples. Unlike a JOIN based on equality, the JOIN order for an OUTER JOIN is vitally important. I discussed search expressions such as LIKE and the issues of trailing blanks. Aggregate functions were presented, again with a discussion of how NULL must be understood for proper use of these functions. I presented the CUBE and ROLLUP OLAP extensions to the standard GROUP BY for use with aggregate functions with examples, and I gave you some pragmatic tips and techniques for using these capabilities.

Although this chapter is far from a complete treatise on the SQL language in general, or on all of SQL Server's capabilities, I hope it has provided some insight into how facilities and extensions in SQL Server help you solve real-world problems and write better applications.

8

Modifying Data

Introduction

In Chapter 7, we looked at how to query data. In this chapter, I'll discuss inserting, updating, and deleting data in tables. I'll touch on the basic SQL commands for these operations but focus on SQL Server–specific behaviors. This chapter will consider each statement as an independent, atomic operation. The ability to group multiple statements into an all-or-nothing atomic operation (that is, a *transaction*) is presented in Chapter 10, "Batches, Transactions, Stored Procedures, and Triggers." Chapter 6, "Tables," examined various types of constraints. Although using constraints is closely related to any discussion of modifying data to maintain focus, all information and examples about modifying data presented in this chapter are based on the assumption that any constraints on the table are already satisfied.

Basic Modification Operations

SQL has three basic data modification statements: INSERT, UPDATE, and DELETE. In previous chapters, I've already used some of these in examples, without comment, because I've assumed that you are already familiar with them. Here, I'll quickly review the most typical operations. INSERT, UPDATE, and DELETE are referred to as DML (data manipulation language). SELECT is often lumped in as DML, although it doesn't modify anything. (Create operations such as CREATE TABLE are DDL—data definition language—while security operations such as GRANT/REVOKE are DCL—data control language.)

INSERT

INSERT is generally used to add one row to a table. Here's the most common form of INSERT:

```
INSERT [INTO]  {table_name|view_name} [(column_list)]
VALUES value_list
```

In SQL Server, the use of INTO is always optional. ANSI SQL specifies using INTO, however. If you are providing a value for every column in the table and the values appear in the exact order in which the columns were defined, the column list is optional. If you omit a value for one or more columns or if the order of your values differs from the order in which the columns were defined for the table, you must use a named columns list. If you do not provide a value for a particular column, that column must allow NULL or it must have a default declared for it. (You can use the keyword DEFAULT as a placeholder.) NULL can be *explicitly entered* for a column, or NULL can be *implicitly entered* for an omitted column for which no default value exists.

An INSERT statement can be issued to a view, but the row is always added to only one underlying table. (Remember that views do not maintain stored data.) You can insert data into a view, as long as values (or defaults) are provided for all the columns of the underlying table. This implies that the view is based on one table only, although this is not always true—you could have a join to another table that allows all NULL values or has default values declared.

Following are some simple examples of using INSERT statements in a table that is similar to *publishers* in the *pubs* sample database. The CREATE TABLE statement is shown so that you can easily see column order and so that you can see which columns allow NULL and which have defaults declared.

```
CREATE TABLE publishers2
(
    pub_id        int            NOT NULL PRIMARY KEY IDENTITY,
    pub_name      varchar(40)    NULL DEFAULT ('Anonymous'),
    city          varchar(20)    NULL,
    state         char(2)        NULL,
    country       varchar(30)    NOT NULL DEFAULT('USA')
)
GO

INSERT publishers2 VALUES ('AAA Publishing', 'Vancouver', 'BC',
'Canada')

INSERT INTO publishers2 VALUES ('Best Publishing', 'Mexico City',
NULL, 'Mexico')

INSERT INTO publishers2 (pub_name,city,state,country)
VALUES ('Complete Publishing', 'Washington', 'DC', 'United States')

INSERT publishers2 (state,city) VALUES ('WA','Redmond')

INSERT publishers2 VALUES (NULL, NULL, NULL, DEFAULT)

INSERT publishers2 VALUES (DEFAULT, NULL, 'WA', DEFAULT)
```

```
INSERT publishers2 VALUES (NULL, DEFAULT, DEFAULT, DEFAULT)

INSERT publishers2 DEFAULT VALUES
GO
```

The table has these values:

pub_id	pub_name	city	state	country
0001	AAA Publishing	Vancouver	BC	Canada
0002	Best Publishing	Mexico City	NULL	Mexico
0003	Complete Publishing	Washington	DC	United States
0004	Anonymous	Redmond	WA	USA
0005	NULL	NULL	NULL	USA
0006	Anonymous	NULL	WA	USA
0007	NULL	NULL	NULL	USA
0008	Anonymous	NULL	NULL	USA

These INSERT examples are pretty self-explanatory, but you should be careful of the following:

- If a column is declared to allow NULL and it also has a default bound to it, omitting the column entirely from the INSERT statement results in the default value being inserted, not the NULL value. (This is also true if the column is declared NOT NULL.)

- Other than for quick-and-dirty, one-time usage, you're better off providing the column list to explicitly name the columns. Your INSERT statement will still work even if a column is added via ALTER TABLE.

- Had one of the INSERT statements in this example failed, the others would have continued and succeeded. Even if I wrapped multiple INSERT statements in a BEGIN TRAN/COMMIT TRAN block (and did nothing more than that), a failure of one INSERT (because of an error such as a constraint violation or duplicate value) would not cause the others to fail. This is expected and proper behavior. If you want all the statements to fail when one statement fails, you must add error handling. (I'll discuss this in depth in Chapter 13.)

- Think of the special form of the INSERT statement using DEFAULT VALUES and no column list as a shorthand method that enables you to avoid supplying the keyword DEFAULT for each column.

- You cannot specify the column name for a column that has the Identity property, and you cannot use the DEFAULT placeholder for a column with the Identity property. (I agree that this would be nice, but SQL Server does not currently work this way.) You must completely omit a reference to the Identity column. To explicitly provide a value for the column, you must use *SET IDENTITY_INSERT ON*. You can use the default VALUES clause, however.

Behavior of DEFAULT and NULL

It is important that you understand the general behavior of INSERT regarding NULL and DEFAULT precedence. If a column is omitted from the column list and the values list, it will take on the default value, if one exists. If a default value does not exist, SQL Server tries a NULL value. An error will result if the column has been declared NOT NULL. If NULL is explicitly specified in the values list, a column will be set to NULL (assuming it allows NULL), even if a default exists. When the DEFAULT placeholder is used on a column allowing NULL and no default has been declared, NULL is inserted for that column. An error will result on a column declared NOT NULL without a default if you specify NULL or DEFAULT or if you omit the value entirely.

Table 8-1 summarizes the results of an INSERT statement that omits columns, specifies NULL, or specifies DEFAULT, depending on whether the column is declared NULL or NOT NULL and whether it has a default declared.

	Column Default Status			
	Default Exists		No Default Exists	
	Nullability of Column			
Entry Description	Null	Not Null	Null	Not Null
Value entered for column satisfies all constraints	Value entered	Value entered	Value entered	Value entered
Value entered for column fails some constraint on table	ERROR Default not used even if it exists.	ERROR Default not used even if it exists.	ERROR Default not used even if it exists.	ERROR Default not used even if it exists.
Column omitted	DEFAULT	DEFAULT	NULL	ERROR
Explicitly entered NULL	NULL	ERROR	NULL	ERROR
Explicitly entered DEFAULT	DEFAULT	DEFAULT	NULL	ERROR

Table 8-1. *The effects of an INSERT statement that omits columns, specifies NULL, or specifies DEFAULT.*

Expressions in VALUES clause

So far, the INSERT examples have demonstrated only constant values in the VALUES clause of INSERT. In fact, you can use a scalar expression such as a function, a local variable, or a global variable in the VALUES clause. (I discuss functions and variables in Chapter 9, "Programming with Transact-SQL." Hopefully, the basics are clear. If not, you can take a quick look ahead and then return to this chapter.) You cannot use an entire SELECT statement as a scalar value even if you are certain that it selects only one row and one column. However, you can take the result of that SELECT statement and assign it to a variable, and then you can use that variable in the VALUES clause. I'll show you how a SELECT statement can completely replace the VALUES clause in the next section.

Here's a contrived example that demonstrates how functions, expressions, arithmetic operations, string concatenation, global variables, and local variables are used within the VALUES clause of an INSERT statement:

```
CREATE TABLE mytable
(
int_val         int,
smallint_val    smallint,
numeric_val     numeric(8,2),
tiny_const      tinyint,
float_val       float,
date_val        datetime,
char_strng      char(10)
)
GO

DECLARE @myvar1 numeric(8, 2)
SELECT @myvar1=65.45

INSERT mytable (int_val, smallint_val, numeric_val, tiny_const,
    float_val, date_val, char_strng)
VALUES
(OBJECT_ID('mytable'), @@spid, @myvar1 /
10.0, 5, SQRT(144), GETDATE(), REPLICATE('A',3)+REPLICATE('B',3))
```

Here are the results:

int_val	smallint_val	Numeric_val	tiny_const	float_val
1913057851	10	6.55	5	12.0

date_val	char_string
Jan 22 1997 2:12PM	AAABBB

Multiple-row INSERT statements

The most typical use of INSERT is to add one row to a table. However, using two special forms of INSERT (INSERT/SELECT and INSERT/EXEC), plus a special SELECT statement (SELECT INTO), you can add multiple rows of data at once. Note that you can use the global variable @@ROWCOUNT after all of these statements to find out the number of rows affected.

INSERT/SELECT As I mentioned earlier, you can use a SELECT statement instead of a VALUES clause with INSERT. You get the full power of SELECT, including joins, subqueries, UNION, and all the other goodies. The table you are inserting into must already exist; it can be a permanent table or a temporary table. The operation is atomic, so a failure of one row, such as from a constraint violation, causes all rows chosen by the SELECT statement to be thrown away. An exception to this occurs if a duplicate key is found on a unique index created with the *SET IGNORE_DUP_KEY* option. In this case, the duplicate row is thrown out but the entire statement continues and is not aborted. You can, of course, also use expressions in the SELECT statement, and using the CONVERT function is common if the target table has a datatype that's different from that of the source table.

Here's an example: Suppose that I want to copy the *authors* table (in the *pubs* sample database) to a temporary table. But rather than show the author ID as a *char* field in Social Security–number format with hyphens, I'll strip out those hyphens and store the ID as an *int*. Then I'll use a single name field with the concatenation of the last and first name. I want to record the current date but strip off the time so that the internal time is considered midnight. (If you're working only with dates, this is a good idea because it avoids issues that occur when the time portions of columns are not equal.) I'll also record each author's area code—the first three digits of their phone number. I need the author's state, but if it is NULL I'll use WA instead.

```
CREATE TABLE #authors
(
    au_id           int                 PRIMARY KEY,
    au_fullname     varchar(60)         NOT NULL,
    date_entered    smalldatetime       NOT NULL,
    area_code       char(3)             NOT NULL,
    state           char(2)             NOT NULL
)
GO

INSERT INTO #authors
SELECT
CONVERT(int, SUBSTRING(au_id, 1, 3) + SUBSTRING(au_id, 5, 2)
    + SUBSTRING(au_id, 8, 4)),
au_lname + ', ' + au_fname,
```

```
CONVERT(varchar, GETDATE(), 102),
CONVERT(char(3), phone),
ISNULL(state, 'WA')
FROM authors

SELECT * FROM #authors
```

Here is the result:

```
au_id       au_fullname        date_entered          area_code   state
---------   ----------------   -------------------   ---------   -----
172321176   White, Johnson     Jan 22 1997 12:00AM   408         CA
213468915   Green, Marjorie    Jan 22 1997 12:00AM   415         CA
238957766   Carson, Cheryl     Jan 22 1997 12:00AM   415         CA
267412394   O'Leary, Michael   Jan 22 1997 12:00AM   408         CA
274809391   Straight, Dean     Jan 22 1997 12:00AM   415         CA
341221782   Smith, Meander     Jan 22 1997 12:00AM   913         KS
409567008   Bennet, Abraham    Jan 22 1997 12:00AM   415         CA
427172319   Dull, Ann          Jan 22 1997 12:00AM   415         CA
472272349   Gringlesby, Burt   Jan 22 1997 12:00AM   707         CA
486291786   Locksley, Charlene Jan 22 1997 12:00AM   415         CA
527723246   Greene, Morningstar Jan 22 1997 12:00AM  615         TN
648921872   Blotchet-Halls,    Jan 22 1997 12:00AM   503         OR
            Reginald
672713249   Yokomoto, Akiko    Jan 22 1997 12:00AM   415         CA
712451867   del Castillo, Innes Jan 22 1997 12:00AM  615         MI
722515454   DeFrance, Michel   Jan 22 1997 12:00AM   219         IN
724089931   Stringer, Dirk     Jan 22 1997 12:00AM   415         CA
724809391   MacFeather, Stearns Jan 22 1997 12:00AM  415         CA
756307391   Karsen, Livia      Jan 22 1997 12:00AM   415         CA
807916654   Panteley, Sylvia   Jan 22 1997 12:00AM   301         MD
846927186   Hunter, Sheryl     Jan 22 1997 12:00AM   415         CA
893721158   McBadden, Heather  Jan 22 1997 12:00AM   707         CA
899462035   Ringer, Anne       Jan 22 1997 12:00AM   801         UT
998723567   Ringer, Albert     Jan 22 1997 12:00AM   801         UT
```

INSERT/EXEC You can use INSERT with the results of a stored procedure taking the place of the VALUES clause. (SQL Server version 6.5 added this powerful extension to ANSI SQL.) This procedure is similar to the INSERT/SELECT form, except that EXEC *procedure_name* is used instead. The procedure should return exactly one result set with types that match the table you have set up for it. You can pass parameters, use EXEC(*'string'*), or even call out to extended procedures (your own custom DLLs) or to remote procedures on other servers. By calling to a remote procedure on another server, putting the data into a temporary table, and then joining on it, you get the capabilities of a distributed join, a feature that SQL Server currently does not directly provide.

An example will explain this better: suppose that I want to store the results of the **sp_configure** stored procedure in a temporary table. (You can also do this with a permanent table.)

```
CREATE TABLE #config_out
(
name_col      varchar(50),
minval        int,
maxval        int,
configval     int,
runval        int
)

INSERT #config_out
    EXEC sp_configure

SELECT * FROM #config_out
```

Here's the result:

```
name_col                 minval   maxval       configval    runval
--------------------     ------   ----------   ---------    --------
Affinity mask            0        2147483647   0            0
Allow updates            0        1            0            0
Backup buffer size       1        10           1            1
Backup threads           0        32           5            5
Cursor threshold         -1       2147483647   -1           -1
Database size            2        10000        2            2
Default language         0        9999         0            0
Default sortorder id     0        255          52           52
fill factor              0        100          0            0
Free buffers             20       524288       2048         2048
Hash buckets             4999     265003       7993         7993
Language in cache        3        100          3            3
LE threshold maximum     2        500000       200          200
LE threshold minimum     2        500000       20           20
LE threshold percent     1        100          0            0
Locks                    5000     2147483647   20000        20000
Logwrite sleep (ms)      -1       500          0            0
Max async IO             1        255          8            8
Max lazywrite IO         1        255          8            8
Max text repl size       0        2147483647   2147483647   2147483647
Max worker threads       10       1024         255          255
Media retention          0        365          0            0
Memory                   2800     1048576      40960        40960
Nested triggers          0        1            1            1
Network packet size      512      32767        4096         4096
```

Open databases	5	32767	20	20
Open objects	100	2147483647	1500	1500
Priority boost	0	1	0	0
Procedure cache	1	99	30	30
RA cache hit limit	1	255	4	4
RA cache miss limit	1	255	3	3
RA delay	0	500	15	15
RA pre-fetches	1	1000	3	3
RA slots per thread	1	255	5	5
RA worker threads	0	255	3	3
Recovery flags	0	1	0	0
Recovery interval	1	32767	5	5
Remote access	0	1	1	1
Remote conn timeout	-1	32767	10	10
Remote login timeout	0	2147483647	5	5
Remote proc trans	0	1	0	0
Remote query timeout	0	2147483647	0	0
Remote sites	0	256	10	10
Resource timeout	5	2147483647	10	10
set working set size	0	1	0	0
Show advanced options	0	1	1	1
SMP concurrency	-1	64	0	1
Sort pages	64	511	64	64
Spin counter	1	2147483647	10000	0
Tempdb in ram (MB)	0	2044	0	0
Time slice	50	1000	100	100
User connections	5	32767	200	200
User options	0	4095	0	0

If I want to execute the procedure against the remote server named "dogfood," that's almost as easy. Assuming the same table *#config_out* exists:

```
INSERT #config_out
    EXEC dogfood.master.dbo.sp_configure
```

SELECT INTO   SELECT INTO is in many ways similar to INSERT/SELECT, but it directly builds the table rather than requiring that the table already exist. In addition, SELECT INTO operates with a special nonlogged mode, which makes it faster. To use SELECT INTO to populate a permanent table, the database must have the **select into/bulkcopy** option enabled (for example, *EXEC sp_dboption pubs,'select into/bulkcopy',true*). Note that if you use SELECT INTO with a permanent table, you must do full database backups because transaction log backups will not have the records for these operations. I always advise using any nonlogged operations with care—think about their effects on your backup and restore plans before you launch such an operation.

You can also use SELECT INTO with temporary tables (# and ## prefixed) without enabling the **select into/bulkcopy** option. Because temporary tables do not have to be recovered, not logging their operation is not a problem. (A user executing SELECT INTO must have permission to select from the target database and also have CREATE TABLE permission, because this statement does both actions.)

SELECT INTO is handy. It is commonly used to easily copy a table or perhaps to drop a column that is no longer needed. In the latter case, you'd simply omit the unnecessary column from the select list. Or you can change the names of columns by aliasing them in the select list.

To illustrate SELECT INTO, here's an equivalent operation to the earlier INSERT/SELECT example. The results, including the column names of the new temporary table, appear identical to those produced using INSERT/SELECT.

```
SELECT
CONVERT(int, SUBSTRING(au_id, 1, 3) + SUBSTRING(au_id, 5, 2)
+ SUBSTRING(au_id, 8, 4)) AS au_id,
au_lname + ', ' + au_fname AS au_fullname,
CONVERT(varchar, GETDATE(), 102) AS date_entered,
CONVERT(char(3), phone) AS area_code,
ISNULL(state, 'WA') AS state

INTO #authors
FROM authors
```

There's one important difference between the two procedures—the datatypes of the table created automatically are slightly different from those I declared explicitly using INSERT/SELECT. If the exact datatypes were important to me, I could use CONVERT to cast them to the types I want in all cases or I could create the table separately and then use INSERT/SELECT.

Utilities related to multiple-row insert

INSERT is not the only way to get data into SQL Server tables. SQL Server also provides some utilities for bulk loading of tables. Because the focus of this book is not on the utilities and tools, I won't describe them in detail, but I'd be remiss if I didn't at least mention them.

Bulk copy libraries, SQL-DMO object, and BCP.EXE   The DB-Library for the C programming interface has a special set of functions known as the bulk copy library and typically referred to as the **bcp** functions. The BCP.EXE command-line utility invokes these libraries. The utility has little code other than that accepting various command-line parameters and then invoking the functions of the **bcp** library. I won't go into the workings of BCP.EXE here, except to say that it was built for function, not form. It is totally command-line driven. If you're a fan of UNIX utilities, you'll love it!

The SQL-DMO BulkCopy object ultimately invokes these same **bcp** functions, but it provides some higher level methods and ease of use within the world of COM (Component Object Model) objects. SQL Enterprise Manager puts an easy-to-use graphical interface on top of this object to make it easy to transfer data between SQL Server installations. However, SQL Enterprise Manager does not yet provide a "graphical **bcp**" to make it simple to load different data files or data sources into SQL Server. Flexible **bcp** is a good tool to use in batch programs. The *SQL Server Administrator's Companion* does a good job of explaining the **bcp** options and provides several examples.

Many custom loader applications have been written that use the **bcp** libraries directly. And some commercial products have been built using the **bcp** libraries to provide data loading services. Even though the same libraries (and DLLs) are used for the BCP.EXE utility, custom loaders can often perform much faster than the utility. The BCP.EXE utility is a general-purpose tool—it doesn't do anything fancy. It does not use multiple threads or do double-buffering. It must perform a lot of dynamic memory allocations since it never knows in advance what type of data it will be reading or writing. Because they can employ these techniques, custom loaders written for a specific application or data can sometimes be much faster. The bottleneck in load speed typically occurs at the client application (which might be the BCP.EXE utility), not the SQL Server engine.

A good approach, if you write your own loader, is to overlap the reading of your data source with the writing of the data to the SQL Server back-end. Ideally, you should use separate threads to read the source data, complete whatever transformations are necessary, and write the data to the SQL Server. Use a double-buffering approach so that you can be filling one buffer while another is being dispatched to SQL Server. And if the source data is from a file, you might want to open the file as a memory-mapped file to speed the file pointer operations.

When possible, you should make your loader service multiple tables in parallel. A **bcp** operation effectively locks a single table, making it impossible to have multiple connections loading the same table. But it can be a big win to load multiple tables at the same time: it can make sense to distribute the client work to many different machines, each loading one table to the SQL Server. In this case, of course, you'll be working via the network. When possible, and if only one client is performing the loads, you should avoid using the network and install the loader application on the same machine as the SQL Server engine. The job of the **bcp** libraries is basically to transform the data into SQL Server format and then hand the data over to the server. Because the client doing the **bcp** operation is doing most of the work, that's almost always where the bottleneck occurs.

Whether you use the **bcp** libraries through the BCP.EXE utility, SQL-DMO, the transfer functions of SQL Enterprise Manager, or through a custom loader, you should be aware of a few **bcp** specifics. First, **bcp** has two main forms, fast and standard. Fast **bcp** is unlogged. As is true with any unlogged job, you must deal manually with any failures while the load is in progress. If that's not possible, you should use standard **bcp**, in which all activity is logged and therefore re-coverable. If you can start everything over, including the table creation, use fast **bcp**. With fast **bcp**, the table must not have any indexes (which also means that it cannot have a PRIMARY KEY or UNIQUE constraint). And the database must have the **select into/bulk copy** option enabled. If a table has no indexes but the **select into/bulk copy** option is not enabled, SQL Server will issue a warning message stating that fast **bcp** mode cannot be used:

```
Warning, reverting to standard bulk copy on table 'authors' because
BULKCOPY option not set in database 'pubs.'
```

This could be exactly what you want—perhaps you didn't set the option because you wanted to ensure that the changes were logged. The warning alerts you in case you simply forgot to set the option.

If you cannot use fast **bcp**, you should use standard **bcp**, which is logged. (Standard **bcp** is still faster than a standard INSERT statement because it comes in at a lower level within SQL Server.) Standard **bcp** will be used whenever a table has indexes.

Whenever you use **bcp** you should also be aware that CHECK and FOREIGN KEY constraints are not enforced and that a trigger on the table will not fire. This is because **bcp** calls directly into the internal **insert()** functions and an execution plan is not built for it as would be the case with the INSERT statement. Recall that the execution plan contains all the steps necessary to carry out CHECK, FOREIGN KEY constraints, and branches to triggers. Because **bcp** uses no such plan, SQL Server performs only the **insert()** step, which might be just a small part of the full plan that would be created if a regular INSERT statement were used. Even if standard **bcp** is used, you should be aware that shortcuts are taken for the sake of bulk-loading performance. If you don't want shortcuts, you should use regular INSERT statements.

LOAD TABLE LOAD TABLE is an often misunderstood SQL Server feature. We added LOAD TABLE to version 6.5 mostly as a disaster-recovery tool. In earlier versions, the LOAD statement was always performed for the complete database or transaction log. Having LOAD work at the database level could sometimes put you between a rock and a hard place. For example, suppose that you just accidentally clobbered an important table in the database. You have a backup (dump) of the database, but it is three days old. If you load the backup database, you will restore the clobbered table to its earlier state, but you'll also restore the three-day-old version of every other table in the database. Those three days might represent a lot of important data that you can't afford to lose. You must decide which is more painful: to lose three days' work in *every* table or to lose *all* the work from the one clobbered table. (As is often the case in the real world, proper backups were not being done in this example.)

> **NOTE** LOAD TABLE helps this situation because it allows a single table to be loaded from the dump of the entire database. We originally conceived that LOAD TABLE would not have a corresponding DUMP TABLE (only DUMP DATABASE). We intentionally designed it not to be orthogonal.

Let's go back to our example. When you use LOAD TABLE, there is no guarantee that FOREIGN KEY constraints are preserved. The data in the other tables, of course, has changed in the three intervening days. Also, LOAD TABLE will not recover transactions from the transaction log of the database dump file. This means that LOAD TABLE will not be exactly up-to-date with the data for that table existing when the DUMP DATABASE was performed if update activity was occurring simultaneously with the dump process. (In a normal LOAD DATABASE operation, after all the data-base pages are reapplied, the transaction log in the dump is also recovered to ensure that everything is up-to-date.)

LOAD TABLE can go a long way in getting you back in business, and then you can fix up your integrity constraints using queries and DML statements, as I'll discuss later in this chapter under "Reenabling integrity constraints" on page 374. LOAD TABLE is not perfect, but it's a lot better than having to restore from outdated backups. Still, you do not want to use LOAD TABLE as your main restore strategy.

Contrary to our original plan, we also added a DUMP TABLE statement. Its development came almost for free as a side effect of developing LOAD TABLE. Some internal tests show that the combination of DUMP TABLE and LOAD TABLE could be several times faster for transferring data between tables at different sites than doing **bcp**-out and **bcp**-in operations. However, except in cases for which you'd use DUMP TABLE as an alternative to **bcp** for, say, moving a table's data between your sites, you should not use the DUMP TABLE and LOAD TABLE combination as part of your normal operation. Otherwise, about the only time you'd use LOAD TABLE is in the disaster recovery situation I described, when the cost of recovering (and overwriting) all the other tables would be more painful than it's worth. If you use DUMP TABLE, do it when no update activity is occurring in the database and after issuing a checkpoint on the database.

From the Author...

Some comments in the version 6.5 documentation suggest that LOAD TABLE should be used only from DUMP TABLE, not DUMP DATABASE, operations. The documentation makes this point because a DUMP TABLE operation would be assumed to be a true snapshot, whereas a DUMP DATABASE operation might result in changes in the log of the dump that will not get applied. As described earlier, this is not quite correct, and I think the documentation still misses the main point I describe here as to why we added LOAD TABLE. Don't make DUMP TABLE/LOAD TABLE part of your normal backup strategy. If you get into the difficult situation described in the example above, it makes perfect sense to use LOAD TABLE from a backup produced with DUMP DATABASE.

UPDATE

UPDATE, the second DML statement, is used to change existing rows. Usually, UPDATE contains a WHERE clause that limits the update to only a subset of rows in the table. (The subset could be a single row, which would generally be accomplished by testing for equality to the primary key values in the WHERE clause.) If no WHERE clause is provided, every row in the table is changed by UPDATE. You can use the @@ROWCOUNT global variable to verify the number of rows that were updated.

Here's the basic UPDATE syntax:

```
UPDATE {table_name|view_name}
SET column_name1 = {expression1|NULL|DEFAULT|(SELECT)}
    [, column_name2 = {expression2|NULL|DEFAULT|(SELECT)}
WHERE {search_conditions}
```

Columns are set to an expression. The expression can be almost any type that returns a scalar value—a constant, another column, an arithmetic expression, a bunch of nested functions that end up returning one value, a local variable, or a global variable. A column can be set to a value conditionally determined using the CASE expression or to a value returned from a subquery. Columns can also be set to NULL (if the column allows it) or to DEFAULT (if a default is declared or if the column allows NULL), much like with the INSERT statement.

You can set multiple columns in a single UPDATE statement. Like a multiple-row INSERT, an UPDATE that affects multiple rows is an atomic operation—if a single UPDATE statement affects multiple rows and one row fails a constraint, all the changes made by that statement are rolled back.

Like INSERT, the single exception to this atomicity occurs if you set the *SET IGNORE_DUP_KEY* option. You need to be careful when using this option: with UPDATE, "ignoring" a preexisting row is tantamount to deleting it. Therefore, I recommend that you avoid the *SET IGNORE_DUP_KEY* option except perhaps for a one-time "scrubbing" of newly imported data.

Here are some simple UPDATE statements that should be self-explanatory. Later in this chapter, I'll show you some that aren't this simple and intuitive.

```
-- Change a specific employee's last name after her marriage
UPDATE employee
    SET lname='Ashworth-Jenkins'
WHERE emp_id='VPA30890F'


-- Raise the price of every title by 12%
-- No WHERE clause so it affects every row in the table
UPDATE titles
    SET price=price * 1.12


-- Publisher 1389 was sold, changing its name and location.
-- All the data in other tables relating to pub_id 1389 is
-- still valid; only the name of the publisher and its
-- location have changed.
UPDATE publishers
    SET pub_name='Oh Canada Publications',
        city='Vancouver',
        state='BC',
        country='Canada'
WHERE pub_id='1389'


-- Change the phone number of authors living in Gary, IN,
-- back to the DEFAULT value
UPDATE authors
    SET phone=DEFAULT
WHERE city='Gary' AND state='IN'
```

More Information...

Notice the use of the keyword DEFAULT in the last example. Sometimes you'll want to stamp a table with the name of the user who last modified the row or with the time it was last modified. You can use system functions, such as SUSER_NAME() or GETDATE(), as the DEFAULT value and then restrict all data modification to be done via stored procedures that explicitly update such columns to the DEFAULT keyword. Or you could make it policy that such columns must always be set to the DEFAULT keyword in the UPDATE statement, and then you could monitor this by also having a CHECK constraint on the same column that insists that the value be equal to that which the function returns. (If you use GETDATE(), you probably want to use it in conjunction with other string and date functions to strip off the milliseconds and avoid the possibility that the value from the DEFAULT might be slightly different than that in the CHECK.) Here's a sample using SUSER_NAME():

```
CREATE TABLE update_def
(
up_id       int            PRIMARY KEY,
up_byname   varchar(30)    NOT NULL DEFAULT SUSER_NAME()
    CHECK (up_byname=SUSER_NAME())
-- Assume other columns would be here
)
GO

UPDATE update_def
SET
-- SET other columns to their value here, and then append the
-- following
up_byname=DEFAULT
WHERE up_id=1
GO
```

More advanced UPDATE examples

You can go well beyond these UPDATE examples, however, and use subqueries, the CASE statement, and even joins in specifying search criteria. (I'll discuss CASE in depth in Chapter 9.) For example, the following UPDATE statement is like a correlated subquery. It sets the *ytd_sales* field of the *titles* table to the sum of all *qty* fields for matching titles:

```
UPDATE titles
SET titles.ytd_sales=(SELECT SUM(sales.qty) FROM sales
    WHERE titles.title_id=sales.title_id)
FROM sales,titles
```

In the next example, you can use the CASE expression with an UPDATE to selectively give pay raises based on an employee's review rating. Assume that reviews have been turned in and big salary adjustments are due. A review rating of 4 should double the employee's salary. A rating of 3 should increase the salary by 60 percent. A 2 should increase the salary by 20 percent, and a rating lower than 2 does not change the salary.

```
UPDATE employee_salaries
    SET salary =
        CASE review
            WHEN 4 THEN salary * 2.0
            WHEN 3 THEN salary * 1.6
            WHEN 2 THEN salary * 1.2
            ELSE salary
        END
```

DELETE

DELETE, the third DML statement, removes rows from a table. Once the action is committed, no undelete action is available. (If not wrapped in a BEGIN TRAN/ COMMIT TRAN block, the COMMIT, of course, occurs by default as soon as the statement completes.) Because you delete only rows, not columns, you never specify column names in a DELETE statement as you do with INSERT or UPDATE. But in many other ways, DELETE acts much like UPDATE—you specify a WHERE clause to limit the delete to certain rows. If you omit the WHERE clause, every row in the table will be deleted. The global variable @@ROWCOUNT keeps track of the number of rows that were deleted. You can delete through a view but only if the view is based on a single table (because there is no way to specify to delete only certain rows in a multiple-table view). However, you can use DELETE when the search criteria uses a view. If you delete through a view, all the underlying FOREIGN KEY constraints on the table must still be satisfied for the delete to succeed.

Here's the general form of DELETE:

```
DELETE [FROM] {table_name | view_name} [WHERE clause]
```

The FROM preposition is ANSI standard, but its inclusion is always optional in SQL Server (similar to INTO with INSERT). The preposition must be specified per ANSI SQL. If the preposition is always needed, it is logically redundant, which is why SQL Server doesn't require it.

Here are some simple examples:

```
DELETE discounts
-- Deletes every row from the discounts table but does not
-- delete the table itself. An empty table remains.
```

```
DELETE FROM sales WHERE qty > 5
-- Deletes those rows from the sales table that have a value for
-- qty of 6 or more

DELETE FROM WA_stores
-- Attempts to delete all rows qualified by the WA_stores view,
-- which would delete those rows from the stores table that have
-- state of WA. This delete is correctly stated but would fail
-- because of a foreign key reference.
```

TRUNCATE TABLE

In the first example, *DELETE discounts* deletes every row of that table. Every row is fully logged. SQL Server provides a much faster way to purge all the rows from the table: TRUNCATE TABLE empties the table by deallocating all the table's pages. TRUNCATE TABLE is orders of magnitude faster than an unqualified DELETE against the whole table. A delete trigger on the table will not fire (because the rows deleted are not individually logged), and TRUNCATE TABLE will still work. If a foreign key references the table to be truncated, however, TRUNCATE TABLE will not work. And if the table is publishing data for replication, which requires the log records, TRUNCATE TABLE will not work.

Despite some information to the contrary, TRUNCATE TABLE is not really an unlogged operation. The deletions of rows are not logged because they don't really occur. Rather, entire pages are deallocated. But the page deallocations *are* logged. If TRUNCATE TABLE were not logged, it could not be used in a rollback transaction. A simple example will demonstrate that the action can be rolled back:

```
BEGIN TRAN
-- Get the initial count of rows
SELECT COUNT(*) FROM titleauthor
    25

TRUNCATE TABLE titleauthor

-- Verify that all rows are now gone
SELECT COUNT(*) FROM titleauthor
    0

-- Undo the truncate operation
ROLLBACK TRAN

-- Verify that rows are still there after the undo
SELECT COUNT(*) FROM titleauthor
    25
```

Modifying Data Through Views

You can specify INSERT, UPDATE, and DELETE statements on views as well as on tables, although you should be aware of some restrictions and other issues. Modifications through a view end up modifying the data in an underlying "base" table (and only one such table) because views do not store data. All three types of data modifications work easily for single-table views, especially in the simplest case in which the view exposes all the columns of the base table. But a single-table view does not necessarily have to expose every column of the base table—it could restrict the view to a subset of columns only. For any modification, all the underlying constraints of the base table must still be satisfied. For example, if a column in the base table is defined as NOT NULL and does not have a DEFAULT declared for it, the column must be visible to the view and the insert must supply a value for it. If the column were not part of the view, an insert through that view could never work because the NOT NULL constraint could never be satisfied. And, of course, you cannot modify or insert a value for a column that is derived by the view, such as an arithmetic calculation or concatenation of two strings of the base table. (You can still modify the nonderived columns in the view, however.)

Basing a view on multiple tables is far less straightforward. You can issue an UPDATE statement against a view that is a join of multiple tables, but only if all columns being modified are part of the same base table. An INSERT statement can also be performed against a view that does a join if one table allows all NULL columns, because again, all columns modified in the view must be part of the same base table. A DELETE statement cannot be executed against a view that is a join, because entire rows are deleted and modifications through a view can affect only one base table. (Because no columns are specified in a delete, from which table would the rows be deleted?)

In the real world, you probably wouldn't use an INSERT statement against a view with a join because you wouldn't usually have a table in which every column allows NULL. (For one thing, every table really should have a primary key, which cannot be NULL.) But the insert is possible. The following simple example illustrates this:

```
CREATE TABLE one
(
col11     int     NOT NULL,
col12     int     NOT NULL
)

CREATE TABLE two
(
col21     int     NOT NULL,
col22     int     NOT NULL
)
GO
```

```
CREATE VIEW one_two
AS
(SELECT col11, col12, col21, col22
FROM one LEFT JOIN two ON (col11=col21))
GO

INSERT one_two (col11, col12)
VALUES (1, 2)

SELECT * FROM one_two
```

Here is the result set:

```
col11     col12    col21    col22
-----     -----    -----    -----
1         2        (null)   (null)
```

Notice that this insert specifies values only for columns from table *one.* Selecting from the view produces the row only because LEFT OUTER JOIN is specified in the view. Because table *two* contains no actual rows, a simple equijoin would have found no matches. Although the row would still have been inserted into table *one,* it would have seemingly vanished from the view. You could specify the view as an equijoin and use WITH CHECK OPTION to prevent an insert that would not find a match. But the insert must still affect only one of the tables, so matching rows would already need to exist in the other table. I'll come back to WITH CHECK OPTION in the next section; for now I'll simply show you how this would be specified:

```
CREATE VIEW one_two_equijoin
AS
(SELECT col11, col12, col21, col22
FROM one JOIN two ON (col11=col21))
WITH CHECK OPTION
GO
```

If I try to specify all columns with either view formulation, even if I simply try to insert NULL values into the columns of table *two,* an error results because the single INSERT operation cannot be performed on both tables. (Admittedly, the error message is slightly misleading.)

```
INSERT one_two (col11, col12, col21, col22)
VALUES (1, 2, NULL,NULL)
Msg 4405, Level 16, State 2
View 'one_two' is not updatable because the FROM clause names
multiple tables.
```

Similarly, a DELETE against this view with a join will be disallowed and results in the same message:

```
DELETE one_two
Msg 4405, Level 16, State 2
View 'one_two' is not updatable because the FROM clause names
multiple tables.
```

The UPDATE case is not common, but it is somewhat more realistic. I'm not a fan of allowing updates through views that do joins, and I'll demonstrate why. Given the following view:

```
CREATE VIEW titles_and_authors
AS
(
SELECT A.au_id, A.au_lname, T.title_id, T.title
FROM
authors AS A
FULL OUTER JOIN titleauthor AS TA ON (A.au_id=TA.au_id)
FULL OUTER JOIN titles AS T ON (TA.title_id=T.title_id)
)
```

Selecting from the view

```
SELECT * FROM titles_and_authors
```

yields this:

au_id	au_lname	title_id	title
172-32-1176	White	PS3333	Prolonged Data Deprivation: Four Case Studies
213-46-8915	Green	BU1032	The Busy Executive's Database Guide
213-46-8915	Green	BU2075	You Can Combat Computer Stress!
238-95-7766	Carson	PC1035	But Is It User Friendly?
267-41-2394	O'Leary	BU1111	Cooking with Computers: Surreptitious Balance Sheets
267-41-2394	O'Leary	TC7777	Sushi, Anyone?
274-80-9391	Straight	BU7832	Straight Talk About Computers
409-56-7008	Bennet	BU1032	The Busy Executive's Database Guide
427-17-2319	Dull	PC8888	Secrets of Silicon Valley
472-27-2349	Gringlesby	TC7777	Sushi, Anyone?
486-29-1786	Locksley	PC9999	Net Etiquette
486-29-1786	Locksley	PS7777	Emotional Security: A New Algorithm

648-92-1872	Blotchet-Halls	TC4203	Fifty Years in Buckingham Palace Kitchens
672-71-3249	Yokomoto	TC7777	Sushi, Anyone?
712-45-1867	del Castillo	MC2222	Silicon Valley Gastronomic Treats
722-51-5454	DeFrance	MC3021	The Gourmet Microwave
724-80-9391	MacFeather	BU1111	Cooking with Computers: Surreptitious Balance Sheets
724-80-9391	MacFeather	PS1372	Computer Phobic AND Non-Phobic Individuals: Behavior Variations
756-30-7391	Karsen	PS1372	Computer Phobic AND Non-Phobic Individuals: Behavior Variations
807-91-6654	Panteley	TC3218	Onions, Leeks, and Garlic: Cooking Secrets of the Mediterranean
846-92-7186	Hunter	PC8888	Secrets of Silicon Valley
899-46-2035	Ringer	MC3021	The Gourmet Microwave
899-46-2035	Ringer	PS2091	Is Anger the Enemy?
998-72-3567	Ringer	PS2091	Is Anger the Enemy?
998-72-3567	Ringer	PS2106	Life Without Fear
341-22-1782	Smith	(null)	(null)
527-72-3246	Greene	(null)	(null)
724-08-9931	Stringer	(null)	(null)
893-72-1158	McBadden	(null)	(null)
(null)	(null)	MC3026	The Psychology of Computer Cooking

(30 rows affected)

The following UPDATE statement works fine because only one underlying table, *authors,* is affected. This example changes the author's name from "DeFrance" to "DeFrance-Macy."

```
UPDATE TITLES_AND_AUTHORS
SET au_lname='DeFrance-Macy'
WHERE au_id='722-51-5454'
(1 row(s) affected)
```

This UPDATE statement yields an error, however, because two tables from a view cannot be updated in the same statement:

```
UPDATE TITLES_AND_AUTHORS
SET au_lname='DeFrance-Macy', title='The Gourmet Microwave Cookbook'
WHERE au_id='722-51-5454' and title_id='MC3021'

Msg 4405, Level 16, State 2
View 'TITLES_AND_AUTHORS' is not updatable because the FROM clause
names multiple tables.
```

If you created the view, it might seem obvious that the UPDATE statement above will not be allowed. But if the person doing the update is not aware of the underlying tables, which a view does a great job of hiding, it will *not* be obvious why one UPDATE statement works and the other one doesn't.

In general, I think it's a good idea to avoid allowing updates (and inserts) on views that do joins. Such views are extremely useful for querying, and I strongly advocate their use to make querying simpler and less prone to bugs from misstating joins. But modifications against them are problematic. If you do allow an update on a view that is a join, you should be sure that the relationships are properly protected via FOREIGN KEY constraints or triggers or you'll run into bigger problems. Suppose, for example, that I wanted to change only the *au_id* column in the example view above. If the existing value in the underlying *authors* table is referenced by a row in *titleauthor,* such an update will not be allowed because it would orphan the row in *titleauthor.* The FOREIGN KEY constraint protects against the modification. But here I'll temporarily disable the FOREIGN KEY constraint between *titleauthor* and *titles*:

```
ALTER TABLE titleauthor    -- This disables the constraint
    NOCHECK CONSTRAINT ALL
```

Notice that although I will be updating the *authors* table, the constraint I am disabling (the constraint that would otherwise be violated) is on the *titleauthor* table. New users often forget that a FOREIGN KEY constraint on one table is essentially a constraint on *both* the referencing table (here *titleauthors*) and on the referenced table (here *titles*). With the constraint now disabled, I change the value of *au_id* through the view for the author Anne Ringer:

```
-- With constraint now disabled, the following update succeeds:
UPDATE titles_and_authors
SET au_id='111-22-3333'
WHERE au_id='899-46-2035'
```

But look at the effect on the same SELECT of all rows in the view:

au_id	au_lname	title_id	title
172-32-1176	White	PS3333	Prolonged Data Deprivation: Four Case Studies
213-46-8915	Green	BU1032	The Busy Executive's Database Guide
213-46-8915	Green	BU2075	You Can Combat Computer Stress!
238-95-7766	Carson	PC1035	But Is It User Friendly?
267-41-2394	O'Leary	BU1111	Cooking with Computers: Surreptitious Balance Sheets
267-41-2394	O'Leary	TC7777	Sushi, Anyone?
274-80-9391	Straight	BU7832	Straight Talk About Computers

```
409-56-7008   Bennet          BU1032   The Busy Executive's Database Guide
427-17-2319   Dull            PC8888   Secrets of Silicon Valley
472-27-2349   Gringlesby      TC7777   Sushi, Anyone?
486-29-1786   Locksley        PC9999   Net Etiquette
486-29-1786   Locksley        PS7777   Emotional Security: A New Algorithm
648-92-1872   Blotchet-Halls  TC4203   Fifty Years in Buckingham Palace
                                       Kitchens
672-71-3249   Yokomoto        TC7777   Sushi, Anyone?
712-45-1867   del Castillo    MC2222   Silicon Valley Gastronomic Treats
722-51-5454   DeFrance-Macy   MC3021   The Gourmet Microwave
724-80-9391   MacFeather      BU1111   Cooking with Computers:
                                       Surreptitious Balance Sheets
724-80-9391   MacFeather      PS1372   Computer Phobic AND Non-Phobic
                                       Individuals: Behavior Variations
756-30-7391   Karsen          PS1372   Computer Phobic AND Non-Phobic
                                       Individuals: Behavior Variations
807-91-6654   Panteley        TC3218   Onions, Leeks, and Garlic: Cooking
                                       Secrets of the Mediterranean
846-92-7186   Hunter          PC8888   Secrets of Silicon Valley
(null)        (null)          MC3021   The Gourmet Microwave
(null)        (null)          PS2091   Is Anger the Enemy?
998-72-3567   Ringer          PS2091   Is Anger the Enemy?
998-72-3567   Ringer          PS2106   Life Without Fear
111-22-3333   Ringer          (null)   (null)
341-22-1782   Smith           (null)   (null)
527-72-3246   Greene          (null)   (null)
724-08-9931   Stringer        (null)   (null)
893-72-1158   McBadden        (null)   (null)
(null)        (null)          MC3026   The Psychology of Computer Cooking
(31 rows affected)
```

Although I have not added or deleted any rows, instead of producing 30 rows total from the view, as was the case earlier, the view now produces 31 rows. This is because the outer-join fabricates a row for the new *au_id* that has no match in the *titles* table (it appears with null title fields). Also notice that the two titles that matched the old *au_id* now have nulls in their author fields. This might be understandable to someone who has detailed understanding of the tables, but if the view is the only window that exists for updating the table, it will be extremely confusing. If, in future releases, referential actions are added that allow updates to cascade, I might temper my recommendation to not use updates against views based on joins; you'd still have the problem of affecting columns from more than one table without being able to know which are which. (I'll discuss implementing referential actions via triggers in Chapter 10.) Theoretically, it is possible to update many more views, such as joins, than SQL Server currently allows. But until these additional algorithms for updatability of views make their way into a future release, it is simply best to avoid the problem.

WITH CHECK OPTION

Earlier, I said that modifying data with views based on one table is pretty straight-forward—but there is one "gotcha" to think about. I think of this as the issue of "disappearing rows." By default, a view can allow an UPDATE or an INSERT, even if the result is that the row no longer qualifies for the view. Consider the following view that qualifies only stores in the state of Washington:

```
CREATE VIEW WA_stores AS
SELECT * FROM stores
WHERE state='WA'
GO

SELECT stor_id, stor_name, state
FROM WA_stores
```

Here's the result:

```
stor_id    stor_name                                   state
-------    ------------------------------------        -----
6380       Eric the Read Books                         WA
7131       Doc-U-Mat: Quality Laundry and Books        WA
(2 rows affected)
```

The following UPDATE statement changes both of the qualifying rows so that they no longer qualify from the view and have seemingly disappeared.

```
UPDATE WA_stores
SET state='CA'
SELECT stor_id, stor_name, state
FROM WA_stores
```

And the result:

```
stor_id    stor_name      state
-------    ---------      -----
(0 rows affected)
```

Modifications made against a view without WITH CHECK OPTION can result in rows being added or modified in the base table, but the rows cannot be selected from the view because they don't meet the view's criteria. The rows seem to disappear, as the example above illustrates.

If you allow data to be modified through a view that uses a WHERE clause, I recommend that you use WITH CHECK OPTION when specifying the view. I don't think you should ever need to specify WITH CHECK OPTION. It should be the default behavior. But the behavior described above is in accordance with the ANSI and ISO SQL standards, and the expected result is that the disappearing row phenomenon can occur unless WITH CHECK OPTION is specified. Of course, any modifications made through the view must also satisfy the constraints of the underlying table or the statement will be aborted. This is true whether or not WITH CHECK OPTION is declared.

This example shows how WITH CHECK OPTION protects against the disappearing rows phenomenon:

```
CREATE VIEW WA_stores AS
SELECT * FROM stores
WHERE state='WA'
WITH CHECK OPTION
GO

UPDATE WA_stores
SET state='CA'
```

Here's the result:

```
Msg 550, Level 16, State 2
The attempted insert or update failed because the target view either
specifies WITH CHECK OPTION or spans a view which specifies WITH
CHECK OPTION and one or more rows resulting from the operation did
not qualify under the CHECK OPTION constraint.
Command has been aborted.

SELECT stor_id, stor_name, state
FROM WA_stores
```

And the final result:

```
stor_id    stor_name                                 state
-------    ------------------------------------      -----
6380       Eric the Read Books                       WA
7131       Doc-U-Mat: Quality Laundry and Books      WA
(2 rows affected)
```

Reenabling integrity constraints

To demonstrate a point in the preceding section, I disabled foreign key checks on the *titleauthor* table. When you're reenabling constraints, you should make sure that no rows violate the constraints. By default, when you add a new constraint, SQL Server automatically checks for violations and the constraint will not be added until the data is cleaned up and such violations are eliminated. You can suppress this check by using the NOCHECK option. With this option, when you reenable an existing constraint that has just been disabled, SQL Server does not recheck the constraint's relationships. FOREIGN KEY constraints can also be compromised if you use the special bulk loading utility BCP.EXE or a custom program that uses the special bulk loading libraries (as BCP.EXE does). Because the objective of **bcp** is to quickly load data, it is designed to skip constraint checking. A LOAD TABLE option can also result in data in which constraints are not satisfied. (As I said earlier, LOAD TABLE is meant to be used as a disaster recovery tool—for those times when only one table needs to be restored. It is not meant to be used as a method on which you base your backup strategy. DUMP and LOAD of complete databases and transaction logs are required to ensure that your integrity constraints are part of your backup strategy.)

After reenabling a disabled constraint, adding a new constraint with the NO-CHECK option, performing a bulk load operation, or performing a LOAD TABLE operation, you should check to see that constraints have been satisfied. Otherwise, the next time a row is updated, you might get an error suggesting that the constraint has been violated, even if the update at that time seems to have nothing to do with that specific constraint.

You can query for constraint violations using subqueries of the type discussed in Chapter 7, "Querying Data." You must formulate a separate query to check for every constraint, which can be tedious if you have many constraints. It is sometimes easier to issue a "dummy update," setting the columns equal to themselves, to be sure that all constraints are valid. If the table has many constraints and you think that none are likely to have been violated, doing the dummy update can be a convenient way to confirm, in one fell swoop, that all constraints are satisfied. If no errors result, you know that *all* constraints are satisfied. Note that if FOREIGN KEY constraints exist, the dummy update actually resets the values. This update is performed as a delete/insert operation (which I'll explain a bit later in this chapter). Although a dummy update can be a convenient way to test all constraints, it might not be appropriate for your environment because a lengthy operation could fill up the transaction log. If a violation occurs, you will still need to do queries to pinpoint the violation. The dummy update does not isolate the offending row(s)—it only tells you that a constraint was violated.

In an earlier example, I disabled the constraints on the *titleauthor* table and updated one row in such a way that the FOREIGN KEY constraint was violated. Here's an example in which I reenable the constraints on *titleauthor* and then do a dummy update, which reveals the constraint failure:

```
-- Reenable constraints. Note this does not check the validity
-- of the constraints.
ALTER TABLE titleauthor
    CHECK CONSTRAINT ALL
GO

-- Do a "Dummy Update" to check the constraints
UPDATE titleauthor
SET au_id=au_id, title_id=title_id
```

```
Msg 547, Level 16, State 2
UPDATE statement conflicted with COLUMN FOREIGN KEY constraint
'FK__titleauth__au_id__1312E04B'. The conflict occurred in database
'pubs', table 'authors', column 'au_id'
Command has been aborted.
```

The constraint failure occurred because of the foreign key reference to the *authors* table. I know that it must be a case of an *au_id* value in the *titleauthor* table that has no match in *authors,* but I don't know which are the offending row(s). Chapter 7 shows you a few approaches for finding such nonmatching rows. The approach I find most useful is to use an outer join and then restrict the results to show only the rows that had to be fabricated for preservation on the outer-join side. These are the nonmatching rows—exactly the ones I'm interested in:

```
SELECT A.au_id, TA.au_id
FROM authors AS A RIGHT OUTER JOIN titleauthor
    AS TA ON (A.au_id=TA.au_id)
WHERE A.au_id IS NULL

au_id     au_id
-----     -----
(null)    899-46-2035
(null)    899-46-2035
```

Internal and Performance Considerations

In Chapter 6, I showed you the details of how SQL Server stores data. Now I'll show you how SQL Server modifies data and optimizes performance.

Row Placement

I've already discussed (in Chapters 3 and 6) clustered indexes and how they are crucial to effective space management within SQL Server. As a rule of thumb, you should *always* have a clustered index on a table. I can think of only a couple of cases when you'd *not* have one: One case is a specialized use of a small table in which practically no data modification takes place. The other occurs when you have a perpetually growing history or audit table in which no rows are deleted and new rows are always added sequentially to the end. This audit table would need to be one that is never queried for specific rows—it would always be scanned in its entirety when accessed.

When a table has no clustered index, a new row is always inserted at the end of the table, even if free slots (from rows that have been deleted) are available within the table. Space management is obviously not efficient. Some marketing propaganda from competitors makes this inefficiency seem like a major concern. But I view it as practically a nonissue. Every significant table has a clustered index because the index provides a big performance win. With a clustered index that is, practically speaking, always in existence, SQL Server space management is excellent and reorganization of the database is required less often than in most (if not all) competing products.

A table that has no clustered indexes is sometimes referred to as a *heap*. You might run into this term in articles about SQL Server.

A clustered index directs an insert to a specific page. This occurs when the new row is the direct result of an INSERT statement or when it is the result of an UPDATE statement executed via a delete-followed-by-insert (delete/insert) strategy. New rows are inserted into their clustered position, splicing in a page via a page split if the current page has no room. If the table has duplicate key values and all the rows that should be pointed to on one page won't fit, *overflow pages* are used. Overflow pages are needed only for clustered, nonunique indexes. This situation never occurs with a nonclustered index: with a nonclustered index, there is no "correct" page for the data because the index doesn't drive the placement of the actual data. And a clustered unique index, of course, would not duplicate keys in the first place.

If a new page must be allocated, it will be allocated (if possible) from the same extent as the other pages to which it will be linked (whether these are normal data pages, overflow pages, or index pages). This helps keep pages contiguous for more efficient I/O, especially during read-ahead operations. If SQL Server cannot keep pages contiguous because the extent is full, a new extent (8 pages, or 16 KB) is allocated and SQL Server attempts to allocate the extent from the same allocation unit as the other pages. (Recall that an allocation unit is a chunk of 256 contiguous 2-KB pages, or 0.5 MB. That's why a database is always altered or created in no less than 0.5-MB chunks at a time.)

Standard INSERT, UPDATE, and DELETE statements are always logged to ensure atomicity, and logging of these cannot be disabled. The modification must be known to be safely on disk in the transaction log (write-ahead logging) before the commit of the statement or transaction can be acknowledged to the calling application. Page allocations and deallocations, including those done by TRUNCATE TABLE, are also logged. You can specify a few unlogged operations by enabling the **select into/bulk copy** option. These unlogged operations are available for faster bulk loading of data.

Chapter 3 discusses in detail the Index Manager and how pages are split and overflow pages are managed. It also gives details about logging and recovery. If you are still unsure of how these mechanisms work, I urge you to go back to that chapter. Here I'll discuss the functional aspects of SQL Server and cover only those internal characteristics that your actions and designs will directly influence.

Update Strategies

SQL Server performs updates in multiple ways. SQL Server automatically and invisibly chooses the fastest update strategy that can be applied for the specific operation. In determining the strategy, SQL Server evaluates how much information must be logged for the update, how the row will be accessed (via a scan or an index retrieval, and which index), and whether the row might need to be moved to a different page. SQL Server uses these factors to decide *when* to make the update and *how* to perform the update.

Deferred updates

Updates can be direct (immediate) or deferred (in a moment). A deferred update is always performed as a delete of the original row followed by an insert of the new image of the row. Typically, you'd use a deferred update if the update could modify the primary key of multiple rows; otherwise you could run into the "Halloween problem." (See Chapter 3 for information on the Halloween problem.) Or *interim violations* might occur, in which a temporary duplicate value would exist but be remedied by the time the statement finished executing. (Recall the example in Chapter 3, in which primary keys were incremented by 1. Remember that a temporary duplicate would exist for each number as it is incremented, resulting in the Halloween problem.)

Using a trigger to subsequently update a table avoids the Halloween problem. The original update is guaranteed to behave as though it ran before the trigger update, and the trigger update is guaranteed to behave as though it ran after the original update (which is what actually occurs). Because the selection criteria that drives the trigger update can be based on the before image or after image of the complete update but not on some intermediate state of the table, the Halloween problem cannot occur solely on the basis of a trigger.

> **NOTE** The execution plan for a trigger is not compiled into the execution plan for the statement. Rather, think of the execution plan as simply branching to the trigger plan just before the statement completes. In this way, the trigger plan can remain cached and reusable, and it does not need to be recompiled and brought into memory for every statement. Constraints, on the other hand, have steps added directly to the execution plan.

Because deferred updates use a two-step logging mechanism and a delete of the original row image followed by an insert of the new image, first the row IDs (RIDs) of each qualifying row are logged. (The full image of the original row is not logged.) The record for each of these rows identifies it to be deleted in a deferred update. This record is called a DNOOP (Delete-No-Op). I'll show you the sequence of log records in a moment. Then the after image of the same row is logged as an INOOP (Insert-No-Op) record. When all qualifying rows have been identified and the new after images have been recorded, SQL Server uses the RIDs in the DNOOP log records to delete all qualifying rows. This is the delete operation that generates DELETE log records. The before-image records are logged for the deletes, but because the DNOOP log records contain only row IDs, little rework is required. SQL Server then inserts the new images using a special INSIND (Insert-Indicator) log record. The INSIND record does not contain the row data—it contains a pointer to the INOOP log record that contains the row data.

This is all fairly complex, so hopefully an example will make it clearer. Suppose that I perform an update requiring a deferred update on a table with three rows and a unique clustered index on the column being updated:

```
UPDATE t1 SET c1=c1+1
```

These log records are required for this update:

```
BEGINXACT    Start the (implicit) transaction.
DNOOP        Logical RID of original 1st row.
INOOP        Complete new after image of 1st row.
DNOOP        Logical RID of original 2nd row.
INOOP        Complete new after image of 2nd row.
DNOOP        Logical RID of original 3rd row.
INOOP        Complete new after image of 3rd row.
DELETE       Delete logical RID specified by 1st DNOOP (physical
                 before image data is logged).
DELETE       Delete RID specified in 2nd DNOOP (physical location
                 of 2nd row now slot1 since row 1 is gone).
DELETE       Delete RID specified in 3nd DNOOP (physical location
                 of 3rd row is now slot1 since rows 1 & 2 are gone).
INSIND       Log physical location of new 1st row but not data.
                 Log a pointer to 1st INOOP which contains the
                 after image.
INSIND       Log physical location of new 2nd row and a pointer to
                 2nd INOOP.
INSIND       Log physical location of new 3rd row and a pointer to
                 3rd INOOP.
ENDXACT      End of Transaction.
```

Direct updates

If an update is not deferred, it is direct. A common misconception is that a direct update means "update-in-place." An update-in-place *is* always a direct update, but some direct updates are delete/insert operations, not update-in-place operations. Direct updates differ from deferred updates in that the DNOOP and INOOP logging steps are not required. In a direct update, the log records for the changes are written (without the first DNOOP and INOOP steps) and then the data page(s) are modified. Most commonly, a direct update is chosen duri compile time (when the execution plan is created), when SQL Server determines that only a single row will qualify for the update (for example, when the WHERE clause produces an exact match on a unique index). In releases earlier than 6.5, any update that could affect multiple rows was always deferred; in version 6.5, additional optimizations allow the direct update mode to be used even if multiple rows are affected when SQL Server determines that there is no risk of the Halloween problem or of interim constraint violations. A direct update can be used in these circumstances:

- If the update does not affect any column that is part of a FOREIGN KEY constraint (either referencing another table or being referenced by another table).

- If the update does not affect any key columns in the clustered index.

- When columns will not be updated in the index used to find the qualifying rows (classic potential Halloween problem).

- When variable-length fields are not being updated. (If no variable-length columns are affected, the row cannot change in size, which could force it to move to another page, introducing the Halloween problem.)

These requirements ensure that the same row cannot be affected more than once. Searched updates using joins and subqueries with IN revert to a deferred update, because they could result in the same row being visited more than once.

Remember, in addition to *when* the update is made, *how* the update is made is important. A deferred update is always a delete/insert (and it also has the additional logging steps discussed earlier). A direct update can use any of the following four strategies: update-in-place, direct-field-update, on-page delete/insert, or full delete/insert.

Update-in-place Update-in-place is a highly efficient form of update because it requires a single simple MODIFY log record; the changed value for the row overwrites the previous values in the same slot on the same data page. Update-in-place is used only when the update mode is direct and the row length of the new image is the same as that of the previous image. This method cannot be used if the table is being replicated (with continuous replication—snapshots are OK) or if the table has an update trigger. Both continuous replication and update triggers require both delete and insert log records (before images and after images), so the MODIFY log record produced by an update-in-place would not be sufficient. Contrary to some folklore, neither replication nor the existence of an update trigger requires all updates to be deferred, but they both require that updates occur with the delete/insert strategies described a bit later.

These general conditions must be satisfied for an update-in-place:

- The update mode is direct. That is, there must be no possibility that the Halloween problem or an interim violation of a unique index could occur. (These conditions would cause the update mode to be deferred, which is always a delete/insert operation with the additional logging steps discussed earlier.)

- The table cannot contain an update trigger.

- The table cannot be marked for continuous replication.

- Only one table can be involved in the execution plan for the UPDATE statement.

- The column(s) being updated cannot be part of the clustered index key.

- The column(s) being updated must be fixed-length, or, if only one row is affected, the columns can be variable-length but only if the net row size remains the same.

- The new row image cannot be "too different" from the previous row image. That is, the number of differing bytes cannot be more than one-half the total row size, and more than 24 discontiguous differing blocks of bytes cannot appear in the row.

A column that is part of a nonclustered index key can be updated without breaking the rules, as long as that index won't be used to drive the search for the qualifying rows (which could cause the Halloween problem) and as long as the column is not also part of the clustered index key. If these criteria are met, there is no risk that updating the column would cause the row to move to another page and perhaps be revisited. For single-row updates, this criteria can go even a step further: if the index is unique and the optimizer is able to determine that at most one row can qualify (because of the unique index being used), the column being updated can be part of the key of the nonclustered index that drives the search for the qualifying row. Multiple rows can be updated in place if all the criteria listed above are met but also only if the updated columns are all of fixed-length types (which means they cannot be NOT NULL in definition).

Logging for update-in-place is simple. For a single row being updated, the following log records are produced. This is as simple as it gets—any update will always have at least these three log records:

```
BEGINXACT    Begin (implicit) transaction
MODIFY       Change the column for the row in place
ENDXACT      End (commit) the transaction
```

A MODIFY record is written for every column that actually changes and for every row that is affected. For example, if you change two columns and two rows are affected, four MODIFY records will be written. If a column is set to its previous value, no MODIFY record is written for it.

Direct-field-update   SQL Server provides another relatively small optimization for update-in-place (although it doesn't change the logging steps), known as a direct-field-update. Normally, for update-in-place, a copy of the row must be made in memory, the fields are updated in the copy, and then the copy of the row is laid on the original row. In a direct-field-update, the values are directly overlaid on the previous values, eliminating the need for the memory copy. This is the most efficient update mode.

I could argue that this is not actually a separate update method because I think the distinction between this and typical update-in-place is pretty subtle. Direct-field-update is a relatively small performance optimization to save some memory operations. No change to the log records must be written for index maintenance. You can do a direct-field-update in cases that are even more restrictive than a typical update-in-place. In addition to the restrictions for update-in-place, a direct-field-update adds these restrictions:

- All the columns being updated must be fixed-length types (even for the single-row case).

- The sum of the length of the fixed-length fields being updated must be less than or equal to half the entire row size.

- No more than five columns in the table are being updated. (This is just a heuristic to prevent excessive time from being spent in trying to decide whether this method can be used. You wouldn't want to check 30 columns and then find out on the thirty-first that you have to fall back to "normal" update-in-place because of the previous half-row length limit.)

On-page delete/insert   With on-page delete/insert, the old row value is deleted and the new value is inserted. The new copy of the row goes on the same page as the old row. This method isn't as good as update-in-place, but it is substantially better than a full delete/insert that requires that two pages be operated on (for the old and new page). A full delete/insert requires that every index be updated, because the row probably is reinserted on another page. With an on-page delete/insert, the index does not need to be updated (assuming that the index key is not updated) since the index points to the page and the page does not change for this method. On-page delete/insert is used when the update mode is direct but when one or more of the requirements for update-in-place is not met. Commonly, this mode of direct update is used (rather than in-place) when the row changes in size but still fits on the same page, when an update trigger occurs, or when the table is being replicated.

An on-page delete/insert generates far fewer log records then an update-in-place. To update one row with this method, the log records appear as shown in the following fragment (assuming that no columns that are keys of any index are updated). Clearly, this is much less work than the deferred update, although both are a form of delete/insert.

```
BEGINXACT    Start of the (implicit) transaction
DELETE       Delete of the data row
INSERT       Insert of the data row
ENDXACT      Completion of transaction
```

Full delete/insert As the name implies, full delete/insert involves the deletion of the original row and the insertion of a new row. The insert goes to wherever the clustered index takes it—not necessarily the same page. All deferred updates are full delete/inserts, but they must perform the two-set logging process described earlier, first writing the DNOOP/INOOP log records. A direct update that is still a full delete/insert does not need the extra NOOP logging step. With full delete/insert, because the row might end up on a different page, all the indexes for the table are updated. An update that is performed as a full delete/insert performs all the steps that a delete of that row would require *plus* the steps that an insert of that row would require, except that all the steps are done within the context of a single transaction. All indexes must be adjusted for a full delete/insert, just as they would for only a delete or only an insert.

A direct update is typically done as a full delete/insert when update-in-place cannot be used because one or more requirements is not met and when an on-page delete/insert is not possible because the row will not fit on the same page. If you update a column that is part of the key of the clustered index, a full delete/insert will be performed. However, a full delete/insert would occur regardless, since updates of columns in the clustered index key must be done as deferred updates to avoid the Halloween problem or interim constraint failures (and since the primary key is often also the clustered index). And you'll recall that a deferred update is always a delete/insert operation, although it generates the additional two-step log operations (DNOOP, INOOP, and so forth).

Determining which update strategy to use

You can use SET SHOWPLAN ON to see the execution plan for any statement, including an update. But if you use SET SHOWPLAN ON to watch your update strategy, it shows the update simply as either deferred or direct. SHOWPLAN represents only the plan prepared at compile time. (The deferred versus direct decision is made at compile time.) The exact direct update strategy to be used cannot be made until runtime, and it is not part of the execution plan so it is unavailable to SHOWPLAN. Sometimes the plan produced during compile time might be for a direct update, but at runtime, when it becomes apparent that there is a possibility of the Halloween problem occurring, the plan is altered back to deferred.

The best way to see the update mode and method actually used is to enable trace flag 323. Trace flag 323 was implemented by one of our developers for his own use in checking his code while making additional update strategy optimizations for SQL Server 6.0. Trace flag 323 was never documented because it was never thought of as a feature. (It could change or go away in the future, so don't build this trace flag into your application!) But trace flag 323 can be useful if you want to see the update strategies being used. Note that this trace flag doesn't provide output in the case of the direct-field-update special optimization for update-in-place. That direct-field-update optimization causes the code to branch off and miss the *printf* function that is otherwise executed when trace flag 323 is enabled. That is the only case in which output is not given, so the absence of output tells you that direct-field-update was the mode and method used. Remember to also turn on trace flag 3604 so that the output is sent back to the calling application.

> **NOTE** For trace flag 323, additional internal messages are written to the SQL Server output when SQL Server is started with trace 323 from the command line; these internal messages are not written when trace 323 is enabled from a connection.

Following are several examples that use trace flag 323 to show the update strategies employed. Questions and misconceptions about update-in-place are common even among experienced users. At the risk of overdoing it, I'll show you a variety of examples with an explanation for each as to why a particular method was chosen or not chosen. In addition, I'll show the log records produced by the various updates that I obtained by selecting from the *syslogs* table, decoding the *op* code of *syslogs* as shown, and looking at the last transaction. Note, however, that these log records are sure to change in subsequent SQL Server releases, and *syslogs* might not continue to be exposed. Although this information is useful here and you might want to look at *syslogs* later, you should not depend on this SELECT statement in future SQL Server releases.

```
-- Decode log records
SELECT
xactid AS TRAN_ID,
CASE op
    WHEN 0   THEN 'BEGINXACT'     -- Start Transaction
    WHEN 1   THEN 'Not Used'
    WHEN 2   THEN 'Not Used'
    WHEN 3   THEN 'Not Used'
    WHEN 4   THEN 'INSERT'        -- Insert row
    WHEN 5   THEN 'DELETE'        -- Delete row
    WHEN 6   THEN 'INSIND'        -- Deferred update step 2 insert record
    WHEN 7   THEN 'IINSERT'       -- NC index insert
    WHEN 8   THEN 'IDELETE'       -- NC index delete
```

```
WHEN 9  THEN 'MODIFY'       -- Modify row
WHEN 10 THEN 'NOOP'         -- NOOP
WHEN 11 THEN 'INOOP'        -- Deferred update step 1 insert record
WHEN 12 THEN 'DNOOP'        -- Deferred update step 1 delete record
WHEN 13 THEN 'ALLOC'        -- Allocation
WHEN 14 THEN 'DBNEXTID'     -- Extent allocation
WHEN 15 THEN 'EXTENT'       -- Extent allocation
WHEN 16 THEN 'SPLIT'        -- Page split
WHEN 17 THEN 'CHECKPOINT'   -- Checkpoint
WHEN 18 THEN 'SAVEXACT'     -- Savepoint
WHEN 19 THEN 'CMD'
WHEN 20 THEN 'DEXTENT'      -- Deallocate extent
WHEN 21 THEN 'DEALLOC'      -- Deallocate page
WHEN 22 THEN 'DROPEXTS'     -- Delete all extents on alloc pg
WHEN 23 THEN 'AEXTENT'      -- Alloc extent - mark all pgs used
WHEN 24 THEN 'SALLOC'       -- Alloc new page for split
WHEN 25 THEN 'Not Used'
WHEN 26 THEN 'Not Used'
WHEN 27 THEN 'SORT'         -- Sort allocations
WHEN 28 THEN 'SODEALLOC'    -- Related to sort allocations
WHEN 29 THEN 'ALTDB'        -- Alter database record
WHEN 30 THEN 'ENDXACT'      -- End transaction
WHEN 31 THEN 'SORTTS'       -- Related to sort allocations
WHEN 32 THEN 'TEXT'         -- Log record of direct TEXT insert
WHEN 33 THEN 'INOOPTEXT'    -- Log record for deferred TEXT insert
WHEN 34 THEN 'DNOOPTEXT'    -- Log record for deferred TEXT delete
WHEN 35 THEN 'INSINDTEXT'   -- Indirect insert log record
WHEN 36 THEN 'TEXTDELETE'   -- Delete text log record
WHEN 37 THEN 'SORTEDSPLIT'  -- Used for sorted splits
WHEN 38 THEN 'CHGINDSTAT'   -- Incremental sysindexes stat changes
WHEN 39 THEN 'CHGINDPG'     -- Direct change to sysindexes
WHEN 40 THEN 'TXTPTR'       -- Info log row WHEN retrieving TEXTPTR
WHEN 41 THEN 'TEXTINFO'     -- Info log for WRITETEXT/UPDATETEXT
WHEN 42 THEN 'RESETIDENT'   -- Used WHEN a truncate table resets an
                               identity value
WHEN 43 THEN 'UNDO'         -- Compensating log record for Insert
                               Only Row Locking (IORL)
WHEN 44 THEN 'INSERT_IORL'  -- Insert with row locking record
WHEN 45 THEN 'INSIND_IORL'  -- INSIND with IORL
WHEN 46 THEN 'IINSERT_IORL' -- IINDEX with IORL
WHEN 47 THEN 'SPLIT_IORL'   -- Page split with IORL
WHEN 48 THEN 'SALLOC_IORL'  -- Alloc new page for split with IORL
WHEN 49 THEN 'ALLOC_IORL'   -- Allocation with IORL
WHEN 50 THEN 'PREALLOCLOG'  -- Preallocate log space for CLRs
ELSE 'Unknown Type' END  AS LOG_RECORD
FROM syslogs
```

Examples

Now that you've seen the method for viewing the log records, let's look at some lengthy examples. I hope they'll illustrate update behavior and show you clearly how updates are processed.

EXAMPLE 1

This example shows a simple update in which only one row is affected. A fixed-length field is being changed. It is exactly qualified with a primary key, so only one row can be affected. No indexed fields are affected, no update trigger is used, and the table is not being replicated. The field being updated is 8 bytes, less than half the row length, and the field is not part of a FOREIGN KEY constraint.

```
UPDATE titles
SET pubdate='1997/1/1' WHERE title_id='BU1111'

(1 row(s) affected)
```

The conditions here are as good as it gets, and hence so is the update strategy. This update was done as an update-in-place using the further direct-field-update optimization. (Recall that there is no trace flag 323 output for the direct-field-update optimization.) This is the simplest possible update (in which a value changes). Here are the log records:

```
0x130300000b00      BEGINXACT
0x130300000b00      MODIFY
0x130300000b00      ENDXACT
```

EXAMPLE 2

This update qualifies the same row that was qualified in Example 1. No indexed fields are being updated, there is no trigger, and the table is not being published for continuous replication. But I am updating a variable-length field. (Note that my server is case-sensitive, so uppercase and lowercase are considered different values.) Update-in-place can still be used, but the additional direct-field-update is not used since the field being updated is variable-length (although it is clearly not changing size).

```
UPDATE titles
SET
title=UPPER(title)
WHERE title_id='BU1111'
```

Because the strategy is update-in-place, but not the direct-field-update optimization, I now get output from trace flag 323:

```
Update: in-place, clust, safeind[0]=0x1

(1 row(s) affected)
```

The *title* column is the key of a nonclustered index. Hence, the log records reflect both the MODIFY of the row's data as well as the adjustment to the nonclustered index on *title*:

```
0x120300000f00    BEGINXACT       -- Start transaction
0x120300000f00    IDELETE         -- Nonclustered (NC) index delete
0x120300000f00    MODIFY          -- Change of data row values
0x120300000f00    IINSERT         -- NC index insert
0x120300000f00    ENDXACT         -- Transaction committed
```

EXAMPLE 3

This update affects one row. There is no update trigger, and the update does not affect a column that is part of the clustered index key. The changed value is not identical to the original, and the column will change (reduce) in size. The column being updated is a key in a nonclustered index, but it is the change in field length, not the nonclustered index, that makes this update become an on-page delete/insert. Even though the field is reduced in size, it must be deleted/inserted to reclaim space on the page.

```
UPDATE authors
SET au_lname='Jones' WHERE au_id='527-72-3246'
Update: on-page delete/insert, clust, safeind[0]=0x1

(1 row(s) affected)
```

The log records reflect the delete/insert for the data as well as the fix-up for the nonclustered index on *au_lname*:

```
0x0c0300000a00    BEGINXACT
0x0c0300000a00    IDELETE     -- Delete for the NC index
0x0c0300000a00    DELETE      -- Delete for the old image of data row
0x0c0300000a00    INSERT      -- Insert for the new image of data row
0x0c0300000a00    IINSERT     -- Insert for the NC index
0x0c0300000a00    ENDXACT
```

EXAMPLE 4

This update affects one small fixed-length field for one row only. The row is exactly qualified using the primary key. No indexes are updated. However, there is an update trigger on the table, so update-in-place cannot be used. The update becomes an on-page delete/insert.

```
UPDATE employee
SET job_lvl=12
WHERE emp_id='AMD15433F'

Update: on-page delete/insert, clust, safeind[0]=0x1

(1 row(s) affected)
```

The log records below show that an on-page delete/insert does not have to fix up any indexes if no columns are being updated that are part of an index key, as in this case.

```
0x0a0300000000      BEGINXACT
0x0a0300000000      DELETE
0x0a0300000000      INSERT
0x0a0300000000      ENDXACT
```

EXAMPLE 5

This update affects an integer column of only one row, and the column is not indexed. The row is exactly qualified using the primary key. Any non-null integer value takes 4 bytes of storage, so the row length is unchanged. It would seem this update could be an update-in-place and that it would also use the further direct-field-update optimization. But the integer column allows NULL and hence is internally variable-length, which means direct-field-update cannot be used. It can still be performed as an update-in-place.

```
UPDATE titles
SET royalty=royalty+1
WHERE title_id='BU1111'

Update: in-place, clust, safeind[0]=0x1

(1 row(s) affected)
```

The log records are simple:

```
0x0b0300001c00    BEGINXACT
0x0b0300001c00    MODIFY
0x0b0300001c00    ENDXACT
```

EXAMPLE 6

This update looks almost like the update in Example 5. A single column that is variable-length is updated, but it is not changing in length since it is set to itself (a dummy update). There is no update trigger, and the row is obviously not changing size. No indexed column is being changed. At a glance, all looks good for update-in-place. But the column being updated is part of a FOREIGN KEY constraint and references another table. Updating a column that is part of a FOREIGN KEY constraint (even if the value doesn't change and only one row is affected) always becomes a deferred update. (This will likely be further optimized for a future release and possibly for a service pack for version 6.5.)

```
UPDATE titles
SET pub_id=pub_id
WHERE title_id='BU1111'

Update: full delete/insert, deferred mode, clust,
    safeind[0]=0xfe

(1 row(s) affected)
```

The log records reflect that this is the two-step deferred method and that all indexes must be fixed up since the update is a full delete/insert:

```
0x090300000b00    BEGINXACT
0x090300000b00    DNOOP
0x090300000b00    INOOP
0x090300000b00    IDELETE
0x090300000b00    DELETE
0x090300000b00    INSIND
0x090300000b00    IINSERT
0x090300000b00    ENDXACT
```

To check to be sure that the FOREIGN KEY constraint is the reason the update is deferred, I'll simply disable the constraint and do the same update:

```
ALTER TABLE titles
    NOCHECK CONSTRAINT ALL
GO
```

```
UPDATE titles
SET pub_id=pub_id
WHERE title_id='BU1111'
GO

Update: in-place, clust, safeind[0]=0x1

(1 row(s) affected)
```

Trace flag 323 output shows that now the update was performed in place. (Since the column being updated is variable-length, direct-field-update was not possible.) The log records also show that the update was in-place, but they also reveal something else: No MODIFY record exists because no column's value changed. Only begin and end transaction records appear in the log. Since the column was set to itself—a dummy update—nothing needed to be logged.

```
0x230300000a00    BEGINXACT
0x230300000a00    ENDXACT
```

Foreign keys can alternately be enforced via triggers. You probably won't \frequently update a column that is part of a FOREIGN KEY constraint, and I recommend using constraints for this purpose rather than triggers. (I discuss this topic in Chapter 6, "Tables," and in Chapter 10, "Batches, Transactions, Stored Procedures, and Triggers.") But if there is some special circumstance in your application that makes it likely that columns in a foreign key relationship would be frequently updated, you might want to use triggers instead of constraints. In the example below, I create a trigger to enforce the relationship. When I do the same update, I see that it does not need to be performed with a deferred update.

> **NOTE** The trigger used in this example doesn't do the whole job of the FOREIGN KEY constraint, because it protects the referencing *titles* table but not the referenced *publishers* table, as a FOREIGN KEY constraint would. So to replace the constraint, I also need a trigger on *publishers* to ensure that updates there won't orphan any titles.

```
CREATE TRIGGER INS_UPD_titles
    ON titles
    FOR INSERT, UPDATE
AS
-- Do any rows exist in the inserted table that do not have a
-- matching pub_id in publishers?
 IF EXISTS
    (SELECT * FROM inserted WHERE inserted.pub_id NOT IN
    (SELECT publishers.pub_id FROM publishers))
```

```
    BEGIN
        RAISERROR('No matching publisher found. Statement will
            be aborted.', 16, 1)
        ROLLBACK TRAN
    END
GO

UPDATE titles
SET pub_id=pub_id
WHERE title_id='BU1111'
GO

Update: on-page delete/insert, clust, safeind[0]=0x1

(1 row(s) affected)
```

As the trace flag 323 output reveals, with the foreign key, the update did not have to be deferred. The trigger requires the update be delete/insert without the two-step logging process. There was room on the page, so the update was an on-page delete/insert, which means that no index maintenance was required since the row did not move and no columns used in an index key were updated. The log records show this operation is simpler than the previous deferred update:

```
0x270300000d00    BEGINXACT
0x270300000d00    DELETE
0x270300000d00    INSERT
0x270300000d00    ENDXACT
```

EXAMPLE 7

This update affects every row in the table to show that update-in-place can be used even for multiple-row updates. The field being updated is fixed-length, so rows cannot grow. The field being updated is only 2 bytes, and the total row length is at a minimum 16 bytes, so the update cannot affect half the row. No indexed fields are updated, and no update trigger exists.

```
UPDATE sales
SET qty=qty + 2

(21 row(s) affected)
```

There is no trace flag 323 output because this update used direct-field-update. The log records show 21 MODIFY records since 21 rows have had the value of one column changed:

```
0x140300000d00    BEGINXACT
0x140300000d00    MODIFY
```

```
0x140300000d00      MODIFY
0x140300000d00      MODIFY
0x140300000d00      MODIFY
0x140300000d00      MODIFY
0x140300000d00      MODIFY
0x140300000d00      MODIFY
0x140300000d00      MODIFY
0x140300000d00      MODIFY
0x140300000d00      MODIFY
0x140300000d00      MODIFY
0x140300000d00      MODIFY
0x140300000d00      MODIFY
0x140300000d00      MODIFY
0x140300000d00      MODIFY
0x140300000d00      MODIFY
0x140300000d00      MODIFY
0x140300000d00      MODIFY
0x140300000d00      MODIFY
0x140300000d00      MODIFY
0x140300000d00      MODIFY
0x140300000d00      MODIFY
0x140300000d00      ENDXACT
```

Create table *t1* for Examples 8 through 11

For these examples, I'll move out of the normal *pubs* tables to update a table that
has more fixed-length columns. First I'll create table *t1*:

```
CREATE TABLE t1
(
c1          int             NOT NULL PRIMARY KEY,
c2          smallint        NOT NULL DEFAULT 2,
c3          tinyint         NOT NULL DEFAULT 3,
c4          char(4)         NOT NULL DEFAULT 'col4',
c5          char(5)         NULL DEFAULT 'col5',
c6          varchar(6)      NOT NULL DEFAULT 'col 6',
c7          datetime        NOT NULL DEFAULT GETDATE(),
c8          char(8)         NOT NULL DEFAULT 'col 8',
c9          char(9)         NOT NULL DEFAULT 'col 9',
c10         char(10)        NOT NULL DEFAULT 'col 10',
c11         char(11)        NOT NULL DEFAULT 'col 11',
c12         varchar(255)    NULL DEFAULT REPLICATE('A', 60)
-- Put 60 A chars here by default
)
GO

CREATE NONCLUSTERED INDEX ind_t1 ON t1 (c4)
GO
```

```
INSERT t1 VALUES
    (1, DEFAULT, DEFAULT, DEFAULT, DEFAULT, DEFAULT, DEFAULT,
    DEFAULT, DEFAULT, DEFAULT, DEFAULT, DEFAULT)
INSERT t1 VALUES
    (2, DEFAULT, DEFAULT, DEFAULT, DEFAULT, DEFAULT, DEFAULT,
    DEFAULT, DEFAULT, DEFAULT, DEFAULT, DEFAULT)
INSERT t1 VALUES
    (3, DEFAULT, DEFAULT, DEFAULT, DEFAULT, DEFAULT, DEFAULT,
    DEFAULT, DEFAULT, DEFAULT, DEFAULT, DEFAULT)
GO
```

EXAMPLE 8

This example shows an unqualified update, which affects all rows. (Here it affects only three rows, but that's enough.) All five columns being updated are fixed-length, and none are keys of an index. The row length is about 126 bytes, so the modifications to these five fields still affect well less than half the total length. Nothing here prevents update-in-place and the direct-field-update optimization, despite the fact that the update affects multiple rows:

```
UPDATE t1
SET c2=200, c3=20, c7=GETDATE(), c8='new 8', c9='new 9'

(3 row(s) affected)
```

Because direct-field-update was used here, no trace flag 323 output appears. Note that the 15 MODIFY log records reflect five columns that are being updated in-place for three rows. (Remember that an update-in-place generates a MODIFY record for every column of every row that changes value.)

```
0x340300002100      BEGINXACT
0x340300002100      MODIFY
0x340300002100      MODIFY
0x340300002100      MODIFY
0x340300002100      MODIFY
0x340300002100      MODIFY
0x340300002100      MODIFY
0x340300002100      MODIFY
0x340300002100      MODIFY
0x340300002100      MODIFY
0x340300002100      MODIFY
0x340300002100      MODIFY
0x340300002100      MODIFY
0x340300002100      MODIFY
0x340300002100      MODIFY
0x340300002100      MODIFY
0x340300002100      ENDXACT
```

EXAMPLE 9

Similar to the update in Example 8, this example updates a sixth fixed-length column. An update-in-place is not prevented, but the direct-field-update optimization can no longer be used since more than five columns are being updated. Notice that trace flag 323 produces output for every row updated:

```
UPDATE t1
SET c2=200, c3=20, c7=GETDATE(), c8='new 8', c9='new 9',
    c10='new 10'

Update: in-place, clust, safeind[0]=0x1
Update: in-place, clust, safeind[0]=0x1
Update: in-place, clust, safeind[0]=0x1

(3 row(s) affected)
```

The log records have three rows by six columns, so you might expect a total of 18 MODIFY records. However, only two columns are being changed because of the update done in Example 8. Column $c7$ is set to the current datetime, which will be a different value. And column $c10$ is changed. But all the other columns are set to the same value that was updated in Example 8. Because only two columns are being changed, for three rows, only 6 MODIFY records are written:

```
0x0d0300000e00        BEGINXACT
0x0d0300000e00        MODIFY
0x0d0300000e00        MODIFY
0x0d0300000e00        MODIFY
0x0d0300000e00        MODIFY
0x0d0300000e00        MODIFY
0x0d0300000e00        MODIFY
0x0d0300000e00        ENDXACT
```

To further emphasize the point that MODIFY records do not get written if an update-in-place doesn't result in a changed value for a column, here is the Example 9 update, but without changing the value of $c7$ and doing a dummy update of it back to its current value:

```
UPDATE t1
SET c2=200, c3=20, c7=c7, c8='new 8', c9='new 9',
    c10='new 10'

Update: in-place, clust, safeind[0]=0x1
Update: in-place, clust, safeind[0]=0x1
Update: in-place, clust, safeind[0]=0x1

(3 row(s) affected)
```

In this case, the only log records written are the BEGIN and END transactions. There was no delete/insert of the row, and no column values changed, so MODIFY records did not need to be written for them.

```
0x0d0300001700      BEGINXACT
0x0d0300001700      ENDXACT
```

EXAMPLE 10

In this example, the Halloween problem resulting from updating the primary key requires that this update be deferred:

```
UPDATE t1 SET c1=c1 + 1
Update: full delete/insert, deferred mode, clust, safeind[0]=0xfe
Update: full delete/insert, deferred mode, clust, safeind[0]=0xfe
Update: full delete/insert, deferred mode, clust, safeind[0]=0xfe

(3 row(s) affected)
```

The log records reflect the two-step logging of the deferred update. Because a deferred update is always a full delete/insert, the nonclustered index must also be adjusted, even though its key field is not being updated. The need to fix up all indexes is one of the main reasons an on-page delete/insert can be significantly more efficient than a full delete/insert:

```
0x1a0300001500      BEGINXACT    -- Start transaction
0x1a0300001500      DNOOP        -- First row delete-NOOP 1st step for
                                    deferred delete/insert
0x1a0300001500      INOOP        -- First row insert-NOOP 1st step for
                                    deferred delete/insert
0x1a0300001500      DNOOP        -- Second row delete-NOOP 1st step for
                                    deferred delete/insert
0x1a0300001500      INOOP        -- Second row delete-NOOP 1st step for
                                    deferred delete/insert
0x1a0300001500      DNOOP        -- Third row delete-NOOP 1st step for
                                    deferred delete/insert
0x1a0300001500      INOOP        -- Third row delete-NOOP 1st step for
                                    deferred delete/insert
0x1a0300001500      IDELETE      -- The nonclustered index entry is deleted
                                    for 1st row
0x1a0300001500      DELETE       -- Actual delete of first row
0x1a0300001500      IDELETE      -- The nonclustered index entry is deleted
                                    for 2nd row
0x1a0300001500      DELETE       -- Delete of second row
0x1a0300001500      IDELETE      -- The nonclustered index entry is deleted
                                    for 3rd row
0x1a0300001500      DELETE       -- Delete of third row
```

```
0x1a0300001500      INSIND      -- Step 2 insert of 1st row
0x1a0300001500      IINSERT     -- The nonclustered index entry is inserted
                                   for 1st row
0x1a0300001500      INSIND      -- Step 2 insert of 2nd row
0x1a0300001500      IINSERT     -- The nonclustered index entry is inserted
                                   for 2nd row
0x1a0300001500      INSIND      -- Step 2 insert of 3rd row
0x1a0300001500      IINSERT     -- The nonclustered index entry is inserted
                                   for 3rd row
0x1a0300001500      ENDXACT     -- Transaction commits
```

EXAMPLE 11

Full delete/insert isn't limited only to deferred updates. If a direct update makes the row no longer able to fit on the page, the update must also be performed as a full delete/insert, even though it will not have the two-step logging process of a deferred update. For this example, I need to fill up some pages by adding more data rows so that a row being updated grows significantly and will no longer fit on the same page:

```
DECLARE @mycounter smallint
SELECT @mycounter=5
WHILE (@mycounter <= 20)
BEGIN
    INSERT t1 VALUES
        (@mycounter, DEFAULT, DEFAULT, DEFAULT, DEFAULT,
        DEFAULT, DEFAULT, DEFAULT, DEFAULT, DEFAULT,
        DEFAULT, DEFAULT)
    SELECT @mycounter=@mycounter + 1
END
```

The following update could be done as on-page delete/insert if it would fit—but it won't. It can still be a direct update (as opposed to deferred), but it must be a full delete/insert:

```
UPDATE t1
SET c2=c2 + 1, c3=20 + 1, c8='even newer 8', c7=GETDATE(),
    c9='even newer 9', c10='even newer 10',
    c12=REPLICATE('B', 255)
WHERE c1=14

Update: full delete/insert, old/new rowlen=136/331,
    freespace=130,
clust, safeind[0]=0x1

(1 row(s) affected)
```

This is not a deferred update, but since there is no longer room for the page, a full delete/insert must be done and all indexes must also be fixed up. In this case, a page split is necessary to allocate a new page:

```
0x140300001300    BEGINXACT
0x140300001300    IDELETE      -- Delete from nonclustered index
0x140300001300    DELETE       -- Delete of data
0x140300001300    SALLOC       -- Allocation for page split
0x140300001300    INSERT       -- Insert of data
0x140300001300    IINSERT      -- Insert of nonclustered index
0x140300001300    IINSERT      -- Free slot in nonclustered index
0x140300001300    CHGINDSTAT   -- Index fixup for split
0x140300001300    ENDXACT
```

> **NOTE** If the last row on a data page is deleted, that page is *deallocated*. (If the page is the only one remaining in the table, it is not deallocated. A table always contains at least one page, even if it is empty.) Index pages are deallocated if a row is deleted (which again might occur as part of a delete/insert update strategy), leaving only one entry on the index page. That entry will be moved to its neighboring page, and then the empty page will be deallocated.

Locking

Any data modification must always be protected with some form of exclusive lock. In Chapter 13, "Locking," I'll discuss the different types of locks and their compatibility. Although I won't repeat that information here, I want to point out some key items to remember about data modification and locking:

- Every type of data modification performed in SQL Server will require some form of exclusive lock (EX_PAGE, IX_PAGE, EX_TAB). For UPDATE and INSERT operations, page locking will be most common, but if many locks are required, this could escalate to a table lock.

- Update locks (UP_PAGE) can be used to signal the intention to do an update and are important to avoid deadlock conditions. But ultimately the UPDATE operation requires that an exclusive lock be performed. The update lock serializes access to ensure that an exclusive lock will be able to be acquired, but the update lock is not sufficient by itself.

- Exclusive locks must always be held until the end of a transaction in case the transaction needs to be undone (unlike shared locks, which can be released as soon as the scan moves off the page, assuming READ COMMITTED isolation is in effect).

■ If a full table scan must be employed to find qualifying rows for an update or a delete, an exclusive table lock is required to be held for the duration of your transaction. It is important to make sure that your UPDATE and DELETE statements are bounded with a WHERE clause that can limit the search to relatively few rows. Doing full table scans to update rows is not going to result in a high-concurrency environment.

SUMMARY

In this chapter, we discussed data modification within SQL Server. Most data modification is made with the three SQL DML statements: INSERT, UPDATE, and DELETE. Although you can typically think of INSERT as affecting only one row, SQL Server provides several forms of INSERT that can insert an entire result set at once. In addition, SQL Server offers utilities and interfaces for fast bulk loading of data. UPDATE and DELETE operations can be searched, bringing to bear all the power of the SQL query.

I also showed you some internal considerations, including the placement of rows in tables, logging, locking, and space utilization. The possible update modes and methods (such as update-in-place versus delete/insert) were also discussed, with examples illustrating the various update strategies.

Now we'll move on to aspects of using the Transact-SQL extensions that offer the kind of power that is normally associated with programming languages.

9

Programming
with Transact-SQL

Introduction

Transact-SQL allows you to use standard SQL as a programming language to write logic that can execute within the database engine. This extremely powerful capability is one of the keys to the success and growth of Microsoft SQL Server. Transact-SQL simplifies application development and reduces the amount of conversation necessary between the client application and the server by allowing more code to be processed at the server.

In this book, I will not delve into all the available syntax of the Transact-SQL language. I'll leave that to the SQL Server documentation. Instead, I'll present the significant programming constructs available, make some comments, and show you some examples. In Chapter 7, "Querying Data," I showed you details of the SELECT statement, which is the foundation for effective use of Transact-SQL. Before reading any further, be sure you have a good understanding of the concepts presented in that chapter.

This chapter focuses on the Transact-SQL programming extensions, such as control of flow, looping, error handling, and environment-specific options. These extensions allow you to easily write complex routines entirely in SQL, and they provide the basis for the additional power of Transact-SQL over standard SQL. In Chapter 10, I will cover batches, transactions, stored procedures, and triggers. Chapter 11 deals with scrollable cursors, which bridge the set-based world of SQL with sequential processing. In Chapter 12, I'll show some extensive Transact-SQL examples that use Transact-SQL in sometimes nonintuitive ways. For those of you interested in developing applications using SQL Server, all of these chapters will provide important information.

Transact-SQL as a Programming Language

Is Transact-SQL really a programming language? On the "No" side, I do not claim that Transact-SQL is an alternative to C, C++, Microsoft Visual Basic, COBOL, Fortran, or such 4GL development environments as PowerBuilder or Delphi. I can't think of a substantial application that I could write entirely in Transact-SQL, and every one of those other languages or tools exist to do exactly that. Also, Transact-SQL offers no user interface and no file or device I/O, and the programming constructs are simple and limited. But I still argue that the answer is basically "Yes." Transact-SQL is a specialized language that is best used in addition to one of those other languages or tools. It allows SQL Server to be programmed to execute complex tasks requiring branching and looping without the need for code to be written in another language. Transact-SQL provides the services to declare and set variables, to branch, to loop, and to check errors. I can write reusable routines that I subsequently invoke and pass variables to. I can introduce bugs if I make an error in logic or syntax. My Transact-SQL code can quickly get so complicated that I am thrilled that I now can use the same debugger I use for C, C++, and Java development to step into and debug Transact-SQL routines.

With Transact-SQL routines, conditional logic executes within the SQL Server engine and even within an executing SQL statement. This can greatly improve performance—the alternative would be message passing between the client process and the server. In today's increasingly networked world, reducing those round-trip conversations is key to developing and deploying efficient applications. Some might claim that the emergence of the Internet makes client/server computing irrelevant. But in fact, the typically slow network conditions found in Internet applications make client/server computing *more important*—operations should be written so that the client/server conversation is minimized. There's no better way to do this than to use the programming aspects of Transact-SQL to let whole routines execute remotely, without the need for intermediate processing at the client. The corresponding performance gains are phenomenal.

In addition, by having SQL Server (rather than the application) handle the database logic, applications can often better insulate themselves from change. An application can execute a procedure simply by calling it and passing some parameters, and then the database structure or the procedure can change radically while the application remains entirely unaffected. So long as the inputs and outputs of the procedure are unchanged, the application is shielded from underlying changes to the database. Being able to encapsulate the database routines can result in a more efficient development environment for large projects in which the application programmers are often distinct from the database experts.

The three-tier model has gained supporters who view the model as preferable, for some applications, to the more traditional two-tier client/server model. Figures 9-1 and 9-2 show both models.

Two-Tier Model

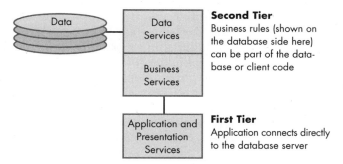

Second Tier
Business rules (shown on the database side here) can be part of the database or client code

First Tier
Application connects directly to the database server

Figure 9-1. *The two-tier model.*

Three-Tier Model

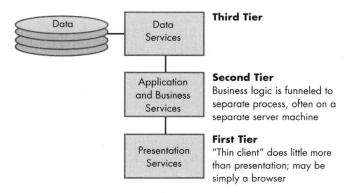

Third Tier

Second Tier
Business logic is funneled to separate process, often on a separate server machine

First Tier
"Thin client" does little more than presentation; may be simply a browser

Figure 9-2. *The three-tier model.*

The two-tier model has a client (first tier) and a server (second tier); the client handles application and presentation logic, and the server handles data services and business services. The two-tier model uses the so-called *fat client*—the client does a large amount of application processing locally. Many solutions deployed today use this topology; certainly the lion's share of today's non-Internet client/server solutions are two-tier.

In the three-tier model, a *thin client* handles mostly presentation tasks. Supporters of the three-tier approach point out that this model allows the client computer to be less powerful; allows a variety of different client operating environments (obviously the case with Internet browsers); and reduces the complexity of installing, configuring, and maintaining software at the client. The client connects to an application server that handles the application process. The application server then connects to the database server, handling data services. The application server typically is a more powerful machine than the client, and it has all the issues of application code maintenance, configuration, operations, and so on. Because there are presumably many fewer application servers then clients, basic arithmetic says that these server costs and issues should be reduced in the three-tier model. (The three tiers are logical concepts; the actual number of computers involved might be more or less than three.) Typically, you are part of a three-tier model when you use the Internet with a browser and access a Web page residing on an Internet server that performs database work. For example, a mail-order company's Web page that checks current availability by accessing its inventory in SQL Server via ODBC calls is a three-tier application.

I'm not emotionally tied to either two-tier or three-tier solutions, and I prefer to stay out of the debate. Both have advantages and disadvantages, and I view each as a potential solution to a given problem, since I've seen excellent solutions using both approaches. I believe that the specifics of the problem and the constraints imposed by the environment (including costs, hardware, and expertise of both development staff and user community) should drive the solution's overall design. I do, however, take exception to those who claim that a three-tier solution means that such capabilities as stored procedures, rules, constraints, or triggers are no longer important or shouldn't be used. In a three-tier solution, the "middle" tier doing application logic is still a client from the perspective of the database services (that is, SQL Server). Consequently, for that tier it is still preferable that remote work be done close to the data. If the data can be accessed by servers other than the application server, integrity checking must be done at the database server as well as in the application. (Otherwise, you've left a gaping hole for the integrity checks in the application to be circumvented.)

From the Author...

Perhaps the single most successful three-tier solution available today is R/3 from SAP. The financial and operations capabilities provided by R/3 use a three-tier model, with a terminal-like interface connected to the R/3 application server, which then accesses Microsoft SQL Server. (R/3 supports several databases, but here I'm emphasizing the solution's topology when using SQL Server.) The R/3 application server wisely and heavily uses stored procedures that provide both performance gains and development efficiency.

Throughout this book, unless otherwise noted, I refer to *client* from the perspective of SQL Server. The client sends the commands and processes the results, and it makes no difference to SQL Server if this is done by an application server process or by the process that the end user is running directly. The benefits of the programmable server provide much more efficient network usage and better abstraction of data services from the application and application server.

Transact-SQL Programming Constructs—The Basics

Transact-SQL extends standard SQL by adding many useful programming constructs. These constructs will look familiar to developers experienced with C/C++, Basic/Visual Basic, Fortran, Java, Pascal, and similar languages. The Transact-SQL extensions are wonderful additions to the original SQL standard. Before the extensions were available, requests to the database were always simple, single statements. Any conditional logic had to be done by the calling application. With a slow network or via the Internet, this would be disastrous, requiring many trips across the network—more than are needed by simply letting conditions be evaluated at the server and allowing subsequent branching of execution.

Variables

Without variables, a programming language would not be very useful; Transact-SQL is no exception. Variables that you declare are *local variables,* having scope and visibility only within the declaring connection. In code, the @ character designates a local variable. Transact-SQL also provides *global variables,* which are designated by @@.

Global variables

In Transact-SQL, global variables, such as @@ERROR (the last return code generated for the connection) and @@ROWCOUNT (the number of rows selected or affected by the last statement), are built in. All connections have access to these variables. The term "global" is different from what you might assume if you are coming from a background of such programming languages as C/C++ or Visual Basic. A better name might have been "automatic variables," because every connection can automatically see each of the global variables. However, the scoping of the value the connection sees is often limited to that connection. For example, @@ERROR represents the last error number generated for a specific connection, not the last error number in the entire system. Currently, a user connection cannot declare a global variable; global variables are predefined, preexisting, automatic values. User-declared global variables would be a nice enhancement that I hope we'll see in a future release. Until then, temporary tables provide a decent alternative for sharing values among connections.

> ### More Information...
>
> For more information about SQL Server's built-in global variables, refer to the Appendix section of this book. This information was extracted from the SQL Server documentation, which also appears on the CD-ROM in this book.

Local variables

You declare local variables at the beginning of a batch or a stored procedure. (The batch or stored procedure can be part of a transaction as well.) You can subsequently assign values to local variables with the SELECT statement, using an equal (=) operator. The values assigned can be constants, other variables, or expressions, and they are typically selected from a column in a table. Variables can be returned in a result set using a standard SELECT statement.

In the following simple example, I declare two variables, assign values to them, and then select their values as a result set. (Note that a single statement can declare multiple variables or assign values to the variables. This group declare/assign approach is usually the preferable method, but the steps can also be done separately.)

```
DECLARE @min_range int, @hi_range int          -- Variables declared
SELECT  @min_range=0,                           -- Variables assigned
        @hi_range=MAX(hirange) FROM roysched
SELECT  @min_range, @hi_range                   -- Variables selected
```

Be careful when assigning variables by selecting a value from the database—you want to ensure that the SELECT statement will return only one row. It is perfectly legal to assign a variable to a SELECT statement that will return multiple rows, but its value is probably not what you expect: no error message is returned, and the variable will have the value of the last row returned.

For example, suppose that the following *stor_name* values exist in the *stores* table of the *pubs* database:

```
stor_name
---------
Eric the Read Books
Barnum's
News & Brews
Doc-U-Mat: Quality Laundry and Books
Fricative Bookshop
Bookbeat
```

The following assignment will run without error but is probably a mistake:

```
DECLARE @stor_name varchar(30)
SELECT @stor_name=stor_name FROM stores
```

The resulting value of *@stor_name* is the last row, *Bookbeat*. But consider the order returned, without an ORDER BY clause, as a chance occurrence. Assigning a variable to a SELECT statement that returns more than one row would usually not be intended, and it is probably a bug introduced by the developer. To avoid this situation, you should qualify the SELECT statement with an appropriate WHERE clause to limit the result set to the one row that meets your criteria. Often this is an aggregate function, such as MAX(), MIN(), or SUM(). Then you can select only the value you want. If you want the assignment to be to only one row of a SELECT statement that might return many rows, you should at least use *SET ROWCOUNT 1* to avoid the effort of gathering many rows, with all but one row thrown out. (In this case, the first row would be returned, not the last. You could use ORDER BY to explicitly indicate what row should be first.) You might also consider checking the value of @@ROWCOUNT immediately after the assignment and, if it is greater than 1, branch off to an error routine.

You can also assign a value to a variable in an UPDATE statement. This approach can be useful and more efficient than using separate statements to swap values. For example, suppose that in the *jobs* table I realize the *min* and *max* columns have accidentally been reversed. The following UPDATE statement efficiently swaps all the values. (To run this example, you must disable the CHECK constraints on the *min_lvl* and *max_lvl* columns.)

```
DECLARE @tmp_val tinyint
BEGIN TRAN
UPDATE jobs SET @tmp_val=min_lvl, min_lvl=max_lvl,
    max_lvl=@tmp_val
```

Control-of-Flow Tools

Like any programming language worth its salt, Transact-SQL provides a decent set of control-of-flow tools. (True, Transact-SQL has only a handful of tools, perhaps not as many as you would like; but they're enough to make it dramatically more powerful than standard SQL.) The control-of-flow tools include conditional logic (IF...ELSE and CASE), loops (only WHILE, but it comes with CONTINUE and BREAK options), unconditional branching (GOTO), and the ability to RETURN a status value to a calling routine. Here is a quick summary of these control-of-flow constructs, which I'll use at various times in this book:

Construct	Description
BEGIN...END	Defines a statement block. Using BEGIN...END allows a group of statements to be executed. Typically, BEGIN immediately follows IF, ELSE, or WHILE. (Otherwise, only the next statement will be executed.) For C programmers, BEGIN...END is similar to using a {..} block after IF.

(continued)

continued

Construct	Description
GOTO label	Continues processing at the statement following the label: as defined by the label.
IF...ELSE	Defines conditional and, optionally, alternate (ELSE) execution when a condition is false.
RETURN [*n*]	Exits unconditionally. Typically used in a stored procedure (although it can also be used in a batch). Optionally, a whole number *n* (positive or negative) can be set as the return status, which can be assigned to a variable when executing the stored procedure.
WAITFOR	Sets a time for statement execution. The time can be a delay interval or a specified time to execute (a specified time of day). The time can be passed as a literal or with a variable.
WHILE	The basic looping construct for SQL Server. Repeats a statement (or block) while a specific condition is true.
...BREAK	Exits the innermost WHILE loop.
...CONTINUE	Restarts a WHILE loop.

CASE

The CASE expression is enormously powerful. Although CASE is part of the ANSI SQL-92 specification, it is not required for ANSI compliance certification, and few products other than Microsoft SQL Server have implemented it. If you have experience with an SQL database other than Microsoft SQL Server, chances are you haven't used CASE. If that's the *case* (pun intended), you should get familiar with it now. It is time well spent. We added CASE in version 6.0, and sometimes I wonder how I managed without it.

CASE is conceptually a simpler way to do IF-ELSE IF-ELSE IF-ELSE IF-ELSE type operations. It is roughly equivalent to a "switch" statement in C. However, CASE is far more than a shorthand for IF—in fact, it's not really even that. CASE is an expression, not a control-of-flow keyword, which means that it can be used *only* in SELECT or UPDATE statements. (IF cannot be used in either.)

Here's a simple example of CASE. Suppose that I want to classify books in the *pubs* database by price. I want to segregate them as low priced, moderately priced, or expensive. And I'd like to do this with a single SELECT statement and not use UNION. Without CASE, I can't do it. With CASE, it's a snap:

```
SELECT
title,
price,
'classification'=CASE
```

```
    WHEN price < 10.00 THEN "Low Priced"
    WHEN price BETWEEN 10.00 AND 20.00 THEN 'Moderately Priced'
    WHEN price > 20.00 THEN 'Expensive'
    ELSE 'Unknown'
    END
FROM titles
```

(Notice that even in this example I need to worry about NULL, since a NULL price won't fit into any of the category buckets.)

Here are the abbreviated results:

```
title                                   price   classification
-------------------------------------   ------  -----------------
The Busy Executive's Database Guide      19.99   Moderately Priced
Cooking with Computers: Surreptitious    11.95   Moderately Priced
Balance Sheets
You Can Combat Computer Stress!           2.99   Low Priced
Straight Talk About Computers            19.99   Moderately Priced
Silicon Valley Gastronomic Treats        19.99   Moderately Priced
The Gourmet Microwave                     2.99   Low Priced
The Psychology of Computer Cooking      (null)   Unknown
But Is It User Friendly?                 22.95   Expensive
```

If you want to compare the value in the CASE statement to a constant, you can use an even simpler form so that you don't have to keep repeating the expression. You might recall that in Chapter 8, "Modifying Data," I displayed the log records generated for various updates. I did this via a query that decoded the *op* code field of the *syslogs* table to the log record type. This was just one big CASE statement, as shown below.

> **NOTE** The log records themselves will surely change in the future, and *syslogs* as a partially exposed table will probably go away, too. You'll likely find this example valuable, but please don't base your application on it because the underlying components will change.

```
SELECT
xactid AS TRAN_ID,
CASE op
    WHEN 0   THEN 'BEGINXACT'      -- Start transaction
    WHEN 1   THEN 'Not Used'
    WHEN 2   THEN 'Not Used'
    WHEN 3   THEN 'Not Used'
    WHEN 4   THEN 'INSERT'         -- Insert row
    WHEN 5   THEN 'DELETE'         -- Delete row
    WHEN 6   THEN 'INSIND'         -- Deferred update step 2 insert record
    WHEN 7   THEN 'IINSERT'        -- NC index insert
```

```
    WHEN 8   THEN 'IDELETE'        -- NC index delete
    WHEN 9   THEN 'MODIFY'         -- Modify row
    WHEN 10  THEN 'NOOP'           -- Noop
    WHEN 11  THEN 'INOOP'          -- Deferred update step 1 insert record
    WHEN 12  THEN 'DNOOP'          -- Deferred update step 1 delete record
    WHEN 13  THEN 'ALLOC'          -- Allocation
    WHEN 14  THEN 'DBNEXTID'       -- Extent allocation
    WHEN 15  THEN 'EXTENT'         -- Extent allocation
    WHEN 16  THEN 'SPLIT'          -- Page split
    WHEN 17  THEN 'CHECKPOINT'     -- Checkpoint
    WHEN 18  THEN 'SAVEXACT'       -- Savepoint
    WHEN 19  THEN 'CMD'
    WHEN 20  THEN 'DEXTENT'        -- Deallocate extent
    WHEN 21  THEN 'DEALLOC'        -- Deallocate page
    WHEN 22  THEN 'DROPEXTS'       -- Delete all extents on alloc pg
    WHEN 23  THEN 'AEXTENT'        -- Alloc extent - mark all pgs used
    WHEN 24  THEN 'SALLOC'         -- Alloc new page for split
    WHEN 25  THEN 'Not Used'
    WHEN 26  THEN 'Not Used'
    WHEN 27  THEN 'SORT'           -- Sort allocations
    WHEN 28  THEN 'SODEALLOC'      -- Related to sort allocations
    WHEN 29  THEN 'ALTDB'          -- Alter database record
    WHEN 30  THEN 'ENDXACT'        -- End transaction
    WHEN 31  THEN 'SORTTS'         -- Related to sort allocations
    WHEN 32  THEN 'TEXT'           -- Log record of direct TEXT insert
    WHEN 33  THEN 'INOOPTEXT'      -- Log record for deferred TEXT insert
    WHEN 34  THEN 'DNOOPTEXT'      -- Log record for deferred TEXT delete
    WHEN 35  THEN 'INSINDTEXT'     -- Indirect insert log record
    WHEN 36  THEN 'TEXTDELETE'     -- Delete text log record
    WHEN 37  THEN 'SORTEDSPLIT'    -- Used for sorted splits
    WHEN 38  THEN 'CHGINDSTAT'     -- Incremental sysindexes stat changes
    WHEN 39  THEN 'CHGINDPG'       -- Direct change to sysindexes
    WHEN 40  THEN 'TXTPTR'         -- Info log row WHEN retrieving TEXTPTR
    WHEN 41  THEN 'TEXTINFO'       -- Info log for WRITETEXT/UPDATETEXT
    WHEN 42  THEN 'RESETIDENT'     -- Used WHEN a truncate table resets an
                                      identity value
    WHEN 43 THEN 'UNDO'            -- Compensating log record for Insert
                                      Only Row Locking (IORL)
    WHEN 44 THEN 'INSERT_IORL'     -- Insert with row locking record
    WHEN 45 THEN 'INSIND_IORL'     -- INSIND with IORL
    WHEN 46 THEN 'IINSERT_IORL'    -- IINDEX with IORL
    WHEN 47 THEN 'SPLIT_IORL'      -- Page split with IORL
    WHEN 48 THEN 'SALLOC_IORL'     -- Alloc new page for split with IORL
    WHEN 49 THEN 'ALLOC_IORL'      -- Allocation with IORL
    WHEN 50 THEN 'PREALLOCLOG'     -- Preallocate log space for CLRs
    ELSE 'Unknown Type' END  AS LOG_RECORD
FROM syslogs
GO
```

You can use CASE in some unusual places; because it is an expression, you can use it anywhere an expression is legal. You can use CASE in the SET statement of UPDATE, in WHERE clauses, in GROUP BY/HAVING clauses, in subqueries, and in views. Using CASE in a view is a nice technique that can make your database more usable to others. For an example, in Chapter 7, I used CASE in a view using CUBE to shield users from the complexity of "grouping NULL" values. Using CASE in an UPDATE statement can make the update easier, and, more important, it can allow you to make changes in a single pass of the data that otherwise would require that you do multiple UPDATE statements, each of which would have to scan the data. The Transact-SQL documentation has a nice conceptual example that I'll reproduce here. Although it works fine and illustrates CASE, the second example shows the UPDATE statement rewritten with an equivalent formulation that I think is more intuitive.

```
-- In this example, reviews have been turned in and big salary
-- adjustments are due. A review rating of 4 will double the
-- worker's salary, 3 will increase it by 60 percent, 2 will
-- increase it by 20 percent, and a rating lower than 2 results
-- in no raise. A raise will not be given if the employee has
-- been at the company for less than 18 months.
UPDATE employee_salaries
    SET salary=
        CASE
            WHEN (review=4 AND
                (DATEDIFF(month, hire_date, GETDATE()) >= 18))
                THEN salary * 2.0
            WHEN (review=3 AND
                (DATEDIFF(month, hire_date, GETDATE()) >= 18))
                THEN salary * 1.6
            WHEN (review=2 AND
                (DATEDIFF(month, hire_date, GETDATE()) >= 18))
                THEN salary * 1.2
            ELSE salary
        END

-- This second formulation is identical, but I think it is more
-- intuitive and clearer
UPDATE employee_salaries
    SET salary=
        CASE review
            WHEN 4 THEN salary * 2.0
            WHEN 3 THEN salary * 1.6
            WHEN 2 THEN salary * 1.2
            ELSE salary
        END
    WHERE (DATEDIFF(month, hire_date, GETDATE()) > 18)
```

Cousins of CASE

SQL Server provides three nice shorthand derivatives of CASE: COALESCE, NULLIF, and ISNULL. COALESCE and NULLIF are both part of the ANSI SQL-92 specification; we added them to version 6.0 at the same time that we added CASE. ISNULL() is a longtime SQL Server function. Following is the syntax for these functions.

COALESCE

```
COALESCE (expression1, expression2, ... expressionN)
```

This statement is equivalent to a searched CASE expression that returns the first NOT NULL expression in a list of expressions. If no non-null values are found, CASE returns NULL (which is what *expressionN* was, given there were no non-null values). Written as a CASE expression, COALESCE looks like this:

```
CASE
    WHEN expression1 IS NOT NULL THEN expression1
    WHEN expression2 IS NOT NULL THEN expression2
⋮
ELSE expressionN
END
```

NULLIF

```
NULLIF(expression1, expression2)
```

This is equivalent to a searched CASE expression in which NULL is returned if *expression1 = expression2*. If the expressions are not equal, *expression1* is returned. In Chapter 7, I showed how NULLIF can be handy if you use dummy values instead of NULL but you don't want those dummy values to skew the results produced by aggregate functions. Written using CASE, NULLIF looks like this:

```
CASE
    WHEN expression1=expression2 THEN NULL
    ELSE expression1
END
```

ISNULL

```
ISNULL(expression1, expression2)
```

This is almost the mirror of NULLIF. ISNULL allows you to easily substitute an alternative expression or value for an expression that is NULL. In Chapter 7, I made use of ISNULL to substitute the string *'ALL'* for a grouping NULL when using CUBE and I used a string of question marks, *'????'* for a NULL value. By doing this, I made the results more clear and intuitive to users. Written instead using CASE, ISNULL looks like this:

```
CASE
    WHEN expression1 IS NULL THEN expression2
    ELSE expression1
END
```

The SQL Server documentation implies that ISNULL can be used only to return a constant value. In fact, ISNULL can be an expression or even a SELECT statement. Say, for example, that I want to query the *titles* table. If a title has NULL for *price,* I want to instead use the lowest price that exists for any book. Without CASE or ISNULL, this is not an easily written query. With ISNULL, it's easy:

```
SELECT title, pub_id, ISNULL(price, (SELECT MIN(price)
    FROM titles)) FROM titles
```

For comparison, here's an equivalent SELECT statement written with the long-hand CASE formulation:

```
SELECT title, pub_id,
    CASE WHEN price IS NULL THEN (SELECT MIN(price) FROM titles)
    ELSE price
    END
FROM titles
```

Comments

As you've seen in examples throughout this book, you can put comments almost anywhere within a SQL Server batch file. You can add comments to explain a subtle query or to explain why a constraint is being added to CREATE TABLE, or you can comment out a line in a query while you're debugging it. As is true with programming in general, you should use comments generously in your SQL code to make it clear and easy to maintain.

Comments do have some disadvantages, however: Because they are sent from the client to the server, they increase network traffic somewhat. And there is a limit of about 64 KB for how much text a stored procedure can contain, of which comments are part. In typical use, however, neither of these limitations is much of a worry.

SQL comments come in two forms: C-style blocks of /*...*/ delineate a block of comments, and the double-hyphen (--), which is the ANSI standard, precedes the comment on that line only. The double-hyphen is analogous to the double-slash (//) used in comments in the C++ language.

> **NOTE** The text limit in stored procedures is a result of the fact that the text of a stored procedure, view, and trigger is kept in *syscomments,* in a *varchar(255)* field, with a row sequencing column, *colid,* which is a *tinyint* (maximum value of 255). Hence, there can be 255 × 255 bytes of text (65,025 total). At the time *syscomments* was originally designed, there was no *text* datatype, which would have been the natural thing to use. The designers, unfortunately, were a bit short-sighted in making *colid* only a *tinyint*. This limitation will be eliminated in a future version of SQL Server. Earlier, the compiled plan was limited to 64, 2-KB pages (128 KB total), but that limit was eliminated in version 6.0.

PRINT and RAISERROR

Transact-SQL, like other programming languages, provides printing capability through the PRINT and RAISERROR statements.

PRINT

PRINT is the most basic way to display a character string of a maximum of 255 characters. You can display a literal character string or a variable of type *char* or *varchar*. PRINT takes a single parameter: the literal string or the variable. This means that you cannot use string functions or the concatenation operator directly in the PRINT statement. You can use string functions and the concatenation operator when you assign the string to a variable, and then simply print the variable, however, as I'll show you in a moment.

Seems as though every time you learn a new programming language, the first assignment is to write the "Hello World" program. Using TRANSACT-SQL, it couldn't be easier:

```
PRINT 'Hello World'
```

PRINT is extremely simple, both in its use and in its capabilities. It is not nearly as powerful as, say, *printf()* in C. You can't give positional parameters, concatenate strings, or control formatting. For example, you *cannot* do this:

```
PRINT 'Today is ' + GETDATE()
```

Or this:

```
PRINT 'Today is %s', GETDATE ()
```

But you can accomplish the same purpose by using a variable. When assigning the variable, you can use string functions to format it, concatenate strings, or use functions. For example:

```
DECLARE @display_date char(20)
SELECT @display_date='Today is ' +
CONVERT(varchar(11), GETDATE(), 100)
PRINT @display_date
```

The string from PRINT is returned to the client, but notice that it is returned as a message (or as an "error" of severity 0), not as a result set. If you are writing an ODBC program, this means the results of a PRINT statement get handled by **SQLError()**; in DB-Library, they get handled by the message handler installed with **dbmsghandle()** (that is, your handler will be called). If you want to return a string as a standard result set, not as a message, you simply select the string. This example returns a result set of one row having one column (of type *varchar*):

```
SELECT 'Today is '+CONVERT(varchar(11), GETDATE(), 100)
```

I can easily give the column an explicit name, such as *today_is*:

```
SELECT today_is='Today is '+CONVERT(varchar(11), GETDATE(), 100)
```

RAISERROR

RAISERROR is similar to PRINT but can be much more powerful than its partner. RAISERROR also sends a message (not a result set) to the client, but it allows you to specify the specific error number and severity of the message. It also allows you to reference an error number, the text for which you can add to the *sysmessages* table. RAISERROR makes it easy for you to develop international versions of your software. Rather than have multiple versions of your SQL code when you want to change the language of the text, you need only one version. You can simply add the text of the message in multiple languages. The user will see the message in the language used by the particular connection. Unlike PRINT, RAISERROR accepts *printf*-like parameter substitution as well as formatting control. RAISERROR also can allow messages to be logged to the Windows NT event service, making them visible to the Windows NT event viewer, and it allows alerts to be configured for these events. All in all, RAISERROR is preferable to PRINT, and I use PRINT only for "quick-and-dirty" situations. For production-caliber code, RAISERROR is a better choice. Here's the syntax:

```
RAISERROR ({msg_id | msg_str}, severity, state[, argument1
[, argument2]])
[WITH LOG]
```

After calling RAISERROR, the global variable @@ERROR will have the value passed as *msg_id*. If no ID is passed, the error will be raised with error number 50000 and @@ERROR will be set to that number. You can also set the severity level; an informational message should be considered severity 0 (or severity 10; 0 and 10 are used interchangeably for a historical reason that's not important here).

Only the system administrator (SA) can raise an error with a severity of 19 or higher. (The SA can also create a stored procedure that can raise such an error, and then grant permission to execute the procedure to someone else.) Errors of severity 20 and higher are considered *fatal,* and the connection to the client will automatically be terminated.

The WITH LOG option must be used for all errors of severity 19 or higher. For such high-severity errors, the message text is not returned to the client. Instead, it is returned to the SQL Server error log and the error number, text, severity, and state are written to the Windows NT event log. The SA can use the WITH LOG option with any error number or any severity level.

Errors written to the Windows NT event log from RAISERROR go to the application event log, with MSSQLServer as the source and Server as the category. These errors have event ID 17060. (Errors that SQL Server raises can have different event IDs, depending on which component they come from.) The type of message in the Windows NT event log depends on the severity used in the RAISERROR statement. Messages with severity 14 and lower are recorded as *informational messages,* severity 15 messages are *warnings,* and severity 16 and higher messages are *errors.* Note that the severity that is recorded in the event log is the number that is passed to RAISERROR, regardless of the stated severity in *sysmessages.* So, although I don't recommend it, you can raise a serious message as informational or a noncritical message as an error. If you look at the data section of the Windows NT event log for a message raised from RAISERROR, or you are reading from it in a program, you'll notice that the error number appears first, followed by the severity level.

You can use any number from 1 through 127 as the *state* parameter. You might pass a line number that tells where the error was raised. But the *state* has no real relevance to SQL Server.

> **TIP** There is a little-known way to cause ISQL.EXE (the command-line version, not the Windows-based version, ISQLW.EXE) to terminate. Raising any error with *state* 127 causes ISQL.EXE to immediately exit, with a return code to the operating system of whatever the error number was. (You can determine the error number from a batch command file with ERRORLEVEL.) You could write your application so that it does something similar—it's a simple change to the error-handling logic. This ISQL.EXE trick can be a useful way to terminate a set of scripts that would be run through ISQL. I've seen some people do this by raising a high severity error to terminate the connection. But using a *state* of 127 is actually simpler, and no scary message will be written to the error log or event log for what is a planned, routine action.

You can add your own messages and text for a message in multiple languages by using the **sp_addmessage** stored procedure. By default, SQL Server uses U.S. English, but you can add languages. (SQL Server distinguishes U.S. English from British because of locale settings, such as currency. The text of messages is the same.) The script \MSSQL\INSTALL\INSTLANG.SQL adds locale settings for nine more languages but not the actual translated messages. By convention, you should consider error numbers lower than 50000 reserved for SQL Server use, so choose a higher number for your own messages.

Suppose that I want to rewrite "Hello World" to use RAISERROR, and I want to make it possible to have the text of the message appear in both U.S. English and German (language ID of 1). Here's how:

```
EXEC sp_addmessage 50001, 10, 'Hello World', @replace='REPLACE'
-- New message 50001 for U.S. English
EXEC sp_addmessage 50001, 10, 'Hallo Welt' , @lang='Deutsch',
    @replace='REPLACE'
-- New message 50001 for German
```

When RAISERROR is executed, the text of the message will be dependent on the SET LANGUAGE setting of the connection. If the connection does a SET LANGUAGE Deutsch, the text returned for RAISERROR (50001, 10, 1) will be *Hallo Welt*. If the text for a language does not exist, the U.S. English text (by default) will be returned. For this reason, the U.S. English message must be added before the text for another language is added. If no entry exists, even in U.S. English, error 2758 results:

```
Msg 2758, Level 16, State 1
RAISERROR could not locate entry for error n in Sysmessages.
```

I can easily enhance the message to say who the "Hello" is from by providing a parameter marker and passing it when calling RAISERROR. (For illustration, I use some *printf*-style formatting, *#6x*, to make the process number be displayed in hexadecimal format.)

```
EXEC sp_addmessage 50001, 10,
    'Hello World from: %s, process id: %#6x', @replace='REPLACE'
```

When user ronsou executes

```
DECLARE @parm1 varchar(30), @parm2 int
SELECT @parm1=USER_NAME(), @parm2=@@spid
RAISERROR (50001, 15, -1, @parm1, @parm2)
```

this error is raised:

```
Msg 50001, Level 15, State 1
Hello World from: ronsou, process id: 0xc
```

Operators

Transact-SQL provides a large collection of operators for doing arithmetic, comparing values, doing bit operations, and concatenating strings. These operators are similar to those you might be familiar with in other programming languages. You can use Transact-SQL operators in any expression, including in the select list of a query, in the WHERE or HAVING clause of queries, in UPDATE and IF statements, and in CASE.

Arithmetic operators

I won't go into much detail here because this is pretty standard stuff. If you need more information on arithmetic operators, see the *Transact-SQL Reference* in the documentation. These are the arithmetic operators:

Symbol	Operation	Used with These Datatypes
+	Addition	*int, smallint, tinyint, numeric, decimal, float, real, money,* and *smallmoney*
–	Subtraction	*int, smallint, tinyint, numeric, decimal, float, real, money,* and *smallmoney*
*	Multiplication	*int, smallint, tinyint, numeric, decimal, float, real, money,* and *smallmoney*
/	Division	*int, smallint, tinyint, numeric, decimal, float, real, money,* and *smallmoney*
%	Modulo	*int, smallint,* and *tinyint*

As with other programming languages, in Transact-SQL you need to consider the datatypes you are using when performing arithmetic operations or you might not get the results you expect. For example, which of the following is correct?

$$1 \div 2 = 0$$

$$1 \div 2 = 0.5$$

If the underlying datatypes are both integers (including *tinyint* and *smallint*), the correct answer is 0. If one or both are *float* (including *real*) or *numeric/decimal* with a nonzero scale, the correct answer is 0.5 (or 0.50000, depending on the precision and scale of the datatype). When doing arithmetic operations, SQL Server implicitly forces the result of the operation to that datatype having the largest scale and precision. For example, an *int* multiplied by a *float* produces a *float*. You can explicitly convert to a given datatype by using the handy CONVERT() function. CONVERT() can act nearly identically to a CAST operation as specified in ANSI SQL-92 (although it's not implemented as such in SQL Server or in most other major products yet).

The addition (+) operator is also used to concatenate character strings. In this example, I want to concatenate last names, followed by a comma, followed by first names from the *authors* table (in *pubs*), and then return the result as a single column:

```
SELECT 'author'=au_lname + ',' + au_fname FROM authors
```

Here's the abbreviated result:

```
author
------
White,Johnson
Green,Marjorie
Carson,Cheryl
O'Leary,Michael
```

Bit operators

These are the SQL Server bit operators:

Symbol	Meaning	Used with These Datatypes
&	Bitwise AND (two operands)	*int, smallint,* or *tinyint* only
|	Bitwise OR (two operands)	*int, smallint,* or *tinyint* only
^	Bitwise exclusive OR (two operands)	*int, smallint,* or *tinyint* only
~	Bitwise NOT (one operand)	*int, smallint, tinyint,* or *bit* only

It's often necessary to keep a lot of indicator-type values in a database, and bit operators make it easy to set up bit masks with a single column to do this. The SQL Server system tables use bit masks. For example, the *status* field in the *sysdatabases* table is a bit mask. If I wanted to see all databases marked as read-only, which is the tenth bit or decimal 1024 (2^{10}), I could use this query:

```
SELECT "read only databases"=name FROM master..sysdatabases
WHERE status & 1024 > 0
```

I use this example for illustration only. In general, it is not a good idea to query the system catalogs directly. Sometimes the catalogs need to change between product releases, and if you query directly, your applications can break because of these required changes. Instead, you should use the provided system catalog stored procedures, which return catalog information in a standard way. If the underlying catalogs change in subsequent releases, the stored procedures are also updated, insulating your application from unexpected changes.

Note that keeping such indicators as *bit* datatype columns can be a better approach than using an *int* as a bit mask. This approach is more straightforward—you do not always need to look up your bit-mask values for each indicator. To write the query above, I had to check the documentation for the bit-mask value for "read only." And many developers, not to mention end users, are not that comfortable using bit operators and are likely to use them incorrectly. From a storage perspective, *bit* columns do not require more space than creating equivalent bit-mask columns requires. (Eight *bit* fields can share the same byte of storage.) True, there are a couple of restrictions on *bit* columns that you don't have if you create a bit mask as an integer and use bit operators: for example, you cannot use NULL or create an index on a *bit* column. But you'd not typically want to do these operations with a "yes/no" indicator field anyway. If you have a huge number of indicator fields, using bit-mask columns of integers instead of *bit* columns might be your only alternative, since a given table in SQL Server can have at most 250 columns. If you frequently add new indicators, using a bit mask on an integer might be better. To add a new indicator, you can make use of an unused bit of an integer status field rather than do an ALTER TABLE and add a new column (which you must do if you use a *bit* column). The case for using a *bit* column boils down to clarity. If the *sysdatabases* table used *bit* columns for its status indicators and had a column called *database_is_readonly,* I could easily and intuitively do the equivalent query in the following manner, and I would not have to check the documentation for the bit-mask value:

```
SELECT "read only databases"=name FROM master..sysdatabases
WHERE database_is_readonly=1
```

Comparison operators

These are the SQL Server comparison operators:

Symbol	Meaning
=	Equal to
>	Greater than
<	Less than
>=	Greater than or equal to
<=	Less than or equal to
< >	Not equal to (ANSI standard)

Symbol	Meaning
!=	Not equal to (not ANSI standard)
!>	Not greater than (not ANSI standard)
!<	Not less than (not ANSI standard)

Comparison operators are straightforward. I can think of only two related issues that might be confusing to a novice SQL Server user:

- When dealing with NULL, remember the issues with three-value logic and the truth tables that were discussed in Chapter 7. Also understand that NULL is an unknown.

- Comparisons of *char* and *varchar* data will depend on the sort order at the SQL Server installation. Whether comparisons evaluate to TRUE depends on the sort order installed. Review the discussion of sort orders in Chapter 4, "Planning for and Installing SQL Server."

Logical and grouping operators (parentheses)

The three logical operators (AND, OR, and NOT) are vitally important in expressions, especially in the WHERE clause. You can use parentheses to group expressions and then apply logical operations to the group. In many cases, it's impossible to correctly formulate a query without using parentheses. In other cases, it might be possible to avoid them, but it's not very intuitive and it could result in bugs. You might construct a convoluted expression using some combination of string concatenations or functions, bit operations, or arithmetic operations instead of using parentheses. But there is no good reason to do this. Using parentheses can make your code more clear, less prone to bugs, and more easily maintained. Because there is no performance penalty beyond parsing in using parentheses, I encourage you to use them liberally. Below is an example query that I could not write intuitively without using parentheses. This is a simple query, and in English the request is easily understood. But this query is also easy to get wrong in Transact-SQL if you're not careful, and it clearly illustrates just how easy it is to make a mistake.

```
Find authors who do not live in either Salt Lake City, UT, or Oakland, CA.
```

Following are four examples that attempt to formulate this query. Three of them are wrong. Test yourself: which one is correctly stated? (As is usually the case, multiple correct formulations are possible—not just the one presented here.)

EXAMPLE 1

```
SELECT au_lname, au_fname, city, state FROM authors
WHERE
city <> 'OAKLAND' AND state <> 'CA'
OR
city <> 'Salt Lake City' AND state <> 'UT'
```

EXAMPLE 2

```
SELECT au_lname, au_fname, city, state FROM authors
WHERE
(city <> 'OAKLAND' AND state <> 'CA')
OR
(city <> 'Salt Lake City' AND state <> 'UT')
```

EXAMPLE 3

```
SELECT au_lname, au_fname, city, state FROM authors
WHERE
(city <> 'OAKLAND' AND state <> 'CA')
AND
(city <> 'Salt Lake City' AND state <> 'UT')
```

EXAMPLE 4

```
SELECT au_lname, au_fname, city, state FROM authors
WHERE
NOT
(
(city='OAKLAND' AND state='CA')
OR
(city='Salt Lake City' AND state='UT')
)
```

Hopefully you can see that only Example 4 operates as wanted. This query would be impossible to write without some combination of parentheses, NOT, OR (including IN, a shorthand for OR), and AND.

You can also use parentheses to change the order of precedence in mathematical and logical operations. These two statements return different results:

```
SELECT 1.0 + 3.0 / 4.0      -- Returns 1.75
SELECT (1.0 + 3.0) / 4.0    -- Returns 1.00
```

The order of precedence is similar to what you learned back in algebra class (except for the bit operators). Operators of the same level are evaluated left to right. You use parentheses to change precedence levels to suit your needs, when you're unsure, or when you simply want to make your code more readable. Groupings with parentheses are evaluated from the innermost grouping outward. Here's the order of precedence (from highest to lowest):

Operation	Operators
Bitwise NOT	~
Multiplication/division/modulo	* / %
Addition/subtraction	+ −
Bitwise exclusive OR	^
Bitwise AND	&
Bitwise OR	|
Logical NOT	NOT
Logical AND	AND
Logical OR	OR

From the Author...

If you didn't pick the correct example, you should easily see the flaw in Examples 1, 2, and 3 by examining the output. Both Examples 1 and 2 return every row. *Every* row is either not in CA or not in UT, since a row can be in only one or the other. A row in CA is not in UT, so the expression returns TRUE. Example 3 is too restrictive—for example, what about the rows in San Francisco, CA? The condition (*city* <> *'OAKLAND'* and *state* <> *'CA'*) would evaluate as (TRUE and FALSE) for San Francisco, CA, which, of course, is FALSE, so the row would be rejected when it *should* be selected according to the desired semantics.

Scalar Functions

In Chapter 7, I discussed aggregate functions, such as MAX(), SUM(), and COUNT(). These functions operate on a set of values to produce a single aggregated value. In addition to aggregate functions, SQL Server provides *scalar functions,* which operate on a single value. "Scalar" is just a fancy term for "single value." You can also think of the value in a single column of a single row as a *scalar*. Scalar functions are enormously useful—the "Swiss Army knife" of SQL

Server. (You've probably noticed that I've used several in examples already— I'd be lost without them.)

Scalar functions can be used anywhere an expression is legal, such as:

- In the select list

- In a WHERE clause, including one defining a view

- Inside a CASE expression

- In a CHECK constraint

- In the VALUES clause of an INSERT statement

- In an UPDATE statement to the right of the SET clause

- With a variable assignment

- As a parameter inside another scalar function

SQL Server provides too many scalar functions. (By "too many," I mean that it's difficult to remember them all.) The best you can do is to familiarize yourself with those that exist, and then, when you encounter a problem and a light bulb goes on in your head to remind you about a function that will help, you can reach for the *Transact-SQL Reference* for details. Even with so many functions available, I often wish for some functions that still do not exist. (I'd have that dilemma even if another couple-hundred functions were added.) I seem to frequently have a specialized need that would benefit from a specific function, and I think it would be great if I could write and add my own libraries of scalar functions. Stored procedures and extended stored procedures come somewhat close and are extraordinarily useful, but even they fall short of the capability provided by scalar functions. And unlike scalar functions, stored procedures or extended stored procedures can't be used in a select list, in a view, or in a WHERE clause. But take heart—we appreciate the need for user-defined functions, and no doubt user-defined functions will make their way into some future SQL Server release. Until then, as I said earlier, you should familiarize yourself with the functions provided and remember that functions can be nested within other functions—sometimes providing what virtually amounts to a separate function.

In the following sections, I'll briefly list the scalar functions that currently exist, comment on them, and give some examples of how they're used. First I'll spend time on the CONVERT() function because it is especially important.

Conversion functions

SQL Server provides two functions for converting datatypes: the generalized CONVERT() function and the more specialized STR() function. CONVERT() is possibly the most useful function in all of SQL Server. It allows you to change the datatype when you select a field, which can be essential for concatenating strings, joining columns that were not initially envisioned as related, performing mathematical operations on columns that were defined as character but which actually contain numbers, and other similar operations. If you are a C programmer, think of CONVERT() as being a CAST operator and conversion function similar to *itoa()* or *atof()*, all rolled into one. Like C, SQL is a fairly strongly typed language. Some languages, such as Microsoft Visual Basic or PL/1 (Programming Language 1), allow you to almost indiscriminately mix datatypes. If you mix datatypes in SQL, however, you will often get an error. (Some conversions are implicit, so, for example, you can add or join a *smallint* and an *int* without any such error; trying to do the same between an *int* and a *char,* however, produces an error.) Without a way to convert datatypes in SQL, you would have to return the values back to the client application, convert them there, and then send them back to the server. You might need to create temporary tables just to hold the intermediate converted values. All of this would be cumbersome and inefficient.

Recognizing this inefficiency, the ANSI committee added the CAST operator to SQL-92. Few, if any, mainstream products today have implemented CAST, but my reading of the SQL-92 specification for CAST tells me that CONVERT() provides a superset of CAST functionality. (It should be easy pickings to make some parser changes that map CAST to CONVERT() in order to support CAST in a future release.) I asked a member of the ANSI SQL committee to tell me which new features in SQL-92 are the most useful and powerful. His reply was "CASE and CAST," and he lamented that few products had implemented either. Fortunately, SQL Server has included CASE since version 6.0, and it has all the functionality of CAST via the CONVERT() function. (It's a good bet that the CAST syntax will also be adopted in the next major release.) The CONVERT() syntax is simple:

```
CONVERT (convert_to_data type[(length)], from_expression
    [, style])
```

Suppose that I want to concatenate the *job_id* (*smallint*) column of the *employee* table with the *lname* (*varchar*) column. Without CONVERT(), this would be impossible (unless I did it in my application). With CONVERT(), it's trivial:

```
SELECT lname + '-' + CONVERT(varchar(2), job_id) FROM employee
```

Here's the abbreviated output:

```
Accorti-13
Afonso-14
Ashworth-6
Bennett-12
Brown-7
Chang-4
```

```
Cramer-2
Cruz-10
Devon-3
 ⋮
```

Specifying a length shorter than the column or expression is a useful way to truncate the column. (You could use the SUBSTRING() function for this equally well, but since I use CONVERT() so frequently, it seems more intuitive to me to do it this way.) Specifying a length when converting to *char, varchar, decimal,* or *numeric* is not required, but I recommend it. Specifying a length better shields you from possible behavioral changes in newer releases of the product.

> **NOTE** Although behavioral changes would generally not occur by design, it is difficult to ensure 100-percent consistency of subtle behavior changes between releases. The development team strives for such consistency, but it is nearly impossible to ensure that no behavioral side effects result when new features and capabilities are added. There is little point in relying on the current default behavior when you can just as easily be explicit about what you expect.

I tend to avoid CONVERT() when converting *float* or *numeric/decimal* values to character strings if I expect to see a certain number of decimal places. CONVERT() does not currently provide formatting capabilities for numbers. Formatting floating-point numbers and such when converting to character strings is another area that's ripe for subtle behavior differences. So when I need to transform a floating-point number to a character string in which I expect a specific format, I use the other conversion function, STR(). The STR() function is a specialized conversion function that always converts from a number (*float, numeric,* and so on) to a character datatype, but it allows you to explicitly specify the length and number of decimal places that should be formatted for the character string. Here's the syntax:

```
STR(float_expression, character_length, number_of_decimal_places)
```

Remember that *character_length* must include room for a decimal point and a negative sign if they might exist. Also be aware that STR() rounds the value to the number of decimal places requested, while CONVERT() simply truncates the value if the character length is smaller than the size required for full display. Here's an example of STR():

```
SELECT discounttype, "Discount"=STR(discount, 7, 3) FROM discounts
```

And here's the output:

```
discounttype        Discount
------------        --------
Initial Customer    10.500
Volume Discount      6.700
Customer Discount    5.000
```

You can think of the ASCII() and CHAR() functions as special type-conversion functions, but I'll cover them later in this chapter as string functions. For now, we'll go back to CONVERT(), which is the workhorse function.

CONVERT() has an optional third parameter, *style*. Currently, this parameter is used only when converting an expression of type *datetime* or *smalldatetime* to type *char* or *varchar*. If not specified, such a conversion will format the date with the default SQL Server date format (for example, Oct 3 1997 2:25PM). By specifying a *style* type, I can format the output as I want. I can also specify a shorter length for the character buffer being converted to, in order to perhaps eliminate the time portion or for other reasons.

Style No. without Century (yy)	Style No. with Century (yyyy)	Type	Output Style
–	0 or 100	Default	mon dd yyyy hh:miAM (or PM)
1	101	USA	mm/dd/yyyy
2	102	ANSI	yyyy.mm.dd
3	103	British/French	dd/mm/yyyy
4	104	German	dd.mm.yyyy
5	105	Italian	dd-mm-yyyy
6	106	–	dd mon yyyy
7	107	–	mon dd, yyyy
–	8 or 108	–	hh:mm:ss
–	9 or 109	–	mon dd yyyy hh:mi:ss:mmmAM (or PM)
10	110	USA	mm-dd-yy
11	111	JAPAN	yy/mm/dd
12	112	ISO	yymmdd
–	13 or 113	–	dd mon yyyy hh:mi:ss:mmm (24h)
14	114	–	hh:mi:ss:mmm (24h)

Note that as we approach the new millennium, using two-character formats for the year can be a bug in your application just waiting to happen! Unless you have a compelling reason not to do so, you should always use the full year (yyyy) for both the input and output formatting of dates to prevent any ambiguity. SQL Server has no problem dealing with the year 2000—in fact, the change in century isn't even a boundary condition in SQL Server's internal representation of dates. But if you represent a year by specifying only the last two digits, the inherent ambiguity might cause your application to make an incorrect assumption. On input of a date formatted that way, a two-digit year is always interpreted as 19yy if the value is greater than or equal to 50 and as 20yy if the value is less than 50. That might be OK now, but by the year 2051 you won't want a two-digit year of 51 to be interpreted as 1951 instead of 2051. (If you assume that your application will have been long since retired, think again. I'll bet a lot of COBOL programmers in the 1960s didn't worry about the year 2000.)

CONVERT() can also be useful if you insert the current date using the GETDATE() function but don't consider meaningful the time elements of the *datetime* datatype. (Remember that SQL Server doesn't currently have separate date and time datatypes.) You can use CONVERT() to format and insert *datetime* data with only a date element. Without the time specification in the GETDATE() value, it will consistently be stored as 12:00AM for any given date. That eliminates problems that can occur when searching or joining between columns of *datetime*: for example, if the date elements are equal between columns but the time element is not, an equality search will fail. You can eliminate this equality problem by making the time portion consistent. (I like to use style 102, ANSI, when inserting dates. This style is always recognizable, no matter what the SQL Server default language and no matter what the DATEFORMAT setting.) Consider this:

```
CREATE TABLE my_date (Col1 datetime)
INSERT INTO my_date VALUES (CONVERT(char(10), GETDATE(), 102))
```

You should be aware that when you use CONVERT(), the conversion occurs on the server and the value is sent to the client application in the converted datatype. Of course, it's also common for applications to convert between datatypes, but conversion at the server is completely separate from conversion at the client. For example, if I use the GETDATE() function to select the current date, it will be returned to the client application as a *datetime* datatype. The client application will likely convert that internal date representation to a string for display. On the other hand, if I use GETDATE() but also explicitly use CONVERT() to make the *datetime* character data, the column is sent to the calling application as a character string already.

Here's a way to illustrate this: Select GETDATE() both with and without CONVERT() from ISQLW.EXE. The ISQLW.EXE (and ISQL.EXE) program is currently a DB-Library program and uses functions in DB-Library for binding columns to character strings. (Note that ISQLW.EXE—and possibly ISQL.EXE—will probably be changed in a future release to use ODBC instead of DB-Library.) DB-Library allows such bindings to automatically pick up locale styles based on the settings of the workstation running the application. (The option Use International Settings in the Client Configuration Utility must be checked for this to occur by default.) So a column returned internally as a *datetime* datatype would be converted by ISQLW.EXE into the same format as the locale setting of Windows. A column containing a date representation as a character string would not, of course, be reformatted.

When I issue the following SELECT with the SQL Server configured for U.S. English as the default language and with Windows NT on the client configured as English (United States), the date and string look alike:

```
SELECT
'returned as date'=GETDATE(),
'returned as string'=CONVERT(varchar(20), GETDATE())

returned as date      returned as string
-----------------     ------------------
Dec 3 1996  3:10PM    Dec  3 1996  3:10PM
```

But if I change the locale in the Regional Settings applet of the Windows NT Control Panel to French (Standard), the same SELECT statement returns this:

```
returned as date      returned as string
-----------------     ------------------
3 déc. 1996 15:10     Dec  3 1996  3:10PM
```

You can see that the value returned to the client in internal date format was converted at the client workstation in the format chosen by the application. The conversion that uses CONVERT() was formatted at the server.

> **NOTE** Although I have used dates in these examples, the discussion is also relevant to formatting numbers and currency.

Some conversions are automatic and implicit, and using CONVERT() is unnecessary (although OK). For example, converting between numbers with types *int, smallint, tinyint, float, numeric,* and so on happens automatically and implicitly so long as an overflow does not occur, in which case you would get an error for arithmetic overflow. Converting numbers with decimal places to integer datatypes results in the truncation of the values to the right of the decimal point—without warning. (Converting between decimal or numeric datatypes requires that you explicitly use CONVERT() if a loss of precision is possible.) Other conversions, such as between character and integer data, can be performed explicitly only by using CONVERT(). Conversions between certain datatypes are nonsensical—for example, between a *float* and a *datetime*—and attempting such an operation results in error 529, which states that the conversion is impossible.

Table 9-1, reprinted from the SQL Server documentation, is one that you will want to refer to periodically for conversion issues:

To:

From:	binary	varbinary	tinyinit(INT1)	smallinit(INT2)	int(INT4)	float	real	char	varchar	money	smallmoney	bit	datetime	smalldatetime	text	image	decimal	numeric
binary	–	I	I	I	I	N	N	I	I	I	N	I	N	N	N	I	E	E
varbinary	I	–	I	I	I	N	N	I	I	I	N	I	N	N	N	I	E	E
tinyinit(INT1)	I	I	–	I	I	I	I	E	E	I	I	I	N	N	N	N	I	I
smallinit(INT2)	I	I	I	–	I	I	I	E	E	I	I	I	N	N	N	N	I	I
int(INT4)	I	I	I	I	–	I	I	E	E	I	I	I	N	N	N	N	I	I
float	N	N	I	I	I	–	I	E	E	I	I	I	N	N	N	N	I	I
real	N	N	I	I	I	I	–	E	E	I	I	I	N	N	N	N	I	I
char	E	E	E	E	E	E	E	–	I	E	E	E	I	I	I	I	E	E
varchar	E	E	E	E	E	E	E	I	–	E	E	E	I	I	I	I	E	E
money	I	I	I	I	I	I	I	I	I	–	I	I	N	N	N	N	I	I
smallmoney	I	I	I	I	I	I	I	I	I	I	–	I	N	N	N	N	I	I
bit	I	I	I	I	I	I	I	I	I	N	N	–	N	N	N	N	I	I
datetime	E	E	N	N	N	N	N	I	I	N	N	N	–	I	N	N	N	N
smalldatetime	E	E	N	N	N	N	N	E	E	N	N	N	I	–	N	N	N	N
text	N	N	N	N	N	N	N	E	E	N	N	N	N	N	–	N	N	N
image	E	E	N	N	N	N	N	N	N	N	N	N	N	N	N	–	N	N
decimal	I	I	I	I	I	I	I	E	E	I	I	I	N	N	N	N	–	*
numeric	I	I	I	I	I	I	I	E	E	I	I	I	N	N	N	N	*	–

Key:		
	I	Implicit conversion
	E	Explicit conversion; CONVERT() function must be used
	N	Conversion not allowed
	*	May be Implicit but requires CONVERT() when a loss of precision or scale will occur
	–	Conversion of a datatype to itself; syntactically allowed, but a NOOP

Table 9-1. *Conversion table from the SQL Server documentation.*

Date and time functions

Operations on *datetime* values are common, such as "get current date and time," "do date arithmetic—50 days from today is what date," or "find out what day of the week falls on a specific date."

Programming languages such as C or Visual Basic are loaded with functions for operations like these. Transact-SQL also provides a nice assortment to choose from:

Date Function	Return Type	Description
DATEADD(*datepart, number, datetime*)	*datetime*	Produces a date by adding an interval to a specified date
DATEDIFF(*datepart datetime1, datetime2*)	*int*	Returns the number of *datepart* "boundaries" crossed between two specified dates
DATENAME(*datepart, datetime*)	*varchar*	Returns a character string representing the specified *datepart* of the specified date
DATEPART(*datepart, datetime*)	*int*	Returns an integer representing the specified *datepart* of the specified date
GETDATE()	*datetime*	Returns the current system date and time in the SQL Server standard internal format for *datetime* values

The *datetime* parameter is any expression with a SQL Server *datetime* datatype or one that can be implicitly converted, such as an appropriately formatted character string like "1996.10.31". The *datepart* parameter uses the following encodings. Either the *FullName* or the *Abbreviation* can be passed as a parameter:

datepart (FullName)	Abbreviation	Values
year	Yy	1753–9999
quarter	Qq	1–4
month	Mm	1–12
dayofyear	Dy	1–366
day	Dd	1–31
week	Wk	1–53
weekday	Dw	1–7 (Sun.–Sat.)
hour	Hh	0–23
minute	Mi	0–59
second	Ss	0–59
millisecond	Ms	0–999

As do other functions, the date functions provide more than simple convenience. Suppose that I needed to find all records entered on the second Tuesday of every month and all records entered within 48 weeks of today. Without SQL Server date functions, the only way I could accomplish such a query would be to select all the rows and return them to my application and then filter them there. With a lot of data and a slow network, this can get ugly. With the date functions, the process is simple and efficient and only the rows that meet this criteria are selected. For this example, assume that my table, *records,* includes these columns:

```
Record_number     int
Entered_on        datetime

SELECT Record_number, Entered_on
FROM records
WHERE
DATEPART(WEEKDAY, Entered_on)=3
-- Tuesday is 3rd day of week (in USA)
AND
DATEPART(DAY, Entered_on) BETWEEN 8 AND 14
-- The 2nd week is from the 8th to 14th
AND
DATEDIFF(WEEK, Entered_on, GETDATE()) <= 48
-- Within 48 weeks of today
```

> **NOTE** The day of the week that is considered "first" is locale-specific and depends on the DATEFIRST setting.

Math functions

Transact-SQL math functions are straightforward and typical. Many are specialized and of the type you learned about in trigonometry class. (If you don't have an engineering or mathematical application, you probably won't use those.) A handful of math functions are useful in general types of queries in applications that are not mathematical in nature. I find ABS(), CEILING(), FLOOR(), and ROUND() most useful for general queries to find values within a certain range.

I also frequently use the random number function, RAND(), to generate test data or conditions. (I'll show examples of RAND() in Chapter 12, "Examples and Brain-teasers with Transact-SQL.")

Following is the complete list of math functions and a few simple examples. (Some of the examples use other functions in addition to the math ones to illustrate how to use functions within functions.)

Function	Parameters	Result
ABS	(*numeric_expr*)	Absolute value of the numeric expression. Results returned are of the same type as *numeric_expr*.
ACOS	(*float_expr*)	Angle (in radians) whose cosine is the specified approximate numeric (*float*) expression.
ASIN	(*float_expr*)	Angle (in radians) whose sine is the specified approximate numeric (*float*) expression.
ATAN	(*float_expr*)	Angle (in radians) whose tangent is the specified approximate numeric (*float*) expression.
ATN2	(*float_expr1, float_expr2*)	Angle (in radians) whose tangent is (*float_expr1/float_expr2*) between two approximate numeric (*float*) expressions.
CEILING	(*numeric_expr*)	Smallest integer greater than or equal to the numeric expression. Result returned is the integer portion of the same type as *numeric_expr*.
COS	(*float_expr*)	Trigonometric cosine of the specified angle (in radians) in an approximate numeric (*float*) expression.
COT	(*float_expr*)	Trigonometric cotangent of the specified angle (in radians) in an approximate numeric (*float*) expression.
DEGREES	(*numeric_expr*)	Degrees converted from radians of the numeric expression. Results are of the same type as *numeric_expr*.
EXP	(*float_expr*)	Exponential value of the specified approximate numeric (*float*) expression.
FLOOR	(*numeric_expr*)	Largest integer less than or equal to the specified numeric expression. Result is the integer portion of the same type as *numeric_expr*.
LOG	(*float_expr*)	Natural logarithm of the specified approximate numeric (*float*) expression.
LOG10	(*float_expr*)	Base-10 logarithm of the specified approximate numeric (*float*) expression.
PI	( )	Constant value of 3.141592653589793.
POWER	(*numeric_expr, y*)	Value of numeric expression to the power of *y*, where *y* is a numeric datatype (*decimal, float, int, money, numeric, real, smallint, smallmoney,* or *tinyint*). Result is of the same type as *numeric_expr*.

(continued)

continued

Function	Parameters	Result
RADIANS	(*numeric_expr*)	Radians converted from degrees of the numeric expression. Result is of the same type as *numeric_expr*.
RAND	([*seed*])	Random approximate numeric (*float*) value between 0 and 1, optionally specifying an integer expression as the *seed*.
ROUND	(*numeric_expr, length*)	Numeric expression rounded off to the *length* (or precision) specified as an integer expression (*tinyint, smallint,* or *int*). Result is of the same type as *numeric_expr*. ROUND() always returns a value even if the *length* is illegal. If the specified *length* is positive and longer than the digits after the decimal point, 0 is added after the fraction digits. If the *length* is negative and larger than or equal to the digits before the decimal point, ROUND() returns 0.00.
SIGN	(*numeric_expr*)	Returns the positive (+1), zero (0), or negative (−1) sign of the numeric expression. Result is of the same type as *numeric_expr*.
SIN	(*float_expr*)	Trigonometric sine of the specified angle (measured in radians) in an approximate numeric (*float*) expression.
SQRT	(*float_expr*)	Square root of the specified approximate numeric (*float*) expression.
TAN	(*float_expr*)	Trigonometric tangent of the specified angle (measured in radians) in an approximate numeric (*float*) expression.

The following examples show some of the math functions at work:

EXAMPLE 1

Produce a table with the cosine, sine, and tangent of all angles in multiples of 10, from 0 through 180. Format the return value as a string of six characters, with the value rounded to four decimal places.

```
DECLARE @angle smallint
SELECT @angle=0
WHILE (@angle <= 180)
BEGIN
```

```
    SELECT
    ANGLE=@angle,
    SINE=STR(SIN(@angle), 7, 5),
    COSINE=STR(COS(@angle), 7, 5),
    TANGENT=STR(TAN(@angle), 7, 5)

    SELECT @angle=@angle + 10
END
```

NOTE This example actually produces 19 different result sets because the SELECT statement is issued once for each iteration of the loop. These separate result statements are concatenated and appear as one result set in this example. That works fine for illustration purposes, but I'd avoid doing an operation like this in the real world, especially on a slow network. Every one of the result sets carries with it metadata to describe itself to the client application. I'll show a better technique in Chapter 12.

And here are the results concatenated as a single table:

```
ANGLE   SINE     COSINE    TANGENT
-----   -------  -------   -------
0        0.0000   1.0000    0.0000
10      -0.5440  -0.8391    0.6484
20       0.9129   0.4081    2.2372
30      -0.9880   0.1543   -6.4053
40       0.7451  -0.6669   -1.1172
50      -0.2624   0.9650   -0.2719
60      -0.3048  -0.9524    0.3200
70       0.7739   0.6333    1.2220
80      -0.9939  -0.1104    9.0037
90       0.8940  -0.4481   -1.9952
100     -0.5064   0.8623   -0.5872
110     -0.0442  -0.9990    0.0443
120      0.5806   0.8142    0.7131
130     -0.9301  -0.3673    2.5323
140      0.9802  -0.1978   -4.9554
150     -0.7149   0.6993   -1.0223
160      0.2194  -0.9756   -0.2249
170      0.3466   0.9380    0.3696
180     -0.8012  -0.5985    1.3387
```

EXAMPLE 2

Express in whole dollar terms the range of prices (non-null) of all books in the *titles* table. This example combines the scalar functions FLOOR() and CEILING() inside the aggregate functions MIN() and MAX():

```
SELECT 'Low End'=MIN(FLOOR(price)),
    'High End'=MAX(CEILING(price))
FROM titles
```

And the result:

```
Low End    High End
-------    --------
2.00       23.00
```

EXAMPLE 3

Use the same *records* table that was used earlier in the date functions example. Find all records within 150 days of Sept. 30, 1997. Without the absolute value function ABS(), it would be necessary to use BETWEEN or to provide two search conditions and OR them to account for both 150 days earlier and 150 days later than that date. ABS() lets you easily reduce that to a single search condition.

```
SELECT Record_number, Entered_on
FROM records
WHERE
ABS(DATEDIFF(DAY, Entered_on, '1997.09.30')) <= 150
-- Plus or minus 150 days
```

String functions

String functions make it easier to work with character data. They let you slice and dice character data, search it, format it, and alter it. Like other scalar functions, string functions allow you to perform functions directly in your search conditions and SQL batches that would otherwise need to be returned to the calling application for further processing. (Also remember the concatenation operator, +, for concatenating strings. You'll use this operator often in conjunction with the string functions.)

Following are the string functions. For more detailed information, consult the documentation on the companion CD-ROM.

Function	Parameters	Returns
ASCII	(*char_expr*)	Indicates the numeric code value of the leftmost character of a character expression.
CHAR	(*integer_expr*)	Character represented by the ASCII code. The ASCII code should be a value from 0 through 255; otherwise, NULL is returned.
CHARINDEX	(*'pattern'*, *expression*)	Returns the starting position of the specified *exact pattern*. A *pattern* is a *char_expr*. The second parameter is an *expression*, usually a column name, in which SQL Server searches for the *pattern*.
DIFFERENCE	(*char_expr1*, *char_expr2*)	Shows the difference between the values of two character expressions as returned by the SOUNDEX function. DIFFERENCE compares two strings and evaluates the similarity between them, returning a value 0 through 4. The value 4 is the best match.
LOWER	(*char_expr*)	Converts uppercase character data to lowercase.
LTRIM	(*char_expr*)	Removes leading blanks.
PATINDEX	(*'%pattern%'*, *expression*)	Returns the starting position of the first occurrence of *pattern* in the specified expression, or 0 if the pattern is not found.
REPLICATE	(*char_expr*, *integer_expr*)	Repeats a character expression a specified number of times. If *integer_expr* is negative, NULL is returned.
REVERSE	(*char_expr*)	Returns the *char_expr* backwards. This function takes a constant, variable, or column as its parameter.
RIGHT	(*char_expr*, *integer_expr*)	Part of a character string starting *integer_expr* characters from the right. If *integer_expr* is negative, NULL is returned.
RTRIM	(*char_expr*)	Removes trailing blanks.
SOUNDEX	(*char_expr*)	Returns a four-character (SOUNDEX) string to evaluate the similarity of two strings. The SOUNDEX function converts an alpha string to a four-digit code used to find similar-sounding words or names.
SPACE	(*integer_expr*)	Returns a string of repeated spaces. The number of spaces is equal to *integer_expr*. If *integer_expr* is negative, NULL is returned.

(continued)

continued

Function	Parameters	Returns
STR	(*float_expr* [, *length* [, *decimal*]])	Returns character data converted from numeric data. The *length* is the total length, including decimal point, sign, digits, and spaces. The *decimal* value is the number of spaces to the right of the decimal point.
STUFF	(*char_expr1*, *start*, *length*, *char_expr2*)	Deletes *length* characters from *char_expr1* at *start* and then inserts *char_expr2* into *char_expr1* at *start*.
SUBSTRING	(*expression*, *start*, *length*)	Returns part of a character or binary string. The first parameter can be a character or binary string, a column name, or an expression that includes a column name. The second parameter specifies where the substring begins. The third parameter specifies the number of characters in the substring.
UPPER	(*char_expr*)	Converts lowercase character data to upper-case.

ASCII() and CHAR() functions

The function name ASCII() is really a bit of a misnomer. ASCII is only a 7-bit character set and hence can deal with only 128 characters. The character parameter to this function does not need to be an ASCII character. The ASCII function returns the code point for the character set installed with SQL Server, so the return value can be from 0 through 255. For example, if SQL Server is installed with the ISO 8859-1 (Latin-1) character set, the statement

```
SELECT ASCII('Ä')
```

returns 196. (The character *Ä* is not an ASCII character.)

The CHAR() function is handy for generating test data, especially when combined with RAND() and REPLICATE(). (I'll show you an example in Chapter 12.) CHAR() is also commonly used for inserting control characters such as tabs and carriage returns into your character string. Suppose, for example, that I want to return authors' last names and first names concatenated as a single field, but with a carriage return (0x0D, or decimal 13) separating them so that without further manipulation in my application, the names occupy two lines when displayed. The CHAR() function makes this simple:

```
SELECT 'NAME'=au_fname + CHAR(13) + au_lname
FROM authors
```

Here's the abbreviated result:

```
NAME
--------
Johnson
White
Marjorie
Green
Cheryl
Carson
Michael
O'Leary
Dean
Straight
Meander
Smith
Abraham
Bennet
Ann
Dull
```

UPPER() and LOWER() functions

The UPPER() and LOWER() functions are useful if you must perform case-insensitive searches on a server that is case-sensitive. On my case-sensitive server, for example, this query finds no rows even though author name Cheryl Carson is included in that table:

```
SELECT COUNT(*) FROM authors WHERE au_lname='CARSON'
```

If I change the query to the following, the row will be found:

```
SELECT COUNT(*) FROM authors WHERE UPPER(au_lname)='CARSON'
```

If the value to be searched might be of mixed case, you need to use the function on both sides of the equation. This query would find the row on the case-sensitive server:

```
DECLARE @name_param varchar(30)
SELECT @name_param='cArSoN'
SELECT COUNT(*) FROM authors WHERE UPPER(au_lname)=UPPER(@name_param)
```

In these examples, even though I have an index on *au_lname,* it will not be useful because the index keys are not uppercase. (However, it would be possible to use triggers to maintain an uppercase copy of the column, index it, and then use it for searching.)

You'll also often want to use UPPER( ) or LOWER( ) in stored procedures in which character parameters are used. For example, in a procedure that expects *Y* or *N* as a parameter, you will likely want to use one of these functions in case *y* is entered instead of *Y.*

TRIM functions

The functions LTRIM( ) and RTRIM( ) are handy for dealing with leading or trailing blanks. Recall that by default (and if you do not enable the ANSI_PADDING setting) a *varchar* datatype is automatically right-trimmed of blanks, but a fixed-length *char* is not. Suppose that I want to concatenate the *type* column and the *title_id* column from the *titles* table, with a colon separating them but with no blanks. The following query does not work because the trailing blanks are retained from the *type* column:

```
SELECT type + ':' + title_id FROM titles
```

This returns (in part):

```
-------------------
business    :BU1032
business    :BU1111
business    :BU2075
business    :BU7832
mod_cook    :MC2222
mod_cook    :MC3021
UNDECIDED   :MC3026
popular_comp:PC1035
popular_comp:PC8888
popular_comp:PC9999
```

But RTRIM( ) returns what I want:

```
SELECT RTRIM(type) + ':' + title_id FROM titles
```

And the result (in part):

```
-------------------
business:BU1032
business:BU1111
business:BU2075
business:BU7832
mod_cook:MC2222
mod_cook:MC3021
UNDECIDED:MC3026
popular_comp:PC1035
popular_comp:PC8888
popular_comp:PC9999
```

String manipulation functions

Functions such as SUBSTRING(), CHARINDEX(), PATINDEX(), STUFF(), RE-
VERSE(), and REPLICATE() are useful for searching and manipulating partial
strings. CHARINDEX() and PATINDEX() are similar, but CHARINDEX() demands an exact match and PATINDEX() works with a regular expression search.
(You could use one or both of these functions as a replacement for LIKE as well.
For example, instead of saying *WHERE name LIKE '%SMITH%'*, you could say
WHERE CHARINDEX('Smith', name) > 0. Before version 6.0, the CHARINDEX()
formulation above was much faster than LIKE for an exact pattern match query
such as this. But this is no longer true—they are now equal in performance.)

Suppose that I want to change occurrences of the word "computer" within the
notes field of the *titles* table and replace it with "Hi-Tech-Computers." Assume
that the SQL Server is case-sensitive and, for simplicity, that I know that "computer" won't appear more than once per column. I want to be careful that the
word "computers," which is already plural, is not also changed. I can't just rely
on searching on "computer" with a trailing blank, because the word might fall
at the end of the sentence followed by a period or a comma. The regular expression *computer[^s]* always finds the word "computer" and ignores "computers,"
so it will work perfectly with PATINDEX().

Here's the data before the change:

```
SELECT title_id, notes
FROM titles
WHERE notes LIKE '%[Cc]omputer%'


title_id   notes
--------   ----------------------------------------------------------
BU7832     Annotated analysis of what computers can do for you: a
           no-hype guide for the critical user.
PC8888     Muckraking reporting on the world's largest computer
           hardware and software manufacturers.
PC9999     A must-read for computer conferencing.
PS1372     A must for the specialist, this book examines the
           difference between those who hate and fear computers
           and those who don't.
PS7777     Protecting yourself and your loved ones from undue
           emotional stress in the modern world. Use of computer
           and nutritional aids emphasized.


UPDATE titles
SET notes=STUFF(notes, PATINDEX('%computer[^s]%', notes),
    DATALENGTH('computer'), 'Hi-Tech-Computers')
WHERE  PATINDEX('%computer[^s]%', notes) > 0
```

Here's the data after the change:

```
SELECT title_id, notes
FROM titles
WHERE notes LIKE '%[Cc]omputer%'

title_id    notes
--------    -----------------------------------------------------------
BU7832      Annotated analysis of what computers can do for you: a
            no-hype guide for the critical user.
PC8888      Muckraking reporting on the world's largest Hi-Tech-
            Computers hardware and software manufacturers.
PC9999      A must-read for Hi-Tech-Computers conferencing.
PS1372      A must for the specialist, this book examines the
            difference between those who hate and fear computers
            and those who don't.
PS7777      Protecting yourself and your loved ones from undue
            emotional stress in the modern world. Use of Hi-Tech-
            Computers and nutritional aids emphasized.
```

Of course, I could have simply provided 8 as the *length* parameter of the string "computer" to be deleted. But I used yet another function, DATALENGTH(), which would be more realistic if I were creating a general purpose search-and-replace procedure. Note that DATALENGTH() returns NULL if the expression is NULL, so in your applications, you might go one step further and use DATA-LENGTH() inside the ISNULL() function to return 0 in the case of NULL.

The REPLICATE() function is useful for adding filler characters—such as for test data. (I don't know many other practical uses for it.) The SPACE() function is a special-purpose version of REPLICATE(): it's identical to using REPLICATE with the space character. REVERSE() reverses a character string (a standard programming puzzle, for sure, but not too common in production applications). I have seen REVERSE() used in a few cases to store and, more importantly, to index a character column backward to get more selectivity from the index. But in general, I rarely use these three functions. (I like to refer to the REVERSE() function as the Harry Caray function. For those of you who aren't Chicago Cubs fans, the Hall of Fame baseball announcer likes to tell listeners how a player's name would be pronounced spelled backward. For example, did you know that MARK GRACE's name backward is ECARG KRAM?)

SOUNDEX() and DIFFERENCE() functions

If you've ever wondered how telephone operators are able to give you telephone numbers so quickly when you call directory assistance, chances are they are using a SOUNDEX algorithm. The SOUNDEX() and DIFFERENCE() functions let you search on character strings that sound similar when spoken. SOUNDEX() converts each string to a four-digit code. DIFFERENCE() can then be used to evaluate the level of similarity between the SOUNDEX values for two strings as returned by SOUNDEX(). For example, you could use these functions if you wanted to look at all rows that sound like "Erickson," and they would find "Erickson," "Erikson," "Ericson," "Ericksen," "Ericsen," and so on.

SOUNDEX is a standard algorithm in the database business. The first character of the four-character SOUNDEX code is the first letter of the word, and the remaining three characters are single digits that describe the phonetic value of the first three syllables of the word (or more accurately, what the function interprets as syllables). If there is no second or subsequent syllable, the phonetic value for it is 0. It should be clear that only nine phonetic values are possible in this scheme. And SOUNDEX() is not sophisticated in dealing with consonant or vowel blends; it provides only an approximation.

DIFFERENCE() internally compares two SOUNDEX values and returns a score from 0 through 4 to indicate how close the match is. A score of 4 is the best match, and 0 means no matches were found. Executing *DIFFERENCE(a1, a2)* first generates the four-character SOUNDEX values for a1 (call it sx_a1) and a2 (call it sx_a2). Then if all four values of the SOUNDEX value sx_a2 match the values of sx_a1, the match is perfect and the level is 4. Note that this compares the SOUNDEX values by character position, not by actual characters. For example, the names "Smythe" and "Smith" both have a SOUNDEX() value of S530, so their difference level is 4, even though the spellings differ. Otherwise, if the first character (a letter, not a number) of the SOUNDEX value sx_a1 is the same as the first character of sx_a2, the starting level is 1. If the first character is different, the starting level is 0. Then each character in sx_a2 is successively compared to all characters in sx_a1. When a match is found, the level is incremented and the next scan on sx_a1 starts from the location of the match. If no match is found, the next sx_a2 character is compared to the entire four-character list of sx_a1.

The above description of the algorithms should make it clear that SOUNDEX() will at best provide an approximation. Even so, sometimes it works extremely well. Suppose that I want to query the *authors* table for names that sound similar to "Larsen." I'll define *similar* to mean "have a SOUNDEX() value of 3 or 4":

```
SELECT au_lname,
Soundex=SOUNDEX(au_lname),
Diff_Larsen=DIFFERENCE(au_lname, 'Larson')
FROM authors
WHERE
DIFFERENCE(au_lname, 'Larson') >= 3
```

Here's the result:

```
au_lname    Soundex    Diff_Larsen
--------    -------    -----------
Carson      C625       3
Karsen      K625       3
```

I'm quite pleased because I found two names that rhyme with "Larsen" and I didn't get any bad hits of names that don't seem close. Sometimes you'll get odd results, but if you follow the algorithms above, you'll understand how these oddities occur. For example, do you think "Bennet" and "Smith" sound similar? Me neither, but SOUNDEX() does. When you investigate, you can see why the two names have a similar SOUNDEX() value. The SOUNDEX values have a different first letter, but the *m* and *n* sounds are considered close; the *i* and *e* sounds are similar, and both names include a *t*. Hence the match. This type of situation happens often with SOUNDEX()—you'll get hits on values that don't seem close, although usually you won't miss the ones that are similar. So if I query the *authors* table for similar values (with a DIFFERENCE() value of 3 or 4) as "Smythe," I get a perfect hit on "Smith" as I'd expect, but I'd also get a close match for "Bennet," which is far from obvious:

```
SELECT au_lname,
Soundex=SOUNDEX(au_lname),
Diff_Smythe=DIFFERENCE(au_lname, 'Smythe')
FROM authors
WHERE
DIFFERENCE(au_lname, 'Smythe') >= 3

au_lname    Soundex    Diff_Smythe
--------    -------    -----------
Smith       S530       4
Bennet      B530       3
```

Sometimes SOUNDEX() misses close matches altogether. This happens when consonant blends are present. For example, I might expect to get a close match between "Knight" and "Nite." But I get a low value of 1 in the DIFFERENCE() between the two:

```
SELECT
"SX_KNIGHT"=SOUNDEX('Knight'),
"SX_NITE"=SOUNDEX('Nite'),
"DIFFERENCE"=DIFFERENCE('Nite', 'Knight')

SX_KNIGHT    SX_NITE    DIFFERENCE
---------    -------    ----------
K523         N300       1
```

System functions

System functions are most useful for returning certain metadata or configuration settings. These are the built-in SQL Server system functions. For more information, see the documentation on the companion CD-ROM.

Function	Parameters	Returns
APP_NAME	NONE	Returns the program name for the current connection if one has been set by the program before logging on.
COALESCE	(*expression1, expression2, ... expressionN*)	A specialized form of the CASE statement. Returns the first non-null expression.
COL_LENGTH	(*'table_name', 'column_name'*)	The defined (maximum) storage length of a column.
COL_NAME	(*table_id, column_id*)	The name of the column.
DATALENGTH	(*'expression'*)	The length of an expression of any datatype.
DB_ID	([*'database-_name'*])	The database identification number.
DB_NAME	([*database_id*])	The database name.
GETANSINULL	([*'database-_name'*])	The default nullability for the database. Returns 1 when the nullability is the ANSI NULL default.
HOST_ID	NONE	The workstation identification number.
HOST_NAME	NONE	The workstation name.
IDENT_INCR	(*'table_or_view'*)	The increment value specified during creation of an identity column of a table or view that includes an identity column.
IDENT_SEED	(*'table_or_view'*)	The seed value specified during creation of an identity column of a table or view that includes an identity column.
INDEX_COL	(*'table_name', index_id, key_*id)	The indexed column name(s).
ISDATE	(*expression_of-_possible _date*)	Checks whether an expression is a *datetime* datatype or a string in a recognizable *datetime* format. Returns 1 when the expression is compatible with the *datetime* type; otherwise returns 0.

(continued)

continued

Function	Parameters	Returns
ISNUMERIC	(*expression_of-_possible_number*)	Checks whether an expression is number-type datatype or a string in a recognizable number format. Returns 1 when the expression is compatible with arithmetic operations; otherwise returns 0.
ISNULL	(*expression, value*)	Replaces NULL entries with the specified value.
NULLIF	(*expression1, expression2*)	A specialized form of CASE. The resulting expression is NULL when *expression1* is equivalent to *expression2*.
OBJECT_ID	('*object_name*')	The database object identification number.
OBJECT_NAME	(*object_id*)	The database object name.
STATS_DATE	(*table_id, index_id*)	The date that the statistics for the specified index (*index_id*) were last updated.
SUSER_ID	([*'login_name'*])	The user's login ID number.
SUSER_NAME	([*server_user_id*])	The user's login name.
USER_ID	([*'user_name'*])	The user's database ID number.
USER_NAME	([*user_id*])	The user's database username.

> **NOTE** You can think of the statements COALESCE, NULLIF, and ISNULL as functions, so I've included them in this table. But they are basically options in the SELECT statement, as discussed in Chapter 7.

The DATALENGTH() function is most often used with variable-length data, especially character strings, and it tells you the actual storage length of the expression (typically a column name). In addition to the obviously variable-length datatypes *varchar, varbinary, text,* and *image,* recall that a fixed-length datatype that allows NULL is internally variable-length. DATALENGTH() returns the storage size for these datatypes. A fixed-length datatype always returns the storage size of its defined type (which is also its actual storage size), which makes it identical to COL_LENGTH() for such a column.

The DATALENGTH() of any NULL expression returns NULL. But if you are using DATALENGTH() to perform an operation such as computing a row length, you might prefer that DATALENGTH() return 0 instead of NULL so that you can add the results. To accomplish this, you can use ISNULL() with DATALENGTH() for any columns that allow NULL. For example, you can use this query to find the average storage length of the data in the *discounts* table, which contains some NULL columns. This example returns the integer 21.

```
SELECT 'Avg_DataLength_of_Discounts'=
    AVG(
        DATALENGTH(discounttype) +
        ISNULL(DATALENGTH(stor_id), 0) +
        ISNULL(DATALENGTH(lowqty), 0) +
        ISNULL(DATALENGTH(highqty), 0) +
        DATALENGTH(discount)
    )
FROM discounts
```

The OBJECT_ID(), OBJECT_NAME(), SUSER_ID(), SUSER_NAME(), USER_ID(), USER_NAME(), COL_NAME(), DB_ID(), and DB_NAME() functions are commonly used to more easily eliminate the need for joins between system catalogs and to get run-time information dynamically. (However, you're still better off using the catalog stored procedures for system catalog information whenever possible.) Although not a function, the global variable @@spid, the process ID for the current connection, is often similarly used and is used in conjunction with these functions. (Note that such a global variable cannot be used in a constraint as a system function can.)

For example, recognizing that an object name is unique within a database for a specific user, I can use the following statement to determine whether an object by the name "foo" exists for my current user ID; if so, I can drop it (assuming that I know it's a table):

```
IF (SELECT id FROM sysobjects WHERE id=OBJECT_ID('foo')
    AND uid=USER_ID() AND type='U') > 0
    DROP TABLE foo
```

Or I can get information from the *sysprocesses* table in the *master* database for any connections made by the login ID *john*:

```
SELECT * FROM master..sysprocesses WHERE suid=SUSER_ID('john')
```

System functions can be handy with constraints and views. Recall that a view can benefit from the use of system functions. For example, if my *accounts* table includes a column that is the system login ID of the user to whom the account belongs, I can create a view of the table that allows the user to work only with his or her own accounts. I do this simply by making the WHERE clause of the view something like this:

```
WHERE system_login_id=SUSER_ID()
```

Or if I want to ensure that updates on a table occur only from an application named CS_UPDATE.EXE, I can use a CHECK constraint in the following way:

```
CONSTRAINT APP_CHECK (APP_NAME()='CS_UPDATE.EXE')
```

For this particular example, the check is by no means foolproof, as the application must set the *app_name* in its login record. A rogue application could simply lie. To prevent casual use by someone running an application like ISQL.EXE, the above formulation might be just fine for your needs. But if you are worried about hackers, this formulation would not be appropriate. Other functions, such as SUSER_ID(), have no analogous way to be explicitly set, so they are better for security operations like this.

The ISDATE() and ISNUMERIC() functions can be useful to determine whether data is appropriate for an operation. For example, suppose that your predecessor didn't know much about using a relational database and defined a column as type *char* and then stored values in it that were naturally of type *money*. Then your predecessor compounded the problem by encoding letter codes in the same field at times as notes. You're trying to work with the data as is (eventually you'll clean it up, but you have a deadline to meet) and you need to get a sum and average of all the values, whenever a value that makes sense to use is present. (If you think this is a contrived example, talk to a programmer in an MIS shop of a Fortune 1000 company with legacy applications and ask if this sounds like an uncommon situation.) Suppose that the table has a *varchar(20)* column named *acct_bal* with these values:

```
acct_bal
--------
205.45
E
(NULL)
B
605.78
32.45
8
98.45
64.23
8456.3
```

If you try to simply use the aggregate functions directly, you'd get error 409:

```
SELECT SUM(acct_bal), AVG(acct_bal)
FROM bad_column_for_money

Msg 409, Level 16, State 2
The sum or average aggregate operation cannot take a varchar
data type as an argument.
```

If you try to use CONVERT( ), the columns that contain alphabetic characters will cause the CONVERT( ) to fail:

```
SELECT
"SUM"=SUM(CONVERT(money, acct_bal)),
"AVG"=AVG(CONVERT(money, acct_bal))
FROM bad_column_for_money

Msg 235, Level 16, State 0
Cannot convert CHAR value to MONEY. The CHAR value has incorrect
syntax.
```

But if you use both CONVERT( ) in the select list and ISNUMERIC( ) in the WHERE clause to choose only those values for which a conversion would be possible, everything works great:

```
SELECT
"SUM"=SUM(CONVERT(money, acct_bal)),
"AVG"=AVG(CONVERT(money, acct_bal))
FROM bad_column_for_money
WHERE ISNUMERIC(acct_bal)=1

SUM        AVG
--------   --------
9,470.66   1,352.95
```

Niladic functions

ANSI SQL-92 has a handful of what it calls *niladic* functions—a fancy way to indicate that these functions do not accept any parameters. Niladic functions were implemented for version 6.0 and map directly to one of SQL Server's system functions. Frankly, they were added to SQL Server 6.0 because they are mandated for conformance to the ANSI SQL-92 standard—all of their functionality was already provided.

Niladic Function	Equivalent SQL Server System Function
CURRENT_TIMESTAMP	GETDATE( )
SYSTEM_USER	SUSER_NAME( )
CURRENT_USER	USER_NAME( )
SESSION_USER	USER_NAME( )
USER	USER_NAME( )

If you execute the following two SELECT statements, you'll see that they return identical results:

```
SELECT CURRENT_TIMESTAMP, USER, SYSTEM_USER, CURRENT_USER,
SESSION_USER

SELECT GETDATE(), USER_NAME(), SUSER_NAME(),
USER_NAME(), USER_NAME()
```

SUMMARY

This chapter discussed the programming extensions beyond typical implementations of SQL that make Transact-SQL a specialized programming language. These extensions include control of flow, conditional branching, looping, variables, logical operations, bitwise operations, and a variety of scalar functions. The extensions let you write sophisticated routines directly in Transact-SQL and execute them directly in the SQL Server engine. Without them, much more logic would need to be written into client applications, which would reduce performance as more "conversation" would need to take place across the network. Having now discussed in some depth the basics of the SQL language and the Transact-SQL extensions, let's move on to using these extensions in stored procedures and triggers: Chapter 10.

10

Batches, Transactions, Stored Procedures, and Triggers

Introduction

In this chapter, I'll discuss using Transact-SQL for more than interactive queries. When you send a query to the server, you are sending a command batch to SQL Server. But you can do more! I'll show you how to wrap up commands in a module that can be stored and cached at the server for later reuse (stored procedures), and I'll demonstrate how you can create modules that will automatically execute when some event occurs (triggers). Although I've briefly discussed transaction boundaries earlier in the book, in this chapter I'll help you better understand them and the effects of changes by multiple users.

Batches

A *batch* is one or several SQL Server commands that are dispatched and executed together. Because every batch sent from the client to the server requires hand-shaking between the two, sending a batch instead of sending separate commands can prove to be more efficient. Even a batch that does not return a result set (for example, a single INSERT statement) requires at least an acknowledgment that the command was processed and offers a status code for its level of success. At the server, the batch must be received, queued for execution, and so on.

Although commands are grouped and dispatched together for execution, each command is distinct from the others. Let's look at an example. Suppose that you need to execute 150 INSERT statements. Executing all 150 statements in one batch requires the processing overhead once, rather than the overhead incurred 150 times. I know of a real-life situation in which an application that took 5 to 6 seconds to complete 150 individual INSERT statements was changed so that all 150 statements were sent as one batch. The processing time decreased to well under 0.5 second, more than a tenfold improvement. And this was on a LAN, not on a slow network like a WAN or the Internet where the improvement would have been even more pronounced. (Try running an application with 150 batches to insert 150 rows over the Internet, and you'll be really sorry!)

Using a batch is a huge win. By using the Transact-SQL constructs that I presented in Chapter 9, such as conditional logic and looping, you can often perform sophisticated operations within a single batch and eliminate the need to carry on an extensive conversation between the client and the server. Those operations can also be saved on the server as a stored procedure, which allows them to execute even more efficiently. Using batches and stored procedures to minimize the client/server conversations is crucial for achieving high-performing applications. And now that more applications are being deployed on slower networks—such as WANs, the Internet, and dial-up systems—instead of on LANs only, using batches and stored procedures is crucial.

Every SELECT statement (except for those used for assigning a value to a variable) generates a result set. Even a SELECT statement that finds zero rows returns a result set that describes the columns that were selected. Every time the server sends a result set back to the client application, it must send *metadata* as well as the actual data. The metadata describes the result set to the client. You can think of metadata in this way: "Here is a result set with eight columns. The first column is named *last_name* and is of type *char(30)*. The second column is...."

Obviously, then, executing a single SELECT statement with a WHERE clause formulated to find (in one fell swoop) all 247 rows that meet your criteria is much more efficient than separately executing 247 SELECT statements that each returns one row of data. In the former case, one result set is returned. In the latter case, 247 result sets are returned—the performance difference is striking. Using batches might seem like a painfully obvious necessity, yet many programmers still write applications that perform poorly because they do not use batches. The problem is especially common for developers who have worked on ISAM or similar sequential files doing row-at-a-time processing. Unlike ISAM, SQL Server works best with *sets* of data, not individual rows of data, so that you can minimize conversations between the server and the client application.

Following is a simple batch, issued from ISQL. Even though three unrelated operations are being performed, I can package them in a single batch to conserve bandwidth.

```
INSERT authors VALUES(etc.)
SELECT * FROM authors
UPDATE publishers SET pub_id= (etc.)
GO
```

NOTE GO is not an SQL command. It is the end-of-batch signal that tells ISQL and ISQL/w that everything since the last GO should be sent to the server for execution. All commands between GOs are sent together in a batch for execution. There is nothing special about the word GO—the end-of-batch signal is specific to the front-end tool (ISQL and ISQL/w use GO), and the server is not aware of it. With a custom application, a batch is executed with a single **dbsqlexec** from DB-Library or **SQLExecute** from ODBC.

Transactions

Like a batch, a user-declared *transaction* typically consists of several SQL commands that read and update the database. But unlike a batch, a transaction doesn't make any permanent changes until a COMMIT statement is issued, or a transaction can undo its changes when a ROLLBACK statement is issued. With a batch, each command is separately and automatically committed. When a transaction is declared or SQL Server is configured for *implicit transactions,* commands are performed as a unit. Usually, both batches and transactions contain multiple commands dispatched together. A single transaction can span across batches (although that's a bad thing to do from a performance perspective), and a batch can contain multiple transactions.

Following is a simple transaction. The BEGIN TRAN and COMMIT TRAN statements cause the commands between them to be performed as a unit.

```
BEGIN TRAN
INSERT authors VALUES(etc.)
SELECT * FROM authors
UPDATE publishers SET pub_id= (etc.)
COMMIT TRAN
GO
```

Transaction processing in SQL Server assures that all commands within a transaction are performed as a unit—even in the presence of a hardware or general system failure. Such transactions are referred to as having the ACID properties (atomicity, consistency, isolation, and durability). (For more information about the ACID properties, refer to pages 38 and 39 in Chapter 2, "A Tour of Microsoft SQL Server.")

Explicit and Implicit Transactions

By default, SQL Server treats each statement, whether dispatched individually or as part of a batch, as independent and immediately commits it. If you want multiple statements to be part of a transaction, you must wrap the group of statements within BEGIN TRANSACTION and COMMIT or ROLLBACK TRANSACTION statements. You can also configure SQL Server to implicitly start a transaction by using *SET IMPLICIT_TRANSACTIONS ON* or by turning the option on globally using **sp_configure 'user options', 2**. More precisely, take the previous value for the *'user options'* setting and OR it with (decimal) 2, which is the mask for IMPLICIT_TRANSACTIONS. For example, if the previous value was (decimal) 8, you'd set it to 10, since 8|2 is 10. If bit operations like 8|2 are somewhat foreign to you, let SQL Server do the work. You can issue a *SELECT 8|2* in ISQL/w and the row returned will be 10. (But be careful not to assume that you just add 2 to whatever is already there—for example, 10|2 is 10, not 12.)

If implicit transactions are enabled, all statements are considered part of a transaction and no work is committed until and unless an explicit COMMIT TRAN (or synonymously, COMMIT WORK or simply COMMIT) is issued. This is true even if all the statements in the batch have executed: you must issue a COMMIT in a subsequent batch before any work is made permanent.

Error Checking in Transactions

One of the most common mistakes that developers make with SQL Server is to assume that *any* error within a transaction will cause the transaction to automatically roll back. If conditional action should result from a possible error, your multistatement transactions should check for errors by selecting the value of @@ERROR after each statement. If a nonfatal error is encountered and you do not take action on it, processing moves on to the next statement. Only fatal errors cause the batch to be automatically aborted.

> **TIP** Neither a query that finds no rows meeting the criteria of the WHERE clause nor a searched UPDATE statement that affects no rows is an error, and @@ERROR is not set to a nonzero value for either case. If you want to check for "no rows affected," use @@ROWCOUNT, not @@ERROR.

Syntax errors will always cause the entire batch to be aborted, as will references to objects that don't exist (for example, a SELECT from a table that doesn't exist). Typically, you'll work out syntax errors and correct references to objects before you put an application into production, so these won't be much of an issue. However, a syntax error on a statement dynamically built and executed using EXECUTE('*string*') cannot be caught until execution, so this type of syntax error does not abort the batch and processing proceeds to the next statement.

Errors that occur in a production environment are typically resource errors that should be encountered infrequently, especially if you have sufficiently tested to make sure that your configuration settings and environment are appropriate. Out-of-resource errors occur when the system runs out of locks, when there is not enough memory to run a procedure, and so on. For these types of fatal errors, conditional action based on @@ERROR is moot since the batch will automatically be aborted.

The following errors are common:

- Lack of permissions on an object
- Constraint violations
- Duplicates encountered while trying to update or insert a row
- Deadlocks with another user
- NOT NULL violations
- Illegal values for the current datatype

Following is a SQL Server chat group posting from a user who encountered a nonfatal execution error and assumed that the entire transaction should have been automatically aborted. When that didn't happen, the user assumed that SQL Server must have a grievous bug. Here's the posting:

> Using SQL 6.5 in the example below, the empty tables *b* and *c* each get an insert within one tran. The insert into table *c* is fine, but the insert to *b* fails a DRI reference, but the table *c* still has a row in it. Isn't this a major bug?! Should the tran not have been rolled back implicitly!?
>
> —*Keith*

```
create table a (
a char(1) primary key)

create table b (
b char(1) references a)

create table c (
c char(1))
go

create proc test as
begin transaction
insert c values ( 'X' )
Insert b values ( 'X' )   --Fails reference
commit transaction
go

exec test
go

select *
from c  --Returns 'X'  !!
```

The statements, however, are performing *as expected;* the bug is in the way the user wrote the transaction. The transaction has not checked for errors for each statement and *unconditionally* commits at the end. So even if one statement fails with a nonfatal execution error like a constraint or permissions violation, execution proceeds to the next statement. Ultimately the COMMIT is executed, so all the statements without errors are committed. *That's exactly what the procedure has been told to do.* If you want to roll back a transaction if *any* error occurs, you must check @@ERROR or use SET XACT_ABORT.

Here is an example of the procedure rewritten to perform error checking, with a branch to perform a rollback if any error is encountered:

```
CREATE PROC test as
BEGIN TRANSACTION
INSERT c VALUES ('X')
    IF (@@ERROR <> 0) GOTO on_error
INSERT b VALUES ('X')   -- Fails reference
    IF (@@ERROR <> 0) GOTO on_error
COMMIT TRANSACTION
RETURN(0)


on_error:
ROLLBACK TRANSACTION
RETURN(1)
```

This simple procedure illustrates the power of Transact-SQL. The global variable @@ERROR is set for the connection after each statement. A value of 0 for @@ERROR means no error occurred. Given the data the user provided, the INSERT statement on table *b* will fail with a foreign key violation. The error message for that type of failure is error 547, with text such as this:

```
INSERT statement conflicted with COLUMN FOREIGN KEY constraint
'FK__b__b__723BFC65'. The conflict occurred in database 'pubs',
table 'a', column 'a'
```

Consequently, @@ERROR would be set to 547 following that INSERT statement. Therefore, the *IF (@@ERROR <> 0)* statement evaluates as TRUE, and execution follows the *GOTO* to the *on_error:* label. Here, the transaction is rolled back. The procedure terminates with a return code of 1 because the *RETURN(1)* statement was used. Had the branch to *on_error:* not been followed (by virtue of @@ERROR not being 0), the procedure would have continued line-by-line execution. It would have reached *COMMIT TRANSACTION,* and then it would have returned value 0 and never made it all the way to the *on_error:* section.

As you do with most programming languages, you should make sure that a status is returned from a procedure to indicate success or failure (and/or other possible outcomes) and that those return status codes are checked from the calling routines. In Keith's original code, an "EXEC test" invoked the procedure. This approach is perfectly legal and could be done equally well with a procedure that returns 0 for SUCCESS and 1 for FAILURE. However, simply using "EXEC test" will not directly provide information about whether the procedure performed as expected. A better method is to use a local variable to examine the return code from that procedure:

```
DECLARE @retcode int
EXEC @retcode=test
```

Following execution of the test procedure, the local variable *@retcode* will have the value 0 (if no errors occurred in the procedure) or 1 (if execution branched to the *on_error:* section).

We added the SET XACT_ABORT option in version 6.5 to help users like Keith. If this option is set, any error, not just a fatal error (equivalent to checking *@@ERROR <> 0* after every statement), will terminate the batch. Here is another way to ensure that *nothing* is committed if *any* error is encountered:

```
CREATE PROC test AS
SET XACT_ABORT ON
BEGIN TRANSACTION
INSERT c VALUES ('X')
INSERT b VALUES ('X')  -- Fails reference
COMMIT TRANSACTION
GO

EXEC test
GO

SELECT * FROM c
```

The output:

```
(0 rows affected)
```

Note that the name of the XACT_ABORT option is a bit of a misnomer because the current batch, not simply the transaction, will be immediately aborted if an error occurs, just as it is when a fatal resource error is encountered. This has consequences that might not be immediately apparent. For example, if you issued two transactions within one batch, the second transaction would never be executed because the batch would be aborted before the second transaction got a chance to execute. More subtly, suppose that I wanted to use good programming practice and check the return status of the procedure above. (Note that even though it does not explicitly do a RETURN(), every procedure has a return status by default, with 0 indicating SUCCESS.)

I'd write a batch like this:

```
DECLARE @retcode int
EXEC @retcode=test
SELECT @retcode
```

Yet there is a subtle but important problem here. If the procedure has an error, the SELECT @RETCODE statement will never be executed: the entire batch will be aborted by virtue of the SET XACT_ABORT statement. This is why I recommend checking @@ERROR instead of using SET XACT_ABORT. Checking @@ERROR after each statement is a bit more tedious, but it gives you finer control of execution in your procedures.

No doubt, error handling will be improved in future releases. Unfortunately, error handling in SQL Server 6.5 can be somewhat messy and inconsistent. For example, there is no way to install a routine that means "Do this on any error" (other than SET XACT_ABORT, which aborts but does not let you specify the actions to be performed). Instead, you must use something similar to the preceding examples that check @@ERROR and then do a GOTO. In addition, there is currently no easy way to determine in advance which errors might be considered fatal so that the batch can be aborted, versus which errors are nonfatal so that the next statement can be executed. In most cases, an error with severity level of 16 or higher is fatal and the batch will be aborted. But syntax that refers to nonexistent functions are level 15 errors, yet the batch is still aborted. Although you can use an @@ERROR to return the specific error number, no global variable such as @@SEVERITY is available to indicate the error's severity level. Instead, you must subsequently select from the *sysmessages* table to see the severity level of the last error. To further complicate matters, some level 16 errors are not fatal. Following is a list of the most common nonfatal level 16 errors:

Error	Error Message
515	Attempt to insert the value NULL into column '%.*s', *table* '%.*s'; column does not allow nulls. %s fails.
544	Attempt to insert explicit value for identity column in table '%.*s' when IDENTITY_INSERT is set to OFF.
547	%s statement conflicted with %s %s constraint '%.*s'. The conflict occurred in database '%.*s', table '%.*s'%s%.*s%s.
550	The attempted insert or update failed because the target view either specifies WITH CHECK OPTION or spans a view which specifies WITH CHECK OPTION and one or more rows resulting from the operation did not qualify under the CHECK OPTION constraint.

Admittedly, the rules are hardly consistent, and this area is ripe for some attention in future releases. As you write your procedures, you should keep in mind that they could be automatically aborted due to an unexpected fatal error or you can cause them to abort with a nonfatal error. In many applications, you should add retry logic to your error handler to attempt to reexecute a command if it is aborted due to a deadlock (error 1205).

Transaction Isolation Levels

The isolation level at which your transaction runs determines your application's sensitivity to changes made by others, and consequently it also determines how long your transaction will need to hold locks to potentially protect against changes made by others. SQL Server 6.5 offers three isolation-level behaviors (although syntactically four options are available, if REPEATABLE READ is included):

- READ UNCOMMITTED (dirty read)

- READ COMMITTED (default—READ COMMITTED is equivalent to the term CURSOR STABILITY, which is used by several other products such as IBM DB/2)

- SERIALIZABLE

Your transactions will behave differently depending on which isolation level is set. The saying "Not to decide *is* to decide" applies here, because *every transaction has an isolation level whether you've specified it or not*. It makes sense for you to understand the levels and choose the one that best fits your needs.

> **NOTE** The syntactical options listed above correspond to the SQL standard isolation levels, which are discussed in detail in the Chapter 3 section entitled "The Transaction Manager." In this section, I will discuss only information that wasn't covered earlier. See Chapter 3 if you need to refresh your memory.

When using the READ UNCOMMITTED option, keep in mind that you should deal with inconsistencies that might result from dirty reads. Because share locks are not issued and exclusive locks of other connections are not honored (that is, the data pages can be read, even though they are supposedly locked), it is possible to get some spurious errors during execution when using the READ UNCOMMITTED option. A moment later, reexecuting the same command is likely to work without error. To shield your end users from such errors, your applications using isolation level 0 (dirty read) should be prepared to retry due to spurious 605, 606, 624, or 625 errors. One of these errors might get raised to falsely indicate that the database is inconsistent. In such a case, what frequently happens is that an update or insert has been rolled back along with its page allocations, so you've read data pages that no longer exist and logically never did. Ordinarily, locking will prevent such inconsistencies, but READ UNCOMMITTED takes some short-cuts and the errors can still occur. The retry logic should be identical to the logic that would be used to retry on a deadlock condition (error 1205).

> **NOTE** Of course, you don't *have* to add retry logic, but without it the command will be aborted and your end user might see a scary and confusing message. Adding a good error handler can make your application much better behaved by enabling an automatic retry, and the user will never know when such an error is raised.

Phantoms

SQL Server allows you to specify REPEATABLE READ, but this is currently simply a synonym for SERIALIZABLE. As currently implemented in SQL Server, both the SERIALIZABLE and REPEATABLE READ options prevent phantoms from occurring. (As you'll recall from Chapter 3, phantoms occur when updated rows suddenly appear in data when it is revisited during a query or another transaction.) I wouldn't use SERIALIZABLE and REPEATABLE READ as interchangeable terms, however. A future SQL Server release will likely loosen the consistency characteristics of REPEATABLE READ and phantoms will be possible. I recommend instead that you specify the isolation level that best fits your current needs. In some operations, REPEATABLE READ might be all you require, and protecting against phantoms might incur an additional and unnecessary penalty on concurrency in the future.

The Future...

Suppose that you're working with Jane Doe's records, and when you issue a requery you need to ensure that only her records haven't been changed. In future releases, it might be possible to lock the range of records with the Jane Doe key (called a *key range*). This would be a preferable situation if SQL Server had to scan data to solve a join, for example. The scan wouldn't have to place locks that would prevent other transactions from inserting new rows into the ranges they scanned indirectly.

In version 6.5, *all* the scanned data would have to be kept locked and new rows could not be inserted. The current locking is more coarse than you might require, and thus concurrency is reduced more than is necessary. Because this situation is likely to change in a future release, you should be aware that the semantics of REPEATABLE READ might allow phantoms in the future.

Nothing illustrates the differences and effects of isolation levels like seeing them for yourself with some simple examples. I urge you to run the following examples. To do so, you'll need to establish two connections to SQL Server. Remember that each connection is *logically* a different user, even if both connections use the same login ID. (Locks made by one connection affect the other connection, even if both are logged in as the same user.) In case you can't run these examples, I'll show the SQL scripts and output here.

EXAMPLE 1

This example shows a dirty read. A simple command file on the accompanying CD-ROM, RUN_ISOLATION1.CMD spawns two simultaneous ISQL.EXE sessions, running the scripts ISOLATION_CNX1.SQL and ISOLATION_CNX2.SQL. Following are the scripts and the output (in bold) as contained in the output files ISOLATION_CNX1.OUT and ISOLATION_CNX2.OUT.

> **NOTE** The procedures **sem_set** and **sem_wait** provide a simple synchronization mechanism between the two connections. They do nothing more than set a value and then poll for a value—a handy technique. You can create these procedures by running the SEMAPHORE.SQL script, which is included on the companion CD-ROM.
>
> But this mechanism won't always do the job as it does in this case. For example, if I put **set_sem** within a transaction, it could be aborted or rolled back. Also, for illustration purposes, I sometimes use simple delays here to coordinate the two scripts. Relying on timing like this creates the potential for a race condition, and it's not how you'd want to program a production application.

```
-- ISOLATION_CNX2.SQL
USE pubs
GO

EXEC sem_wait 1    -- Wait until other connection says can start
BEGIN TRAN
    UPDATE authors SET au_lname='Smith'
    -- Give other connection chance to read uncommitted data
    WAITFOR DELAY "000:00:20"
ROLLBACK TRAN

EXEC sem_set 0     -- Tell other connection done
```

(23 rows affected)

459

```
-- ISOLATION_CNX1.SQL
-- Illustrate Read Uncommitted (aka "Dirty Read")
--
USE pubs
GO
EXEC sem_set 0     -- Clear semaphore to start
GO

-- First verify there's only one author named 'Smith'
SELECT au_lname FROM authors WHERE au_lname='Smith'
GO
```

```
au_lname
-------------------------
Smith
```

(1 row affected)

```
SET TRANSACTION ISOLATION LEVEL READ UNCOMMITTED

-- Signal other connection that it's ok to update, and then wait
-- for it to proceed. (Obvious possible race condition here
-- this is just for illustration.)

EXEC sem_set 1
-- Wait 10 secs for other connection to update
WAITFOR DELAY "000:00:10"
-- Check again for authors of name 'Smith'.  Now find 23 of them,
-- even though the other connection doesn't COMMIT the changes.
SELECT au_lname FROM authors WHERE au_lname='Smith'
```

```
au_lname
-------------------------
Smith
Smith
Smith
Smith
Smith
Smith
Smith
Smith
Smith
Smith
Smith
Smith
Smith
```

```
Smith
Smith
Smith
Smith
Smith
Smith
Smith
Smith
Smith
Smith
```

(23 rows affected)

```
IF (@@ROWCOUNT > 0)
    PRINT 'Just read uncommitted data !!'
```

Just read uncommitted data !!

```
-- Now the other connection will roll back its changes:
EXEC sem_wait 0

-- Now check again for authors of name 'Smith'.
-- Find only one now, because other connection did a rollback.
SELECT au_lname FROM authors WHERE au_lname='Smith'
```

au_lname
```
-------------------------
```
Smith

(1 row affected)

The scripts above, running simultaneously, illustrate that by setting the isolation level to READ UNCOMMITTED, you can read data that logically never existed (a dirty read). The update to *Smith* was never committed by the ISOLATION-_CNX2.SQL script, yet the other connection read it. Not only did the connection read the update, it did so immediately and did not have to wait for the exclusive lock of the second connection updating the data to be released. In this example, concurrency is very high, but consistency of the data is not maintained. By changing the isolation level back to the default (READ COMMITTED), the same scripts would never see more than one row containing *Smith*. But with READ COMMITTED, the connection reading the data must wait until the updating transaction is done, and this is the tradeoff: higher consistency is achieved (the uncommitted rows are not seen by others), but concurrency is reduced.

EXAMPLE 2

This example illustrates the semantic differences between selecting data under
the default isolation level of READ COMMITTED (cursor stability) and under the
isolation level of SERIALIZABLE. Use the command file RUN_ISOLATION3.CMD
to run these two scripts simultaneously. Output will be written to ISOLATION3-
_CNX1.OUT and ISOLATION3_CNX2.OUT.

```
-- ISOLATION3_CNX2.SQL

USE pubs
GO

-- Wait until other connection says can start, then sleep 10 secs
EXEC sem_wait 1

WAITFOR DELAY "000:00:10"
GO
UPDATE authors SET au_lname='Smith'
GO
(23 rows affected)

EXEC sem_set 0     -- Tell other connection done with first part
EXEC sem_wait 1    -- Wait until other connection says can start,
                   -- then sleep 10 secs
GO

WAITFOR DELAY "000:00:10"
GO

UPDATE authors SET au_lname='Jones'
GO
(23 rows affected)

-- ISOLATION3_CNX1.SQL
-- Illustrate Read Repeatable/Serializable (aka level 2 & 3)
USE pubs
GO

UPDATE authors SET au_lname='Doe' -- Make sure no Smith or Jones
(23 rows affected)

EXEC sem_SET 0    -- Clear semaphore to start
GO

-- First verify there are no authors named 'Smith'
SELECT au_lname FROM authors WHERE au_lname='Smith'
GO
```

```
au_lname
--------------------
```

(0 rows affected)

```
SET TRANSACTION ISOLATION LEVEL READ COMMITTED
GO

-- Signal other connection it's ok to update, then wait for it to
-- proceed. (Obvious possible race condition here - this is just
-- for illustration.)
EXEC sem_SET 1
GO

BEGIN TRAN
SELECT au_lname FROM authors WHERE au_lname='Smith'
GO
```

```
au_lname
--------------------
```

(0 rows affected)

```
WAITFOR DELAY "000:00:15"
```

```
SELECT au_lname FROM authors WHERE au_lname='Smith'
```

```
au_lname
--------------------
 Smith
 Smith
 Smith
 Smith
 Smith
 Smith
 Smith
 Smith
 Smith
 Smith
 Smith
 Smith
 Smith
 Smith
 Smith
 Smith
 Smith
```

```
  Smith
  Smith
  Smith
  Smith
  Smith

(23 rows affected)

COMMIT TRAN
GO

EXEC sem_wait 0
EXEC sem_SET 1
GO

-- Now do the same thing, but with SERIALIZABLE isolation

SET TRANSACTION ISOLATION LEVEL SERIALIZABLE
GO

BEGIN TRAN
SELECT au_lname FROM authors WHERE au_lname='Jones'
GO

au_lname
--------------------

(0 rows affected)

-- Wait for other connection to have a chance to make and commit
-- its changes
WAITFOR DELAY "000:00:15"

SELECT au_lname FROM authors WHERE au_lname='Jones'

au_lname
--------------------

(0 rows affected)

COMMIT TRAN
GO

-- Now notice that Jones updates have been done
SELECT au_lname FROM authors WHERE au_lname='Jones'
GO
```

```
au_lname
--------------------
Jones
Jones
Jones
Jones
Jones
Jones
Jones
Jones
Jones
Jones
Jones
Jones
Jones
Jones
Jones
Jones
Jones
Jones
Jones
Jones
Jones
Jones
Jones

(23 rows affected)

EXEC sem_SET 0    -- Tell other connection done
```

As you can see, when the isolation level was set to READ COMMITTED, doing the same SELECT twice within a transaction yielded totally different results: first no Smiths were found, and then 23 of them appeared. If this were a banking transaction, these results would be unacceptable. For applications that are less sensitive to minor changes, or when business functions guard against such inconsistencies in other ways, this behavior might be acceptable.

After changing the isolation level to SERIALIZABLE, I got the same result (no Joneses) with both SELECT statements. Immediately after the transaction has committed, the other connection updated all the names to Jones. So when I again selected for Jones (immediately after the transaction was committed), the update took place—but at some cost. In the first case, the other connection was able to do the update as soon as the first SELECT was processed. It did not have to wait for the second query and subsequent transaction to complete. In the second case, that second connection had to wait until the first connection completed the transaction in its entirety. In this example, concurrency was significantly reduced but consistency was perfect.

Additional Characteristics of Transactions

In addition to isolation levels, it is important to understand the following characteristics of transactions.

First, a single UPDATE, DELETE, or INSERT/SELECT statement that affects multiple rows is always an atomic operation and must complete without error or it is automatically rolled back. For example, if you did a single UPDATE statement that updated all rows, but one row failed a constraint, the operation would be terminated with no rows updated. Because there is no way to do error checking for each row within such a statement, any error rolls back the statement. However, the batch is not aborted. Execution proceeds to the next available statement in the batch. This will occur even in INSERT operations that are based on a SELECT statement (INSERT/SELECT or SELECT INTO).

Like the statements mentioned above, modifications made by a trigger are always atomic with the underlying data modification statement. For example, if an update trigger attempts to update data but fails, the underlying data modification operation is rolled back. Both operations must succeed or neither does.

It might not be obvious, but Example 2 (the SERIALIZABLE example) shows that a transaction can affect pure SELECT operations in which no data is modified. The transaction boundaries define the statements between which a specified isolation level will be assured. Two identical SELECT statements might behave differently if they were executed while wrapped by BEGIN TRAN/COMMIT TRAN with an isolation level of REPEATABLE READ than they would behave if they were executed together in the same batch, but not within a transaction.

Finally, another point that might not seem obvious: the SET TRANSACTION ISOLATION LEVEL setting applies to the entire batch, no matter where or in what order it appears in the batch. For example, if you have been operating with REPEATABLE READ, but you want to change the setting to READ COMMITTED, it would seem natural to put the READ COMMITTED statement at the end of your batch. However, doing so would change the entire batch to READ COMMITTED—including the statements that appeared before it.

Stored Procedures

Now that you've learned about batches and transactions, it's time to discuss another important capability of Transact-SQL. *Stored procedures* enable you to cache commands at the server for later use. To create a stored procedure, you take a batch and wrap it inside a CREATE PROCEDURE *proc_name* AS statement. After that, you use Transact-SQL with nothing special except for declaring what parameters will be passed to the procedure.

To demonstrate how easy it is to create a stored procedure, I've written a simple procedure called **get_author** that takes one parameter, the *author_id,* and returns the names of any authors that have IDs equal to whatever character string is passed to the procedure.

```
CREATE PROC get_author @au_id varchar(11)
AS
SELECT au_lname, au_fname
FROM authors
WHERE au_id=@au_id
```

This procedure can be subsequently executed with syntax like this:

```
EXEC get_author '172-32-1176'
EXEC get_author @au_id='172-32-1176'
```

You can see that the parameters can be passed anonymously by including values in order, or the parameters can be explicitly named so that the order in which they are passed is not important.

If the procedure is the first statement in the batch, using EXEC is optional. However, I think it's always best to use EXEC so that later you won't wind up scratching your head with confusion, wondering why your procedure won't execute (only to realize later that it is no longer the first statement of the batch).

In practice, you'll probably want a procedure like the one above to be a bit more sophisticated. Perhaps you'd want to search for author names that begin with a partial ID that you pass. If you choose not to pass anything, rather than give you an error message stating that the parameter is missing, the procedure should show all authors. And maybe you'd like to return some value as a variable, distinct from the result set returned and from the return code, that you would use to check for successful execution.

You can do this by passing an *output* parameter, which has a *pass-by reference* capability. Passing an output parameter to a stored procedure is similar to passing a pointer when calling a function in C. Rather than passing a value, you pass the address of a storage area in which the procedure will cache a value. That value is subsequently available to the SQL batch after the stored procedure has executed. For example, I might want an output parameter to tell me the number of rows returned by a SELECT statement. While the @@ROWCOUNT global variable has this information, it is maintained only for the last statement executed. If the stored procedure executed many statements, I'd need to put this value away for safekeeping. An output parameter provides an easy way to do this.

Here's a simple procedure that selects all the rows from the *authors* table and all the rows from the *titles* table. It also sets an output parameter for each table based on @@ROWCOUNT. This value is subsequently available to the calling batch by checking the variables passed as the output parameters.

```
CREATE PROC count_tables @authorcount int OUTPUT,
@titlecount int OUTPUT
AS
SELECT * FROM authors
SELECT @authorcount=@@ROWCOUNT
SELECT * FROM titles
SELECT @titlecount=@@ROWCOUNT
RETURN(0)
```

The procedure would then be executed like this:

```
DECLARE @a_count int, @t_count int
EXEC count_tables @a_count OUTPUT, @t_count OUTPUT
```

> **TIP** Variables are always local, so I could have used the same names for both the variables in the procedure and those passed by the batch as output parameters. In fact, this is probably the most common way to invoke them. I chose not to do this here to make it clear that the variables don't need to have the same name. Even with the same name, they are in fact different variables because their scoping is different.

This procedure will return all the rows from both tables. In addition, the variables *@a_count* and *@t_count* will retain the row counts from the *authors* and *titles* tables, respectively.

```
SELECT authorcount=@a_count, titlecount=@t_count
```

Here's the output:

```
authorcount    titlecount
-----------    ----------
23             18
```

When creating a stored procedure, you can reference a table, a view, or another stored procedure that does not currently exist. (In the latter case, you'll get a warning message informing you that a referenced object does not exist. As long as the object exists at the time the procedure is executed, all will be fine.)

Nested Stored Procedures

Stored procedures can be nested and can call other procedures. A procedure invoked from another procedure can also then invoke yet another procedure. In such a transaction, the top-level procedure has a nesting level of 1. The first subordinate procedure has a nesting level of 2. If that subordinate procedure subsequently invokes another stored procedure, the nesting level will be 3, and so on, to a limit of 16 nesting levels. If the 16-level limit is reached, a fatal error will result, the batch will be aborted, and any open transactions will be rolled back. The nesting-level limit prevents stack overflows that can result from procedures recursively calling themselves infinitely. The limit allows a procedure to recursively call itself only 15 subsequent times (for a total of 16 procedure calls). To determine how deeply a procedure is nested at runtime, you can select the global variable @@NESTLEVEL.

Unlike nesting levels, SQL Server has no practical limit on the number of stored procedures that can be invoked from a given stored procedure. For example, a main stored procedure could invoke hundreds or more subordinate stored procedures. If the subordinate procedures don't invoke other subordinate procedures, the nesting level never reaches a depth greater than 2.

An error in a nested (subordinate) stored procedure is not necessarily fatal to the calling stored procedure. When invoking a stored procedure from another stored procedure, it's a good idea to use a RETURN statement and check the return value in the calling procedure. In this way, you can conditionally work with error situations (as shown in the factorial example below).

Recursion in Stored Procedures

Stored procedures can perform nested calls to themselves, a technique known as *recursion*. Only powerful programming languages such as C—and Transact-SQL—support recursion. Recursion is a technique by which the solution to a problem can be expressed by applying the solution to subsets of the problem. Programming instructors usually demonstrate recursion by having students write a factorial program using recursion to display a table of factorial values for *0!* through *10!*. Recall that a factorial of a positive integer *n,* written as *n!,* is the multiplication of all integers from 1 through *n*. For example:

```
8!    = 8 x 7 x 6 x 5 x 4 x 3 x 2 x 1 = 40320
```

(Zero is a special case—*0!* is defined as equal to 1.)

I can write a stored procedure that computes factorials, and I can do the recursive programming assignment in Transact-SQL.

NOTE I'm not saying recursion is the best way to solve this problem. An iterative (looping) approach is probably better. This example is simply for illustration purposes.

```
-- Use Transact-SQL to recursively calculate factorial
-- of numbers between 0 and 12
-- Parameters greater than 12 are disallowed as result
-- overflows the bounds of an int

CREATE PROC factorial @param1 int
AS
DECLARE @one_less int, @answer int
IF (@param1 < 0 OR @param1 > 12)
    BEGIN
        -- Illegal parameter value. Must be between 0 and 12.
        RETURN -1
    END

IF (@param1=0 or @param1=1)
    SELECT @answer=1
ELSE
    BEGIN
    SELECT @one_less=@param1 - 1
    EXEC @answer=factorial @one_less -- Recursively call itself
    IF (@answer= -1)
        BEGIN
            RETURN -1
        END

    SELECT @answer=@answer * @param1
        IF (@@ERROR <> 0)
            RETURN -1
    END

RETURN(@answer)
```

Note that when the procedure is initially created, a warning message like the one shown below will indicate that the procedure is referencing a procedure that doesn't currently exist (which is itself in this case):

```
Cannot add rows to Sysdepends for the current stored procedure
because it depends on the missing object 'factorial'. The stored
procedure will still be created.
```

Once the procedure exists, I can use it to display the standard factorial table that students generate in C programming classes:

```
DECLARE @answer numeric, @param int
SELECT @param=0
WHILE (@param <= 12)
BEGIN EXEC @answer=factorial @param IF (@answer= -1) BEGIN
RAISERROR('Error executing factorial procedure.', 16, -1) RETURN END
SELECT CONVERT(varchar, @param) + '! = ' + CONVERT(varchar, @answer)
SELECT @param=@param + 1
END
```

Here's the return table:

```
0! = 1
1! = 1
2! = 2
3! = 6
4! = 24
5! = 120
6! = 720
7! = 5040
8! = 40320
9! = 362880
10! = 3628800
11! = 39916800
12! = 479001600
```

I stopped at *12!* in the **factorial** procedure because *13!* is 6,227,020,800, which exceeds the range of a 32-bit (4-byte) integer. However, even without the range limit, I could have gone only to *15!* because I'd have reached the maximum nesting depth of 16, which includes recursive calls. The procedure would have then terminated with error 217:

```
Maximum stored procedure nesting level exceeded (limit 16)
```

Notice too that I return −1 if the procedure results in an error or is passed an illegal parameter. This return code can then be checked for an error.

In C, you need to be sure that you don't overflow your stack when you use recursion. Using Transact-SQL shields you from that concern, but it does so by steadfastly refusing to nest calls more than 16 levels deep. You can also watch @@NESTLEVEL and take appropriate action before reaching the hard limit. As is often the case with a recursion problem, an iterative solution could be performed without the restriction of nesting or worries about the stack.

Here is an iterative approach. To illustrate that there is no restriction of 16 levels since it is simple iteration, I take this exercise further, to *33!*. The value from a RETURN statement, however, is always an *int*. So this version uses an output parameter declared as *numeric(38,0)* instead of *int*. (This example also illustrates that a numeric datatype with scale of 0 can be used as an alternative to *int* for integer operations that require values larger than the 4-byte *int* can handle.) I stop at *33!* because *34!* would overflow the precision of a *numeric(38,0)* variable. (Note that SQL Server must be started with the **-p38** flag to increase the maximum precision to 38 digits instead of the default of 28.) Here's the iterative solution:

```
-- Alternative iterative solution does not have the restriction
-- of 16 nesting levels
CREATE PROC factorial2 @param1 int, @answer NUMERIC(38,0) OUTPUT
AS
DECLARE @counter int
IF (@param1 < 0 OR @param1 > 33)
    BEGIN
    RAISERROR ('Illegal Parameter Value. Must be between 0 and 33',
        16, -1)
    RETURN -1
    END

SELECT @counter=1, @answer=1

WHILE (@counter < @param1 AND @param1 <> 0 )
    SELECT @answer=@answer * (@counter + 1), @counter=@counter + 1

RETURN
GO

DECLARE @answer numeric(38, 0), @param int
SELECT @param=0
WHILE (@param <= 33)
BEGIN
    EXEC factorial2 @param, @answer OUTPUT
    SELECT CONVERT(varchar(45), @param) + '! = '
        + CONVERT(varchar(45), @answer)
    SELECT @param=@param + 1
END
```

And here's the output table:

```
0! = 1
1! = 1
2! = 2
3! = 6
4! = 24
5! = 120
6! = 720
7! = 5040
8! = 40320
9! = 362880
```

```
10! =  3628800
11! =  39916800
12! =  479001600
13! =  6227020800
14! =  87178291200
15! =  1307674368000
16! =  20922789888000
17! =  355687428096000
18! =  6402373705728000
19! =  121645100408832000
20! =  2432902008176640000
21! =  51090942171709440000
22! =  1124000727777607680000
23! =  25852016738884976640000
24! =  620448401733239439360000
25! =  15511210043330985984000000
26! =  403291461126605635584000000
27! =  10888869450418352160768000000
28! =  304888344611713860501504000000
29! =  8841761993739701954543616000000
30! =  265252859812191058636308480000000
31! =  8222838654177922817725562880000000
32! =  263130836933693530167218012160000000
33! =  8683317618811886495518194401280000000
```

Nested Transaction Blocks

It is syntactically acceptable for blocks of BEGIN TRANSACTION followed by COMMIT or ROLLBACK to be nested within other such blocks. This kind of nesting can also be done with calls to nested stored procedures. However, the semantics of such a formulation might not be what you would expect if you think that the transactions are truly nested: they are not. But the behavior is reasonable and predictable. A ROLLBACK rolls back all levels of the transaction, not only its inner block. A COMMIT TRAN does nothing to commit the transaction if the statement is not part of the outermost block, in which case it commits all levels of the transaction. So the behavior of a COMMIT or a ROLLBACK is not too orthogonal when the transaction blocks are nested. Only the outermost COMMIT is able to commit the transaction, but any ROLLBACK will roll back the entire transaction at all levels. If this were not true, a ROLLBACK in an outer transaction would not be able to perform its job, because the data would have already been committed. This behavior allows stored procedures (and triggers) to be executed automatically and in a predictable way without your needing to check the transaction state. A nested stored procedure that does a ROLLBACK will roll back the entire transaction, including work done by the top-level procedure. At this point, you will get a message similar to the one on the following page that warns of a mismatch of transaction blocks.

```
Msg 266, Level 16, State 1
Transaction count after EXECUTE indicates that a COMMIT or ROLLBACK
TRAN is missing. Previous count = 1, Current count = 0.
```

In addition, the blocks of BEGIN TRAN and COMMIT or ROLLBACK are determined only by what actually executes, not by what is present in the batch. If conditional branching occurs (via IF statements, for example) and one of the statements doesn't execute, the statement is not part of a block.

A common misconception about ROLLBACK is that it changes the flow of control, causing, for example, an immediate return from a stored procedure or a batch. However, flow of control continues to the next statement, which, of course, could be an explicit RETURN. ROLLBACK affects only the actual data; it does not affect local variables or SET statements. If local variables are changed during a transaction or if SET statements are issued, those variables and options *do not* revert to the values they had before the transaction started. Variables and SET options are not part of transaction control.

The global variable @@TRANCOUNT keeps count of the depth of executed BEGIN TRAN blocks. You can think of the behavior of COMMIT and ROLLBACK in this way: ROLLBACK performs its job for all levels of transaction blocks whenever @@TRANCOUNT is 1 or greater. A COMMIT commits changes *only* when @@TRANCOUNT is 1.

> **NOTE** Beginning on page 476, I'll show you several examples of nesting transaction blocks. For illustration, I've noted the value of @@TRANCOUNT in the comments. If this discussion isn't totally clear to you, I suggest that you work through these examples by hand to understand why the value of @@TRANCOUNT is what it is, why it changes, and why the behavior of COMMIT or ROLLBACK acts in a way that depends on the @@TRANCOUNT value.

Executing a BEGIN TRAN statement always increments the value of @@TRANCOUNT. If no transaction is active, @@TRANCOUNT is 0. Executing a COMMIT TRAN decrements the value of @@TRANCOUNT. Executing a ROLLBACK TRAN rolls back the entire transaction and sets @@TRANCOUNT to 0. Executing either a COMMIT or a ROLLBACK when there is no open transaction (@@TRANCOUNT is 0) results in error 3902 or 3903, which states that the COMMIT or ROLLBACK request has no corresponding BEGIN TRANSACTION. In this case, @@TRANCOUNT is not decremented, so it can never go below 0.

Other errors, not of your making, are fatal as well—for example, out of memory, out of locks, or termination due to a deadlock. Such errors cause an open transaction to automatically roll back. If that occurs, @@TRANCOUNT is set to 0, signaling that no open transaction exists. The following incidents cause fatal errors:

- The system runs out of resources such as locks.

- The log runs out of space.

- Deadlock conditions exist.

- Protection exceptions occur (that is, sufficient permissions are unavailable on an object).

- A stored procedure cannot run (for example, it is not present or you don't have privileges).

- Reading or writing a stored procedure or trigger from the *sysprocedures* table or the cache is not possible because the system is out of memory or a procedure cache is too small.

- The maximum nesting level of stored procedure executions has been reached.

You can't plan precisely for all of these situations, and even if you could, a new release could likely add another one. In a production environment, fatal errors should be few and far between. But as is true in nearly all programming, it's up to you to decide whether you want to try to plan for every conceivable problem that could happen and then deal with each specifically, or whether you will accept the system default behavior. In SQL Server, the default behavior would typically be to raise an error for the condition encountered and then, when the COMMIT or ROLLBACK is executed, raise another that says it has no corresponding transaction. For my program, I would probably consider writing some retry logic in my ODBC or DB-Library application to deal with a possible deadlock condition. For the other error conditions, I'd probably go with the default error behavior. If I deploy my application with proper system management, such errors should be nonexistent or rare. I could also check @@TRANCOUNT easily enough before executing a ROLLBACK or COMMIT to ensure that a transaction on which to operate is open.

The nesting of transaction blocks provides a good reason for you *not* to name the transaction in a ROLLBACK statement. If, in a rollback, any transaction other than the top-level transaction is named, error 6401 will result:

```
Cannot rollback XXX - no transaction or savepoint of that name found.
```

It's fine to name the transaction in the BEGIN TRAN block, however. A COMMIT can also be named, and it won't prompt an error if it is not paired in the top-level branch since it basically is a NOOP in that case anyway (except that it decrements the value of @@TRANCOUNT). You might choose sometimes to name the transaction so that you can see which transactions were automatically rolled back and rolled forward at system startup if you set *recovery flags* to 1 using **sp_configure**. The error log and event log will then include useful messages similar to those shown on the next page.

```
96/11/06 10:52:10.04 spid1    Recovering database 'pubs'.
96/11/06 10:52:10.20 spid1    Recovery dbid 4 ckpt (1039,20) oldest
                              tran=(1044,12).
96/11/06 10:52:10.20 spid1    Roll forward transaction 'TRAN_B' in dbid 4.
96/11/06 10:52:10.44 spid1    Roll back transaction 'TRAN_A' - was
                              aborted in dbid 4.
96/11/06 10:52:10.53 spid1    1 transactions rolled forward in dbid 4.
96/11/06 10:52:10.53 spid1    1 transactions rolled back in dbid 4.
```

The following batch will result in an error. The statement *ROLLBACK TRAN B* will fail, with error 6401. The subsequent *ROLLBACK TRAN A* will succeed because it is the top-level transaction block:

```
-- To start with, verify @@TRANCOUNT is 0
SELECT @@TRANCOUNT
BEGIN TRAN A
    -- Verify @@TRANCOUNT is 1
    SELECT @@TRANCOUNT
    -- Assume some real work happens here
    BEGIN TRAN B
        -- Verify @@TRANCOUNT is 2
        SELECT @@TRANCOUNT
        -- Assume some real work happens here
    ROLLBACK TRAN B
-- @@TRANCOUNT is still 2, because the previous ROLLBACK
-- failed due to error 6401
SELECT @@TRANCOUNT -- Assume some real work happens here
ROLLBACK TRAN A
-- This ROLLBACK succeeds, so @@TRANCOUNT is back to 0
SELECT @@TRANCOUNT
```

The following example is arguably an improvement over the previous attempt. The first ROLLBACK will execute but will still result in an error. The second ROLLBACK will fail, with error 3903:

```
-- The ROLLBACK transaction request has no corresponding BEGIN
-- TRANSACTION. The first ROLLBACK did its job and there is no open
-- transaction.
-- To start with, verify @@TRANCOUNT is 0
SELECT @@TRANCOUNT
BEGIN TRAN A
    -- Verify @@TRANCOUNT is 1
    SELECT @@TRANCOUNT
    -- Assume some real work happens here
    BEGIN TRAN B
        -- Verify @@TRANCOUNT is 2
        SELECT @@TRANCOUNT
    -- Assume some real work happens here
```

```
    ROLLBACK TRAN -- Notice the tran is unnamed but works
    -- That ROLLBACK terminates transaction. @@TRANCOUNT is now 0.
    SELECT @@TRANCOUNT
-- The following ROLLBACK will fail because there is no open
-- transaction (that is, @@TRANCOUNT is 0)
ROLLBACK TRAN
-- @@TRANCOUNT does not go negative. It remains at 0.
SELECT @@TRANCOUNT
```

In the following example, the second ROLLBACK will not execute because @@TRANCOUNT is 0 following the prior ROLLBACK. If you syntactically nest transactions, be careful not to nest multiple ROLLBACK statements in a way that would allow more than one to execute. To illustrate that COMMIT behaves differently than ROLLBACK, note that the following example will run without error. However, the statement *COMMIT TRAN B* does not commit any changes. It does have the effect of decrementing @@TRANCOUNT, however.

```
-- To start with, verify @@TRANCOUNT is 0
SELECT @@TRANCOUNT
BEGIN TRAN A
    -- Verify @@TRANCOUNT is 1
    SELECT @@TRANCOUNT
    -- Assume some real work happens here
        BEGIN TRAN B
            -- Verify @@TRANCOUNT is 2
            SELECT @@TRANCOUNT
            -- Assume some real work happens here
        COMMIT TRAN B
-- The COMMIT didn't COMMIT anything, but does decrement
-- @@TRANCOUNT
    -- Verify @@TRANCOUNT is back down to 1:
    SELECT @@TRANCOUNT
    -- Assume some real work happens here
COMMIT TRAN A
-- The COMMIT on previous line does commit the changes and
-- closes the transaction
-- Since there's no open transaction, @@TRANCOUNT is again 0
SELECT @@TRANCOUNT
```

In summary, nesting transaction blocks is perfectly valid, but you must understand the semantics as I've discussed and shown above. If you understand when @@TRANCOUNT is incremented, decremented, and set to 0, and you know the simple rule for COMMIT and ROLLBACK, you can pretty simply produce the effect you want.

Savepoints

Often, users will nest transaction blocks, only to find that the behavior is not what they want. What they *really* want is for a *savepoint* to occur in a transaction. A savepoint provides a point up to which a transaction can be undone—it might have been more accurately named a "rollback point." A savepoint does not commit any changes to the database—only a COMMIT statement can do that.

SQL Server allows you to use savepoints via the SAVE TRAN statement, which doesn't affect the @@TRANCOUNT value. A rollback to a savepoint (not a transaction) does not affect the @@TRANCOUNT either. However, the rollback must explicitly name the savepoint: using ROLLBACK without a specific name will roll back the entire transaction.

In the first nested transaction block example shown on the preceding pages, a rollback to a transaction name failed with error 6401 because the name was not the top-level transaction. Had the name been a savepoint instead of a transaction, no error would result, as this example shows:

```
--To start with, verify @@TRANCOUNT is 0
SELECT @@TRANCOUNT
BEGIN TRAN A
    -- Verify @@TRANCOUNT is 1
    SELECT @@trancount
    -- Assume some real work happens here
    SAVE TRAN B
-- Verify @@TRANCOUNT is still 1. A savepoint does not affect it.
        SELECT @@TRANCOUNT
        -- Assume some real work happens here
    ROLLBACK TRAN B
-- @@TRANCOUNT is still 1, because the previous ROLLBACK
-- affects just the savepoint, not the transaction
SELECT @@TRANCOUNT
-- Assume some real work happens here
ROLLBACK TRAN A
-- This ROLLBACK succeeds, so @@TRANCOUNT is back to 0
SELECT @@TRANCOUNT
```

Stored Procedure Parameters

Stored procedures take parameters, and you can give parameters default values. If you do not supply a default value, a specific parameter will be required. If you do not pass a required parameter, an error like this will result:

```
Msg 201, Level 16, State 2
Procedure sp_passit expects parameter @param1, which was not supplied.
```

You can pass values by explicitly naming the parameters or by furnishing all the parameter values anonymously but in correct positional order. You can also use the keyword DEFAULT as a placeholder in passing parameters. NULL can also be passed as a parameter (or defined to be the default). Here's a simple example with results in bold:

```
CREATE PROCEDURE pass_params
@param0 int=NULL,    -- Defaults to NULL
@param1 int=1 ,      -- Defaults to 1
@param2 int=2        -- Defaults to 2
AS
SELECT @param0, @param1, @param2
GO

EXEC pass_params              -- PASS NOTHING - ALL Defaults
(null)    1    2

EXEC pass_params 0, 10, 20    -- PASS ALL, IN ORDER
0    10    20

EXEC pass_params @param2=200, @param1=NULL
-- Explicitly identify last two params (out of order)
(null)    (null)    200

EXEC pass_params 0, DEFAULT, 20
-- Let param1 default. Others by place.
0    1    20
```

Executing Batches, or What's Stored About a Stored Procedure?

Typically, when a batch of Transact-SQL commands is received from a client connection, the following high-level actions are performed:

Step 1: Parse commands and create the sequence tree.   The command parser checks for proper syntax and translates the Transact-SQL commands into an internal format that can be operated on. The internal format is known as a *sequence tree* or *query tree*. The command parser handles these language events.

Step 2: Compile the batch.   An execution plan is generated from the sequence tree. The entire batch is compiled, queries are optimized, and security is checked. The execution plan contains the necessary steps to check any constraints that exist. If a trigger exists, the call to that procedure is appended to the execution plan. (Recall that a trigger is really a specialized type of stored procedure. Its plan is cached, and the trigger does not need to be recompiled every time data is modified).

The execution plan includes:

- The complete set of necessary steps to carry out the commands in the batch or stored procedure

- The steps needed to enforce constraints (for example, for a foreign key, this would involve checking values in another table)

- A branch to the stored procedure plan for a trigger, if one exists

Step 3: Execute.   During execution, each step of the execution plan is dispatched serially to a "manager" that is responsible for carrying out that type of command. For example, a data definition command (in DDL), such as CREATE TABLE, is dispatched to the DDL Manager. DML statements, such as SELECT, UPDATE, INSERT, and DELETE, go to the DML Manager. Miscellaneous commands, such as DBCC and WAITFOR, go to the Utility Manager. Calls to stored procedures (for example, EXEC **sp_who**) are dispatched to the Stored Procedure Manager. A statement with an explicit BEGIN TRAN interacts directly with the Transaction Manager.

Contrary to what many people think, stored procedures do not permanently store the execution plan of the procedure. (*This is a feature*—the execution plan is relatively dynamic.) Think for a moment about why it is important for the execution plan to be dynamic. As new indexes are added, preexisting indexes are dropped, constraints are added or changed, and triggers are added or changed; or as the amount of data changes, the plan can easily become obsolete.

So, what's stored about a stored procedure?

The sequence tree and the SQL statements that were used to create the procedure are stored, eliminating the need to reparse the Transact-SQL statements and re-create the sequence tree. The first time a stored procedure is executed after SQL Server was last restarted, the sequence tree is retrieved and an execution plan is compiled. The execution plan resides in the portion of memory known as the *procedure cache*. The execution plan is then cached, and it remains in the procedure cache for possible reuse until it is forced out in a least recently used (LRU) manner. Hence, a subsequent execution of the stored procedure can skip not only Step 1, *parsing,* but also Step 2, *compiling,* and go directly to Step 3, *execution*. Steps 1 and 2 always add some overhead and sometimes can be as costly as actually executing the commands. Obviously, if you can eliminate the first two steps in a three-step process, you've done well. That's what stored procedures let you do.

As I mentioned above, the execution plan of a stored procedure resides in the portion of SQL Server's cache known as the procedure cache. The procedure cache must be big enough to store at least one copy of the biggest execution plan you will execute. If it is not big enough, you will get an error stating that insufficient memory is available to run the procedure.

NOTE The SQL Server cache is composed of the procedure cache, which keeps execution plans of stored procedures, and the data cache. The amount of space that is allocated to each area is a function of the **sp_configure 'procedure cache'** setting, which is expressed as a percentage of available cache rather than as a specific amount. The remaining memory is then made available for data caching.

When you execute a stored procedure, if a valid execution plan exists in the procedure cache, it will be used (eliminating the parsing and sequencing steps). When the server is restarted, no execution plans will be in the cache, so the first time the server is restarted a stored procedure will be compiled.

TIP You can preload your procedure cache with execution plans for stored procedures by defining a startup stored procedure that executes the procedures you want to have compiled and cached.

After a procedure executes, its plan remains in the procedure cache and is reused the next time any connection executes the same procedure. However, an execution plan is not *reentrant*: that is, a copy of the plan must be available for every connection attempting to execute the procedure. So if you expect 10 different connections to simultaneously execute a stored procedure, you should expect 10 copies of the execution plan to be in memory (provided that you have sufficient space in the procedure cache).

Figures 10-1 and 10-2 show execution with and without a stored procedure:

EXECUTE Stored Procedure

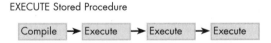

Figure 10-1. *Execution is more efficient with a stored procedure.*

EXECUTE Batch (Without Stored Procedure)

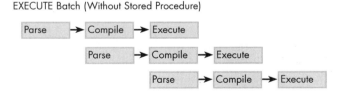

Figure 10-2. *Execution is less efficient without a stored procedure.*

Step 4: Recompile execution plans.   By now it should be clear that sequence trees persist in the database but execution plans do not. Execution plans are cached in memory (in the procedure cache). But sometimes they can be invalidated and a new plan generated.

So, when is a new execution plan compiled?

■ When a copy of the execution plan is not available in memory.

■ When an index on a referenced table is dropped.

■ When a table referenced in the procedure is altered using ALTER TABLE. This includes adding datatypes or adding, changing, or dropping constraints. Any changes to the table results in the schema column of the *sysobjects* table being incremented. If the schema value changes after the execution plan is created, the plan will be invalidated at runtime and then re-created.

■ When a rule or default is bound to the table or column. This is basically the same as altering a table. Binding a rule or default increments the schema column of *sysobjects* for the given table, invalidating the plans of any procedures that reference the table.

■ When the table has been specifically identified, using **sp_recompile**, to force recompilation of any stored procedures referencing it. The system procedure **sp_recompile** increments the schema column of *sysobjects* for a given table. This invalidates any plans that reference the table, as described in the examples above. You do not specify a specific procedure to be recompiled—instead, you simply supply the name of a table to **sp_recompile** and all execution plans or procedures referencing the table will be invalidated. If you add a new index or update statistics on the data, it is a good idea to execute **sp_recompile** if you want the new options or information to be considered. (If it's practical to do so, you can simply restart SQL Server. All stored procedures will then get new execution plans the next time they are run.)

■ When the stored procedure was created using the WITH RECOMPILE option. A stored procedure can be created using WITH RECOMPILE to ensure that its execution plan will be recompiled for every call and will never be reused. Using WITH RECOMPILE is not common, but it can be useful if the procedures take parameters and the values of the parameters differ widely, resulting in a need for different execution plans to be formulated. For example, if a procedure is passed a value to be matched in the WHERE clause of a query, the best way to carry out that query can depend on the value passed. SQL Server keeps a page of sample data for each index as a histogram to help it decide whether the index is selective enough to be useful.

For a given value, while an index might be highly selective, distribution statistics might indicate that only 5 percent of the rows have that value. Although the index would need to be visited, it would exclude many pages of data from having to be visited. Using the index would still be a good strategy. Using another value, the index might not be so selective. Rather than use only the index to visit most of the data pages (ultimately doing more I/O, since you're reading both the index and the data), you'd be better off simply scanning the data and not reading the index.

For example, suppose that I have an index on the *color* column of my *automobile* table. Forty percent of the cars are blue, 40 percent are red, and 5 percent each are yellow, orange, green, and purple. It is likely that a query based on color should table scan if the color being searched on is blue or red; but it should use the index for the other colors. Without using the WITH RECOMPILE option, the execution plan created and saved would be based on the color value the first time the procedure was executed. So if I passed *blue* to the procedure the first time it executed, I would get a plan that table scanned. Subsequently, if I pass *yellow,* I might be able to use the previous plan that was created for *blue.* In this case, however, I'd be doing a table scan, when I'd be better off using the index. In such a case, when there is a lot of variance in the distribution of data and execution plans are based on the parameters passed, it makes sense to use the WITH RECOMPILE option.

This example should also make it clear that two execution plans for the same procedure can be different. Suppose that I am not using WITH RECOMPILE, and I execute the procedure for both *blue* and *green* simultaneously from two different connections. Assume for a moment that no plan is cached (each will generate a new plan, but one plan will use the index and the other will not). When a subsequent request for *red* arrives, the plan it would use is a matter of chance. And if two simultaneous calls come in for *red* and each plan is available, the two equivalent requests will execute differently because they'll use different plans. If, as you're processing queries, you see significant deviations in the execution times of apparently identical procedures, think back to this example.

- When the stored procedure is executed using the WITH RECOMPILE option. This case is similar to the preceding one, except that here the procedure isn't created with the option, but rather the option is specified when the procedure is called. The WITH RECOMPILE option can always be added on execution, forcing a new execution plan to be generated. The new plan is then available for subsequent executions (not using WITH RECOMPILE). Executing using the WITH RECOMPILE option can be appropriate if there are significant deviations in parameters being passed or if you want a new plan to be generated because the histogram of distribution was updated (UPDATE STATISTICS) or new indexes that you think might help were added.

Storage of Stored Procedures

With each new stored procedure, a row is created in the *sysobjects* table, as occurs for all database objects. Information about the sequence tree that is used internally by SQL Server is stored in the *sysprocedures* table. The actual binary representation of the sequence tree is not exposed as part of the table—think of it as a hidden column of *sysprocedures*. The text of a stored procedure (including comments) is stored in *syscomments,* which is typically useful. This allows procedures like **sp_helptext** to display the source code of a stored procedure so that you can understand what's going on, and it allows stored procedure editors and debuggers to exist.

For most users and developers, the fact that the full text of a procedure is stored in English text is clearly a feature of SQL Server. But this text storage can also become the factor limiting how big a procedure can be. Prior to version 6.0, if you hit a size limit for your procedure, the execution plan was likely the cause. The execution plan was limited to 64 pages (128 KB, given 2-KB pages). Version 6.0 eliminated that limit, and as long as the procedure cache is big enough to hold one copy of the plan, it can execute. However, the size of a stored procedure might still be constrained due to the amount of text that can be stored in *syscomments* for a given stored procedure.

In the *syscomments* table, a throwback to the days before the *text* datatype existed, the text of procedures is kept in a column named *text*—but the *text* column is defined as *varchar(255)*. Any given procedure can have many rows in *syscomments,* with comment chunks in lengths of up to 255 characters, and those chunks are sequenced by the *colid* field. But *colid* was rather shortsightedly defined as a *tinyint* to ostensibly save a byte. Because the maximum value a *tinyint* can take is 255, up to 255 chunks of text can be included, each of which can be up to 255 bytes in size. Hence, the maximum size of the text used to create a stored procedure is 255 × 255, or 65,025 bytes (roughly 64 KB).

Remember that comments are also stored—so in a pinch, you can strip the comments from your procedures. A better solution, though, is to break up your stored procedure into multiple stored procedures, since procedures can call other procedures. Not only does this get you past the 64-KB text limit, but it makes your code more maintainable since smaller, more discreet modules are preferable to a single huge module.

Encrypting Stored Procedures

With the rollout of version 6.0, we learned somewhat painfully that some users did not appreciate as a feature the ability to store the text of stored procedures. Several independent software vendors (ISVs) had already built integrated solutions or tools that created stored procedures to use with earlier versions of SQL Server. In most cases, these solutions were sophisticated applications, and the ISVs viewed the source code as their proprietary intellectual property. They had correctly noticed that the text of the procedure in *syscomments* didn't seem to do anything. If they set the text field to NULL, the procedure still ran fine—so that's what these ISVs did. In this way, they wouldn't be publishing their procedure source code with their applications. Unfortunately, when it came time to upgrade a database to version 6.0, this approach exposed a significant problem for their applications. The internal data structures for the sequence plans had changed between versions 4.2 and 6.0. ISVs had to re-create procedures, triggers, and views to generate the new structure. Although our Setup program was designed to do this automatically, it accomplished the tasks by simply extracting the text of the procedure from *syscomments* and then dropping and re-creating the procedure using the extracted text. It's no surprise that this automatic approach failed for procedures in which the creator had deleted the text.

The truth is that we were simply not aware of the number of ISV application designers who had deleted the text in this way. When we learned of this problem after we released our beta version, we immediately understood why developers had felt compelled to delete the text. Nonetheless, we could not undo the work that had already been done. Developers with these ISVs had to dig out their original DDL scripts and manually drop and re-create all their procedures. While perhaps possible, it wasn't really practical for us to create a converter program that would operate purely on the internal data structures used to represent procedures and views. Attempting this would have been like developing a utility to run against an executable program and have it backward engineer the precise source code (more than a disassembly) that was used to create the binary. The SQL source code compilation process is designed to be a descriptive process that produces the executable, not an equation that can be solved for either side.

Following the 6.0 beta release, but before the final release of version 6.0, we added the ability to *encrypt* the text stored in *syscomments* for stored procedures, triggers, and views. This allowed programmers to protect their source code, without making it impossible for our upgrade process to re-create stored procedures, triggers, and views in the future. You can now protect your source by simply adding the modifier WITH ENCRYPTION to CREATE. No decrypt function is exposed (which would defeat the purpose of hiding the textlike source code). Internally, SQL Server can read this encrypted text and upgrade the sequence trees when necessary. Because the text is not used at runtime, no performance penalty is associated with executing procedures created using WITH ENCRYPTION.

NOTE You give up some capabilities when you use WITH ENCRYPTION. For example, you can no longer use the **sp_helptext** stored procedure or object editors that display and edit the text of the stored procedure, and you cannot use a source-level debugger for Transact-SQL, like the one available in Microsoft Visual C++ Enterprise Edition. Unless you are concerned about someone seeing your procedures, you shouldn't use the WITH ENCRYPTION option.

If a procedure, trigger, or view is created using WITH ENCRYPTION, the *texttype* column of *syscomments* will have its third bit set to ON. (It will be OR'ed with decimal number 4.) For now, this simply means that the decimal value of *texttype* would be 6—the only other bit to be set would be the second one (decimal 2), indicating that the text in that procedure resulted from a CREATE statement and not a user-supplied comment. If you want to programmatically determine whether a procedure is encrypted, it is safer to check the value of the third bit by AND'ing it with 4 than it is to look for the value of 6. New bits could get added in the future, and the value of 6 might no longer be accurate.

To illustrate their effects on *syscomments,* two procedures—one encrypted and one not—are created in the following example:

```
CREATE PROCEDURE cleartext
AS
SELECT * FROM authors
GO

CREATE PROCEDURE hidetext WITH ENCRYPTION
AS
SELECT * FROM authors
GO

SELECT sysobjects.name, syscomments.* FROM syscomments, sysobjects
WHERE sysobjects.id=syscomments.id AND
(
sysobjects.id=OBJECT_ID('hidetext') OR
sysobjects.id=OBJECT_ID('cleartext')
)
```

Here's the output:

name	id	number	colid	texttype	language	text
cleartext	364528332	1	1	2	0	CREATE PROCEDURE cleartext AS SELECT * FROM authors

```
hidetext    380528389  1       1       6       0       Lýsåvù00éf:3j"ØË/
                                                        @âËAx+"Z%ÙX3ÔÏ2Då
                                                        &UÓ4ÏtRh]ÅÑn² ^
                                                        •2Zò{'õÎÛvv,D"
```

To find created objects that have encrypted text, you can use a simple query:

```
-- Find the names and types of objects that have encrypted text
SELECT name, type FROM syscomments, sysobjects
WHERE sysobjects.id=syscomments.id
AND texttype & 4 > 0
```

Here's the output:

```
name      type
--------  ----
hidetext  P6
```

If you try to run **sp_helptext** against an encrypted procedure, it will return a message stating that the text is encrypted and cannot be displayed:

```
EXEC sp_helptext 'hidetext'
The object's comments have been encrypted.
```

Temporary Stored Procedures

Temporary stored procedures allow a sequence tree to be set up and an execution plan to be cached, but the object's existence, the sequence tree, and the text of the procedure are stored in the temporary database (*tempdb*) system tables—in *sysobjects, sysprocedures,* and *syscomments*. Recall that *tempdb* is re-created every time the server is restarted, so these objects do not exist after SQL Server is shut down. During a given SQL Server session, you can reuse the procedure without permanently storing it. If you are familiar with the PREPARE/EXECUTE model used by several other products, especially with the Embedded SQL programming paradigm, you'll know that temporary procedures use a similar model. The SQL Server ODBC driver, in fact, creates and executes temporary stored procedures when **SQLPrepare** and **SQLExecute** are performed.

Typically, you'll use a temporary stored procedure when you want to regularly execute the same task several times in a session, although you might use different parameter values, and you don't want to permanently store the task. You could conceivably use a permanent stored procedure and drop it when you are finished, but you'd inevitably run into cleanup issues if a stored procedure was still hanging around and the client application terminated without dropping the procedure. Because temporary stored procedures are deleted automatically when SQL server is shut down (and *tempdb* is created anew at startup), cleanup is not an issue. (And if you explicitly drop your temporary objects when you're finished with them, you might be able to keep *tempdb* at a smaller size.)

Just as SQL Server has three types of temporary tables, it also has three types of temporary stored procedures: *private, global,* and those created from direct use of *tempdb.*

Private temporary stored procedures

By adding a single pound sign (#) at the beginning of the stored procedure name (for example, *CREATE PROC #get_author AS…*), you can create the procedure from within any database as a private temporary stored procedure. Only the connection that created the procedure can execute it, and you cannot grant privileges on it to another connection. The procedure exists for the life of the creating connection only; that connection can explicitly use DROP PROCEDURE on it to clean up sooner. Because the scoping of a private temporary table is specific only to the connection that created it, you will not encounter a name collision should you choose a procedure name that's used by another connection. As with local variables, you use your private version and what occurs in other connections is irrelevant.

Global temporary stored procedures

By prefixing two pound signs (##) to the stored procedure name (for example, *CREATE PROC ##get_author AS…*), you can create the procedure from within any database as a global temporary stored procedure. Any connection can subsequently execute that procedure without EXECUTE permission being specifically granted. Unlike private temporary stored procedures, only one copy of a global temporary stored procedure exists for all connections. If another connection created a procedure with the same name, the two names will collide and the CREATE PROCEDURE statement will fail. A global temporary stored procedure exists until the creating connection terminates and all current execution of the procedure completes. Once the creating connection terminates, however, no further execution is allowed. Only those connections that have already started executing are allowed to finish.

Procedures created from direct use of *tempdb*

Realizing that *tempdb* is re-created every time SQL Server is started, you can create a procedure in *tempdb* that fully qualifies objects in other databases. Procedures created in *tempdb* in this way can exist even after the creating connection is terminated, and the creator can specifically grant and revoke execute permissions to specific users. To do this, the creator of the procedure must have CREATE PROCEDURE privileges in *tempdb.* Privileges in *tempdb* can be set up in one of two ways: you can set your privileges in *model* (the template database) so that they will be copied to *tempdb* when it is created at system restart, or you can set up an *autostart* procedure to set the *tempdb* privileges every time SQL Server is started. Here's an example of creating a procedure in *tempdb* and then executing it in the *pubs* database:

```
USE tempdb
GO

CREATE PROC testit AS
SELECT * FROM pubs.dbo.authors
GO

-- Executing the procedure created above from the pubs database
USE pubs
EXEC tempdb..testit
```

While we're on the subject of temporary objects, keep in mind that a private temporary table created within a stored procedure is not visible to the connection after the creating procedure completes. It is possible, however, to create a local temporary table before executing a stored procedure and make the table visible to the stored procedure. The scoping of the temporary table extends to the current statement block and all subordinate levels.

> **NOTE** You can use the @@NESTLEVEL global variable to check for the visibility of temporary tables. A temporary table created at nest level 0 will be visible to all further levels on that connection. A table created within a procedure at nest level 1, for example, will not be visible when execution returns to the calling block at nest level 0. A global temporary table, or a table directly created in *tempdb* without using either # or ##, will be visible no matter what the nesting level.

System Stored Procedures and the Special *sp_* Prefix

SQL Server installs a large number of system stored procedures that are used mostly for administrative and informational purposes. In many cases, these are called behind the scenes by the SQL-DMO objects used by SQL Enterprise Manager and other applications. But the system stored procedures can also be called directly, and only a few years ago, doing so was the primary mechanism by which SQL Server was administered. Old-time SQL Server users (like me) were indoctrinated into using system stored procedures, and I confess that my primary administration tool for SQL Server remains using these system stored procedures directly, even though I recognize that the administration tools of today make things much easier. (I have made some headway into the modern era though. I now use the more graphical ISQLW.EXE instead of the character-based ISQL.EXE!) With the great tools and interfaces that are a core part of SQL Server today, there is not much reason to work with these system stored procedures directly anymore. But it's good to be familiar with them—understanding them can help you understand the operations that occur on the system tables and can take much of the mystery out of what's going on behind the scenes with the graphical tools.

All of the system stored procedure names begin with *sp_*, and most exist in the *master* database. This is more than just a convention. A procedure created in the *master* database that begins with *sp_* is uniquely able to be called from any other database without the necessity of fully referencing the procedure with the database name. This can be useful for procedures you create as well. The *sp_* magic works even for *extended stored procedures,* which are user-written calls to dynamic link libraries (DLLs). By convention, extended stored procedure names begin with *xp_*, but the *sp_* prefix and its special property can be applied to them as well (but only when added to the *master* database). In fact, some extended procedures that are supplied as part of the product, such as those used to create Automation objects (for example, **sp_OACreate**), use the *sp_* prefix so that they can be called from anywhere, although they are actually functions in a DLL, not a Transact-SQL stored procedure.

If you look carefully through the SQL Server system tables, you will find procedures beginning with *sp_* that are not among the documented system stored procedures. Typically, these procedures exist to be called by some other system stored procedure that is exposed; to support some SQL Server utility, such as SQL Enterprise Manager; or to provide statistics to the Windows NT Performance Monitor. These procedures are not documented for direct use because they exist only to support functionality exposed elsewhere—they do not provide that functionality independently. There is nothing secret about these procedures, and their text is exposed clearly in *syscomments*. You are welcome to explore them to see what they do and use them if you want. But unlike the documented stored procedures, maintaining system stored procedures or striving to make them exhibit exactly consistent behavior is not a commitment in future releases. Of course, if your applications were to become dependent on one of these procedures, you could certainly maintain your own version of it to perform exactly as you specify, or you could use one of them as a starting point and customize it to suit your needs (under a different name).

The *SQL Server Transact-SQL Reference* explains the specifics of each system stored procedure, so there is no need to restate those specifics here. I'll just categorize and enumerate most of them to give you a general understanding of the types and number of procedures that exist. The name of the procedure usually reveals its purpose. But first, I'll show you how to autostart stored procedures.

Autostart Stored Procedures

Version 6.0 introduced the handy ability to mark a stored procedure as *autostart*. Autostart stored procedures are useful if you regularly want to perform housekeeping functions or if you have a background daemon procedure that is expected always to be running. Another handy use for an autostart procedure is to have it assign some privileges in *tempdb*. Or the procedure can create a global temporary table and then sleep indefinitely using WAITFOR. This will ensure that such a temporary table will always exist, because the calling process is the first thing executed and it never terminates.

It is simple to make a stored procedure start automatically—you use the system stored procedure **sp_makestartup** *procname* and pass the name of the procedure you want to start. You can remove the *autostart* attribute using **sp_unmakestartup**, or you can use **sp_helpstartup** to enumerate which procedures have been so marked. A procedure that is autostarted runs in the context of the SA (system administrator) account. (The procedure can use SETUSER to impersonate another account.) An autostarted procedure is launched asynchronously, and it can execute in a loop for the entire duration of the SQL Server process. This allows several such procedures to be launched simultaneously at startup. While a startup procedure is active, it consumes one of the configured user connections (from **sp_configure**).

A single startup procedure can nest calls to other stored procedures, consuming only a single user connection. Such execution of the nested procedures is synchronous, as would normally be the case. (That is, execution in the calling procedure does not proceed until the procedure being called completes.) Typically, a stored procedure that is autostarted will not generate a lot of output. Errors, including those raised with RAISERROR, will be written to the SQL Server error log, and any result sets generated will seemingly vanish. If you need the stored procedure to return result sets, you should use a stored procedure that calls the main stored procedure with INSERT/EXEC to insert the results into a table.

If you want to prevent a procedure marked as autostart from executing, you can start the server using trace flag 4022 or as a minimally configured server using the **-f** switch to SQLSERVR.EXE. (Add **-T4022** or **-f** as a parameter to SQL Server using the Setup program's Server Options dialog box.) These safeguards allow you to recover from problems. (Consider the perhaps absurd but illustrative example of someone including a procedure that executes the SHUTDOWN command. If such a procedure were marked for autostart, SQL Server would immediately shut itself down before you could do anything about it!)

The following sections discuss the broad categories for grouping stored procedures: System, Catalog, SQL Executive, Replication, and Extended.

System Stored Procedures

System stored procedures aid in the administration of your system, and they sometimes modify the system tables. You should not configure the system to allow direct modification of the system tables, since a mistake can render your database useless. That's why direct modification of system tables is prohibited by default. If modification is necessary, a system stored procedure is provided that is known to do the job correctly. Below are the SQL Server system stored procedures. Each procedure's name gives you a clue as to its function.

sp_addalias	sp_dropdevice	sp_helpsort
sp_addextendedproc	sp_dropextendedproc	sp_helpsql
sp_addgroup	sp_dropgroup	sp_helpstartup
sp_addlanguage	sp_droplanguage	sp_helptext
sp_addlogin	sp_droplogin	sp_helpuser
sp_addmessage	sp_dropremotelogin	sp_lock
sp_addremotelogin	sp_dropsegment	sp_lock2
sp_addsegment	sp_dropserver	sp_lockinfo
sp_addserver	sp_droptype	sp_logdevice
sp_addumpdevice	sp_dropuser	sp_makestartup
sp_adduser	sp_dropwebtask	sp_makewebtask
sp_altermessage	sp_extendsegment	sp_monitor
sp_bindefault	sp_fallback_activate_svr_db	sp_objcheck
sp_bindrule	sp_fallback_deactivate_svr_db	sp_objectsegment
sp_certify_removable	sp_fallback_enroll_svr_db	sp_password
sp_change_users_login	sp_fallback_help	sp_placeobject
sp_changedbowner	sp_fallback_permanent_svr	sp_recompile
sp_changegroup	sp_fallback_upd_dev_drive	sp_remoteoption
sp_check_removable	sp_fallback_withdraw_svr_db	sp_rename
sp_coalesce_fragments	sp_help	sp_renamedb
sp_configure	sp_helpconstraint	sp_runwebtask
sp_create_removable	sp_helpdb	sp_server_info
sp_dbinstall	sp_helpdevice	sp_serveroption
sp_dboption	sp_helpextendedproc	sp_setlangalias
sp_dbremove	sp_helpgroup	sp_setnetname
sp_db_upgrade	sp_helpindex	sp_spaceused
sp_defaultdb	sp_helplanguage	sp_special_columns
sp_defaultlanguage	sp_helplog	sp_sproc_columns
sp_depends	sp_helplogins	sp_unbindefault
sp_devoption	sp_helpremotelogin	sp_unbindrule
sp_diskdefault	sp_helprotect	sp_unmakestartup
sp_dropalias	sp_helpsegment	sp_who
sp_droparticle	sp_helpserver	sp_who2

Catalog Stored Procedures

Applications and development tools commonly need access to information about table names, column types, datatypes, constraints, privileges, and configuration options. All this information is stored in the system tables (system catalogs). But system tables might require changes between releases to support new features, so your directly accessing the system tables could result in your application breaking from a new SQL Server release. For this reason, SQL Server provides catalog stored procedures, a series of stored procedures that extract the information from the system tables, providing an abstraction layer that insulates your application. If the system tables are changed, the stored procedures that extract and provide the information will also be changed to ensure that they operate consistently from an external perspective from one release to another. Many of these procedures also map nearly identically with an ODBC call. The SQL Server ODBC driver calls these procedures in response to those function calls. While it is fine to directly query the system catalogs for ad hoc use, if you are deploying an application that needs to get information from the system tables, use these catalog stored procedures:

sp_column_privileges	sp_special_columns
sp_columns	sp_sproc_columns
sp_databases	sp_statistics
sp_datatype_info	sp_stored_procedures
sp_fkeys	sp_table_privileges
sp_pkeys	sp_tables
sp_server_info	

SQL Executive Stored Procedures

SQL Executive stored procedures are used by SQL Enterprise Manager to set up alerts and to schedule tasks for execution. If your application needs to carry out tasks like these, the following procedures can be called directly. They must be called from the *msdb* database.

Here are the alert stored procedures:

sp_addalert	sp_helpalert
sp_addnotification	sp_helpnotification
sp_addoperator	sp_helpoperator
sp_dropalert	sp_updatealert
sp_dropnotification	sp_updatenotification
sp_dropoperator	sp_updateoperator

And here are the scheduling stored procedures:

sp_addtask	**sp_helptask**
sp_droptask	**sp_purgehistory**
sp_helphistory	**sp_updatetask**

Replication Stored Procedures

Replication stored procedures are used to set up and manage publication and sub-scription tasks. SQL Enterprise Manager typically provides a front-end to these, but you can also call them directly. SQL Server has many replication stored procedures, and frankly it is hard to manually use replication with these procedures. (It *can* be done though, if you're bound and determined.) Everything SQL Enterprise Manager does (and makes it easy to do) ultimately uses these system stored procedures. Especially for replication, I urge you to use SQL Enterprise Manager or SQL-DMO if you need to customize replication administration into your application. Following are the replication stored procedures, by function. First, here are the server configuration and replication monitoring stored procedures:

sp_addpublisher	**sp_MSkill_job**
sp_addsubscriber	**sp_replcleanup**
sp_changesubscriber	**sp_replcmds**
sp_dboption	**sp_replcounters**
sp_distcounters	**sp_repldone**
sp_dropsubscriber	**sp_replica**
sp_helpdistributor	**sp_replsync**
sp_helpserver	**sp_repltrans**
sp_helpsubscriberinfo	

Here are the publication stored procedures:

sp_articlecolumn	**sp_helppublication**
sp_changearticle	**sp_helppublicationsync**
sp_changepublication	**sp_helpreplicationdb**
sp_droparticle	**sp_replflush**
sp_droppublication	**sp_replstatus**
sp_enumfullsubscribers	

And these are the subscription stored procedures:

sp_addsubscription	**sp_helpreplicationdb**
sp_changesubscription	**sp_helpsubscription**
sp_changesubstatus	**sp_subscribe**
sp_dropsubscription	**sp_unsubscribe**

Extended Stored Procedures

Extended stored procedures allow you to create your own external routines in a language such as C and have SQL Server automatically load and execute those routines just like a regular stored procedure. As you can with stored procedures, you can pass parameters to extended stored procedures and they can return results and/or return status. This allows you to extend the capabilities of SQL Server in powerful ways. Many features in the SQL Server product that have been introduced in the last couple of years have been implemented using extended stored procedures. These features include additions to SQL Enterprise Manager, the ability to send or receive e-mail messages, login integration with Windows NT domain security, and the ability to create a Web page based on a query.

Extended stored procedures are DLLs that SQL Server can dynamically load and execute. Extended stored procedures are not separate processes spawned by SQL Server—they run directly in the address space of SQL Server. The DLLs are created using the Open Data Services API, which SQL Server also uses.

Writing an extended stored procedure sounds harder than it really is, which is probably why these procedures are somewhat underused. But writing one can be as simple as writing a wrapper around a C function. For example, consider the formatting capabilities in SQL Server's PRINT statement, which are limited and do not allow parameter substitution. The C language provides the **sprintf** function, which is powerful for formatting a string buffer and includes parameter substitution. It is easy to wrap the C **sprintf** function and create an extended stored procedure that calls it, resulting in the procedure **xp_sprintf**. To show you how easy this is, below is the entire source code for the procedure **xp_sprintf**. Note that most of this code is setup code, and at the heart is the call to the C run-time function **sprintf()**:

```
// XP_SPRINTF
//
// Format and store a series of characters and values into an
// output string using sprintf
//
// Parameters:
//     srvproc - the handle to the client connection
//
// Returns:
//     XP_NOERROR or XP_ERROR
//
// Side Effects:
//
//
```

```
SRVRETCODE xp_sprintf( SRV_PROC * srvproc )
{
    int numparams;
    int paramtype;
    int i;
    char string [MAXSTRLEN];
    char format[MAXSTRLEN];
    char values[MAXARGUMENTS][MAXSTRLEN];
    char szBuffer[MAXSTRLEN];

    // Get number of parameters
    //
    numparams=srv_rpcparams(srvproc);

    // Check number of parameters
    //
    if (numparams < 3)
    {
        // Send error message and return


        //
        LoadString(hModule, IDS_ERROR_PARAM, szBuffer,
            sizeof(szBuffer));
        goto ErrorExit;
    }

    paramtype=srv_paramtype(srvproc, 1);
    if (paramtype != SRVVARCHAR)
    {
        // Send error message and return
        //
        LoadString(hModule, IDS_ERROR_PARAM_TYPE, szBuffer,
            sizeof(szBuffer));
        goto ErrorExit;
    }

    if (!srv_paramstatus(srvproc, 1))
    {
        // Send error message and return
        //
        LoadString(hModule, IDS_ERROR_PARAM_STATUS, szBuffer,
            sizeof(szBuffer));
        goto ErrorExit;
    }
```

```
for (i = 2; i <= numparams; i++)
{
    paramtype=srv_paramtype(srvproc, i);

    if (paramtype != SRVVARCHAR)
    {
        // Send error message and return
        //
        LoadString(hModule, IDS_ERROR_PARAM_TYPE, szBuffer,
            sizeof(szBuffer));
        goto ErrorExit;
    }
}

for (i=0; i < MAXARGUMENTS; i++)
{
    memset(values[i], 0, MAXSTRLEN);


    srv_bmove(srv_paramdata(srvproc, i + 3),
            values[i],
            srv_paramlen(srvproc, i + 3));
}

memset(string, 0, MAXSTRLEN);
srv_bmove(srv_paramdata(srvproc, 2), format,
    srv_paramlen(srvproc, 2));
format[srv_paramlen(srvproc, 2)]='\0';

// This is the heart of the function -- it simply wraps sprintf
// and passes back the string
sprintf(string, format,
    values[0],  values[1],  values[2],  values[3],  values[4],
    values[5],  values[6],  values[7],  values[8],  values[9],
    values[10], values[11], values[12], values[13], values[14],
    values[15], values[16], values[17], values[18], values[19],
    values[20], values[21], values[22], values[23], values[24],
    values[25], values[26], values[27], values[28], values[29],
    values[30], values[31], values[32], values[33], values[34],
    values[35], values[36], values[37], values[38], values[39],
    values[40], values[41], values[42], values[43], values[44],
    values[45], values[46], values[47], values[48], values[49]);

srv_paramset(srvproc, 1, string, strlen(string));

return XP_NOERROR;
```

```
ErrorExit:
    srv_sendmsg(srvproc,
                SRV_MSG_ERROR,
                SPRINTF_ERROR,
                SRV_INFO,
                (DBTINYINT) 0,
                NULL,
                0,
                0,
                szBuffer,
                SRV_NULLTERM);

    return XP_ERROR;
}
```

Because extended stored procedures run in the same address space as SQL Server, they can be efficient; however, although unlikely, a badly behaved extended stored procedure could theoretically crash SQL Server. A server crash would more likely result from someone's maliciousness rather than carelessness. But this is a definite area for concern, and you should understand the issues that I'll discuss in the rest of this section.

An extended stored procedure runs on the thread that called it. Each calling thread executes using the Windows NT structured exception handling constructs (most notably *try-except*). When a thread is badly written and does a bad thing, such as trying to reference memory outside its address space, it is terminated. But only that single connection is terminated, and SQL Server remains unaffected. Any resources held by the thread, such as locks, are automatically released.

In actual usage, I've seen that extended stored procedures do not introduce significant stability issues into the environment. Nonetheless, it certainly is theoretically possible for an extended stored procedure to twiddle some data structure within SQL Server (which it would have access to since the procedure is part of the SQL Server's address space) that could disrupt SQL Server's operation or conceivably even corrupt data. This could happen as a chance occurrence as a result of a bug in the extended stored procedure if you're unlucky, but it is more likely that the procedure would cause an access violation and have its thread terminated with no ill effects. A malicious procedure could conceivably cause data corruption, but such data structures are not exposed publicly so it would not be easy to write a malicious procedure. It is possible, however, and given the propensity of some social misfits to create viruses, I wouldn't rule out this problem (although I don't know of a single instance of this happening). The ultimate responsibility for protecting your data has to rest with your SA, who has control over which, if any, extended stored procedures can be added to the system.

Only the SA can register an extended stored procedure with the system (using **sp_addextendedproc**), and only the SA can grant others permission to execute the procedure. Extended stored procedures can be added only to the *master* database (eliminating their ability to be transferred simply to other systems via dump/load of databases, for example). The SA should allow use of only the procedures that have been thoroughly tested and proven to be safe and nondestructive. Ideally, the SA could also have access to the source code and build environment of the extended stored procedure to verify that it bears no malicious intent. (Some people have told me that they don't even want their SA to be able to do this—because the SA might not be trustworthy. If that's the case, you have bigger problems. If you can't trust your SA, you'd better get a new one.)

Even without extended stored procedures, the SA can disrupt a SQL Server environment in many ways. (Munging the system tables would be a good start.) Of course, you can decide that extended stored procedures will never be added to your system. That's certainly a safe approach, but you give up powerful capability by taking this route. (It's kind of like deciding never to ride in a car to avoid having an accident.) Even if you prohibit foreign extended stored procedures from your system, you should not go overboard and make this a sweeping rule that would prevent use of even the procedures provided by Microsoft to implement new features. Could one of these procedures have a bug that could disrupt SQL Server? Sure, but it's no more likely to occur than if the code for them had simply been statically linked into the SQLSERVR.EXE file rather than implemented as a DLL and loaded on demand. (Of course, the Microsoft procedures are thoroughly tested before their release. The chance of a catastrophic bug is pretty low.) The fact that these are *extended* stored procedures in no way increases the risk of bugs. It's an engineering decision, and a smart one, that allows additional features to be added to the product in a way that doesn't require extra change to the core product nor additional resource use by environments that don't call these features.

By convention, most of the extended stored procedures provided as part of the product begin with **xp_**. Unlike the **sp_** prefix, no special properties are associated with **xp_**. In fact, several extended stored procedures begin with *sp_* (for example, *EXEC* **sp_name**), which allows them to be called from any database without being fully qualified (for example, *EXEC master.dbo.***xp_name**). To ascertain whether a procedure is a regular stored procedure or an extended stored procedure, you shouldn't rely on the name's prefix. Instead, check the *type* column of *sysobjects,* which will show *P* for stored procedures or *X* for extended stored procedures.

As was the case with stored procedures, some extended stored procedures that are installed are not documented for direct use. These procedures exist to support functionality elsewhere, especially for SQL Enterprise Manager, SQL-DMO, and replication, rather than to provide features directly themselves.

Following are the extended stored procedures that are provided and documented for direct use. First, here are the general extended stored procedures:

xp_cmdshell

xp_sprintf

xp_sscanf

Here are the administration and monitoring extended stored procedures:

xp_logevent

xp_msver

xp_snmp_getstate

xp_snmp_raisetrap

xp_sqlinventory

xp_sqltrace

These are the integrated security related extended stored procedures:

xp_enumgroups

xp_grantlogin

xp_loginconfig

xp_logininfo

xp_revokelogin

And finally, the SQL mail-related extended stored procedures:

xp_deletemail

xp_findnextmsg

xp_readmail

xp_sendmail

xp_startmail

xp_stopmail

Triggers

A *trigger* is a special type of stored procedure that is fired on an event-driven basis rather than by a direct call. Here are some common uses for triggers:

- To maintain data integrity rules that extend beyond simple referential integrity

- To keep running totals updated

- To keep a computed column updated

- To implement a referential action, such as cascading deletes

- To maintain an audit record of changes

- To invoke an external action, such as begin a reorder process if inventory falls below a certain level or send e-mail or a pager notification to someone who needs to perform an action because of data changes

A trigger can be set up to fire when data is changed in some way—that is, via an INSERT, an UPDATE, or a DELETE statement. Only one trigger can be defined for each event, although a trigger can invoke many stored procedures and different actions can be specified by evaluating the values of a given column of data. While it is true that a table is "limited" to three triggers, because of the ability to call an almost unlimited number of stored procedures, this should not really be a limitation in any way. (The nesting depth limit is still 16, however.) In fact, some might consider having the three triggers a feature because it forces you to properly think through and specify the ordering of the actions. Rather than simply defining, say, five stored procedures that should fire given a data change, this "limitation" also ensures that the order of trigger firing is exactly specified, which, of course, can greatly affect the results of the trigger.

A single trigger can be created to execute for any or all of the INSERT, UPDATE, and DELETE actions, which modify data. Currently, SQL Server offers no trigger on a SELECT statement, since SELECT does not modify data. In addition, triggers can exist only on base tables, not on views. (Of course, data modified on a view does cause a trigger on the underlying base table to fire.)

A trigger is executed once for each UPDATE, INSERT, or DELETE statement, regardless of the number of rows it affects. Although it is sometimes thought that a trigger is executed once per row or once per transaction, neither of these assumptions is correct, strictly speaking. However, if a statement affects only one row or is a transaction unto itself, the trigger will exhibit the *characteristics* of per-row or per-transaction execution. For example, if a WHILE loop were set up to perform an UPDATE statement repeatedly, an update trigger would execute each time the UPDATE statement was executed in the loop.

A trigger fires after the data modification statement has performed its work but before that work is committed to the database. Both the statement and any modifications made in the trigger are implicitly a transaction (whether or not an explicit BEGIN TRANSACTION was declared). Therefore, the trigger can roll back the work. A trigger has access to the before image and after image of the data via the special pseudotables *inserted* and *deleted*. These two tables have the same set of columns as the underlying table being changed. You can check the before and after values of specific columns and take action depending on what you encounter. These tables are not physical structures—SQL Server constructs them from the transaction log. This is why an unlogged operation such as a bulk copy or SELECT INTO does not cause triggers to fire. For regular logged operations, a trigger will always fire if it exists. A trigger cannot be circumvented (short of dropping it).

The *inserted* and *deleted* pseudotables cannot be modified directly because they don't actually exist. As I mentioned earlier, the data from these tables can be queried only. The data they appear to contain is based entirely on modifications made to data in an actual, underlying base table. The *inserted* and *deleted* pseudotables will contain as many rows as the INSERT, UPDATE, or DELETE statement affected. Sometimes it is necessary to work on a row-by-row basis within the pseudotables, although, as usual, a set-based operation is generally preferable to row-by-row operations. You can perform row-by-row operations by executing the underlying INSERT, UPDATE, or DELETE in a loop so that any single execution affects only one row, or you can perform the operations by opening a cursor on one of the *inserted* or *deleted* tables within the trigger. The need to reconstruct the *inserted* and *deleted* pseudotables from the log is the primary reason why an update on a table having an update trigger always needs to generate delete and insert log records—and why update-in-place is not possible when an update trigger exists.

Rolling Back a Trigger

Executing a ROLLBACK from within a trigger is different from executing a ROLLBACK from within a nested stored procedure. In a nested stored procedure, a ROLLBACK will cause the outermost transaction to abort, but the flow of control continues. However, if a trigger results in a ROLLBACK (whether because of a fatal error or from an explicit ROLLBACK command), the entire batch is aborted.

> **NOTE**   In the final release of version 6.5, a ROLLBACK in a trigger did not abort the batch and flow of control continued. This was due to a bug, not an intentional change. You could argue that the "buggy" behavior is more desirable than the expected behavior, but the expected behavior was added back in Service Pack 1 to provide backward compatibility. In Service Pack 1 and all subsequent service packs, a rollback in the transaction aborts the batch as it always did in releases earlier than version 6.5.

Suppose that the following pseudocode batch is issued from ISQL.EXE:

```
begin tran
delete....
update....
insert....  -- This starts some chain of events that fires a trigger
            -- that rolls back the current transaction
```

```
update.... -- Execution never gets to here - entire batch is
            -- aborted because of the rollback in the trigger
if....commit  -- Neither this statement nor any of the following
              -- will be executed
else....rollback
begin tran....
insert....
if....commit
else....rollback

GO              -- isql batch terminator only

select ...   -- Next statement that will be executed is here
```

As you can see, once the trigger in the first INSERT statement aborts the batch, SQL Server not only rolls back the first transaction but skips the second transaction completely and continues execution following the GO.

Misconceptions about triggers include the belief that the trigger cannot do a SELECT statement that returns rows and that it cannot execute a PRINT statement. Although you can use SELECT and PRINT in a trigger, doing these operations is usually dangerous practice unless you control all the applications that will work with the table that includes the trigger. Otherwise, applications not written to expect a result set or a print message following a change in data might fail because that unexpected behavior occurs anyway.

Be aware that if a trigger modifies data on the same table on which the trigger exists, that trigger does not fire again. (This could easily lead to an infinite loop.) However, if separate triggers exist for INSERT, UPDATE, and DELETE statements, one trigger on a table could cause a different trigger on the same table to fire (but only if **sp_configuration 'nested triggers'** is set to 1, as I'll discuss in a moment).

A trigger can also modify data on some other table. If that other table has a trigger, whether or not that trigger also fires depends on the current **sp_configuration** value for the **nested triggers** option. If that option is set to 1 (TRUE), which is the default setting, triggers will cascade to a maximum chain of 16. If an operation would cause more than 16 triggers to fire, the batch will be aborted and any transaction will be rolled back. This prevents an infinite cycle from being encountered. If your operation is hitting the limit of 16 firing triggers, you should probably look at your design—you've reached a point at which there are no longer any simple operations, so you're probably not going to be ecstatic with the performance of your system. If your operation truly is so complex that you need to perform further operations on 16 or more tables to modify any data, you could call stored procedures to perform the actions directly rather than enabling and using cascading triggers. Although valuable, overused cascading triggers can make your system a nightmare to maintain.

Debugging Stored Procedures and Triggers

By now, it should be obvious that stored procedures and triggers can represent a significant portion of your application's code. Even so, for a long time, no decent debugger support existed for stored procedures. (The typical debugging tool was the liberal use of PRINT statements.) Some ISVs jumped in and helped by adding some "pseudo-debugging" products—but these products didn't have access to the actual SQL Server execution environment. They typically added debugging support by doing tricks behind the scenes, such as adding additional PRINT statements or adding SELECT statements to get the current values of variables. Although some of these products were helpful, they had significant limitations: typically, they couldn't step into nested stored procedures or into triggers. A Transact-SQL debugger was always prominent on the wish list of SQL Server customers. I know firsthand how frustrating it was not to have a proper debugger, and I've spent many late nights putting PRINT statements into stored procedures.

Still, it didn't make sense for us to write a new SQL Server–specific debugger because there were already too many debuggers on the market. If you're like most programmers, you want to do your work in one development environment. For example, if you are a C programmer, you probably want to use the same debugger on your SQL code that you use on your C code. Or if you program in Microsoft Visual Basic, you probably want to use the Visual Basic development environment for debugging. Fortunately, this environment-specific debugging capability now exists and its availability is rapidly expanding. If you are a developer in Microsoft Visual C++, Microsoft Visual J++, or Visual Basic, you can now debug Transact-SQL using the same debugger you use in those environments.

To accomplish this, we defined a DLL and a set of callbacks that SQL Server 6.5 would load and call at the beginning of each SQL statement. In essence, we defined a set of debug events that would allow us to control the execution on a statement-by-statement basis within SQL Server. This has come to be known as the SQL Server Debug Interface, or SDI. The interface that shipped with the version 6.5 release was a work in progress. SDI's first customer was Visual C++ version 4.2. SQL Server 6.5 shipped several months before Visual C++ 4.2, and, of course, we didn't get the interface quite right. Specs are never perfect, and they nearly always get tweaked—at a minimum—during implementation. This was certainly true for SDI, so to use it with Visual C++ version 4.2 and later you need SQL Server version 6.5 with Service Pack 1 or later. We debugged the debugging interface using the Visual C++ team as guinea pigs, and now other development tools are also adding support for SDI. By the time you read this, I expect SDI to be available with Visual C++, Visual Basic, Visual J++, and other development tools from Microsoft. (The exact packaging is always subject to change, but in general, the debugger support for Transact-SQL is available only in each product's Enterprise Edition.)

Although the interface is quite likely to change in future releases, it is also made available via a technical note to ISVs that want to add SQL Server debugger support. SDI is a specialized interface that is of interest only to those writing debuggers, so it is not considered a general feature of SQL Server.

With the existence of SDI, and using the Microsoft Developer Studio debugging environment of Visual C++ Enterprise Edition, you now have a real debugging environment for Transact-SQL. For example, as a C/C++ developer using Developer Studio (Visual C++ Enterprise Edition), you can:

- Do line-by-line debugging of all your Transact-SQL code.

- Step directly from your C code executing on your client machine into the Transact-SQL code executing remotely at the SQL Server machine.

- Remotely debug your procedures, with the actual execution of the procedures happening at the SQL Server machine and your debugging environment happening locally. (Or if you prefer, you can do it all from one machine.)

- Set breakpoints anywhere in your SQL code.

- Watch the contents of SQL local and global variables. You can even watch global variables that are not used in your SQL code: for example, you can watch current status codes using @@ERROR or the number of rows selected using @@ROWCOUNT.

- Modify the values of most variables in a watch window, testing conditional logic in your code more easily. (Note that variables with datatypes for which there is no direct mapping in C cannot be edited in a watch window.)

- Examine the values of parameters passed to stored procedures.

- Step into or over nested procedures. And if a statement causes a trigger to fire, you can even step into the trigger.

- Use Microsoft Developer Studio to edit your procedures and save them to the server. This makes it easy to fix bugs on the fly. SQL keywords and comments in your code are color coded, as they would be in C, to make them easier to spot.

- Optionally send results of your SQL statements to the result window directly in Developer Studio.

The SDI is implemented via the pseudo–extended stored procedure **sp_sdi-debug**. (The *sp_* convention was used so that the procedure could be called from any database without being fully qualified.) By *pseudo,* I mean that, like a normal extended stored procedure, you will see an entry in the *sysobjects* table of type *X* for **sp_sdidebug**. But unlike a normal extended stored procedure, the code for **sp_sdidebug** is internal to the SQL Server and does not reside in a separate DLL. This is true for a few other procedures as well, such as the remote cursor calls made by ODBC and DB-Library cursor functions. This was done so that we could add a new capability to the server without having to change the tabular data stream (TDS) protocol that describes result sets back to the client application. It also eliminates the need for new keywords (potentially breaking a few applications) when the commands are of the sort that would not be executed directly by an application anyway.

You should never call **sp_sdidebug** directly. The procedure exists to load a DLL that the provider of the debugger would write and to toggle debugging on and off for the specific SQL Server connection being debugged. The debug DLL for Visual C++ is SQLSDI.DLL. When debugging is enabled, SQLSDI.DLL is given access to internal state information for the SQL Server connection being debugged. All of the APIs defined in the interface are synchronous calls, and they are called in the context of the thread associated with the connection, which allows for callbacks to SQL Server to occur in the context of the client's thread. The internal Process Status Structure (PSS) holds status information for the connection being debugged, and the DLL is then able to read this structure to determine local variable, parameter, global variable, and symbol information.

The debugging support in Visual C++ Enterprise Edition seems pretty normal if you are already familiar with the environment. Typically, the biggest problem people have with debugging Transact-SQL is getting it configured in the first place. Here are some tips that might help to you in debugging Transact-SQL from Developer Studio:

- You must use the Enterprise Edition of Visual C++ 4.2 or later, not the Professional or Standard edition. You must have run Setup from Visual C++ to install the SQL Server debugging components. Setup also installs SQL Server version 6.5 Service Pack 1 (SP1), and this version or a later one is also required for debugging support.

- You must use the SP1 or later components of DB-Library and/or the SQL Server ODBC driver to be able to step from your C++ or Java source code to stored procedure code and back. For DB-Library, you need version 6.50.212 or later; for the ODBC driver, you need version 2.50.0212 or later.

- I recommend that you use Windows NT 4.0. If you use Windows NT 3.51, you must apply Windows NT 3.51 Service Pack 4. You can debug from Windows 95 as well, but you must use remote debugging because SQL Server does not currently run on Windows 95.

- Run SQL Server under a user account, not as Local System. (You can change this in the Services applet of the Windows NT Control Panel.) If SQL Server is running under the local account, breakpoints are ignored. When debugging on a machine also running SQL Server, you should run SQL Server under the same user context used for running the debugger. (Make sure that you can run SQL Server from the command line rather than as a service—for example, *C:\MSSQL\BINN\SQLSERVER.EXE -c.*)

- Extended error information regarding debugging can be written to the Windows NT event log. The events are written to the application log under MSDEVSDI. For example, *Event ID 11,* which relates directly to the previous tip (running SQL Server under a user account), will be written there:

```
Event ID #11: SQL Server when started as service must not log
on as System Account. Reset to logon as user account using
Control Panel.
```

- SQL Server Debugging must be enabled in Developer Studio. To enable this option in Developer Studio 97, from the Tools menu, select Options. In the Options dialog box, click on the Data View tab, and then click the SQL Server Debugging check box.

- Text, numeric/decimal, and float datatypes cannot be edited in a watch window.

- Do not debug on a production server. Due to the added overhead and break-in nature of the debugging product, you could adversely affect other users.

- String and text values larger than 255 bytes are shown as NULL in the watch window.

- Right-click the mouse, and then click the Refresh option to obtain object changes in DDL from other clients.

- If you delete all characters from a string in the watch window, the value will show NULL. If the variable does not allow NULL, the next step operation will reset the value to its previous value.

- Only the first 64 bytes of a text column are displayed in the output window, even if more data is contained in the actual column.

For simple debugging, you might find yourself still using PRINT; for tougher problems, you might come to regard the new debugging capability as a lifesaver. I demonstrated this capability at the SQL Server Professional Developer Conference in September 1996, and this 5-minute sidebar of my 2-hour presentation seemed to generate more interest than anything else I covered!

Execute("*any string*")

The ability to formulate and then execute a string dynamically in SQL Server is a subtle but powerful capability. Using this capability, you can avoid additional round-trips to the client application by formulating a new statement to be executed directly on the server. You can pass a string directly, or you can pass a local variable of type *char* or *varchar*. This capability is especially useful if you need to pass an object name to a procedure or if you want to build an SQL statement from the result of another SQL statement. For example, suppose that I had partitioned my database to have multiple tables similar to the *authors* table. I could write a procedure like the one shown below to pass the name of the table I want to insert into. The procedure would then formulate the INSERT statement by concatenating strings, and then it would execute the string it formulated:

```
CREATE PROC add_author
@au_id char(11),
@au_lname varchar(20),
@au_fname varchar(20),
@tabname varchar(30) AS

BEGIN
DECLARE @insert_stmt varchar(255)
SELECT @insert_stmt="INSERT " + @tabname + " (au_id,
    au_lname, au_fname, contract) VALUES ('" + @au_id +
    "','" + @au_lname + "','" + @au_fname + "', 1)"
EXECUTE (@insert_stmt)
END

EXEC add_author '999-99-1234', 'Soukup', 'Ron', 'authors'
```

Working with Text and Image Data

SQL Server provides binary large object (BLOB) support via the *text* and *image* datatypes. If you work with these datatypes, you might want to use the additional statements provided by SQL Server along with the standard SELECT, INSERT, UPDATE, and DELETE statements. Because a single text column can be as large as 2 GB, you frequently need to work with text data in chunks, and these additional statements (which I'll discuss in a moment) can help. (I might have discussed this topic earlier, when I discussed Transact-SQL programming. However, because you need some knowledge of isolation levels, transactions, and consistency issues to understand this topic, I decided to wait until after I had covered those issues.)

For simplicity's sake, I'll frame this discussion mostly in terms of the *text* datatype. But everything here is also relevant to the *image* datatype. These two datatypes are essentially the same internally. Recall that *text* and *image* datatypes are unique in that they are not stored on the same data page as the rest of the row. Instead, a pointer to a separate chain of pages for the text/image data is stored in the row. A separate chain of pages exists for each *text* (or *image*) column, and these pages are not shared when several such columns are present. This means that an entire 2-KB page must be used to store the first single byte of data plus the 16-byte text pointer that is written on the data page. If another row with 1 byte of text were added, another entire 2-KB page would be needed to store the data. An initially NULL text column (occurring either by omission of the column in the INSERT statement or by specifying NULL in the VALUES clause) does not require an entire page for storage, so until data is written to the *text* column, no storage for it is consumed. Although you can think of *text* and *image* as variable-length datatypes, their storage size is a step function. The effective storage size can be 0 bytes if the value is implicitly NULL, but then storage increases in 2-KB increments as each new page is required. (Plus, when the column is not NULL, an additional 16 bytes is required for the text pointer. About 1800 bytes of data can actually be stored per page.)

Clearly, the space required by *text* and *image* for small amounts of data is inefficient. But there are also functional drawbacks. Although you can indeed use standard INSERT, UPDATE, DELETE, and SELECT statements with a *text* or *image* column, some significant restrictions apply. In a WHERE clause, you can search on the *text* column only with the LIKE operator or with a function such as PATINDEX( ). *Text* and *image* variables cannot be manipulated. You can declare a parameter in a stored procedure to be of type *text* or *image,* but you can't do much besides pass a value to the procedure initially. For example, you cannot subsequently assign different values to the parameter. Because of the space usage and functional drawbacks, you'll want to use *text* or *image* only when another datatype isn't a reasonable option. If a *varchar(255)* column can work for you, you can use it and avoid *text* altogether. But if you absolutely need a memo field, for example, and 255 characters are not enough, you'll need to use *text* (or denormalize and use multiple *varchar* columns).

If a *text* column makes the most sense for you despite its drawbacks, you need to understand how to work effectively with text. When you can, it is easiest to work with *text/image* datatypes using standard SELECT, INSERT, UPDATE, and DELETE statements. But if your text data gets large, you're going to run into issues, such as how big a string your application can pass, that might make it necessary for you to deal with chunks of data at a time instead of the entire column.

The special statements for working with text data are WRITETEXT, READTEXT, and UPDATETEXT. Both READTEXT and UPDATETEXT let you work with chunks of a *text* column at a time. The WRITETEXT statement does not let you deal with chunks but rather with the entire column only. WRITETEXT and UPDATETEXT will not log the text operations by default, although they can be instructed to log them. (The database must have the **select into/bulkcopy** option enabled for nonlogged operations.) An INSERT, UPDATE, or DELETE statement will always be logged, but these special text statements can be run without logging.

I don't encourage nonlogged operations for general use because they can compromise your database backup strategy. The situation is similar to nonlogged bulk copy. Nonlogged operations cannot be recovered at startup. A terminated nonlogged operation will leave the database in the state it was in before the operation began because logging (and hence rollback) of extent allocations still occurs. But the biggest downside to this is that in the face of a failure after a nonlogged operation, your database is only as good as your last full backup and transaction dumps up to the issuance of the nonlogged operation. You can't do further transaction dumps after a nonlogged operation is performed. So think carefully about the appropriateness of nonlogged text and image operations. Also, if you use SQL Server replication to replicate *text* or *image* columns, the operations *must* be logged because the replication process looks for changes based on the transaction log.

The WRITETEXT, READTEXT, and UPDATETEXT statements all work with a *text pointer*. A text pointer is a unique *varbinary(16)* value for each *text* or *image* column of each row.

WRITETEXT

WRITETEXT completely overwrites an existing *text* or *image* column. You provide the column name (qualified by the table name), the text pointer for the specific column of a specific row, and the actual data to be written. The WITH LOG clause is optional, although I will always use it in the examples presented here. It might seem like a catch-22 when using WRITETEXT immediately, because you need to pass it a text pointer—but if the column is initially NULL, there *is* no text pointer. So how do you get one? You SELECT it with the TEXTPTR() function. But if the *text* column has not been initialized, the TEXTPTR() function returns NULL. To initialize a text pointer for a column of a row with *text* or *image* data, you can do some variation of the following:

- Explicitly insert a non-null value in the *text* column when you use an INSERT statement. Recognize that WRITETEXT will completely overwrite the column anyway, so the value can always be something like *A* or a blank space.

- Define a default on the column with a non-null value like *A*. Then when you do the insert, you can specify DEFAULT or omit the column, which will result in the default value being inserted and the text pointer being initialized.

- Explicitly update the row after inserting it, and then set the column to NULL (or to anything else).

No matter how you initialize the text pointer, as soon as you do it, at least one data page will be consumed for the column of that row, even if you initialize the value to NULL or to a single character.

You then select the text pointer into a variable declared as *varbinary(16)* and pass that to WRITETEXT. You can't use SELECT statements or expressions in the WRITETEXT statement. This means that the statement is limited to being executed one row at a time (although it can be done from within a cursor). The SELECT statement that gets the text pointer should be known to return only one row, preferably by using an exact match on the primary key value in the WHERE clause, because that will ensure that at most one row can meet the criteria. You can, of course, use @@ROWCOUNT to check this if you are not absolutely sure that the SELECT statement can return only one row. Before using the WRITETEXT statement, you should also ensure that you have a valid text pointer. If you find a row with the criteria you specified and the text pointer for that row was initialized, it will be valid. You can check it as a separate statement using the TEXTVALID() function. Or you can check that you do not have a NULL value in your variable that was assigned the text pointer, as I'll show in the following example. Make sure that you don't have an old text pointer value from a previous use, which would make the IS NOT NULL check be TRUE. In this example, I do one variable assignment and the variable starts out NULL, so I am sure that a non-null value means I have selected a valid text pointer:

```
-- WRITETEXT with an unprotected text pointer
DECLARE @mytextptr varbinary(16)
SELECT @mytextptr=TEXTPTR(pr_info)
    FROM pub_info WHERE pub_id='9999'
IF @mytextptr IS NOT NULL
    WRITETEXT pub_info.pr_info @mytextptr WITH LOG 'Hello Again'
```

In this example, the text pointer is not protected from changes made by others. Therefore, it is possible that the text pointer will no longer be valid by the time the WRITETEXT operation is performed. Suppose that you get a text pointer for the row with *pub_id='9999'*. But before you use it with WRITETEXT, another user deletes and reinserts the row for publisher 9999. In that case, the text pointer you are holding will no longer be valid. In the example above, the window for this happening is small, since I do the WRITETEXT immediately after getting the text pointer. *But there is still a window.* In your application, the window may be wider. If the text pointer is not valid when you do the WRITETEXT operation, you will get an error message like this:

```
Msg 7123, Level 16, State 1
Invalid text pointer value 000000000253f380.
```

You can easily see this for yourself if you add a delay (for example, *WAITFOR DELAY "00:00:15"*) after getting the text pointer and then delete the row from another connection. You'll get error 7123 when the WRITETEXT operation executes. If you think the chances of getting this error are slim, you can choose to simply deal with the error when and if it occurs. Frankly, because this seems to be what most applications that use text do, *text* columns are used in mostly low-concurrency environments. But even so, I don't think it's good practice. (More likely, this is the general usage because we haven't sufficiently explained the concurrency issue.)

I recommend that you instead use transaction protection to ensure that the text pointer will not change from the time you read it until you use it, and to serialize access for updates so that you do not encounter frequent deadlocks. Many applications use TEXTVALID() to check right before operating—that's the right idea, but it's hardly foolproof. There is still a window between the TEXTVALID() operation and the use of the text pointer, during which the text pointer may be invalidated. The only way to close the window is to make both operations part of an atomic operation. This means using a transaction and having SQL Server protect the transaction with a lock. (For more about locking, see Chapter 13. You might want to read that chapter and then return to this section.)

By default, SQL Server will operate with Read Committed isolation and release a share (READ) lock after the page has been read. So simply putting the pointer in a transaction with the READ COMMITTED isolation level, which is SQL Server's default, is not enough. You need to ensure that the lock is held until the text pointer is used. You could change the isolation level to Repeatable Read, which is not a bad solution, but this changes the isolation behavior for all operations on that connection and so it might have a more widespread effect than you intend. (Although you could, of course, then change it right back.) But even this is not ideal. This approach doesn't guarantee that you will subsequently be able to get the exclusive lock required to do the WRITETEXT operation; it ensures only that when you get to the WRITETEXT operation, the text pointer will still be valid. You won't be sure that you're not in the lock queue behind another connection waiting to update the same row and column. In that case, your transaction and the competing one would both hold a share lock on the same page and would both need to acquire an exclusive lock. Since both transactions are holding a share lock, neither can get the exclusive lock, and a *deadlock* results in one of the connections having its transaction automatically aborted. (In Chapter 13, you'll see that this is an example of a *conversion deadlock*.) If multiple processes are intending to modify the text and all transactions first request an update lock in a transaction when selecting the text pointer, conversion deadlocks will be avoided because only one process will get the update lock and the others will queue for it. But those users' transactions that need only to read the page will not be affected, since an update lock and a share lock are compatible.

Using the update lock on the text pointer is good for serializing access to the actual text pages, even though the lock on the text page is distinct from the lock or the text pointer. In this case, you essentially use the update lock on a text pointer as you'd use an intent lock for the text page. This is conceptually similar to the intent locks that SQL Server uses on a table when a page-locking operation for that table will take place. That operation recognizes that pages and tables have an implicit hierarchy. You can think of text pointers and text pages as having a similar hierarchy and use the update lock on the text pointer to protect access to the associated text pages. Following is the improved version that protects the text pointer from getting invalidated and also reserves my transaction's spot in the queue so that it will get the exclusive lock that's necessary to change the column. This approach will avoid conversion deadlocks on the text pages:

```
-- WRITETEXT with a properly protected text pointer
BEGIN TRAN
DECLARE @mytextptr varbinary(16)
SELECT @mytextptr=TEXTPTR(pr_info)
    FROM pub_info (UPDLOCK) WHERE pub_id='9999'
IF @mytextptr IS NOT NULL
    WRITETEXT pub_info.pr_info @mytextptr WITH LOG 'Hello Again'
COMMIT TRAN
```

READTEXT

READTEXT is used in a similar way to WRITETEXT, except that READTEXT allows you to specify a starting position and the number of bytes to read. Here is its basic syntax:

```
READTEXT [[database.]owner.]table_name.column_name
    text_ptr offset size [HOLDLOCK]
```

Unlike with WRITETEXT, with READTEXT I do not need to work with the entire contents of the data. I can specify the starting position (*offset*) and the number of bytes to read (*size*). READTEXT is often used with the PATINDEX() function to find the offset at which some string or pattern exists, and it's also used with DATALENGTH() to determine the total size of the text column. But these functions cannot be used as the offset parameter directly. Instead, you must execute them beforehand and keep their values in a local variable, which you then pass. As mentioned in the discussion of WRITETEXT, you'll want to protect your text pointer from becoming invalidated. In the next example, you'll read text without updating it. So you can use the HOLDLOCK lock hint on the SELECT statement for the text pointer (or set the isolation level to Reapeatable Read).

Sometimes people think that transactions are used only for data modifications, but notice that in this case you use a transaction to ensure read repeatability (of the text pointer) even though you are not updating anything. You can optionally add HOLDLOCK to the READTEXT statement to ensure that the text doesn't change until the transaction has completed. But in the example below, I read the entire contents with just one read and I will not be rereading the contents, so there is no point in using HOLDLOCK here. This example finds the pattern *Washington* in the *pr_info* column for *pub_id* 0877 and returns the contents of that column from that point on:

```
-- READTEXT with a protected text pointer
BEGIN TRAN
DECLARE @mytextptr varbinary(16), @sizeneeded int, @pat_offset int
SELECT @mytextptr=TEXTPTR(pr_info),
    @pat_offset=PATINDEX('%Washington%',pr_info) - 1,
    @sizeneeded=DATALENGTH(pr_info) -
        PATINDEX('%Washington%',pr_info) - 1
    FROM pub_info (HOLDLOCK) WHERE pub_id='0877'

IF @mytextptr IS NOT NULL AND @pat_offset >= 0 AND
    @sizeneeded IS NOT NULL
    READTEXT  pub_info.pr_info @mytextptr @pat_offset @sizeneeded

COMMIT TRAN
```

The offset returned by PATINDEX() and the offset used by READTEXT unfortunately are not consistent. READINDEX treats the first character as offset *0*. (This makes sense to me since I think of an offset as how many characters you have to move to get to the desired position—to get to the first character, you don't need to move at all.) But PATINDEX() returns the value in terms of position, not really as an offset, and so the first character for it would be *1*. (I'd call this a minor bug. But people have adapted to it, so changing it would cause more problems than it would solve at this point. You should assume that this acts as intended and adjust for it.) You need to fix this discrepancy by taking the result of PATINDEX() and subtracting *1* from it. PATINDEX() returns *−1* if the pattern is not found. Since I subtract *1* from the value returned by patindex(), if the pattern were not found, the variable @pat_offset would be *−2*. I simply check that @pat_offset is not negative.

You also need to specify how many bytes you want to read. If you want to read from that point to the end of the column, for example, you can take the total length as returned from DATALENGTH() and subtract the starting position, as shown in the example above. You cannot simply specify a buffer that you know is large enough to read the rest of the column into; that will result in error 7124:

```
The offset and length specified in the READTEXT command is greater
than the actual data length of %d.
```

If you could always perform a single READTEXT to handle your data, you'd probably not use it; instead, you could use SELECT. You need to use READTEXT when a *text* column is too long to reasonably bring back with just one statement. For example, the text size of the *pr_info* field for publisher 1622 is 18,518 bytes. I can't select this value in a program like ISQL/w because it's longer than the maximum expected row length for a result set, so it would be truncated. But I can set up a simple loop to show the text in pieces. To understand this process, you need to be aware of the global variable @@TEXTSIZE, which is the maximum amount of text or image data that you can retrieve in a single statement. (Of course, you need to make sure that the buffer in your application will also be large enough to accept the text.) You can read chunks smaller than the @@TEXT-SIZE limit, but not larger.

You can change the value of @@TEXTSIZE for your connection by using SET TEXTSIZE *n*. The default value for @@TEXTSIZE is 64 KB. I suggest that you read chunks whose size is based on the amount of space available in your application buffer and based on the network packet size so that the text will fit in one packet, with an allowance for some additional space for metadata. For example, with the default network packet size of 4192 bytes (4 KB), a good read size would be about 4100 bytes, assuming that your application could deal with that size. You should also be sure that @@TEXTSIZE is at least equal to your read size. You can either check to determine its size or explicitly set it as I do in the example below. Also notice the handy use of the CASE statement for a variable assignment to initialize the @readsize variable to the smaller of the total length of the column and the value of @@TEXTSIZE. (In this example, I make my read size only 100 characters so that it displays easily in an ISQL/w or in a similar query window. But this is too small for most applications and is used here for illustration only.)

```
-- READTEXT in a loop to read chunks of text
-- Instead of using HOLDLOCK, use SET TRANSACTION ISOLATION LEVEL
-- REPEATABLE READ (equivalent). Then SET it back when done but
-- be sure to do so in a separate batch.
SET TRANSACTION ISOLATION LEVEL REPEATABLE READ
SET TEXTSIZE 100    -- Just for illustration.  Too small for
                    -- real world.  4000 would be a better value.
BEGIN TRAN

DECLARE @mytextptr varbinary(16), @totalsize int,
    @lastread int, @readsize int

SELECT
    @mytextptr=TEXTPTR(pr_info), @totalsize=DATALENGTH(pr_info),
    @lastread=0,
    -- Set the readsize to the smaller of the @@TEXTSIZE setting
    -- and the total length of the column
    @readsize=CASE WHEN (@@TEXTSIZE < DATALENGTH(pr_info)) THEN
        @@TEXTSIZE ELSE DATALENGTH(pr_info) END
    FROM pub_info WHERE pub_id='1622'
```

```
IF @mytextptr IS NOT NULL AND @readsize > 0
    WHILE (@lastread < @totalsize)
    BEGIN
        READTEXT pub_info.pr_info @mytextptr @lastread @readsize
        IF (@@error <> 0)
            BREAK    -- Break out of loop if an error on read
        -- Change offset to last char read
        SELECT @lastread=@lastread + @readsize
        -- If read size would go beyond end, adjust read size
        IF ((@readsize + @lastread) > @totalsize)
            SELECT @readsize=@totalsize - @lastread
    END

COMMIT TRAN
GO
-- Set it back, but in a separate batch
SET TRANSACTION ISOLATION LEVEL READ COMMITTED
```

Notice that in this example I need to ensure not only that the text pointer is still valid when I get to READTEXT but also that the column did not get changed *between* iterations of READTEXT. (If another connection simply updated the text in place, the text pointer would still be valid, although my read would be messed up since the contents and length were changed.) I could use HOLDLOCK both on the READTEXT statement as well as for protecting the text pointer. But for illustration, I instead chose to change the isolation level to REPEATABLE READ.

UPDATETEXT

UPDATETEXT, added in version 6.0, is a big improvement to text processing. In earlier versions, you were stuck with only WRITETEXT, which meant that to make even a minor change, you needed to completely rewrite the entire column. UPDATETEXT lets you work with text in pieces to insert, overwrite, or append data. Or you can copy data from another *text* column and append it or overwrite the column with it. Because of its additional capability and flexibility, the syntax for UPDATETEXT is a bit more complex:

```
UPDATETEXT table_name.dest_column_name dest_text_ptr
    offset delete_length [WITH LOG] [inserted_data |
    table_name.src_column_name src_text_ptr ]
```

The destination column name and text pointer parameters point to the column that you will be updating; these parameters are always used. Like you would with WRITETEXT, you should use the UPDLOCK hint to protect the text pointer from becoming invalid and to serialize access to the text pages to prevent a conversion deadlock. The source column name parameters are used only when you are copying data from another *text* column. Otherwise, you directly include in that spot the data you'll be adding or you omit the parameter if you are deleting data.

The *offset* is the position at which you start your data modification. It should be *NULL* if you are appending to the current contents and *0* if you are starting from the beginning of the column. The *delete_length* parameter tells you how many bytes to delete (if any) starting from the offset parameter. Use *NULL* for this parameter if you will delete all contents from the offset up to the end of the column, and use *0* if you will delete no bytes. As with READTEXT, the first character of the column is considered to have a 0 offset.

UPDATETEXT can do everything, and it can do much more than WRITETEXT can do. So you might choose to use only READTEXT and UPDATETEXT and forget about WRITETEXT. (WRITETEXT existed in versions before UPDATETEXT appeared, so the former is maintained for backward compatibility, but there isn't much need for it now.)

Following are some examples that will illustrate the use of UPDATETEXT better than further explanation.

EXAMPLE 1

Use UPDATETEXT to completely replace the contents of a column:

```
-- Use UPDATETEXT to completely overwrite a text column.
-- Alternative to WRITETEXT.
DECLARE @mytextptr varbinary(16)
BEGIN TRAN

SELECT @mytextptr=TEXTPTR(pr_info) FROM pub_info (UPDLOCK) WHERE
    pub_id='9999'
IF @mytextptr IS NOT NULL
    UPDATETEXT pub_info.pr_info @mytextptr 0 NULL WITH LOG
        "New text for 9999"

COMMIT TRAN
```

EXAMPLE 2

Use UPDATETEXT to delete characters off the end; first notice that publisher 0877, Binnet, has the following contents in the text column *pr_info*:

```
This is sample text data for Binnet & Hardley, publisher 0877 in
the pubs database. Binnet & Hardley is located in Washington,
D.C.
This is sample text data for Binnet & Hardley, publisher 0877 in
the pubs database. Binnet & Hardley is located in Washington,
D.C.
```

```
This is sample text data for Binnet & Hardley, publisher 0877 in
the pubs database. Binnet & Hardley is located in Washington,
D.C.
This is sample text data for Binnet & Hardley, publisher 0877 in
the pubs database. Binnet & Hardley is located in Washington,
D.C.
This is sample text data for Binnet & Hardley, publisher 0877 in
the pubs database. Binnet & Hardley is located in Washington,
D.C.
```

Because the text is repeated several times, I want to delete all characters that follow the first occurrence of *D.C.* Here's how:

```
DECLARE @mytextptr varbinary(16), @pat_offset int
BEGIN TRAN
SELECT @mytextptr=TEXTPTR(pr_info),
    @pat_offset=PATINDEX('%D.C.%', pr_info)-1+4
    -- For offset, subtract 1 for offset adjust but add 4 for
    -- length of "D.C."
    FROM pub_info (UPDLOCK) WHERE pub_id='0877'

IF @mytextptr IS NOT NULL AND @pat_offset >= 0
    UPDATETEXT pub_info.pr_info @mytextptr @pat_offset NULL WITH LOG

COMMIT TRAN
```

The column now has these contents (only):

```
This is sample text data for Binnet & Hardley, publisher 0877 in
the pubs database. Binnet & Hardley is located in Washington, D.C.
```

EXAMPLE 3

With the small amount of text here, it wouldn't be bad to simply rewrite the column with new text. But if this were a large *text* column (you could literally store the contents of *War and Peace* in a single *text* column), it would be extremely inefficient to rewrite the entire column just to make a minor change. In this example, I want to add the text "Mary Doe is president of the company." to the current contents. I'll use UPDATETEXT to append text to the column:

```
DECLARE @mytextptr varbinary(16)
BEGIN TRAN
SELECT @mytextptr=TEXTPTR(pr_info) FROM pub_info (UPDLOCK)
    WHERE pub_id='0877'
```

```
IF @mytextptr IS NOT NULL
    UPDATETEXT pub_info.pr_info @mytextptr NULL NULL WITH LOG
        "Mary Doe is president of the company."

COMMIT TRAN
```

And the result:

```
This is sample text data for Binnet & Hardley, publisher 0877 in
the pubs database. Binnet & Hardley is located in Washington,
D.C.Mary Doe is president of the company.
```

That worked exactly as I specified, but I really wish I had skipped a line and then included a tab before adding the new sentence. I can easily add both a vertical and a horizontal tab, as you can see in Example 4.

EXAMPLE 4

Use UPDATETEXT to insert some characters:

```
DECLARE @mytextptr varbinary(16), @pat_offset int,
    @mystring char(2)
BEGIN TRAN
SELECT
@mystring=char(13) + CHAR(9),    -- Vertical tab is code point 13.
                                 -- Tab is 9.
@pat_offset=PATINDEX('%Mary%', pr_info)-1,
@mytextptr=TEXTPTR(pr_info) FROM pub_info (UPDLOCK)
    WHERE pub_id='0877'

IF @mytextptr IS NOT NULL AND @pat_offset >= 0
    UPDATETEXT pub_info.pr_info @mytextptr @pat_offset 0 WITH LOG
        @mystring

COMMIT TRAN
```

And the result:

```
This is sample text data for Binnet & Hardley, publisher 0877 in
the pubs database. Binnet & Hardley is located in Washington,
D.C.
    Mary Doe is president of the company.
```

Oops! I just learned that the president is *Marie Dow*, not *Mary Doe*. I need to fix that.

EXAMPLE 5

Use UPDATETEXT for search and replace:

```
-- UPDATETEXT for Search and Replace
DECLARE @mytextptr varbinary(16), @pat_offset int,
    @oldstring varchar(255), @newstring varchar(255),
    @sizeold int

BEGIN TRAN
SELECT @oldstring="Mary Doe", @newstring="Marie Dow"

SELECT @sizeold=DATALENGTH(@oldstring),
@pat_offset=PATINDEX('%' + @oldstring + '%', pr_info)-1,
@mytextptr=TEXTPTR(pr_info)
FROM pub_info (UPDLOCK) WHERE pub_id='0877'

IF @mytextptr IS NOT NULL AND @pat_offset >= 0
    UPDATETEXT pub_info.pr_info @mytextptr @pat_offset @sizeold
        WITH LOG @newstring

COMMIT TRAN
```

And the result:

```
This is sample text data for Binnet & Hardley, publisher 0877 in
the pubs database. Binnet & Hardley is located in Washington,
D.C.
    Marie Dow is president of the company.
```

I used variables above and figured lengths and offsets using SQL Server's built-in functions. By doing this, I ensured that the procedure is pretty generic and that it can deal with changing the string to another string that is either longer or shorter than the original.

EXAMPLE 6

Suppose that I want to append the contents of the text for publisher Scootney (*pub_id* 9952) to the text for Binnet (*pub_id* 0877). If I did not have this option in UPDATETEXT, it would be necessary to bring all that text back to the client application, append it, and then send it back to the server. Over a slow network like the Internet, this would not be practical if the *text* columns were large. But with UPDATETEXT, the whole operation is done on the server. In this example, notice that I protect the text pointer for the target with UPDLOCK, since I'll be updating that row, but I use HOLDLOCK for the source row since I am reading it only and I want to ensure that it hasn't changed.

I'll use UPDATETEXT to copy and append one text column to another:

```
-- UPDATETEXT to copy and append another text column
DECLARE @target_textptr varbinary(16),
    @source_textptr varbinary(16)
BEGIN TRAN

SELECT @target_textptr=TEXTPTR(pr_info) FROM pub_info (UPDLOCK)
WHERE pub_id='0877'
SELECT @source_textptr=TEXTPTR(pr_info) FROM pub_info (HOLDLOCK)
WHERE pub_id='9952'

IF @target_textptr IS NOT NULL AND @source_textptr IS NOT NULL
    UPDATETEXT pub_info.pr_info @target_textptr NULL NULL
        WITH LOG pub_info.pr_info @source_textptr

COMMIT TRAN
```

Environmental Concerns

To finish this discussion of Transact-SQL programming, I'll introduce some of the environmental concerns that you need to be aware of in your programming—for example, case sensitivity, which can greatly affect your applications. I'll also discuss nullability issues and ANSI compatibility.

Case Sensitivity

Various options and settings affect the semantics of your Transact-SQL statements. You must be sure that your Transact-SQL code can work regardless of the setting, or you must control the environment so that you know what the setting is.

Case sensitivity is by far the most common environmental problem, and it is simple to avoid. I recommend that you do most of your development in a case-sensitive environment, even if you will deploy your application mostly in a case-insensitive environment. The reason is simple: nearly all operations that work in a case-sensitive environment will also work in a case-insensitive environment, but the converse is not true. For example, if I write the statement *select * from authors* in the *pubs* database of a case-sensitive environment, it will work equally well in a case-insensitive environment. On the other hand, the statement *SELECT * FROM AUTHORS* will work fine in a case-insensitive environment but will fail in a case-sensitive environment. The table in *pubs* is actually named *authors,* which is lowercase. The only instance I can think of that would work in a case-sensitive environment but would fail in a case-insensitive environment is in the declaration of an object name, a column name, or a variable name. For example, with the statement *declare @myvar int,* using *@MYVAR int* would work fine in a case-sensitive environment because the two names are distinct, but it would fail in a case-insensitive environment because the names would be considered duplicates.

The easiest way to determine whether your environment is case-sensitive is to do a SELECT statement with a WHERE clause that compares a lowercase letter with its uppercase counterpart—you wouldn't need to access a table to do this. The following simple SELECT statement returns 1 if the server is case-sensitive and 0 if the server is case-insensitive:

```
SELECT CASE
    WHEN ('A'='a') THEN 0
    ELSE 1
END
```

Case sensitivity is just one of the issues surrounding the character set used by SQL Server. The character set choice will affect both the rows selected and their ordering in the result set for a query such as this:

```
SELECT au_lname, au_fname FROM authors
    WHERE au_lname='Josè'
ORDER BY au_lname, au_fname
```

If you never use characters that are not in the standard ASCII character set, case sensitivity is really your primary issue. But if your data has special characters like the *è* in this example, be sure that you understand character-set issues. (For more information, see Chapter 4, "Planning for and Installing SQL Server.")

Nullability and ANSI Compliance Settings

In order to pass the NIST test suite for ANSI SQL-92 compliance, various options had to be enabled in version 6.5 because of subtle differences in semantics between the traditional SQL Server behavior and what is mandated by ANSI. I have discussed the majority of these issues in earlier chapters. To preserve backward compatibility, the prior behavior couldn't simply be changed. So we added options (or in a few cases, previous options were toggled on) to change the semantics to comply with the ANSI SQL requirements. These options are summarized below. (I've also listed the statement used to change the behavior.)

- Disable SQL Server's = NULL extension (*SET ANSI_NULLS ON*).

- Automatically display a warning if a truncation would occur because the target column is too small to accept a value. By default, SQL Server truncates without any warning (*SET ANSI_WARNINGS ON*).

- Always right-pad *char* columns, and don't trim trailing blanks that were entered in *varchar* columns, as SQL Server would do by default (*SET ANSI_PADDING ON*).

- Make statements implicitly part of a transaction, requiring a subsequent COMMIT or ROLLBACK (*SET IMPLICIT_TRANSACTIONS ON*).

■ Terminate a query if an overflow or divide-by-zero error occurs (*SET ARITHABORT ON*). By default, SQL Server returns NULL for these operators, issues a warning message, and proceeds.

■ Close any open cursors upon COMMIT of a transaction. By default, SQL Server keeps the cursor open so that it can be reused without incurring the overhead of reopening it (*SET CURSOR_CLOSE_ON_COMMIT ON*).

■ Allow identifier names to include SQL Server keywords if the identifier is included in double quotation marks, which by default is not allowed. This causes single and double quotation marks to be treated differently (*SET QUOTED_IDENTIFIER ON*).

■ By default, create as NOT NULL a column in a CREATE TABLE statement that is not specified as NULL or NOT NULL. *SET ANSI_NULL-_DFLT_ON ON* toggles this so that the column can be created with NULL. (I recommend that you always specify NULL or NOT NULL so that this setting option is irrelevant.) The nullability of a column not explicitly declared is determined by the setting at the time the table was created, which could be different from the current setting.

All of the above options can be set individually, but I'd avoid doing that because there are 256 (2^8) permutations to consider. You might want to set a few of the options individually, such as *SET ARITHABORT* or *SET ARITHIGNORE*. But by and large, I'd either leave them all at their default settings (my preference) or change them as a group to the ANSI SQL-92 behavior. These options can be enabled as a group by setting *SET ANSI_DEFAULTS ON*.

The ability to set these options on a per-connection basis makes life "interesting" for you as a SQL Server application programmer. Your challenge is to recognize and deal with the fact that these settings will change the behavior of your code. Basically, that means that you need to adopt some form of the following four strategies:

■ The Optimistic Approach. Hope that none of your users or the person doing database administration will change such a setting. Augment your optimism by educating users not to change these settings.

■ The Flexible Approach. Try to write all your procedures as to accommodate all permutations of the settings of all the various options (usually not practical).

■ The Hard-Line Approach. Explicitly set your preferences at startup and periodically recheck them to determine that they have not been subsequently altered. Simply refuse to run if the settings are not exactly what you expect.

- The Clean Room Approach. Have a "sealed" system that prevents any-one from having direct access to change such a setting.

Whichever of these approaches you take is your choice, but recognize that if you don't think about the issue at all, you have basically settled for the Optimistic Approach. This approach is certainly adequate for many applications for which it's pretty clear that the user community would have neither the desire nor the ability to make environmental changes. But if you are deploying an application and the SQL Server will be accessed by applications that you do not control, it is probably an overly simplistic approach. Philosophically, the Flexible Approach is nice, but I don't think it's realistic unless the application is quite simple.

You can change the SQL Server default values for the server as a whole by us-ing **sp_configure 'user options'**. A specific user connection can then further refine the environment by issuing one of the specific SET statements discussed above. The global variable @@OPTIONS can then be queried by any connection to see the current settings for that connection. The @@OPTIONS variable and the value to be set using **sp_configure 'user options'** are a bit mask with the following values:

Decimal Value	Hex Value	Option and Description
1	0x0001	DISABLE_DEF_CNST_CHK. Controls interim constraint checking.
2	0x0002	IMPLICIT_TRANSACTIONS. Controls whether a transaction is started implicitly when a statement is executed.
4	0x0004	CURSOR_CLOSE_ON_COMMIT. Controls behavior of cursors once a commit has been performed.
8	0x0008	ANSI_WARNINGS. Controls truncation and NULL in aggre-gate warnings.
16	0x0010	ANSI_PADDING. Controls padding of variables.
32	0x0020	ANSI_NULLS. Controls NULL handling by using equality operators.
64	0x0040	ARITHABORT. Terminates a query when an overflow or divide-by-zero error occurs during query execution.
128	0x0080	ARITHIGNORE. Returns NULL when an overflow or divide-by-zero error occurs during a query.
256	0x0100	QUOTED_IDENTIFIER. Differentiates between single and double quotation marks when evaluating an expression, allowing object names to include characters that would other-wise not conform to naming rules or would collide with a reserved word or a keyword.

Decimal Value	Hex Value	Option and Description
512	0x0200	NOCOUNT. Turns off the message returned at the end of each statement that states how many rows were affected by the statement.
1024	0x0400	ANSI_NULL_DFLT_ON. Alters the session's behavior to use ANSI compatibility for nullability. New columns defined without explicit nullability will be defined to allow NULLs.
2048	0x0800	ANSI_NULL_DFLT_OFF. Alters the session's behavior to not use ANSI compatibility for nullability. New columns defined without explicit nullability will be defined not to allow NULLS.

By default, none of these options is enabled. So in a brand-new SQL Server 6.5 installation, the run value for **sp_configure 'user options'** will be 0. The SA can set this so that all connections have the same initial default settings. If you query the value of @@OPTIONS from an application that has not modified the environment, the value will also be 0. However, be aware that many applications, or even the SQL Server ODBC driver that the application uses, might have changed the environment. For example, if you use ISQLW.EXE, you may well see a value of 512 for @@OPTIONS if you have the No Count Display option checked under Query Options. If you are using an ODBC-based application, you might have options 256 (QUOTED_IDENTIFIER) and 16 (ANSI_PADDING) set.

To change the default behavior, simply set the corresponding bit by doing a bitwise OR with the previous value. For example, suppose that your run value is 512, which indicates that NOCOUNT is the only option turned on. You want to leave NOCOUNT enabled, but you also want to enable option number 1, which turns off the ability to deal with interim constraint violations. You'd simply pass the decimal value 513 (or 0x201) to **sp_configure 'user options'**, which is the result of doing a bitwise OR between the two options (for example, SELECT 1 | 512).

You can examine current options that have been set using *DBCC USER OPTIONS*. The output is similar to this:

```
Set Option    Value
----------    ----------
textsize      64512
language      us_english
dateformat    mdy
datefirst     7
arithabort    SET
nocount       SET
```

This DBCC command shows only options that have been set—it doesn't show all the current settings for **sp_configure 'user options'**. But you can also decode your current connection settings pretty easily from @@OPTIONS using something like this:

```
SELECT "DISABLE_DEF_CNST_CHK" AS "OPTION",
    "SETTING"=CASE WHEN (@@OPTIONS & 0x0001 > 0) THEN 'ON' ELSE 'OFF'
    END
UNION
SELECT "IMPLICIT TRANSACTIONS", CASE WHEN
    (@@OPTIONS & 0x0002 > 0) THEN 'ON' ELSE 'OFF' END
UNION
SELECT "CURSOR_CLOSE_ON_COMMIT", CASE WHEN
    (@@OPTIONS & 0x0004 > 0) THEN 'ON' ELSE 'OFF' END
UNION
SELECT "ANSI_WARNINGS",CASE WHEN (@@OPTIONS & 0x0008 > 0) THEN
    'ON' ELSE 'OFF' END
UNION
SELECT "ANSI_PADDINGS", CASE WHEN (@@OPTIONS & 0x0010 > 0) THEN
    'ON' ELSE 'OFF' END
UNION
SELECT "ANSI_NULLS", CASE WHEN (@@OPTIONS & 0x0020 > 0) THEN 'ON'
    ELSE 'OFF' END
UNION
SELECT "ARITHABORT", CASE WHEN (@@OPTIONS & 0x0040 > 0) THEN 'ON'
    ELSE 'OFF' END
UNION
SELECT "ARITHIGNORE", CASE WHEN (@@OPTIONS & 0x0080 > 0)
    THEN 'ON' ELSE 'OFF' END
UNION
SELECT "QUOTED_IDENTIFIER", CASE WHEN (@@OPTIONS & 0x0100 > 0)
    THEN 'ON' ELSE 'OFF' END
UNION
SELECT "NOCOUNT", CASE WHEN (@@OPTIONS & 0x0200 > 0) THEN 'ON'
    ELSE 'OFF' END
UNION
SELECT "ANSI_NULL_DFLT_ON", CASE WHEN (@@OPTIONS & 0x0400 > 0)
    THEN 'ON' ELSE 'OFF' END
UNION
SELECT "ANSI_NULL_DFLT_OFF", CASE WHEN (@@OPTIONS & 0x0800 > 0)
    THEN 'ON' ELSE 'OFF' END
ORDER BY "OPTION"
```

Here's the result:

```
OPTION                        SETTING
----------------------        -------
ANSI_NULL_DFLT_OFF            OFF
ANSI_NULL_DFLT_ON             OFF
ANSI_NULLS                    OFF
ANSI_PADDINGS                 OFF
ANSI_WARNINGS                 OFF
ARITHABORT                    OFF
ARITHIGNORE                   OFF
CURSOR_CLOSE_ON_COMMIT        OFF
DISABLE_DEF_CNST_CHK          ON
IMPLICIT TRANSACTIONS         OFF
NOCOUNT                       ON
QUOTED_IDENTIFIER             OFF
```

Locale-Specific SET Options

Beware of the locale-specific SET options. *SET DATEFORMAT* and *SET DATE-FIRST* change the recognized default date format. If DATEFORMAT is changed to *dmy* instead of the (U.S.) default *mdy,* a date such as *'12/10/96'* will be interpreted as October 12, 1997. I think a good strategy for dates is to always use the ANSI format yyyy.mm.dd, which is recognized no matter what the setting is of DATEFORMAT.

DATEFIRST affects what is considered the first day of the week. By default (in the U.S.), it has the value 7 (Sunday). Date functions that work with the day-of-week as a value between 1 and 7 will be affected by this setting. These day-of-week values can be confusing, since their numbering depends on the DATE-FIRST value; but the values for DATEFIRST don't change. For example, as far as DATEFIRST is considered, Sunday's value is always 7. But having then designated Sunday (7) as DATEFIRST, if you did a *SELECT DATEPART(dw,GETDATE())* and your date falls on a Sunday, the statement will return 1. You just defined Sunday to be the first day of the week, so 1 is correct.

SUMMARY

Transact-SQL statements can be grouped together in batches, they can persist in the database, they can repeatedly execute as stored procedures, and they can be made to automatically fire as triggers. It is essential that you understand the differences between these functions and that you understand that their actions are not mutually exclusive.

Transact-SQL stored procedures can be quite complex, and they can become a significant portion of your application's source code. Fortunately, Microsoft Developer Studio provides debugging support for SQL Server stored procedures.

Programming effectively with Transact-SQL also requires that you understand transactional topics, such as when transactions will be committed and when they can be rolled back. Since you'll likely be working in a multiuser environment, it is vital that you make the appropriate concurrency and consistency choices to suit the isolation level for your environment. Understanding isolation levels is also important for working with BLOBs in SQL Server using the special operators READTEXT, WRITETEXT, and UPDATETEXT. And no matter what task you are performing, it is important to realize that you must plan for various environmental options that will affect the behavior and semantics of your Transact-SQL code.

11

Cursors

Introduction

A relational database like Microsoft SQL Server is naturally *set oriented*. This means that a given statement, such as SELECT, will return a *set of results*—often more than one row of data. On the other hand, most programming languages and many applications tend ultimately to be *record based*. For example, take an application that displays a list of customers. Users scroll through the list and periodically drill down to get more detail about the customer and perhaps make some modifications. Then a user might proceed to the next customer and do the operation again, and so on, one record at a time.

The incongruity between the set-oriented approach and the record-based approach is sometimes referred to as an *impedance mismatch* in industry parlance. So how do you deal with this mismatch? SQL Server provides a significant bridge between the two models: cursors.

You can think of a cursor as a named result set in which a current position is always maintained as you move about through the result set. For example, as you visually scan names in a printed phone book, you likely run your finger down the entries. Your finger acts like a cursor—it maintains a pointer to the current entry out of the many entries you have in front of you. You can use your finger to scroll up or down the list, looking for records of interest to you. Think of the entries on the current page of the phone book as the result set from your query. The action of moving your finger through the listings on that page is similar to the action of a *scrollable cursor*—it moves forward and backward or up and down at different times, but it always maintains a current position on one row.

SQL Server has different types of cursors that you can choose from based on your scrolling requirements and on how insulated you want the cursor to be from data changes made by others. Special cursor libraries in ODBC and DB-Library have network optimizations that prevent each row *fetched* in a cursor from incurring the overhead of its own network conversation. Figure 11-1 on the next page shows how a cursor works.

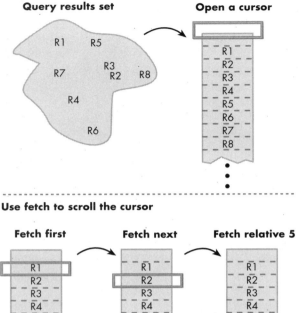

Figure 11-1. *SQL Server cursors bridge set-based and record-based models.*

Cursor Basics

Working with cursors involves a few basic steps. First you declare the cursor, and then you open it, fetch rows in the cursor, and then (optionally) update or delete rows in the table that have the cursor. Finally you close the cursor and clean up.

1. Declare the cursor. Using the DECLARE statement, you name the cursor. You choose the appropriate cursor based on how sensitive to the changes of others the cursor should be while it is open and based on what level of scrolling should be allowed. Then you specify the SELECT statement that will produce the cursor's result set. Often, the rows in the result set will be explicitly sorted via the ORDER BY clause.

   Most database systems that provide cursors allow you to move only forward through the result set. SQL Server's scrollable cursors allow you to reposition the cursor to any row. SQL Server cursors are also fully updateable.

2. Open the cursor. You can think of this step as executing the DECLARE statement from step 1.

3. Fetch rows in the cursor. While fetching (getting) rows, the cursor position moves within the result set to get the next row or the previous row, to go back five rows, to get the last row, and so on. Typically, the FETCH statement is executed many times—at least once for every row in the result set. (The other cursor statements tend to be executed only once per cursor.) In SQL Server, you typically check the @@FETCH_STATUS global variable after each fetch. A 0 status value indicates that the fetch was successful. A –1 value indicates that there are no more rows—that is, the fetch would move the cursor beyond the result set, either past the last row or before the first row. And –2 indicates that the row no longer exists in the cursor—it has been deleted from the base table after the cursor has been opened, or it was updated in a way that no longer meets the criteria of the SELECT statement that generated the result set.

4. Update/delete the table where the cursor is positioned. This step is optional; you can update or delete rows from the table on which the cursor is positioned. Here's the syntax:

```
UPDATE/DELETE table WHERE CURRENT OF cursor_name
```

After the cursor is positioned at a specific row, that row is usually updated or deleted. Instead of supplying a WHERE clause that identifies a row in the table via values such as the primary key for the UPDATE or DELETE statement, you identify the row to be operated on by specifying CURRENT, which is the row the cursor points to. This type of operation is known as a *positioned update* (or a *positioned delete*).

5. Close the cursor. Closing the cursor ends the active cursor operation. The cursor is still declared, so it can simply be reopened without your having to declare it again.

6. Deallocate the cursor. Because internal data structures consume memory in the procedure cache, you should use the DEALLOCATE statement to clean up after you're done with the cursor. Think of DEALLOCATE as essentially "UNDECLARE"—the opposite of DECLARE, as CLOSE is the opposite of OPEN. Following is an example of a simple cursor that fetches forward through the *authors* table and retrieves each row one by one. (For now, just note that this is slightly pseudocode—and highly inefficient. I don't want to get immersed in the details quite yet.)

```
DECLARE au_cursor CURSOR FOR
SELECT * FROM authors ORDER by au_lname

OPEN au_cursor

WHILE (more rows)
FETCH NEXT FROM au_cursor     -- Do until end
CLOSE au_cursor
DEALLOCATE au_cursor
```

Of course, if I wanted to get all the rows from the *authors* table, it would have been a lot easier to issue the SELECT statement directly, which would return all the rows in one set. Using a cursor to return a simple result set is inappropriate. I'll discuss uses of cursors next.

Important! Cursors and ISAMs

Before you proceed, I want to be sure that you understand something crucial about using cursors: *don't let cursors turn SQL Server into a network ISAM.*

If you read about the history of SQL Server in the first chapter of this book, you might recall that the initial grand plan for SQL Server called for it to be a higher performance back-end for Ashton-Tate's dBASE IV. dBASE was really a record-oriented, ISAM-like (that is, it did sequential, row-by-row processing) data management system. It was not set-based. At that time, SQL Server didn't use cursors, which made a difficult task even more difficult. The original plan to make the two record-oriented and set-based systems totally compatible and seamlessly interchangeable was doomed from the outset because of the inherent differences in the models. Had the original SQL Server the rich cursor model it has now, cursors would have been heavily used to build the dBASE IV front-end from the start. But I do not lament this, because I think it was probably better that the impedance mismatch became obvious. It forced us to reexamine the basic goals and dramatically change our plans for the better. It also emphasized the importance of orienting oneself to work with sets of data, not individual records as one would do with an ISAM. Had cursors existed then, they probably would have been abused, with the result being a bad SQL Server front-end.

Cursors can be an important tool when used prudently. However, because cursors are record-oriented, using them often seems natural to those who have backgrounds with ISAM systems (such as IMS, dBASE, VSAM, or the Microsoft Jet database engine used in Microsoft Access). It is tempting for such programmers to use cursors to port an application from an ISAM system to SQL Server. Such a port can be done quickly, but this is also one of the fastest ways to produce a *truly bad* SQL Server application. In the basic cursor example shown previously, the operation to fetch each row of the *authors* table is much like an ISAM operation on the *authors* file. This example cursor would be an order of magnitude less efficient than simply using a single SELECT statement to get all authors. But this type of cursor misuse, rather than using a SELECT statement, is more common than you'd think. Whenever I hear of an application with an ISAM as its origin that is being ported to SQL Server, I get worried. If you need to do this, do a *deep port*—that is, go back and look at the basic design of the application and the data structures before you do the port. A *shallow port*—making SQL Server mimic an ISAM—is appropriate only for those programmers who believe that there's never time to do the port right but there's always time to do it over.

For example, even a modestly experienced SQL Server programmer who wants to show authors and their corresponding book titles would write a single SELECT statement similar to the one shown below that joins the appropriate tables. This SELECT statement is likely to yield subsecond response time even if all the tables are large, assuming appropriate indexes exist on the tables.

```
SELECT A.au_id, au_lname, title
FROM authors A
JOIN titleauthor TA ON (A.au_id=TA.au_id)
JOIN titles T ON (T.title_id=TA.title_id)
ORDER BY A.au_id, title
```

> **NOTE** When I refer to response time, I mean the time it takes to begin sending results back to the client application. In other words, how long it takes until the First Row Returned.

In this example, all the join processing is done at the back-end and a single result set is returned. Minimal conversation occurs between the client application and the server—only the single request is received and all the qualifying rows are returned as one result set. SQL Server decides on the most efficient order in which to work with the tables and projects a single result set to satisfy the request.

An ISAM programmer who doesn't know about an operation like a join would approach the same problem by opening the *authors* "file" (as an ISAM programmer would think of it) and then iterating for each author by scanning the *titleauthor* "connecting file." This crack programmer would then traverse into the *titles* file to retrieve the appropriate records. So rather than write the simple and efficient SQL join shown above, the ISAM programmer might see cursors as the natural solution and write the code shown below. This solution works in a sense: it produces the correct results. But it is truly horrific in both relative complexity to write and relative performance, compared to the set-based join operation. The join would be more than 100 times faster than this query:

```
DECLARE @au_id char(11), @au_lname varchar(40), @title_id char(6),
    @au_id2 char(11), @title_id2 char(6), @title varchar(80)

DECLARE au_cursor CURSOR FOR
    SELECT au_id, au_lname FROM authors ORDER BY au_id
```

```
DECLARE au_titles CURSOR FOR
    SELECT au_id, title_id FROM titleauthor ORDER BY au_id

DECLARE titles_cursor CURSOR FOR
    SELECT title_id, title FROM titles ORDER BY title

OPEN au_cursor
FETCH NEXT FROM au_cursor INTO @au_id, @au_lname

WHILE (@@FETCH_STATUS=0)
    BEGIN
    OPEN au_titles
    FETCH NEXT FROM au_titles INTO @au_id2, @title_id


    WHILE (@@FETCH_STATUS=0)
        BEGIN
        -- If this is for the current author, then get
        -- titles too
        IF (@au_id=@au_id2)
            BEGIN
            OPEN titles_cursor
            FETCH NEXT FROM titles_cursor INTO
                @title_id2, @title

            WHILE (@@FETCH_STATUS=0)
                BEGIN
                -- If right title_id, then display the values
                IF (@title_id=@title_id2)
                    SELECT @au_id, @au_lname, @title

                FETCH NEXT FROM titles_cursor INTO
                    @title_id2, @title
                END
                CLOSE titles_cursor
            END
        FETCH NEXT FROM au_titles INTO @au_id2, @title_id
        END

    CLOSE au_titles
    FETCH NEXT FROM au_cursor INTO @au_id,@au_lname
    END
CLOSE au_cursor

DEALLOCATE titles_cursor
DEALLOCATE au_titles
DEALLOCATE au_cursor
```

Although this cursor solution is technically correct and is much like how ISAM processing would be written, if your developers are writing SQL Server applications like this, *stop them immediately* and get them better educated.

It might be easy for a developer who is familiar with SQL to see that the join is much better, but a developer who is steeped in ISAM operations might see the cursor solution as more straightforward, even though it is more verbose. Again, I want to emphasize that this is more than just a style issue. Even for this trivial example from *pubs* with only 25 rows of output, the join solution is orders of magnitude faster. SQL Server is designed for set operations, so whenever possible, you should perform set operations instead of sequential row-by-row operations. In addition to the huge performance gain, join operations are simpler to write and they are far less likely to introduce a bug.

Programmers familiar with the ISAM model do positioned updates. That is, they seek (or position) to a specific row, modify it, seek to another row, update it, and so forth. Cursors also offer positioned updates. But positioned update performance will be far below what could be achieved by using a single UPDATE statement that simultaneously affects multiple rows. Although the previous example showed a SELECT operation, updates and deletes can also be searched using subquery and join operations. (For details, review Chapter 8, "Modifying Data.")

The following sections discuss the main problems with this ISAM style of writing applications for SQL Server.

ISAM: Excessive Commands and Network Traffic

The ISAM-style operation makes excessive requests to the SQL Server. When cursor operations are done in the client application, a huge increase in network traffic results. In the join solution example above, one request was made to the server: the SQL query doing the join. But in ISAM-style code, if every OPEN and FETCH presents a command to the server, this simple example that produces fewer than 30 rows of output results in more than 1000 commands being sent to the SQL Server!

> **NOTE** For illustration, I wrote the procedure entirely with Transact-SQL cursors. But cursors are typically written from a client application, and every OPEN and every FETCH would indeed be a separate command and a separate network conversation. The number of commands grows large because of all the nested iteration that happens with the series of inner loops, as you'll see if you trace through the commands. Although I wrote this procedure in a pretty convoluted way, such solutions are not unlike ones that I've seen in some real applications.

ISAM: Excessive Use of Server Resources

It is almost always more expensive to use a cursor than it is to use set-oriented SQL to accomplish a given task. ISAM's only form of update is the positioned update, but a positioned update always requires at least two round-trips to the server—one to position on the row and another to then change it. In set-oriented SQL, the client application tells the server that it wants to update the set of records that meet specified criteria. Then the server figures out how to accomplish the update as a single unit of work. When using a cursor, the client doesn't allow the server to manage retrieving and updating records. In addition, using a cursor implies that the server is maintaining client "state" information, such as the user's current result set at the server, usually in *tempdb,* as well as consumption of memory for the cursor itself. Maintaining this state unnecessarily for a large number of clients is a waste of server resources. A better strategy for using SQL Server (or in fact any server resource) is for the client application to get a request in and out as quickly as possible, minimizing the client state at the server between requests. Set-oriented SQL supports this strategy, which makes it ideal for the client/server model.

ISAM: Unnecessarily Long Transactions

The ISAM-style application example uses a conversational style of communicating with the server, often involving many network round-trips within the scope of a single transaction. The effect is that transactions take longer. Transactions handled in this way can require seconds, minutes, or *worse* between the BEGIN TRANSACTION and COMMIT TRANSACTION statements. These long-running transactions might work fine for a single user, but they scale much too poorly for multiple users if any update activity occurs.

To support transactional consistency, the database must hold locks on shared resources from the time the resources are first acquired within the transaction until the commit time. Other users must wait to access the same resources. If one user holds these locks longer, that user is going to affect other users more as well as increase the possibility of a deadlock. (For more on locking, see Chapter 13.)

Designing Efficient Applications

The focus of this book is on the SQL Server back-end capabilities, but I urge you to read Peter Hussey's whitepaper, "Developing Efficient SQL Server Applications." This paper discusses the various programming interfaces that can be used for SQL Server development, and it covers such issues as appropriate uses of cursors. It is freely downloadable from http://www.microsoft.com/sql. For your convenience, I have also included a copy of this paper on the companion CD.

Cursor Models

The subject of cursors confuses many people, at least in part because there are several different cursor models and those models have different options and capabilities. I like to narrow it down to three main cursor models: *Transact-SQL cursors, API server cursors,* and *client cursors.*

Transact-SQL Cursors

You use Transact-SQL cursors within SQL typically within a stored procedure or a batch that needs to do row-by-row processing. Transact-SQL cursors use the familiar statements DECLARE CURSOR, OPEN *cursor,* and FETCH. At times we have referred to Transact-SQL cursors as "ANSI cursors" because the syntax and capabilities of Transact-SQL cursors fully implement—and go well beyond—the scrollable cursor functionality specified by ANSI SQL-92. The ANSI specification states that scrollable cursors are read-only. This isn't the way applications work, of course, so fortunately SQL Server allows scrollable cursors that can be updated. SQL Server provides backward scrolling, relative and absolute positioning within the result set, and many options regarding sensitivity to changes made by others, as well as positioned updates and deletes. I am not aware of any other product that has implemented even the ANSI specification for scrollable, read-only cursors, let alone a cursor model as rich as SQL Server's. I know of no other mainstream RDBMS that provides more than simple forward-scrolling cursors.

The cursor functionality of SQL Server is without question the richest in the industry. We've generally stopped using the term "ANSI cursor" because it implies a feature that is commonplace in the industry; the extensive cursor functionality is unique to SQL Server and greatly supersedes that specified by ANSI.

API Server Cursors

The ODBC driver for SQL Server and the DB-Library programming libraries have special cursor functions that are optimized for cursor operations and much better network utilization between a client application and a server application. For a high-performance application, it is important that there be no excessive conversation between the client and the server. The hallmark of client/server computing is to issue a single, brief command and then have the server respond. If every row fetched in a cursor had to be individually requested over the network and had to provide all the metadata to describe the row fetched, performance would be abysmal.

The ODBC driver that Microsoft provides for SQL Server fully implements these special cursor commands, as does the DB-Library programming interface. Higher level interfaces, such as RDO and DAO via ODBCDirect, also implement these functions. Rather than refer to these capabilities with the cumbersome names "ODBC server cursors," "DB-Library server cursors," "RDO server cursors," and so on, we've recently begun to refer to them as *API server cursors*.

API server cursors enable smarter communication between the calling client application and the SQL Server back-end. Central to this is the capability of this interface to specify a "fat" cursor. That is, instead of thinking of a cursor as pointing to a single row, imagine the cursor pointing to multiple rows. Take, for example, an application that displays a list box of 20 customers at a time. As the user scrolls through the list box, a FETCH would request the next 20 rows. Or perhaps it would fetch the previous 20 rows, the last 20 rows, or the 20 rows thought to be about three-fourths of the way through the result set. The interface here is provided by such function calls as **SQLExtendedFetch** and **SQLSetPos** for ODBC and **dbcursorfetch** for DB-Library. These functions make sense within those programming environments, and they are used instead of sending SQL commands like DECLARE CURSOR and FETCH. These API functions allow options and capabilities, such as defining the "width" of the cursor (the number of rows), that cannot be expressed with Transact-SQL cursor syntax. Another important performance optimization of API server cursors is that metadata is sent only once for the cursor and not with every FETCH operation, as is the case with a Transact-SQL cursor statement.

Besides offering performance advantages (especially for operations across a network), API server cursors have other capabilities that Transact-SQL cursors do not have. API server cursors can be declared on a stored procedure as long as the procedure contains only one SELECT statement. You will use API server cursors mostly in your application code.

> **NOTE** Because multiple APIs provide access to API server cursors (ODBC, DB-Library, RDO, ADO, and DAO with ODBCDirect), throughout this chapter I will discuss cursor capabilities primarily in the context of Transact-SQL cursor syntax, which is the most widely readable syntax. But when a capability is available only via API server cursors, I will point that out. The information discussed in terms of Transact-SQL cursors is relevant to all forms of API server cursors as well. After reading the information here, you can consult the programming reference for the specific API you use to better understand the capabilities offered.

Client Cursors

If you consider that the job of a cursor is to set a position within a result set, it should be clear to you that this task could be performed (although possibly less efficiently) within the client application with no assistance from the server. SQL Server originally had no cursor support, and many application designers wrote their own client-side cursor libraries to do this type of operation. While version 4.2 did not yet have cursor support in the engine, we provided a rich set of cursor functions for DB-Library rather than have many applications reinvent the wheel. These functions were implemented entirely on the client. No magic was performed, and these functions did nothing that other ISVs couldn't do (although with considerable effort—our functions were quite sophisticated and it would have been difficult for others to do this type of work). But when we designed this cursor library, we knew from the outset that we eventually wanted cursor support in the engine. The API was designed so that the bulk of the work could eventually be executed remotely at the server and so that a new API or substantial changes to applications using the API would not be necessary.

In version 6.0, we introduced scrollable cursor support directly in the SQL Server engine. With this support, applications that had been written using the DB-Library version 4.2 cursor library typically worked without any changes. In fact, they worked quite a bit better because of the server-side assistance that they got. With version 6.0, we also provided an optimized ODBC driver that fully exploited SQL Server's support for scrollable cursors. With database management systems other than SQL Server (most of which do not have scrollable cursors), it's not unusual for an ODBC driver to take on these cursor functions in a way that's similar to how DB-Library used to do it for SQL Server. But with the Microsoft-provided ODBC driver that ships with SQL Server, cursor operations use the back-end engine's capabilities.

With SQL Server, you tend to make use of cursors on the server. Because client cursors are more of a programming convenience, I won't discuss them in much depth. Instead, I'll focus on the server. But be aware that you can still use the ODBC cursor library to do the cursor operations for you (using client cursors) instead of having them processed at the server. (To use client cursors, include the SQL_ODBC_CURSORS constant in a call to **SQLSetConnectOption**.) Although DB-Library now automatically uses the server cursor features, the client cursor code from the version 4.2 days can still be enabled with the DBCLIENT-CURSORS constant via **dbsetopt**.

Some people consider client cursors obsolete now that server cursors are available. But client cursors can make a lot of sense when properly used. For example, if you want your user interface to provide forward and backward scrolling, but you want to use the more efficient default result set rather than a server cursor, you need a local buffering mechanism to cache the entire result set and provide the scrolling operations. You can write this mechanism yourself, but client cursors already provide it. Also, the emergence of the Internet brings new issues and challenges for "stateless" management of data. (That is, the connection to SQL Server is not persistent.) Client cursors can play a major part in these solutions. Although we viewed server cursors in version 6.0 as practically making client cursors obsolete, the Internet will probably drive future work into new and more sophisticated client-cursor solutions.

Default Result Set

Do not fall into the habit of thinking that every result set is a cursor, at least of the type previously discussed, or you'll inch toward the dark side—always using cursors. Earlier I said that you can think of a cursor as a named result set. I think of rows not returned in a cursor as the *default result set* or as just a result set. I don't consider a default result set to be a cursor. You can think of a default result set as a fourth type of cursor as long as you remember that no cursor functionality at the server is involved.

Despite the differences, a default result set is frequently referred to as a *firehose cursor* in discussions of the cursor capabilities of ODBC. Within the SQL Server ODBC driver, you use the same function call, **SQLExtendedFetch**, to process rows from SQL Server whether they emanate from a cursor operation or simply from a default result set. With ODBC, if you request a cursor that is forward-only and read-only, with a rowset size of 1, the driver doesn't ask for a cursor at all. Instead, it asks for a default result set, which is much more efficient than a cursor. The term "firehose" reflects the way that the server blasts rows to the client as long as the client keeps processing them so that there is room in the network buffer to send more results. In Chapter 3, I discussed how sending results from the server to the client works, and this is exactly what happens with a firehose cursor. The fact that the same ODBC functions work for both cursor and noncursor results is a nice programming simplicity, so I have no objection to using the term "firehose cursor." Just remember that from the SQL Server engine's perspective, this is not a cursor.

API Server Cursors vs. Transact-SQL Cursors

Although this book is not about ODBC or DB-Library programming, cursors are intrinsically related to those programming interfaces. This news shouldn't be too surprising, since you know that a key motivation for including cursors was to bridge the impedance mismatch between the set operations of SQL Server and the ISAM operations of traditional programming languages. And traditional programming languages use ODBC or DB-Library (or higher level interfaces that build on them, such as RDO or DAODirect). The most complete description I have seen regarding API server cursors is found in *Inside ODBC* (Microsoft Press, 1995) by Kyle Geiger. Kyle's discussion is obviously centered around ODBC, but he goes into significant depth to show the interaction between the ODBC calls and the server cursor functions. If you program with ODBC, Kyle's book is a must-read. But even if you use DB-Library or another interface that uses cursor functionality, such as RDO (which sits on top of ODBC), I think there is plenty to be gained from Kyle's discussion.

Some History...

See Chapter 6, "A Tour of the Microsoft SQL Server ODBC Driver," in Kyle's book. Kyle and I worked together for several years at Microsoft, and we remain friends. He was one of the five people already in the SQL Server group when I joined. Although he was originally part of the SQL Server group, he was fully involved with the early efforts to get ODBC adopted as an industry standard. It became clear that for ODBC to be adopted as a standard, it could not continue to exist within the SQL Server group, so Kyle formed the ODBC group within Microsoft. Kyle truly is the father of ODBC, which is clearly the most successful database call-level interface ever adopted. I have tremendous respect for Kyle and the work he did in bringing ODBC to fruition.

SQL Server provides some specialized cursor functions that are called only internally by the ODBC driver or by DB-Library (and surely in the future by an OLE-DB interface to SQL Server). These functions look like stored procedures and have stubs in the *sysobjects* table, so you might see their names there (for example, **sp_cursor**). If you trace the functions going to SQL Server (using SQL Trace or perhaps a network sniffer), you will see these functions flowing from the client application. In fact, you can execute them directly from ad hoc tools like ISQLW.EXE, although they should not be called directly from your applications.

These functions are not really stored procedures. Instead, they are capabilities implemented directly in SQL Server. The code is compiled into SQLSERVR.EXE— it is not a stored procedure or an extended stored procedure. I will refer to them as "pseudo–stored procedures." The stubs in *sysobjects* were used to make cursor execution mimic that of a stored procedure so that there was no need to make any major changes to the tabular data stream (TDS) between client and server. Remember that when we implemented server cursor support (in version 6.0), a major goal was to work seamlessly with applications that had written to the client cursor functions of DB-Library version 4.2, so implementing cursors without changing the TDS was a clever idea. These functions are not intended, or supported, for direct use by an application. They are invoked directly by the ODBC driver, by the DB-Library programming libraries, and in the future, by the native OLE-DB interface to SQL Server. These functions could also be used directly by some ISV trying to provide a gateway to another data source, if that ISV wanted the gateway to include support for scrollable cursors. It would be possible for the gateway to trap these calls and then mimic them in whatever way makes sense to the final destination. To my knowledge, no such gateway yet achieves the level of transparency we've achieved with ODBC and DB-Library.

(Doing so would be far from trivial, since writing a cursor library takes some significant work. And such an effort would require technical assistance from Microsoft, since the interface hasn't been supported for third-party development. But since products like gateways tend to be relatively expensive, high-level capabilities are expected, and I think such a capability would be highly valued.)

Transact-SQL cursors and API server cursors use the same code within SQL Server, although the Transact-SQL cursors do not directly call the pseudo–stored procedures. Because the procedures exist only for the sake of remoting the work from ODBC and DB-Library, an SQL statement, which is already executing inside the engine, has no need to call the routines in that way. While Transact-SQL and API server cursors execute the same code and have many similarities, you should not think of them as alternate ways to do the same thing.

Appropriate Use of Cursors

When should you use cursors? My somewhat simplistic answer is "Only when you have to." I'm not being totally facetious, because as a rule of thumb, if I can think of a set-based solution to a problem and avoid using a cursor, I do that. Ordinarily, when approaching a problem, cursors should be near the bottom of your list of possible solutions, not at the top. Remember that SQL Server is a relational database, so it is inherently set-based. As I showed you earlier, if you overuse cursors, you turn SQL Server into an ISAM-like product and severely cripple its power.

Although I have gone to great lengths to warn you about cursor abuse, you should not interpret this as a blanket statement that you should never use cursors. Scrollable cursors were, in fact, near the top of my wish list of features for several years. More important, cursors were near the top of the developer community's wish list. I *use* cursors—I just take care not to *misuse* them. Cursors are extremely powerful and provide SQL Server capabilities that cannot be achieved with other products. So now, rather than talk about situations in which to avoid them, I'll show you some situations in which cursors provide a great benefit.

Row-by-Row Operations

Transact-SQL cursors are great when you need to do row-by-row operations with a stored procedure or a single batch. For example, suppose that I have some financial data that includes cash flows, and for each row of that data, I want to return only rows having an internal rate of return (IRR) of more than 20 percent. IRR is a pretty involved financial function that requires iterating and converging to an answer, and I can't simply express it in the SELECT statement. But suppose that I write an extended stored procedure for IRR so that I can pass it my cash flows and it will return the IRR. Then for each row qualified by a query, I will calculate the IRR using columns in the row as input to my IRR extended procedure. And then I'll return only rows in which the IRR would be 20 percent or more. This is an appropriate use of Transact-SQL cursors. If I could not use a cursor, I would have to return all the rows across the network to the client application so that I could do the IRR operation there. (Or consider other, more complex, situations that could occur if cursors weren't available, such as problems that could arise by having another program running on the server.)

Because the cursor allows individual rows to be examined entirely at the server, I avoid sending multiple requests from the client. Because a SELECT statement will not work for this situation, the cursor allows the operation to return to the client only those rows in which the IRR value is greater than 20 percent—not all the rows. If I had wanted to return all the rows, I could have simply returned the raw data to the client and computed the IRR with a client function. In the future, when SQL Server provides support for user-defined functions (UDFs), this problem could be solved without the cursor. This is one reason (of many) that UDFs are high on my list of desirable future enhancements.

With Transact-SQL cursors, FETCH is almost always done in a loop and the cursor is used to perform row-by-row processing on the entire result set. But you should not use Transact-SQL cursors across multiple batches. For example, don't issue singular FETCH commands as their own batches. If your application fetches rows, does some work, fetches more rows, and so on, you should be using API server cursors, not Transact-SQL cursors.

Query Operations

I frequently use Transact-SQL cursors in conjunction with EXECUTE('*string*') to write and execute SQL statements based on the results of some query. For example, suppose that I wanted to issue an UPDATE STATISTICS command for every table in a database. Using Transact-SQL cursors, I can use the following generic batch to do the entire operation—without needing to return the names of the tables to the calling client application, only to be reformatted into the correct commands and sent back to the server. Instead, the entire operation is done at the server; only the initial request is sent from the client application.

```
DECLARE tables_curs CURSOR FOR
    SELECT name FROM sysobjects WHERE type='U'
OPEN tables_curs
DECLARE @tablename varchar(30), @output_msg varchar(80)
FETCH NEXT FROM tables_curs INTO @tablename
WHILE (@@FETCH_STATUS=0 )
    BEGIN
    EXEC ("UPDATE STATISTICS " + @tablename)
        IF (@@ERROR=0)
            SELECT @output_msg=
                'Statistics successfully updated on table '
                + @tablename
```

```
        ELSE
            SELECT @output_msg=
                'Failed to Update Statistics on table '
                + @tablename + ' @@ERROR=' +
                CONVERT(varchar, @@ERROR)
        PRINT @output_msg
        FETCH NEXT FROM tables_curs INTO @tablename
        END
CLOSE tables_curs
DEALLOCATE tables_curs
```

Scrolling Applications

The need for Transact-SQL cursors was not the biggest motivation for adding cursors to SQL Server. Rather, the crying need was for API server cursors to support what I refer to as "scrolling applications." Many of these applications originated from ISAM applications, or they started as single-user FoxPro or dBASE applications. Or even if they did not originate as such, they follow that paradigm—you know the type I mean.

Think of an address book of the type used in your e-mail program, for example. The user opens the address book and scrolls up or down to view the list of names. The user drags the scroll bar slider to the bottom and expects to be positioned at the last record. Dragging the slider to the beginning of the list, the user expects to be repositioned at the first record. Is this an appropriate use for a cursor? The answer depends on what you want to do with the information in the list. Here are some examples that show how I'd think about the problem.

EXAMPLE 1

This is an example of a situation in which a cursor is unnecessary. First I consider the size of the address book and whether I want changes in data to be immediately reflected. I will not use a cursor if the address book includes only a few hundred entries, if it will be read-only, or if I'm not concerned with sensitivity to changes in data (that is, I'm not concerned whether the most up-to-date copy of the data is necessarily available). After the user's list box is initially populated, a few new names might be added or the information might change in some way. But for my purposes, it is unnecessary for the list box to exhibit dynamic behavior such as names appearing, disappearing, or changing as the user scrolls through the list. In this case and with these requirements, I would simply issue my query and get the results. I could easily buffer a few hundred rows of information on the client, so there is no need for cursors.

EXAMPLE 2

This example describes a situation in which using an API server cursor would be appropriate. Suppose that the address book has 100,000 entries. The user will probably look at only a few dozen entries and then quit. Should I select all 100,000 rows to populate my list box so that the user can see only a few dozen? In most cases, the answer is no. Using a cursor would be reasonable in this situation; I would use an API server cursor.

Suppose that the list box can display 20 names at a time. I'd probably set my cursor width to 20 (a fat cursor) so that with any fetch forward or backward I'd get one list box worth of data. Or perhaps I might fetch 60 or 80 rows at a time so that the user can scroll by a few screenfuls within the application without having to ask the server for more rows. If the user moves the scroll bar slider to the bottom of the list, I fetch the bottom 20 rows, using LAST. If the user moves the slider to the top, I fetch the top 20 rows, using FIRST. And if the slider is moved three-fourths of the way down the list, I do some quick division and scroll to that point, using ABSOLUTE n. (For example, I can easily determine the total number of qualifying rows. If 100,000 rows are available and I want to scroll approximately three-fourths of the way down, I'd do a *FETCH ABSOLUTE 75000.*)

If you have to provide this type of scrolling application with a large amount of data, using a cursor makes good sense. Of course, it might have been better in the first place had the user been required to type in a few characters—that would have allowed the application to qualify the result set of the cursor. If I knew that the user was interested in only names starting with *S*, for example, I could have significantly reduced the size of the cursor by adding the appropriate criteria (for example, *name like 'S%'*) in the cursor SELECT statement.

Choosing a Cursor

Although it might seem that you have an overabundance of choices in the cursor model, the decision-making process is fairly straightforward. Follow these guidelines to choose the appropriate cursor for your situation:

- If you can do the operation with a good set-oriented solution, do so and avoid using a cursor. (In ODBC parlance—use a firehose cursor.)

- If you have decided that a cursor is appropriate and you will be doing multiple fetches over the network (such as to support a scrolling application), use an API server cursor. You'll use ODBC, RDO, DB-Library, ADO, DAO with ODBCDirect, or another API as your application needs dictate.

■ For the most part, avoid using client-side cursors and products or libraries that heavily perform cursor operations in the client application. Such applications tend to make excessive requests to the server and use the server inefficiently, since the multitude of network round-trips makes for a slow, sluggish application.

Table 11-1 compares the ways cursors are declared and opened and how operations are performed in Transact-SQL cursor statements, their rough equivalents among the pseudo–stored procedures used by the ODBC driver and DB-Library, and the ODBC and DB-Library cursor functions.

Transact-SQL Cursor Statement	Pseudo–Stored Procedure	ODBC Cursor Function	DB-Library Cursor Function
DECLARE/OPEN	**sp_cursoropen**	**SQLSetStmtOption** (SQL_CURSOR_TYPE)	**dbcursoropen**
		SQLSetStmtOption (SQL_CONCURRENCY)	
		SQLExecDirect()	
		SQLRowCount()	
FETCH	**sp_cursorfetch**	**SQLSetStmtOption** (SQL_ROWSET_SIZE)	**dbcursor-fetchex**
		SQLExtendedFetch()	
UPDATE/DELETE (positioned)	**sp_cursor**	**SQLSetPos()**	**dbcursor**
CLOSE/DEALLOC	**sp_cursorclose**	**SQLFreeStmt** (SQL_CLOSE)	**dbcursorclose**

Table 11-1. *Equivalent Transact-SQL cursor statements, pseudo–stored procedures, ODBC cursor functions, and DB-Library cursor functions.*

Cursor Membership, Scrolling, and Sensitivity to Change

In addition to understanding the cursor model (that is, Transact-SQL or API server cursors), you need to understand some other key options. These options deal with the "membership" of the cursor and the behavior the cursor will exhibit as you scroll through the result set.

Transact-SQL cursors use the ANSI-specified syntax with INSENSITIVE and SCROLL options that you can specify when you declare the cursor. The ANSI specification does not define standards for several semantic issues regarding sensitivity to changes made by others. (When the specification was written, it is likely that no one involved had implemented scrollable cursors. Even today, SQL Server is the only widely used product with scrollable cursors.) The issue of sensitivity to changes is further complicated in the client/server environment, since using a FETCH means fetching across the network.

When we set about to implement cursors, we had to make a lot of decisions about some subtle behavioral issues. We wanted efficient scrollable cursors that could be used for updating in a networked client/server environment. However, according to the ANSI specification, scrollable cursors are read-only![1] Fortunately, we were able to go way beyond the specification when we implemented scrollable, updateable cursors.

We came up with numerous cursor models that were useful in different scenarios. In doing so, we decided on terminology that describes the cursor types and works better than what can be described with the ANSI SQL syntax. SQL Server uses four main cursor models (static, keyset, dynamic, and forward-only) to describe how membership in the cursor is maintained (that is, which rows qualify), what scrolling capabilities are possible, and the sensitivity to change that the cursor will exhibit.

From the Author...

Rick Vicik conceived of the initial cursor specification for DB-Library, which held up remarkably well when the capabilities were added directly to the engine. Rick had to be truly forward-thinking in the original specification for this to be the case. The DB-Library specification also largely influenced the ODBC cursor specification. (It is always much easier to write a good spec with a working reference model, which Rick's work provided to ODBC.) Lale Divringi almost single-handedly implemented scrollable cursors both for DB-Library in version 4.2 and for the engine in version 6.0. She, of course, also worked out kinks in the spec, with Rick's input. Also providing substantial input were Peter Hussey and Kerry Chesbro, who developed the ODBC driver for SQL Server that utilized the engine cursor functionality. Implementing scrollable cursors in the database engine was a daunting task—tantamount to writing a database management system inside a database management system. Lale's accomplishment is truly impressive.

Static cursors

A static cursor is attached to a snapshot of the data that qualified for the cursor. The snapshot of the data is stored in *tempdb*. A static cursor is read-only, and the rows in the cursor and the data values of the rows never change as you fetch

---

1. American National Standard X3.135-1992, Section 13.1, p. 308. Regarding <Declare Cursor>, "5) If either Insensitive, Scroll, or Order By is specified...READ ONLY is implicit."

anywhere in the cursor because you operate on a private, temporary copy of the data. As such, it should be clear that membership in a static cursor is fixed—that is, as you fetch in any direction, new rows cannot qualify and old rows cannot change in such a way that they no longer qualify.

Before you use a static cursor, you should ask yourself whether you need to use a cursor at all. If the data is static and read-only, it probably makes more sense to process it all in the client application as a default result set and not use a cursor. If the number of rows is too large to reasonably process on the client, creating this temporary table on the server will also prove to be an expensive undertaking.

If you use Transact-SQL cursors and specify the modifier INSENSITIVE, the cursor will be static. A private temporary table will be created for the SELECT statement you specify. Note that even the cursor cannot do positioned updates or deletes on this snapshot of data in the temporary table.

You might want to use a static cursor for some "What If"–type operations on the data, when you know the changes will never be reflected in the base tables. If you want to do this type of operation, you can do a SELECT INTO in a temporary table and then declare a cursor on that table without specifying INSENSITIVE. If you specify a query that performs an aggregate function (such as SUM, MIN, MAX, GROUP BY, or UNION), the cursor might also need to be materialized in a temporary table and therefore will be a static cursor.

Keyset cursors

For a keyset cursor, a list is kept in *tempdb* of all the key values for the rows that meet the SELECT statement criteria. For example, if you declare a scrollable cursor on the *customer* table, the keyset would be a list of those *cust_id* values that qualified for membership in the SELECT statement when the cursor was opened. For example, suppose that when the cursor was opened, the SELECT statement used to declare the cursor had a WHERE clause in this form:

```
WHERE cust_balance > 100000
```

Then suppose that customers 7, 12, 18, 24, and 56 (that is, rows with *cust_id* of those values) qualified. These keys are subsequently used whenever fetching is performed. Conceptually, further selection for the cursor is of the form

```
WHERE cust_id IN (7,12,18,24,56)
```

rather than this form

```
WHERE cust_balance > 100000
```

(Internally, the SELECT statement is not issued again. This is for illustration only.) Membership in the keyset cursor is *fixed*: that is, these five identified rows are part of the cursor and no other rows will be seen in subsequent fetching. Even if other rows that meet the SELECT statement criteria are subsequently inserted or updated, they will not be seen by this cursor after it is opened.

In a keyset cursor, as opposed to a static cursor, I can see changes to the data in the rows that meet the SELECT criteria when the cursor is opened. For example, if another user modifies the customer balance while I hold the cursor open and I then fetch the row again, I will see those changes (unless I hold locks to prevent such changes). In fact, even if the modification causes the row to no longer satisfy the criteria of *cust_balance > 100000*, I will still see the row in a subsequent fetch. The row will disappear only if it is actually deleted. The key value will still exist because it was squirreled away in *tempdb,* but the row will be gone. Default values, NULL values, blank spaces, or zeros (as appropriate) are supplied for the column values. But more importantly, the global variable @@FETCH_STATUS returns a value of −2 for this case, indicating that the row no longer exists.

Because the keys are gathered when the cursor is open and membership is fixed, keyset cursors are able to fetch to an absolute position within the result set. For example, it is reasonable to fetch to row 104 of the cursor:

```
FETCH ABSOLUTE 104 FROM cursor
```

It shouldn't come as a surprise that a keyset cursor demands that a unique index exist on every table used in the SELECT statement for the cursor. The unique index is necessary to identify the keys. The index could be created directly (with CREATE INDEX), or it could exist as a result of a PRIMARY KEY or UNIQUE constraint.

Dynamic cursors
Think of a dynamic cursor as a cursor in which the SELECT statement is again applied in subsequent FETCH operations. That is, the cursor does not refetch specific rows, as in this statement:

```
WHERE cust_id IN (12,18,24,56,7)
```

Instead, conceptually, the WHERE clause is reapplied. For example:

```
WHERE cust_balance > 100000
```

This means that membership is *not* fixed—subsequent fetches might include newly qualifying rows, or previously qualifying rows might disappear. This can occur due to changes you have made within the cursor, but it also could be due to changes made by others. If the cursor has not locked the rows of the result set (which is dependent on the concurrency options selected, as I'll come to in a moment), the changes made by others will be seen in your cursor when you do a subsequent fetch on the cursor. You see such changes only on a subsequent fetch. The *image* of data in the buffer from the last fetch is just that—a copy in memory of what the row(s) looked like when the last fetch was performed. (This is not specific to dynamic cursors. The fourth cursor type, forward-only, is a subtype of the dynamic cursor that is restricted to allow only FETCH NEXT—not PRIOR, ABSOLUTE *n,* and so on. "Dynamic" and "forward-only" are not options explicitly used in the Transact-SQL cursor interface. They are fully available with the API server cursor interfaces and can do operations such as FETCH PRIOR, FIRST, and so on. The exception is FETCH ABSOLUTE, which is not supported for dynamic cursors, even using API server cursors.)

Since membership in a dynamic cursor is not fixed, there is no guarantee that subsequent fetches will always bring up the same information. It doesn't make sense, for example, to simply fetch to row 104 if every subsequent fetch brings up a row 104 that contains different information. However, FETCH RELATIVE is supported with dynamic cursors, which sometimes surprises people. When used with a dynamic cursor, FETCH RELATIVE *n* starts fetching from the first row in the current cursor set and skips the first *n* rows from that point.

A cursor declared with an ORDER BY clause can be dynamic only if an index contains keys that match the ORDER BY. If no index exists, the cursor automatically converts to a keyset cursor.

Forward-only cursors

Typically, Transact-SQL cursors are forward-only cursors. As I mentioned above, forward-only cursors are dynamic cursors that allow only a FETCH type of NEXT. I think it's OK for you to think of SQL Server as having only *three* types of cursors (static, keyset, and dynamic). In fact, that's how I think about cursors. I treat forward-only as its own type here because API server cursors specify forward-only at the same level as keyset and dynamic. When the INSENSITIVE, SCROLL, or FOR READ ONLY options are not specified, a forward-only cursor will be used (with one exception: if the query uses an aggregate function, such as GROUP BY or UNION, the cursor must be created as static).

Forward-only scrolling is consistent with Transact-SQL cursors' recommended use of providing row-by-row processing within a stored procedure or batch. Such processing would usually be from start to end—one way, so that rows are never refetched. If you are using Transact-SQL cursors appropriately, typically you are scrolling forward-only to do a row-by-row operation and you are not revisiting rows. Forward-only cursors are usually the fastest type of cursor, but a standard SELECT statement (not a cursor) will still be significantly faster.

Cursor keys

Keyset cursors demand a unique index, and the columns that are defined as keys for the index used are the *cursor keys.* Dynamic cursors also process along an index if possible, although that is not mandatory. If multiple indexes are used, an index is chosen according to the rules described below.

Index selection rules If a suitable index is specified as an optimizer hint, that index is used. For a dynamic cursor, the index does not have to be unique if it is clustered. These index selection rules are listed in order for a dynamic (including forward-only) cursor:

1. The primary key index is used if it matches the ORDER BY in the SELECT statement, or this index might be used if no ORDER BY clause is present. (See step 5.)

2. The lowest numbered unique index that matches the ORDER BY clause is used.

3. The lowest numbered unique index is used if no ORDER BY clause is present.

4. A clustered nonunique index that matches the ORDER BY clause (if one is present) is used.

5. If none of the above criteria are satisfied but a primary key index is present, it will be used. But if the index does not match a specified ORDER BY clause, the cursor will be converted to a keyset cursor and is not dynamic.

6. The lowest unique index is used. (Again, the cursor is converted to a keyset cursor if the index does not match the ORDER BY clause, if specified.)

7. If no suitable index exists, the dynamic cursor does a table scan. The cursor still allows FETCH operations other than NEXT, but unless your table is very small, you don't want a table scan to be used for most cursor operations.

A keyset cursor must always have a unique index for every table. If no such index exists, a cursor that would otherwise be created as KEYSET is converted to INSENSITIVE. The index selection rules for dynamic cursors can sometimes result in less than ideal query plans, especially on queries that want to use a nonunique index. In those cases, you might want to check the query plan using *SET SHOWPLAN ON* with a simple SELECT statement, and if possible, you should use an optimizer hint for index selection to most closely emulate the (noncursor) query plan. In future SQL Server releases, index selection for a cursor will be more tightly integrated with the query optimizer.

Following are the index selection rules for a keyset cursor:

1. Use a user-specified (via optimizer hint) unique index, if provided.

2. Choose the primary key index.

3. Otherwise, choose the lowest numbered unique index.

4. If there is no unique index, the cursor will still be created but it must be converted to INSENSITIVE since a keyset cursor always requires a unique index.

Transact-SQL Cursor Syntax and Behavior

The syntax for Transact-SQL cursors almost exactly matches that specified by ANSI SQL-92 for scrollable cursors. We've also included some extensions—most notably, scrollable cursors are also updateable. The ANSI syntax is used nearly verbatim except for DEALLOCATE, which is SQL Server–specific syntax for performing internal resource cleanup. The ANSI specification is pretty loose about issues regarding membership of the cursor, likely because no mainstream products had implemented scrollable cursors when the ANSI specification was written. Many such issues are *implementation defined* (which means no standard exists for these important details). I know of no other mainstream products that have fully implemented scrollable cursors directly in the engine, and there is no test for scrollable cursors in any ANSI conformance certification suite.

In the following sections, I'll briefly discuss the cursor syntax supported before making comments about behavioral issues that you need to be aware of. After discussing syntax and options, I'll detail how the syntax relates to whether the cursor is static, keyset, or dynamic. I'll also address issues of locking and concurrency control. Throughout this discussion, I'll refer to cursor functionality that is present in the server, which in some cases is available only through API server cursors.

DECLARE

Here's the syntax to declare a cursor with a given name:

```
DECLARE cursor_name [INSENSITIVE][SCROLL] CURSOR
    FOR select_statement
    [FOR {READ ONLY | UPDATE [OF column_list]}]
```

A cursor is always private in scope to the connection declaring it. Although named, the cursor is not visible to other connections, and other connections can have cursors of the same name. (This is not quite analogous to the way a local variable works. A cursor is global to the connection; local-variable names are scoped by the procedure or batch that contains them.) A Transact-SQL cursor always has its result set generated from a SELECT statement. The SELECT statement can be ordered (ORDER BY), and that's often the case. An API server cursor can also be declared with the result set being the result of a stored procedure. This powerful capability, which is important for scrolling applications, is not available via the Transact-SQL syntax.

If the cursor is declared as SCROLL, every table listed in the SELECT statement must have a unique index; otherwise, the cursor will convert to INSENSITIVE and be read-only. If INSENSITIVE is specified, the results are copied into a temporary table when OPEN CURSOR is called. From then on, the results are returned from the temporary table in the server and the updates done by other users are not reflected in the cursor rows. If SCROLL is specified, all forms of FETCH are legal. If this option is not specified, only FETCH NEXT is allowed.

If INSENSITIVE is specified, the cursor is read-only and cannot be updated. If none of the READ ONLY, FOR UPDATE, or INSENSITIVE modifiers are specified, the cursor will allow updates if the underlying SELECT statement doesn't prevent it. (Such a SELECT might specify an aggregate function or use UNION and hence not be updateable.) If you specify FOR UPDATE and the underlying SELECT statement is of a type that cannot be updated, you will get an error immediately and the DECLARE statement will fail. If FOR UPDATE is not specified, the DECLARE statement will succeed, but if you later attempt an update, you will get an error. So if you are intending to do an update (or delete) via the cursor, you should specify FOR UPDATE during the DECLARE so that any inability to modify the row is detected right up front.

It is worth pointing out here that if the DECLARE statement includes a local variable, its value is captured at declare time, not at open time. In the following example, the cursor will use a WHERE clause of *qty > 30*, not *qty > 5*:

```
DECLARE @t smallint
SELECT @t=30

DECLARE c1 SCROLL CURSOR FOR SELECT ord_num, qty FROM sales
    WHERE qty > @t

DECLARE @ordnum varchar(20), @qty smallint

SELECT @t=5
OPEN c1
```

OPEN

The OPEN cursor syntax opens the cursor, generating and populating temporary tables if needed:

```
OPEN cursor_name
```

If the cursor is keyset-based, the keys are also retrieved when the cursor is opened. Subsequent update or fetch operations on a cursor are illegal unless the cursor opened successfully. You can use the global variable @@CURSOR_ROWS subsequent to the OPEN to retrieve the number of qualifying rows in the last opened cursor. Depending on the number of rows expected in the result set, SQL Server may choose to populate the keyset cursor asynchronously on a separate thread. This allows fetches to proceed immediately, even if the keyset cursor is not fully populated. The following table shows the values returned by using @@CURSOR_ROWS and a description of each value.

Value	Description
-1	The cursor is dynamic. @@CURSOR_ROWS is not applicable.
$-m$	A keyset cursor is still in the process of being populated asynchronously. This value refers to the number of rows in the keyset so far. The negative value indicates that the keyset is still being retrieved. A negative value (asynchronous population) can be returned only with a keyset cursor.
n	This value refers to the number of rows in the cursor.
0	No cursors have been opened, or the last opened cursor has been closed.

To set the threshold at which SQL Server will generate keysets asynchronously (and potentially return a negative value), use the **cursor threshold** configuration option with **sp_configure**. Note that this is an "advanced option" and not visible unless Show Advanced Options is also enabled with **sp_configure**. By default, the setting for this cursor threshold is −1, which means that the keyset will be fully populated before the OPEN statement completes. (That is, the keyset generation is synchronous.) With asynchronous keyset generation, OPEN completes almost immediately and you can begin fetching rows while other keys are still being gathered. However, this can lead to some potentially puzzling behaviors. For example, you can't really FETCH LAST until the keyset is fully populated. Unless you are generating large cursors, it's not usually necessary to set this option—synchronous keyset generation works fine and the behavior is more predictable. If you need to open a large cursor, however, this is an important capability for maintaining good response times.

FETCH

The FETCH syntax fetches a row from the cursor in the specified direction:

```
FETCH [row_selector FROM] cursor_name [INTO @v1. @v2...]
```

A successful fetch results in the global variable @@FETCH_STATUS being set to 0. If the cursor is declared with the SCROLL option, the *row_selector* can be NEXT, PRIOR, FIRST, LAST, ABSOLUTE *n,* or RELATIVE *n*. If no *row_selector* is specified, the default is NEXT. FETCH NEXT operations are by far the most common type of fetch for Transact-SQL cursors. This is consistent with their recommended use when row-by-row processing is needed with a stored procedure or batch. Such processing would nearly always be from start to finish.

But more exotic forms of fetch are also supported. ABSOLUTE *n* returns the *n*th row in the result set, with a negative value representing a row number counting backward from the end of the result set. RELATIVE *n* returns the *n*th row relative to the last row fetched, and a negative value indicates the row number is counted backward starting from the last row fetched. Fetches using NEXT, PRIOR, or RELATIVE operations are done in respect to the current cursor position.

RELATIVE 0 means "refetch the current row." This can be useful to "freshen" a "stale" row. The row number *n* specified in RELATIVE and ABSOLUTE fetch types can be a local variable or a parameter of type *integer, smallint,* or *tinyint*.

The ANSI SQL-92 specification states that you cannot specify SCROLL and FOR UPDATE together. According to the specification, SCROLL forces a cursor to be read-only. I don't see any rational explanation for this, except that it was considered too hard to implement to put into the standard. Fortunately, SQL Server scrollable cursors are indeed updateable—a quantum leap forward from what the standard specifies!

If the SCROLL option is not specified, only NEXT *row_selector* (or no explicit parameter, which amounts to the same thing) is legal. When the cursor is opened and no fetch is done, the cursor is positioned before the first row—that is, FETCH NEXT returns the first row. When some rows are fetched successfully, the cursor will be positioned on the last row fetched. When a FETCH request causes the cursor position to exceed the given result set, the cursor will be positioned after the last row—that is, a FETCH PRIOR returns the last row. A fetch that causes the position to go outside the cursor range (before the first row or after the last row) causes the global variable @@FETCH_STATUS to be set to −1. Probably the most common and appropriate use of Transact-SQL cursors is to FETCH NEXT within a loop until @@FETCH_STATUS EQUALS −1 (or <> 0).

If a row is fetched but no longer exists with a keyset cursor, it is considered "missing" and @@FETCH_STATUS returns −2. The row might have been deleted by some other user or by an operation within the cursor. A missing row has been deleted, not simply updated so that it no longer meets the criteria of the SELECT statement. (If that's the semantic you want, you should use a dynamic cursor.)

Missing rows apply to keyset cursors only. A static cursor, of course, never changes—it is merely a snapshot of the data stored in a temporary table and cannot be updated. A dynamic cursor does not have fixed membership. There is no expectation for a row to be part of a dynamic cursor since rows come and go as the cursor is fetched, depending on what rows currently meet the query criteria. So there is no concept of a missing row for a dynamic cursor. With Transact-SQL cursors, since the dynamic cursor is forward-only, there is no way to refetch a row anyway.

If an INTO clause is provided, the data from each column in the SELECT list is inserted into the specified local variable; otherwise, the data is sent to the client as a normal result set with full metadata using TDS. In other words, the result set of a Transact-SQL cursor is the same as any other result set. But doing 50 fetches back to the application in this way produces 50 result sets, which is inefficient. An error occurs from the fetch if the datatypes of the column being retrieved and the local variable being assigned are incompatible or if the length of the local variable is less than the maximum length of the column. It is also necessary for the number of variables and their order to exactly match those of the selected columns in the SELECT statement that defines the cursor.

UPDATE

The UPDATE syntax updates the table row corresponding to the given row in the cursor:

```
UPDATE table_name SET assignment_list WHERE CURRENT OF cursor_name
```

This is referred to as a *positioned update*. Using Transact-SQL cursors, a positioned update (or *positioned delete*) operates only on the last row fetched and can affect only one row. (API server cursors can update multiple rows in a single operation. Think of this capability as an array of structures that can all be applied in one operation. This is a significant capability, but it makes sense to use it only from an application programming language. The SQL-92 syntax provides no mechanism for this type of multiple-row update via a cursor.)

An update involving a column that is used as a key value will be treated internally as a delete/insert, as though the row with the original key values was deleted and a new row with the modified key value(s) was inserted into the table.

DELETE

The following is a positioned delete:

```
DELETE FROM table_name WHERE CURRENT OF cursor_name
```

This statement deletes from the given table the row corresponding to the current position of the cursor. This is similar to a positioned update. There is no positioned insert capability, however. Since a cursor can be thought of as a named result set, it should be clear that you do not insert into a cursor but into the table (or view).

CLOSE

The CLOSE syntax closes the cursor:

```
CLOSE cursor_name
```

After it is closed, the cursor can no longer be fetched from or updated/deleted. Closing the cursor deletes its keyset while leaving the definition of the cursor intact. (That is, a closed cursor can be reopened without being redeclared.) The keyset will be regenerated during the next OPEN. Similarly, closing a static cursor deletes the temporary table of results, which can be regenerated when the cursor is reopened. Closing a dynamic cursor doesn't have much effect because neither the data nor the keys are materialized.

From the Author...

ANSI specifies that cursors are closed when a COMMIT is issued. I don't understand the value of this. For the types of applications in which cursors are most appropriate (what I call scrolling applications), it is common to make a change and want to commit it but to keep working within the cursor. Having the cursor close whenever a COMMIT is issued seems inefficient to me, and rather pointless. But if you want to be consistent with ANSI on this, a SET option provides this "feature":

```
SET CURSOR_CLOSE_ON_COMMIT ON
```

Note that when using API server cursors with ODBC, the default is to close the cursor on COMMIT; ODBC followed the ANSI lead here. But the SQL Server driver provides a specific connection option, SQL_PRESERVE_CURSORS, so that cursors are not closed on COMMIT.

DEALLOCATE

DEALLOCATE, not part of the ANSI specification, is a cleanup command:

```
DEALLOCATE cursor_name
```

DEALLOCATE releases all the data structures associated with the cursor and removes the definition of the cursor. Once a cursor is deallocated, it cannot be opened until a new DECLARE statement is issued. Although it's considered standard practice to close a cursor, if you DEALLOCATE an open cursor it is automatically closed. The existence of DEALLOCATE is basically a performance optimization. Without it, when would a cursor's resources be cleaned up? How would SQL Server know you are really done using the cursor? Probably the only alternative would be to do the cleanup anytime a CLOSE is issued. But then all the overhead of a new DECLARE would be necessary before a cursor could be opened again. Although it is yet another command to issue, DEALLOCATE allows us to provide a way to close and reopen a cursor without redeclaring it.

Transact-SQL Cursor Behavior

I think it confuses many users that we describe cursors as static, keyset, dynamic, and forward-only, yet these options are not directly exposed via the Transact-SQL DECLARE CURSOR statement. Because pseudo–stored procedures have clear parameters, API server cursors can be more direct in their declarations. Transact-SQL cursors use the ANSI syntax, which doesn't provide as rich a set of capabilities as those provided by API server cursors. In addition, the mapping of capabilities provided by SQL Server to those from the ANSI specification is not one-for-one. As I have already mentioned, several capabilities of SQL Server cursors are exposed only via the API server interfaces (ODBC, DB-Library, and so on).

Table 11-2 shows the types of cursors that will be used depending on the specific Transact-SQL cursor syntax used. The table does not include every possible combination and certainly not combinations that do not make sense, such as INSENSITIVE and FOR UPDATE used together. Such combinations result in errors stating that the cursor is read-only when the DECLARE CURSOR statement executes. Table 11-2 is intended to show the typical cases. Some SELECT statements, such as those using an aggregate function (UNION and so on), can use a cursor only by materializing a temporary table. Hence, cursors declared with such a SELECT statement are always converted to INSENSITIVE and therefore are read-only.

DECLARE Statement	Comment	Updateable? (Assume Successful DECLARE)	Cursor Type*
DECLARE cursor_name CURSOR FOR select	Default syntax; no optional modifiers used	Typically yes, but since neither FOR UPDATE nor FOR READ ONLY specified, depends on SELECT**	Forward-only (dynamic)
DECLARE cursor_name CURSOR FOR select FOR UPDATE	Default syntax; no optional modifiers used	Yes	Forward-only (dynamic)
DECLARE cursor_name SCROLL CURSOR FOR select	Assume unique index exists for all tables in SELECT	Typically yes, but since neither FOR UPDATE nor FOR READ ONLY specified depends on SELECT**	Keyset
DECLARE cursor_name SCROLL CURSOR FOR select FOR READ ONLY	Assume unique index exists for all tables in SELECT	No (cursor declared READ ONLY)	Keyset
DECLARE cursor_name SCROLL CURSOR FOR select	Assume no unique index exists for one or more tables in SELECT	No (cursor static due to lack of unique index)	Static (cursor READ ONLY might not be apparent until update attempted)
DECLARE cursor_name SCROLL CURSOR FOR select FOR UPDATE	Assume no unique index exists for one or more tables in SELECT	No (cursor not created since DECLARE fails)	Error (DECLARE fails because cursor not updateable due to lack of unique index)
DECLARE cursor_name SCROLL CURSOR FOR select FOR UPDATE	Unique index exists for all tables in SELECT	Yes (advantage over ANSI SQL-92 spec)	Keyset
DECLARE cursor_name INSENSITIVE CURSOR FOR select		No	Static
DECLARE cursor_name INSENSITIVE SCROLL CURSOR FOR select		No	Static
DECLARE cursor_name CURSOR FOR select FOR READ ONLY		No	Forward-only (dynamic)
DECLARE cursor_name CURSOR FOR select	Assume SELECT includes ORDER BY that doesn't match unique index or nonunique clustered index; unique index exists on every table involved	Yes (if none of conditions in footnote apply)**	Keyset

*Assume for this table that the SELECT statement does not use an aggregate function, such as AVG() or SUM(), or does not otherwise use a GROUP BY, UNION, HAVING, or DISTINCT clause. If the SELECT statement uses one of these clauses, the data is copied to a temporary table at open time and the cursor will be static.

**The cursor will not be updateable if the SELECT statement uses an aggregate function, such as AVG() or SUM(), or otherwise uses a GROUP BY, UNION, HAVING, or DISTINCT clause.

Table 11-2. *Transact-SQL syntax and the resulting cursor types.*

Simplest Cursor Syntax

In its simplest form, with no other options declared, this example cursor will be forward-only (a dynamic cursor subtype):

```
DECLARE my_curs CURSOR FOR SELECT au_id, au_lname FROM authors
```

If you tried any fetch operation other than FETCH NEXT (or simply FETCH, since NEXT is the default if no modifier is specified), you would get an error like this:

```
Msg 16911, Level 16, State 1
fetch: The fetch type FETCH_LAST cannot be used with forward only cursors
```

Transact-SQL cursors can scroll only to the NEXT row (forward-only) unless the SCROLL option is explicitly stated (even if the cursor is INSENSITIVE). Such a cursor will be keyset, based on whether you use the SCROLL modifier and whether a unique index exists for every table used in the cursor. Then *any* fetch operation will be legal. Transact-SQL cursors that are forward-only are never scrollable (other than FETCH NEXT). However, API server cursors can be both dynamic and scrollable with some limits. (For example, absolute positioning cannot be supported since there is no fixed position of rows.)

Fully Scrollable Transact-SQL Cursors

Here is a an example of a fully scrollable Transact-SQL cursor:

```
DECLARE my_curs SCROLL CURSOR FOR SELECT au_id, au_lname
    FROM authors
OPEN my_curs
FETCH ABSOLUTE 6 FROM my_curs
```

Here's the output:

```
au_id           au_lname
------------    --------------
341-22-1782     Smith
```

> **NOTE** To keep the examples here focused on the central point, I don't check @@FETCH_STATUS or @@ERROR. Real production-caliber code, of course, *would* check.

If the cursor is declared as SCROLL but not every table listed in the SELECT statement has a unique index, the cursor will be created as a static (read-only) cursor, although it will still be scrollable. The results of the SELECT statement will be copied into a temporary table when the cursor is opened. Unless the FOR UPDATE OF clause is used, you will receive no warning that this will occur. In that case, an error will result after the DECLARE cursor statement is issued:

```
CREATE TABLE foo
(col1    int,
col2     int)
-- No indexes on this table
GO

DECLARE my_curs2 SCROLL CURSOR FOR SELECT col1, col2 FROM foo
FOR UPDATE OF col1
```

This returns:

```
Msg 16929, Level 16, State 1
Cursor is read only
```

Some options don't make sense when used together. For example, you can't both declare a cursor to be INSENSITIVE and use FOR UPDATE OF. This will generate an error message when the cursor is declared. Remember that the INSENSITIVE option and FOR READ ONLY are not quite equivalent. When INSENSITIVE is specified, the results are copied into a temporary table when OPEN CURSOR is called. From then on, the results are returned from this temporary table in the server and the updates done by other users are not reflected in the cursor rows. But a dynamic cursor that is not INSENSITIVE or that does not use the SCROLL modifier or a keyset cursor (scroll cursor with unique index existing) can be READ ONLY but not INSENSITIVE. As you scroll, you might see values that have been changed by other users since the time the cursor was opened. A cursor declared with these characteristics doesn't allow positioned updates or deletes via the cursor, but it doesn't prevent those updates or deletes made by others from being visible. (As mentioned earlier, the case of a dynamic cursor refetching rows and seeing different values or different rows will happen only with API server cursors. All dynamic Transact-SQL cursors are forward-only, so a row is never refetched.)

Concurrency Control with Transact-SQL Cursors

If you use a cursor that's not in the scope of a transaction, by default, locks will not be held for long durations. A shared lock will be briefly requested for the fetch operation and then will be immediately released. If you subsequently attempt to update through the cursor, *optimistic concurrency control* (OPTCC) is used to ensure that the row being updated is still consistent with the row you fetched into the cursor.

```
DECLARE my_curs SCROLL CURSOR FOR SELECT au_id, au_lname
FROM authors
OPEN my_curs
FETCH ABSOLUTE 6 FROM my_curs
-- This would return: 341-22-1782 Smith
```

```
-- Assume some other user modifies this row between this and
-- the next statement:
UPDATE authors SET au_lname='Donaldson' WHERE CURRENT OF my_curs
```

This returns:

```
Msg 16934, Level 16, State 1
Optimistic concurrency check failed, the row was modified outside
of this cursor
```

With optimistic concurrency control, locks are not held on the data that's selected. Because no locks are held, concurrency is increased. Then, at the time of the update, the current row in the table is compared to the row that had been fetched into the cursor. If nothing has changed, the update occurs. If a change is detected, the update will not occur and error message 16934 will be returned. The term "optimistic" is meant to convey that the update will be attempted with the *hope* that nothing has changed. A check is made at the time of the update to ensure that, in fact, nothing has changed. (It's *not* so optimistic that it forgoes the check.) In this case, although a change will be detected and the update will be refused, no locks have been issued to prevent such a change. I could decide to go ahead and update the row, even though it failed the optimistic concurrency check. To do so, I fully qualify the update but I don't do a positioned update (*WHERE CURRENT OF my_curs*). Rather, I do a standard update from the same connection, exactly qualifying the row via the unique key. For example:

```
UPDATE authors
SET au_lname='from proc with cursor, but not via a cursor'
WHERE au_id='648-92-1872'
```

Although here I am describing this situation via the Transact-SQL syntax, you are much more likely to encounter this situation using API server cursors in the real world. In such a case, you might use optimistic concurrency control. If a conflict is encountered, you can display a message to your end user—something like: "The row has subsequently changed. Here is the new value [which you could refetch to get]. Do you still want to go ahead with your update?"

There are actually two types of optimistic concurrency. With Transact-SQL cursors, if the table has a timestamp column defined, a cursor update will use it to determine whether the row has been changed since it was fetched. (Recall that a timestamp column is an automatic increasing value that is updated for any change to the row. It is unique within the database, but it bears no relationship to the system's or the calendar's date and time.) When the update is attempted, the current timestamp on the row is compared to the timestamp that was present when the row was fetched. The timestamp will be automatically and invisibly fetched into the cursor even though it was not declared in the select list. Be aware that an update will fail the optimistic concurrency check even if a column not in the cursor has been updated since the row was fetched. The update to that column (not in the cursor) will increase the timestamp, making the comparison fail. But this happens only if a timestamp column exists on the table being updated.

If there is no timestamp column, optimistic concurrency control silently reverts to a "by-value" mode. Since no timestamp exists to indicate whether the row has been updated, the values for *all* columns in the row are compared to the current values in the row at the time of the update. If the values are identical, the update is allowed. Notice that an attempt to update a column in a row that is not part of the cursor will cause optimistic concurrency control to fail, whether it is timestamp-based or value-based. You can also use traditional locking in conjunction with a cursor to prevent other users from changing the data that you fetch.

Optimistic concurrency control works quite well in environments with relatively low update contention. When high update activity occurs, optimistic concurrency control might not be appropriate; for example, you might not be able to get an update to succeed because the row is being modified by some other user. Whether optimistic or pessimistic (locking) concurrency control is more appropriate depends on the nature of your application. An address book application, with few updates, is likely well-suited to optimistic concurrency control. An application used to sell a product and keep track of inventory is probably not well-suited to optimistic concurrency control.

For example, if I am writing an application to sell reserved tickets for a flight, and sales are brisk, optimistic concurrency control is probably not appropriate. Here is what the dialog between the ticket agent and customer calling on the telephone might sound like if I used optimistic concurrency control:

> *Caller: "I'd like two tickets to Honolulu for January 15."*
>
> *Ticket Agent: "OK, I have two seats on flight number 1 leaving at 10 A.M."*
>
> *Caller: "Great, I'll take them."*
>
> *Ticket Agent: "Oops. I just tried to reserve them, and they've been sold by another agent. Nothing else seems to be available on that date."*

If it's not sufficient to simply hope that no updates have occurred since a row was last fetched, optimistic concurrency control is probably not suitable. You need to be pessimistic and prevent others from making updates by using locking.

NOTE Locking is discussed in detail in Chapters 13 and 14.

If you want to make sure that no other users have changed the data you have fetched, you will want to hold shared locks on data that is fetched while the cursor is open. You can do this by setting TRANSACTION ISOLATION LEVEL to RE-PEATABLE READ or by using the lock hint HOLDLOCK in the SELECT portion of the DECLARE CURSOR statement. Used outside of cursors, lock hints and the effects of transaction isolation levels come into play only if a transaction is in effect (BEGIN TRAN or *SET IMPLICIT_TRANSACTIONS ON*). But with cursors, the shared locks would be held until the cursor is closed in these cases, even if an explicit transaction is pending. Here is an example of a cursor that will hold shared locks while the cursor is open, ensuring that another user cannot update the fetched row:

```
SET TRANSACTION ISOLATION LEVEL REPEATABLE READ
DECLARE my_curs SCROLL CURSOR FOR SELECT au_id, au_lname
    FROM authors
OPEN my_curs
FETCH ABSOLUTE 12 FROM my_curs
-- Pause to create window for other connection.
-- From other connection, try to update the row. E.g.,
-- UPDATE authors SET au_lname='Newest val' WHERE au_id='648-92-1872'
-- The update will be blocked by a SH_PAGE lock until this cursor is
-- closed. Refetch the row next and see that it has not changed.
-- The CLOSE cursor will release the SH_PAGE lock.
WAITFOR DELAY "00:00:20"
FETCH RELATIVE 0 FROM my_curs
-- RELATIVE 0 = "freshen" current row
CLOSE my_curs
DEALLOCATE my_curs
```

In this example, I am reading data only, not modifying it. If you are doing positioned updates or deletes, you will often want to group all the cursor operations as a single transaction. To do that, you use an explicit BEGIN TRAN. The fetch will request a shared lock, and the lock will be retained only if the isolation level is Repeatable Read (or higher) or if the HOLDLOCK hint is used. If neither of those is the case, you will still be operating under optimistic concurrency control.

The following example shows optimistic concurrency control within a transaction. I added a couple of delays so that you can go to another connection and watch the locks. You'll see that the SH_PAGE (shared page) locks are not held, although, of course, the EX_PAGE (exclusive page) locks, once issued, are held until the cursor completes. This example also terminates the cursor and rolls back the transaction if either of the two update or fetch operations fail.

```
-- Be sure the default setting is in effect
SET TRANSACTION ISOLATION LEVEL READ COMMITTED
DECLARE my_curs SCROLL CURSOR FOR SELECT au_id, au_lname
    FROM authors
OPEN my_curs
BEGIN TRAN

FETCH FIRST FROM my_curs
IF (@@FETCH_STATUS <> 0) -- If not a valid fetch, get out
    GOTO OnError
-- Delay for 10 secs so can verify from another connection
-- and see no lock held using sp_lock
WAITFOR DELAY "00:00:10"

UPDATE authors SET au_lname='Row1 Name' WHERE CURRENT OF my_curs

IF (@@ERROR <> 0)
    GOTO OnError

FETCH LAST FROM my_curs

IF (@@FETCH_STATUS <> 0) -- If not a valid fetch, get out
    GOTO OnError

-- Delay for 10 secs so can verify from another connection
-- and see holding the EX_PAGE lock from previous update
WAITFOR DELAY "00:00:10"

UPDATE authors SET au_lname='LastRow Name' WHERE CURRENT OF my_curs
IF (@@ERROR <> 0)
    GOTO OnError
COMMIT TRAN
IF (@@ERROR=0)
PRINT 'Committed Transaction'
GOTO Done
OnError:
PRINT 'Rolling Back Transaction'
ROLLBACK TRAN
Done:
CLOSE my_curs
DEALLOCATE my_curs
```

The above example uses a transaction, but it still uses optimistic concurrency control. If you want to be sure that a row doesn't change once you've fetched it, you need to hold the shared locks. You can do this either via the HOLDLOCK hint in the SELECT statement or by setting the isolation level to Repeatable Read (or Serializable), as in the example on the following page.

```
SET TRANSACTION ISOLATION LEVEL REPEATABLE READ
DECLARE my_curs SCROLL CURSOR FOR SELECT au_id, au_lname
    FROM authors
OPEN my_curs
BEGIN TRAN

FETCH FIRST FROM my_curs
IF (@@FETCH_STATUS <> 0) -- If not a valid fetch, get out
    GOTO OnError
-- Delay for 10 secs so can verify from another connection
-- and see SH_PAGE lock is held
WAITFOR DELAY "00:00:10"

UPDATE authors SET au_lname='Newer Row1 Name'
    WHERE CURRENT OF my_curs

IF (@@ERROR <> 0)
    GOTO OnError

FETCH LAST FROM my_curs

IF (@@FETCH_STATUS <> 0) -- If not a valid fetch, get out
    GOTO OnError

-- Delay for 10 secs so can verify from another connection
-- and see holding the EX_PAGE lock from previous update, and
-- SH_PAGE from most recent FETCH
WAITFOR DELAY "00:00:10"

UPDATE authors SET au_lname='Newer LastRow Name'
    WHERE CURRENT OF my_curs
IF (@@ERROR <> 0)
    GOTO OnError

COMMIT TRAN
IF (@@ERROR=0)
    PRINT 'Committed Transaction'
GOTO Done

OnError:
PRINT 'Rolling Back Transaction'
ROLLBACK TRAN

Done:
CLOSE my_curs
DEALLOCATE my_curs
```

In this example, because I hold shared locks, I can be sure that a row I fetch will not be changed by another user while the transaction is in process. However, I cannot be sure that I will be able to update the row. If you take the example above and run it simultaneously in two ISQLW.EXE windows, you'll almost certainly get the following error in one of the two windows:

```
Msg 1205, Level 13, State 2
Your server command (process id 14) was deadlocked with another
process and has been chosen as deadlock victim. Re-run your command
```

This is a classic *conversion deadlock,* which occurs when each process holds a shared lock on a page and each needs an exclusive lock on the same page. Neither can get the exclusive lock because of the other process's shared lock. No matter how long the two processes wait, no resolution will occur, because neither can ever get the lock it needs. SQL Server will terminate one of the processes so that the other can conclude. (Chapter 13, "Locking," describes such deadlocks in considerably more detail.) To avoid conversion deadlocks, you should use update locks instead of shared locks for any data you are reading if you intend to update it later. An update lock does not prevent another process from reading the data, but it ensures that the holder of the update lock is next in line for an exclusive lock for that resource and thus eliminates the conversion deadlock problem by serializing access for the update lock resource.

Here is a modification to the previous example that now uses update locks, not shared locks, with the UPDLOCK hint in the SELECT statement. If I run 2 (or even 200) instances of this simultaneously, I will not get a deadlock. The update lock makes the multiple instances run serially, since they must queue and wait for the update lock:

```
-- I will use update locks, which are held until the end regardless.
-- So I do not require REPEATABLE READ.
SET TRANSACTION ISOLATION LEVEL READ COMMITTED

DECLARE my_curs SCROLL CURSOR FOR SELECT au_id, au_lname
    FROM authors (UPDLOCK)
OPEN my_curs
BEGIN TRAN

FETCH FIRST FROM my_curs
IF (@@FETCH_STATUS <> 0) -- If not a valid fetch, get out
    GOTO OnError
-- Delay for 10 secs to increase chances of deadlocks
WAITFOR DELAY "00:00:10"

UPDATE authors SET au_lname='Newer Row1 Name'
    WHERE CURRENT OF my_curs
```

```
IF (@@ERROR <> 0)
    GOTO OnError

FETCH LAST FROM my_curs

IF (@@FETCH_STATUS <> 0) -- If not a valid fetch, get out
    GOTO OnError

-- Delay for 10 secs to increase chances of deadlocks
WAITFOR DELAY "00:00:10"

UPDATE authors SET au_lname='Newer LastRow Name'
    WHERE CURRENT OF my_curs
IF (@@ERROR <> 0)
    GOTO OnError

COMMIT TRAN
IF (@@ERROR=0)
    PRINT 'Committed Transaction'
GOTO Done

OnError:
PRINT 'Rolling Back Transaction'
ROLLBACK TRAN

Done:
CLOSE my_curs
DEALLOCATE my_curs
```

NOTE If you didn't do an explicit BEGIN TRAN in the example above, you would still get a UPD lock on the page under the most recently fetched row. This lock would then move to subsequent pages as the fetch continued.

Choosing optimistic currency control or locking

Whether you choose to use optimistic concurrency control, hold shared locks, or hold update locks will depend on the degree to which you are experiencing update conflicts or deadlocks. If the system is lightly updated or the updates tend to be quite dispersed and few conflicts occur, optimistic concurrency control gives the best concurrency since locks are not held. But some updates will be rejected, and you'll have to decide how you want to deal with that issue. If updates are frequently being rejected, you'll likely move to the more pessimistic and traditional mode of locking. Holding shared locks prevents rows from being changed by someone else, but it could well lead to deadlocks. If you are getting frequent deadlocks, you should probably move to using update locks.

Note that the FOR UPDATE OF modifier of the DECLARE statement does not affect locking behavior, and it does not mean that update locks will be used. The modifier's only purpose in version 6.5 is to allow you to ensure that the cursor will be updateable and that the user has the necessary permissions to make updates. If a cursor cannot be updated, you'll get an error message when a cursor is declared with FOR UPDATE. I would prefer that if FOR UPDATE OF is specified, update locks rather than shared locks would be requested on the fetched data, although there is certainly a case to be made for not doing it this way. Although FOR UPDATE OF is specified, an update might never be actually made. If no update occurs, using shared locks is a win because someone else can still declare the same cursor and there is no need to serialize the running of that batch. Concurrency is therefore increased.

You should also realize that you do not have to issue the modifier FOR UPDATE OF to be able to do positioned updates via the cursor. You can update a cursor that did not have the FOR UPDATE OF modifier specified as long as the underlying declared cursor is updateable. As I mentioned earlier, a SELECT statement cannot be updated if it uses an aggregate function such as GROUP BY, HAVING, UNION, or CASE. But you will not get an error message stating that the SELECT statement cannot be updated until you actually try to do an update. By specifying FOR UPDATE OF in the DECLARE statement, you'll find out right away if the SELECT cannot be updated. I recommend that you always specify FOR UPDATE OF for any cursor that you might later update.

If you will usually be updating fetched rows and there is contention for updates, I suggest that you use the UPDLOCK hint to make it clear that you want update locks to be allowed. Yes, this will serialize access to that resource, but the alternative is a high incidence of rejected updates with optimistic concurrency control or deadlocks with holding shared locks. Both of those will require a lot of retries, which is wasteful. Using update locks in this type of scenario probably will be both the simplest application to write and will give you the best throughput for your system.

A final comment regarding concurrency options. If you use FOR UPDATE, you can update any column in the cursor. (And you might be able to update any column if you don't specify the option at all, but you won't know that until you try the positioned update.) But if you use the FOR UPDATE OF *column_list* syntax and then try to update a column that is not in your specified list, you will get error message 16932.

SUMMARY

This chapter described scrollable cursors in detail. Cursors are important tools that help you bridge the gap of impedance mismatch between the set-oriented world of SQL Server and traditional record-oriented programming languages. Used properly, cursors are invaluable. Overused or used inappropriately, they can cause you to have a bad experience with SQL Server. SQL Server provides fully scrollable, updateable cursors. Typically, other mainstream products provide only forward-only cursors; if they do allow full scrolling, they do not allow updates. The cursor capabilities in SQL Server are far richer than any other RDBMS as of this writing. SQL Server cursors implement and go well beyond all the functionality in ANSI SQL-92, which specifies that a scrollable cursor must be read-only, a limitation that's not present in SQL Server.

SQL Server has four main cursor models: static, keyset, dynamic, and forward-only. Cursors can be accessed via syntax used directly in Transact-SQL or via function calls used in the programming interfaces to SQL Server (ODBC, DB-Library, and so on). These two types of cursors are called Transact-SQL cursors and API server cursors. Transact-SQL cursors are typically used if a batch or stored procedure must do some row-by-row processing. API server cursors are often used and are often appropriate for scrolling applications. Cursors allow positioned updates and deletes. They can use optimistic concurrency control or locking (also known as pessimistic concurrency control). This chapter focused on the Transact-SQL syntax as a general discussion of the capabilities of cursors. However, the key points are relevant no matter what cursor interface you use with SQL Server. After reading this chapter, you should have better insight into cursors, their capabilities, and their suggested uses.

12

Transact-SQL Examples and Brainteasers

Introduction

In this chapter, I'll present some examples of relatively common programming needs that aren't necessarily as simple as you might hope. If you find a solution here for something you need to do, that's great. But my real hope is that you gain some insight into the power and flexibility of Transact-SQL. For some examples, I show multiple solutions, often with different performance characteristics. Keep in mind in your own work that there often are many different ways to solve a problem.

Using Triggers to Implement Referential Actions

As was discussed in Chapter 6, SQL Server implements FOREIGN KEY (or REFERENCES) constraints. If you attempt a data modification that would break a relationship—for example, you attempt to delete the primary key row[1] while foreign key references exist—the data modification is disallowed and the command is aborted. In other words, no action is taken—in fact, ANSI SQL-92 refers to this as the NO ACTION referential action. (Colloquially, NO ACTION is often referred to as RESTRICT, although technically this is incorrect. ANSI uses the term "RESTRICT" for some security and permissions issues.) Three additional referential actions are included in the SQL-92 specification for UPDATE and DELETE operations; the four actions are NO ACTION, SET NULL, SET DEFAULT, and CASCADE.

---

1. A FOREIGN KEY constraint can of course be directed toward a UNIQUE constraint, not just a PRIMARY KEY constraint. But there is no performance difference if the referenced table is instead declared using UNIQUE. In this section, I will refer only to PRIMARY KEY in the referenced table for simplicity.

- NO ACTION *Don't allow the action to be performed if the FOREIGN KEY constraint would be violated.* This is the only referential action implemented by SQL Server 6.5 for a declared FOREIGN KEY constraint, and it's the only action that must be implemented for a product to claim to be "SQL-92 conformant."

- SET NULL *Instead of preventing the data modification from occurring, update the referencing table so that the foreign key columns are set to NULL.* Obviously, this requires that the columns were defined to allow NULL.

- SET DEFAULT *Instead of preventing the data modification from occurring, update the referencing table so that the foreign key columns are set to their DEFAULT values.* The columns must have had DEFAULT values defined.

- CASCADE *Instead of preventing the data modification from occurring, update the referencing table so that the foreign key columns are set to the same values that the primary key was changed to, or delete the referencing rows entirely if the primary key row is deleted.*

A declared FOREIGN KEY constraint, rather than a trigger, is generally your best choice to implement the NO ACTION case. I recommend using the constraint for ease of use and to eliminate the possibility of a bug in a trigger that you write. Although no significant performance difference will usually exist between using a constraint or using a properly written trigger, sometimes the trigger can be faster. This is because any update of a column involved in a declared FOREIGN KEY constraint results in a deferred update, while you can often still use a Direct mode delete/insert with a trigger that enforces the constraint. (See Chapter 8, "Modifying Data," for more information.) Triggers can be used to implement any of the other referential actions not currently available with declared FOREIGN KEY constraints.

> **NOTE** Using a trigger also offers the ability to specially customize the tables at hand. For example, you can customize the error messages to make them more informative than the generic messages you'll receive with a violation of a declared constraint.

Recall that constraint violations are tested before triggers fire. If a constraint violation is detected, the statement is aborted and execution never gets to the trigger (and the trigger will never fire). Therefore, you cannot use a declared FOREIGN KEY constraint to ensure that a relationship will never be violated and then also use a trigger to perform a cascading action (or other such action). To make this possible, triggers would need to both take on enforcement of the FOREIGN KEY relationship and carry out the referential action. You can and should still declare PRIMARY KEY or UNIQUE on the table to be referenced, however. It's relatively simple to write triggers to perform referential actions, as I will show in the examples here. And for readability, you can still declare the FOREIGN KEY constraint in your CREATE TABLE scripts but then alter it to NO CHECK so that it is not enforced. By doing this, you will ensure that the constraint will still appear in the output of *sp_help <table>* and similar procedures.

> **NOTE** Although I'm about to show you how to write triggers to perform referential actions, I want to first urge you to consider another option altogether. If you want to define constraints and still also have update and delete capability beyond NO ACTION, a good alternative to using triggers is to use stored procedures that exclusively perform the update and delete operations. A stored procedure could easily perform the referential action desired (within the scope of a transaction) before the constraint would be violated. No violation of the constraint would occur since the corresponding "fix-up" operation would have already been performed in the stored procedure. If an INSERT or UPDATE statement were directly issued (and that could be prevented in the first place by not granting such permissions), the FOREIGN KEY constraint would still ensure that the relationship was not violated.

It's important that you remember that a FOREIGN KEY constraint affects *two* tables, not just one. It affects the *referenced* table (the table with the primary key that is being pointed to) as well as the *referencing* table (the table with the foreign key pointing to the other table). While the constraint is declared on the referencing table, a modification that affects the primary key of the referenced table is always checking to determine whether the constraint has been violated. A declared foreign key results in checks of the following conditions any time a data modification occurs in either the referencing or referenced table. None of the following actions is allowed by a FOREIGN KEY constraint:

- Inserting a row in a referencing table so that the value of a foreign key does not match a primary key value in the referenced table.

- Updating a foreign key value in a row in a referencing table when no matching primary key value is in the referenced table.

- Updating a primary key value in a row in a referenced table so that a foreign key in a row in the referencing table no longer has a matching primary key value.

- Deleting a row in a referenced table so that a foreign key in a row in the referencing table no longer has a matching primary key value.

As an example of using triggers to implement a referential action, suppose rather than just implementing NO ACTION I want to implement ON DELETE CASCADE and ON UPDATE SET DEFAULT for the foreign key relationship between *titleauthor* and *titles*. I would need to create the following three triggers (or suitable alternatives):

```
-- 1. INSERT and UPDATE trigger on referencing table.
-- Disallow any insert or update if the foreign key title_id
-- here in the referencing table titleauthor does not match
-- the primary key title_id in the referenced table titles.
CREATE TRIGGER INS_UPD_titleauthor
    ON titleauthor
    FOR INSERT, UPDATE
AS
-- Do any rows exist in the inserted table that do not have
-- a matching id in titles?
IF EXISTS
    (SELECT * FROM inserted WHERE inserted.title_id NOT IN
        (SELECT titles.title_id FROM titles) )
    BEGIN
    RAISERROR('No matching title found. Statement will be
aborted.', 16, 1)
    ROLLBACK TRAN
    END
GO


-- 2. If primary key in referenced table titles is changed,
-- update any rows in titleauthor to the DEFAULT value.
-- This implements ON UPDATE SET DEFAULT. Notice this trigger could
-- be easily changed to set the column to NULL instead of DEFAULT,
-- which would implement ON UPDATE SET NULL.
CREATE TRIGGER UPD_titles
    ON titles
    FOR UPDATE
AS
    DECLARE @counter int
    IF UPDATE(title_id)
        BEGIN
        UPDATE titleauthor
        SET titleauthor.title_id=DEFAULT
        FROM titleauthor, deleted
        WHERE titleauthor.title_id=deleted.title_id

        SELECT @COUNTER=@@ROWCOUNT
        -- If the trigger resulted in modifying rows of
        -- titleauthor, raise an informational message
```

```
    IF (@counter > 0)
        RAISERROR('%d rows of titleauthor were updated to
DEFAULT title_id as a result of an update to titles table',
10, 1, @counter)
        END
GO


-- 3. DELETE of referenced table titles will CASCADE to referencing
-- table titleauthor and delete any rows that referenced the row
-- deleted
CREATE TRIGGER DelCascadeTrig
    ON titles
    FOR DELETE
AS
    DECLARE @counter int
    DELETE titleauthor
    FROM titleauthor, deleted
    WHERE titleauthor.title_id=deleted.title_id
    SELECT @counter=@@ROWCOUNT

    IF (@counter > 0)
        RAISERROR('%d rows of titleauthor were deleted as a result
of a delete to the titles table', 10, 1, @counter)
GO
```

> **NOTE** In order for these examples to run, you would need to drop or suspend the existing FOREIGN KEY constraints on these two tables as well as on a couple of others (*sales* and *roysched*) that reference them. The sample code on the accompanying CD-ROM does this.

The following example shows a cascading update trigger on the *titles* (referenced) table that updates all rows in the *titleauthor* table with matching foreign key values. The cascading update is tricky. It requires that you associate both the before and after values (from the inserted and deleted pseudotables) to the referencing table. In a cascading update, you are by definition changing that primary key or unique value. This means that typically the cascading update will work only if one row of the referenced table is updated. If you change the values of multiple primary keys in the same update statement, you will have lost the ability to correctly associate the referencing table. You can easily restrict an update of a primary key to not affect more than one row using the @@ROWCOUNT global variable, as shown on the following page.

```
CREATE TRIGGER UpdCascadeTrig1
    ON titles
    FOR UPDATE
AS
    DECLARE @num_affected int, @title_id varchar(11),
        @old_title_id varchar(11)
    SELECT @num_affected=@@ROWCOUNT
    IF (@num_affected=0)     -- No rows affected, so nothing to do
        RETURN

    IF UPDATE(title_id)
        BEGIN
        IF (@num_affected=1)
            BEGIN
            SELECT @title_id=title_id FROM inserted
            SELECT @old_title_id=title_id FROM deleted
            UPDATE titleauthor
            SET title_id=@title_id
            FROM titleauthor
            WHERE titleauthor.title_id=@old_title_id
            SELECT @num_affected=@@ROWCOUNT
            RAISERROR ('Cascaded update in titles of Primary Key
from %s to %s to %d rows in titleauthor', 10, 1, @old_title_id,
@title_id, @num_affected)
            END
        ELSE
            BEGIN
            RAISERROR ('Cannot update multiple Primary Key values
                in a single statement due to Cascading Update
                trigger in existence.', 16, 1)
            ROLLBACK TRANSACTION
            END
        END
```

The inability to update more than one primary key value at a time is not a limitation—if anything, it might save you from making a mistake. You would not typically want to make mass updates to a primary key. If you have declared a PRIMARY KEY or UNIQUE constraint (as you should), mass updates would usually not work because of the constraint's need for uniqueness. Although such an update would be rare, you might want to set the value to some expression, such as multiplying all Customer ID values by 1000 in order to renumber them. For such unusual cases, you could easily perform the UPDATE in a loop, one row at a time, and use a cascading trigger.

Although it is logically the correct thing to do, you are not required to create a PRIMARY KEY or UNIQUE constraint on a referenced table. And there is no hard-and-fast requirement that the constraint be unique. (However, not making it unique would violate the logical relationship.) I bring this up only to point out that the "one row only" restriction in the cascading trigger above is a tad more restrictive than is necessary. If uniqueness were not required on *title_id,* the restriction could be eased a bit to allow the update to affect more than one row in the *titles* table, as long as all affected rows are updated to the same value for *title_id.* When uniqueness on *titles.title_id* is required (as should usually be the case), the two restrictions are actually redundant. Since all affected rows will be updated to the same value for *title_id,* I no longer have to worry about associating the new value in the referencing table, *titleauthor.* There would be only one value. The trigger would look like this:

```
CREATE TRIGGER UpdCascadeTrig2
    ON titles
    FOR UPDATE
AS
    DECLARE @num_distinct int, @num_affected int,
        @title_id varchar(11)
    SELECT @num_affected=@@ROWCOUNT

    IF (@num_affected=0)     -- No rows affected, so nothing to do
        RETURN

    IF UPDATE(title_id)
        BEGIN
        SELECT @num_distinct=COUNT(DISTINCT title_id) FROM inserted
        IF (@num_distinct=1)
            BEGIN
            -- Temporarily make it return just one row
            SET ROWCOUNT 1
            SELECT @title_id=title_id FROM inserted
            SET ROWCOUNT 0       -- Revert ROWCOUNT back
            UPDATE titleauthor
            SET titleauthor.title_id=@title_id
            FROM titleauthor, deleted
            WHERE titleauthor.title_id=deleted.title_id
            SELECT @num_affected=@@ROWCOUNT
            RAISERROR ('Cascaded update of Primary Key to value in
titles to %d rows in titleauthor', 10, 1, @title_id, @num_affected)
            END
        ELSE
            BEGIN
            RAISERROR ('Cannot cascade a multi-row update that
changes title_id to multiple different values.', 16, 1)
            ROLLBACK TRANSACTION
            END
        END
```

Using *COUNT(DISTINCT title_id) FROM inserted* ensures that even if multiple rows were affected they all were set to the same value. So *@title_id* can pick up the value of *title_id* for any row in the inserted table. I use the *SET ROWCOUNT 1* statement to limit the subsequent SELECT to only the first row. This is not required, but it's better practice and a small optimization. If I didn't use *SET ROWCOUNT 1*, the assignment would still work correctly, but every inserted row would be selected and I'd end up with the value of the last row (which, of course, is the same value as any other row). It's not good practice to do a SELECT or a variable assignment that assumes just one row is returned unless you're sure only one row *can* be returned. I could have also assured a single returned row by doing the assignment like this:

```
SELECT @title_id=title_id FROM titles GROUP BY title_id HAVING
    COUNT(DISTINCT title_id)=1
```

Because the previous IF allows only one distinct *title_id* value, I am assured that the SELECT statement above will return only one row.

In the two triggers in the code on the previous page, I first check to determine whether any rows were updated; if none were updated, I do a RETURN. This illustrates something that might not be obvious: a trigger fires even if no rows were affected by the update. Recall that the plan for the trigger is appended to the rest of the statements' execution plan. You won't know the number of rows affected until execution. This is a feature, not a bug; it allows you to take action when you expect some rows to be affected but none are. Recall that having no rows affected is not an error in this case. However, you can use a trigger to return an error when this occurs. The two triggers in the above examples use RAISERROR to provide either a message that indicates the number of rows cascaded or an error message. If no rows were affected, I wouldn't want any messages to be raised, so I opted to return from the trigger immediately.

Brainteasers

Sometimes a reasonable and straightforward question posed in English can be difficult to write in SQL. In Chapter 7, "Querying Data," I provided my favorite illustration of this—the query, "Show me the stores that have sold every book title." Although it's an extremely simple question in English, it's quite tricky to get right in SQL. If you think this example reveals some deficiencies in SQL as a query language, I agree with you. But enhancements to the SQL standard, many of which have not yet been implemented, as well as existing and future extensions unique to SQL Server keep shortening the list of deficiencies. The addition of CASE, allowing the use of DISTINCT and UNION in views and subqueries, and full outer-join support in the last two releases dramatically chopped down my complaint list. In this section, I will show some more examples based on real-world queries that I've encountered. When applicable, I'll try to show both a formulation that uses pure ANSI-standard SQL as well as one that might use a SQL Server extension.

Generating Test Data

Nothing tricky here, but because generating test data is a common need and some of the later solutions depend on such test data, I'll show a few simple techniques that I'll use, without further comment. (Of course, it's preferable to use an actual data set of representative values for testing rather than using generated test data before deploying a production application. But sometimes generating test data is much more practical and suited to the need for something "quick and dirty.")

If you need a bunch of rows and you don't care about their distribution of values, it's easy to create a table using default values for every column and the Identity property on a column that would act as the primary key. You can then set a counter to loop as many times as necessary to achieve the number of rows you want, and then execute the special INSERT...DEFAULT VALUES statement. Here is an example that will create 1000 rows in table *xyz*:

```
-- Method 1.  Simple DEFAULT values on table.
CREATE TABLE xyz
(
col1    int             PRIMARY KEY IDENTITY(1, 1) NOT NULL,
col2    int             NOT NULL DEFAULT 999,
col3    char(10)        NOT NULL DEFAULT 'ABCEFGHIJK'
)
GO

DECLARE @counter int
SELECT @counter=1
WHILE (@counter <= 1000)
    BEGIN
    INSERT xyz DEFAULT VALUES
    SELECT @counter=@counter+1
    END
```

```
SELECT * FROM xyz

col1    col2    col3
----    ----    ----------
1       999     ABCEFGHIJK
2       999     ABCEFGHIJK
3       999     ABCEFGHIJK
4       999     ABCEFGHIJK
5       999     ABCEFGHIJK
⋮
999     999     ABCEFGHIJK
1000    999     ABCEFGHIJK
```

Usually, you want some distribution in the data values; the RAND() function, the modulo operator, and the functions CONVERT(), CHAR(), and REPLICATE() come in handy. The RAND() function is a standard random number generator that's just like the function used in C, which RAND() calls. Because RAND() returns a *float* with a value between 0 and 1, you typically will multiply it and convert the result to an integer so that you can use the modulo operator to indicate the range of values. For example, if I want a random integer from 0 through 9999, the following expression will work nicely:

```
(CONVERT(int, RAND() * 100000) % 10000)
```

If I want to include negative numbers (for example, a range from −9999 through 9999), I can use RAND() to flip a coin to generate 0 or 1 (by doing modulo 2) and then use CASE to multiply half of the numbers by −1.

```
CASE
WHEN CONVERT(int, RAND() * 1000) % 2 = 1 THEN
    (CONVERT(int, RAND() * 100000) % 10000 * -1)
ELSE CONVERT(int, RAND() * 100000) % 10000
END
```

To use character data, you should generate a random number from 0 through 25 (since the alphabet has 26 letters) and add that number to 64, which is the ASCII value for *A*. The result is then the ASCII value for a character from *A* through *Z*. You can perform this operation a specified number of times or in a loop to generate as many characters as you want. Usually, after you've indicated a few lead characters, you can use filler characters for the rest of a field. The REPLICATE() function is a nice tool to use for the filler. (If you want to be sure that different executions of the routine return different random numbers, you should *seed* the RAND() function by including an integer value between the parentheses. You can use @@spid, the *object_id* of the newly created table, or any other "almost-random" integer value.)

The most common way to generate character data is to use local variables for the generated data inside a WHILE loop that does INSERT statements using the variables. Here is an example:

```
-- Method 2.    Generate random data in a loop.
IF (ISNULL(OBJECT_ID('random_data'), 0)) > 0
    DROP TABLE random_data
GO

CREATE TABLE random_data
(
col1        int PRIMARY KEY,
col2        int,
col3        char(15)
)
GO

DECLARE @counter int, @col2 int, @col3 char(15)
/* Insert 1000 rows of data  */
-- Seed random generator
SELECT @counter=0, @col2=RAND(@@spid + cpu + physical_io)
FROM master..sysprocesses where spid=@@spid

WHILE (@counter < 1000)
    BEGIN
    SELECT @counter=@counter + 10,    -- Sequence numbers by 10
    @col2=
        CASE          -- Random integer between -9999 and 9999
            WHEN CONVERT(int, RAND() * 1000) % 2 = 1
            THEN (CONVERT(int, RAND() * 100000) % 10000 * -1)
            ELSE CONVERT(int, RAND() * 100000) % 10000
        END,
    @col3=        -- Four random letters followed by random fill letter
        CHAR((CONVERT(int, RAND() * 1000) % 26 ) + 65) -- 65 is 'A'
            + CHAR((CONVERT(int, RAND() * 1000) % 26 ) + 65)
            + CHAR((CONVERT(int, RAND() * 1000) % 26 ) + 65)
            + CHAR((CONVERT(int, RAND() * 1000) % 26 ) + 65)
            + REPLICATE(CHAR((CONVERT(int, RAND() * 1000) % 26 )
            + 65), 11)

    INSERT random_data VALUES (@counter, @col2, @col3)
    END
GO
```

```
-- Limit number of rows for illustration only
SELECT * FROM random_data WHERE COL1 < 200

col1    col2    col3
----    -----   ----------------
10      -5240   LXDSGGGGGGGGGGGG
20      9814    TTPD00000000000
30      3004    IEYXEEEEEEEEEEEE
40      -9377   MITDAAAAAAAAAAAA
50      -3823   ISGMUUUUUUUUUUUU
60      -4249   DHZQQQQQQQQQQQQQ
70      2335    XBJKEEEEEEEEEEEE
80      -4570   ILYWNNNNNNNNNNNN
90      4223    DHISDDDDDDDDDDDD
100     -3332   THXLWWWWWWWWWWWW
110     -9959   ALHFLLLLLLLLLLLL
120     4580    BCZNGGGGGGGGGGGG
130     6072    HRTJ00000000000
140     -8274   QPTKWWWWWWWWWWWW
150     8212    FBQABBBBBBBBBBBB
160     8223    YXAPLLLLLLLLLLLL
170     -9469   LIHCAAAAAAAAAAAA
180     -2959   GYKRZZZZZZZZZZZZ
190     7677    KWWBJJJJJJJJJJJJ
```

You can also set up the table with a DEFAULT that includes the random data expression and then use the DEFAULT VALUES statement. This method is sort of a combination of the above two methods. With this method, all the complexity of the random values is segregated to the CREATE TABLE command and the INSERT is again a simple loop using DEFAULT VALUES. Notice in the example below that it is possible to use a CASE statement in a DEFAULT clause of a CREATE TABLE command:

```
-- Method 3.   Generate random values for DEFAULT.
CREATE TABLE random_data
(
col1    int     PRIMARY KEY IDENTITY(10,10) NOT NULL,
col2    int     NOT NULL DEFAULT CASE
                -- Random integer between -9999 and 9999
                WHEN CONVERT(int, RAND() * 1000) % 2 = 1
                THEN (CONVERT(int, RAND() * 100000) % 10000 * -1 )
                ELSE CONVERT(int, RAND() * 100000) % 10000
                END,
```

```
col3    char(15) NOT NULL DEFAULT
                 CHAR((CONVERT(int, RAND() * 1000) % 26 ) + 65)
                 -- 65 is 'A'
                 + CHAR((CONVERT(int, RAND() * 1000) % 26 ) + 65)
                 + CHAR((CONVERT(int, RAND() * 1000) % 26 ) + 65)
                 + CHAR((CONVERT(int, RAND() * 1000) % 26 ) + 65)
                 + REPLICATE(CHAR((CONVERT(int, RAND() * 1000)
                    % 26) + 65), 11)
)
GO

DECLARE @counter int
SELECT @counter=1
WHILE (@counter <= 1000)
    BEGIN
    INSERT random_data DEFAULT VALUES
    SELECT @counter=@counter + 1
    END

-- Limit number of rows for illustration only
SELECT * FROM random_data WHERE COL1 <= 200


col1    col2    col3
----    -----   ---------------
10      -6358   LCNLMMMMMMMMMMM
20      -2284   SSAITTTTTTTTTTT
30      -1498   NARJAAAAAAAAAAA
40      -1908   EINLZZZZZZZZZZZ
50      -716    KNIOFFFFFFFFFFF
60      -8331   WZPRYYYYYYYYYYY
70      -2571   TMUBEEEEEEEEEEE
80      -7965   LILNCCCCCCCCCCC
90      9728    IXLOBBBBBBBBBBB
100     878     IPMPPPPPPPPPPPP
110     -2649   QXPAPPPPPPPPPPP
120     -4443   EBVHKKKKKKKKKKK
130     6133    VRJWXXXXXXXXXXX
140     -5154   HMHXLLLLLLLLLLL
150     -480    RNLVQQQQQQQQQQQ
160     -2655   SEHXTTTTTTTTTTT
170     -8204   JVLHZZZZZZZZZZZ
180     -3201   PTWGBBBBBBBBBBB
190     -7529   TDCJXXXXXXXXXXX
200     2622    ANLDHHHHHHHHHHH
```

Getting Top *n* Values

The standard MAX() and MIN() aggregate functions make it simple to get the maximum or minimum value of a data set. But it's not so simple to get, for example, the top five or bottom five values using standard SQL. By performing a rank ordering of the values by nesting a SELECT inside the select list, you can accomplish such a task. For each row in the outer SELECT, the inner SELECT returns the number of rows in the table with an equal or greater value in the column being ranked. This "rows rank" value is then correlated back to the main query. Having materialized the rank as a value, you can restrict its value in the WHERE clause to the number in which you're interested. Here is a view using standard SQL to assign ranks to each row in the table. The view can be queried to obtain any rank.

```
CREATE VIEW ranked_sales (rank, title_id, ytd_sales, title)
AS
SELECT (SELECT COUNT(DISTINCT ISNULL(T2.ytd_sales, -1))
FROM titles AS T2
WHERE ISNULL(T1.ytd_sales, -1) <= ISNULL(T2.ytd_sales, -1))
    AS rank,
T1.title_id,
ytd_sales,
T1.title
FROM titles AS T1
GO

SELECT title_id, ytd_sales, title FROM RANKED_SALES WHERE rank <= 5
    ORDER BY rank
GO
```

```
title_id    ytd_sales    title
--------    ---------    ----------------------------------------
MC3021      22246        The Gourmet Microwave
BU2075      18722        You Can Combat Computer Stress!
TC4203      15096        Fifty Years in Buckingham Palace Kitchens
PC1035      8780         But Is It User Friendly?
BU1032      4095         The Busy Executive's Database Guide
BU7832      4095         Straight Talk About Computers
PC8888      4095         Secrets of Silicon Valley
TC7777      4095         Sushi, Anyone?
```

The view above is not needed; I used it for readability. Instead, this operation can be performed in a single SELECT statement, although this makes it more difficult to compute the rank column and then not select it. You can treat the view as a derived table (which I like to think of as an *unnamed view*) and eliminate the rank column. By doing so, you don't need to create the view and performance is the same. Here is the solution, without the view, which returns the same result set as the previous solution:

```
SELECT
Z.title_id,
Z.ytd_sales,
Z.title
FROM
(SELECT (SELECT COUNT(DISTINCT ISNULL(T2.ytd_sales, -1))
    FROM titles AS T2
WHERE ISNULL(T1.ytd_sales, -1) <= ISNULL(T2.ytd_sales, -1))
    AS rank,
T1.title_id,
ytd_sales,
T1.title
FROM titles as T1) AS Z
WHERE Z.rank <= 5
ORDER BY Z.rank
GO
```

Notice that to get accurate results I had to decide what to do with a NULL value for *ytd_sales*. (Those NULLs always complicate things!) In this example, I treated a NULL as less than zero, using the handy ISNULL() function. Be aware that this query can return more than five rows, as it did here. (Multiple rows might be tied for fifth—or whatever—place, so all tied rows are returned.) This query performs acceptably well with the small *titles* table. But with a large table, you wouldn't be happy with the results. The query nested within the select list is essentially executed for every row of the table. (You can see this by watching the scan count when turning on the STATISTICS IO SET option.) This is an expensive operation and of course, the query is not too intuitive in the first place. There is a better way. SQL Server has an extension, *SET ROWCOUNT n*, that greatly simplifies this type of query. If you order on the columns for which you want to query and use SET ROWCOUNT to indicate the number of places you're interested in, it will be much faster to find the top five rows than it would be using the tricky correlated view or derived table query presented above. (Note that you can easily change the problem to BOTTOM *n* by changing the ORDER BY to ASCENDING rather than DESCENDING.)

```
SET ROWCOUNT 5    -- Limit to first five rows
SELECT
title_id,
ytd_sales,
title
FROM titles ORDER BY ytd_sales DESC
```

```
SET ROWCOUNT 0     -- Revert setting

title_id    ytd_sales    title
--------    ---------    ----------------------------------------
MC3021      22246        The Gourmet Microwave
BU2075      18722        You Can Combat Computer Stress!
TC4203      15096        Fifty Years in Buckingham Palace Kitchens
PC1035      8780         But Is It User Friendly?
BU1032      4095         The Busy Executive's Database Guide
```

Because NULL sorts low by default in SQL Server, you don't need to do anything special to deal with it if you're looking for the five highest values. But regardless of NULL, the semantics of this query are not quite the same as those of the prior query. The ROWCOUNT query will never return more than five rows, even if ties exist. This approach is best suited to queries in which no ties exist, for queries in which you have additional column(s) in the ORDER BY to break the ties, or for those in which you simply don't care about ties. (There is a ROWCOUNT solution that you can use for ties as well, as you'll see in a moment.)

The SET ROWCOUNT approach is much faster than the approach with a SELECT nested within the select list that correlates back to the main query. In addition to not needing to iterate on the inner nested SELECT (the chief reason for the performance advantage), SET ROWCOUNT can be further optimized internally. To resolve the query for all rows in the table (not just the top five), SQL Server might have chosen to scan the table and then perform a sort, even if an index existed that could eliminate the sort. This is because it would be more expensive to visit the leaf page of the index—and then go to a data page, back to an index page, back to a data page, and so on—than it would be to simply make one pass through the data.

If only a few rows at the top of the requested result set will be needed, however, the strategy of using the index will usually be the better one. The SQL Server optimizer will automatically consider the setting of SET ROWCOUNT in formulating its query plan, and the setting can influence the optimizer to choose the index strategy. Even if this did not occur, execution would stop when the number of chosen rows equals the ROWCOUNT value. SQL Server does not resolve the entire query and then just throw away rows past n. Once it reaches n, it stops.

I can easily modify this query to return the bottom five rows rather than the top five. I simply change the *ORDER BY <column> DESC* to *ORDER BY <column> ASC*. (If you do this, you will need to consider NULL, because NULL sorts low. You can filter NULL out, treat it as low, or do whatever makes sense for your required semantics. I, of course, would define the column to not allow NULL in the first place, making this concern moot.)

As I mentioned before, the ROWCOUNT query does not deal with ties. If you want to show all rows with values greater than or equal to the fifth value, you can still use SET ROWCOUNT in a somewhat different way. Recall that it's legal, but often a mistake, to assign a value to a variable from a query that can return more than one row. The variable will retain the value of the last row returned. You can take advantage of this by first using SET ROWCOUNT, assigning the variable, and then querying based on that value. (It's probably a good idea to add a comment to your query that makes it clear that you are intentionally allowing the assignment to be done on a query returning multiple rows. That might save someone else from thinking it's a bug later.) For example, to find the top five *ytd_sales* values, and considering the possibility of ties, I can declare a variable and then set its value with a query ordered by *ytd_sales* with *SET ROWCOUNT 5*. At the end of the assignment, the variable retains the value of the fifth row of that query. I can then query all rows that have a value greater than or equal to the value of the variable:

```
DECLARE @ytd_sales money
SET ROWCOUNT 5    -- I want the following variable to take on the
                  -- value of the fith row
SELECT @ytd_sales=ytd_sales FROM titles ORDER BY ytd_sales DESC
SET ROWCOUNT 0    -- Revert setting
SELECT
title_id, ytd_sales, title
FROM titles WHERE ytd_sales >= @ytd_sales
ORDER BY ytd_sales DESC
GO
```

```
title_id    ytd_sales    title
--------    ---------    -----------------------------------------
MC3021      22246        The Gourmet Microwave
BU2075      18722        You Can Combat Computer Stress!
TC4203      15096        Fifty Years in Buckingham Palace Kitchens
PC1035      8780         But Is It User Friendly?
BU1032      4095         The Busy Executive's Database Guide
BU7832      4095         Straight Talk About Computers
PC8888      4095         Secrets of Silicon Valley
TC7777      4095         Sushi, Anyone?
```

Getting Rankings

The rankings problem is closely related to the previous Top *n* example. In fact, a common and workable (although slow) solution for rankings is simply a slight variation of the query that used a correlated SELECT in the select list in the previous example. There is no SET ROWCOUNT magic bullet for rankings; however, some other clever solutions are available, so I'll treat this case independently and present a few new and different solutions here.

Let's look again at the *titles* table. Suppose I want to assign a rank value to all rows in the table based on their *ytd_sales* values (with the highest value getting the top rank). In the Top *n* example, I assumed there was a need to show *n* number of rows, but I did not assign a rank number. In this example, I want to assign a rank number. The two approaches differ in how they deal with ties, and before choosing the approach you'll use, you need to decide how you want to treat ties (if ties are possible).

Approach 1: The standard SQL approach using a view

This is the same view presented as the first Top *n* example. Performance will suffer on large tables because a table must be successively scanned for every row. Ties will be assigned equal rank—unique numbers are not guaranteed unless the column(s) you are ranking on are known to be unique. In this example, the next nontie value's rank will be one higher, not lower. Notice that in this case I have altered the view to completely disregard rows with NULL values for *ytd_sales*.

```
CREATE VIEW ranked_sales (rank, title_id, ytd_sales, title)
AS
SELECT
(SELECT COUNT(DISTINCT T2.ytd_sales) FROM titles AS T2
    WHERE T2.ytd_sales >= T1.ytd_sales ) AS rank,
title_id,
ytd_sales,
title
FROM titles AS T1 WHERE ytd_sales IS NOT NULL
GO

SELECT * FROM ranked_sales ORDER BY rank
GO
```

rank	title_id	ytd_sales	title
1	MC3021	22246	The Gourmet Microwave
2	BU2075	18722	You Can Combat Computer Stress!
3	TC4203	15096	Fifty Years in Buckingham Palace Kitchens
4	PC1035	8780	But Is It User Friendly?
5	BU1032	4095	The Busy Executive's Database Guide
5	BU7832	4095	Straight Talk About Computers
5	PC8888	4095	Secrets of Silicon Valley
5	TC7777	4095	Sushi, Anyone?

6	PS3333	4072	Prolonged Data Deprivation: Four Case Studies
7	BU1111	3876	Cooking with Computers: Surreptitious Balance Sheets
8	PS7777	3336	Emotional Security: A New Algorithm
9	PS2091	2045	Is Anger the Enemy?
10	MC2222	2032	Silicon Valley Gastronomic Treats
11	PS1372	375	Computer Phobic AND Non-Phobic Individuals: Behavior Variations
11	TC3218	375	Onions, Leeks, and Garlic: Cooking Secrets of the Mediterranean
12	PS2106	111	Life Without Fear

Approach 2: The standard SQL approach without a view

This approach is basically the same as the view approach, but it saves you the step of creating the view, at the possible cost of it being a bit harder to understand. Instead of a view, a derived table is used (by adding a SELECT in the FROM clause). Performance is identical to the view approach, however (that is, it's not too good). The results are identical to the result set of the view approach, so I won't bother repeating them here:

```
SELECT rank, title_id, ytd_sales, title
FROM (SELECT
    T1.title_id,
    ytd_sales,
    T1.title,
        (SELECT COUNT(DISTINCT T2.ytd_sales) FROM titles AS T2
        WHERE T1.ytd_sales <= T2.ytd_sales) AS rank
        FROM titles AS T1) AS X
    WHERE ytd_sales IS NOT NULL
    ORDER BY rank
```

Approach 3: The temp table with identity approach and all unique rankings

If you want to assign a unique number even in the case of ties, or if you know that ties will not occur, you can create a temporary table with an identity column and then SELECT into the temporary table in an ordered fashion. This gives you a materialized table with rankings. This approach is conceptually easy to understand and it's fast. Its only downside is that it will not recognize tied values. It's not ANSI-standard SQL, but instead the approach takes advantage of SQL Server–specific features. This approach can prove useful with other sequential operations, as I'll show later.

```
CREATE TABLE #ranked_order
(
rank            int         IDENTITY NOT NULL PRIMARY KEY,
title_id        char(6)     NOT NULL,
ytd_sales       int         NOT NULL,
title           varchar(80) NOT NULL
)
GO

INSERT #ranked_order
    SELECT title_id, ytd_sales, title FROM titles WHERE ytd_sales
    IS NOT NULL ORDER BY ytd_sales DESC

SELECT * FROM #ranked_order

DROP TABLE #ranked_order

rank  title_id  ytd_sales  title
----  --------  ---------  ----------------------------------
1     MC3021    22246      The Gourmet Microwave
2     BU2075    18722      You Can Combat Computer Stress!
3     TC4203    15096      Fifty Years in Buckingham Palace
                           Kitchens
4     PC1035    8780       But Is It User Friendly?
5     BU1032    4095       The Busy Executive's Database Guide
6     BU7832    4095       Straight Talk About Computers
7     PC8888    4095       Secrets of Silicon Valley
8     TC7777    4095       Sushi, Anyone?
9     PS3333    4072       Prolonged Data Deprivation: Four Case
                           Studies
10    BU1111    3876       Cooking with Computers: Surreptitious
                           Balance Sheets
11    PS7777    3336       Emotional Security: A New Algorithm
12    PS2091    2045       Is Anger the Enemy?
13    MC2222    2032       Silicon Valley Gastronomic Treats
14    PS1372    375        Computer Phobic AND Non-Phobic
                           Individuals: Behavior Variations
15    TC3218    375        Onions, Leeks, and Garlic: Cooking
                           Secrets of the Mediterranean
16    PS2106    111        Life Without Fear
```

Approach 4: The temp table with identity approach and ties

Depending on how you want to deal with ties, the temporary table with identity approach can be slightly changed to make a nice fit. With standard SQL solutions, if the query focused on four rows and two rows tied for second rank, one row would have the rank of first, two rows second, and one row third. No row would be fourth, even though four rows exist. A reasonable alternative way to rank them would be to make one row first, two rows second, no row third, and one row fourth. This, for example, is how the standings in a golf tournament would be posted if two players tied for second place. The standard SQL solutions do not rank in this way, but the temporary-table approach can be made to do so quite easily. After populating the temporary table, you can query the table for the lowest rank for a given value and correlate that value back to the main query with a nested SELECT. This approach is efficient and might be ideal if you prefer to deal with ties in this way:

```
-- Approach 4A.  Create a temp table with an identity, and then do
-- an ordered select to populate it.
-- Do a nested select correlated back to itself to find the lowest
-- rank for a given value.
CREATE TABLE #ranked_order
(
rank        int         IDENTITY NOT NULL,
title_id    char(6)     NOT NULL,
ytd_sales   int         NOT NULL,
title       varchar(80) NOT NULL
)
GO

INSERT #ranked_order
    SELECT title_id, ytd_sales, title FROM titles WHERE ytd_sales
        IS NOT NULL ORDER BY ytd_sales DESC


SELECT B.rank, A.title_id, B.ytd_sales , A.title
FROM
(SELECT MIN(T2.rank) AS rank, T2.ytd_sales FROM #ranked_order AS T2
    GROUP BY T2.ytd_sales) AS B,
#ranked_order AS A
WHERE A.ytd_sales=B.ytd_sales
ORDER BY B.rank

DROP TABLE #ranked_order

rank title_id ytd_sales title
---- -------- --------- ----------------------------------------
1    MC3021   22246     The Gourmet Microwave
2    BU2075   18722     You Can Combat Computer Stress!
3    TC4203   15096     Fifty Years in Buckingham Palace Kitchens
4    PC1035   8780      But Is It User Friendly?
```

```
5      BU1032    4095      The Busy Executive's Database Guide
5      BU7832    4095      Straight Talk About Computers
5      PC8888    4095      Secrets of Silicon Valley
5      TC7777    4095      Sushi, Anyone?
9      PS3333    4072      Prolonged Data Deprivation: Four Case
                           Studies
10     BU1111    3876      Cooking with Computers: Surreptitious
                           Balance Sheets
11     PS7777    3336      Emotional Security: A New Algorithm
12     PS2091    2045      Is Anger the Enemy?
13     MC2222    2032      Silicon Valley Gastronomic Treats
14     PS1372    375       Computer Phobic AND Non-Phobic
                           Individuals: Behavior Variations
14     TC3218    375       Onions, Leeks, and Garlic: Cooking
                           Secrets of the Mediterranean
16     PS2106    111       Life Without Fear
```

I can slightly modify the SELECT on the temporary table and explicitly indicate where ties exist and how many values were tied. (The creation and population of the temporary table are identical here, so I'll show just the SELECT statement.)

```
-- Approach 4B. Same as above, explicitly noting the ties.
SELECT B.rank,
CASE B.number_tied
    WHEN 1 THEN ' '
    ELSE '('+ CONVERT(varchar, number_tied) + ' Way Tie)'
    END AS tie,
A.title_id,
B.ytd_sales,
A.title
FROM
(SELECT MIN(T2.rank) AS rank, COUNT(*) AS number_tied, T2.ytd_sales
FROM #ranked_order AS T2 GROUP BY T2.ytd_sales) AS B,
#ranked_order AS A
WHERE A.ytd_sales=B.ytd_sales
ORDER BY B.rank
```

```
rank   tie            title_id   ytd_sales   title
----   -----------    --------   ---------   --------------------------
1                     MC3021     22246       The Gourmet Microwave
2                     BU2075     18722       You Can Combat Computer
                                             Stress!
3                     TC4203     15096       Fifty Years in Buckingham
                                             Palace Kitchens
4                     PC1035     8780        But Is It User Friendly?
```

5	(4 Way Tie)	BU1032	4095	The Busy Executive's Database Guide
5	(4 Way Tie)	BU7832	4095	Straight Talk About Computers
5	(4 Way Tie)	PC8888	4095	Secrets of Silicon Valley
5	(4 Way Tie)	TC7777	4095	Sushi, Anyone?
9		PS3333	4072	Prolonged Data Deprivation: Four Case Studies
10		BU1111	3876	Cooking with Computers: Surreptitious Balance Sheets
11		PS7777	3336	Emotional Security: A New Algorithm
12		PS2091	2045	Is Anger the Enemy?
13		MC2222	2032	Silicon Valley Gastronomic Treats
14	(2 Way Tie)	PS1372	375	Computer Phobic AND Non-Phobic Individuals: Behavior Variations
14	(2 Way Tie)	TC3218	375	Onions, Leeks, and Garlic: Cooking Secrets of the Mediterranean
16		PS2106	111	Life Without Fear

Approach 5: The cursor approach

As a rule, I try to perform an operation using a set operation (preferably using a single SELECT statement) wherever possible. The nonprocedural set operation is usually simpler to write (which means there's less chance of introducing a bug), and it lets the SQL Server optimizer find an efficient way to carry out the request. This usually makes the set operation more efficient. In some cases, however, the problem is a naturally sequential operation. The SELECT statement (set operation) might require a correlated subquery or self-join to solve the problem, such that data is visited multiple times to provide the result. This kind of problem lends itself well to a cursor approach, since it can be solved with one pass through the data. Using a cursor can be a more efficient solution than using the single SELECT statement for sequential operations like these. The ranking operation is such a case. (However, it is not faster than the temporary table solutions.) The cursor solution is a more programmatic, procedural solution than the SELECT statements used in Approaches 1 and 2. It takes more work to correctly program it, but the solution allows you considerable control and flexibility. In the approaches discussed above, I have identified three rules for dealing with ties. Using a cursor approach, I can choose any of the three rules to best fit my needs, making only a small change.

1. Give ties a duplicate rank value, and rank the next nonduplicate value one higher.

2. Always assign a unique rank value even in the case of ties.

3. Assign a duplicate rank value, but rank the next nonduplicate value according to its overall standing, not simply one higher.

Approach 5A: Cursor with Rule 1 for ties

```
-- Approach 5A.  Use cursors and deal with ties like the standard
-- SQL approaches did.
-- Assign a duplicate rank value, and simply increment the next
-- nonduplicate.
DECLARE @rank int, @title_id char(6), @ytd_sales int,
    @title varchar(80), @last_rank int, @last_ytd_sales money,
    @counter int
SELECT @rank=1, @last_rank=1, @last_ytd_sales=0, @counter=1
DECLARE rank_cursor CURSOR FOR SELECT title_id, ytd_sales,
    title FROM titles WHERE ytd_sales IS NOT NULL
    ORDER BY ytd_sales DESC
OPEN rank_cursor
FETCH NEXT FROM rank_cursor INTO @title_id, @ytd_sales, @title
WHILE (@@FETCH_STATUS <> -1)
BEGIN

    IF (@counter=1)     -- For first row, just display values
                        -- and set last values
        BEGIN
        SELECT rank=@rank, title_id=@title_id,
            ytd_sales=@ytd_sales, title=@title
        END
    ELSE
        BEGIN
        -- If current sales is same as last, assign the same rank
        IF (@ytd_sales=@last_ytd_sales)
            SELECT rank=@last_rank, title_id=@title_id,
                ytd_sales=@ytd_sales, title=@title
        ELSE    -- Otherwise, increment the rank
            BEGIN
            SELECT rank=@last_rank+1, title_id=@title_id,
                ytd_sales=@ytd_sales, title=@title
            SELECT @rank=@last_rank + 1
            END
        END
```

```
-- Set values to current row
SELECT @counter=@counter + 1, @last_rank=@rank,
    @last_ytd_sales=@ytd_sales
FETCH NEXT FROM rank_cursor INTO @title_id, @ytd_sales, @title
END

CLOSE rank_cursor
DEALLOCATE rank_cursor
```

rank	title_id	ytd_sales	title
1	MC3021	22246	The Gourmet Microwave
2	BU2075	18722	You Can Combat Computer Stress!
3	TC4203	15096	Fifty Years in Buckingham Palace Kitchens
4	PC1035	8780	But Is It User Friendly?
5	BU1032	4095	The Busy Executive's Database Guide
5	BU7832	4095	Straight Talk About Computers
5	PC8888	4095	Secrets of Silicon Valley
5	TC7777	4095	Sushi, Anyone?
6	PS3333	4072	Prolonged Data Deprivation: Four Case Studies
7	BU1111	3876	Cooking with Computers: Surreptitious Balance Sheets
8	PS7777	3336	Emotional Security: A New Algorithm
9	PS2091	2045	Is Anger the Enemy?
10	MC2222	2032	Silicon Valley Gastronomic Treats
11	PS1372	375	Computer Phobic AND Non-Phobic Individuals: Behavior Variations
11	TC3218	375	Onions, Leeks, and Garlic: Cooking Secrets of the Mediterranean
12	PS2106	111	Life Without Fear

Approach 5B: Cursor with Rule 2 for ties

```
-- Approach 5B.  Use cursors and always assign next row an
-- incremented rank value, even if it's a tie.
DECLARE @rank int, @title_id char(6), @ytd_sales int,
    @title varchar(80)
SELECT @rank=1
DECLARE rank_cursor CURSOR FOR SELECT title_id, ytd_sales, title
FROM titles WHERE ytd_sales IS NOT NULL ORDER BY ytd_sales DESC
OPEN rank_cursor
FETCH NEXT FROM rank_cursor INTO @title_id, @ytd_sales, @title
```

```
WHILE (@@FETCH_STATUS <> -1 )
    BEGIN
    SELECT rank=@rank, title_id=@title_id, ytd_sales=@ytd_sales,
        title=@title
    SELECT @rank=@rank + 1
FETCH NEXT FROM rank_cursor INTO @title_id, @ytd_sales, @title
END

CLOSE rank_cursor
DEALLOCATE rank_cursor
```

rank	title_id	ytd_sales	title
1	MC3021	22246	The Gourmet Microwave
2	BU2075	18722	You Can Combat Computer Stress!
3	TC4203	15096	Fifty Years in Buckingham Palace Kitchens
4	PC1035	8780	But Is It User Friendly?
5	BU1032	4095	The Busy Executive's Database Guide
6	BU7832	4095	Straight Talk About Computers
7	PC8888	4095	Secrets of Silicon Valley
8	TC7777	4095	Sushi, Anyone?
9	PS3333	4072	Prolonged Data Deprivation: Four Case Studies
10	BU1111	3876	Cooking with Computers: Surreptitious Balance Sheets
11	PS7777	3336	Emotional Security: A New Algorithm
12	PS2091	2045	Is Anger the Enemy?
13	MC2222	2032	Silicon Valley Gastronomic Treats
14	PS1372	375	Computer Phobic AND Non-Phobic Individuals: Behavior Variations
15	TC3218	375	Onions, Leeks, and Garlic: Cooking Secrets of the Mediterranean
16	PS2106	111	Life Without Fear

Approach 5C: Cursor with Rule 3 for ties

```
-- Approach 5C.  Use cursors and deal with ties by assigning a
-- duplicate rank value, but then make the next nonduplicate
-- value its overall standing, not simply a rank of one higher.
-- For example, if 2 rows qualify for rank #1, then the 3rd row
-- will be #3 and no row will have rank #2.
```

```
DECLARE @rank int, @title_id char(6), @ytd_sales int,
    @title varchar(80), @last_rank int, @last_ytd_sales money,
    @counter int
SELECT @rank=1, @last_rank=1, @last_ytd_sales=0, @counter=1
DECLARE rank_cursor CURSOR FOR SELECT title_id, ytd_sales, title
FROM titles WHERE ytd_sales IS NOT NULL ORDER BY ytd_sales DESC
OPEN rank_cursor
FETCH NEXT FROM rank_cursor INTO @title_id, @ytd_sales, @title
WHILE (@@FETCH_STATUS <> -1)
    BEGIN

    IF (@counter=1)       -- For first row, just display values and
                          -- set last values
        BEGIN
        SELECT rank=@rank, title_id=@title_id,
            ytd_sales=@ytd_sales, title=@title
        END
    ELSE
        BEGIN
        -- If current sales are same as last, assign the same rank
        IF (@ytd_sales=@last_ytd_sales)
            SELECT rank=@last_rank, title_id=@title_id,
                ytd_sales=@ytd_sales, title=@title
        ELSE      -- Otherwise, set the rank to the overall
                  -- counter of how many rows have been visited
            BEGIN
            SELECT @rank=@counter
            SELECT rank=@rank, title_id=@title_id,
                ytd_sales=@ytd_sales, title=@title
            END
        END
    -- Set values to current row
    SELECT @counter=@counter+1, @last_rank=@rank,
        @last_ytd_sales=@ytd_sales
    FETCH NEXT FROM rank_cursor INTO @title_id, @ytd_sales, @title
    END

CLOSE rank_cursor
DEALLOCATE rank_cursor
GO
```

```
rank   title_id   ytd_sales   title
----   --------   ---------   ----------------------------------------
1      MC3021     22246       The Gourmet Microwave
2      BU2075     18722       You Can Combat Computer Stress!
3      TC4203     15096       Fifty Years in Buckingham Palace Kitchens
4      PC1035     8780        But Is It User Friendly?
5      BU1032     4095        The Busy Executive's Database Guide
5      BU7832     4095        Straight Talk About Computers
5      PC8888     4095        Secrets of Silicon Valley
5      TC7777     4095        Sushi, Anyone?
9      PS3333     4072        Prolonged Data Deprivation: Four Case
                              Studies
10     BU1111     3876        Cooking with Computers: Surreptitious
                              Balance Sheets
11     PS7777     3336        Emotional Security: A New Algorithm
12     PS2091     2045        Is Anger the Enemy?
13     MC2222     2032        Silicon Valley Gastronomic Treats
14     PS1372     375         Computer Phobic AND Non-Phobic
                              Individuals: Behavior Variations
14     TC3218     375         Onions, Leeks, and Garlic: Cooking
                              Secrets of the Mediterranean
16     PS2106     111         Life Without Fear
```

From the Author...

Here's a warning regarding the cursor solution: Unlike the other approaches, the cursor solution results in multiple result sets because of the multiple FETCH operations. This means that there are as many result sets as rows (16 in the example here). Every result set requires that metadata is passed between the server and client. With a slow network connection, this will become a notice-able problem that will be a drag on performance. The cursor solution could be a good performer when executed on the SQL Server or on your LAN, but it will be a poor performer over your dial-up lines if the result set contains many rows.

Of the approaches presented above, I'd recommend that you use the temporary table approaches, if they meet your needs for dealing with ties. They are intui-tive and efficient, and they return a single result set. The temporary table solu-tions are the fastest of those presented here. I'm not aware of faster solutions, but I don't claim that there cannot be other, even better, solutions. If you find one, please let me know.

Time Series Problems: Finding Differences Between Intervals

Suppose I have recorded data for measured temperatures in a table with two columns. The first column is the datetime at which the measurement was taken, and the second column is the temperature that was measured. I'd like to find the change in temperature between one interval and the next, and I want it expressed as the absolute value of the number of degrees that changed per minute. There is no preexisting primary key, such as *measurement_id*. It's unlikely that duplicate measurements exist for any single time (that is, it's likely that the datetime field is unique), but we don't know this for sure. And the durations between data measurements are not consistent. In fact, the data was not inserted in order (although a clustered index exists, so if data were selected without an ORDER BY, the data would seem to be in order). Like the rankings problem presented earlier, this problem can be solved using standard (but tricky) SQL, by using a temporary table, or by using cursors. In fact, you can think of this as another type of rankings problem—but in this problem, you want to see the differences between adjacent ranks.

First I'll set up the table with some fairly random data. I don't care about the realism of the temperature values or about how much they might fluctuate in even a few minutes. (So if you run this example and see temperatures of −100° F or a 40-degree change in temperature in five minutes, don't worry about it. I never said these readings were being done on Earth, did I?)

NOTE I think it's worthwhile to set up the routine to generate test data, even though in this case I could manually insert 20 rows of data faster than it took to do the routine to generate the data. However, once the routine is working and you've checked your solution on the small table, its easy to change the constant in the WHILE loop to add much more data. This is important, since many solutions seem to perform well for small amounts of data but can degrade badly with large amounts of data. (This can be especially true if a solution uses correlated subqueries or self-joins, or if it does table scans.)

```
-- diff_intervals.sql
IF NULLIF(OBJECT_ID('measurements'), 0) > 0
    DROP TABLE measurements
GO

CREATE TABLE measurements
(
when_taken      datetime      NOT NULL,
temperature     numeric(4, 1)  -- (Fahrenheit)
)
```

```
CREATE CLUSTERED INDEX measurements_idx01
    ON measurements (when_taken)
GO

DECLARE @counter int, @whendate datetime, @val numeric(4, 1)
    @randdiff smallint, @randmins smallint
SELECT @counter=1, @whendate=GETDATE(), @val=50.0
/* Insert 20 rows of data.  Change constant if you want more.   */
WHILE (@counter <= 20)
    BEGIN
    INSERT measurements VALUES (@whendate, @val)
    -- Get a random number between -20 and 20 for change in
    -- temperature. This will be added to the previous value,
    -- plus RAND() again to give a fractional component.
      SELECT
      @randdiff=CASE
      WHEN CONVERT(int, RAND() * 100) % 2 = 1 THEN
          CONVERT(int, RAND() * 1000) % 21 * -1
      ELSE CONVERT(int, RAND() * 1000) % 21
      END,
    -- Get a random number between 0 and 10080 (the number of mins
    -- in a week). This will be added to the current GETDATE()
    -- value. Since GETDATE() returns a value to the millisecond,
    -- it's very unlikely there will ever be a duplicate, though it
    -- is possible if the result of the addition and the current
    -- GETDATE() value happen to collide with the addition in
    -- another row. (I am intentionally letting that be the case;
    -- not assuming that dups are automatically prevented.)
        @randmins=CONVERT(int, RAND() * 100000) % 10080
    SELECT @counter=@counter + 1,
    @whendate=DATEADD(mi, @randmins, GETDATE()),
    @val=@val + @randdiff + RAND()
    END

SELECT * FROM measurements

when_taken                 temperature
-------------------        -----------
Nov 21 1996 12:05PM        50.0
Nov 21 1996 1:36PM         13.5
Nov 21 1996 3:16PM         46.3
Nov 21 1996 7:49PM         -15.0
Nov 22 1996 12:44AM        32.1
Nov 22 1996 11:37AM        -21.1
Nov 22 1996 5:46PM         12.3
Nov 22 1996 7:52PM         -16.5
Nov 23 1996 3:49AM         7.6
Nov 23 1996 12:31PM        -15.9
```

```
Nov 23 1996 2:12PM     -13.2
Nov 23 1996 7:24PM     -13.0
Nov 24 1996 6:37AM      36.7
Nov 25 1996 10:49PM     -3.6
Nov 27 1996 3:51AM      46.7
Nov 27 1996 7:12AM      -2.6
Nov 27 1996 12:00PM    -13.6
Nov 27 1996 2:37PM      59.0
Nov 27 1996 9:35PM      -8.3
Nov 27 1996 11:58PM     55.1
```

Approach 1: Standard SQL

This approach is similar to the rankings solution. I assign a ranking and then join it back to itself by the ranking value less 1. If duplicate datetime values exist, this approach would still compute the differential to the previous (nonduplicate) measurement, which might or might not be how you'd want to deal with it. As was the case in the rankings solution, I can use this approach either as a view or as a derived table. I think it's easier to understand it as a view, so I'll present it that way here.

As in the Top *n* and rankings problems, this approach is a good brainteaser, but it's not a good performer if the table is anything but very small. (And this approach would be problematic if duplicate datetime values could exist.)

```
CREATE VIEW rankdates (when_taken, temperature, daterank)
AS
SELECT when_taken, temperature,
    (SELECT COUNT(DISTINCT when_taken) FROM measurements AS T1
    WHERE T1.when_taken <= T0.when_taken) AS rank
FROM measurements AS T0
GO

SELECT * FROM rankdates ORDER BY daterank
GO
```

```
when_taken              temperature  daterank
-------------------     -----------  --------
Nov 21 1996 12:05PM     50.0         1
Nov 21 1996  1:36PM     13.5         2
Nov 21 1996  3:16PM     46.3         3
Nov 21 1996  7:49PM    -15.0         4
Nov 22 1996 12:44AM     32.1         5
Nov 22 1996 11:37AM    -21.1         6
Nov 22 1996  5:46PM     12.3         7
Nov 22 1996  7:52PM    -16.5         8
Nov 23 1996  3:49AM      7.6         9
Nov 23 1996 12:31PM    -15.9         10
Nov 23 1996  2:12PM    -13.2         11
```

```
Nov 23 1996  7:24PM    -13.0        12
Nov 24 1996  6:37AM     36.7        13
Nov 25 1996 10:49PM     -3.6        14
Nov 27 1996  3:51AM     46.7        15
Nov 27 1996  7:12AM     -2.6        16
Nov 27 1996 12:00PM    -13.6        17
Nov 27 1996  2:37PM     59.0        18
Nov 27 1996  9:35PM     -8.3        19
Nov 27 1996 11:58PM     55.1        20
```

```
-- Correlate each value with the one right before it
SELECT
P1_WHEN=V1.when_taken, P2_WHEN=V2.when_taken,
P1=V1.temperature, P2=V2.temperature,
DIFF=(V2.temperature - V1.temperature)
FROM rankdates AS V1 LEFT OUTER JOIN rankdates AS V2
ON (V2.daterank=V1.daterank + 1)
GO
```

P1_WHEN	P2_WHEN	P1	P2	DIFF
Nov 21 1996 12:05PM	Nov 21 1996 1:36PM	50.0	13.5	-36.5
Nov 21 1996 1:36PM	Nov 21 1996 3:16PM	13.5	46.3	32.8
Nov 21 1996 3:16PM	Nov 21 1996 7:49PM	46.3	-15.0	-61.3
Nov 21 1996 7:49PM	Nov 22 1996 12:44AM	-15.0	32.1	47.1
Nov 22 1996 12:44AM	Nov 22 1996 11:37AM	32.1	-21.1	-53.2
Nov 22 1996 11:37AM	Nov 22 1996 5:46PM	-21.1	12.3	33.4
Nov 22 1996 5:46PM	Nov 22 1996 7:52PM	12.3	-16.5	-28.8
Nov 22 1996 7:52PM	Nov 23 1996 3:49AM	-16.5	7.6	24.1
Nov 23 1996 3:49AM	Nov 23 1996 12:31PM	7.6	-15.9	-23.5
Nov 23 1996 12:31PM	Nov 23 1996 2:12PM	-15.9	-13.2	2.7
Nov 23 1996 2:12PM	Nov 23 1996 7:24PM	-13.2	-13.0	0.2
Nov 23 1996 7:24PM	Nov 24 1996 6:37AM	-13.0	36.7	49.7
Nov 24 1996 6:37AM	Nov 25 1996 10:49PM	36.7	-3.6	-40.3
Nov 25 1996 10:49PM	Nov 27 1996 3:51AM	-3.6	46.7	50.3
Nov 27 1996 3:51AM	Nov 27 1996 7:12AM	46.7	-2.6	-49.3
Nov 27 1996 7:12AM	Nov 27 1996 12:00PM	-2.6	-13.6	-11.0
Nov 27 1996 12:00PM	Nov 27 1996 2:37PM	-13.6	59.0	72.6
Nov 27 1996 2:37PM	Nov 27 1996 9:35PM	59.0	-8.3	-67.3
Nov 27 1996 9:35PM	Nov 27 1996 11:58PM	-8.3	55.1	63.4
Nov 27 1996 11:58PM	(null)	55.1	(null)	(null)

NOTE If you're interested in the derived table solution, go back to the rankings problem and note the difference between a view and a derived table; it should be easy to see how the derived table solution can be done here as well.

Approach 2: Materialize rankings, and then self-join

Conceptually, this solution is similar to the standard SQL approach. But rather than use a true view, I materialize the rankings as a temporary table, similar to the approach in one of the rankings solutions. Once created, I do the self-join with the temporary table. The advantage, of course, is that I create the rankings only once instead of many times. And creating them once is faster since the identity value simply assigns the rank in the order that the rows are presented.

This solution is an order of magnitude faster than the standard SQL solution. The results are the same, so I won't bother repeating the output. The standard SQL approach takes more than 1700 logical I/Os with this dataset, whereas the temporary table approach here takes only 21 logical I/Os. For anyone who thinks that only physical I/Os are important and that "logical I/Os are free," this is a good example to correct your thinking. Because so little data is involved, only one physical I/O will occur in either of these solutions. But the significant difference in the number of logical I/Os is extremely noticeable; you don't need to time the approaches to see that one is much faster than the other.

```
CREATE TABLE #rankdates (
when_taken datetime,
temperature numeric(4, 1),
daterank int IDENTITY PRIMARY KEY)
GO

INSERT #rankdates (when_taken, temperature)
    SELECT when_taken, temperature
    FROM measurements
    ORDER BY when_taken ASC
GO

SELECT
P1_WHEN=V1.when_taken, P2_WHEN=V2.when_taken,
P1=V1.temperature, P2=V2.temperature,
DIFF=(V2.temperature - V1.temperature)
FROM #rankdates AS V1 LEFT OUTER JOIN #rankdates AS V2
ON (V2.daterank=V1.daterank + 1)
GO
```

Approach 3: Using a cursor

Since Approach 3 truly is a sequential operation, you might expect a cursor to work well here, and it does:

```
DECLARE @lastval int, @currdate datetime, @currval numeric(4, 1),
    @counter int
SELECT @counter=1
DECLARE diffprev CURSOR
FOR SELECT when_taken, temperature FROM measurements
    ORDER BY when_taken ASC
```

```
OPEN diffprev
FETCH NEXT FROM diffprev INTO @currdate, @currval
WHILE (@@FETCH_STATUS <> -1)
BEGIN
    IF (@counter=1)    -- For first row, just get value and return
            SELECT WHEN_TAKEN=@currdate, "CURR_VALUE"=@currval,
                RANK=@counter, "PREV_VALUE"=NULL, "DIFF"=NULL
        ELSE
            SELECT WHEN_TAKEN=@currdate, "CURR_VALUE"=@currval,
                RANK=@counter, "PREV_VALUE"=@lastval,
                "DIFF"=@currval - @lastval
    SELECT @lastval=@currval, @counter=@counter + 1
    FETCH NEXT FROM diffprev INTO @currdate, @currval
END

CLOSE diffprev
DEALLOCATE diffprev
GO
```

From the perspective of logical I/Os, the cursor approach is nearly as efficient as Approach 2, which materializes the rankings using a temporary table and an identity value and then does a self-join. However, over a slow network, the performance of Approach 2 will appear to be an order of magnitude faster than this cursor approach. In this solution, each FETCH is treated as a separate result set; so 20 result sets, each with one row, are present instead of just one result set with 20 rows as in Approach 2. The cursor approach does, however, give you ultimate flexibility. For example, suppose that the time differential between two points is less than five seconds, and you want to throw out that point and use the differential to the next point instead. This would be difficult to write in pure SQL, but it is easy with a cursor.

Keeping Running Totals

The running totals problem can be solved by making some small changes to the techniques used for the time series problems—it's much the same sort of problem. Consider the following table:

```
col1    value    running_tot
----    -----    -----------
1       10       0
2       15       0
3       63       0
4       72       0
5       75       0
```

```
6      20      0
7      21      0
8      34      0
9      76      0
10      2      0
```

I would like to store the running total of the *value* column in the *running_tot* column:

```
col1    value    running_tot
----    -----    -----------
1       10       10
2       15       25
3       63       88
4       72       160
5       75       235
6       20       255
7       21       276
8       34       310
9       76       386
10       2       388
```

You can adapt any of the solutions for the time series problem to work for this problem. But I discovered another solution, a "side-effect" that is known to work with version 6.5—not a committed and documented feature. (In the real world, I'd use this solution with care, since it might not work in a future version.) This highly efficient solution uses only one logical I/O to compute all the values. (No solution can do fewer than one logical I/O.) It uses a single update statement and, within the same statement, increments the column value by the value of the local variable; then it sets the local variable to the resulting current column value. Since processing of the expressions in the UPDATE statement is done left-to-right, this works. And since the rows are scanned and updated in clustered index order, they are processed in the order expected. As I've mentioned, it's always dangerous to rely on any ordering that is not explicit. But this solution will work for version 6.5, and while I would not build it into a production application, it can be useful for ad hoc data-scrubbing–type operations:

```
-- running_tot.sql
DECLARE @run_total int
SELECT @run_total=0
UPDATE running_tot
    SET RUNNING_TOT=value + @run_total, @run_total=RUNNING_TOT
FROM running_tot (1)
-- Used the (1) hint to ensure processing done along the clustered
-- index
```

Sampling Every *n* Rows

I'll leave it as an exercise for the reader to see that the previous time series and difference between interval problems can also be easily adapted for this sampling problem. In this problem, you want to check the value of every *n*th row. For example, suppose you want to find every fifth row. By using a solution that materializes the rankings in a temporary table, you can select from the temporary table with modulus 5. Or, using a cursor solution, you can use *FETCH RELATIVE 5*. Note that the idea of sampling is not too "relational," since there is no logically implied order of rows stored in the table (although physically this exists if a clustered index is present).

Finding Rows with Matching Columns

Suppose you want to look in a table for all rows that have duplicate values in multiple nonkey columns. For example, in the following table, *match_cols,* you want to find duplicate rows (except for *row_num*). It isn't enough to simply identify the *col2* and *col3* values that are duplicates (COUNT and GROUP BY would make that a piece of cake); you must identify the specific rows that contain the duplicates. This is a pretty common need for data-scrubbing–type solutions. In the example below, rows 3 and 10 are such duplicates. (Note that *row_num* is a primary key, so the entire row is never a duplicate. You want to find duplicates across only the other columns.) With only 10 rows in the example below, you can easily spot the other duplicates (rows 4 and 6). But the example on the CD-ROM creates 5000 rows of data, again with letters for *col2* and *col3* of *A* through *D*. (Since there are four letters and two columns, there are 4^2—or 16—possible combinations.) Depending on which solution you choose, this operation can prove expensive for even 5000 rows—not to mention real-world–size datasets of perhaps 5 million rows!

```
row_num    col2    col3
-------    ----    ----
1          A       A
2          C       C
3          B       D
4          D       B
5          D       C
6          D       B
7          A       C
8          A       D
9          B       A
10         B       D
```

Approach 1: The self-join

I find the self-join solution the most intuitive. If I were to try to find matching columns between two different tables, I would almost surely reach for a join, not a subquery, even though I could do it either way. The solution below seems simple to me. Unfortunately, with larger amounts of data, it is not so efficient. It does nested iteration, and the second virtual table must be scanned for each row in the first. With no useful index available for the duplicate columns, this is a full table scan and is unacceptable. Even with a useful index, as exists for the example on the CD-ROM, the second virtual table must be scanned for each row in the first (and "scanned" here does not refer to a full table scan—the index is used), and this is expensive. A table of 5000 rows results in 5000 scans and more than 19,000 logical I/Os. Response time isn't too bad with this number of rows—the results return within a few seconds. But this is a costly solution, and we can do better, as our alternative approaches will show.

```
-- The self-join solution
SELECT DISTINCT A.row_num, A.col2, A.col3
FROM match_cols AS A, match_cols AS B
WHERE A.col2=B.col2 AND A.col3=B.col3 AND A.row_num <> B.row_num
ORDER BY A.col2, A.col3
```

Approach 2: The correlated subquery

I mentioned in describing the problem that using COUNT and GROUP BY makes it easy to find values that are known to have duplicates. So you can use GROUP BY...COUNT as an inner query to identify known duplicate values and then correlate the query to an outer query of the same table to find the specific rows with those values known to have a count greater than 1 (and that, therefore, are duplicates). With few rows (say, a few hundred), the self-join (Approach 1) is faster than this solution. But when querying large numbers of rows, this solution is much faster. The scan counts are about the same for both solutions, but the amount of logical I/Os in Approach 2 is much less. Because the inner query uses the EXISTS operator, the optimizer knows that as soon as one value is found, it can return TRUE. This limits the scan to a great extent. With 5000 rows, the scan count is still a bit more than 5000 (since every row must be correlated to the outer query). But logical I/Os are down to about 10,000—about half that of Approach 1.

```
-- The subquery solution
SELECT A.row_num, A.col2, A.col3 FROM match_cols AS A
WHERE EXISTS
(SELECT B.col2, B.col3 FROM match_cols AS B
    WHERE B.col2=A.col2
    AND   B.col3=A.col3
    GROUP BY B.col2, B.col3 HAVING COUNT(*) > 1)
ORDER BY A.col2, A.col3
```

Approach 3: Materializing the nonunique values, and then joining to the result

Earlier I said that I try to find join solutions rather than subquery solutions and that correlated subquery solutions can be expensive. For this problem, I'd like to have a table with just the known nonunique columns and do a simple equijoin to it. This approach is kind of a hybrid between the self-join and the correlated subquery solutions. Using a temporary table, I can easily do this. (But using a temporary table feels like "cheating" here. So stay tuned for another approach.)

```
-- The temp table solution - materialize rows that are known to
-- have dups
SELECT col2, col3 INTO #mytemp
FROM match_cols
GROUP BY col2, col3 HAVING COUNT(*) > 1

-- Now simply do an equijoin to the temp table
SELECT #mytemp.col2, #mytemp.col3, match_cols.row_num
FROM #mytemp
JOIN match_cols
ON (#mytemp.col2=match_cols.col2 AND #mytemp.col3=match_cols.col3)
ORDER BY 1, 2, 3
```

This solution is fast. Since there are just 16 possible combinations, and thus 16 ways to make duplicates, the temporary table contains only 16 rows. This becomes the outer table for the join. Then the main table, *match_cols,* is scanned (using an index) once for each of those 16 rows. So rather than the scan counts of 5000 we saw in the previous solutions, the scan count here is only 16. And only about 64 logical I/Os occur, far lower than the 10,000 or 19,000 I/Os of the previous solutions. This solution is by far the fastest yet. But it's a procedural solution, and it would be much more satisfying to do this with a pure SQL query that is also efficient.

Approach 4: Using derived tables

This fast, pure SQL solution is conceptually like the prior solution that used a temporary table. But rather than explicitly create and populate the temporary table, a derived table is used. The derived table performs the query for the duplicate values (again finding 16). Then *match_cols* is joined to the derived table. After the optimizer chooses the best join order, the table is processed internally, almost identically to the temporary table situation. Using derived tables is a great solution. If this solution immediately came to your mind, you get a gold star.

```
-- The derived table solution
SELECT A.row_num, A.col2, A.col3 FROM match_cols AS A
-- Join the table to a virtual table that has one row for any row
-- combinations known not to be unique (count greater than 1)
```

```
JOIN
(SELECT col2, col3 FROM match_cols AS B
              GROUP BY col2, col3 HAVING COUNT(*) > 1) AS B
ON (A.col2=B.col2 AND A.col3=B.col3)
ORDER BY A.col2, A.col3, A.row_num
```

Related Approach: Data scrubbing

Often, a problem such as "find rows with duplicate columns and delete duplicates" is used for data scrubbing—simply to eliminate duplicate rows. If you want to delete duplicate rows, you can create a new table that has a unique index, with the IGNORE_DUP_KEY option on the columns to be checked for duplicates. Then use the INSERT...SELECT command to populate the new table and discard all the duplicate rows. This is a fast and easy solution. (This solution won't work if you want to identify the rows and not delete them, however. To identify and not delete, you could use the previous solutions and convert them to DELETE operations.) This solution gets rid of duplicates but doesn't identify them:

```
-- Data scrubbing
-- Use a unique index with IGNORE_DUP_KEY to throw out the duplicate
-- rows. This isn't quite a solution to the problem at hand, as it
-- doesn't identify the duplicate rows, but it does eliminate them.
CREATE TABLE #match_cols
(
row_num      int,
col2         char(1),
col3         char(1)
)
GO

CREATE UNIQUE INDEX #match_col2_idx ON #match_cols (col2, col3) WITH
IGNORE_DUP_KEY
GO

-- Note many dups in original table
SELECT "COUNT(*)"=COUNT(*), col2, col3
FROM match_cols
GROUP BY col2, col3
```

COUNT(*)	col2	col3
264	A	A
339	A	B
304	A	C
334	A	D
329	B	A
309	B	B

```
319        B        C
341        B        D
312        C        A
320        C        B
300        C        C
341        C        D
297        D        A
297        D        B
304        D        C
290        D        D


-- Supposedly selects ALL from the original table,
-- but duplicates will get silently thrown away
INSERT #match_cols
    SELECT * FROM match_cols


-- No dups in new table
SELECT "COUNT(*)"=COUNT(*), col2, col3
FROM #match_cols
GROUP BY col2, col3


COUNT(*)    col2    col3
--------    ----    ----
1           A       A
1           A       B
1           A       C
1           A       D
1           B       A
1           B       B
1           B       C
1           B       D
1           C       A
1           C       B
1           C       C
1           C       D
1           D       A
1           D       B
1           D       C
1           D       D
```

Putting Data on a Web Page—The Fast Way

Need a fast way to copy data to a simple but functional Web page? You can choose from among several third-party tools that can do this, but a simple (and free) way is to use the special stored procedure **sp_makewebtask** (which wraps the extended stored procedure, **xp_makewebtask**). This procedure has a GUI front-end—SQL Server Web Assistant—but you can also call it directly. Here I show a simple use of the solution to present a table of authors on a Web page, although you can get as fancy as you want. (Several optional parameters are discussed in the online documentation.) To use this solution, you specify the name of the HTML file to be created and write a query to get the data. You can also specify several formatting options, links to other URLs, and links to pages of related text or image data contained for each row. In this example, the entries in the *pr_info* and *logo* columns are hyperlinks to the actual text and image data:

```
sp_makewebtask @outputfile="c:\tmp\pub_info.htm",
@query="SELECT pub_id, pr_info, pub_id, logo, pub_id FROM pub_info",
@blobfmt="%2%FILE=c:\tmp\pubtxt_.html%4%FILE=c:\tmp\pubimg_.gif"
```

Here's how it looks in Microsoft Internet Explorer:

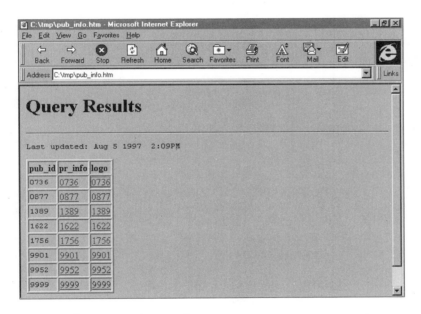

Expanding a Hierarchy— a.k.a. The Bill of Materials Problem

Let's say you want to expand a hierarchy, such as an organization chart; prepare a bill of materials; or navigate a tree structure. This problem doesn't lend itself naturally to standard SQL usage. Suppose I have a simple table of employees. It uses a self-reference such that each employee is associated with his or her manager's row in the same table.

```
CREATE TABLE emp_mgr
(
emp_no        int            NOT NULL PRIMARY KEY,
emp_name      varchar(25)    NOT NULL,
emp_title     varchar(25)    NOT NULL,
mgr_no        int            REFERENCES emp_mgr (emp_no)
)
```

If I want to provide a list of employees, with each employee's manager name and title on the same line, it's easy. A self-join works like this:

```
SELECT
E.emp_no, E.emp_name AS Employee, E.emp_title,
M.mgr_no, M.emp_name AS Manager, M.emp_title AS Mgr_title
FROM
     emp_mgr AS E
JOIN
     emp_mgr AS M
ON (E.mgr_no=M.emp_no)
ORDER BY E.emp_no
```

emp_no	Employee	emp_title	mgr_no	Manager	Mgr_title
16	Dave Edgerton	VP-Operations	99	Mark Burke	President
73	Rick Eckhart	Albany Plant Manager	16	Dave Edgerton	VP-Operations
99	Mark Burke	President	10050	John Smith	CEO
643	Greg Chapman	VP-Sales & Marketing	99	Mark Burke	President
692	Ethel Knoll	Staff Accountant	7437	Rachel Hunt	Senior Cost Accountant
865	Ron Simms	Terre Haute Plant Manager	16	Dave Edgerton	VP-Operations
935	Deb Kerns	Mechanical Engineer	86145	Adam Smale	Chief Engineer
1803	John Jacobs	Cash Flow Management	9543	Jill Hansen	Treasurer
2037	Keith Teeter	Civil Engineer	28762	Jeff Cullerton	Electrical Engineer
2345	Mike Jackson	Charlotte Plant Manager	16	Dave Edgerton	VP-Operations
3260	Lee Chao	VP-R&D	99	Mark Burke	President
4096	Hillary Loews	Staff Accountant	7437	Rachel Hunt	Senior Cost Accountant

4318	Phyllis Brown	VP-Human Resources	99	Mark Burke	President
4378	Kurt Phillips	Electrical Engineer	86145	Adam Smale	Chief Engineer
4673	Kurt Johansen	Fremont Plant Manager	16	Dave Edgerton	VP-Operations
6298	Wes Thomas	Mechanical Engineer	8548	Lee Roberts Johnson	Chief Engineer
6578	Karl Johnson	Chief Engineer	4673	Kurt Johansen	Fremont Plant Manager
7210	Ajay Kumar	Electrical Engineer	9763	Takeshi Sato	Chief Engineer
7437	Rachel Hunt	Senior Cost Accountant	8576	Phil Kertzman	Corporate Controller
8548	Lee Roberts Johnson	Chief Engineer	865	Ron Simms	Terre Haute Plant Manager
8576	Phil Kertzman	Corporate Controller	20240	Sue Ferrel	VP-Finance
9543	Jill Hansen	Treasurer	20240	Sue Ferrel	VP-Finance
9763	Takeshi Sato	Chief Engineer	2345	Mike Jackson	Charlotte Plant Manager
9871	Mike Baker	Staff Accountant	1803	John Jacobs	Cash Flow Management
10050	John Smith	CEO	10050	John Smith	CEO
11456	Paul Good	Civil Engineer	935	Deb Kerns	Mechanical Engineer
20240	Sue Ferrel	VP-Finance	99	Mark Burke	President
23756	Pete Fuller	Civil Engineer	56432	Walt White	Mechanical Engineer
28762	Jeff Cullerton	Electrical Engineer	8548	Lee Roberts Johnson	Chief Engineer
56432	Walt White	Mechanical Engineer	6578	Karl Johnson	Chief Engineer
84521	Leland Teng	Civil Engineer	9763	Takeshi Sato	Chief Engineer
86145	Adam Smale	Chief Engineer	73	Rick Eckhart	Albany Plant Manager
92314	Billy Bob Jones	Mechanical Engineer	7210	Ajay Kumar	Electrical Engineer

From the Author...

This solution is credited to Rick Vicik—at least I learned the technique from him. It uses a temporary table as a stack to keep track of all the items for which processing has begun but is not complete. When an item has been fully traversed, it is removed from the stack. This is a nice approach because it can work to an arbitrary and unknown number of levels. And by slightly modifying it (or making it a procedure and passing parameters), you can start at a given level and end at a given level.

Rick's original solution to this problem can be found in the SQL Server documentation under the topic "Expanding Hierarchies." The following approach is a bit of a refinement that I've made to his solution. Rick's solution was from several years back, before the existence of IDENTITY. It relied on multiple PRINT statements to present the output.

If I want to show the hierarchy and the reporting relationships, it's not so easy. As I've mentioned, returning a bunch of result sets back to the client application is inefficient and should be avoided whenever possible. In the old days, you couldn't really avoid doing it this way. Now, however, I can use a temporary table and sequence it with IDENTITY to hold the order of the reporting relationship. When I finish traversing the hierarchy, I need to join to that temporary table with a single, simple SELECT. (I make use of the SPACE() function and string concatenation to produce a simple report of the following form, showing each employee's reporting relationship. This is not central to the main solution, of course.)

```
Manager -> Employees
John Smith,   CEO
    Mark Burke,   President
        Dave Edgerton,   VP-Operations
            Rick Eckhart,   Albany Plant Manager
                Adam Smale,   Chief Engineer
                    Deb Kerns,   Mechanical Engineer
                        Paul Good,   Civil Engineer
                    Kurt Phillips,   Electrical Engineer
            Ron Simms,   Terre Haute Plant Manager
                Lee Roberts Johnson,   Chief Engineer
                    Wes Thomas,   Mechanical Engineer
                    Jeff Cullerton,   Electrical Engineer
                        Keith Teeter,   Civil Engineer
```

```
        Mike Jackson,   Charlotte Plant Manager
            Takeshi Sato,   Chief Engineer
                Ajay Kumar,   Electrical Engineer
                    Billy Bob Jones,   Mechanical Engineer
                Leland Teng,   Civil Engineer
        Kurt Johansen,   Fremont Plant Manager
            Karl Johnson,   Chief Engineer
                Walt White,   Mechanical Engineer
                    Pete Fuller,   Civil Engineer
    Greg Chapman,   VP-Sales & Marketing
    Lee Chao,   VP-R&D
    Phyllis Brown,   VP-Human Resources
    Sue Ferrel,   VP-Finance
        Phil Kertzman,   Corporate Controller
            Rachel Hunt,   Senior Cost Accountant
                Ethel Knoll,   Staff Accountant
                Hillary Loews,   Staff Accountant
        Jill Hansen,   Treasurer
            John Jacobs,   Cash Flow Management
                Mike Baker,   Staff Accountant
```

Here is the batch, with comments, that produced this hierarchy:

```sql
-- Variables to keep track of reporting level and the current emp
DECLARE @level int, @current int

-- This table will act as a stack. We push employees onto the stack
-- until we process all their reports.
CREATE TABLE #stack
(depth_level int, emp_no int)

-- This temp table will be used to hold the reporting chain.
-- The identity automatically sequences it and allows us to
-- ultimately return the hierarchy as just a single result set.
CREATE TABLE #orgchart
(seq_no      int     IDENTITY
org_level    int     NOT NULL
emp_id       int     NOT NULL
)

-- Assume I know with certainty that only one employee
-- (the CEO) can have himself as manager
-- Can change this however makes sense - but need some way to
-- know where to start
```

```
-- I'll set ROWCOUNT to 1 to be sure - but it is not necessary
-- since I know this
-- In this batch, we'll assume we start with level 1 as the
-- depth_level
SET ROWCOUNT 1
SELECT @level=1, @current=emp_no FROM emp_mgr WHERE emp_no=mgr_no
SET ROWCOUNT 0

INSERT INTO #stack (depth_level, emp_no) VALUES (@level, @current)

WHILE (@level > 0)    -- Do if any levels remain
    BEGIN

    -- See if any rows for the level we're on
    IF EXISTS (SELECT * FROM #stack WHERE depth_level=@level)
        BEGIN

        -- Get FIRST emp_no at current level
        SET ROWCOUNT 1
        SELECT @current=emp_no FROM #stack
        WHERE depth_level=@level
        SET ROWCOUNT 0

        -- Put the employee in a temp table so
        -- we can later do a single select and join
        -- I could SELECT here for every employee, but
        -- all those result sets are inefficient
        -- The orgchart temp table is automatically sequenced
        -- via an identity. That's the key to the temp table
        -- providing a solution here.
        INSERT INTO #orgchart (ORG_LEVEL, EMP_ID)
            SELECT @level, @current

        -- Delete row just processed from the stack
        DELETE FROM #stack
        WHERE depth_level=@level AND emp_no=@current

        -- Get new rows for stack by finding anyone reporting to
        -- current: except for the top employee who reports to self
        INSERT INTO #stack
            SELECT @level + 1, emp_no
            FROM emp_mgr
            WHERE mgr_no=@current
            AND mgr_no <> emp_no

        -- If any rows were found and inserted, there is a level
        -- below this employee, so increment level
```

```
    IF @@ROWCOUNT > 0
        SELECT @level=@level + 1

    END
ELSE
    -- There are no levels below this employee, so pop up one
    SELECT @level=@level - 1
END
```

```
-- Now just join to the #org_chart to get emp_names & titles.
-- Concatenate employees and managers into one string, indented by
-- level. Use SPACE()*level*5 to indent 5 spaces per level, except
-- for level 1.
SELECT "Manager -> Employees"=
SPACE((O.org_level - 1) * 5) + E.emp_name + ',     '+ E.emp_title
FROM #orgchart AS O
JOIN emp_mgr AS E ON (E.emp_no=O.emp_id)
ORDER BY O.SEQ_NO

DROP TABLE #stack, #orgchart
```

This problem can also be solved in a straightforward, but tedious, way by using cursors. You simply FETCH through the chain for each employee to find all employees who report to him or her. However, this solution needs to do many fetches, which of course creates many result sets.

> **NOTE** David Rozenshtein has written extensively on the topic of tree processing in SQL. (His book *Optimizing Transact-SQL* is on the Suggested Reading list near the end of this book.) It's possible that one of his solutions is more efficient than this. However, the solution presented above is quite efficient, and I doubt there is great room for improvement.

Select Instead of Iterating

It's common to need to perform some operation for every value, from *1* to *n*. In Chapter 9, I wanted to use the trigonometry functions to produce a listing of sine/cosine/tangent for every 10 degrees between 0 and 180. So I took the obvious route and wrote a simple loop. However, using that approach results in every row being its own result set. As I've mentioned many times, sending many result sets when one will do is inefficient, and it is also more cumbersome to process in the client application. To refresh your memory, the solution from Chapter 9 is shown on the following page.

```
DECLARE @angle smallint
SELECT @angle=0
WHILE (@angle <= 180)
BEGIN

    SELECT
    ANGLE=@angle,
    SINE=STR(SIN(@angle), 7, 4),
    COSINE=STR(COS(@angle), 7, 4),
    TANGENT=STR(TAN(@angle), 7, 4)

    SELECT @angle=@angle + 10
END
```

Since it's common to iterate in this way, a simple table of ordered numbers can come in handy. (In fact, I wish this were an "automatic" table so that I wouldn't have to decide what number to start and finish with and I could simply count on the table always being there.)

```
-- Create the seq_num table
CREATE TABLE seq_num
(seq_num INT PRIMARY KEY NOT NULL)

-- Populate the seq_num table with values from -500 through 500
DECLARE @counter int
SELECT @counter= -500
WHILE (@counter <= 500)
    BEGIN
    INSERT seq_num VALUES (@counter)
    SELECT @counter=@counter + 1
    END

-- If doing this for real, you might as well set FILLFACTOR to 100.
-- I won't bother here.
UPDATE STATISTICS seq_num
```

When this handy *seq_num* table is around, I can select or join to this table rather than iterating. The following solution runs much faster than the solution from Chapter 9, and it returns a single result set—and it's easier to write:

```
SELECT
    ANGLE=seq_num * 10,
    SINE=STR(SIN(seq_num * 10), 7, 4),
    COSINE=STR(COS(seq_num * 10), 7, 4),
    TANGENT=STR(TAN(seq_num * 10), 7, 4)
FROM seq_num
WHERE seq_num BETWEEN 0 AND 18
```

```
ANGLE    SINE     COSINE   TANGENT
-----    -------  ------   -------
0        0.0000   1.0000   0.0000
10      -0.5440  -0.8391   0.6484
20       0.9129   0.4081   2.2372
30      -0.9880   0.1543  -6.4053
40       0.7451  -0.6669  -1.1172
50      -0.2624   0.9650  -0.2719
60      -0.3048  -0.9524   0.3200
70       0.7739   0.6333   1.2220
80      -0.9939  -0.1104   9.0037
90       0.8940  -0.4481  -1.9952
100     -0.5064   0.8623  -0.5872
110     -0.0442  -0.9990   0.0443
120      0.5806   0.8142   0.7131
130     -0.9301  -0.3673   2.5323
140      0.9802  -0.1978  -4.9554
150     -0.7149   0.6993  -1.0223
160      0.2194  -0.9756  -0.2249
170      0.3466   0.9380   0.3696
180     -0.8012  -0.5985   1.3387
```

Getting a Row Count of a Table—The Fast Way

Let's say you want to get the number of rows in a table, without qualification. Using the *seq_num* table of the last example, the obvious way to check the number of rows is to do this:

```
SELECT COUNT(*) FROM seq_num
```

While this is the most obvious solution, it's not the fastest one. The table still requires a scan (via some index or a full table scan). The number of rows in the table is maintained, and can be relied on to be accurate, in the *sysindexes* table. Recall that every table will have at least one entry, and the entry will have a value of *0* for *indid* if no clustered index is present. If a clustered index exists, the table will have a value of *1* for *indid*. It will not have both values, although it will of course include other rows for all nonclustered indexes. You can put together a fast, simple query to find the number of rows by searching on the table in question and the *indid* of *0* or *1* (knowing that both cannot be present). This approach will execute with only two or three logical I/Os—even for very large tables:

```
-- Faster way to get count of all rows in table
SELECT rows
FROM sysindexes
WHERE id=OBJECT_ID("seq_num")
```

```
AND indid < 2    -- If the table has no clustered index, the entry
                 -- will be 0 for the table. If the table has a
                 -- clustered index, the entry will instead be 1 for
                 -- the clustered index. So it will be either 0 or 1,
                 -- not both. Hence, specifying it as < 2 finds it
                 -- either way.
```

Of course, if you need to qualify the count (for example, get the count for all rows with positive values), you can do this only with COUNT(*). The *sysindexes.rows* trick works only to get a count of *all* rows in the table, without qualification.

Stored, Computed Columns

In this example, you select a column that is the result of a computation on data in other columns (for example, *SELECT QTY, PRICE, REV = QTY * PRICE*). SQL makes this simple; you can do it either directly with the SELECT statement or as a view. However, since the computed column is not physically stored, it cannot be indexed. If you find that you frequently search on a column value that is logically computed, you might want to have an index on that computed value to speed retrieval. (For example, you might want to maintain a customer's current balance in the specific customer row rather than recompute it each time it's needed. Or you might need to maintain and index on a SOUNDEX() value if your telephone operators use it for information retrieval.) Here is an example of a trigger that maintains a SOUNDEX() value. The table is clustered to enable names that *sound* similar to be stored together. Whenever the *cust_name* column is changed or a new customer is added, the SOUNDEX() value is updated.

```
-- soundex_trig.sql
CREATE TABLE customer_sx
(
cust_name       char(20)
soundex_value   char(4)     NULL
)
CREATE CLUSTERED INDEX sounds_like ON customer_sx (soundex_value)
GO

CREATE TRIGGER maintain_soundex ON customer_sx
FOR INSERT, UPDATE
AS
    UPDATE soundex_name SET soundex_value=SOUNDEX(inserted.cust_name)
        FROM customer_sx, inserted
        WHERE customer_sx.cust_name=inserted.cust_name
GO
```

Pivot Tables—a.k.a Cross-Tabs

Suppose you have a simple table called *cross_tab* with sales values for different years and quarters:

year	qtr	value		year	qtr	value
1990	1	15		1993	1	20
1990	2	26		1993	2	35
1990	3	37		1993	3	47
1990	4	48		1993	4	58
1991	1	19		1994	1	25
1991	2	25		1994	2	36
1991	3	37		1994	3	49
1991	4	48		1994	4	50
1992	1	15		1995	1	31
1992	2	29		1995	2	45
1992	3	32		1995	3	57
1992	4	44		1995	4	68

You are asked to provide summary data—one line for each year, values for all four quarters in the year, and the year's total. This query will do the trick:

```
SELECT year,
q1=(SELECT value FROM cross_tab WHERE year=c.year AND qtr=1),
q2=(SELECT value FROM cross_tab WHERE year=c.year AND qtr=2),
q3=(SELECT value FROM cross_tab WHERE year=c.year AND qtr=3),
q4=(SELECT value FROM cross_tab WHERE year=c.year AND qtr=4),
total=(SELECT SUM(value) FROM cross_tab WHERE year=c.year)
FROM cross_tab c
GROUP BY year
```

year	q1	q2	q3	q4	total
1990	15	26	37	48	126
1991	19	25	37	48	129
1992	15	29	32	44	120
1993	20	35	47	58	160
1994	25	36	49	50	160
1995	31	45	57	68	201

If multiple data points existed for a given year and quarter (which in this case isn't possible since those two columns make up the primary key in the *cross_tab* table), you could slightly modify the query to use SUM for each quarter, not just for the total. On the next page is the modified query, which works for the case in which multiple entries can exist for any year/quarter combination. It works fine on the *cross_tab* table, too, but contains extra SUMs.

```
SELECT year,
q1=(SELECT SUM(value) FROM cross_tab WHERE year=c.year AND qtr=1),
q2=(SELECT SUM(value) FROM cross_tab WHERE year=c.year AND qtr=2),
q3=(SELECT SUM(value) FROM cross_tab WHERE year=c.year AND qtr=3),
q4=(SELECT SUM(value) FROM cross_tab WHERE year=c.year AND qtr=4),
total=(SELECT SUM(value) FROM cross_tab WHERE year=c.year)
FROM cross_tab c
GROUP BY year
```

I used this solution prior to CASE being added to SQL Server. But all those SE-LECT statements do not make for a highly efficient solution. In fact, running this query with just the 24 data rows in this example requires more than 85 scans (not full table scans) and more than 150 logical I/Os.

Using CASE, the following solution makes only a single pass through the *cross_tab* table. Its scan count is two (one for *cross_tab* and one for a worktable), and its logical I/O count is only 14. Obviously, this solution is much more efficient:

```
SELECT
year=c.year,
SUM(CASE qtr WHEN 1 THEN value ELSE 0 END) AS q1,
SUM(CASE qtr WHEN 2 THEN value ELSE 0 END) AS q2,
SUM(CASE qtr WHEN 3 THEN value ELSE 0 END) AS q3,
SUM(CASE qtr WHEN 4 THEN value ELSE 0 END) AS q4
FROM cross_tab c
GROUP BY year
```

Unfortunately, this solution doesn't quite meet the original specifications of the query: it doesn't calculate the total for the year. If you're going to throw the results in a spreadsheet, it's OK as it is—you can let the spreadsheet calculate that total value for the year based on the previous four columns.

It would be nice to do something like the following, but it's not supported—you can't treat a column heading as a column name as this example does:

```
/* The syntax below would be nice, but it does not work:
SELECT
year=c.year,
SUM(CASE qtr WHEN 1 THEN value ELSE 0 END) AS q1,
SUM(CASE qtr WHEN 2 THEN value ELSE 0 END) AS q2,
SUM(CASE qtr WHEN 3 THEN value ELSE 0 END) AS q3,
SUM(CASE qtr WHEN 4 THEN value ELSE 0 END) AS q4
SUM (q1 + q2 + q3 + q4) AS total
FROM cross_tab c
GROUP BY year
*/
```

We need to find a hybrid of the two methods. Here is the obvious solution: use the more efficient CASE solution, and, for the *total* column that can't be solved with the single CASE pass, do a SELECT inside the SELECT.

```
SELECT
year=c.year,
SUM(CASE qtr WHEN 1 THEN value ELSE 0 END) AS q1,
SUM(CASE qtr WHEN 2 THEN value ELSE 0 END) AS q2,
SUM(CASE qtr WHEN 3 THEN value ELSE 0 END) AS q3,
SUM(CASE qtr WHEN 4 THEN value ELSE 0 END) AS q4,
(SELECT SUM(value) FROM cross_tab WHERE year=c.year) AS total
FROM cross_tab c
GROUP BY year
```

This adds 12 to the scan count and another 36 logical I/Os. But it's still much more efficient than the first solution, and it now meets the query specification. It's a pretty good solution.

Still, I know there's an easy way to compute the total for one year. It's a simple query to write:

```
SELECT year, SUM(value)
FROM cross_tab
GROUP BY year
```

I'd really like to use the result of this query and join it to the fast query. Then I'd have the best of both worlds. Here I will do just that—making the query for the year totals a derived table and then joining to it:

```
SELECT
c.year AS year,
SUM(CASE qtr WHEN 1 THEN value ELSE 0 END) AS q1,
SUM(CASE qtr WHEN 2 THEN value ELSE 0 END) AS q2,
SUM(CASE qtr WHEN 3 THEN value ELSE 0 END) AS q3,
SUM(CASE qtr WHEN 4 THEN value ELSE 0 END) AS q4,
MIN(y.VAL) AS total
FROM cross_tab AS c
JOIN
    (SELECT year, SUM(value) AS VAL
    FROM cross_tab c
    GROUP BY year) AS y
    ON (y.year=c.year)

GROUP BY c.year
```

This works and is the most efficient solution I can come up with. (I don't know that it's the fastest one that exists. You might be more clever than I.) Note one tricky thing here: I used *MIN(y.VAL)* instead of *SUM(y.VAL)* as you might have expected. Had I used SUM, I'd get four times the value for each year, because the row from the derived table would be projected to every row for each year— and there are four quarters for each year. I don't want the sum of all yearly totals; I just want one total for the entire year. But I can't mix nonaggregates in the

SELECT list because I need to use GROUP BY. So the solution is to use one value for each year, which I do by using MIN. MAX would work just as well. The MIN, MAX, and AVG for each year's total will of course be the same, since only one total can exist for the year.

Finally, I know of one more solution to this problem. The idea comes from an article Steve Roti wrote back in about 1990 in *DBMS* magazine. He constructed a "unit matrix" table that looks like this:

```
Qtr    Q1    Q2    Q3    Q4
---    --    --    --    --
1      1     0     0     0
2      0     1     0     0
3      0     0     1     0
4      0     0     0     1
```

Having constructed and carefully populated the table, (named *pivot* in the example that follows), you can use it to join to the *cross_tab* table via the *Qtr* column. The value for each column can be multiplied by its respective quarter. For example, since only one quarter in any given row has a value of 1 and each of the others has the value of 0, multiplying will yield the desired result. The column retains the value (by multiplying it by 1) for the respective quarter but sets it to 0 (by multiplying by 0) for a different quarter. This is a clever and efficient solution, though not as efficient as the CASE and derived table solution. And it does require that you fabricate the unit matrix table, although this is not difficult to do. Without CASE, this is probably the solution I'd use:

```
SELECT year,
q1=SUM(value * Q1),
q2=SUM(value * Q2),
q3=SUM(value * Q3),
q4=SUM(value * Q4),
total=SUM(value)
FROM cross_tab JOIN pivot
ON (cross_tab.qtr=pivot.Qtr)
GROUP BY year
```

Integrating SQL Server with E-Mail

SQL Server has a unique capability to directly send and receive e-mail. At first blush, many people don't grasp the significance of this. But this feature can perform such operations as alerting you of an important data value or perhaps automatically generating a new order to your supplier when inventory reaches a certain level. SQL Server can also receive mail—you can e-mail a query to SQL Server and it will return the results to you via a reply, or you can have the body of the e-mail message stored in a database for later use.

Automatically sending mail based on an event

Following is a trigger I use for the bug database (called RAID) that we use in developing the SQL Server product. If a "severity 1" (bad) bug is found in a shipping version, I want to know about it right away. So I added a trigger to the database that sends me e-mail whenever such a bug is entered or when an existing bug is elevated to "sev 1."

```
-- raidtrigger.sql
CREATE trigger OnCheckBugs ON Bugs
 FOR INSERT, UPDATE, DELETE
 AS
  DECLARE @test int
  DECLARE @recipients varchar(255), @message varchar(255),
      @subject varchar(50)
 -- Send mail for any newly activated sev 1 bugs on a version
 -- that has been released
 IF EXISTS (SELECT * FROM inserted WHERE
    inserted.Severity='1' AND inserted.Status='ACTIVE')

    BEGIN
    -- If row was already sev 1 and ACTIVE (and is just being
    -- edited), don't resend mail
    IF EXISTS (SELECT * FROM deleted WHERE
        deleted.Severity='1' AND deleted.Status='ACTIVE')
        RETURN

    -- UPDATE NEXT LINE FOR ALL WHO SHOULD GET THE MAIL
    -- Separate with semicolons
    SELECT @recipients='ronsou;johnsmith;janedoe'

    -- Make subject line of mail the severity, bug number,
    -- & bug database
    SELECT @subject='Sev' + inserted.Severity + '  Bug ' +
        CONVERT(varchar(6), inserted.BugID)
        + ' activated in ' + DB_NAME() FROM inserted

    -- Make message the component area, who opened bug, & its title
    SELECT @message='Component: ' + RTRIM(Component) +
        ' Opened By: ' + RTRIM(inserted.OpenedBy) +
        'Version: ' + OpenedRev + char(13) +
        'Title: ' + RTRIM(inserted.Title) FROM inserted

    EXECUTE master..xp_sendmail     @recipients= @recipients,
                                    @message=    @message,
                                    @subject=    @subject,
                                    @no_output=  TRUE

    END

  RETURN
```

Processing incoming mail

We've had a tradition in the SQL Server group that once a week each developer sends a brief e-mail message to everyone in the group reporting about what he or she is working on. I wanted to keep this e-mail train but didn't want it cluttering up my e-mail Inbox folder. I also wanted to be able to query on it in a structured way. Basically, I wanted the mail to be automatically put into a SQL Server database. We could have created a form that people use to populate a database, but the e-mail tradition was well established, informal, and well liked (as much as any demand for status reports is ever liked). I didn't want to make a new procedure; I just wanted to get the text into a SQL Server database.

I wrote the following procedure using the **xp_readmail** capabilities of SQL Server 6.5. It processes mail and reads only mail with the string "stat" (written as uppercase, lowercase, or mixed case) in the subject line. It then inserts attributes such as the sender, datetime sent, and exact subject line into a table. The body of the message is inserted into a text column.

```
USE pubs   -- For example case, make table in pubs database
GO
CREATE TABLE mailstore
(
Msg_ID    varchar(64)  NOT NULL PRIMARY KEY,
Sent_By   varchar(20)  NOT NULL,  -- REFERENCES employees(emp_email)
Subject   varchar(40)  NOT NULL DEFAULT 'No Subject',
Recvd     datetime     NOT NULL DEFAULT GETDATE(),
Msg_Text  text         NULL
)
GO

USE MASTER
GO

DROP PROCEDURE sp_status_mail
GO

CREATE PROCEDURE sp_status_mail
    -- Process only unread mail
    @unread_msgs_only varchar(5)='false',
    -- Delete processed mail
    @delete_after_reading varchar(5)='false',
    -- Do not change mail read status
    @do_not_change_read_status varchar(5)='true',
    -- Only Process "Stat" mail
    @only_read_stat_mail varchar(5)='true'

AS
DECLARE @status int,              -- MAPI Status
```

```
        @msg_id varchar(64),      -- MSG ID for each mail
        @originator varchar(255), -- MAIL FROM
        @msgsubject varchar(255), -- MAIL SUBJECT
        @msgtext varchar(255),    -- BUFFER FOR MAIL TEXT
        @messages int,            -- Counter for messages processed
        @mapifailure int,         -- Indicator if MAPI error
        @maildate varchar(255),   -- MAIL SENT Date
        @skip_bytes int,          -- Pointer for where to read next
                                  -- text chunk
        @msg_length int,          -- Total size of message text
        @textptr varbinary(16)    -- TextPointer

SELECT @messages=0
SELECT @mapifailure=0

WHILE (1=1)
    BEGIN  -- BEGIN NEXT MSG LOOP
        EXEC @status=master.dbo.xp_findnextmsg
            @msg_id=@msg_id OUTPUT,
            @unread_only=@unread_msgs_only

        IF @status <> 0
        BEGIN
            SELECT @mapifailure=1
            BREAK    -- If any MAPI error, bail out
        END

        IF (@msg_id IS NULL)   -- If msg_id is NULL, it's not a
                               -- valid received message so continue
                               -- with the next message
        BREAK

        SELECT @skip_bytes=0, @msg_length=0

        EXEC @status=master.dbo.xp_readmail
            @msg_id=@msg_id,
            @originator=@originator OUTPUT,
            @subject=@msgsubject OUTPUT,
            @date_received=@maildate OUTPUT,
            @message=@msgtext OUTPUT,
            @skip_bytes=@skip_bytes OUTPUT,
            @msg_length=@msg_length OUTPUT,
            @peek=@do_not_change_read_status

        IF @status <> 0
            BEGIN
                SELECT @mapifailure=1
                BREAK     -- If any MAPI error, bail out
            END
```

```
-- If flag is set, care only about mail that has "stat" in the
-- subject line. So forget rest and continue.
-- Do not count an "uninteresting" message as one processed.

    IF (LOWER(@only_read_stat_mail)='true' AND
        LOWER(@msgsubject) NOT LIKE '%stat%')
        CONTINUE

    -- Count how many messages processed
    SELECT @messages=@messages + 1

    -- The sender field might be an address or a name.
    -- If it's a name, get the address. Must turn off expand
    -- to friendly names. Then, if there is a < in originator,
    -- parse for the address using only charindex.

    SELECT @originator=CASE
        WHEN (@originator NOT LIKE '%<%' OR @originator
            NOT LIKE '% %')
            THEN @originator
        ELSE SUBSTRING(@originator,
            (charindex('<', @originator) + 1),
            (charindex('@', @originator) -
            (charindex('<', @originator) + 1)))
        END

    -- Insert message into a table

    INSERT pubs.dbo.mailstore
        (Sent_By, Msg_ID, Subject, Recvd, Msg_Text)
    VALUES (@originator, @msg_id, @msgsubject, @maildate,
            @msgtext)

    -- If MSG_ID already there, then continue and try the next
    -- message: error 2627 is a violation of a unique or PK
    -- constraint due to duplicates, and error 2601 is same but
    -- just due to a unique index

    IF (@@ERROR IN (2627, 2601))
        BEGIN
            RAISERROR ('MSG ID: %s already exists. Skipping to
next message.', 16, 1, @msg_id)
            CONTINUE
        END
```

```
        -- Get the textptr from last row inserted
        SELECT @textptr=TEXTPTR(Msg_Text)
        FROM pubs.dbo.mailstore WHERE Msg_ID=@msg_id

        -- If a non-null textptr and skip_bytes shows there is more
        -- to read, then keep reading message text until done, and
        -- append with UPDATETEXT

        WHILE ((@textptr IS NOT NULL) AND
            (@skip_bytes < @msg_length))
            BEGIN    -- BEGIN READ-ALL-TEXT-LOOP
                EXEC @status=master.dbo.xp_readmail
                    @msg_id=@msg_id,
                    @message=@msgtext OUTPUT,
                    @skip_bytes=@skip_bytes OUTPUT,
                    @msg_length=@msg_length OUTPUT

                IF @status <> 0
                    BEGIN
                        SELECT @mapifailure=1
                        BREAK    -- If any MAPI error, bail out
                    END

                UPDATETEXT pubs.dbo.mailstore.Msg_Text
                    @textptr  NULL  0  WITH LOG  @msgtext
            END    --   END READ-ALL-TEXT-LOOP

        -- If broke out of text loop because of MAPI failure,
        -- then break out of next message processing too

        IF @mapifailure=1
            BREAK

        -- If delete flag is ON, delete this message

        IF (LOWER(@delete_after_reading)='true')
            BEGIN
                EXEC @status=master.dbo.xp_deletemail @msg_id
                IF @status <> 0
                    BEGIN
                        SELECT @mapifailure=1
                        BREAK    -- If any MAPI error, bail out
                    END
            END

    END -- END NEXT MSG LOOP

/* Finished examining the contents of inbox */
```

```
    IF @mapifailure=0      -- No MAPI errors. Success!
        BEGIN
            RAISERROR(15079, -1, -1, @messages)
            RETURN(0)
        END
    ELSE                      -- MAPI Errors. Bailed out.
        BEGIN
            RAISERROR ('MAPI Error. Terminated Procedure', 16, 1)
            RETURN(-100)
        END
```

Mimicking a Distributed Query

SQL Server does not currently provide a built-in, seamless way to perform a single distributed query between servers. But that doesn't mean it can't be done. The key to doing this is to combine the use of INSERT/EXEC PROC, the special stored procedure **sp_sqlexec**, and a temporary table. The procedure **sp_sqlexec** is simply a stored procedure wrapper over the *EXECUTE(@string)* capability. (This is true since version 6.5. In prior versions, **sp_sqlexec** was a special internal function in ODS. The functionality worked equivalently, however.)

To show how simple **sp_sqlexec** is, here is the entire procedure:

```
CREATE PROCEDURE sp_sqlexec @p1 text
AS EXEC(@p1)
```

This procedure accepts a single parameter of text (an SQL command) and executes it. By wrapping it as a stored procedure, it can be executed remotely. And since it's a stored procedure, it can also be used with INSERT/EXEC to have its results populate a table.

Let's assume I want to find out if my *authors* table at a remote server has any rows that are not present in my local table. I execute **sp_sqlexec** against my remote server (named RONSOU9 in this example) and bring the results back to a temporary table on my local server. Once there, I can perform any query I want—a join, a subquery, a union, or so on. And I certainly could have supplied a WHERE clause with **sp_sqlexec** to limit the rows to some criteria rather than retrieve them all as I do in this example:

```
-- spsqlexec.sql
-- Mimic a distributed query.
-- Get authors from RONSOU9 into a temp table on local server.
-- Then do a standard query on the local server to find authors on
-- remote server that are NOT in local server. Could also of course
-- just join them or do any other type of operation.

-- Do a SELECT INTO guaranteed not to find any rows
-- simply as an easy way to auto-generate the table.
-- Put the @@SERVERNAME on the SELECT in case want to see
-- what server the rows were really from.
```

```
SELECT @@SERVERNAME AS SERVERNAME, *
    INTO #all_authors
    FROM authors
    WHERE 1=2      -- Dummy WHERE clause that can never be satisfied

-- Populate the local temp table with the data from the remote
-- server (RONSOU9). Pass SQL statement via the special procedure
-- sp_sqlexec.

INSERT #all_authors
    EXEC RONSOU9.pubs.dbo.sp_sqlexec
        'SELECT @@SERVERNAME, * FROM authors'

-- Now do a standard query. This finds authors in the remote server
-- that are NOT in the local server.

SELECT * FROM #all_authors A
WHERE A.au_id NOT IN (SELECT B.au_id FROM authors B)
GO
```

This is certainly not as elegant as just issuing a single query against two (or more) servers simultaneously. However, it is functional, and it's not difficult by any means. And it is fast. I've showed this solution to some people whose reactions were along the lines of "...but that copies the rows back locally." Of course it does—any distributed query capability must do that. If it's efficient, it will restrict the copy to only the subset of the rows and columns it needs. You can certainly do this by providing a WHERE clause and specifying the exact columns you need in the SELECT list.

Mimicking a Distributed, Partitioned Insert

This example is related to the distributed query example above. Suppose I want to decide at runtime which server and table a row should be stored in based on its values. For example, SERVER1 gets any customer whose name begins with a letter preceding *N*, and SERVER2 gets customers *N* onward. If all data modification is done via a stored procedure, this is pretty simple to do. I could even later change the partitioning by changing the procedure, and the application would be unaffected. Here is a simple example to illustrate the concept. I build up the INSERT statement dynamically, including conditionally deciding on the server name, and then I execute it with **sp_sqlexec**.

```
-- spsqlexec_ins.sql
CREATE PROC add_author
@au_id char(11),
@au_lname varchar(20) AS

DECLARE @server_name varchar(30),
    @insert_stmt varchar(128),
    @retstat smallint
```

```
IF (@au_lname < 'N')
    SELECT @server_name='SERVER1'
    ELSE
    SELECT @server_name='SERVER2'

SELECT @insert_stmt=@server_name +
    "..sp_sqlexec INSERT pubs.dbo.authors VALUES
    ('" + @au_id + "','" + @au_lname + ")"
EXECUTE (@insert_stmt)
```

Copying Text to Sequenced *varchar* Columns

The text datatype is sometimes awkward to work with. Many functions don't operate against text, stored procedures are limited in what they can do with text, and some tools don't deal with it well. Instead of having a single, huge text column, sometimes it's easier to work with a sequenced set of rows with a *varchar(255)* column. But how, then, can you copy a text column to multiple *varchar(255)* columns and make sure they are sequenced correctly within a single SQL batch? You could, of course, read the data out to a program and then reinsert it. But then you would need to do a lot of copying of large amounts of data between processes. This is far from ideal.

When I needed to do this, I thought of a clever solution (in my humble opinion) using INSERT/EXEC and READTEXT. However, it turned out that INSERT/EXEC didn't work with a procedure doing READTEXT. So we added support for this in Service Pack 2 for version 6.5. To use this technique, you must be running 6.5 Service Pack 2 or later.

This procedure operates on the *pub_info* table from the *pubs* database. For a given *pub_id,* the procedure takes the text column of the row and does successive READTEXT operations in chunks of 255 until the entire text column has been read. Having created the procedure, I use a cursor to iterate for each row of *pub_info* and copy the text column into multiple rows of a temporary table. When I'm done for a given *pub_id,* I then take the temporary table's contents and add it to the permanent table. I truncate the temporary table and move on to the next *pub_id* value:

```
-- copy_text_to_varchar.sql
-- Be sure the pub_info table has the text columns added.
-- If necessary, run \MSSQL\INSTALL\PUBTEXT.BAT to add the text
-- columns. (Run from that directory.)
--
-- Proc get_text does READTEXT in a loop to read chunks of text
-- no larger than 255, or the column size or @@TEXTSIZE, and
-- produces as many rows as necessary to store the text column
-- as a series of sequenced varchar(255) rows
```

```
CREATE PROC get_text @pub_id char(4)
AS

DECLARE @mytextptr varbinary(16), @totalsize int, @lastread int,
    @readsize int
-- Use a TRAN and HOLDLOCK to ensure that textptr and text are
-- constant during the iterative reads
BEGIN TRAN
SELECT @mytextptr=TEXTPTR(pr_info), @totalsize=DATALENGTH(pr_info),
    @lastread=0,
    -- Set the readsize to the smaller of the @@TEXTSIZE settings,
    -- 255, and the total length of the column
    @readsize=CASE WHEN (255 < DATALENGTH(pr_info)) THEN 255
    ELSE DATALENGTH(pr_info) END
    FROM pub_info (HOLDLOCK) WHERE pub_id=@pub_id

-- If debugging, uncomment this to check values
-- SELECT @mytextptr, @totalsize, @lastread, @readsize

-- Do READTEXT in a loop to get next 255 characters until done
IF @mytextptr IS NOT NULL AND @readsize > 0
    WHILE (@lastread < @totalsize)
    BEGIN
        -- If readsize would go beyond end, adjust readsize
        IF ((@readsize + @lastread) > @totalsize)
            SELECT @readsize = @totalsize - @lastread

        -- If debugging, uncomment this to check values
        -- SELECT 'valid ptr?'=textvalid('pub_info.pr_info',
        --     @mytextptr), 'totalsize'=@totalsize,
        --     'lastread'=@lastread, 'readsize'=@readsize

        READTEXT pub_info.pr_info @mytextptr @lastread @readsize
        IF (@@ERROR <> 0)
            BREAK    -- Break out of loop if an error on read
        -- Change offset to last char read
        SELECT @lastread=@lastread + @readsize

    END

COMMIT TRAN
GO

IF EXISTS (SELECT * FROM tempdb.dbo.sysobjects
    WHERE name='##mytmptext' AND type='U')
    DROP TABLE ##mytmptext
GO
```

```
-- Intermediate temp table that READTEXT will use.
-- This table is truncated after each pub_id value, so the Identity
-- property sequences the rows for each publisher separately.
CREATE TABLE ##mytmptext
(
seq_no          int       IDENTITY,
text_chunk      text
)
GO

IF EXISTS (SELECT * FROM sysobjects
    WHERE name='newprinfo' AND type='U')
    DROP TABLE newprinfo
GO

-- This is the new table that pub_info is copied to.
-- It keeps chunks of text and is sequenced for each pub_id.
CREATE TABLE newprinfo
(
pub_id          char(4)    NOT NULL,
seq_no          int        NOT NULL,
text_chunk      varchar(255),
CONSTRAINT PK PRIMARY KEY (pub_id, seq_no)
)
GO

-- Having created the procedure get_text, iterate for each pub_id
-- value, temporarily sequencing them in the temp table. Once done
-- for a given pub_id, copy them to the new permanent table. Then
-- truncate the temp table for use with reseeded Identity for next
-- pub_id row.
DECLARE @pub_id char(4)
DECLARE iterate_prinfo CURSOR FOR
    SELECT pub_id FROM pub_info ORDER BY pub_id

OPEN iterate_prinfo
    FETCH NEXT FROM iterate_prinfo INTO @pub_id
    WHILE (@@FETCH_STATUS <> -1)
        BEGIN
        TRUNCATE TABLE ##mytmptext

        INSERT ##mytmptext
            EXEC get_text @pub_id

        INSERT newprinfo (pub_id, seq_no, text_chunk)
            SELECT @pub_id, SEQ_NO,
            CONVERT(varchar(255), TEXT_CHUNK)
```

```
            FROM ##mytmptext ORDER BY SEQ_NO

        FETCH NEXT FROM iterate_prinfo INTO @pub_id
        END

CLOSE iterate_prinfo
DEALLOCATE iterate_prinfo
GO

-- Simply verify contents of the new table
SELECT * FROM newprinfo ORDER BY pub_id,seq_no
GO
```

A subset of the output looks like the following:

```
pub_id   seq_no    text_chunk
------   ------    ------------------------------------------------
0736     1         This is sample text data for New Moon Books,
                   publisher 0736 in the pubs database. New Moon
                   Books is located in Boston,
0736     2         Massachusetts.
                   This is sample text data for New Moon Books,
                   publisher 0736 in the pubs database. New Moon
                   Books is located in Boston, Massachusetts. This
                   is sample text data for New Moon Books,
                   publisher 0736 in the pubs database. New Moon
                   Books is
0736     3         located in Boston, Massachusetts.
```

Instantiating and Executing an Automation Object

SQL Server doesn't (yet) support user-defined functions (UDF). It does let you write call-outs to extended procedures, which are your own DLLs written via the ODS API. Writing extended procedures isn't too difficult to do, but it's still too daunting a task for many programmers.

Many development tools, such as Microsoft Visual Basic 5.0 or Microsoft Visual C++ 5.0, make it easy to create Automation objects. Using Visual Basic, it can be as easy as calling one of the built-in Visual Basic functions and saving it as an Automation procedure. If you can do that, you can run that Automation procedure from SQL Server.

At the SQL Server Professional Developer Conference in September 1996, I demonstrated how you could use Visual Basic to create an internal rate of return (IRR) function. For those non-MBAs, IRR is a financial term representing the percentage return, based on a set of cash flows, that would be required for the cash flows to have a net present value (NPV) of 0. In other words, the IRR is the interest rate implicitly earned on an investment consisting of payments (negative values) and income (positive values) that occur at regular periods, such that total income equals total payments. Calculating IRR is not easy, and it requires an iterative solution—you start with a guess and move toward the solution. Visual Basic provides a load of nice financial functions; SQL Server does not. So it is natural to want to use one of these Visual Basic functions, and this is what the following example does. This solution assumes that you have previously used Visual Basic to create the object GET_IIR used here (which takes about three mouse clicks to do—you simply load the IRR function provided by the software).

```
-- VB_IRR.SQL
-- Use an OLE object named GET_IIR previously created from VB
-- as an internal rate of return (IRR) function
DECLARE
@pObj int,     -- Will be used as an OUTPUT parameter to hold
               -- the object token when the object is created
@hr int        -- Return code

DECLARE @source varchar(30)     -- Output variable for source of an
                                -- error
DECLARE @desc varchar(200)      -- Output variable for error string
DECLARE @IRR float              -- Output variable for IRR value
                                -- (VB doesn't have a decimal)

-- Instantiate the object
EXEC @hr=sp_OACreate "GetIRR.CGetIRR", @pObj OUT
    IF @hr <> 0 GOTO Err

-- Call the IRR method
-- Takes variable number of parameters as cash flows
EXEC @hr=sp_OAMethod @pObj, "GetIRR", @IRR OUT,
            -900, 100, 300, 300, 200, 200
    IF @hr <> 0 GOTO Err

-- Convert the float column to a decimal
SELECT "IRR"=CONVERT(DECIMAL(5, 3), @IRR)
GOTO Done

Err:
    RAISERROR ('Error in calculating Net Present Value. ', 16, 1)
    -- Get error info from OLE object
    EXEC sp_OAGetErrorInfo NULL, @source OUT, @desc OUT
    SELECT hr=CONVERT(BINARY(4), @hr), source=@source,
        description=@desc

Done:
    -- Destroy the object instance
    EXEC sp_OADestroy @pObj
```

Because most of the preceding code is template code, you can cut and paste it for use with another object (except for the call to **sp_OAMethod**, of course). The ability to use Automation gives you a lot of flexibility. However, these procedures are not particularly fast when they are run from within the SQL Server context. Because of reentrancy issues within SQL Server's threaded environment, they must be protected with mutexes, so really only one such procedure runs at a given time and other executions for that same object get serialized. For many uses, though, this will suffice just fine, and it fills a nice niche until true UDFs are available.

SUMMARY

This chapter covered many problems and approaches to solve those problems. It discussed how to implement referential actions via triggers, how to generate test data, and how to solve various types of statistical or time series problems. It showed standard SQL solutions as well as how SQL Server extensions could be used. It presented solutions to problems that are difficult to solve in SQL, such as expanding a hierarchy or pivoting a table. Real-world solutions for use of the **xp_mail** functionality were presented, as was an example for running an Automation object from SQL Server. A solution was shown that mimics a distributed query, and another example offered a solution for cracking a text column into multiple sequenced rows of *varchar* datatypes.

13

Locking

Introduction

Locking is a crucial function of any multiple-user database system, including SQL Server. As you've learned earlier, SQL Server manages multiple users simultaneously and ensures that all transactions observe the properties of the chosen isolation level. At the highest isolation level, Serializable, SQL Server must make the multiple-user system yield results that are indistinguishable from those of a single-user system. To do this, SQL Server provides isolation to protect data that is being used by multiple simultaneous users. Isolation automatically locks data to prevent changes made by one user from having an unexpected effect on work being done by another user on the same database at the same time.

The Lock Manager

SQL Server can hold several types of locks. For example, read operations acquire *shared locks,* and write operations acquire *exclusive locks. Update locks* are created at the page level and are acquired during the initial portion of an update operation when the pages are being read or by cursors opened with pessimistic concurrency.

The *Lock Manager* acquires and releases these locks. It also manages the compatibility between lock types, resolves deadlocks, and escalates locks if necessary. The Lock Manager controls locks on tables, on the pages of a table, and on *system data* (data that's private to the database system, such as page headers and indexes). SQL Server's Lock Manager provides two separate locking systems. The first system affects all fully shared data and provides page locks and table locks for tables, data pages, text pages, and leaf-level index pages. The second locking system is used internally, for restrictively used system data only, to protect root and intermediate index pages while indexes are being traversed. This internal mechanism uses *resource locks,* or *rlocks*, which provide performance optimization. The first type of locks, "full-blown" locks, could be used for all locking, but because of their complexity, they would slow the system down if they were used for these internal needs. If you examine locks by using the **sp_lock** system stored procedure or by using a similar mechanism that gets its information from the *syslocks* table, you will not be able to see rlocks—you'll see only information about locks for fully shared data.

The Lock Manager and Isolation Levels

SQL Server supports all four transaction isolation levels as specified by ANSI and ISO: Repeatable Read, Serializable, Committed Read, and Uncommitted Read. (You can review Chapter 3, "SQL Server Architecture," and Chapter 10, "Batches, Transactions, Stored Procedures, and Triggers," for details.) As you'll recall from earlier chapters, Repeatable Read and Serializable currently behave in an equivalent way, and phantoms are prevented even at the Repeatable Read level. For the Serializable isolation level, phantoms must be prevented, since the transaction's behavior must be identical to that which would have occurred had the transaction been run on a single-user system. SQL Server provides serializability through the HOLDLOCK option, or it can be set via *SET TRANSACTION ISOLATION SERIALIZABLE*. To support serializability, SQL Server locks index ranges until the end of the transaction to prevent phantoms. If no index exists, the Lock Manager will use a table lock to guarantee serializability. The page and table locks support multiple levels of access (shared, exclusive, intent-to-update, and so on).

The Lock Manager provides fairly standard *two-phase locking* (2PL) services.[1] In two-phase locking, a transaction has a "growing" phase, during which it acquires locks, and a "shrinking" phase, during which it releases locks. To achieve serializability, all acquired locks are held until the end of the transaction and then dropped at once. For a lower isolation level, such as Committed Read, locks can be released sooner when the use of the object is completed. For example, if a range of data is being queried in the table, there likely will be shared page locks outstanding. With Committed Read isolation, a shared page lock will be released as soon as the scan moves off that page and on to the next. Exclusive locks, on the other hand, are always held until the end of the transaction so that the transaction can be rolled back, if necessary. If the isolation level is Serializable (or Repeatable Read), those shared locks must be held until the end of the transaction to guarantee that the data that was read will not change or that new rows meeting the criteria of the query cannot be added while the transaction is in progress. Like a shared lock, rlocks are not tied to the boundaries of a transaction, since rlocks are used to provide mutual exclusion (mutex) functionality rather than to directly lock data. For example, during a row insert in a table with a clustered index, the nearby index page is rlocked to prevent other inserts from colliding. The rlocks are needed to provide mutual exclusion only during "long" periods of time (that is, periods of time with more than a few instruction cycles).

---

1. Although the names are similar, two-phase locking (2PL) and the two-phase commit (2PC) protocol are not directly related, other than by the obvious fact that 2PC must use 2PL services.

Spinlocks

For even shorter term needs, mutual exclusion is usually obtained through a *latch,* a lightweight mechanism implemented in SQL Server with a *spinlock.* A spinlock is used purely for mutual exclusion and is never used to lock user data. Spinlocks are even more lightweight than rlocks, which are lighter than the full locks used for data and index leaf pages. The spinlock in SQL Server is the only place in which processor-specific assembly language is used. A spinlock is implemented in a few lines of assembly language specific to each processor type (*x*86/Pentium, Alpha, and so on). The requester of a spinlock repeats its request if the lock is not immediately available. (That is, the requestor "spins" on the lock until it is free.) Spinlocks are often used as mutexes within SQL Server for cases in which a resource is usually not busy. If a resource is busy, the duration of a spinlock is short enough to make it better to retry rather than to wait and be rescheduled by Windows NT, resulting in context switching between threads. Spinning is preferable to having the thread scheduled out because the savings in context switches more than offsets the cost of spinning, provided that you don't have to spin too long. Spinlocks are used for situations in which the wait for a resource is expected to be brief (or, typically, no wait should occur).

Deadlocks

A *deadlock* occurs when two processes are waiting for a resource and neither process can advance because the other process prevents it from getting the resource. A true deadlock is a catch-22 in which, without intervention, neither process will ever be able to progress. When a deadlock occurs, SQL Server intervenes automatically.

> **NOTE** A simple wait for a lock is *not* a deadlock. When the process that's holding the lock completes, the waiting process gets the lock. Lock waits are normal, expected, and necessary in multiple-user systems.

In SQL Server, two main types of deadlocks can occur: a *cycle deadlock* and a *conversion deadlock.* Figure 13-1 on the following page shows an example of a cycle deadlock. In the figure, process A starts a transaction, acquires an exclusive table lock on the *customer* table, and requests an exclusive table lock on the *parts* table. Simultaneously, process B starts a transaction, acquires an exclusive lock on the *parts* table, and requests an exclusive lock on the *customer* table. **Stop!** The two processes are now deadlocked, caught in a "deadly embrace." Each process holds a resource that's needed by the other process. Neither can progress, and, without intervention, both would be stuck in deadlock forever.

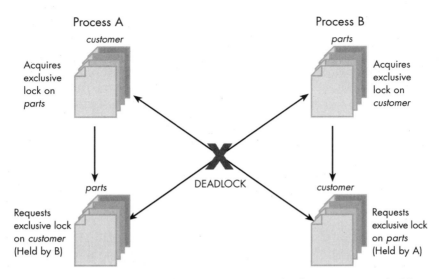

Figure 13-1. *A cycle deadlock occurs when each of two processes holds a resource needed by the other.*

Figure 13-2 shows an example of a conversion deadlock. Suppose that process A and process B each hold a shared lock on the same page within a transaction. Each process wants to promote its shared lock to an exclusive lock but cannot do so because of the other process's lock. Again, intervention is required.

SQL Server automatically detects deadlocks and intervenes through the Lock Manager, which provides deadlock detection for both regular locks and rlocks. When SQL Server detects a deadlock, it chooses a process and then terminates that process's batch, rolling back the transaction and releasing all that process's locks to resolve the deadlock. Typically, the process chosen as the "victim" is the one that made the lock request that "closed the loop" and started the deadlock. In SQL Server releases prior to version 6.5 and in internal builds that were never released, we used other algorithms to choose the deadlock victim (such as choosing the process that had consumed fewer CPU cycles). Those attempts were noble, but they often resulted in another deadlock, since yet another process might have been queued for the same resource that was part of the deadlock circular chain of lock requests. That type of approach set off a chain reaction. We have since found empirically that the best way to resolve the deadlock is to terminate the process that closed the loop in lock requests.

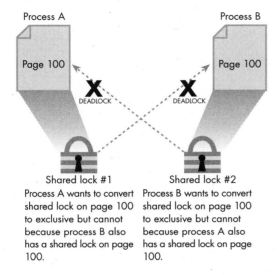

Process A   Process B

Page 100   Page 100

X   **X**
DEADLOCK   DEADLOCK

Shared lock #1   Shared lock #2

Process A wants to convert   Process B wants to convert
shared lock on page 100   shared lock on page 100
to exclusive but cannot   to exclusive but cannot
because process B also   because process A also
has a shared lock on page   has a shared lock on page
100.   100.

Figure 13-2. *A conversion deadlock occurs when each of two processes holds a shared lock on the same resource within a transaction and both need to promote the shared lock to an exclusive lock.*

Using the *SET DEADLOCK_PRIORITY LOW | NORMAL* statement, you can make a process "sacrifice" itself as the victim if a deadlock is detected. If a process has a deadlock priority of LOW, it will terminate when a deadlock is detected, even if it is not the process that closed the loop.

NOTE The lightweight spinlocks used internally do not have deadlock detection services. Instead, deadlocks on spinlocks are *avoided* rather than *resolved*. Avoidance is achieved via strict programming guidelines used by the SQL Server development team—spinlocks must be acquired in a hierarchy, and a process must not have to wait for a regular or resource lock while holding a spinlock. A spinlock is strictly a "get-in-and-get-out" mutex. For example, one coding rule is that a process holding a spinlock must never directly wait for a lock or call another service that might have to wait for a lock, and a request can never be made for a spinlock that is higher in the acquisition hierarchy. Establishing similar guidelines for your development team for the order in which SQL Server objects are accessed can go a long way toward avoiding deadlocks in the first place.

In the deadlock examples shown in Figures 13-1 and 13-2, the cycle deadlock ("deadly embrace") could have been avoided had both process A and process B decided on a protocol beforehand—perhaps, for example, that they would always access the *customer* table first and the *parts* table second (or vice versa). Then one of the processes would get the initial exclusive lock on the table being accessed first, and the other process would wait for the lock to be released. One process waiting for a lock is normal and natural. (Remember, waiting is not a deadlock.) You should always try to have a standard protocol for the order in which processes will access tables. In the conversion deadlock example, if you knew that the processes might need to later update the row after reading it, they should have initially requested an update lock, not a shared lock.

I'll discuss compatibility of locks a little later in this chapter, and even more information on deadlocks is presented in Chapter 14. For now, trust me when I say that if both processes had requested an update lock rather than a shared lock, the process that was granted an update lock would have been assured that the lock could later be traded in for an exclusive lock. The other process requesting an update lock would have had to wait. The use of an update lock serializes the requests for an exclusive lock. Other processes needing to read the data only would still have been able to get their shared locks and read. Since the holder of the update lock would have been guaranteed an exclusive lock, the deadlock would have been avoided.

Although not specifically related to deadlocking, the time that your process holds locks should be minimal so that other processes aren't waiting too long for the locks to be released. Although you don't usually invoke locking directly, you can influence locking by keeping transactions as short as possible. For example, don't ask for user input in the middle of a transaction. Instead, get the input first and then quickly perform the transaction.

Locks and Memory

Locks are not on-disk structures—you won't find a lock field directly on a data page or a table header—because it would be too slow to do disk I/O operations for locking operations. Locks are *internal memory structures* (they consume part of the memory configured for SQL Server) of approximately 28 bytes each. They contain fields that identify the process ID of the requester and the database ID, object ID, row number (if applicable), and type of lock. Beyond the lock (or *lock block*) itself, each locked resource (a page or a table) also requires a *resource lock block,* another in-memory structure of 28 bytes. The process owning a lock also must have a *lock owner block* of about 32 bytes. (Sometimes a single transaction can have multiple lock owner blocks, as a scrollable cursor sometimes uses several.)

NOTE In this context, I am referring to a "process" as a SQL Server subtask. Every user connection is referred to as a process, as are the Checkpoint Manager, the Lazywriter, and the Read Ahead Manager. But all of these are only subtasks within SQL Server, not processes from the perspective of Windows NT, which considers the entire SQL Server engine to be a single process with multiple threads.

Lock Types for User Data

SQL Server can lock user data (not system resources, which are protected with rlocks) at the table level, the page level, the extent level, or the row level for most insert operations. As I mentioned earlier, SQL Server uses several types of locks, including shared locks, exclusive locks, update locks, and intent locks. Shared locks are used when data will be read-only and not changed. Exclusive locks are needed when data is to be modified.

Update locks prevent the conversion deadlock situation I showed in Figure 13-2, and they provide compatibility with other current readers of data, allowing the process to later modify data with the assurance that the data hasn't been changed since it was last read. An update lock is not sufficient to allow you to change the data—all modifications require that the object being modified has an exclusive lock. Instead, an update lock acts as a serialization gate to queue future requests for the exclusive lock. (Many processes can hold shared locks for a resource, but only one process can hold an update lock.) As long as a process holds an update lock on a resource, no other process can acquire an update lock or an exclusive lock for that same resource; instead, another process requesting an update or exclusive lock for the same resource must wait. The process holding the update lock will be able to acquire an exclusive lock on that resource because the update lock will prevent lock incompatibility with any other processes. You can think of update locks as "intent-to-update" locks, which is essentially the role they perform. Used alone, update locks are insufficient for updating data—an exclusive lock is still required for updates. Serializing access for the exclusive lock enables you to avoid conversion deadlocks.

Intent locks are placed on tables; they signal the intention to place either shared or exclusive locks on pages within that table. Contrary to popular belief, an intent lock on a table does *not* signal an intention to acquire a lock on the entire table. Intent locks bridge the hierarchy of tables and pages, as shown in the table on the next page, which shows the types and descriptions of locks SQL Server supplies for user data.

Abbreviation	Lock Type	Description
SH_TAB	Shared table	Allows other processes to read but not change the table. Used for read operations that scan the entire table or when numerous shared page locks escalate to a table-level shared lock.
EX_TAB	Exclusive table	Prevents another process from modifying or reading data in the table (unless the process is set to the Read Uncommitted isolation level). Used to modify data when the entire table will be affected or scanned or when numerous exclusive page locks escalate to an exclusive table lock.
SH_INT	Shared table intent	Signals a process's intention to do shared page locking later on this table.*
EX_INT	Exclusive table intent	Signals a process's intention to do page locking (non-shared) on this table.**
SH_PAGE	Shared page	Used for read operations. Locks a single page so that other processes can read but not change the data.
UP_PAGE	Update page	Locks a single page; can be obtained while other processes hold shared locks on the same page. These locks prevent conversion deadlocks because they serialize access to the exclusive lock needed to make updates to data.†
EX_PAGE	Exclusive page	Locks a page being updated. Other processes cannot read or modify the data while this lock is held (unless another process is operating with Read Uncommitted isolation).
IX_PAGE	Insert page for insert row level locking (IRL)	Locks a page for an insert action only, allowing other processes to simultaneously insert to the same page.
LN_PAGE	Link page for IRL	Prevents further IX_PAGE locks from being granted if no more room is available on the page and a new page must be allocated.

* Although its name might seem to imply it, this type of lock does *not* signal the intention of issuing a shared lock on the entire table. Rather, it is used because table and page locks implicitly represent a hierarchy. If a single page of a table is locked by one process, another process cannot get an exclusive lock on the entire table. Intent locks protect this hierarchy by placing the table lock first.

** Although its name might seem to imply it, this type of lock does *not* signal the intention of issuing an exclusive lock on the entire table. Rather, it is used because table and page locks implicitly represent a hierarchy. Conceptually, EX_INT is like SH_INT, but EX_INT protects the hierarchy when the page lock to be requested will be an exclusive page lock (EX_PAGE), an update page lock (UP_PAGE), or a row-level lock (IX_PAGE or LN_PAGE).

† Once obtained, an UP_PAGE update page lock still allows other processes to be granted shared locks to read the page. But if an UP_PAGE is held, another process will not be granted either an exclusive lock or an update lock for that page. This ensures that once a process holds an update page lock, no other process will be able to jump in front of it and obtain an exclusive lock. In other words, the holder of an update page lock is guaranteed that it can later "promote" the lock to an EX_PAGE should the process decide to modify the page. In the meantime, processes wanting to read the data can do so.

Viewing Locks

To see the locks currently outstanding in the system as well as those that are being waited for, look at the *syslocks* system table or execute the system stored procedure **sp_lock**. (The *syslocks* table is not really a system table. It is not maintained on disk because locks are not maintained on disk. Rather, *syslocks* is materialized in table format based on the Lock Manager's current accounting of locks each time *syslocks* is queried.) An even better way to watch locking activity is with the excellent graphical representation of locking status provided by SQL Enterprise Manager. (Even non-GUI dinosaurs like me can appreciate SQL Enterprise Manager's view of locking.)

Locking is also done on *extents* (units of disk space that are 16 KB in size—eight pages of 2 KB each). This kind of locking automatically occurs when a table or an index needs to grow and a new extent must be allocated. Think of an extent lock as another type of special purpose resource lock. Extents can have both shared extent (SH_EXT) and exclusive extent (EX_EXT) locks. Other types of extent locks are used to serialize access of extent allocation—UP_EXT (update extent) to serialize suballocation of extents, NX_EXT (next extent), and PR_EXT (previous extent). Generally, you won't need to be concerned with extent locking, but I mention these lock types because you might see them if you are running **sp_lock** or perusing *syslocks*.

Lock Compatibility

Two locks are compatible if one lock can be granted while another lock on the same object by a different process is outstanding. On the other hand, if a lock requested for an object is not compatible with a lock currently being held, the requesting connection must wait for the lock. For example, if a shared page lock exists on a page, another process requesting a shared page lock for the same page will be granted the lock because these two lock types are compatible. But a process that requests an exclusive lock for the same page would not be granted the lock, because an exclusive lock is not compatible with the shared lock already held.

Table 13-1 summarizes the compatibility of page locks in SQL Server, and Table 13-2 summarizes the compatibility of table locks in SQL Server. Both tables appear on the following page.

Page Lock Held	Page Lock Requested				
	EX_PAGE	IX_PAGE	LN_PAGE	UP_PAGE	SH_PAGE
EX_PAGE	No	No	No	No	No
IX_PAGE	No	Yes	Yes	No	No
LN_PAGE	No	No	No	No	No
UP_PAGE	No	No	No	No	Yes
SH_PAGE	No	No	No	Yes	Yes

Table 13-1. Yes *indicates that the page lock held is compatible with the page lock requested;* No *means they're not compatible.*

Table Lock Held	Table Lock Requested			
	SH_TAB	EX_TAB	SH_INT	EX_INT
SH_TAB	Yes	No	Yes	No
EX_TAB	No	No	No	No
SH_INT	Yes	No	Yes	Yes
EX_INT	No	No	Yes	Yes

Table 13-2. Yes *indicates that the table lock held is compatible with the table lock requested;* No *means they're not compatible.*

Lock compatibility comes into play between locks of the same type, such as table locks or page locks. A table and a page obviously represent an implicit hierarchy since a table is made up of multiple pages. If an exclusive page lock (EX_PAGE) is held on one page of a table, another process cannot get even a shared table lock (SH_TAB) for that table. This hierarchy is protected via intent table locks (SH_INT and EX_INT). A process acquiring an EX_PAGE, UP_PAGE, IX_PAGE, or LN_PAGE lock will first acquire an EX_INT lock on the table, signaling its intention to modify a portion of the table. Granting the EX_INT lock prevents another process from acquiring the SH_TAB lock on that table. (Remember, EX_INT and SH_TAB are not compatible.) Similarly, a process acquiring an SH_PAGE lock must first acquire an SH_INT lock for the table, which would prevent another process from acquiring an EX_TAB lock. Or if the EX_TAB lock already existed, the SH_INT lock would not be granted and the SH_PAGE lock would have to wait until the EX_TAB lock was released. Without intent locks, process A could lock a page in a table with an exclusive page lock, while process

B could place an exclusive table lock on the same table and hence think it has rights to modify the entire table, including the page that process A has exclusively locked.

At the risk of stating the obvious, compatibility of locks is an issue only when the locks affect the same object. For example, two or more processes can each hold exclusive page locks simultaneously, as long as the locks are on different pages.

Even though two locks may be compatible, the requester of the second lock might still have to wait if an incompatible lock is already waiting. For example, suppose that process A holds an SH_PAGE lock. Process B requests an EX_PAGE lock and must wait because SH_PAGE and EX_PAGE are not compatible. Process C requests a SH_PAGE lock that is compatible with the SH_LOCK already outstanding to process A. However, the SH_PAGE lock cannot be immediately granted. Process C must wait for the SH_PAGE lock, because process B is ahead of it in the lock queue with a request (EX_PAGE) that is not compatible.

By examining the compatibility of locks not only to those processes granted but also to those processes waiting, SQL Server prevents *lock starvation*. Lock starvation results if overlapping requests for shared locks keep occurring, so the request for the exclusive lock would never be able to be granted. (It would be starved.)

Bound Connections

Remember that the issue of lock *contention* applies only between different processes (also called *connections*). A process holding locks on a resource does not lock itself from the resource—only other processes are prevented access. But any other process (or connection to SQL Server) could actually execute as the same application and user. It is common for applications to have more than one connection to SQL Server. Every such connection is treated as an entirely different SQL Server process, and by default no sharing of the "lock space" occurs between connections, even if they belong to the same user and the same application. (Again, in this context, "process" means a SQL Server subtask, not a Windows NT process.)

Beginning with version 6.5, however, it is possible for two different connections to share a lock space and hence not lock each other out. This capability is known as a *bound connection*. With a bound connection, the first connection asks SQL Server to give out its *bind token*. The bind token is passed by the application (using a global variable, shared memory, or another method) for use in subsequent connections. The bind token acts as a "magic cookie" so that those other connections can share the lock space of the original connection. Locks held by bound connections do not lock each other. (The **sp_getbindtoken** and **sp_bindsession** system stored procedures get and use the bind token.) Bound connections are especially useful if you are writing an extended stored procedure, which is a function you've written in your own DLL, and that extended stored procedure needs to call back into the database to do some work. Without a bound connection, the extended stored procedure would collide with its own calling process's locks. When multiple processes share a lock and transaction space by using bound connections, a COMMIT or ROLLBACK affects all the participating connections.

Row-Level Locking vs. Page-Level Locking

The debate over whether row-level locking is better than page-level locking or vice versa is one of those near-religious wars and warrants a few comments here. Despite those who would have you believe that one is always better, it's not really that simple.

Locking isn't free. Considerable resources are required to manage locks. Recall that a lock is an in-memory structure of about 28 bytes. If you needed a lock for every row and you were scanning a million rows, more than 25 MB of RAM would be required just to hold locks for that one process. In practice, the memory needs are even greater when you include the resource lock blocks and the lock owner block.

Beyond the memory consumption issues, locking is a fairly processing-intensive operation. Managing locks requires substantial bookkeeping. (Recall that, internally, SQL Server uses a lightweight mutex called a spinlock to guard resources, and it uses rlocks—also lighter than full-blown locks—to protect non–leaf level B-Tree pages. These are performance optimizations used to avoid the overhead of full locking.) If a page of data contains 50 rows of data, all of which will be used, it is obviously much more efficient to issue and manage one lock on the page than it would be to manage 50. That's the obvious benefit of page locking—a reduction in the number of lock structures that must exist and that must be managed.

If two different processes each need to update a few separate rows of data, and some of the rows needed by each process happen to exist on the same page, one process must wait until the page locks of the other process are released. If, in this case, you used row-level locking instead of page-level locking, the other process would not have to wait. The finer granularity of the locks means that no conflict occurs in the first place because each process is concerned with different rows. That's the obvious benefit of row-level locking. Which of these "obvious benefits" wins? Well, it's not clear cut, and it depends on the application and the data. Each type of locking can be shown to be superior for different types of applications and usage.

You can expect that in a future release, SQL Server will determine at runtime whether to page lock or row lock. The type of locking chosen will be based on the number of rows and pages to be scanned, the number of rows on a page, the isolation level in effect, the update activity going on, and so on. Perhaps the best of both worlds would be to "deescalate" locks—that is, start at a coarser level of locking and change to more granular locks if and only if there is a conflict for the coarse lock. For example, suppose that you have two processes that will each update a few rows. Process A might start with page locking. If no other process requests a lock of the same page, no contention occurs, so the additional overhead of doing locking for every row does not happen. But if process B asks for a lock on one of the pages locked by process A, those held locks could be deescalated to row locks for only the rows that are actually needed. Having failed to obtain the page-level lock, process B could then also try to get a lock on only the specific rows it needs, rather than on the entire page. If the rows needed are not the same between the processes, there is no contention and each gets its own row locks. But when there is no contention for rows, the reduced overhead of only locking at the page level can be realized. You could begin the locking at an even coarser level, such as at the table level, and deescalate as needed to a page, and then further to a row, and conceptually even further to perhaps a column level, although this might be stretching the model. A deescalation locking strategy is being studied for future releases in the long term, although its inclusion is far from definite. As of version 6.5, SQL Server uses predominantly page-level locking, although it offers row-level locking for insert operations, which I'll discuss next.

Insert Row-Level Locking

The most common situation in which page-level locking causes lock contention is during insert operations, and insert row-level locking (IRL) can help. But first I'll describe the problem. Insert operations are prone to develop "hot spots" for page locking, which can occur when records are inserted and one of the following conditions exists:

- A table does not have a clustered index. In this case, all inserts go to the last page of the table, and the last page becomes the hot spot, often referred to as the *last-page collision*.

- A table has a clustered index with a sequential key value, such as an identity column. Figure 13-3 on the next page shows an example. The *cust_num* column is the primary key of a table. *cust_num* is an auto-sequencing identity column and has a clustered index. In this case, *cust_num* 51 would try to fit on the same page as 50, and 52 would try to fit on the same page as 51, and so on. This causes a last-page collision, since the sequential key value of the clustered index makes all insert operations compete for space on the last page.

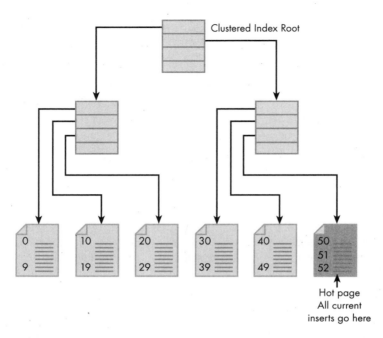

Clustered Index Root

Hot page
All current
inserts go here

Figure 13-3. *Hot spots can occur when a table has a clustered index with a sequential key.*

- A table has a nonclustered index on a sequential key value, as shown in Figure 13-4. In this case, it appears that the database designer recognized the issue of the last-page collision caused by a clustered index on a column like *cust_num*. So the designer intelligently decided to make the clustered index on a column with a wider range of values, such as *cust_name*. But because the designer still wants fast access on exact matches on the *cust_id*, the designer chose to also add a nonclustered index on *cust_id*, which results in the nonclustered index becoming the hot spot. An insert operation would still need to lock the leaf page of the nonclustered index containing the *cust_id* value. Because that value is sequential, the nonclustered index page becomes a hot spot even though there is no longer a last-page collision on the data page.

Insert row-level locking, added in version 6.5, can often eliminate hot-spot pages that result from insert operations in the situations described above. However, if the table has a clustered index (and most tables should), IRL can be used only if the clustered index is also a unique index (as would be true in the case of a primary key, for example). Because applications created in versions earlier than 6.5 could experience behavioral differences because of suddenly locking rows (not pages, as was formerly the case), IRL is turned off by default and must be explicitly enabled for a table. You can enable IRL for all insert activity for a specific table by using the **sp_tableoption** system stored procedure, or you can use DBCC ROWLOCK and immediately enable IRL only for a specific connection.

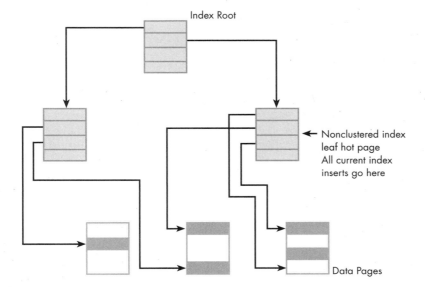

Figure 13-4. *Hot spots can occur when a table has a nonclustered index on a sequential key.*

If you understand the lock-compatibility concepts that were presented earlier in this chapter, IRL should be easy to understand. Simply remember that there are two additional types of page locks: IX_PAGE (insert page) and LN_PAGE (link page). These then become part of a hierarchy of page locks that allow two locks to simultaneously exist on the same page so long as both processes are doing an insert operation. You'll notice that protecting a specific row during insert activities occurs through a special hierarchy of page locks. There is no explicit ROW lock type—rather, these page locks include row *slot* information and have clear compatibility behaviors with other page locks.

Insert page locks

Multiple transactions can obtain an insert page lock on a page while concurrently inserting data. An IX_PAGE is compatible only with other IX_PAGE locks and is held until the transaction completes. The lock structure records the row number or slot being used so that two processes, each with an IX_PAGE, don't compete for the same slot in which to put the row.

Link page locks

An LN_PAGE is obtained by the first process that detects that the current page is full and that a new page needs to be allocated and linked to the current page. The transaction's IX_PAGE is upgraded to an LN_PAGE. Each subsequent request for an IX_PAGE is blocked until the transaction owning the LN_PAGE completes.

Lock Escalation

SQL Server automatically *escalates* page locks to coarser table locks as appropriate. This escalation protects system resources—it prevents the system from running out of locks and increases efficiency. For example, after a query acquires many page locks, the lock level can be escalated to a table lock. If every page in a table needs to be visited, it probably makes more sense to do a single table lock than to do many page locks. Then a single table lock would be acquired and the many page locks would be released. This escalation to a table lock reduces the locking overhead and also keeps the system from running out of locks. (Recall that a lock is a memory structure. Because there is a finite amount of memory, there must be a finite number of locks. You configure SQL Server for the maximum number of locks your system is expected to need.)

You can specify the point at which locks are escalated as either a specific number of locks or as a percentage of how many pages a table has. (For example, you might choose to escalate to a table lock if more than 40 percent of the table must be scanned.) The default configuration is to escalate from page locks to table locks if more than 200 page locks for an object are acquired. If you are running out of locks, you can configure the system to escalate sooner, you can use the **sp_configure** system stored procedure to configure more locks in the first place, or you can do both. Keep in mind that the configuration for the locks uses memory and that the memory is allocated (and hence not available for other things) whether or not a lock is used. Ideally, you want to configure for plenty of locks and related lock structures, but you shouldn't overdo it.

The ***sp_configure*** *'locks'* setting allocates not only the number of locks but also an equal number of resource lock blocks and lock owner blocks. Given the respective size of these structures (28, 28, and 32 bytes for a total of 88 bytes), configuring for 10,000 locks would use 880,000 bytes of memory (0.84 MB). That's not bad, and 10,000 locks are enough for most systems. But the only reason 10,000 are enough for most cases is the availability of lock escalation. Without escalation, you'd likely need 30 to 40 times more locks in a system.

Lock Hints and Application Issues

Just as you can specify hints on queries to direct the optimizer to choose a certain index or strategy in its query plan, you can also specify hints for locking. For example, if you know that your query will scan so many rows that its page locks will escalate to table locks, you can direct the query to use table locks in the first place, which would be more efficient. I'll detail the use of lock hints and locking contention issues in Chapter 14, "Design and Query Performance Implications."

For now, armed with the knowledge of locking you've gained here, you might want to watch the locking activity of your system to understand how and when locks are occurring. Trace flag 1204 provides detailed information about deadlocks, and this information can help you understand why locks are occurring and how you might change the order of access to objects to reduce them. Trace flag 1200 provides detailed locking information as every request for a lock is made. (But be prepared, the output of 1200 is voluminous.)

SUMMARY

SQL Server allows you to manage multiple users simultaneously and ensure that transactions observe the properties of the chosen isolation level—this is a key feature. Locking is used to guard data and the internal resources that make it possible for a multiple-user system to operate with behavior like that of a single-user system. In this chapter, I discussed the locking mechanisms within SQL Server, including full locking for data and leaf-level index pages and lightweight locking mechanisms for internally used resources.

I also discussed the types and granularities of locks as well as lock compatibility and lock escalation. It is important to understand the issues of lock compatibility to design and implement high-concurrency applications. I introduced you to deadlocks and showed you how to avoid them. I commented on the row-level locking versus page-level locking "holy war," and I discussed the SQL Server development team's philosophy about this contentious issue. A good understanding of locking is important so that you can design, develop, and deploy applications that perform as you want them to in multiple-user environments.

PART

FOUR

Performance and Tuning

14

Design and Query Performance Implications

Introduction

If you want to end up with a poorly performing application or a complete project failure, you should wait until the end of the project to deal with performance concerns. If, however, you want your application to be the best it can be, it is crucial that you consider performance *throughout the development cycle*. In fact, you really must consider performance before you write your first line of code.

Throughout this book, I have included performance information and insights to some extent in nearly every discussion. If you've turned directly to this chapter in hopes of finding the secret recipe to reform your lackluster application, you will be disappointed. Truth is, there are no magic ingredients. Instead, there are guidelines that you need to keep in mind—in this chapter, I will present many of them, with some pointers that refer back to information I already covered or to other materials that you might find useful.

SQL Server can be a brilliantly fast system with a well-designed, well-implemented application. I know of many customer success stories and production systems that support workloads of the type and size that I never dreamed possible back in 1988 when I started working with SQL Server. And performance on industry-standard benchmarks and on various review benchmarks also bear out its superb relative performance characteristics. But with a poorly planned or poorly implemented system, SQL Server can perform horribly. Having worked in the database industry for many years, I know that DBMS's tend to get blamed for bad applications. Statements like "SQL Server is slow" are not uncommon. (Nor are such statements about other database products.) Anytime I hear this from someone who has deployed a production application, I immediately assume that the person has dropped the ball somewhere along the line. Had the project been properly planned, performance issues and problems would have been identified up front—or perhaps SQL Server's unsuitability to the task at hand would have been realized. (Although SQL Server today can handle a large percentage of systems, some systems are still beyond its reach. For example, I would not urge United Airlines to rewrite its reservation system to use SQL Server today, but in a few years my opinion might well be different.)

This chapter presents a list of items that you should keep in mind, followed by a discussion of each item and, in some cases, suggestions about where to go to get more information—back to an earlier chapter, to an external source, or to a topic covered later in this chapter or later in the book. If this is the first chapter you've turned to, please stop now and go back at least to Chapter 3, "SQL Server Architecture." All the chapters from Chapter 3 up to this one are relevant to performance issues. You might also be well served to reread Chapter 11, "Cursors," (if you use them) and Chapter 13, "Locking," if you are not very familiar with these topics. A thorough understanding of cursors and locking is a prerequisite for understanding the material in this chapter.

Performance Guidelines

Take a look at a quick checklist of the steps you need to include when planning and implementing good performance in your system (on the facing page). I'll explain these items in detail later in this chapter and in Chapter 15.

Develop Expertise on Your Development Team

There is a high correlation between a software project's success and the experience and skill levels of the staff developing it. Your second SQL Server development project will be better than your first, no matter how smart you are, so don't make your first SQL Server project one that will demand thousands of concurrent users, manage tens of gigabytes of data, and replicate data to 10 other servers. If you tackle such an extensive project your first time out, chances are you'll fail (or in the best case, you'll finish over schedule and over budget). Whenever I see proposals for big projects, one of the first questions I ask is about the prior experience of members of the development team. The difference between success and failure usually hinges on the people involved. One of the biggest mistakes I see people make is overestimating their skill. It's useful to have experience working with other systems and environments, because those skills will help you use SQL Server. But even with those skills, you can't expect a 100 percent direct transformation to successful SQL Server development.

- ✔ Develop expertise on your development team
- ✔ Understand that there is no substitute for solid application and database design
- ✔ State performance requirements for peak, not average, use
- ✔ Consider perceived response time for interactive systems
- ✔ Prototype, benchmark, and test throughout the development cycle
- ✔ Create useful indexes
- ✔ Choose appropriate hardware
- ✔ Use cursors judiciously
- ✔ Use stored procedures almost always
- ✔ Minimize network round-trips
- ✔ Understand update modes (direct and deferred)
- ✔ Understand concurrency and consistency trade-offs
- ✔ Analyze and resolve locking (blocking) problems
- ✔ Analyze and resolve deadlock problems
- ✔ Monitor and tune queries
- ✔ Review/adjust Windows NT settings
- ✔ Review/adjust SQL Server configuration settings
- ✔ Measure using Performance Monitor
- ✔ Make only one change at a time and measure its effect
- ✔ Do periodic database maintenance

I think companies are smartest when they decide to start with a small, less-than-mission-critical system before eventually moving many applications over to SQL Server. Staff members can learn a tremendous amount from developing and working with their first system, so it's best to make a mission-critical system the second system developed, not the first one. If your management will not allow you the luxury of having a "practice," you should at least try to augment your team with an experienced consultant or two. Look for someone who, at a minimum, is a Microsoft Certified Professional (MCP) in SQL Server. I don't think this alone guarantees that the person is truly an expert, but it at least raises the bar. I encourage you to make it a goal that every member of your development team be able to pass, handily, the SQL Server MCP exams.

Of course, before you begin that first project, you need to educate yourself and your staff. Experience will build on education, and some education will "click" only after you have gained some experience. But you need *both* to succeed in large-scale development projects. This book, while hopefully useful, can't replace all other training. And skills such as database design, which transcend SQL Server specifically, are nonetheless essential for a project's success. Near the end of this book, I list some suggested reading that I have found useful, and certainly there are many other good sources of information.

More Information...

The course "Performance Tuning and Optimization of Microsoft SQL Server 6.5" (course number 665) is worthwhile. Microsoft develops this course with input from the development group. In fact, some information in this chapter regarding the query optimizer and configuration settings comes from that course material. Microsoft makes the course available at Authorized Technical Education Centers (ATECs). For more information on ATECs and classes, visit the Web page at http://www.microsoft.com/atec.

Enforce Solid Application and Database Design

The biggest performance gains come from changes to the application and database design. For example, you might change your configuration settings and add heftier hardware and be thrilled when performance doubles. But changes to the application can often result in even larger performance increases. The potential pot of gold lies in the application.

There are as many approaches to software development as there are pages in this book. I have my own opinions as to how to approach development, and they've served me well. I'll recommend some guidelines here, but keep in mind that no single approach is the right approach—yours must be tailored to the size of the project, the team on hand, and the skill level of the team.

Normalize Your Database

I assume that if you're reading this book, you understand the concept of *normalization* and terms such as *third normal form*. (If you don't know these concepts, it is crucial that you stop now and learn about them. I recommend Candace Fleming and Barbara Von Halle's book on database design and Pat O'Neil's *Database* textbook, both of which are included in the suggested reading list. A plethora of other books about database design and normalization are also available.)

A *normalized database* eliminates functional dependencies in the data so that updating the database is easy and efficient. But querying from that database might require a lot of joins between tables, so common sense comes into play. If the most important and time-critical function your system must perform is fast querying, it often makes sense to consciously back off from a normalized design to one that has some functional dependencies. (That is, the design is not in third normal form or higher.) Think of normalization as typically being good for updating but potentially bad for querying. Start with a normalized design, and then look at all the demands that will be placed on the system.

From the Author...

I'm being a bit loose with terminology here. There really isn't a binary concept of being "normalized" or "not normalized." There are, of course, degrees of normalization, with *first normal form* not being what most people would call "normalized," since it has repeating groups and functional dependencies. Yet even that level is "normalized"—at the *first level.* Colloquially, it is common to refer to a database that is at least in third normal form as "normalized" and to refer to a database at a lower level of normalization as "denormalized." But since every database has some level of normalization, a term like "denormalized" doesn't really make much sense, strictly speaking. And, of course, levels of normalization beyond third normal form also exist. But to keep the discussion simple, I am using the terms in the way that I think most people think of them, imprecise though it may be. Again, when I refer to a *normalized database,* I mean one that is generally in third normal form (or higher). And when I refer to a *denormalized database,* I mean one that is in first or second normal form. My apologies to those who make their livings doing entity-relationship diagrams and are horrified by my loose use of these terms.

If you understand the data elements that you are going to need to record and you understand data modeling, producing a normalized design is not difficult. It shouldn't take weeks. It is true, however, that the person producing a normalized design might need a considerable amount of time—weeks—to learn about the underlying elements and processes that will need to be recorded in the database. To create a data model for a new system, you should first learn about the way a business operates, and that might take some time. But if you or someone else already understands the underlying processes to be modeled and you know how to do data modeling, the mechanics of producing a normalized database design are quite straightforward. There's no rocket science here, and I think it's rather intuitive (although some do portray it as a kind of mystical art).

Once you have produced a normalized design, which you can also think of as the *logical design,* you need to decide if you can implement the design nearly "as is" or if you will need to modify it to fit your performance characteristics. A lot of people have trouble with this. Rather than try to articulate specific performance characteristics, people generalize and define performance in ways like this—"as fast as possible" or "as many users as we can handle." Although goals can be difficult to articulate precisely, you should at least set relative goals.

Because there are trade-offs to be made between update and query performance, for example, it's important that you understand the relative demands and expectations for each. If, for example, your agent is supposed to call up all of a customer's records while the customer is waiting on the phone, that action had better occur within a few seconds. Or suppose you want to run a bunch of batch processes and reports for your manufacturing operation each night, and you have a window of four hours in which to do it—you have a pretty clear objective that needs to be met.

Evaluate Your Critical Transactions

I recommend that you immediately look at your *critical transactions*—that is, those transactions whose performance will make or break the system. (In this context, I'm using the term "transaction" a bit loosely. I mean any operation on the database.) You should evaluate which tables and joins will be required to run your critical transactions. Are the data accesses going to be straightforward or complicated? For example, say that you have looked at your needs and you realize that it is imperative that a given query must have a 1 to 2 second response time. Your system will access customer records while an agent is on the phone with the customer, so fast response in retrieving those records will make or break the system. But your normalized design will require a seven-way join!

If this particular query is the most important operation in your system, it's worth looking at what *not* being normalized would cost—although it's not necessarily out of the question for the seven-way join to return as fast as you require. That is, if tables are properly indexed, the query is well qualified, the search parameters are quite selective, and not a lot of data needs to be returned, the quick response might be possible. But this situation would stand out for me as a likely trouble area—I'd want to consider other alternatives before I implemented this design. In fact, anytime I get beyond a four-way join, I look for alternatives. For a query like this example, you might find that you could redundantly carry a little extra information on a couple of tables to make it just a three-way join. The cost you'd incur is in terms of the extra overhead that's required to correctly update (including insert and delete activity) the redundant data in multiple places. If update activity is infrequent or less important and the query performance is essential, altering your design is likely worth the cost. You might alternatively decide that rather than compute a customer's balance by retrieving a large amount of data, you can simply maintain summary values. You could use triggers to update these values incrementally anytime a customer's records change. (That is, you could take the old value and add to or average it, or so forth, but not compute the whole thing from scratch each time.) Then when you need the customer balance, it would be available, precomputed. The cost occurs in the extra update overhead needed for the trigger to keep the value up-to-date, as well as in the small amount of additional storage needed.

Creating proper indexes is probably the single most important factor in getting the query performance you need. But you'll have query-versus-update trade-offs, similar to those described above, when you decide on the indexing of tables, because indexes speed retrieval but slow updating. Chapter 8, "Modifying Data," shows the extra work that must be performed and logged when doing updates that require index maintenance. With many indexes, maintenance becomes more substantial than the update of the data itself. Realizing this, I like to lay out my critical transactions and look for the likely problems early on. If I can keep joins on critical transactions to four tables or less, and preferably make them simple equijoins, I know I'm in good shape to proceed.

Nothing in this is new, nor is it specific to SQL Server. We did all this back in the mainframe days. Back then, we used a technique known as *completing a CRUD chart*. CRUD stands for Create-Retrieve-Update-Delete. In SQL, this would translate as ISUD, Insert-Select-Update-Delete. Conceptually, CRUD is pretty simple. You draw a matrix with critical transactions on the vertical axis and tables with their fields on the horizontal axis. The matrix gets real big, real quick, so creating it in Microsoft Excel or in your favorite spreadsheet program can be helpful. For each transaction, note which fields need to be accessed and how they are accessed, and note the access as *I-S-U*-and/or *D,* as appropriate. Make the granularity down to the field level so that you can gain insights into what information you're going after in each table. This is the information you will need if you decide to carry some fields redundantly in other tables to reduce the number of joins required. Of course, some transactions require many tables to be accessed, so be sure to note whether the tables are accessed sequentially or via a join. You should also indicate the frequency and time of day that a transaction runs, what is its expected performance, and how critical it is that the transaction meet the performance metric.

How formal and exhaustive you make this exercise is up to you. I like to get to the level at which I have a clear idea of where my hot spots will likely occur for my critical transactions. Some people like to try to think of every transaction in the system, but I'm not smart enough to think of them all in advance. And what's more, it doesn't matter: only a few critical transactions need special care so that the system handles them in a way that meets your needs. Other transactions can more or less lie where they fall.

I wouldn't worry much about those noncritical reports that will run only in off-hours and that are unlikely to be much of an issue. Instead, you want to identify areas that look like they'll potentially cause problems. For example, if you have to do frequent select operations simultaneously on the tables that are being updated the most, you might be concerned about locking conflicts. What transaction isolation level must you operate with—could your query live with Uncommitted Read and not conflict with the update activity? If your most important performance objective is to allow an agent on the phone to retrieve a customer's records within 2 seconds, you should look at how many tables must be joined to do this. If it requires a join of many tables, you might look at less normalized designs to make the query simpler and to see what that will cost in terms of update performance and complexity.

If you are doing complex joins or expensive aggregate functions—SUM(), AVG(), and so on—for what are common or critical queries, you should explore techniques like the following and you should understand the trade-offs between query performance improvement and the cost to your update processes:

- Add logically redundant columns to reduce the number of tables to be joined.

- Use triggers to maintain aggregate summary data, such as customer balances, the highest value, and so forth. Such aggregates can usually be incrementally computed quickly. The update performance impact can be slight, but the query performance improvement can be dramatic.

Keep Table Row Lengths and Keys Compact

When creating tables, you need to understand the trade-offs of using variable-length columns (and consult Chapter 6, "Tables"). As a general rule, data with substantial variance in the actual storage length and that is not a hot spot for update activity is appropriate for variable-length columns. Also remember that the more compact the row length, the more rows will fit on a given page. Hence, a single I/O operation with compact rows is more efficient than an I/O operation with longer row lengths—it returns a higher number of rows and the data cache allows more rows to fit into the fixed amount of memory. (Review the discussion in Chapter 8, and understand the impact a variable-length column can have on the update strategy that you choose. It can cause your update strategy to change from update-in-place to delete/insert. And recall that any column that allows NULL is variable-length and has the same effect on the update strategy, even if the datatype is not ostensibly a variable-length type.)

As with tables, when creating keys you should try to make primary key field(s) compact. If no naturally compact primary key exists, use an identity column as a surrogate. And recall that if the primary key is a composite of multiple columns, the columns are indexed in the order that they are declared to the key. The order of the columns in the key can greatly affect how selective, and hence how useful, the index is.

Occasionally, a given table will have some columns that are infrequently used or modified, while others are very hot. In such cases, it can make sense to break the single table into two tables; then you can join them back together. This is kind of the reverse of denormalization as you commonly think of it. In this case, you do not carry redundant information to reduce the number of tables; instead, you increase the number of tables to more than is logically called for to put the hot columns into a separate, narrower table. With the more compact row length, you'll get the benefits of more rows per page and potentially a higher cache-hit ratio. As for any movement away from your normalized model, however, you should do this only when you have good reason to do so. After you complete a CRUD chart analysis, you might see that while your customer table is frequently accessed, 99 percent of the time this access occurs just to find out a customer's credit balance. You might decide to maintain this balance via a trigger rather than by recomputing it each time the query occurs. Information such as the customer addresses, phone numbers, e-mail addresses, and so on are large fields that make the table have a wide row length. But all that information is not needed for critical transactions—only the customer balance is needed. In this case, splitting the table into two could result in the difference between fitting, say, 150 rows on a page instead of only 2 or 3 rows. The more narrow table will result in a better likelihood that the customer balance will be able to be read from cache rather than by requiring a physical I/O.

State Performance Requirements for Peak Usage

It is not unusual for someone to ask me a question like, "Do you think SQL Server could handle our system? We do a million transactions a day." Even if I know exactly the transactions they have in mind (which, of course, I usually don't), I can't answer this question as posed because I don't know the system's peak usage. If a million transactions a day are nicely spread out over 24 hours, that's less than 12 transactions per second. Although without more information I still couldn't say with certainty whether SQL Server could handle the load, in general I'd say that a 12-TPS (transaction-per-second) system would be no trouble. But if 90 percent of the million transactions come in between 2 o'clock and 3 o'clock every day, it's a very different situation—with rates of about 275 TPS on average during that hour and probably peaks of more than 350 TPS. At these rates, my answer will be in the "It depends on the nature of the transactions" category. Certainly there are benchmarks, like Debit-Credit, in which SQL Server performs over 1500 TPS, but because all transactions are different, you can't simply extrapolate this TPS number and assume that your system can achieve it. It is meaningless to refer to how many transactions per second SQL Server, *or any system,* can handle without also talking about what specific transactions will occur.

Regardless of the specific transactions, though, you need to design and build your system to handle *peak usage*. In the case above, in which a million transactions a day must be handled, the important consideration is peak usage, which will determine whether you'll target your system to usage rates of about 350 TPS for unevenly distributed usage or to a much lower volume of only 12 TPS with usage spread out evenly. (Most systems experience peaks, and daily usage is not so nicely spread out.)

Consider Perceived Response Time for Interactive Systems

Systems are often built and measured without the appropriate performance goals in mind. In measuring query performance, for example, most designers tend to measure the time that it takes for the query to complete. By default, this is how SQL Server decides to cost query performance. But this might not be the way your users perceive system performance. To users, performance is often measured by the amount of time that passes between pressing the Enter key and getting some data. As a program designer, you can use this to your advantage. For example, you can make your application begin displaying results as soon as the first few rows are returned; if many rows will appear in the result set, you don't have to wait until they are all processed. These differences in approach can be used to dramatically improve the user's perception of the system's responsiveness. So although the time required to get the last row might be about the same with both approaches, the time it takes to get the first row can be different between the two approaches—and the *perceived* difference can translate into the success or failure of the project.

By default, SQL Server optimizes a query based on the total estimated I/O to process the query to completion. If you recall the architectural discussion in Chapter 3, you know that if a significant percentage of the rows in a table must be retrieved, it would be better to scan the entire table than to use a nonclustered index to drive the retrieval. (A clustered index, of course, would be ideal since the data would physically be ordered already. The discussion here pertains only to the performance trade-off of scan-and-sort versus use of a nonclustered index.) Retrieving a page via the nonclustered index requires traversing the B-Tree to get the address of a data page, and then retrieving that page and then traversing the B-Tree to get the address for the next data page and retrieving it, and so on. Many data pages will be read many times each, so the total number of page accesses can easily be more than the total number of pages included in the table. If your data and the corresponding nonclustered index are not highly selective, SQL Server will usually decide not to use that nonclustered index. That is, if the index is not expected to eliminate more than about 80 percent of the pages from consideration, it is typically more efficient to simply scan the table than to do all the extra I/O of reading both B-Tree and data pages. And by following the index, the data pages frequently need to be accessed multiple times each (once for every row pointed to by the index). Subsequent reads are likely to be from cache, not from physical I/O, but they are still much more costly than simply reading the page once for all the rows it contains (as happens in a scan). Scanning the table is the strategy SQL Server chooses in many cases, even if a nonclustered index is available that could be used to drive the query, and even if it would eliminate a sort to return the rows based on an ORDER BY clause. A scan strategy is chosen because it can be much less costly to execute the query in terms of total I/O and time.

However, that choice is based on SQL Server's estimate for how long it takes the query to complete in its entirety, not on the time it takes for the first row to be returned. If an index exists with a key that matches the ORDER BY clause of the query and the index is used to drive the query execution, there will be no need to sort the data to match the ORDER BY clause (because it's already ordered that way). The first row will be returned faster by SQL Server chasing the index, even though the last row returned could take considerably longer than it would take if the table were simply scanned and the chosen rows sorted.

In more concrete terms, let's say that a query that returns many rows takes 1 minute to complete using the scan-and-sort strategy and 2 minutes using a nonclustered index. With the scan-and-sort strategy, the user doesn't see the first row until all the processing is almost done—for this example, in about 1 minute. But with the index strategy, the user sees the first row within a *subsecond*—the time it takes to do, say, three I/O operations (read two levels of the nonclustered index and then read the data page). Scan-and-sort is faster in total time, but the nonclustered index is faster in returning the first row.

SQL Server provides an optimizer hint called FASTFIRSTROW that can be used to let SQL Server know that having the first row returned quickly is more important to your application than the total time, which would be the normal way query plans get costed. Later on, I'll discuss some techniques for speeding up slow queries and describe when it is appropriate to use the optimizer hint. For now, you should understand the issues of *response time* (the time needed to get the first row) versus *throughput* (the time needed to get all rows) when you are thinking about your system and stating your performance goals.

Typically, highly interactive systems should be designed for best response time, and batch-oriented systems should be designed for best throughput. Often, when I've met with a reviewer for a major industry publication who is writing a product review and doing a benchmark test, I've asked the reviewer whether the timed query tests will be based on first row returned or last row returned (or both). In most cases, the reviewer hadn't considered the question, even though it's a vitally important one. Be sure that you think about it when designing and writing your application.

Prototype, Benchmark, and Test Throughout Development

As you make changes in your design, application, hardware, or configuration, it is important that you measure the effects of these changes. A simple-to-run benchmark test that will allow you to take a scientific approach and measure differences is a tremendous asset. You'll want to balance the complexity of the benchmark system, because it has to correlate well with the expected performance of the real system. But it has to be relatively simple and easy to run or it won't be run regularly, which is essential. If you have a development "acceptance test suite" that you run before checking in any significant changes, you'll ideally add the benchmark to that test suite.

> **TIP**   Not measuring performance with at least a proxy test until the system is almost complete is a good recipe for failure. Optimism without data to back it up is usually misguided.

Your benchmark doesn't have to be sophisticated initially. You can create your database and populate it with a nontrivial amount of data at first—*thousands* of rows at a minimum. The data can be randomly generated, although the more representative you can make the data the better. For example, if a particular part represents 80 percent of your orders, you won't want all your test data to be randomly dispersed. Any differences in the selectivity of indexes between your real data and your generated test data will probably cause significant differences in the execution plans you choose. You should also be sure that you have data in related tables if you use FOREIGN KEY constraints. As I explained earlier in this book, the enforcement of FOREIGN KEY constraints requires that those related tables (either referenced or referencing) be accessed if you are modifying data in a column participating in the constraint. So the execution plan is sometimes considerably more complicated due to the constraints than might be apparent, and a plethora of constraints can result in a system that has no simple operations.

As a rule of thumb, you should start with at least enough data so that the difference between selecting a single row based on its primary key by using an index is dramatically faster than selecting such a row by using a table scan. (This assumes that the table in production will be large enough to reflect that difference.) Remember that the system will perform much differently depending on whether I/Os are physical or from the cache. So don't base your conclusions on a system that is getting high cache-hit ratios unless you have enough data to be confident that this behavior also will be true for your production system.

Early on in development, you should identify areas of lock contention between transactions and any specific queries or transactions that take a long time to run. And if table scans will be a drain on the production system, you need to have enough data early on so that the drain is apparent when you scan. If you can run with several thousand rows of data without lock contention problems and with good response time on queries, you're in a good position for proceeding with a successful development cycle. Of course, you need to continue monitoring and making adjustments as you ramp up to the actual system and add more realistic amounts of data and simultaneous users. And, of course, your system test also needs to take place on an ongoing basis before you deploy your application. It's not a one-time thing that you do the night before going live with a new system.

> **TIP** Before you roll out your production system, you must be able to conduct system tests with the same volumes of data and usage that the real system will have when it goes live. Crossing your fingers and hoping will not be good enough.

Obviously, if your smallish prototype is exhibiting lock contention problems or the queries do not fall well within your desired goals, it's not likely that your real, more taxing system will perform as desired. Run the stored procedures that constitute your critical transactions. You can use a simple tool like ISQL.EXE to dispatch them. First run each query or transaction alone—time it in isolation, and check the execution plans (*SET SHOWPLAN ON*). Then run multiple sessions to simulate multiple users. (A bit later, I'll show you how to analyze and improve a slow-running query.)

Also, based on your CRUD chart analysis (or on any other analysis you did of critical transactions), identify tasks that will run at the same time as your critical transactions. Add these other tasks to your testing routine to determine whether they are cause for concern regarding contention while they run simultaneously with your critical transactions. For example, suppose your critical transaction is **proc_take_orders**. When it runs, you also expect some reports and customer status inquiries to run. You should run some mixture of these types of processes while analyzing **proc_take_orders**. This will help you identify potential lock contention issues or other resource issues, such as high CPU usage, low cache hits, or space depletion in *tempdb*.

You might also want to take advantage of the SQL Server benchmark kit, which is available on the CD in this book as well as on the Microsoft Web site at http://www.microsoft.com/sql. Although the transaction in the kit will probably not be directly applicable to your situation, the benchmark framework provides the infrastructure you need to launch and coordinate multiple client tasks simultaneously to time their work for both throughput and response time. The kit also provides some example code for populating the test database. And the price is right—it's free! Other significant tools to help with your custom benchmarking are available from other companies. For example, Dynameasure from Bluecurve, Inc. (at http://www.bluecurve.com), provides tools that aid in performance measurement.

With an easy-to-run benchmark system, you will be equipped to approach your system deployment using the scientific method. You can hypothesize why a given change might make a difference in your system, whether the change occurs in the database design or indexing, application or querying, or hardware or configuration. Then you can test your hypothesis, rather than cross your fingers and hope for the best. Investing in a benchmark system for your application can give you fantastic returns.

A Rant Regarding Development Methodologies

This section might seem off the subject, but it does relate to topics like considering the truly critical transactions early on and the need for prototyping and measurement. It relates to the notion of how you design your system and the design's effect on performance issues. How much you spec, how you spec, when you start coding, and how prototyping factors in are all matters for which there is no consensus, and I truly believe there is no one right answer. What's right for one team or project could be wrong for another.

I like to remind my team that ultimately we ship products, not specs and design documents, so we need to remember the endgame. By that, I mean that the spec's purpose should be kept in perspective—it exists to clearly articulate and document how a module or system should work. It's there to help ensure that we know what we're building—developers know what to develop, testers know how a feature should work so that they can appropriately test it, and the documentation team can correctly describe the project's functionality.

A design document explains the approach and the general formation to accomplish the task at hand. The purpose of the design document is to ensure that the developer thinks through the approach before writing code. The brief design document is also vitally important to others who come in later and are new to the system. It should be written by the developer(s) and used as a tool for the developer to crystallize his or her thoughts. It might also discuss some options that were rejected and the reasons for their rejections. While writing the design document, the developer might have to write some quick prototype code to help think through an issue. Or if not actually including working code in the document, the developer should certainly write some pseudocode and include it as part of the document. I don't care much about format, eloquent introductions, or documents that try to give me pseudocode for every part of the system. But any development task that will take more than a couple of days to implement deserves a simple design document. Writing such a document should not be an academic exercise. I'm a busy guy, and I don't want to read a *book* for a design document; in fact, I simply can't do this, because I have too many time demands, and that's typical for most developers. Those fat specs and design documents tend to sit on a shelf and not be used. I think at most 15 pages, and often about 3 pages, should be sufficient for even a complex component if it's written succinctly. The best design documents can be read in one sitting, and the reader should come away understanding clearly how the system will be built.

After it's written, the design should be reviewed by other developers before coding begins. This is best done in a positive, informal atmosphere in which developers feel as if they are benefiting from the opportunity to have others contribute ideas. And, of course, in a healthy environment, developers are continually bouncing ideas off their peers while thinking of the design up front. Almost daily, I ask someone if I can buy them a cup of coffee (it's Seattle, so it's espresso) and use the person as a sounding board for an idea I have. I want this person to challenge my ideas, think about the cases I missed, and add some good ideas. If your developers don't regularly seek each other out as resources, your organization is somewhat dysfunctional and you need to try to fix this.

The design document should be to the point. Assume that the reader already knows *why* a module or component is needed. The document must provide the *how*. I have seen too many specs that have 40 pages describing the market need for something or why a product could be really cool if it were built, and then 1 page that in essence says, "We'll figure it out when we code it up." In my opinion, this is not useful. Nor are design documents that are copious in detail but don't bear much direct relationship with what actually gets built because issues identified later were not anticipated up front and the document didn't get updated. This usually happens when people who won't be doing the actual development write design documents. I think that most ivory-towered architecture groups tend to be disastrous. Developers *must* be at the core of the design of the system. There may be mentoring by more senior people, of course, but the developer must be involved both for understanding and to buy in that the plan will work and is doable. Forcing ideas down a developer's throat leads to a development fiasco.

I can't write a near-perfect spec up front, and I have not yet met anyone who can. So I think software methodologies that say you do all the spec and design up front and then you code it up don't work too well and usually result in failures or, at best, systems that do not perform well. I think prototyping the spec in an iterative fashion works far better. Areas that are clear don't need a prototype; use prototypes for areas fraught with nagging worries, for your critical transactions, and in a critical area of the system in which multiple approaches are possible or reasonable. For the tricky stuff that you can't describe or predict a best performance, prototypes provide enormous benefits.

A useful prototype can be "quick and dirty." If you don't worry about all the failure cases and every conceivable state in which something can exist, useful prototype code can often be produced in one-twentieth of the time it takes to create production-caliber code (in which you must worry about those things). However, the production code might be 10 times better because you have recognized and corrected deficiencies early on. You'll either junk the prototype code or maybe use it for the skeleton of the real system. Prototyping lets you learn and prove or disprove ideas, and then you can update the spec based on what you learn. And if you're selling your ideas to management or customers, your prototype can be useful to demonstrate proof of your concept.

As I said before, I believe every nontrivial development task deserves a brief design document. You need enough documentation to lay out the framework and system architecture and to detail how pieces fit together. But at the detailed levels, I find it works much better to simply comment the source code liberally and hand in hand with its being written and modified. In my experience, external design documentation rarely gets updated in a timely manner, so it quickly becomes useless. Developers should not be encouraged to write their code and then go back and comment it, even in prototyping. Commenting works only when it is done *as part of coding,* when it can help the programmer better think through issues, and results in more solid code. I have little use for worthless comments (like adding *incrementing i* before the statement *i++* in C). Rather, comments should tell me about the approach and intent of each routine, the expected inputs and outputs, and any side effects that might occur by changing the code. Tell me what operations are doing when it is not obvious. Don't assume that I am as smart as you are and will immediately grasp your subtleties, nuances, and mastery of the programming language. And when you change something after the fact, add a comment as to what you changed, when you changed it, and why you did so. A module should be commented well enough so that a tester or technical writer can get a good understanding of what is going on purely from reading the comments, even if those people are not skilled programmers.

That's it for my rant. As comedian Dennis Miller might say after one of *his* rants, "That's just my opinion. I could be wrong."

Create Useful Indexes

Creating useful indexes is one of the most important tasks you can do to achieve good performance. Creating indexes is part of designing the database, and as I said earlier, the biggest impact to performance is found in your database and application design. Indexes can dramatically speed up data retrieval and selection, but they are a drag on data modification because along with writing the changes to the data, the index entries must also be maintained and those changes logged. (For a refresher on indexes and the effects when modifying data, refer back to Chapter 3, "SQL Server Architecture," and Chapter 8, "Modifying Data.")

The key to creating useful indexes is to understand the system's demands of the data, the types and frequencies of queries performed, and the way indexes can be used by queries. The CRUD chart analysis or a similar technique is invaluable to this effort.

Guidelines for Creating Useful Indexes

As you create indexes, keep the following information in mind.

Choose the clustered index wisely

Clustered indexes are extremely useful for range queries (for example, *WHERE sales_date BETWEEN '1/1/94' and '12/31/94'*) and for queries in which the data must be ordered in a way that matches the clustering key. Only one clustered index can exist per table, since it defines the physical ordering of the data for that table. Since you can have only one clustered index per table, choose it carefully based on the most critical retrieval operations identified.

Because of the clustered index's role in managing space within the table, nearly every table should have one. And if a table will have only one index, it should usually be clustered. An exception to this might be a table that has a large amount of insert activity and little or no update or delete activity (for example, a pure history table).

If a table is declared with a primary key (advised), by default the primary key column(s) will form the clustered index. Again, this is because almost every table should have a clustered index, and if the table will have only one index, it should probably be clustered. But if your table will have several indexes, it is often the case that some other index would better serve as the clustered index. This is often true when you do single-row retrieval by primary key. A nonclustered, unique index works nearly as well in this case and still enforces the primary key. So save your clustered index for something that will benefit more from it by adding the keyword NONCLUSTERED when declaring the PRIMARY KEY constraint.

Make nonclustered indexes highly selective

A query using an index on a large table will often be dramatically faster than a query doing a table scan. But this is not always true, and table scans are not all inherently "evil." Nonclustered index retrieval means reading B-Tree entries to determine the data page that is pointed to and then retrieving the page, going back to the B-Tree, retrieving another data page, and so on, until many data pages are read over and over (subsequent retrievals may be from cache). With a table scan, the pages are read only once. If the index does not disqualify a large percentage of the rows, it is cheaper to simply scan the data pages, reading every page exactly once.

The query optimizer greatly favors clustered indexes over nonclustered indexes, because in scanning a clustered index, the system is already scanning the data pages. Once at the leaf of the index, the system has gotten the data as well. (Recall that the leaf pages of the clustered index are, in fact, the data pages of the table.) So there is no need to read the B-Tree, then read the data page, and so on. This is why nonclustered indexes must be able to eliminate a large percentage of rows to be useful (that is, they must be highly selective), whereas clustered indexes are useful even with less selectivity.

Indexing on columns used in the WHERE clause of frequent or critical queries is often a big win, but this usually depends on how selective the index is likely to be. For example, if a query has the clause *WHERE last_name = 'Stankowski'*, an index on *last_name* is likely to be very useful; it can probably eliminate 99.9 percent of the rows from consideration. On the other hand, a nonclustered index will probably not be useful on a clause of *WHERE sex = 'M'* because it eliminates only about half of the rows from consideration and the repeated steps needed to read the B-Tree entries just to read the data are much greater than simply making one single scan through all the data. So nonclustered indexes are typically not useful on columns that do not have a wide dispersion of values. Think of selectivity as the percentage of qualifying rows in the table (qualifying rows/total rows). If the ratio of qualifying rows to total rows is low, the index is highly selective and is most useful. If the index is used, it can eliminate most of the rows in the table from consideration and greatly reduce the work that must be performed. If the ratio of qualifying rows to total rows is high, the index has poor selectivity and will not be useful. A nonclustered index is most useful when the ratio is around 15 percent or less—that is, if the index can eliminate 85 percent of the rows from consideration. If the index has poorer selectivity than 15 percent, it probably will not be used; either a different index will be chosen as more useful or the table will be scanned. Recall that the first page of an index is a histogram of sampled data values for the index key, which the optimizer uses to estimate whether the index is selective enough to be useful to the query.

Tailor indexes to critical transactions

Indexes speed data retrieval at the cost of additional work for data modification. To determine a reasonable number of indexes, you must consider the frequency of updates versus retrievals and the relative importance of the competing types of work. If your system is almost pure decision-support (DSS) with little update activity, it makes sense to have as many indexes as will be useful to the queries being issued. A DSS might reasonably have a dozen or more indexes on a single table. If you have a predominantly online transaction processing (OLTP) application, you want relatively few indexes on a table—probably just a couple that have been carefully chosen.

The query optimizer usually uses no more than one index per table per query. (Queries with OR can sometimes use multiple indexes per table.) If your most critical transaction is a query with many predicates, don't assume that creating a bunch of indexes for that query will be a win—probably only one of them is useful and the others are overhead. Identify (by testing) the most useful index, and drop the others. It's a good strategy when testing your queries to create a bunch of indexes—do this on all the columns that look like decent candidates. Then see which of the indexes are actually used and drop all the rest. You don't want to keep a bunch of useless indexes around, and they are so easy to create and drop that you shouldn't hesitate to experiment. I cannot predict with high success and regularity the indexes and execution plan that will be chosen, and I doubt you can either, so there is no substitute for empirical testing.

Look for opportunities to achieve *index coverage* in queries, but don't get carried away. An index "covers" the query if it has all the data values needed as part of the index key. For example, if you had a query such as *SELECT emp_name, emp_sex FROM employee WHERE emp_name LIKE 'Sm%'* and you have a non-clustered index on *emp_name,* it might make sense to append the *emp_sex* column to the index key as well. Then the index would still be useful for the selection, but it would also already have the value for *emp_sex.* There would be no need for the optimizer to read the data page for the row to get the *emp_sex* value; the optimizer is smart enough to realize this and simply gets the value from the B-Tree key. The *emp_sex* column is probably a *char(1),* so the column doesn't add greatly to the key length, and this is a win. But some people can go too far and add all types of fields to the index. The net effect is that the index practically becomes a virtual copy of the table, just organized differently: far fewer index entries fit on a page, I/O increases, cache efficiency is reduced, and much more disk space is required. Be aware of the covered queries technique to improve some query performance, but use such queries with discretion.

A unique index (whether nonclustered or clustered), by definition, offers the greatest selectivity (that is, only one row can match), so it is most useful for queries that are intended to return exactly one row. Nonclustered indexes are great for single-row accesses via the PRIMARY KEY or UNIQUE constraint values in the WHERE clause.

Indexes are important for data modifications, not just for queries. Indexes can speed data retrieval—and not just for query operations. Searched update, searched delete, and cursor operations also benefit from good indexes. In fact, if no useful index for such operations exists, the only alternative is for SQL Server to scan the table to look for qualifying rows. This kind of scan is not only a potentially expensive operation, but it can significantly reduce concurrency by causing an exclusive table lock. Update or delete operations on only one row are common; you should do these operations using the primary key (or other UNIQUE constraint index) values to be assured that there is a useful index to that row and no others.

Updating indexed columns can affect the update strategy chosen. For example, updating any column that is part of the key of the clustered index on a table requires that the update be processed as a deferred update rather than as a direct update. In deciding which columns to index, especially which columns to make part of the clustered index, you must consider the effects the index will have on the update method used. (Review the discussion of update strategies in Chapter 8.)

Remember that column order is important

At the risk of stating the obvious, an index can be useful to a query only if the criteria of the query match the columns that are leftmost in the index key. For example, if an index has a composite key of *last_name, first_name*, that index would be useful for a query like *WHERE last_name = 'Smith'* or *WHERE last_name = 'Smith' AND first_name = 'John'*. But it would not be useful for a query like *WHERE first_name = 'John'*. Think of using the index like a phone book. You use a phone book as an index on last name to find the corresponding phone number. But the standard phone book is useless if you know only a person's first name because the first name could be located on any page.

Take care to put the most selective columns leftmost in the key of nonclustered indexes. For example, an index on *emp_name, emp_sex* would be useful for a clause such as *WHERE emp_name = 'Smith' AND emp_sex = 'M'*. However, if the index were defined as *emp_sex, emp_name*, it wouldn't be useful for most retrievals. The leftmost key, *emp_sex*, cannot rule out enough rows to make the index useful. Be especially aware of this regarding the indexes built to enforce a PRIMARY KEY or UNIQUE constraint defined on multiple columns. The index is built in the order the columns are defined for the constraint. So you should adjust the order of the columns in the constraint to make the index most useful to queries; doing so will not affect its duty in enforcing uniqueness.

Index columns used in joins

Index columns are frequently used to join tables. When you create a PRIMARY KEY or UNIQUE constraint, an index is automatically created for you. But no index is automatically created for the referencing columns in a FOREIGN KEY constraint. Such columns are frequently used to join tables, so they are almost always among the most likely candidates on which to create an index. If your primary key and foreign key columns are not naturally compact, consider creating a surrogate key using an identity column (or similar technique). Similar to row length for tables, if you can keep your index keys compact, you can fit many more keys on a given page, resulting in less physical I/O and better cache efficiency. And if you can join tables based on integer values like an identity, you avoid having to do relatively expensive character-by-character comparisons. Ideally, columns used to join tables will be integer columns—fast and compact.

Join density is the average number of rows in the inner table that match a row in the outer table being joined. Density can also be thought of as the average number of duplicates for an index key. A column with a unique index has the lowest possible density (there can be no duplicates) and hence is extremely selective for the join. If a column being joined has a large number of duplicates, it has a high density and is not very selective for joins. Joins are processed most often as nested iterations—basically a loop. For example, if while joining the *orders* table with *order_items,* the system starts with the *orders* table (the outer table), and then for each qualifying order row, the inner table is searched for corresponding rows. Think of the join being processed as "Given a specific row in the outer table, go find all corresponding rows in the inner table." If you think of joins in this way, you should know that it is important to have a useful index on the inner table, which is the one being searched for a specific value. For the most common type of join, an equijoin that looks for equal values in columns of two tables, the optimizer automatically decides which is the inner table and which is the outer table of a join. The table order that you specify for the join doesn't matter in the equijoin case. However, the order for outer joins must match the semantics of the query, so the resulting order is dependent on the order specified. (You can review Chapter 7, "Querying Data," for its discussion of outer joins.)

Create or drop indexes as needed

If you create indexes but find they aren't used, you should drop them. (You can see if the indexes are used by watching the plans produced via *SET SHOWPLAN ON.*) Unused indexes are overhead that slow modifications to data without helping retrieval.

Some batch-oriented processes that are query intensive would benefit from certain indexes. It is often the case that such processes as complex reports or end-of-quarter financial closings run infrequently. If this is the case, remember that creating and dropping indexes is simple. Consider a strategy of creating certain indexes in advance of your batch processes and then dropping them when those batch processes are done. In this way, the batch processes benefit from the indexes yet they do not add overhead to your OLTP usage.

Choose Appropriate Hardware

I don't advise trying to solve your problems solely by "killing them with hardware." You shouldn't hope that by buying a powerful system you can compensate for basic inefficiencies in the application or database design. No matter how fast your hardware is, you're unlikely to be pleased with a poorly designed and implemented database and application.

But having said this, using the appropriate hardware is extremely important. I covered this topic in depth in Chapter 4, "Planning for and Installing SQL Server." Remember that SQL Server performance, from the hardware perspective, is a function of the integer processing (CPU) power, the amount of memory in the system, and the I/O capacity of the system. It is vital that a system be well matched—even a system with tremendous CPU capacity might run SQL Server slower than a system with less CPU power if the first system has too little memory or I/O capacity. And when putting together your system, you should think carefully about not just the I/O capacity required but also about the fault tolerance capabilities needed. RAID solutions provide varying capabilities of increased I/O performance and fault tolerance. You need to decide up front on the appropriate level of RAID for your system. Chapter 4 also discusses your choices for RAID and how to decide which RAID level you need.

Use Cursors Judiciously

If you intend to use cursors heavily in your application, make sure you've closely read Chapter 11, "Cursors." Used properly, cursors are a great asset that provide valuable features not found in any other mainstream database product. But, as I discussed in Chapter 11, I have seen cursors misused in many systems, turning SQL Server into a network ISAM instead of a relational database. This problem is common if a system is being ported from a mainframe using VSAM (or a similar method) or upsized from a data store such as Btrieve or Microsoft FoxPro. In such cases, the cursor model of one-row-at-a-time processing seems familiar to developers with an ISAM background. Converting the ISAM calls to cursor calls looks easy, and it is. But doing so is great way to produce a bad application. You should approach your application in terms of set operations and nonprocedural code, and I strongly warn you to avoid the temptation of simply doing a quick port from an ISAM and using cursors extensively.

Use Stored Procedures Almost Always

While I urge you to think carefully before using cursors, I urge you to use stored procedures rather than dynamic SQL whenever possible. Recall from Chapter 3 the efficiencies that stored procedures bring in terms of not requiring the compilation of an execution plan for each execution. Plans can be reused and stay cached, available for subsequent use. Beyond the significant performance advantages, stored procedures can provide a valuable level of indirection between your applications and the database design. If your application issues a procedure like **get_customer_balance** and expects a result set to be returned, the underlying database can change, and as long as the procedure also changes to return the result set as expected, the application can be totally unaffected and unaware of the change. For example, perhaps you decide to denormalize your database design to provide faster query performance. The stored procedure can be changed to respecify the query. Perhaps many applications call the procedure. You can simply change the stored procedure once and never touch the application. In fact, a running application doesn't even need to be restarted—it would execute the new version of the stored procedure the next time it is called.

Minimize Network Round-Trips

Another good reason to use stored procedures is to minimize round-trips on the network (that is, the conversational TDS traffic necessary between the client application and SQL Server for every batch and result set). If you will take different actions based on data values, make those decisions directly in the procedure whenever possible. (Strictly speaking, you don't need to use a stored procedure to do this—a batch also provides this benefit.) Issue as many commands as possible in a batch. To illustrate this, try a simple test by inserting 100 rows first as a single batch and then as every insert in its own batch (that is, 100 batches). You'll see a performance improvement of an order of magnitude even on a LAN, and on a slow network the improvement will be stunning. While LAN speeds of 10 megabits per second (Mbps) are fast enough so that the network is generally not a significant bottleneck, speeds can be tremendously different on a slow network. A modem operating at 28.8 kilobits per second (Kbps) is roughly 300 times slower than your LAN. Although WAN speeds vary greatly, they typically can be 100 to 200 times slower than a LAN. The fast LAN performance might hide inefficient network use. A prime example of this phenomenon is often exposed while using cursors. Fetching each row individually might be tolerable on a LAN but will be intolerable via dial-up lines.

If a stored procedure has multiple statements, by default SQL Server sends a message to the client application at the completion of each statement to indicate the number of rows affected for each statement. This is known as a DONE_IN_PROC message in TDS-speak. However, most applications do not need DONE_IN_PROC messages, and applications written in DB-Library never use them. So if you are confident that your applications do not need these messages, you can disable them, which can cause a big performance win on a slow network when there is otherwise little network traffic. (I know of an application deployed on a WAN for which suppressing the DONE_IN_PROC messages made an order of magnitude performance improvement and literally was the difference between a successful deployment and a fiasco.)

Using the connection-specific option *SET NOCOUNT ON* disables these messages for the application. Note that while they are disabled, you will not be able to use the DB-Library **dbcount( )** function or the ODBC **SQLRowCount( )** function. However, you certainly can toggle NOCOUNT on and off as you need, and you can use *SELECT @@ROWCOUNT* even when NOCOUNT is on. You can also suppress the sending of DONE_IN_PROC messages by starting the server with trace flag 3640, which lets you suppress what might be needless overhead without touching your application. However, some ODBC applications can depend on the DONE_IN_PROC message, so you need to test your application before using trace flag 3640 in production—it can break applications written implicitly expecting that token, which is why it is safer to write applications specifically to use *SET NOCOUNT ON*. Microsoft Access is a notable application that uses the DONE_IN_PROC message and can break if you enable trace flag 3640.

It's a good idea to keep an eye on the traffic between your client applications and the server. An application designed and tuned for slow networks works great on a fast network, but the reverse is not true. If you use a higher level development tool that generates the SQL statements and issues commands on your behalf, it is especially important to keep an eye on what's moving across the network. The SQL Trace utility that comes with SQL Server lets you watch all traffic into the server. If you want to watch both commands in and responses sent, you can start the server from the command line with trace flags 4032 and 4031, which respectively display the server's receive and send buffers (for example, **sqlservr –c –T4031 –T4032**). Enabling these two flags dumps all conversation to and from the server to standard output for the **sqlservr** process, which will be the monitor if you start it from a console window. (Note that the output can get voluminous.) Whether you use SQL Trace or these trace flags, you can get all the exact commands and data being sent. Just to monitor network traffic, though, this might be overkill; a network sniffer, like Network Monitor (available with Microsoft Windows NT Server and Microsoft Systems Management Server) can work better if you only want to monitor network traffic. Network Monitor is easy to use, and even a neophyte to networking can immediately set it up and do a few mouse clicks to watch the amount of traffic between two machine pairs.

Understand Concurrency and Consistency Trade-Offs

If you are designing a multiple-user application that will both query and modify the same data, a good understanding of concurrency and consistency concepts is vital. *Concurrency* refers to the ability to have many simultaneous users operating at once. The more users who can simultaneously work well, the higher your concurrency. *Consistency* refers to the level at which the data in multiple-user scenarios exhibits the same behavior it would if only one user were operating at a time. Consistency is expressed in terms of isolation levels. Under the most consistent isolation level, Serializable, the multiple-user system behaves semantically identical to what would exist if users submitted their requests serially—that is, as though the system made every user queue up and run operations one at a time (serially). The cost to achieve Serializable results is a greater need to protect resources, which is done by locking and which reduces concurrency. (Be sure you understand locking concepts, discussed in Chapter 13, "Locking." You must also understand transactional concepts, as presented in Chapter 10, "Batches, Transactions, Stored Procedures, and Triggers." Key topics in these chapters deal with the compatibility of locks, transaction isolation levels, deadlocks, and the scope of transactions. You must understand these concepts well to effectively deal with blocking problems. If necessary, please go back and review them.)

In many typical environments, an ongoing struggle occurs between the OLTP demands on the database and DSS demands. Relatively high volumes of transactions that modify data characterize OLTP. The transactions tend to be relatively short and usually don't query large amounts of data. DSS is read-intensive, often with complex queries that can take a long time to complete and thus hold locks for a long time. The exclusive locks needed for data modification with OLTP applications block the shared locks used for DSS. And DSS tends to use many shared locks and often holds them for long periods, stalling the OLTP applications, which then must wait to acquire the exclusive locks required for updating. Beyond locking issues, DSS tends to benefit from many indexes and often from a denormalized database design that reduces the number of tables to be joined. Large numbers of indexes are a drag on OLTP because of the additional work to keep them updated. And denormalization means redundancy—a tax on the update procedures.

You need to understand the isolation level required by your application. Certainly, you do not want to request Serializable (or, equivalently, use the HOLDLOCK hint) if you need only Committed Read, or you would pay a potentially high cost in terms of holding shared locks longer than necessary. And it might become clear that some queries in your application really require only Uncommitted Read (dirty read), since they look for trends and don't need guaranteed precision. If that's the case, you potentially have some nice flexibility in terms of queries not requiring shared locks, which keeps them both from being blocked by processes modifying the database and from blocking those modifying processes. But even if you can live with a dirty-read level, I recommend that you use it only if it proves necessary. This isolation level means that you might read data that logically never existed so it poses some potentially weird conditions to the application. (For example, a row that's just been read seems to vanish because it gets rolled back.) If you find your application can live with dirty-read isolation level, it might be comforting to have that as a fallback. However, I recommend that you first try to make your application work with the standard isolation level of Committed Read and fall back to dirty read (Uncommitted Read) only when necessary.

Analyze and Resolve Locking (Blocking) Problems

Many applications suffer poor performance because processes are backed up waiting to acquire locks or because of deadlocks. A smooth, fast application should minimize the time spent waiting for locks, and it should avoid deadlocks. The most important step you can take is to first really understand how locking works. (See Chapter 13.) It is important that you become comfortable with locking concepts if you are going to resolve locking and deadlock situations.

The term *blocking* refers to the situation that occurs when a process is stalled because it is waiting to acquire a lock that is incompatible with a lock held by some other process. It is often, but erroneously, referred to as a "deadlock." As long as the process being stalled is not, in turn, stalling the offending process—which results in a circular chain that will never work itself out without intervention—you have a blocking problem, not a deadlock. If the blocking process is simply holding on to locks or is itself blocked by some other process, this is not a deadlock either. The process requesting the lock must wait for the other process to release the incompatible lock; but when it does, all will be fine. Of course, if the process holds that lock excessively, performance still grinds to a halt and you must deal with the blocking problem. While your process suffers from bad performance, it might also then be holding locks that are stalling other processes and every system on the network appears to hang.

Guidelines for Resolving Blocking Problems

Keep transactions as short as possible. Ideally, a BEGIN TRAN...COMMIT TRAN block will include only the actual DML statements that must be executed. To the extent possible, do conditional logic, variable assignment, and other "setup" work before the BEGIN TRAN. The shorter the transaction lasts, the shorter the time that locks will be held. Keep the entire transaction within one batch if possible.

Never add a pause within a transaction for user input. This rule is basically a part of the previous statement, but it is especially important. Humans are slow and unreliable compared to computers. Do not add a pause in the middle of the transaction to ask a user to input some value or to confirm an intention to take some action. The human might decide to get up to take a coffee break, stalling that transaction and making it hold locks that cause blocking problems for other processes. If it is imperative that some locks be held until the user provides more information, you should set timers in your application so that even if the user decides to go to lunch, the transaction will be aborted and the locks released. Similarly, give your applications a way to cancel out of a query if such an action is deemed necessary. (Canceling queries should be the *exception,* not the rule. I've seen some applications designed with the intention of explicitly canceling in common cases. This is bad. Cancels are pretty hard on the server in terms of the cleanup it must go through. A good application cancels requests only in unusual situations.)

When processing a result set, process all rows as quickly as possible. Recall from Chapter 3 that an application that stops processing results can impede the server from sending more results and stall the scanning process, which requires locks to be held much longer.

For browsing applications, consider using cursors with optimistic concurrency control. An address book application is a good example of a browsing application: users scroll around to look at data and occasionally update it. But the update activity is relatively infrequent compared to the time spent perusing the data. Using scrollable cursors with optimistic concurrency control (OPTCC) is a good solution for such applications. Instead of locking, the cursor's OPTCC logic determines whether the row has changed from the copy that your cursor read. If the row has not changed, the update is made without holding locks during the lengthy period in which the user is perusing the data. If the row has changed, the UPDATE statement will produce an error and the application can decide how to respond. Although I've strenuously cautioned in Chapter 11 about the misuse of cursors, they are ideally suited to browsing applications.

You can also easily implement your own optimistic concurrency mechanism even without using cursors. Save the values of the data you selected, and add a WHERE clause to your update that checks whether the values in the current data are the same as those you retrieved. Or, rather than use the values of the data, use a SQL Server *timestamp* column—an ever-increasing number that's updated whenever the row is touched, unrelated to the system time. If the values or timestamp are not identical, your update will not find any qualifying row and will not affect anything. You can also detect changes with @@ROWCOUNT and decide to simply abort, or more typically, you can indicate to the user that the values have changed and then inquire whether the update should still be performed. But between the time the data was initially retrieved and the time the update request was issued, shared locks are not held, so the likelihood of blocking issues and deadlocks is significantly reduced.

Analyze and Resolve Deadlock Problems

Deadlocks befuddle many programmers and are the bane of many applications. A deadlock occurs when, without some intervening action, processes could never get the locks they need no matter how long they waited. Simply waiting for locks is *not* a deadlock condition. SQL Server automatically detects the deadlock condition and terminates one of the processes involved to resolve the situation. The process gets the infamous error message 1205 indicating that it was selected as the "victim" and that its batch and the current transaction have been cancelled. The other process is then able to get the locks it needs and can proceed. The two general forms of deadlocks are cycle deadlocks and conversion deadlocks. (You can refer to Chapter 13 for more information about these two kinds of deadlocks.)

Cycle Deadlock Example

If you repeatedly run the following two transactions simultaneously from different ISQL.EXE sessions, you are nearly assured of encountering a "deadly embrace" (cycle deadlock) almost immediately from one of the two processes. It should be clear why: One of the processes gets an exclusive lock on a page in the *authors* table and needs an exclusive lock on a page in the *employee* table. The other process gets an exclusive lock on the page in *employee,* but it needs an exclusive lock for the same page in *authors* that the first process has locked. The result—an immediate deadlock.

```
-- Connection 1
USE pubs
WHILE (1=1)
BEGIN
    BEGIN TRAN
    UPDATE employee SET lname='Smith' WHERE emp_id='PMA42628M'
    UPDATE authors SET au_lname='Jones' WHERE au_id='172-32-1176'
    COMMIT TRAN
END

-- Connection 2
USE pubs
WHILE (1=1)
BEGIN
    BEGIN TRAN
    UPDATE authors SET au_lname='Jones' WHERE au_id='172-32-1176'
    UPDATE employee SET lname='Smith' WHERE emp_id='PMA42628M'
    COMMIT TRAN
END
```

The result is the dreaded error 1205 from one of the connections. The other connection goes along as if no problem exists.

```
Msg 1205, Level 13, State 2
Your server command (process id 12) was deadlocked with another
process and has been chosen as deadlock victim. Re-run your command
```

If you simply rewrite one of the batches so that both batches first update *authors* and then update *employee,* the two connections will run forever without falling into the "deadly embrace" of a cycle deadlock. Or you could first update *employee* and then update *authors* from both connections. Which table you update first doesn't matter, but the updates must be consistent and you must follow a known protocol. If the protocol for accessing the tables is consistently followed, one of the connections gets the exclusive page lock on the first table and the other process must wait for the lock to be released. Simply waiting momentarily for a lock is normal, usually fast, and happens frequently without your realizing it. That is *not* a deadlock.

Conversion Deadlock Example

Run the following transaction simultaneously from two different ISQL.EXE sessions. You're running the same script, so it's obvious that the two processes follow a consistent order for accessing tables. But this example will quickly produce a deadlock. I added a delay so that you'll encounter the race condition more quickly, but the condition is lurking there even without the WAITFOR DELAY—the delay just widens the window.

```
USE pubs
SET TRANSACTION ISOLATION LEVEL REPEATABLE READ
BEGIN TRAN
SELECT * FROM authors WHERE au_id='172-32-1176'
-- Add 5 sec sleep to widen the window for the deadlock
WAITFOR DELAY "00:00:05"
UPDATE authors SET au_lname='Updated by '
    + CONVERT(varchar, @@spid) WHERE au_id='172-32-1176'
COMMIT TRAN
```

You can correct this example in a couple of ways. Does the isolation level need to be Repeatable Read? If Committed Read is sufficient, simply change the isolation level to get rid of the deadlock and to provide better concurrency. By running with Committed Read isolation, the shared locks can be released after the SELECT, and then one of the two processes can acquire the exclusive lock it needs. The other process then waits for the exclusive lock and acquires it as soon as the first process finishes its update. All operations progress smoothly, and the queuing and waiting for locks happen invisibly and so quickly that it is not noticeable to the processes.

But suppose that you need Repeatable Read (or Serializable) isolation. Your solution is to serialize access by using an update lock, which is requested via the UPDLOCK hint. Recall from Chapter 13 that an update lock is compatible with a shared lock for the same page. But two update locks for the same page are not compatible, and update and exclusive locks are also not compatible. Acquiring an update lock does not prevent others from reading the same data, but it does ensure that you are first in line to upgrade your lock to an exclusive lock should you subsequently decide to modify the data on the locked page. (The key is that the exclusive lock will be able to be acquired. So this technique works equally well even if that second statement were a DELETE and not an UPDATE as in this example.) By serializing access to the exclusive lock, you prevent the deadlock situation. The serialization also reduces concurrency, but that's the price you must pay to achieve the high level of transaction isolation. Following is a modified example, and multiple simultaneous instances of this example will not deadlock. Try running about 20 simultaneous instances and see for yourself. You'll note that none deadlock and all complete, but they do run serially. With the built-in 5-second sleep, it takes about 100 seconds for all 20 connections to complete, since one connection completes about every 5 seconds. This illustrates the lower concurrency that results as the need for higher levels of consistency (in this case, Repeatable Read) increases.

```
USE pubs
SET TRANSACTION ISOLATION LEVEL REPEATABLE READ
BEGIN TRAN
SELECT * FROM authors (UPDLOCK) WHERE au_id='172-32-1176'
-- Add 5 sec sleep to widen the window for the deadlock
```

```
WAITFOR DELAY "00:00:05"
UPDATE authors SET au_lname='Updated by '
    + CONVERT(varchar, @@spid) WHERE au_id='172-32-1176'
COMMIT TRAN
```

As a general strategy, add the UPDLOCK hint (or some other serialization) if you discover during your testing that conversion deadlocks are occurring. Or add UPDLOCK from the outset because you expect from your CRUD analysis that deadlocks are likely, and then try backing it off during multiple-user testing to see if it is absolutely necessary. Either approach is viable. If you know that in the majority of cases the read-for-update (discussed later) will follow with an actual update, you might opt for the UPDLOCK hint from the outset and see if perhaps you can back it off later. But if the transaction is short and you will later update the data in most cases, there isn't much point in backing off the update lock. The shared lock will need to upgrade to an exclusive lock, so getting the update lock in the first place makes good sense.

Deadlocks from Page Splits

Occasionally, an application might deadlock due to a high number of page splits. This is pretty uncommon, and the deadlocks in this case are not on the data pages but usually on index pages though the rlocks (resource locks) that protect the intermediate levels of the index structures. (Chapter 8 showed you how to examine the log records to determine whether page splits were occurring.) A high rate of page splits is bad even without deadlocks, so reducing the incidence of splits is the best way to attack this problem. You can consider using a different key for the clustered index, but the best approach is usually to reserve some space on the pages using the FILLFACTOR parameter for CREATE INDEX. And you should also use the PAD_INDEX option, which is a FILLFACTOR for the intermediate levels of the index, not just the leaf levels. Periodically, you can reestablish the FILLFACTOR by rebuilding the indexes via the DBCC REINDEX command.

An application that normally has many connections, which insert into one table that starts out empty and then must rapidly grow, is susceptible to this type of page-split deadlock problem. Since FILLFACTOR applies only to existing data, and in this case the application regularly purges the table, FILLFACTOR does not help. This is a pretty unusual case, but if you are experiencing this problem, the best course of action might be to initially forgo the clustered index. My rule of thumb is that *nearly* every table should have a clustered index. But this type of situation is the exception. The clustered index requires that the pages split as they fill up. Without the clustered index, pages are simply added at the end and no split activity occurs. If you take this route, you can then go ahead and add the clustered index with a FILLFACTOR after you have a significant amount of data, which will give you some free slots and reduce further splits. And recall that if you declare a primary key, by default the index on it will be clustered but you can declare it explicitly as nonclustered.

An application with a clustered index that has a lot of insert and delete activity is not likely to have this problem because page splitting is less likely—the table tends to stay roughly the same size because the two actions offset each other. Page splitting tends to be an issue only when the table is growing at an extremely rapid pace and multiple connections are competing to split pages due to their high insert activity.

Preventing Deadlocks

Deadlocks can usually be avoided, although you might have to do some detailed analysis to resolve the problems that cause them. Sometimes the "cure" is worse than the "ailment," and you're better off handling deadlocks rather than totally preventing them, as I'll discuss in the next section. Preventing deadlocks (especially conversion deadlocks) requires a thorough understanding of lock compatibility. Following is a list of the main techniques you can use to prevent deadlocks:

- To prevent cycle deadlocks, make all processes access resources in a consistent order.

- Reduce the transaction isolation level if it's suitable to the application to do so.

- To prevent conversion deadlocks, explicitly serialize access to a resource.

Deadlock prevention is a good reason to use stored procedures. By encapsulating the data access logic in stored procedures, it's easier to impose consistent protocols for the order in which resources (for example, tables) are accessed, which can help to avoid cycle deadlocks. But in so doing, you are not reducing the likelihood of conversion deadlocks. As noted above, conversion deadlocks are best dealt with by serializing access to a resource or by lowering the transaction isolation level if appropriate for the application. The most common scenario for conversion deadlock is the *read-for-update* situation. If a resource will be read within a transaction requiring Repeatable Read or Serializable isolation and will be updated later, an update lock should be requested on the read using the UPDLOCK hint. The update lock will allow other users to read the data, but it prevents others from updating the data or doing a read-for-update. The net effect is that once the update lock is acquired, you will be assured that the process is next in line for the exclusive lock needed to actually modify it.

Handling Deadlocks Instead of Preventing Them

The cost of serializing access is that other users wanting to read-for-update (or actually update or delete) must wait. If you are not experiencing deadlocks, serializing access might needlessly reduce concurrency. You might experience a case in which a transaction often does a read-for-update but only infrequently does the update. In this case, while deadlocks might exist once in a while, their frequency is quite low. The best course of action in this situation might be *not* to prevent deadlocks, since they don't often occur, and you can simply deal with them when they do.

Preventing deadlocks might significantly reduce concurrency since the read-for-update would be blocked, and if the deadlocks don't often occur, the cure could be worse than the ailment. Instead, you should simply write your applications to handle deadlocking. Check for deadlock message 1205, and simply retry the transaction. With retry logic, you can live with moderate deadlock activity without adding a lot of serialization to the application. It's still a good idea to keep some counter as to how often you are experiencing deadlocks; if the incidence is high, the wasted effort and constant retrying are likely to be worse than the cost of preventing the deadlock in the first place. How you write the deadlock handler will depend on the language or tool you use to build your application. But an application that is prone to deadlocks should have a deadlock handler that retries. Such a handler must be written in the host language. There is no current way to do a retry directly within a stored procedure or a batch, since deadlock error 1205 terminates the batch. Here is an example, from the SQL Server documentation, of a deadlock handler for DB-Library. Even though you might program in ODBC, RDO, or another interface, the concepts are similar and should be apparent:

```
// Deadlock detection:
// In the DBPROCESS structure, save a pointer to a DBBOOL
// variable.
// The message handler sets the variable when deadlock occurs.
// The result processing logic checks the variable and resends
// the transaction in case of deadlock.

// Allocate the space for the DBBOOL variable and save it in
// the DBPROCESS structure.

dbsetuserdata(dbproc, malloc(sizeof(DBBOOL)));

// Initialize the variable to FALSE.
*((DBBOOL *) dbgetuserdata(dbproc)) = FALSE;
// Run queries and check for deadlock.
deadlock:
```

```
// Did the application get here via deadlock?
// If so, the server has already canceled the transaction.
// Start the application again. In a real application,
// the deadlock handling may need to be somewhat more
// sophisticated. For instance, you may want to keep a
// counter and retry the transaction a fixed number
// of times.

if (*((DBBOOL *) dbgetuserdata(dbproc)) == TRUE)
{
    // Reset the variable to FALSE.
    *((DBBOOL *) dbgetuserdata(dbproc)) = FALSE;
}


// Start the transaction.
dbcmd(dbproc, "begin transaction ");

// Run the first UPDATE command.
dbcmd(dbproc, "update ......");
dbsqlexec(dbproc);
while (dbresults(dbproc) ! = NO_MORE_RESULTS)
{
// application code
}


// Did the application deadlock?
if (*(DBBOOL *) dbgetuserdata(dbproc)) == TRUE)
    goto deadlock;

// Run the second UPDATE command.
dbcmd(dbproc, "update ......");
dbsqlexec(dbproc);
while (dbresults(dbproc) ! = NO_MORE_RESULTS)
{
    // application code
}


// Did the application deadlock?
if (*((DBBOOL *) dbgetuserdata(dbproc)) == TRUE)
    goto deadlock;

// No deadlock -- Commit the transaction.
dbcmd(dbproc, "commit transaction");
dbsqlexec(dbproc);
dbresults(dbproc);
```

```
// SERVERMSGS
// This is the server message handler. Assume that the dbmsghandle
// function installed it earlier in the application.

servermsgs(dbproc, msgno, msgstate, severity, msgtext,
    srvname, procname, line)
DBPROCESS      *dbproc;
DBINT          msgno;
int            msgstate;
int            severity;
char           *msgtext;
char           srvname;
char           *procname;
DBUSMALLINT    line;
{

// Is this a deadlock message?
if (msgno = 1205)
{
    // Set the deadlock indicator.
    * ((DBBOOL *) dbgetuserdata(dbproc)) = TRUE;
    return (0);
}

// Normal message handling code here.
}
```

Volunteering to Be the Deadlock Victim

Recall from Chapter 13 that SQL Server chooses the deadlock victim by determining the process that made the final lock request that closed the loop and created a circular chain that would not resolve without intervention. But a process can also "offer to sacrifice itself" as the victim for deadlock resolution. You can make this happen by using the *SET DEADLOCK_PRIORITY LOW | NORMAL* statement. If a process has a deadlock priority of LOW and the other participating process is NORMAL (the default), the LOW process will be chosen as the victim even if it was not the process that closed the loop.

In the deadlock examples shown earlier, you saw that the default victim is the process that you started second, since it closes the loop. However, adding *SET DEADLOCK_PRIORITY LOW* to one of the connections (and not the other) indicates that it will be selected as the victim, even if it was started first. You might find this useful if, for example, you are doing reporting and OLTP on the same database and you occasionally have deadlocks, and you know that one process is more important than the other. You would set the less important process to LOW. It might also be useful if one application was written with a good deadlock handler and the other was not. Until the application without the handler can be fixed, the "good" application can make the simple change of volunteering itself and then handle a deadlock with retry logic when the deadlock occurs later.

Row-Level Locking and Deadlocks

Some people think that deadlocking is an issue unique to page-level locks. That is, they erroneously believe that deadlocks would not occur with row-level locking. It should be obvious that the cycle and conversion deadlock examples above would deadlock with row-level locking, just as they do with page-level locking. Page locking can make the situation worse, because by locking the page, you lock more than just the row you need. If you understand locking, it should take little effort to conceive of a scenario in which you would not deadlock with page locking but you would deadlock with row-level locking. (Here's a hint: Suppose that two rows live on the same page and are to be updated by two different processes, which access them in the opposite order. This would not deadlock with page locking, but it would deadlock with row locking.) Even when SQL Server adds true row-level locking (beyond the insert case) in a future release, you still need to be aware of deadlock issues.

Identifying the Culprit

As with most debugging situations, the hardest part of resolving a problem with locking is understanding the problem. If you get complaints that "the system is hung," it's a good bet that you have a blocking problem. Most blocking problems happen because a single process holds locks for an extended period of time. A classic case (as I discussed earlier) is an interactive application that holds locks until the user at the other end takes an action, like clicking a button to commit the transaction or scrolling to the end of the output, which causes all the results to be processed. If the user goes to lunch and doesn't take that action, everyone else might as well grab lunch too, because they're not going to get much else done. Locks pile up, and the system seems to hang. The locks in the system are reported in the pseudo–system table, *syslocks,* and in the *master* database.

> **NOTE** The pseudo–system table is not maintained as an on-disk structure. Locking and process data are by definition relevant only at runtime. So *syslocks* and *sysprocesses* are presented as system tables, and although they can be queried just like other system tables, they do not have on-disk storage as a normal table does.

A big challenge in trying to identify the cause of blocking is that when you experience such problems, you probably have hundreds or thousands of locks piled up. At these times, it's hard to see the trees through the forest. Usually, you just want to see which process is holding up everyone else. Once identified, of course, the immediate need is to get that process out of the way, either by forcing it to complete or, if necessary, by issuing the KILL command on the connection. The longer term solution is to rework the application so that it will not hold locks indefinitely.

SQL Enterprise Manager, shown in Figure 14-1, provides a graphical way to watch locking activity, and this is the method that I recommend most of the time. (From the Server menu, choose Current Activity.) A tabbed dialog box allows you to look at locks either by user or by object and to quickly move between those views. The color coding makes it apparent which users are being blocked and which user is blocking. You can even double-click on the process in the tree to see the last command the process has issued. And perhaps you can then send a message to the offending user to please complete the transaction (although this is a short-lived solution at best). You can also kill the process from SQL Enterprise Manager—which isn't ideal, but sometimes it's the best short-term course of action.

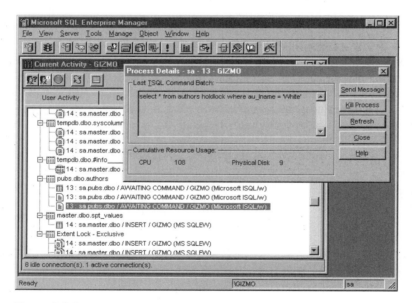

Figure 14-1.
The SQL Enterprise Manager allows you to monitor locking through a color-coded graphical view.

But sometimes even SQL Enterprise Manager might get blocked by locking activity in *tempdb,* so it's useful to know how to do monitor locking the old fashioned way, by using system stored procedures and/or querying directly from the *syslocks* table. The basic place to start is by running **sp_who** and **sp_lock2**. (Most people are familiar with **sp_lock**, but not **sp_lock2**. **sp_lock2** works almost the same way as **sp_lock**, except that it decodes the table name and database names for you, rather than just presenting their IDs. Similarly, **sp_who2** is a bit friendlier and more informative version of **sp_who**.) The *blk* column of the **sp_who** output shows the ID (*spid*) of a blocking process. The procedure **sp_lock2** is a formatted and sorted listing of *syslocks* that decodes the lock types into mnemonic forms (like *update_page* instead of *type 7*). If your users say the system is hung, try to log on and execute **sp_who** and **sp_lock2**. By virtue of being able to log on and execute these procedures, you immediately know the system is not hung. If you see a nonzero *spid* in the *blk* column of the **sp_who** output, or the **-blk** string is appended to a lock type in the **sp_lock2** output, this means that blocking is occurring. It's normal for some blocking to occur— that is just an indication that one process is waiting for a resource held by another. If such contention didn't exist, you wouldn't even need to lock. But if you reissue the query for lock activity a moment later, you expect to find that same specific blockage cleared up. In a smoothly running system, the duration for which locks are held is short, so the long pileups of locks don't occur.

When you have a major lock pileup, you can get a lengthy chain of processes blocking other processes. It can get pretty cumbersome to try to track this manually. You can create a procedure like the following to look for the process that is at the head of the blocking chain:

```
CREATE PROCEDURE sp_leadblocker
AS
IF EXISTS
    (SELECT * FROM master.dbo.sysprocesses
    WHERE spid IN (SELECT blocked FROM master.dbo.sysprocesses))
    SELECT
        spid, status, loginame=SUBSTRING(SUSER_NAME(suid), 1, 12),
        hostname=substring(hostname, 1, 12),
            blk=CONVERT(char(3), blocked),
        dbname=SUBSTRING(DB_NAME(dbid), 1, 10), cmd, waittype
    FROM master.dbo.sysprocesses
    WHERE spid IN (SELECT blocked FROM master.dbo.sysprocesses)
        AND blocked=0
ELSE
SELECT "No blocking processes found!"
```

Once you've identified the connection (*spid*) causing the problem, check to see the specific locks that it is holding. You can query from *syslocks* for this, but simply running **sp_lock2** *spid* will probably give you exactly what you need.

It can also be useful to see the last command issued by the offending process. Use *DBCC INPUTBUFFER (spid)* for this—which is the same thing SQL Enterprise Manager does when you double-click on a specific process. DBCC

INPUTBUFFER reads the memory from within the server that was used for the last command. So DBCC INPUTBUFFER can access whatever command is still in the buffer for a given connection, even if it has already been executed.

One caveat to note regarding DBCC INPUTBUFFER is that a stored procedure issued to SQL Server's RPC handler, not the language event handler, will have no command to display. For example, this will occur if you use **dbrpcexec()** instead of **dbsqlexec()** with DB-Library; or with ODBC, if you construct the statement that uses the ODBC procedure syntax and procedure markings, using **SQLPrepare()**, **SQLBindParameter()**, and then **SQLExecDirect()**. The SQL Trace utility, however, can see RPC events, but it must be running at the time the commands or RPCs are issued since it basically intercepts the commands.

Usually by this point, you have enough of a handle on the problem to turn your attention to the application, which is where the resolution will ultimately lie. But if you need or want to go a bit further, you can find out the depth at which the connection is nested within a transaction (by querying @@TRANCOUNT for some other connection). Blocking problems often result because the connection doesn't realize the depth at which it is nested in a transaction and hasn't applied the correct pairing of COMMIT commands. (Chapter 10, "Batches, Transactions, Stored Procedures, and Triggers," discusses the scoping and nesting levels of transactions.) This is pretty detailed, and it involves dumping out the Process Status Structure (PSS) for the offending connection (*spid*) that is causing the blockage. (Recall from Chapter 3 that the PSS keeps the current state of activity for each connection so that the connection can be worked on for a while, scheduled out, worked on again, and so on.)

The following example syntax checks for depth of nesting, assuming you have already identified the connection (*spid*) at the head of the blocking change with the techniques discussed above:

```
DBCC TRACEON (3604) -- Return subsequent DBCC output to client
GO


-- Find the suid for the offending spid
SELECT suid FROM sysprocesses WHERE spid=<blocking spid number>
GO


-- Dump the PSS for the offending spid
DBCC PSS (suid, spid, 0) -- suid is from above, and spid is the
                         -- blocker

GO
```

The output of the PSS looks similar to this:

```
PSS:
pstat=0x0 pcurdb=1 psuid=1 puid=1
puname= ploginflags=7 prowcnt=0 pstatlist0x0
pnumplan=0,pcurckptdb=0x0
plasterror=0 ppreverror=0 prowcount=1 plastprocid=0
pprocnest=0
pgid=0 phid=0 pspid=12 pkspid=12
poptions=0x400000
poptions2=0x0 poffsets=0 pcurcmd=230
pcputot=20 pcpucur=130 pmemusage=1 pbufread=5
pbufwrite=0 pcmderrs=0 pntext=69 ptext=0x0
donestat=0x0donecurcmd=0 donecount=0
pxcb->xcb_xactcnt=0 ptimeslice=99 pcurcolid=0
pchgsysbuf=0x1441e14
pcompct=0 phdr=0x1496800 pplan=0x1496800
parsinputfn=4394555 parsinput=0 pstackframe=0 pline=1
ptrigdate=0x0
precvbuf=0x144534c psendbuf=0x1445364 pdbtable=0x140a9b0
ppars=0x0
pcurstep=21589166 preswait=0x0 pnetid=0
pdbindex=-1 piscurdba=1 pbackground=0
pactiveRAslots=0

PHDR:
address=0x1496800 p_hdrstep=0x1496c80 p_hdrseq=0x1496b16
p_hdrcrt=0x0
p_hdrpbuf=0x0 p_hdrtmps=0x0
p_hdrcaller=0x0 p_hdrelease=0 p_hdrtabid=0 p_hdrstatus=0x0
p_lastpg=0 p_lastoff=0 p_procnum=0
mempgptr=0x1496800 byte_count=1306 byte_save=606
```

The PSS is an internal structure that SQL Server uses to maintain state for the connection, and the great bulk of information here is not useful to you. But note the **pxcb->xcb_xactcnt = *n*** entry (in boldface in code above), where ***n*** is the @@TRANCOUNT value for the *spid*. This shows the transaction nesting level for the blocking *spid,* which can explain why it is holding locks. If the value is greater than 0, the *spid* is in the midst of a transaction, in which case exclusive and update locks must be held. If the connection is operating with a transaction isolation level of Repeatable Read or Serializable or it is using the HOLDLOCK hint, shared locks also will be held. In the example above, the value is 0, which means that the connection is not in the middle of a transaction.

Watching Locking Activity

Locking problems often result from locks that you don't even realize are being taken. You might be updating only table *A,* yet blocking issues arise on table *B* because of relationships that you don't realize exist. If, for example, a foreign key relationship exists between table *A* and table *B,* the update on *A* is causing some query activity to *B*; some shared locks must exist. Or a trigger or a nested call to another procedure might be causing some locking that isn't obvious to you.

For cases like these, it is crucial that you be able to watch locks to perhaps discover some locking operations you weren't aware of. The graphical lock display of SQL Enterprise Manager is the most convenient way to watch locking in many cases. However, SQL Enterprise Manager provides only a snapshot of the *current* state of locking; you can miss a lot of locking activity that occurs in the time it takes you to refresh the display.

Trace flag 1200—display all locking activity

Sometimes you want to see a history and a record of all locks acquired and released. Trace flag 1200 can be useful for this purpose. But be forewarned that it produces volumes of output. On the facing page is an example of trace flag 1200 output if it is enabled for the entire server. You do this by starting the server from the command line as follows:

```
sqlservr -c -T1200 -T3605 -elocks.out
```

From an ISQLW.EXE connection, do a simple *SELECT * FROM pubs..authors*, and you'll get output similar to the code shown on the facing page that is written to the file LOCKS.OUT. The boldface output shows the *spid* of the connection that requested the lock (for example, *Process 11*) and the type of lock requested (*SH_PAGE*). The two numbers at the end of the lines correspond to *database_id,object_id* for table-level locks (including intent locks) and *database_id,page_number* for page-level locks. From this information, you need to decode the *spid*, *database_id*, *ob-ject_id*, and, in some cases, *page_number*.

Remember that the process ID is not the same as the server login ID. Rather, the process ID for the specific connection ID (the *spid*), and the same user who logs on again later will likely have a different *spid*. The *spid* is mapped to the server user in the *sysprocesses* system table. To translate *spid* to the server login *id,* simply do a query like the one shown below, but remember that this is valid only if the connection that made the lock requests is still connected, since otherwise the process ID is no longer valid.

```
SELECT SUSER_NAME(suid) FROM master..sysprocesses WHERE spid=11
```

```
97/04/24 12:31:27.75 kernel Microsoft SQL Server 6.50 - 6.50.251 (Intel X86)
              Mar 27 1997 11:47:42
              Copyright (c) 1988-1997 Microsoft Corporation
97/04/24 12:31:27.85 kernel Copyright (C) 1988-1994 Microsoft Corporation.
97/04/24 12:31:27.89 kernel All rights reserved.
97/04/24 12:31:27.92 kernel Logging SQL Server messages in file 'Locks'
97/04/24 12:31:27.94 kernel initconfig: number of user connections limited to 15
97/04/24 12:31:27.99 kernel SQL Server is starting at priority class 'normal' with
dataserver semaphore = 1 (1 CPU detected, SMPStat=1).
97/04/24 12:31:28.25 kernel initializing virtual device 0, D:\MSSQL65\DATA\MASTER.DAT
97/04/24 12:31:28.29 kernel Opening Master Database ...
97/04/24 12:31:28.34 spid1 Loading SQL Server's default sort order and character set
97/04/24 12:31:28.39 spid1 Recovering Database 'master'
97/04/24 12:31:28.42 spid1 Recovery dbid 1 ckpt (8512,24) oldest tran=(8512,0)
97/04/24 12:31:28.50 spid1 1 transactions rolled forward
Process 1 clearing all internal xact locks on xdes @0x013D00F8
97/04/24 12:31:29.02 spid1 server name is 'RONSOU8'
97/04/24 12:31:29.05 spid1 Recovering database 'model'
97/04/24 12:31:29.10 spid1 Recovery dbid 3 ckpt (338,36) oldest tran=(338,0)
Process 1 clearing all internal xact locks on xdes @0x013D00F8
97/04/24 12:31:29.35 spid1 Clearing temp db
Process 1 clearing all pss locks
Process 1 clearing locks on xdes @0x013D00F8 chain
Process 1 clearing all pss locks
Process 1 clearing locks on xdes @0x013D00F8 chain
Process 1 clearing all internal xact locks on xdes @0x013D00F8
Process 1 clearing all pss locks
Process 1 clearing locks on xdes @0x013D00F8 chain
Process 1 clearing all pss locks
Process 1 clearing locks on xdes @0x013D00F8 chain
Process 1 clearing all internal xact locks on xdes @0x013D00F8
97/04/24 12:31:30.66 kernel Read Ahead Manager started.
97/04/24 12:31:30.70 kernel Using 'SQLEVN60.DLL' version '6.00.000'.
97/04/24 12:31:30.74 kernel Using 'OPENDS60.DLL' version '6.00.01.02'.
97/04/24 12:31:30.78 kernel Using 'NTWDBLIB.DLL' version '6.50.251'.
97/04/24 12:31:30.81 ods  Using 'SSNMPN60.DLL' version '6.5.0.0' to listen on
'\\.\pipe\sql\query'.
97/04/24 12:31:32.80 spid10 Recovering database 'pubs'
97/04/24 12:31:32.83 spid10 Recovery dbid 5 ckpt (953,22) oldest tran=(953,0)
Process -1 clearing all pss locks
Process 10 clearing all internal xact locks on xdes @0x013E5C2C
97/04/24 12:31:33.10 spid1 Recovery complete.
97/04/24 12:31:33.13 spid1 SQL Server's default sort order is:
97/04/24 12:31:33.15 spid1    'dictionary' (ID = 51)
97/04/24 12:31:33.18 spid1 on top of default character set:
97/04/24 12:31:33.20 spid1    'iso_1' (ID = 1)
Process -1 clearing all pss locks
Process 11 requesting table lock of type SH_INT on 5 3
chaining lock onto PSS chain
Process 11 requesting page lock of type SH_PAGE on 5 317
chaining lock onto PSS chain
Process 11 releasing page lock of type SH_PAGE on 5 317
Process 11 releasing table lock of type SH_INT on 5 3
Process 11 requesting table lock of type SH_INT on 5 3
chaining lock onto PSS chain
Process 11 requesting page lock of type SH_PAGE on 5 317
chaining lock onto PSS chain
Process 11 releasing page lock of type SH_PAGE on 5 317
Process 11 releasing table lock of type SH_INT on 5 3
Process 11 requesting page lock of type SH_PAGE on 5 25
chaining lock onto PSS chain
Process 11 requesting page lock of type SH_PAGE on 5 26
chaining lock onto PSS chain
Process 11 releasing page lock of type SH_PAGE on 5 25
Process 11 releasing page lock of type SH_PAGE on 5 26
Process 11 requesting table lock of type SH_INT on 5 16003088
chaining lock onto PSS chain
Process 11 requesting page lock of type SH_PAGE on 5 360
Process 11 requesting page lock of type SH_PAGE on 5 361
chaining lock onto PSS chain
```

Similarly, you should use functions like DB_NAME() and OBJECT_NAME() to decode the database and table names.

It is usually easier to create a simple procedure similar to the following. And of course, if you want to see additional information from the *sysprocesses* table, such as *host_name, program_name,* or *hostprocess,* you can easily modify this procedure to display such information:

```
CREATE PROC DECODE_LOCKNUMS @spid int, @dbid int, @object_id int
AS
DECLARE @command varchar(255), @dbname sysname,
    @susername sysname
SELECT @susername=SUSER_NAME(suid) FROM master..sysprocesses
    WHERE spid=@spid
SELECT @dbname=DB_NAME(@dbid)
IF @susername IS NULL
    BEGIN
    PRINT "No Username Found. Exiting"
    RETURN (-1)
    END

IF @dbname IS NULL
    BEGIN
    PRINT "No Database Found. Exiting"
    RETURN (-2)
    END

SELECT @command="USE " + @dbname + " SELECT SUSERNAME='"
    + @susername + "', DATA_BASE='" + @dbname
    + "', Object_name=OBJECT_NAME(" + CONVERT(varchar, @object_id)
    + ")"
EXECUTE (@command)
RETURN (0)
```

Then, to decode a line like this

```
Process 11 requesting table lock of type SH_INT on 5 16003088
```

you can simply issue this statement:

```
EXEC decode_locknums 11, 5, 16003088
```

This returns:

```
SUSERNAME    DATA_BASE    Object_name
---------    ---------    -----------
ron          pubs         authors
```

The easiest way to identify to which object a page belongs is to use DBCC PAGE to display just the page header. From the header output, find the *object_id,* and then decode it using the OBJECT_NAME() function. (For details about DBCC PAGE, see Chapter 6, "Tables.") If you do this from ISQL or ISQL/w, be sure to also enable trace flag 3604 to see the output:

```
DBCC TRACEON(3604)
DBCC PAGE(5,361)

PAGE:
Page found in cache.

BUFFER:
Buffer header for buffer 0x10a5540
    page=0x1152000 bdnew=0x10a5540 bdold=0x10a5540 bhash=0x10a1160
bnew=0x10a55a0
    bold=0x10a54e0 bvirtpg=2413 bdbid=5 bpinproc=0 bkeep=0 bspid=0
bstat=0x1004 bpageno=361

PAGE HEADER:
Page header for page 0x1152000
pageno=361 nextpg=0 prevpg=360 objid=16003088 timestamp=0001 0000107d
nextrno=2 level=0 indid=0 freeoff=228 minlen=15
page status bits: 0x100,0x1
```

Then, after identifying the object ID and *indid,* decode the object's name. If the *indid* is 0, the entry is for a data page. This statement determines the object (table) to which the page belongs:

```
SELECT OBJECT_NAME(16003088)
```

It returns:

```
authors
```

A nonzero *indid* indicates that the lock is on an index or a text/image page. If the *indid* is a value other than 0, use a query similar to the following to determine the type of page:

```
SELECT
name,
pagetype=
    CASE
    WHEN indid=0 THEN 'DATA'
    WHEN indid=1 THEN 'CLUST INDEX'
    WHEN indid BETWEEN 2 AND 254 THEN 'NONCLUST INDEX'
```

```
      WHEN indid=255 THEN 'TEXT/IMAGE'
      ELSE 'Not found in sysindexes'
      END
FROM sysindexes
WHERE id=<objid from above> and indid=<nonzero indid from above>
```

Trace flags for analyzing deadlock activity

Trace flags are useful for analyzing deadlock situations. When a process is part of a deadlock, the victim process realizes that the deadlock occurred by getting error message 1205. Any other process participating in the deadlock is unaware of the situation. To resolve the deadlock, you'll probably want to see *both* processes involved, and trace flag 1204 provides this information. Here is a fragment of the output from SQLSERVR.EXE started from the command line using **–T1204**. I've used the conversion deadlock example I used previously—issuing the same batch from two connections—to illustrate the output of trace flag 1204:

```
sqlservr -c -T1204


97/05/15 09:41:21.02 spid11
*** DEADLOCK DETECTED with spid 10 ***
spid 11 requesting UP_PAGE (waittype 0x8007), blocked by:
 SH_PAGE: spid 10, dbid 5, page 0x168, table authors, indid 0
 UP_PAGE: spid 10, dbid 5, page 0x168, table authors, indid 0
 pcurcmd UPDATE(0xc5), input buffer:
SET TRANSACTION ISOLATION LEVEL REPEATABLE READ
BEGIN TRAN
SELECT * FROM aut
spid 10 waiting for EX_PAGE (waittype 0x5), blocked by:
 SH_PAGE: spid 11, dbid 5, page 0x168, table authors, indid 0
 pcurcmd UPDATE(0xc5), input buffer:
SET TRANSACTION ISOLATION LEVEL REPEATABLE READ
BEGIN TRAN
SELECT * FROM aut
VICTIM: spid 11, pstat 0x0000, cputime 0
```

This output shows the *spid* for both processes affected, gives a fragment of their input buffer (but not the entire command), and notes that neither process can upgrade its locks from the shared lock it holds. The output will help you resolve the problem—you now know the processes involved and the locks that could not be acquired, and you have an idea of the commands being executed.

Trace flag 1206 is used in conjunction with trace flag 1204 to provide additional output. Trace flag 1206 shows *all* locks currently held by the processes involved, even locks that are not apparently part of the deadlock situation. This can be helpful because deadlocks tend to cascade. After one deadlock is resolved by SQL Server terminating one of the processes, sometimes another deadlock follows.

By using trace flag 1206 in addition to 1204, you can find out which other locks are affecting a participant in a deadlock. You might prefer to use trace flag 1208, which is similar to 1206 but adds the *hostname* and *progname* values specified by the application to the deadlock information.

> **NOTE** The numbers assigned to trace flags 1204, 1206, and 1208 are intended to help you remember them. Recall that error 1205 is the well-known error message an application receives when it is chosen as the deadlock victim.

This example turns on both trace flags 1204 and 1206 for the specific connection (rather than for the server as a whole). Then the conversion deadlock example is used to produce a deadlock.

```
-- Turn on 1204 and 1206 lock info, display output to client (3604)
DBCC TRACEON (1204, 1206, 3604)
GO

SET TRANSACTION ISOLATION LEVEL REPEATABLE READ
BEGIN TRAN
SELECT * FROM authors WHERE au_id='172-32-1176'
-- Add sleep to widen the window for the deadlock
WAITFOR DELAY "00:00:05"
UPDATE authors SET au_lname='Updated by '
    + CONVERT(varchar, @@spid) WHERE au_id='172-32-1176'
COMMIT TRAN
```

This produces:

```
spid 10 requesting UP_PAGE (waittype 0x8007), blocked by:
 SH_PAGE: spid 11, dbid 5, page 0x168, table authors, indid 0
 UP_PAGE: spid 11, dbid 5, page 0x168, table authors, indid 0
 pcurcmd UPDATE(0xc5), input buffer: SET TRANSACTION ISOLATION LEVEL
REPEATABLE READ


BEGIN TRAN

SELECT * FROM autho
Locks held by spid 10:
 SH_INT: spid 10, dbid 5, table authors
 EX_INT: spid 10, dbid 5, table authors
 SH_PAGE: spid 10, dbid 5, page 0x168, table authors, indid 0
spid 11 waiting for EX_PAGE (waittype 0x5), blocked by:
  pcurcmd UPDATE(0xc5), input buffer: SET TRANSACTION ISOLATION LEVEL
REPEATABLE READ
```

```
BEGIN TRAN

SELECT * FROM autho
Locks held by spid 11:
 SH_INT: spid 11, dbid 5, table authors
 EX_INT: spid 11, dbid 5, table authors
 SH_PAGE: spid 11, dbid 5, page 0x168, table authors, indid 0
 UP_PAGE: spid 11, dbid 5, page 0x168, table authors, indid 0
VICTIM: spid 10, pstat 0x0000 , cputime 110

Msg 1205, Level 13, State 2
Your server command (process id 10) was deadlocked with another
process and has been chosen as deadlock victim. Re-run your command
```

Consider Segregating OLTP and DSS Applications

Sometimes it makes sense to split up your OLTP and DSS applications. For example, this can be an excellent strategy if your DSS applications don't need immediate access to information. This is a key notion behind the recent popularity of data warehousing, data marts, and other data management systems (although these concepts have been around for many years).

You can use a separate database (on the same server or on different servers) for DSS and OLTP, and the DSS database can be much more heavily indexed than the OLTP database. The DSS database will not have exclusive locks holding up queries, and the OLTP database's transactions will not get held up by the shared locks of the DSS. SQL Server's built-in replication capabilities make it relatively easy to *publish* data from the OLTP server and *subscribe* to it from your reporting server. SQL Server's replication capabilities can propagate data in near real time, with latency between the servers of just a few seconds. However, for maintaining a DSS server, it is best to propagate the changes in off-peak hours, such as at night. Otherwise, the locks acquired during propagation at the subscribing site will affect the DSS users as any other update activity would.

Monitor and Tune Queries

Effectively monitoring and tuning your queries is another essential part of effective performance. Insight into how the query optimizer works can make SQL Server less mysterious and can be helpful as you think about how to write a good query or as you choose what indexes to define. However, you should guard against "outsmarting yourself." Here's what I mean: I think it makes sense to treat the optimizer as a "black box" and let it do its thing (even though this book shows you the *inside* of SQL Server). Often, someone will show me a couple of variations in the approach to a query and then ask me which approach will be faster. Well, my success rate at predicting such a thing is not that impressive. I might be right more often than I'm wrong, but I would not skip empirically testing my alternatives. If I fool myself into thinking that I can predict what the optimizer will do, I might miss some good options. I prefer to write a query in the most intuitive way I can, and then I try to tune it only when the query's performance doesn't seem to be good enough.

The big gains in query performance usually do not come from some syntactic change in the query but rather from a change in the database design or in indexing. Gains sometimes come from taking a completely different approach to the query. For example, you might have to choose among writing a pretty complex query using a self-join or multilevel correlated subquery, using a cursor, and creating a solution that involves temporary tables. (I showed you some alternative formulations using these techniques in the Transact-SQL examples in Chapter 12.) Invariably, the only way you can be sure which solution is best is to try all the queries. Often, I'm surprised by the results of testing. If I think I know too much before a test about how a query will operate, I tend to outsmart myself.

Rather than try to know a bunch of tricks up front, I'm much more interested in doing the basics right. That is, I need to be sure that I've set up a good database structure—including perhaps some denormalization based on my CRUD exercise—and that I have created in advance what appear to be useful indexes. From there, I test my queries and study SHOWPLAN output for any queries that seem problematic. This is why I've discussed general strategies on database design and indexing before discussing how the optimizer works.

Having said all this, however, insight into how the optimizer works is certainly useful knowledge. It can take some of the mystery out of the recommendations regarding what indexes to create, and the plans you will examine from SHOW-PLAN will make more sense.

The Optimizer

For each table involved in the query, the query optimizer evaluates the search arguments and considers which indexes are available to narrow the scan of a table. That is, the optimizer evaluates to what extent the index can exclude rows from consideration. The more rows that can be excluded, the better, since that leaves fewer rows to process.

Joins are usually processed via nested iteration. The optimizer decides on the order in which the tables should be accessed. Because a nested iteration is a loop, order is important. The fewer the iterations through the loops, the less processing that is required. So it is useful to start with the table(s) that can exclude the most rows as the outer loops. The general strategy is to make the outer table most limit the search, which results in the fewest total iterations (scans) needing to execute.

For each table, the query optimizer estimates the number of logical I/Os (page accesses) that will be required given a particular access method and the order in which the tables will be processed. Then the optimizer compares the sum of all the estimated logical I/Os for each plan and chooses the plan with the lowest estimate. Query optimization works in three main phases: query analysis, index selection, and join selection. The following sections discuss each phase.

Query analysis

In the first phase of query optimization, *query analysis,* the optimizer looks at each clause of the query and determines whether it can be useful in limiting how much data must be scanned—that is, whether the clause is useful as a search argument (SARG) or as part of the join criteria. A clause that can be used as a search argument is referred to as *sargable,* or sometimes as *optimizable,* and can make use of an index for faster retrieval.

A SARG limits a search because it is specific in the information it requests. It specifies an exact match, a range of values, or a conjunction of two or more items joined by AND. A SARG contains a constant expression (or a variable that is resolved to a constant) that acts on a column by using an operator. It has the form

```
column inclusive_operator <constant or variable>
```

or

```
<constant or variable> inclusive_operator column
```

The column name can appear on one side of the operator, and the constant or variable can appear on the other side. If a column appears on both sides of the operator, the clause is not sargable. Sargable operators include =, >, <, =>, <=, BETWEEN, and sometimes LIKE. LIKE is sargable depending on the type of wildcards (regular expression) used. For example, *LIKE 'Jon%'* is sargable but *LIKE '%Jon%'* is not because the wildcard (%) at the beginning prohibits the usefulness of an index. Here are some SARG examples:

```
name = 'jones'

salary > 40000

60000 < salary

department = 'sales'

name = 'jones' AND salary > 100000

name LIKE 'jon%'
```

A single SARG can include many conditions if they are AND'ed together. This means that one index might be able to operate on all the conditions that are AND'ed together. In the example above, there might be an index on (*name,salary*), so the entire clause *name = 'jones' AND salary > 100000* can be considered one SARG and evaluated for qualifying rows using one index. If OR is used instead of AND in this example, a single index scan cannot be used to qualify both terms. The reason should be clear—if the lead field in the index key is *name,* the index is useful to find just the *'jones'* entries. If the criteria is AND *salary,* the second field of the index also qualifies those rows. But if the criteria is OR *salary,* the index would not be useful since all the rows would need to be examined, not just the *'jones'* entries. Again, the phone book analogy works. If you wanted to find *people with the name "jones" AND that live on 5th Avenue,* using the phone book can greatly assist to reduce the size of your search. But if you want to find *people with the name "Jones" OR that live on 5th Avenue,* you would have to scan every entry in the book. (This assumes that you have only one phone book that is sorted alphabetically by name. If you have two phone books, and one is sorted by name and one is sorted by street, that's another story, which I'll come to in discussing OR.)

An expression that is not sargable cannot limit the search (that is, every row must be evaluated), so an index is not useful to nonsargable expressions. The most typical of such expressions include negation operators such as NOT, !=, <>, !>, !<, NOT EXISTS, NOT IN, and NOT LIKE. Don't extrapolate too far and think that this means using a nonsargable clause is always going to result in a table scan. An index will not be useful to the nonsargable clause, but there might be indexes useful to other SARGs in the query. Queries often have multiple clauses, so a great index for another clause might be available for use. Remember that for queries that do not use OR, only one index per table will be used anyway. Here are some examples of nonsargable clauses:

```
name <> 'jones'

salary !> 40000

NOT(60000 < salary)

name LIKE '%jon%'

name = 'jones' OR salary > 100000
```

> **NOTE** The last example clause shown above is not a single search argument, but each expression on either side of the OR is individually sargable. So a single index won't be used to evaluate both expressions as could occur if the operator was AND. An index can still be useful to one expression or the other.

In some cases, a nonsargable expression can easily be rewritten to be sargable and to perhaps avail itself of an index. (Do not put computations on both sides of the equal sign, since that immediately makes the expression nonsargable.) The following table shows examples of nonsargable expressions and their equivalent sargable expressions.

Nonsargable Expression	Equivalent Sargable Expression
WHERE price * 12.0 = sales/costs	WHERE price = sales/costs/12.0
WHERE salary !> 40000	WHERE salary <= 40000

Index selection

Index selection is the second phase of query optimization. During this phase, the query optimizer determines whether an index exists for a clause, assesses the index's usefulness by determining the selectivity of the clause (that is, how many rows will be returned), and estimates the number of page accesses (or logical I/Os) required to find the qualifying rows. An index is potentially useful if its first column is used in the search argument and the search argument establishes a lower bound, upper bound, or both to limit the search. In the index selection phase, the optimizer finds the potentially useful indexes and then chooses the one it determines is best for each table.

Index statistics After a potentially useful index is found that matches the clause, it is evaluated based on the selectivity of the clause. The optimizer checks the index's statistics—the histogram of values in the index's distribution page. Those values are created when the index is created on existing data, and they are refreshed every time UPDATE STATISTICS runs. If the index is created before data exists in the table, no statistics will appear. The statistics will be misleading if they were generated at a time when the dispersion of data values was significantly different from what appears in the current data in the table. This means that it is important that you periodically run UPDATE STATISTICS to get an accurate picture of the current data.

The *distribution page* is an even sampling of values—a histogram—for the index key, based on the current data. No matter how big the table, the sampling is always stored on just one page. When the statistics are to be generated, SQL Server determines how many entries can fit on one distribution page and then samples the entire table at a consistent interval to gather this number of entries. Each entry is referred to as a *step*.

The distribution page also keeps statistics on the uniqueness of the data values encountered, referred to as the *density,* which provides a measure of how selective the index is. Recall that the more selective an index, the more useful it is, because higher selectivity can eliminate more rows from consideration. A unique index, of course, is the most selective—by definition, each index entry can point to only one row. A unique index has a density value of 1/*number of rows in the table*.

Density values range from 0 through 1. Highly selective indexes will have density values of 0.15 or lower. For example, say a unique index on a table with 8345 rows has a density of 0.00012 (1/8345). If there is a nonunique index with a density of 0.2165 on the same table of 8345 rows, each index key could be expected to point to about 1807 rows (0.2165 × 8345). This is probably not selective enough to be more efficient than just scanning the table, so this index is probably not useful. Because driving the query from a nonclustered index means that the pages must be retrieved in index order, the estimate projects that about 1807 data page accesses (or logical I/Os) will be needed. The only time a data page doesn't need to be reaccessed is for the occasional coincidence that could occur when two adjacent index entries happen to point to the same data page. Assume in this example that about 40 rows fit on a page, so there are about 209 total pages. The chance of two adjacent index entries pointing to the same page is only about 0.5 percent (1/209). The number of logical I/Os for just the data pages, not even counting the index I/O, is likely to be close to 1807. In contrast, the entire table can be scanned with just 209 logical I/Os—the number of pages in the table. In this case, the optimizer will look for a better index or it will decide that a table scan is the best it can do.

The distribution page keeps steps (samples) for only the lead column of the index. This optimization takes into account the fact that an index is useful only if its lead column is specified in a WHERE clause. By keeping just the lead column, the distribution page can include more entries for the most relevant information. However, density is kept for all columns and helps in deciding how useful the index is for joins. Suppose, for example, that an index is composed of three key fields. The density on the first column might be 0.50, which is not too useful. But as you look at more columns in the key, the number of rows pointed to will be fewer (or in the worst case, the same) as that first column, so the density value goes down. If you're looking at both the first and second columns, the density might be 0.25, which is somewhat better. And if three columns are examined, the density might be 0.03, which is highly selective. (Note that it doesn't make sense to refer to the density of only the second column. The lead column density is always needed.)

To determine whether a distribution page has been created for an index, you can query the *distribution* column in the *sysindexes* table. A 0 in the *distribution* column indicates that no statistics are available for that index, which means that the index was created before the table had any data. Any other value indicates the location of the distribution page. Executing UPDATE STATISTICS creates a distribution page for each index on a table.

Here is an example using a *Tasks* table that assigns work items to people. The *Task_ID* column, a 4-byte integer column, has a nonclustered unique index named *NC_IDX02_Tasks*. The table has fewer than 5000 rows, and the *Task_ID* values are sequential from 1 through 5000. This statement

```
DBCC SHOW_STATISTICS(Tasks, NC_IDX02_Tasks)
```

returns this:

```
Updated                 Rows    Steps    Density
------------------      ----    -----    -------
May 28 1997 9:00AM      5000    313      0.0002

All density     Columns
-----------     -------
0.0002          Task_ID

Steps
    1
   17
   33
   49
   65
   81
   97
  113
  129
  145
  161
  177
  193
  209
  225
    ⋮
 4945
 4961
 4977
 4993
```

```
(313 row(s) affected)
```

This output tells me that the statistics for this index were last updated on May 28, 1997. It also tells me that the table currently has 5000 rows. I know that the index is unique and that there are no duplicates, so the density is 1/*number of rows,* or 1/5000, which is 0.0002. The index is highly selective and will be useful to a query that uses WHERE *Task_ID operator.* In fact, because the index is unique, it is *optimally* selective and the optimizer has some shortcuts it can take because it knows only one row can match an index entry. With the 4-byte index key (a single integer column) and 5000 rows of data, 313 data samples (steps) are recorded. The number of steps is a function of the index key and the number of rows in the table, as I'll explain shortly. Given 5000 rows and 313 steps, about every sixteenth row (5000/313) is sampled. That is, the *sampling interval,* also referred to as the *step width,* is 16. In this case, the distribution page's sampling is about 6.3 percent of the entire table (313/5000). Even if the table included a million rows, the statistics are still kept on only one distribution page and would represent only 0.03 percent (313/1,000,000) of the table.

It is correct to infer that query optimization is *probability-based,* which means that its conclusions can sometimes be wrong. The optimizer can sometimes make decisions that are not optimal, even if those decisions are based on a sound principle. The decisions will make sense from a probability standpoint, but the actual data doesn't bear out the prediction. (As an analogy, you can think of national election polls, which show how accurate relatively small samples can be when used to predict results of much larger populations. But the famous headline "Dewey Defeats Truman!" demonstrates that predictions based on sample populations can also be wrong.)

You can view the values of a distribution page by clicking the Distribution button while the Manage Indexes window is displayed in SQL Enterprise Manager. Figure 14-2 shows the example index viewed in this way.

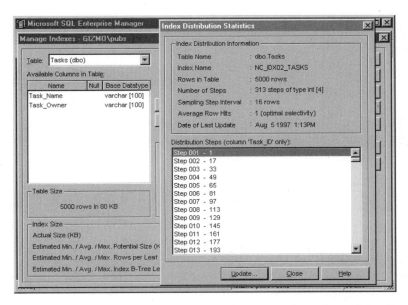

Figure 14-2. *SQL Enterprise Manager shows you the values of the distribution page.*

The number of samples (steps) that will fit on a single distribution page depends on the number of index key columns and the columns' storage lengths. Most pages will contain from 50 to 350 steps. The simplest way to see how many steps are included on a given distribution page is to run DBCC SHOW_STATISTICS.

If you are intent on predicting how many steps will appear on a page, you can determine the value in the following way:

```
#STEPS=CEILING(#ROWS_IN_TABLE/STEPWIDTH)
```

Where:

```
STEPWIDTH=(#ROWS_IN_TABLE + MAXSTEPS - 1)/MAXSTEPS

MAXSTEPS=((PAGESIZE - PAGEHEADSIZE - DENSITY_SIZE -
    DATE_SIZE)/STEP_ROW_SIZE) - 1
```

Several of these values are constants, of course:

```
PAGESIZE=2048
PAGEHEADSIZE=32
DATE_SIZE=8
```

So the formula simplifies to:

```
MAXSTEPS=((2008 - DENSITY_SIZE)/(STEP_ROW_SIZE)) - 1
```

Since density is kept for the entire key and for every subkey combination, 4 bytes are needed for each column that is part of the index, plus 1 byte for the total:

```
DENSITY_SIZE=4 * (#KEY_COLUMNS + 1)
```

The STEP_ROW_SIZE value depends on the length of all the index columns. For variable-length columns, the maximum (declared) size, not the average size, is important. For fixed-length columns:

```
STEP_ROW_SIZE=TOT_COLUMNS_LENGTH + 2
```

For variable-length columns:

```
STEP_ROW_SIZE=MAX_COLUMNS_LENGTH + 7
```

In the example above, using *1* for the number of key columns with a single, fixed-length column of 4 bytes reduces the equation to this:

```
MAXSTEPS=((2008 - (4*(1+1)))/(4+2)) - 1
    = 332
```

Having computed MAXSTEPS and knowing that the table has 5000 rows, the STEPWIDTH is calculated like this:

```
STEPWIDTH    =(#ROWS_IN_TABLE + MAXSTEPS - 1)/MAXSTEPS
             =(5000 + 332 - 1)/332
             =16
```

In this example, DENSITY_SIZE is 4 bytes and STEP_ROW_SIZE is 6 bytes. Plugging in the values for the number of rows and the STEPWIDTH and rounding up the values yields the number of steps, which is 313 for the example:

```
#STEPS    =CEILING(#ROWS_IN_TABLE/STEPWIDTH)
          =CEILING(5000/16)
          =313
```

Based on index statistics, decide whether the index is useful As a second part of determining the selectivity of a clause, the query optimizer calculates the logical I/Os estimated for the various access methods that could be used. Even if a useful index is present, it might not be used if the optimizer determines that index access would not yield the fewest number of logical I/Os. "Logical I/O" refers to the number of page accesses that are needed, whether the pages are already in the memory cache or must be read from disk and brought into the cache. The term is sometimes used to refer to I/O from cache, as if an I/O were either logical or physical, but this is really a misnomer. As I discussed in Chapter 3, pages are *always* retrieved from the cache via a request to the Buffer Manager, so *all I/Os are logical*. If the pages are not already in the cache, they must be brought in first by the Buffer Manager. In those cases, the I/O operation is also physical. Only the Buffer Manager, which serves up the pages, knows whether a page is already in cache or needs to be accessed from disk and brought into cache. The ratio of how much I/O is already in the cache and does not require a physical I/O is referred to as the *cache-hit ratio,* an important metric to watch.

The optimizer evaluates indexes to estimate the number of likely "hits" based on the density and step values in the distribution pages. Based on these values, the optimizer estimates how many rows would qualify for the given SARG and how many logical I/Os would be estimated to retrieve those qualifying rows. It might find multiple indexes that could be chosen to find qualifying rows, or it might determine that just scanning the table and checking all the rows would be best. The optimizer chooses the access method that it predicts will require the fewest logical I/Os to retrieve the qualifying rows.

Whether the access method uses a clustered index, a nonclustered index, a table scan, or another option determines the estimated number of logical I/Os. This number can be very different for each method. Using an index to find qualifying rows is frequently referred to as *an index driving the scan.* When a nonclustered index drives the scan, the query optimizer assumes that the page containing each identified qualifying row is likely not the same page accessed the last time. Because the pages must be retrieved in the order in which the index entries exist, retrieving the next row with a query driven by a nonclustered index will likely require that a different page than the one that contained the previous row must be fetched, since it's unlikely that the two rows reside on the same page. By coincidence, sometimes they will reside on the same page, but the optimizer correctly assumes that typically this will not be the case. (If there are 5000 pages, the chance of this occurring is 1/5000.) If the index is not clustered, data order is random in respect to the index key.

If the scan is driven from a clustered index, it is likely that the next row is located on the same page as the previous row, since the index leaf is, in fact, the data. The only time this will not be the case when using a clustered index is when the last row on a page has been retrieved, so the next page must be accessed, which will contain the next bunch of rows. But moving back and forth between the index and the data pages is not required.

There is, of course, a chance that a specific page might already be in cache when using a nonclustered index, but a logical I/O will still occur, even if the scan does not require a physical I/O (an I/O from disk). Physical I/O is an order of magnitude more costly than I/O from cache. But don't assume that only the cost of physical I/Os matters—I/O operations from the cache are still far from free. In some of the advanced examples in Chapter 12, the small *pubs* database is used. For this database, alternative solutions exist that each use about the same number of physical I/Os, since the tables are small enough to all be cached, but the various solutions have widely different needs for logical I/O and the performance differences are quite dramatic.

As the query optimizer attempts to minimize logical I/O, it tries to produce a plan that will result in the fewest number of page operations. By doing so, it is likely that the optimizer will also minimize physical I/O. As an example, suppose that I need to resolve a query with the following SARG:

```
WHERE Emp_Name BETWEEN 'Smith' AND 'Snow'
```

Here are the relevant index entries:

```
Index_Key (Emp_Name)     Found on Page(s)
-------------------      ----------------
Smith                    867, 984, 10012
Smyth                    867
Snow                     984, 10012
```

Using this nonclustered index, six logical I/Os are required to retrieve the data pages, in addition to the I/O that's necessary to read the index. If none of the pages were already cached, the data access would result in three physical I/Os, assuming that the pages remained in the cache long enough to be reused for the subsequent rows (which is a good bet). Suppose, for example, that all the index entries are on one leaf page and the index has one intermediate level. In that case, three I/Os (logical and probably physical) are necessary to read the index (one root level, one intermediate level, and one leaf level). So chances are that driving this query via the nonclustered index would require about nine logical I/Os, six of which would likely be physical if the cache started out empty. The data pages would be retrieved in the following order:

Page 867 to get row with Smith
Page 984 for Smith
Page 10012 for Smith
Page 867 (again) for Smyth
Page 984 (again) for Snow
Page 10012 (again) for Snow

If a clustered index existed on the *Emp_Name* column, all six of the qualifying rows would likely be located on the same page. The number of logical I/Os will probably be only three (the index root, the intermediate index page, and the leaf index page, which is the data page; plus the final I/O will retrieve all the qualifying rows). This scenario should make it clear to you why a clustered index can be so important to a range query. In this simple example, the query using a clustered index uses only one-third as many logical I/Os as it does using a nonclustered index. The difference gets more pronounced with more data.

If there were no clustered index, the choice would need to be made between doing a table scan and using the nonclustered index. The number of logical I/Os required to do a scan of the table is equal to the number of pages in the table. A table scan starts at the first page and follows the linked list of pages until the scan is done. As the pages are read, the rows are evaluated to see whether they qualify based on the search criteria. Clearly, if the table from the previous example had fewer than nine data pages total, fewer logical I/Os would be necessary to scan the whole thing than would be needed to drive the scan off the nonclustered index (which was estimated to take nine logical I/Os).

The estimates for the logical I/Os necessary to scan for qualifying rows is summarized in the table on the following page. The access method with the estimate for fewest logical I/Os will be chosen based on this information.

Access Method	Logical I/Os Required
Table scan	Total number of data pages in the table.
Clustered index	Number of levels in the index plus the number of data pages to scan (data pages to be scanned = number of qualifying rows / rows per data page).
Nonclustered index	Number of levels in the index, plus the number of leaf pages, plus the number of qualifying rows (a logical I/O for the data page of each qualifying row). The same data pages will often be retrieved (from cache) many times, so the number of logical I/Os can be much higher than the number of pages in the table.
Covering nonclustered index	Number of levels in the index plus the number of leaf pages (qualifying rows / rows per leaf page). The data page does not need to be accessed since all needed information is in the index key.
Unique nonclustered index	Number of index levels plus one data page if the query is searching for an equality on all parts of the key of a unique index.

The table above and the examples that follow assume that you know the number of rows in a table, the number of pages, and the number of levels in the indexes. If these topics are not clear, review Chapter 6, "Tables." Also see Appendix B of *Administrator's Companion* in the SQL Server documentation (on the CD with this book), which shows examples and the steps needed to estimate the number of pages in a table and the number of nonleaf levels in an index.

No statistics are available   If no statistics are available, the server uses fixed percentages, shown in the table below, depending on the operator. These fixed percentages can be grossly inaccurate for your specific data, however, so it is important that you make sure to run UPDATE STATISTICS to get statistics that resemble the distribution of your data.

Operator	Percentage of Rows
=	10%
>	33%
<	33%
BETWEEN	25%

A special case occurs when the optimizer recognizes an equality in the WHERE clause and that the index is unique. Because this combination yields an exact match and always returns one row, the optimizer doesn't have to use statistics.

For queries for one row that use an exact match, such as a lookup by primary key, a unique nonclustered index is highly efficient. In fact, many environments probably shouldn't "waste" their clustered index on the primary key. If access via the complete primary key is common, it might be a big win to specify NON-CLUSTERED when declaring the primary key and save the clustered index for another type of access, such as a range query, that can benefit more from the clustered index.

Processing queries with OR   Multiple indexes can be used if a single table has multiple predicates that are OR'ed together. The results are then UNION'ed together to determine all the qualifying rows. This technique is referred to in SHOWPLAN output as a Dynamic Index. It is also commonly referred to as *index union*. This technique is used only when all the predicates to be OR'ed together pertain to the same table and each one of them would benefit from an index—that is, the indexes are highly selective. In many cases, having multiple predicates on a table will result in the table being scanned, because the optimizer will decide that scanning is the least costly method to check all the criteria.

The predicates can relate to different columns, each of which has a selective index. For example:

```
WHERE name='Jordan' OR number=23
```

It's not too typical for several different nonclustered indexes to be used on a given table. As you know, a nonclustered index must be highly selective to be useful. When considering the use of multiple different indexes with OR'ed predicates, the optimizer will often decide that it would spend so much time traversing indexes that a table scan would be simpler and more efficient. The indexes must be highly selective (or perhaps both unique—the ultimate selectivity) for this strategy to be used.

More common than the case of multiple indexes are queries with multiple OR'ed predicates against the same column. For example:

```
WHERE name='Jordan' OR name='Pippen' OR name='Kukoc'
```

This strategy treats OR and IN identically. The plan would not be different if the clause were instead written like this:

```
WHERE name IN ('Jordan', 'Pippen', 'Kukoc')
```

If the index is highly selective, many terms can be put in the IN clause (or multiple OR's, but that would be clumsy to write) and the Dynamic Index strategy can still be used. As an optimization, the terms in the IN clause are internally sorted before the index is scanned. The index scan can progress from the point of the last term and will not have to rescan for each term.

The Dynamic Index is an internal worktable that is created with the row identifiers (page and row ID) for every row that meets any one of the predicates being OR'ed. After all the indexes are evaluated, the worktable is sorted to remove duplicates (rows that qualify on the basis of meeting multiple criteria). The worktable ends up as a list of all unique row identifiers that meet one or more of the criteria. The list is then used to retrieve the rows, similar to the way the leaf level of a standard B-Tree index is used. When all the rows are retrieved, the worktable is discarded. Essentially, it has resolved the query by using multiple indexes (or the same index multiple times) and then doing a UNION on the result (and eliminating duplicates). Hence, the term "index union" is appropriate.

Note that SQL Server does not currently employ an *index intersection* strategy that might prove useful to queries using AND. Such a technique (using multiple indexes on one table for clauses AND'ed together) might show up in a future version. However, in many cases, the index intersection would be suboptimal. If one index is highly selective, it alone can eliminate the large number of rows from consideration when two predicates are AND'ed (that is, *both* predicates must evaluate as TRUE). If failure to meet just one term eliminates the row, it should be clear that evaluating *both* terms is wasted effort.

Join selection and processing

Join selection is the third major step in query optimization. If the query is a multiple-table query or a self-join, the optimizer will evaluate join selection. The optimizer compares how the clauses are ordered and selects the join plan with the lowest estimated number of I/Os. Joins are usually processed as nested iterations, simply a set of loops that takes a row from the first table and then uses that row to scan the inner table, and so on, until the result that matches is used to scan the last table. The number of iterations through any of the loops equals the number of scans that must be done. (This is not a *table scan*, since it will usually be done via an index. In fact, if no useful index is available to be used for an inner table, nested iteration will probably not be used and reformatting will be used instead, as I'll discuss shortly.) The result set is narrowed down as it progresses from table to table within each iteration in the loop. If you've done any programming with an ISAM-type product, this should look pretty familiar in terms of opening one "file" and then seeking into another in a loop. Pseudocode to process the join

```
WHERE dept.deptno=empl.deptno
```

would look something like this:

```
DO (until no more dept rows);
    GET NEXT dept row;
        {
        begin
```

```
// scan empl, hopefully using an index on empl.deptno
                GET NEXT empl row for given dept
            end
}
```

The plan with the fewest logical I/Os is chosen. Usually, the chosen plan is the one with the fewest scan counts (iterations through the loop).

Join selectivity is used to estimate how many rows from table *A* will join with a single row from table *B*. This is different from determining how many rows match a search argument. The estimate of the number of rows that will match in a nested iteration is essential to determine an efficient order in which to access the tables. If an index with updated statistics on the fields being used to join is available, the selectivity is based on the density of the index. If no such index is available, the density is estimated as the reciprocal of the number of rows in the smaller table.

Join clause example

WHERE dept.deptno=empl.deptno

These are the assumptions for this join clause example:

- One thousand employees appear on 40 data pages (~25 rows per page).

- One hundred departments appear on 5 data pages (~20 rows per page).

- There is a nonclustered unique index on *dept.deptno,* only two levels deep (for nonleaf levels of index—the leaf level is always "level 0"). Retrieving a specific department row via this *deptno* index requires four logical I/Os (two nonleaf pages in the index, one leaf page, and one I/O for the data page pointed to).

- There is a nonclustered nonunique index on *empl.deptno,* two levels deep. Retrieving *empl* rows via an exact search on a specific *deptno* value by using the index requires logical I/Os estimated as *3 + number of qualifying rows.*

- There are no SARGs to limit the search for either table.

- The selectivity for the above WHERE clause is 1/100 (0.01—*1 / number of departments,* since *dept.deptno* is known to be unique, hence ultimate selectivity).

- Given a row in the *dept* table, the estimated average number of rows in the *empl* table to join to it is 10 (1000 × .01).

- Given a row in the *empl* table, the estimated average number of rows in the *dept* table to join to it is 1 (100 × .01).

Following, in pseudocode, are two strategies the optimizer might consider:

OPTION 1

```
// TABLE SCAN on dept as OUTER table, with empl INNER table.
// For each dept row (100 rows over 5 pages. 1 table scan: 5
// logical I/Os).
        {
        Get corresponding empl rows using index on deptno.
// Estimate 10 empl rows will be found for each dept
// Each scan estimated at 3+10 logical I/Os = 13
// (13 = 2 nonleaf index pages + 1 leaf index page + 10 data pages)
// Because there are 100 dept rows, this inner scan needs to be
// executed 100 times - once for each dept
// Total logical I/O of this inner loop then will be
// 100 scans * 13 logical I/O per scan = 1300 logical I/Os
}

Total estimated logical I/O for Option 1 is 1305 (5 + 1300)
Scan Count is 101 (1 + 100)
```

OPTION 2

```
// TABLE SCAN on empl as OUTER table, with dept INNER table.
// For each empl row (of which there are 1000. 1 table scan: 40
// logical I/Os).
        {
        Get corresponding dept rows using unique index on deptno.
// Since unique index, know that only 1 dept row (at most)
// will be found. Each scan for the unique row estimated at
// 4 logical I/Os using the nonclustered unique index.
// (4 = 2 nonleaf level + 1 leaf level + 1 data page)
// Because there are 1000 empl rows, this inner scan needs to be
// executed 1000 times, once for each empl row
// Total logical I/O of this inner loop then will be
// 1000 scans * 4 logical I/O per scan = 4000 logical I/Os
}

Total Estimated Logical I/O for Option 2 is 4040 (40 + 4000)
Scan Count is 1001 (1 + 1000)
```

You can see that it will be much more efficient (requiring far fewer I/Os) to begin the join with *dept* and then make *empl* the inner loop. This is what the optimizer will decide to do.

Another optimizer example   The overall effect of the steps mentioned are that the optimizer evaluates the number of tables, the rows in each table, SARGs, appropriateness of indexes, and the joins to estimate the number of logical I/Os needed to process a query. The optimizer then chooses the plan with the lowest estimate. Here is another example illustrating this process:

```
SELECT t.title, a.au_lname
FROM titles t, authors a, titleauthor ta
WHERE t.title_id=ta.title_id
    AND a.au_id=ta.au_id
    AND a.au_lname='Green'
```

Even a relatively simple query like this can be executed in many ways. But for simplification, I will reduce the choices to two. Consider *titleauthor* to be purely a "connecting" table and probably not one to start with. The two choices for the nested iteration that is needed to process this join are as follows:

- Start the join processing with *titles,* and then for each qualifying row find the corresponding *titleauthor* row via the *title_id* column. Then for each of these *titleauthor* rows find the corresponding row in the *authors* table via the *au_id* column.

- Start the join processing with *authors*. Discard all rows that do not contain the name Green, and for each qualifying row find the corresponding *titleauthor* rows via the *au_id* column. Then for each of these *titleauthor* rows, find the corresponding row in *titles* via the *title_id* column.

The *titles* table has 18 rows (on three data pages), *authors* has 23 rows (on one data page), and *titleauthor* has 25 rows (on one data page). However, this query also contains a SARG, *au_lname = 'Green'*, and an index (nonclustered) exists on *au_lname* that is highly selective (it has a density of less than 0.04). So figuring in the row counts and counting the ability to significantly limit the scan on *authors* via the SARG and the nonclustered index on *au_lname,* the two options can be viewed as follows:

OPTION 1

1. Scan *authors* using the nonclustered index and SARG. This requires one scan (iteration) that likely yields at most one row (0.04 density × 23 rows).

2. For each row of step 1 (estimated to be just one), gather the corresponding rows in *titleauthor* (one scan yields two rows on average) via the *au_id* column.

3. For each row of step 2 (estimated to be two rows), gather the corresponding rows in *titles* via the *title_id* column. (This involves two scans—one for each of the rows gathered in step 2, each yielding one row for a total of two rows.)

The output of SET STATISTICS IO (discussed a bit later) when this join method is used shows the exact scan counts predicted above and the logical I/O counts. (Note that I've removed the physical I/O statistics in this output. The example uses little data, and it's probably all in cache. If you run this example on the *pubs* database in its initial installed state, you might get different physical I/O statistics but the logical I/O output should be the same.)

```
Table: authors scan count 1, logical reads: 2
Table: titleauthor scan count 1, logical reads: 1
Table: titles scan count 2, logical reads: 4
```

As you can see from the output above, the *authors* table is scanned once. There are two logical I/Os for *authors*—one for the nonclustered index page (the table is so small that the entire B-Tree is on one page), and one for the data page. The *titleauthor* table is then scanned once, hence one logical I/O. Then the *titles* table must be scanned twice. Each scan uses two logical I/Os—one for the clustered index root and one for the leaf (data) page. Two scans of two I/Os each yield four logical I/Os. (The optimizer estimates logical I/Os to produce its plans.) By following this join order, a total of four scans and seven logical I/Os occurs. (You could rightly argue that the first scan of *authors* really shouldn't have bothered with the index on *authors,* since the entire table is one data page. But the difference between one or two logical I/Os is trivial, and the optimizer is designed for the general case, in which the index here would be expected to be useful.)

OPTION 2

1. Scan the *titles* table. There is no SARG, so every row qualifies. (One scan yields 18 rows.)

2. For each of the 18 rows in *titles,* gather the corresponding rows in *titleauthor.* (Eighteen scans are *estimated* to each yield 1.3 rows—23/18— on average, but 25 rows are actually found.)

3. For each row gathered in step 2 (typically 1 or 2 per iteration, 1.3 on average), scan for the corresponding row in *authors.* Each scan of the *authors* table is expected to yield 1 row since a unique index exists on *au_id.* This scan needs to be done an estimated 23 times, since that's the estimated number of rows that step 2 will yield. (Twenty-three scans estimated, each yielding 1 row. Step 2 actually finds 25 rows, so the scan count here is 25.)

This option uses pure table scanning. But the number of iterations is higher than you might expect because it was not possible to first trim away the rows, as was done in Option 1. Option 2 found that 44 scans were necessary (close to the 42 that would be estimated), using 46 logical I/Os. Option 1 required only 7 logical I/Os and is clearly better than Option 2.

```
Table: titles scan count 1, logical reads: 3
Table: titleauthor scan count 18, logical reads: 18
Table: authors scan count 25, logical reads: 25
```

The optimizer chooses to process the query using Option 1, having internally calculated estimates along these lines. The statistics shown above are reported after the query has run with each method. (The statistics are the actual values, not the estimates.) (Note that I had to force the second, nonoptimal plan to be chosen using *SET FORCEPLAN ON*, which I'll discuss a bit later.)

Reformatting strategy for joins

SQL Server sometimes resorts to a *reformatting strategy* when joining large tables with no useful index on which to base a nested iteration. If the inner table would need to be scanned many times and is large with no useful index, the reformatting strategy is used to avoid repeated costly table scans of the inner table. The reformatting strategy inserts the rows from the smaller of the two tables into a worktable (an internal temporary table in *tempdb*). A clustered index is created on the worktable, which is used in the join to retrieve the qualifying rows from each table. Although this is costly, it is less costly than the repeated full table scans that would be required by the nested iteration. As a general rule, if an important query is taking too long and you determine that it is being processed via a reformatting strategy, you should try to create an index that will allow an efficient nested iteration strategy to be used instead.

One special case of reformatting can be nicely efficient and certainly not a problem: think of it as a *merge-join,* although SHOWPLAN output will not distinguish it as such. The merge-join strategy is used when no useful indexes are available for the join operation and when the search argument is restrictive (as determined by the index statistics). The process involves using the index to filter out the desired rows into a worktable and then joining that worktable as the outer table to the second, inner, table. The plan is different from the standard reformatting strategy because the new worktable is used as the outer, not the inner, table. You might see a reformatting strategy joining two tables and still get good performance. (In general, of course, you will try to alter the behavior only of queries that are not performing up to par. You would not try to influence the behavior simply because SHOWPLAN indicates that a reformatting strategy was used.)

Joins of many tables

Some folklore insists that SQL Server "does not optimize" joins of more than four tables. This is incorrect. However, SQL Server does evaluate join order using four tables at a time. This is a performance optimization—a pruning technique to keep the decision tree at a manageable size. For example, if you are joining six tables, SQL Server will evaluate how to join the first four. After joining the first four, SQL Server joins this intermediate result to the remaining two tables (and the order of this now three-table join will again be evaluated). As you can see, with more than four tables, the order of the tables in the SELECT statement can make a difference. With four or fewer tables, it shouldn't matter what order the tables appear in the FROM clause.

Monitor Query Performance

Before you think about taking some action to make a query faster, such as adding an index or denormalizing, you should understand how a query is being processed. SQL Server provides these tools (SET options) for monitoring queries:

- STATISTICS IO
- STATISTICS TIME
- SHOWPLAN ON

You enable all of these SET options before running a query, and they will produce additional output. Typically, you will run your query with these options set in a tool like ISQLW.EXE, and then when you are satisfied with your query, you cut and paste it into your application or into the script file that creates your stored procedures. ISQLW.EXE provides checkboxes you can use to turn any or all of these options on and off.

STATISTICS IO

The output from *SET STATISTICS IO ON* includes the values Logical Reads, Physical Reads, Read Ahead Reads, and Scan Count.

Logical Reads

This value indicates the total number of page accesses needed to process the query. Every page is read from the data cache, whether or not it was necessary to bring that page from disk into the cache for any given read. This value is always at least as large and usually larger than the value for Physical Reads. The same page can be read many times (such as when a query is driven from an index), so the count of Logical Reads for a table can be greater than the number of pages in a table.

Physical Reads

This value indicates the number of pages that were read from disk and will always be less than or equal to the value of Logical Reads. The value of the cache-hit ratio can be computed from the Logical Reads and Physical Reads values as follows:

Cache-Hit Ratio = (Logical Reads − Physical Reads)/Logical Reads

Remember that the value for Physical Reads will vary substantially and will decrease substantially with the second and subsequent execution, because the cache is loaded by the first execution. The value is also greatly affected by other SQL Server activity and can also appear low if the page was preloaded by the Read Ahead Manager. For this reason, I don't find it useful to do a lot of analysis of physical I/O on a per-query basis. When looking at individual queries, Logical Reads are usually more interesting since the information is consistent. Physical I/O and achieving a good cache-hit ratio is crucial but is more interesting at the all-server level. Pay close attention to Logical Reads for each important query, and pay close attention to physical I/O and the cache-hit ratio for the server as a whole.

STATISTICS IO acts on a per-table, per-query basis. You might want to see the *physical_io* column in *sysprocesses* corresponding to the specific connection. This column shows the cumulative count of synchronous I/O that has occurred during the *spid*'s existence, regardless of the table. It even includes any Read Ahead Reads that were initiated because of that connection. Read-ahead services requests are associated with each *spid*'s session descriptor of open tables (SDES's), so the physical I/O can be associated with the original requestor.

Read Ahead Reads

This value indicates the number of pages that were read into cache by the Read Ahead Manager while processing this query. These pages are not necessarily used by the query. If a page is ultimately needed, a logical read is counted but a physical read is not. A high number for this value means that the value for Physical Reads is probably lower and the cache-hit ratio is probably higher than if a read ahead was not done. In a situation like this, you shouldn't infer from a high cache-hit ratio that your system wouldn't benefit from additional memory. The high cache-hit ratio might have been achieved solely because the Read Ahead Manager is operating efficiently. That's a good thing, but it would perhaps have been even better had the data simply remained in cache from previous use. The same or an even higher cache-hit ratio might have been achieved without requiring the Read Ahead Reads (which is simply an optimistic form of physical I/O).

Scan Count

This value indicates the number of times that the corresponding table was accessed. Outer tables of a nested iteration (join) have a Scan Count of 1. For inner tables, the Scan Count is the number of times "through the loop" that the table was accessed. (If this doesn't make sense to you, you can review the discussion of join processing and nested iteration earlier in this chapter.) The number of Logical Reads will be determined by the sum of the Scan Count times the number of pages accessed on each scan.

STATISTICS TIME

The output of *SET STATISTICS TIME ON* is pretty self-explanatory. It shows the elapsed and CPU time it took (which in this context means the time not spent waiting for resources such as locks or I/O operations to complete) to process the query. The times are separated into two components: the time required to parse and compile the query, and the time required to execute the query.

SHOWPLAN

The output of *SET SHOWPLAN ON* is your window into the query execution plan. The output shows the order in which tables are accessed and how they are joined, which indexes are used, which tables are scanned, and what worktables (temporary tables) are created. SHOWPLAN is your primary tool to determine which indexes are useful.

It is typical to add an index that you think might help speed up a query and then use SHOWPLAN to see whether the index was actually used. Or you can add several possible indexes and then use SHOWPLAN to see which of them is chosen as "best." If some indexes are never being used (and are not needed to maintain a PRIMARY KEY or UNIQUE constraint), you might as well drop the indexes. If an index is not useful for queries, the index is overhead—a drag on data modification performance with no benefit for queries. (But before deciding that an index is not useful, be sure that you have updated statistics for the table. The optimizer might not be choosing an index because the distribution page doesn't show it to be useful or perhaps a distribution page was never created. If current statistics were reflected in the distribution page, it might be that the index, in fact, *would* be useful.) After adding indexes, be sure to then monitor their effect on your updates, since indexes add overhead to data modification (inserts, deletes, and updates).

SHOWPLAN will show those "nasty" reformatting strategies, so you can try to stamp them out by adding useful indexes. It will also show table scans, of course, but it should be clear by now that not all table scans are bad and should be avoided. For either a problematic table scan or a reformatting strategy, the best approach is to add an index hypothesized to be useful and then see if it is useful to eliminate a table scan or reformatting strategy. If the index *is* useful, also consider whether it is "worth it" in terms of the effect it has on your data modification operations. If a change to indexing alone is not the answer, you need to look at other possible solutions, such as using an index hint or changing the general approach to the query. (In Chapter 12, I showed cases in which several totally different approaches can be useful to some queries—ranging from use of somewhat tricky SQL to use of temporary tables to use of cursors. When those approaches also fail, it is time to consider changes to the database design using the denormalization techniques discussed earlier.)

SHOWPLAN also shows whether an update is being processed via a direct or a deferred strategy. However, the specific direct method choice is not made until the execution of the update, so it is not available in the execution plan or to SHOWPLAN. To analyze updates, I recommend using trace flag 323 (as discussed in Chapter 8) in addition to using SHOWPLAN.

SHOWPLAN is often used in conjunction with *SET NOEXEC ON*—you can see the query execution plan but you don't execute the query. This is useful while experimenting with indexes, but ultimately you'll need to test how the query executes using a representative data set.

Thirty pages of the SQL Server documentation are devoted to explaining SHOWPLAN output. I don't have much to add here, so I'll refer you to the documentation instead. By now, I hope that you understand what makes an index useful, why a table scan can make more sense than using an index, and how joins can be processed. The SHOWPLAN output will give you new insight into what's going on.

Watching the Optimizer's Decision Process

SHOWPLAN reveals the actual plan chosen for the query, and it is the primary tool you'll use to get information about a query. SQL Server also has trace flags that can give some insight into the optimizer's decision process. These trace flags, which exist primarily for use by Microsoft developers working on the optimizer, show information used to cost various strategies. The output isn't pretty, and most of the information relates to values for internal structures in the engine that are for all intents and purposes irrelevant to you. Here is a brief description of the trace flags.

Flag	Description
302	Provides information about index selection decisions, such as indexes considered, selectivity values used (from the distribution page or from the defaults if no distribution page exists), and estimates for I/O if the indexes were used to drive the scan
310	Provides information about join-order possibilities and estimated costs

Again, much of the information provided by these trace flags probably will not be relevant to you, but they contain enough information to help you answer questions like these:

- Was every search argument (SARG) mentioned with the correct operator?

- Was every index considered?

- Is a statistics page available for each index?

- Are the row and page estimates close to reality?

- What join orders were considered?

- Were the appropriate indexes tested with each different join order?

Here is an example of a simple query with these trace flags enabled. The output is voluminous and would be even larger had a more complex query been used. I've marked in boldface type results that will help to answer the questions posed above. Notice that early in the output, each table is assigned a value for *varno* and is subsequently referred to by that value. A single table can be accessed multiple times, so it can have multiple *varno* values. The *crows* value is an estimate of the number of rows expected to satisfy the search or join clause. The *crows* value will be equal to the number of rows in the table if there are no SEARCH clauses on the table. The *crows* information can be seen following the *q_score_join* portion in the "Scoring clause for index" section in the output.

```
DBCC TRACEON (3604, 302 ,310)
GO

SELECT
au_lname, au_fname, title
FROM
        authors AS A
        JOIN titleauthor AS TA ON (A.au_id=TA.au_id)
        JOIN titles AS T ON (T.title_id=TA.title_id)
WHERE
A.state <> 'CA'
ORDER BY au_lname, au_fname
GO


*******************************
Leaving q_init_sclause() for table 'authors' (varno 0).
The table has 23 rows and 1 pages.
Cheapest index is index 0, costing 1 pages per scan.
```

```
******************************
Leaving q_init_sclause() for table 'titleauthor' (varno 1).
The table has 25 rows and 1 pages.
Cheapest index is index 0, costing 1 pages per scan.

******************************
Leaving q_init_sclause() for table 'titles' (varno 2).
The table has 18 rows and 3 pages.
Cheapest index is index 0, costing 3 pages per scan.

******************************
Entering q_score_join() for table 'authors' (varno 0).
The table has 23 rows and 1 pages.
Scoring the join clause:
AND (!:0x1498e6a) (andstat:0x2)
 EQ (L:0x1498e56) ( rsltype(0x2f):CHAR rsllen:255 rslprec:11
 rslscale:0 opstat:0x0)
 VAR (L:0x1498db8) (varname:au_id varno:0 colid:1
 coltype(0x27):VARCHAR colen:11 coloff:-1 colprec:11 colscale:0
 vartypeid:101 varnext:1499052 varusecnt:1 varlevel:0 varsubq:0)
 VAR (R:0x1498e0c) (varname:au_id varno:1 colid:1
 coltype(0x27):VARCHAR colen:11 coloff:-1 colprec:11 colscale:0
 vartypeid:101 varnext:1498f9e varusecnt:1 varlevel:0 varsubq:0)

Unique clustered index found--return rows 1 pages 2
Cheapest index is index 0, costing 1 pages and generating 1 rows per
scan.
Join selectivity is 23.
******************************

******************************
Entering q_score_join() for table 'titleauthor' (varno 1).
The table has 25 rows and 1 pages.
Scoring the join clause:
AND (!:0x1498e6a) (andstat:0x2)
 EQ (L:0x1498e56) ( rsltype(0x2f):CHAR rsllen:255 rslprec:11
 rslscale:0 opstat:0x0)
 VAR (L:0x1498e0c) (varname:au_id varno:1 colid:1
 coltype(0x27):VARCHAR colen:11 coloff:-1 colprec:11 colscale:0
 vartypeid:101 varnext:1498f9e varusecnt:1 varlevel:0 varsubq:0)
 VAR (R:0x1498db8) (varname:au_id right:1498e0c varno:0 colid:1
 coltype(0x27):VARCHAR colen:11 coloff:-1 colprec:11 colscale:0
 vartypeid:101 varnext:1499052 varusecnt:1 varstat:0x884
 varlevel:0 varsubq:0)
```

```
Unique clustered index found--return rows 1 pages 2
Scoring clause for index 1
Relop bits are: 0x1000,0x800,0x80,0x4
Estimate: indid 1, selectivity 6.250000e-002, rows 1 pages 2
Scoring clause for index 2
Relop bits are: 0x1000,0x800,0x80,0x4
Estimate: indid 2, selectivity 6.250000e-002, rows 1 pages 3
Cheapest index is index 0, costing 1 pages and generating 25 rows per
scan.
Cost join selectivity is 1.
Best join selectivity is 16.
*******************************

*******************************
Entering q_score_join() for table 'titleauthor' (varno 1).
The table has 25 rows and 1 pages.
Scoring the join clause:
AND (!:0x1499004) (andstat:0x2)
 EQ (L:0x1498fea) ( rsltype(0x2f):CHAR rsllen:255 rslprec:6
 rslscale:0 opstat:0x0)
 VAR (L:0x1498f9e) (varname:title_id varno:1 colid:2
 coltype(0x27):VARCHAR colen:6 coloff:-2 colprec:6 colscale:0
 vartypeid:102 varusecnt:1 varlevel:0 varsubq:0)
 VAR (R:0x1498f46) (varname:title_id varno:2 colid:1
 coltype(0x27):VARCHAR colen:6 coloff:-1 colprec:6 colscale:0
 vartypeid:102 varnext:1498c24 varusecnt:1 varlevel:0 varsubq:0)

Scoring clause for index 3
Relop bits are: 0x80,0x4
Estimate: indid 3, selectivity 7.142857e-002, rows 1 pages 3
Cheapest index is index 0, costing 1 pages and generating 25 rows per
scan.
Cost join selectivity is 1.
Best join selectivity is 14.
*******************************

*******************************
Entering q_score_join() for table 'titles' (varno 2).
The table has 18 rows and 3 pages.
Scoring the join clause:
AND (!:0x1499004) (andstat:0x2)
 EQ (L:0x1498fea) ( rsltype(0x2f):CHAR rsllen:255 rslprec:6
 rslscale:0 opstat:0x0)
   VAR (L:0x1498f46) (varname:title_id varno:2 colid:1
   coltype(0x27):VARCHAR colen:6 coloff:-1 colprec:6 colscale:0
   vartypeid:102 varnext:1498c24 varusecnt:1 varlevel:0 varsubq:0)
   VAR (R:0x1498f9e) (varname:title_id right:1498f46 varno:1
   colid:2 coltype(0x27):VARCHAR colen:6 coloff:-2 colprec:6
```

```
    colscale:0 vartypeid:102 varusecnt:1 varstat:0x84 varlevel:0
    varsubq:0)
```

Unique clustered index found--return rows 1 pages 2
Cheapest index is index 1, costing 2 pages and generating 1 rows per
scan.
Join selectivity is 18.
```
*******************************
```

QUERY IS CONNECTED

J_OPTIMIZE: Remaining vars=[0,1,2]

permutation: 0 - 1 - 2

NEW PLAN #1 (total cost = 268):
JPLAN (0x253f49c) varno=0 indexid=0 **totcost=16** pathtype=sclause
class=join optype=? **method=NESTED ITERATION outerrows=1 rows=23**
joinsel=1 lp=1 pp=1 cpages=1 ctotpages=1 corder=1 cstat=0x20
maxpages=1 matcost=10144 matpages=1 **crows=23** cjoinsel=1

JPLAN (0x253f500) varno=1 indexid=0 **totcost=60** pathtype=sclause
class=join optype=? **method=NESTED ITERATION outerrows=23 rows=25**
joinsel=16 lp=23 pp=1 cpages=1 ctotpages=1 corder=1 cstat=0x20
maxpages=1 matcost=10168 matpages=2 **crows=25** cjoinsel=1 joinmap=[0]

JPLAN (0x253f564) varno=2 indexid=0 **totcost=192** pathtype=sclause
class=join optype=? **method=NESTED ITERATION outerrows=25 rows=25**
joinsel=14 lp=75 pp=3 cpages=3 ctotpages=3 corder=1 cstat=0x20
maxpages=3 **crows=18** cjoinsel=1 joinmap=[1]

NEW PLAN #2 (total cost = 218):
JPLAN (0x253f49c) varno=0 indexid=0 **totcost=16** pathtype=sclause
class=join optype=? **method=NESTED ITERATION outerrows=1 rows=23**
joinsel=1 lp=1 pp=1 cpages=1 ctotpages=1 corder=1 cstat=0x20
maxpages=1 matcost=10144 matpages=1 **crows=23** cjoinsel=1

JPLAN (0x253f500) varno=1 indexid=0 totcost=60 pathtype=sclause
class=join optype=? method=**NESTED ITERATION outerrows=23 rows=25**
joinsel=16 lp=23 pp=1 cpages=1 ctotpages=1 corder=1 cstat=0x20
maxpages=1 matcost=10168 matpages=2 **crows=25** cjoinsel=1 joinmap=[0]

JPLAN (0x253f564) varno=2 indexid=1 totcost=142 pathtype=join
class=join optype=? method=NESTED ITERATION outerrows=25 rows=25
joinsel=14 lp=50 pp=3 cpages=2 ctotpages=3 corder=1 cstat=0x4
maxpages=3 **crows=1** cjoinsel=18 joinmap=[1] jnvar=1 refindid=0
refcost=0 refpages=0 reftotpages=0 ordercol[0]=1 ordercol[1]=2
```
```

```
WORK PLAN #3 (total cost = 10418):

permutation: 0 - 2 - 1
IGNORING THIS PERMUTATION

permutation: 1 - 0 - 2
WORK PLAN #4 (total cost = 272):
WORK PLAN #5 (total cost = 222):
WORK PLAN #6 (total cost = 10422):

permutation: 2 - 0 - 1
IGNORING THIS PERMUTATION

permutation: 1 - 2 - 0
WORK PLAN #7 (total cost = 272):
WORK PLAN #8 (total cost = 222):
WORK PLAN #9 (total cost = 10392):

permutation: 2 - 1 - 0

NEW PLAN #10 (total cost = 162):
JPLAN (0x253f49c) varno=2 indexid=0 totcost=48 pathtype=sclause
class=join optype=? method=NESTED ITERATION outerrows=1 rows=18
joinsel=1 lp=3 pp=3 cpages=3 ctotpages=3 corder=1 cstat=0x20
maxpages=3 matcost=10119 matpages=1 crows=18 cjoinsel=1

JPLAN (0x253f500) varno=1 indexid=0 totcost=50 pathtype=sclause
class=join optype=? method=NESTED ITERATION outerrows=18 rows=25
joinsel=14 lp=18 pp=1 cpages=1 ctotpages=1 corder=1 cstat=0x20
maxpages=1 matcost=10168 matpages=2 crows=25 cjoinsel=1 joinmap=[2]

JPLAN (0x253f564) varno=0 indexid=0 totcost=64 pathtype=sclause
class=join optype=? method=NESTED ITERATION outerrows=25 rows=25
joinsel=16 lp=25 pp=1 cpages=1 ctotpages=1 corder=1 cstat=0x20
maxpages=1 crows=23 cjoinsel=1 joinmap=[1]

BEST PERMUTATION (total cost = 162):
JPLAN (0x253e7fc) varno=2 indexid=0 totcost=48 pathtype=sclause
class=join optype=? method=NESTED ITERATION outerrows=1 rows=18
joinsel=1 lp=3 pp=3 cpages=3 ctotpages=3 corder=1 cstat=0x20
maxpages=3 matcost=10119 matpages=1 crows=18 cjoinsel=1

JPLAN (0x253e860) varno=1 indexid=0 totcost=50 pathtype=sclause
class=join optype=? method=NESTED ITERATION outerrows=18 rows=25
joinsel=14 lp=18 pp=1 cpages=1 ctotpages=1 corder=1 cstat=0x20
maxpages=1 matcost=10168 matpages=2 crows=25 cjoinsel=1 joinmap=[2]
```

```
JPLAN (0x253e8c4) varno=0 indexid=0 totcost=64 pathtype=sclause
class=join optype=? method=NESTED ITERATION outerrows=25 rows=25
joinsel=16 lp=25 pp=1 cpages=1 ctotpages=1 corder=1 cstat=0x20
maxpages=1 crows=23 cjoinsel=1 joinmap=[1]

TOTAL # COMBINATIONS: 1
TOTAL # PERMUTATIONS: 6
TOTAL # PLANS CONSIDERED: 10

FINAL PLAN (total cost = 162, maxpages = 5):
JPLAN (0x253e7fc) varno=2 indexid=0 totcost=48 pathtype=sclause
class=join optype=SUBSTITUTE method=NESTED ITERATION outerrows=1
rows=18 joinsel=1 lp=3 pp=3 cpages=3 ctotpages=3 corder=1 cstat=0x20
maxpages=3 matcost=10119 matpages=1 crows=18 cjoinsel=1

JPLAN (0x253e860) varno=1 indexid=0 totcost=50 pathtype=sclause
class=join optype=SUBSTITUTE method=NESTED ITERATION outerrows=18
rows=25 joinsel=14 lp=18 pp=1 cpages=1 ctotpages=1 corder=1
cstat=0x20 maxpages=1 matcost=10168 matpages=2 crows=25 cjoinsel=1
joinmap=[2]

JPLAN (0x253e8c4) varno=0 indexid=0 totcost=64 pathtype=sclause
class=join optype=SUBSTITUTE method=NESTED ITERATION outerrows=25
rows=25 joinsel=16 lp=25 pp=1 cpages=1 ctotpages=1 corder=1
cstat=0x20 maxpages=1 crows=23 cjoinsel=1 joinmap=[1]

QUERY IS CONNECTED

J_OPTIMIZE: Remaining vars=[3]

permutation: 3

NEW PLAN #1 (total cost = 32):
JPLAN (0x253f49c) varno=3 indexid=0 totcost=32 pathtype=sclause
class=join optype=? method=NESTED ITERATION outerrows=1 rows=25
joinsel=1 lp=2 pp=2 cpages=2 ctotpages=0 corder=0 cstat=0x1
maxpages=2 crows=25 cjoinsel=1

BEST PERMUTATION (total cost = 32):
JPLAN (0x253e7fc) varno=3 indexid=0 totcost=32 pathtype=sclause
class=join optype=? method=NESTED ITERATION outerrows=1 rows=25
joinsel=1 lp=2 pp=2 cpages=2 ctotpages=0 corder=0 cstat=0x1
maxpages=2 crows=25 cjoinsel=1

TOTAL # COMBINATIONS: 1
TOTAL # PERMUTATIONS: 1
TOTAL # PLANS CONSIDERED: 1
```

```
FINAL PLAN (total cost = 43, maxpages = 2):
JPLAN (0x253e7fc) varno=3 indexid=0 totcost=43 pathtype=sclause
class=join optype=GETSORTED method=NESTED ITERATION outerrows=1
rows=25 joinsel=1 lp=2 pp=2 cpages=2 ctotpages=0 corder=0 cstat=0x1
maxpages=2 crows=25 cjoinsel=1
```

Using Optimizer and Lock Hints

As you know, locking and query optimization is done automatically by SQL Server. But because the optimizer is probability-based, it will sometimes make wrong predictions. For example, to eliminate a deadlock, you might want to force an update lock to be taken. Or you might want to tell the optimizer that you value the first row returned more highly than total throughput. You can specify these and other behaviors by using optimizer and lock hints. The word "hint" is a bit of a misnomer in this context, because using a hint is generally a firm directive to SQL Server—the hint will be handled as a directive rather than as a suggestion. SQL Server provides four general types of hints that specify the following:

■ The order in which tables will be processed for a join.

■ A specific index, if any, that should be used to drive the scan.

■ A particular locking mode that should be used.

■ That the time it takes to return the first row is more important than overall throughput. (This simply gives the optimizer more information with which to make a decision, but the optimizer still makes the decision.)

If you've made it this far in this book, you probably understand the various issues that are related to hints. That is, you should understand locking, how indexes are selected, overall throughput versus the first row returned, and how join order is determined. Understanding these issues is the key to effectively using hints and allows you to intelligently instruct SQL Server to deviate from "normal" behavior when necessary. Hints are simply syntactic hooks that override default behavior; you should now have insight into those behaviors so that you can make good decisions as to when such overrides are warranted.

Optimizer hints should be used for the special case—not as standard operating procedure. When you specify a hint, you constrain SQL Server. For example, suppose you indicate in a hint that a specific index should be used. Later you add another index that would be even more useful, but the hint prevents the optimizer from considering the new index. As new versions of SQL Server are released, you can expect new query optimization strategies, more access methods, and new locking behaviors. If you bind your queries to one specific behavior, you forego your chances of benefiting from such improvements. And perhaps most important, a huge advantage provided by a product like SQL Server is the *nonprocedural development approach*. That is, you don't need to tell SQL Server *how* to do something. Rather, you tell it *what* you want it to do. Hints are quite contrary to this approach. Nonetheless, the reality is that the optimizer isn't perfect and never can be. So using hints judiciously can be a huge win—literally the difference between a project's success and failure.

When you use a hint, you must have a clear vision of how you think it might help. It's a good idea to add a comment to the query to justify the hint. Then test your hypothesis by watching the output of STATISTICS IO, STATISTICS TIME, and SHOWPLAN both with and without your hint.

Specify the order in which tables will be processed for a join

SET FORCEPLAN ON makes SQL Server choose the join order of tables to be the same as the order in which the tables are listed in the FROM clause, rather than have the join order chosen based on Scan Count and logical I/O estimates. *SET FORCEPLAN ON* remains in effect throughout the connection period until *SET FORCEPLAN OFF* is issued. If you use SET FORCEPLAN, be sure to toggle it *ON* immediately before issuing the query that needs the override; then immediately toggle it *OFF*.

Specify an index to be used to drive the scan (INDEX/)

You can direct that a specific index be used by naming it directly in the FROM clause. You can also specify the index by its *indid* value, but practically speaking, this makes sense only when you specify *not* to use an index or to use the clustered index, whatever it is. Otherwise, the *indid* value is prone to change as indexes are dropped and re-created. You can use the value 0 to specify that no index should be used—that is, to force a table scan. And you can use the value 1 to specify that the clustered index should be used regardless of the columns on which it exists. The index hint syntax looks like this:

```
SELECT select_list
FROM table_name [(INDEX = {index_name | index_id})]
```

This example forces the query to do a table scan:

```
SELECT au_lname, au_fname
FROM authors (INDEX=0)
WHERE au_lname LIKE 'C%'
```

This example forces the query to use the clustered index:

```
SELECT au_lname, au_fname
FROM authors (INDEX=1)
WHERE au_lname LIKE 'C%'
```

This example forces the query to use the index named *aunmind*:

```
SELECT au_lname, au_fname
FROM authors (INDEX=aunmind)
WHERE au_lname LIKE 'C%'
```

This example forces the query to use index 2, *aunmind*. Note, however, that identifying an index by *indid* is dangerous and not advised. If an index is dropped and re-created in a different place, that index might take on a different *indid*:

```
SELECT au_lname, au_fname
FROM authors (INDEX=2)
WHERE au_lname LIKE 'C%'
```

Specify that a particular locking mode should be used

You can specify a lock type or duration in a way that is syntactically similar to that used for specifying index hints. Chapter 13, "Locking," explains the compatibility of locks and other issues that are essential to using lock hints properly. Lock hints work only in the context of a transaction, so if you use these hints, you must remember to use BEGIN TRAN/END TRAN blocks (or you must run with implicit transactions set to *ON*). The lock hint syntax is as follows:

```
SELECT select_list
FROM table_name [(LOCKTYPE)]
```

> **TIP**　Remember to put the lock hint in parentheses, or it will be treated as an alias name for the table, instead of as a lock hint.

The lock type can be NOLOCK, HOLDLOCK, UPDLOCK, TABLOCK, PAGLOCK, or TABLOCKX.

NOLOCK　Allows uncommitted, or dirty, reads. Shared locks are not issued by the scan, and the exclusive locks of others are not honored. This option is similar to specifying *SET TRANSACTION ISOLATION LEVEL READ UNCOMMITTED*. However, the SET option prescribes READ UNCOMMITTED behavior for all tables in the query; this hint is specified on a table-by-table basis.

HOLDLOCK　Holds shared locks for the specified table until the end of the transaction. This option is similar to specifying *SET TRANSACTION ISOLATION LEVEL REPEATABLE READ*, except that the SET option would affect all tables, not only the one specified in this hint.

UPDLOCK　Takes update page locks instead of shared page locks while reading the table and holds them until the end of the transaction. Taking update locks can be an important technique to eliminate conversion deadlocks.

TABLOCK Takes a shared lock on the table even if page locks would be taken otherwise. This option is useful when you know you'll escalate to a table lock or if you need to get a complete snapshot of a table. This option can be used with HOLDLOCK if you want the table lock held until the end of the transaction block (REPEATABLE READ).

PAGLOCK Takes shared page locks where a single shared table lock might otherwise be taken. (There is no hint for taking an exclusive page lock. Instead, you would hint to take an update page lock, using UPDLOCK. Once acquired, you know UPDLOCK can be automatically upgraded to an exclusive lock if and when required.)

TABLOCKX Takes an exclusive lock on the table that is held until the end of the transaction block. (All exclusive locks are always held until the end of a transaction, regardless of the isolation level in effect.)

You can combine index and lock hints and use different hints for different tables, and you can combine HOLDLOCK with the level of shared locks (page or table). Here's an example:

```
BEGIN TRAN
SELECT title, au_lname
FROM titles (TABLOCK), titleauthor, authors (PAGLOCK HOLDLOCK
    INDEX=1)
WHERE titles.title_id=titleauthor.title_id
AND authors.au_id=titleauthor.au_id
```

Using the FASTFIRSTROW option

You can use this option to influence the optimizer to drive a scan using a nonclustered index that matches the ORDER BY clause of a query rather than using a different access method and then doing a sort to match the ORDER BY clause. Often, the number of logical I/Os needed to drive a scan from a nonclustered index can be many times greater than the number of pages in the table, because of the optimizer's need to reread pages many times (perhaps once for every row in the table). In this case, the optimizer typically would not use the index and would perform the sort. With the FASTFIRSTROW hint, the optimizer might favor the index, eliminating the sort but with the effect of degrading the total throughput of the query. But by driving the scan from the index, the first row is immediately available with the first data page retrieved—otherwise, if the sort is performed, the first row is not available until the end. Using the index, the first row might be returned with just a handful of I/Os even for large scans (but it might be much more costly to get the *last* row).

Unlike other hints that are really strict directives, FASTFIRSTROW is a true hint. If the query contains a WHERE clause as well as an ORDER BY clause, SQL Server might still use an index that resolves a SARG in the WHERE clause instead of the index that resolves the ORDER BY clause. The decision process is as normal, based on the selectivity of the index. But this hint influences the decision and costing estimates. You can, of course, also provide an index hint by using INDEX/ (really a directive), mentioned a few paragraphs earlier, to ensure that the index matching the ORDER BY is also used to drive the scan, but this option relates to the decision in regards to a nonclustered index. If a clustered index matches the ORDER BY, the sort will be avoided since the rows are already physically in the order wanted.

SUMMARY

This chapter walked you through a checklist of performance-related topics that you should consider while designing and implementing a high-performance application. There are no magic knobs to turn to improve performance. It must be considered from the outset of a project. Because all the information in this book is prerequisite to the topics discussed here, this chapter should not be read in isolation from the rest of the book.

As a starting point, skilled team members are vital to major development tasks. More than anything else, your staff is the best predictor and insurance of a project's success. You must establish performance criteria and prototype, test, and monitor performance throughout development.

In this chapter, I also presented various techniques that you can use in database design and in making indexing decisions. I discussed in detail how to look at lock contention issues and how to resolve deadlocks. I also discussed how the query optimizer chooses a plan and actions you can take to ensure that it performs as well as possible.

As you make and monitor changes, remember to change just one variable at a time. When you change multiple variables at the same time, you'll find that it is impossible to evaluate the effectiveness of any one of them. This goes for all changes, whether they are related to design, indexing, the use of an optimizer hint, or a configuration setting. This is a fundamental aspect of all performance work, but one that people often forget. In the next chapter, I'll discuss configuration and performance monitoring topics.

15

Configuration and Monitoring for Performance

Introduction

In the last chapter, I discussed the most important aspects of performance—those that are affected by your design, prototyping, indexing, and query writing.

Tuning your system configuration can also help you further improve your system performance, but doing so is unlikely to yield the same magnitude of gain that a change to your design might bring. More importantly, you should be sure that your system is not misconfigured. You might see a 10 percent improvement in performance by moving from a reasonable configuration to an ideal configuration. Ten percent is nothing to sneeze at, but it's unlikely to have a make-or-break effect on your application. On the other hand, a badly misconfigured system can absolutely kill your application's performance.

In this chapter, I'll present configuration options for both Microsoft Windows NT and SQL Server. I'll offer guidelines for important values and offer suggestions about improvements that will likely be smaller and more incremental at best. I'll follow this discussion with a summary of how to effectively use Performance Monitor to monitor changes methodically as you make them.

Review and Adjust Windows NT Configuration Settings

In this section, I'll present configuration options in Windows NT. In the next section, I'll cover SQL Server configuration. As I mentioned above, a badly configured system can destroy performance. For example, a system with an incorrectly configured memory setting can break an application. I recommend that you make sure values are set at reasonable levels and spend most of your effort on application and database design, indexing, tuning queries, and other such activities.

Windows NT Task Management

As I discussed in Chapter 3, "SQL Server Architecture," Windows NT schedules all threads in the system for execution. Each thread of every process has a priority, and Windows NT executes the next ready thread with the highest priority. By default, Windows NT gives active applications (that is, applications that a user is currently using) a higher priority to offer better system responsiveness to interactive users. But this priority choice is a bad one for a server application that's running in the background, such as SQL Server. To remedy this situation, SQL Server's Setup program eliminates Windows NT's favoritism of foreground applications by modifying the priority setting. Although SQL Server Setup makes the modification, it's not a bad idea for you to periodically double-check this setting (in case someone sets it back) in the following way: From the Windows NT Control Panel, double-click the System icon. Then, on the Performance tab in the Application Performance section, slide the control labeled Select The Performance Boost For The Foreground Application to the None setting.

Windows NT Server Resource Allocation

A computer running Windows NT Server for file and print services would want to use the most memory for file caching. But if a computer is also running SQL Server, it makes sense that more memory be available for SQL Server's use.

You can configure the server's resource allocation (and associated nonpaged memory pool usage) in the Server dialog box of the Network applet. Double-click the Network icon on the Control Panel, and select the Services tab. The Server dialog box appears, as shown in Figure 15-1.

The setting Maximize Throughput For Network Applications is best for running SQL Server. You need high network throughput, with minimal memory devoted to file caching, so that the most memory is available to SQL Server. With this option set, network applications—such as SQL Server—have priority over the file cache for access to memory. Although you might expect that choosing the Minimize Memory Used option would help, that option minimizes the memory available for some internal network settings that are needed to support a lot of SQL Server users.

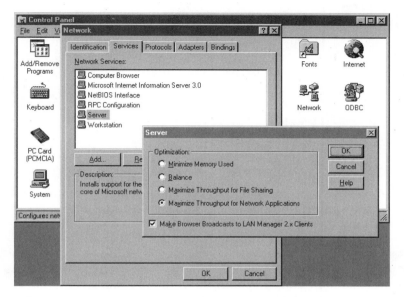

Figure 15-1. *Use the Server dialog box to configure the server service software.*

Windows NT Server PAGEFILE.SYS Location

If possible, you should place the Windows NT page file on a different drive than those files being used by SQL Server. This is vital if your system will be paging. However, an even better approach is for you to add memory and/or change the SQL Server memory configuration to effectively eliminate paging. Then so little page file activity will occur that the file's location will be irrelevant.

Windows NT File System Selection

As I discussed in Chapter 4, "Planning for and Installing SQL Server," whether you use the FAT or the NTFS file system doesn't matter much to system performance. I recommend you use NTFS for most cases for reasons of security and robustness, not performance.

Nonessential Windows NT Services

You should disable any services you don't need via the Services icon on the Control Panel. These unnecessary services add overhead to the system and use resources that could otherwise go to SQL Server. If possible, don't make the Windows NT server that's running SQL Server also be the primary domain controller or backup domain controller (PDC or BDC), the group's file or print server, the Web server, the DHCP server, or so on. You should also consider disabling the Alerter, ClipBook Server, Computer Browser, Messenger, Network DDE, and/ or Schedule services that are enabled by default but not needed by SQL Server.

Windows NT Network Protocols

In general, you should run only the network protocols you actually need for connectivity. Having multiple network protocols (TCP/IP, NWLink, NetBEUI, DLC, Appletalk) on your system is so easy that some systems run protocols that aren't even being used. But this adds overhead to a system. If you legitimately need to use multiple protocols, you should make sure that the highest binding is set for the most often used protocol. Protocols and bind order are set via the Control Panel's Network icon.

Review and Adjust SQL Server Configuration Settings

I've seen more cases of people degrading system performance by thoughtlessly changing configuration settings than cases in which configuration changes really helped. (The **memory** configuration parameter is a notable exception to this—you must make the setting at least reasonable, even if it's not absolutely optimal.) You should change configuration options only when you have a clear reason for doing so, and you should closely monitor the effects of each change so that you can determine whether the change improved or degraded your system's performance. Make and monitor each change one at a time. Otherwise, it's not clear which effect to attribute to which change.

Serverwide Options: sp_configure Settings

Each of the options discussed here are set via the **sp_configure** system stored procedure, or they can be configured serverwide from SQL Enterprise Manager (which simply calls **sp_configure**). No changes take effect until the RECONFIGURE command (or RECONFIGURE WITH OVERRIDE, in some cases) is issued. Some changes take effect immediately (dynamic changes) upon reconfiguration, but others do not take effect until the server is restarted. If an option's *run_value* and *config_value* as displayed by **sp_configure** are different, it means that the server must be restarted for the *config_value* to take effect.

I will not describe every configuration option here—only those that relate directly to performance. I will discuss a few options that you should *not* change in most cases. (I mention these options because people often change them anyway.) Some of these options relate to performance only in that they consume memory (for example, **open objects**). Settings like these are not really *performance* settings—they are *resource* settings. But configured excessively high, they can rob a system of memory and degrade performance.

Rather than describe these **sp_configure** settings in alphabetical order, I've grouped them into three broad categories: options that every site should examine, options needed for adequate resources, and options for fine-tuning. Within each category, I'll discuss the setting in order of general importance. (Such importance, of course, will vary among applications.) I'll provide some guidelines and tips for every setting, but as I like to say (tongue-in-cheek), "*All* generalizations are bad." So treat these options as guidelines, not as hard and fast axioms.

Category 1: Options that every site should examine

This category of options includes those that you absolutely should evaluate: memory and procedure cache.

memory   The **memory** setting, by far the most important configuration setting, is one for which a good default doesn't really exist. After Setup runs, even if hundreds of megabytes of memory are available on your system, SQL Server will *not* be configured to use more than 16 MB of it.

Windows NT provides virtual memory, which is a great feature. But with virtual memory, the aggregate total of all processes' address spaces can actually exceed the amount of RAM on the machine, so any "spillover" is kept on disk in the paging file (PAGEFILE.SYS). (I'm being simplistic here—more than just the spillover is involved. Windows NT keeps a "standby list" that you can page to and from so that you won't always page to and from disk. But the real point here is that memory can be paged, and you want to avoid that because memory paging is very expensive.)

If you configure SQL Server for too much memory, you'll cause page faults, which are requests for virtual memory that is not currently in RAM, so the memory image must be paged in. Generating page faults is much worse than achieving a slightly lower cache-hit ratio, so you shouldn't be super-aggressive and try to get the **memory** setting down to the very last byte. But you do want to get your money's worth out of the memory you have, and more memory can make a dramatic performance difference. Reading data from memory is thousands of times faster than requiring a disk I/O. The memory-configuration guidelines from Chapter 4 suggest general values that will help you realize the most benefits from system memory, but these guidelines are conservative, so you probably won't be paging much due to over-allocation to SQL Server. You can generally be a bit more aggressive than those guidelines suggest—but only while monitoring the system. Remember that it's better to err on the low side than to overcommit memory.

The approach for monitoring and fine-tuning your memory configuration is conceptually simple but will take some time and iteration to get right. The basic strategy is this: Configure SQL Server to use more memory so long as you continue to see a higher cache-hit ratio *and* you do not see an increase in the amount of paging. If possible, keep adding physical memory to the system as long as your cache hits keep improving significantly.

You can watch the cache-hit ratio from the Windows NT Performance Monitor, with the SQLServer object Cache Hit Ratio counter. The value can also be seen by directly executing DBCC PERFMON. In Performance Monitor, use the Memory object and the Pages/sec and Page Faults/sec counters to watch paging. To do this correctly, you have to start Performance Monitor and watch these values for a while (minutes at least, hours preferably, and days sometimes if workloads are uneven) as the system settles into equilibrium. If you've just restarted SQL Server, the cache-hit ratio will, of course, be poor initially, since the cache hasn't yet filled. When you first start monitoring, even the simple actions like moving around your screen groups or clicking with the mouse will cause system activity that might generate page faults. But as the system settles and that activity ceases, the number of page faults should decrease. Ideally, after the system is settled, you should see Page Faults/sec reach or approach 0. If hundreds of page faults per second still occur, even after the system has settled, you'll know that the system memory is overcommitted, and you should lower the **memory** configuration value for SQL Server. Or an even better solution might be to add physical memory to the machine. If you keep getting significantly better cache-hit ratios as you add memory, adding more memory will continue to help. You should keep adding more physical memory (and configuring for it) until the cache-hit ratio stops improving or until you run out of money in your hardware budget, whichever comes first.

The **memory** configuration option controls the total amount of memory SQL Server will allocate. This total includes SQL's Server's executable code (about 2.5 MB, including the DLLs loaded by SQLSERVR.EXE), all its static structures (structures allocated for the number of open objects, open databases, and the maximum number of user connections), various global resources, and locks. After those needs are accounted for, the remaining memory is available for caching stored procedures and data. (The two types of cache are separate, as I'll explain in a moment.) When you alter configuration parameters, be aware that these adjustments can affect the size of the cache since they take memory from it. On the flip side, if you can reduce values for some of those settings, you can free up memory for SQL Server. For most sites though, the cache size will dwarf the memory used for other needs.

Nearly all memory used by SQL Server is suballocated from the chunk specified with **sp_configure memory**, with a few exceptions. If **tempdb in ram** is enabled (as I'll discuss a bit later), that memory is separate, above and beyond that specified by the **memory** option. Also, some dynamic memory allocation is done by the server and relates to cursors and network input and output buffers. Because SQL Server needs to create and destroy Windows NT threads to service different combinations of users, the private stack space for each thread is allocated at that time. By default, Windows NT allocates 1 MB of memory for each thread's stack. If memory is tight and a large number of worker threads must be used, you can use the EDITBIN.EXE utility (supplied with Windows NT) directly on SQLSERVR.EXE to reduce the stack size to perhaps 64 KB. You can go as low as 16 KB, although if this value is set too low, the worker thread will be rudely terminated with a stack overflow exception. These exceptions are pretty small, however, and for the most part, the **sp_configure memory** setting controls all of SQL Server's memory allocation.

Part of the difficulty in estimating memory size requirements is that you must also consider what else is running on the machine. For example, don't try to fine-tune memory while running a bunch of applications that won't be running on your production system (including such applications as SQL Enterprise Manager). But those applications that *will* be running on your system should be running while you're tuning. In short, try to closely approximate the actual environment and workload for your production application before tuning. And before you put your application into production, you must test the system with performance workloads that represent actual usage.

It's a good bet that a future release of SQL Server will "autotune" memory configuration by default. When SQL Server can grab more memory without causing paging and with increased cache hits, it will do so: if the system starts paging, it will trim its needs, and the memory usage will rise and fall dynamically, without your needing to explicitly reconfigure or restart the server.

procedure cache   As I mentioned, after SQL Server's memory needs are met (code, locks, internal resources, and so on), the rest of the memory is then available for cache. The memory for cache is divided between data-caching needs and procedure-caching needs. The **procedure cache** configuration option specifies the percentage that should be given to the procedure cache. The allowed values for this option are 1 through 99—that is, you can never specify this value at either 0 percent or 100 percent, since you always need to specify *some* procedure cache and *some* data cache. A procedure must always be brought into memory and compiled before it runs, and the execution plan must fit into the procedure cache. A data page must always be brought into the data cache to be used. For example, if the value is 30, 30 percent of the memory available for cache (after accounting for the needs of static structures, locks, and so on) will be used for procedure cache and 70 percent will be used for the data cache.

Using a percentage rather than a specific designated size ensures that all memory is fully used, without being overcommitted. However, the fact that the setting is specified as a percentage rather than a specific value can pose a small problem. Assume that you have the procedure cache at the "right" size. If you add and configure more memory to SQL Server with the intent to improve data cache hits, the procedure cache will take its designated percentage of the new memory, which might make it the wrong size. In this case, you might want to decrease the procedure cache percentage to maintain the absolute size of the procedure cache.

When considering the procedure cache, keep in mind that stored procedures are not reentrant, although they can be reused. For example, if 50 users will simultaneously execute a stored procedure named **sp_myproc**, there must be room in the cache for 50 copies of the procedure. That is, if a copy of the procedure is already in cache and is not currently executing, it is available for the next user. But the procedure cache must be big enough to hold a copy of the procedure for each user machine that is simultaneously executing it.

Obviously, the size of the procedure cache should be based on the number and size of the stored procedures that execute concurrently. I can't offer any broad guidelines, except to say that you should leave the procedure cache option at its default of 30 until some data suggests that it should be changed. You can get this data by executing DBCC MEMUSAGE and DBCC PROCCACHE. (Some of these same statistics are also exported to SQL Server's Performance Monitor counters.) You *know* the procedure cache is too small if your users get error 701:

```
There is insufficient system memory to run this query.
```

DBCC MEMUSAGE is useful if you want to see the size of a given procedure and then extrapolate the size that would be necessary to hold as many copies as you want. DBCC MEMUSAGE monitors the 20 largest procedures in the procedure cache and also reports on memory that's currently allocated to code and other resources. The output provides the size of all the procedures in cache, so after you figure out a particular procedure's size, you can estimate its cache-sizing needs by multiplying this size by the number of users you expect to simultaneously execute the procedure.

DBCC PROCCACHE returns useful information about the current contents of the procedure cache. This information is also available via Performance Monitor, using the SQL Server-Procedure Cache object that invokes the DBCC command and does some division to express values as percentages. The table below shows the most important information from this DBCC command and its counterpart in Performance Monitor:

DBCC VALUE (2-KB pages)	Performance Monitor Counter	Description
proc cache size	Procedure Cache Size	The total size of the procedure cache in 2-KB pages
proc cache used	Procedure Cache Used %	The percentage of 2-KB pages in the procedure cache that contain procedures
proc cache active	Procedure Cache Active %	The percentage of 2-KB pages in the procedure cache that contain procedures that are currently executing

You should monitor the system over a period of time—not do just a one-time look. If the value of *proc cache used* is usually much smaller than the *proc cache size* value, your procedures are not filling the cache. You can make the cache smaller if the measured workload was representative of your usual workload. If the *proc cache used* value is 100 percent, adding more memory to your system or allocating more to the procedure cache is a good idea. Ideally, the *proc cache used* value will be about 95 percent of the *proc cache size,* which indicates that your procedure cache size is sufficient but it's not so large that it is wasteful or needlessly depriving the data cache of memory.

The *proc cache active* value is a subset of the *proc cache used* value. (Note that the Performance Monitor value is a percentage of the *proc cache size,* not the *proc cache used.*) If this value is nearly as large as both the *used* and *size* values, that means there is little or no space for an unused procedure to remain waiting to be invoked. In other words, it's possible that your procedures need to be brought into memory and recompiled very often, forgoing the benefits of being reusable and avoiding recompilation. If this is the case, enlarging the procedure cache or adding or configuring more memory will probably be beneficial. It is also possible, although unlikely if you've not been iterating to get the sizing just right, that this state was achieved because the cache is sized perfectly. That is, there is just enough room for all the procedures you want to execute to remain in cache. But pretty much nothing in software ever works out that way, so unless you've been working at it and you methodically arrive at this state, your cache sizing probably could use some work.

The output from DBCC PROCCACHE and DBCC MEMUSAGE also has information about *buffer slots.* This information, however, is less important than other information. As many procedure buffer slots as procedure cache pages are stored in a fixed array. Each procedure buffer slot uses 122 bytes of procedure cache. In DBCC MEMUSAGE output, the space needed to hold the procedure buffer array is called *Proc Headers.* Each used procedure buffer slot points to a *procedure header,* which is the first page of a procedure plan or tree in cache. This first page contains memory management information, such as the addresses of the other pages in the plan or tree. It also contains a pointer to the first statement in the plan as well as the calling procedure (if any). That structure consumes 606 bytes of the first 2-KB page. The rest of the 2-KB page is available for plan or tree use. Depending on the size of the plan or tree, many additional pages might be associated with it. In DBCC MEMUSAGE output, space available to be used as procedure cache is labeled *Proc Cache Bufs.* DBCC MEMUSAGE also gives a detailed breakdown of memory consumed by static structures. If trace flag 3635 is enabled, it will further display the exact size of each structure (in the specific version of SQLSERVR.EXE that is currently running), ending, for all time, debates about the exact amount of memory a configured user connection (PSS structure) takes, for example.

Category 2: Options needed for adequate resources

Increasing the four configuration values—user connections, locks, open databases, and open objects—will not improve performance unless they were badly configured to start with. However, if they are configured too low, you will run out of the respective resource and statements will fail. But since all options use some memory, you don't want to configure them absurdly high. (You can set these options so high that your system won't have enough memory to run. If you inadvertently do this, start SQLSERVR.EXE from the command line with the **−f** minimal configuration parameter. Then you can reconfigure for reasonable settings.) The basic rule is to always have an adequate supply of memory. Don't try to cut your needs extremely close, but also don't be excessive and consume memory that could have been effectively used for caching. In general, I advise not changing SQL Server's default values until and unless you need to—either because you know the counts you need or because it becomes clear via an error message that you are out of the respective resource.

user connections This configuration option allows you to set the maximum allowable number of simultaneous connections to SQL Server. It controls how much memory is reserved for Process Status Structures (PSS) at system startup. Each configured user connection reserves about 27 KB of SQL Server's memory allocation to maintain context for that connection, whether or not it's used. The memory for each PSS is actually allocated/deallocated at user connect/disconnect time, but the computations that size the data and procedure caches from the **sp_configure memory** parameter assume that the maximum configured number of users will ultimately be connected. This is a conservative assumption, since if fewer users are actually connected, the caches could have been sized larger—but then the maximum number of users couldn't connect without exceeding the amount of memory specified by **sp_configure**.

As a rule of thumb, you should estimate that every 40 configured user connections will cost you about a megabyte of memory. This does not include the stack space for worker threads, which ebbs and flows as the users are active or idle. (You can refer back to Chapter 3's discussion about memory use per user connection.) Be aware that this value governs connections, not users. If 10 users are simultaneously running an application that uses 3 connections, you need 30 connections to support this application.

When setting the **user connections** value, remember that rarely will all users actively use the system simultaneously. You need to set the value high enough to accommodate only the number of actual simultaneous users, not every conceivable user. You can use the SQLServer object's Max Users Connected counter in Performance Monitor (or just use the User Connections counter and watch the MAX value in the monitor) to see the highest value reached. (Keep in mind that those counters also include the four system processes—CHECKPOINT, MIRROR

HANDLER, LAZY WRITER, and RA HANDLER—and the Performance Monitor process. But when you configure **user connections**, the value you enter is added to the number of system processes. So the value you see from Performance Monitor is five more than what you really need for **user connections**.

Some sites work too hard, and counterproductively, to keep **user connections** as low as possible. They use a "make-break" strategy in the application—so connections are made, commands are issued, and then connections immediately disconnect. In this scenario, if it's likely that the same user will shortly connect again, this is a bad strategy. The processing overhead to connect and disconnect is far more costly than the 27 KB of memory use for the user context. Let connections hang around for at least a few minutes, even if they're idle, if there's a chance that the application or a user will issue another request. It makes great sense to use a timer so that if the application is idle for 20 or 30 minutes, a disconnect will occur. And don't configure **user connections** right to the edge: If you estimated slightly wrong, your users will be unable to connect. If you think you really need a maximum of 90 user connections, splurge and give yourself *at least* 100.

locks   This configuration option sets the number of available locks (of all types). The default is 5000, and you should increase this value if SQL Server displays a message saying that you have exceeded the number of available locks. Each lock consumes about 30 bytes of memory, so you probably don't need to worry too much about an increase of even several thousand or do too much fine-tuning. (A lock consumes 28 bytes and lock owner blocks are 32 bytes; this configuration option controls both—thus, the 30-byte estimate.) If you run out of locks, try setting the option to 10000. The cost is less than 150 KB for the additional 5000 locks. But use your head—if you ran out of locks with a setting of 5000, don't jump the value up to a million, which will cost about 30 MB. (I am sometimes horrified to see these kinds of things, which happen when people change configuration settings without understanding why they are doing so.)

open databases   This configuration option sets the maximum number of databases that can be open at one time on SQL Server. The default is 20, but you can set this value to the number of databases that you'll actually work with at one time. The memory needed for each database configured is a bit less than 1 KB. A system with 50 simultaneously open databases is fairly unusual, and 100 is very unusual. But even in the 100-open-databases case, this configuration option would consume less than 100 KB, so don't worry. If you're running out of space for open databases, set the option value high enough to handle your needs (without being capricious). If in doubt, just set it to the total number of databases you have on your system, plus a little extra. Unless you have hundreds of databases on one server (atypical), further fine-tuning is not worth it—you have bigger fish to fry.

open objects   This configuration option sets the maximum number of database objects (in *sysobjects*) that can be open at one time on SQL Server. The default is 500, which is too low for many sites. The structure for each configured open object takes only about 70 bytes, so you can add another 100 for a cost of only about 7 KB, or you can double the value to 1000 at a cost of only 35 KB. Again, if you are not getting error messages about being out of open objects, you should leave the setting alone. If you need to increase it, set it high enough to handle your needs, but only by a few hundred at a time if you're unsure of the number required. Memory usage by the **open objects** configuration setting simply isn't significant enough to put a great deal of time into fine-tuning it.

Category 3: Options for fine-tuning only

These are options that you should leave alone unless you have carefully monitored and analyzed your system and have already thoroughly designed your application and database. These settings all have reasonable defaults; you might find that tweaking settings gives you a small performance gain—perhaps a couple of percentage points. But changing them radically without much understanding of what they are for results more often in serious problems and degraded performance. The following options are presented in the order that they should be evaluated.

Lock escalation   SQL Server uses page locking for most operations, but it will escalate page locks to a single table lock to optimize performance. If most of a table will be scanned and will need a large number of page locks, using one table lock instead of lots of page locks requires less overhead in the system.

Deciding when to escalate takes careful consideration. If the escalation occurs too soon, concurrency can be hurt by using table locks rather than just locking a range of pages. If you escalate too late, the system spends time doing locking operations when it would have been better off just getting a table lock early on.

By default, SQL Server escalates to a table lock after 200 page locks on a table have been acquired. This default is just a historical legacy—there's no magic number, and 200 was probably just a random selection made by the original developer. When the ability to configure lock escalation was added in version 6.0, we kept the default at 200 to minimize behavioral changes to users upgrading from earlier versions. But escalating at a fixed number of pages, like 200, is really just arbitrary. If, for example, the table has only 100 pages, the number is not aggressive enough. On the other hand, if a table has 500,000 pages, escalating to a table lock would occur when only 0.04 percent of the table (200/500,000) needed to be scanned, which might be overly aggressive.

Three configuration settings govern lock escalation: **LE threshold maximum**, **LE threshold percent**, and **LE threshold minimum**. These settings apply to the server at large, not just to a table (perhaps unfortunately), and they work in combination with one another, not in isolation.

LE threshold maximum: This value specifies the maximum number of page locks to be held before escalating to a table lock. If the number of page locks is greater than the escalation maximum, a table lock will occur regardless of whether the **LE threshold percent** value has been exceeded. At the default of 200, lock escalation will occur whenever 200 page locks have been acquired, regardless of the size of the table—although escalation might have occurred prior to the 200-lock limit because of the **LE threshold percent** setting. For sites with large tables, you might experiment by making this value considerably higher and relying more on the **LE threshold percent** setting for most escalation.

LE threshold percent: This value specifies the percentage of page locks, rather than a fixed number of pages, needed on a table before a table lock is requested. A value of 0, the default, causes a table lock to occur only when the **LE threshold maximum** value has been reached. You might want to test with a value of about 20, meaning that escalation to a table lock will occur if the number of page locks exceeds 20 percent of the total number of pages in the table.

LE threshold minimum: The **LE threshold minimum** setting determines the minimum number of page locks that must occur before escalating to a table lock, regardless of the **LE threshold percent** setting. Using **LE threshold minimum** makes sense when working with small tables. For example, suppose that your table has only four data pages. With **LE threshold percent** set to 20, only the table lock could exist, since one page is already over the limit—at 25 percent of the entire table.

When the number of page locks exceeds the **LE threshold minimum** value *and* the percentage of page locks exceeds the **LE threshold percent** (or the **LE threshold maximum**), the lock is escalated. The default value is 20, so at least 20 page locks must be acquired before escalation will occur. However, in the example of the small four-page table, lock escalation would not occur because 20 page locks would never be taken, so you'd want to decrease this amount in this case. If you want to delay lock escalation on tables in the 100-page to 200-page size, use this setting rather than **LE threshold percent**. (Obviously, you should make sure that the **LE threshold maximum** value is larger than the **LE threshold minimum** value. However, if you erroneously configured with a minimum value higher than the maximum, SQL Server will use the declared maximum value as the minimum as well.)

The table on the next page illustrates at what point lock escalation will occur. Escalation points are shown for five tables of different sizes and for two different sets of configuration values. The first set of values shows the default settings, and the second set shows alternate values that are reasonable for a lot of sites. You might want to do some empirical testing using values similar to these, adjusted to values appropriate for your table sizes.

Total Number of Pages in Table	Default Values: LE threshold maximum = 200 LE threshold percent = 0 LE threshold minimum = 20	Alternate Values: LE threshold maximum = 2500 LE threshold percent = 20 LE threshold minimum = 15
10	No escalation	No escalation
100	No escalation	20 pages
1000	200 pages	200 pages
10,000	200 pages	2000 pages
500,000	200 pages	2500 pages

sort pages   This value specifies the maximum number of memory pages that will be allocated to sorting per user. Sorting is always a memory-intensive operation, and increasing this number can improve performance on systems that perform large sorts. The default value is 64, which means that a given connection can use up to 64 memory pages (128 KB) for its sort processing. If you do queries that perform large sorts or frequently build indexes (which requires sorting), you can experiment with values of 128, 256, and even the maximum value of 511. Then measure the effects on your operations that require sorts. Large sort operations can be substantially improved using this higher setting. However, the high setting does reduce memory available for the cache, so be sure to also measure your cache-hit ratio and general throughput. If the sorting operations were noticeably improved and your cache-hit ratio not significantly degraded, you've made the right choice. If the sorting operations were improved but the cache-hit ratio suffered, your best action would be to add memory so that you can increase the **sort pages** setting but keep the cache at least as big as it was before the setting was changed.

max worker threads   In Chapter 3, I discussed how SQL Server makes use of the Windows NT thread services by keeping a pool of worker threads that take requests off the queue. With 100 or fewer users, there will usually be as many worker threads as active users (not just connected users who are idle). With a higher number of users, it often makes sense for total throughput to have fewer worker threads than active users. Although some user requests would then need to wait for a worker thread to become available, total throughput would increase because less context switching would occur.

This setting is somewhat autoconfigured. The default is 255, which does not mean that 255 worker threads will be in the pool. Instead, it means that if a connection is waiting to be serviced and no thread is available, a new thread will be created if the thread total is currently below 255. If this setting is configured to 255 but the greatest number of simultaneously executing commands is, say, 125, the actual number of worker threads will not be higher than 125. It might be less than that, since SQL Server destroys and trims away worker threads that are no longer being used. I advise you to leave this setting alone if your system is handling 100 or fewer simultaneous connections. In that case, the worker thread pool is not going to be greater than 100 and will probably be less.

Even systems that handle 4000 or more connected users run fine with the default setting of 255. With more than 255 threads, the system might *thrash* (that is, excessive time will be spent context switching and scheduling in and out threads and not enough time will be spent doing useful work). Even when thousands of users are simultaneously connected, the actual worker thread pool is usually well below 255 since from the back-end database perspective most connections are idle, even though the user might be doing plenty of work in the front-end. This value could also be affected by the number of available processors, since only one thread on the system executes on a given processor at any one time. Unless you have more than two processors in your system, you'll probably want SQL Server to be using fewer than 100 threads.

You can watch the number of active threads in SQL Server by using the Thread Count counter in the Process object of Performance Monitor (instance SQLSERVR). A nearly idle SQL Server process has about 18 active threads. Thread counts higher than 18 predominantly reflect increases in the worker thread pool. If the thread count is 100 or fewer, I wouldn't bother changing from the default. If the count is 100 to 255, you might want to try some fine-tuning. The Performance Monitor counter Net Command Queue Length in the SQLServer object purports to monitor exactly this. But in version 6.5, the worker thread approach changed from a queue to the use of IOCompletion ports. Unfortunately, that counter did not also get updated—with version 6.5, the counter will always display 0 and is useless. Instead, I suggest monitoring based on watching the total thread count, total throughput, and response time to interactive users. Basically, you are experimenting to determine whether funneling the requests to a smaller number of worker threads will be worth it in terms of greater overall throughput. If you see a significant increase in total throughput and response times are still good, you might change the **max worker threads** value. But this is still much in the realm of fine-tuning, and you should make changes only when you have data indicating that it might be a win; and you should always measure to determine whether the change was beneficial. On high-end systems with loads of disks, you probably need more threads to drive the system. We have machines in our performance lab with 180 or more physical disk drives. Setting worker threads too low, to below 100, for example, probably wouldn't use the hardware to its potential.

hash buckets   As I discussed in Chapter 3, locating buffer pages in a large data cache could be a costly operation if you don't do it wisely. SQL Server hashes the pages for fast access (or to determine whether the page is not in cache). The **hash buckets** configuration option sets the number of buckets that will be used for hashing pages to data cache buffers in memory. Specifying more hash buckets allows SQL Server to find a referenced page faster, because it hashes close to the referenced page in the used page list and then traverses the chain until it finds the right page. The goal is to limit the size of the chain for any particular hash bucket. The more buckets, the shorter the chains. Even a large data cache can be searched quickly using only a modest number of hash buckets. Use DBCC BUFCOUNT to determine effectiveness of the current hashing configuration:

```
DBCC TRACEON(3604)
DBCC BUFCOUNT
GO


**** THE 10 LONGEST BUFFER CHAINS ****
    bucket number = 20   chain size = 2
    bucket number = 276   chain size = 2
    bucket number = 532   chain size = 2
    bucket number = 1044   chain size = 2
    bucket number = 1300   chain size = 2
    bucket number = 1556   chain size = 2
    bucket number = 1812   chain size = 2
    bucket number = 2324   chain size = 2
    bucket number = 3092   chain size = 2
    bucket number = 3604   chain size = 2
    The Smallest Chain Size is: 0
    The Average Chain Size is: 0.671668
```

If all the chain sizes equal 4 or less, the configuration is fine. If you have longer chains, try increasing the configuration value. DBCC SQLPERF(HASHSTATS) was added in version 6.5 to make setting hash buckets even easier. It shows the average and maximum synonym chain length for the data-page hash chains as well as for all other types of hash chains, including those that are not configurable, such as lock and DES (descriptor structure for objects like tables) hash chains. Again, if the chains on the data cache are longer than 4, increase the setting.

The number of hash buckets is adjusted by SQL Server to a prime number closest to the entered value. So unless you enter a prime number, the value used won't be exactly the number you entered. (Use of prime numbers in hashing is a standard hashing technique.) The default value is 7993 hash buckets, and the maximum value is 265,003 hash buckets.

set working set size   If you enable this option by setting it to 1, SQL Server calls the Win32 API **SetProcessWorkingSetSize( )** to fix its working set to a size equal to the amount of configured memory, plus the size of *tempdb* if it's configured to be in RAM. This setting defaults to 0, which allows the Windows NT server virtual memory manager to determine the working set size of SQL Server. Setting it to 1 instructs Windows NT not to page any memory from SQL Server. If the Windows NT virtual memory manager must page, it must do so from other processes.

If SQL Server is the most important application in your system, it is a good idea to set this option; but make sure you have an appropriately sized Windows NT paging file. Otherwise, you might get "out of virtual memory" errors, especially if you've configured SQL Server for too much memory. In general, you should make sure that you're doing little paging on the system in the first place. If SQL Server is Number 1 on your system and you have properly configured memory, I advise you to enable this option (set to 1). Then the virtual memory manager of Windows NT will know to leave SQL Server alone and will not try to trim its working set. If you run SQL Server from the command line, rather than as a service, this setting can be pretty important. Beginning with version 4.0, Windows NT aggressively trims the working set of a process that has been minimized from the command window. This feature was added to speed interactive desktop processing. But if you run SQL Server from the command line and then minimize it, its working set will probably be trimmed more than you'd like.

max async IO This option controls how many outstanding I/O operations SQL Server can have at a time. This number is specific to the speed of the I/O system of the hardware. The default setting of 8 is a reasonable choice for most systems, but it is too low to be optimal for systems with good I/O subsystems and high OLTP transaction rates. As usual, you shouldn't change the default capriciously, but this setting probably warrants changing for such systems.

This setting governs the checkpoint and recovery processes (remember that recovery also runs as part of LOAD), since it is only during these operations that multiple outstanding I/Os come into play. (Actually, they affect the Lazywriter too, but it has its own separate configuration setting.) During checkpoint, large numbers of pages might need to be flushed. Recall that asynchronous I/O is never used for writing to the log, since write-ahead logging demands synchronous I/O to ensure recoverability. And a single page write, when a page must be flushed to make room for another, would not typically benefit (since 8 should be plenty for this). If you have a fast RAID system and your checkpoint process flushes many pages (that is, you have a high OLTP-type application), you can try changing this value and then measure the difference by monitoring the throughput of your application or benchmark test. (The SQL Server Benchmark Kit, available on the accompanying CD-ROM, is a good proxy test for this setting, since this setting is more a function of what your hardware can handle rather than specific to your application.) You can see your system's effectiveness with asynchronous I/O during the checkpoint process by watching the I/O Batch Writes/sec counter of the SQLServer object.

On systems with a fast I/O subsystem—multiple disks in a fast RAID environment—the setting of 8 might be too low to fully drive the hardware's capability. A value of 25 to 40 is probably more appropriate, but you should change the setting only if you will empirically measure the result. If you set it too high, you might flood the system and hurt, not help, throughput. When set too high, the large numbers of outstanding write I/Os issued by a checkpoint can result in other read activity being starved, so other activity might be significantly affected during the checkpoint. Correctly setting this value results in throttling the checkpoint process such that you should see less than a 10 percent reduction in throughput even on a heavily loaded OLTP system while the checkpoint process is active.

max lazywrite IO   This setting is similar to **max async IO**, but it relates to the Lazywriter process rather than to the checkpoint process. I recommend that you either leave this setting alone or use the same setting you determined was best for **max async IO**. As of version 6.5, this setting is less important. Improvements to the Lazywriter process make it less important that it's throttled in the same way that you use **max async IO** to throttle the checkpoint.

network packet size   This option sets the serverwide value for the default size of the send-and-receive buffers in SQL Server's network handling. (See Chapter 3 to review how network buffering works.) The client application can override this value. The default is 4096, and I'd leave it alone unless you have a good reason to change it. If you have requests that return little data, you might try reducing it to as low as 512. Or if you return large result sets, do a lot of large text or image processing, or do bulk load operations, you might try increasing the setting to 8192. I don't think you should go higher than 8192, though.

priority boost   If this setting is enabled, SQL Server runs at a higher Windows NT scheduling priority. The default is 0, which means that SQL Server runs at normal priority on a single-processor machine and at a somewhat higher priority on an SMP machine. (To be specific, it runs at priority base 7, NORMAL, if the machine is a single processor. It runs at priority base 15, the high range of "normal," on an SMP machine. Windows NT priority values range from 1, IDLE, to 31, REALTIME TIME_CRITICAL.)

Even if you don't enable this option, SQL Server runs at a slightly boosted priority on SMP hardware to avoid some priority inversion issues. Windows NT by default temporarily boosts the priority of a thread that uses IOCompletion ports, which SQL Server does. (For details, refer to Chapter 3.) With none of the other threads in SQL Server also running at a higher standard priority, the boost in only some of SQL Server's threads causes some priority inversion problems on multiprocessor hardware. The solution is to boost priority a bit when running on an SMP machine. SQL Server automatically detects the number of processors on the hardware at startup and sets its priority accordingly.

I don't see cases for which setting this option makes much difference anymore, so my recommendation is to leave it alone. Back in the days of version 4.2, the settings could make a pretty big difference, but I don't believe that's the case anymore. For example, we no longer set this configuration value when we publish TPC-C benchmarks. Still, some sites claim it makes a difference. But I'm skeptical, and I think those sites are probably basing these statements on behavior back in the days of version 4.2. But if your machine is totally dedicated to running SQL Server, you might want to try enabling this option (setting it to 1) to see for yourself. If you enable this setting, it runs SQL Server at high priority, specifically priority base 15 on a uniprocessor machine and base 24 on an SMP machine. Contrary to some folklore, setting this does not make SQL Server run at the highest Windows NT priority, base 31, REALTIME TIME_CRITICAL.

SMP concurrency   This setting controls the number of threads that SQL Server will allow to simultaneously access data. When operating under its default setting of 0, $n - 1$ threads (where n is the number of processors on the system) are allowed simultaneous access to the dataserver semaphore. This semaphore acts as a throttle to allow only the given number of threads to do low-level data access operations. As with worker threads, by limiting the number of threads, throughput is generally increased. The default uses $n - 1$, rather than just n, to keep one processor free to do important operating system and network functions. If you set an explicit number, that number of threads will be allowed. And setting this value to -1 skips calls related to the dataserver semaphore, which might prove helpful in some cases on SMP machines. If you have a heavily loaded SMP machine with four or more processors, you can change this option to see if performance improves. But measure changes carefully—throughput might go down if the system gets "flooded." For most sites, I'd use the default setting.

free buffers   Recall from Chapter 3 that SQL Server supports a system process called the Lazywriter that exists to maintain a ready supply of clean (free) buffer pages. This process will start flushing buffers automatically when the number of available free buffers falls below the threshold determined by the **free buffers** configuration option. SQL Server does a good job of tuning this parameter, and when you change the memory setting, it tries to make this setting about 5 percent of the available memory—in most cases, that's a good default. You can watch the number of free buffers by using Performance Monitor's Number Of Free Buffers counter under the SQLServer object. If the number goes down to, say, 1 percent of the size of the data cache, you might set **free buffers** higher to try to keep the number of free buffers at least in the 3 to 5 percent range. If you need to change this value, try to set it to as small a value as possible while allowing short, sudden demands for free pages to be covered (without having to do a single page write to free up a page). If the Lazywriter is unable to maintain the supply of free buffers, specifying a larger free buffer pool only postpones the problem.

LogLRU buffers   The **LogLRU buffers** advanced configuration option specifies the number of transaction log buffers to keep in cache, like a private "named cache" for the log. Usually, SQL Server writes to the log but doesn't read from it. Prior to version 6.5, by default, all of the log's pages go through the same Buffer Manager used by regular data pages. But if you always write to but never read from the log, it is wasteful to put log pages on the LRU buffer chain (because you know you won't need them again). Since version 6.5, however, the **LogLRU**

setting allows you to reserve a small portion of cache for the log, and by doing so, you can generally keep log pages from polluting the regular cache. The parameter's default value is 0, which preserves the pre-6.5 behavior of using the same buffer pool for log pages.

You will typically want *some* cache space for the log, because it is not *always* true that the log is only written to and not read from. Deferred updates, triggers (to construct the *inserted* and *deleted* pseudotables), rollback, and replication all need to read the recently created parts of the log. Performance will be better if those log pages are kept in cache rather than read from disk. In addition, the reduction in physical I/O to read the log avoids having to wait for the disk arm to move back—it remains in place to do the next sequential write, which is the main I/O done with the log. That is also why log I/O is *not* random, so I/O rates to a disk dedicated to a log can usually be much higher than the 80 to 90 I/Os per second I use as a rule of thumb for random I/O. By using the cache for log page storage, you basically eliminate the seek time from the I/O and only the data transfer time of the I/O comes into play. (Usually, the seek time is more than the transfer time for an I/O size of 2 KB, which is what SQL Server uses.)

If you don't change the default setting, the log pages almost surely will be in cache. But this might be much more of the log in the cache than you need; in this case, the log pages are robbing the cache of memory that could be more productively used elsewhere. If you do set this value, but you set it too low, you might significantly reduce performance (from having to do physical I/O for log read operations). If you change this value, set it high enough to minimize physical log I/O but not so high that it reduces the number of buffers available to cache normal data pages to the point that the cache-hit ratio is reduced. (As should be clear by now, everything in performance tuning is a trade-off.)

You might start with a setting equal to that used for **free buffers**. Then monitor **LogLRU buffers** effectiveness via DBCC SQLPERF(LRUSTATS2). (LRUSTATS2 was added in Service Pack 2 of version 6.5.) To tune the setting further, keep reducing it (it is dynamic) until DBCC SQLPERF(LRUSTATS2) shows log page reads, and then increase the value until the log page reads go away. LRUSTATS2 reports only physical log reads per second, so this is quite easy to watch. LRU-STATS2 also reports both LogLRU buffers and total log buffers in both caches. The LogLRU cache is for recently created log buffers only. If they are written to disk and later read back in to service a deferred operation, replication, or so on, they will go into the regular cache.

> **NOTE** You must have installed Service Pack 2 or later of SQL Server 6.5 for DBCC SQLPERF(LRUSTATS2) to work.

recovery interval The checkpoint process is a system process that is always running (primarily in a sleep state) on SQL Server. To see the checkpoint process, use the **sp_who** system stored procedure. Once each minute, the checkpoint process wakes up and inspects the transaction log of each database. If the checkpoint system process determines that enough work has occurred since the last checkpoint, SQL Server will issue another checkpoint for that database. (Recall from Chapter 3 that a checkpoint flushes all dirty pages to disk.)

Whether enough work has been done to warrant a checkpoint is determined by the **recovery interval** configuration option. If you want checkpoints to be done less frequently, you can set this value higher. For example, if you are concerned with the relatively small slowdown that occurs during the checkpoint process, you might want to configure for less frequent checkpoints (but they will then tend to be of longer duration when they do occur). Doing less frequent checkpoints will make SQL Server take longer to recover databases at startup when orderly shutdowns were not performed, since there will be more work to undo or redo. In most cases, I think the default setting is just fine.

logwrite sleep SQL Server has a "group commit" performance optimization. When a transaction is ready to commit, SQL Server can wait to see if another transaction also comes in with a commit. If so, both (or potentially even more than two) transactions can get committed with the same I/O to the log. (If the buffer is already full, the transaction does not wait and gets written immediately.) The commit acknowledgement is not given to the waiting transaction *until and unless* the write actually occurs, so there is no danger of not being able to recover because of this delay.

The very slight delay in committing the first transaction can result in much better throughput overall. As an example, imagine that you're a taxi driver transporting three people from point A to point B. Instead of taking the first person as soon as he shows up, you wait a moment. If the other two people arrive soon, you take all three with just one trip and the overall trip time is significantly reduced. If no one shows up within a brief span of time, you take the first person alone. If the taxi is full, you leave immediately and don't wait any longer. This is pretty much what happens with the group commit optimization.

The **logwrite sleep** setting specifies how long the transaction will wait, if the buffer is not already full, to see if another commit arrives. It specifies the delay in milliseconds that can range from −1 through 500. With any value other than −1, a Win32 call to *WaitForSingleObject* is made with the configured value of milliseconds. The default is 0, which causes the server to wait only if other transactions are ready to execute. The special value of −1 means that the log write will not be delayed and every commit will be written immediately. I don't think changing this from the default would benefit most sites.

A **logwrite sleep** of 0 calls *WaitForSingleObject* with a timeout of 0, which would seem like it would be the same as −1 (not calling *WaitForSingleObject* at all). But calling it with 0 yields execution and seems to result in better log packing. The default of 0 seems best for almost all cases, but the value −1 could be better in extremely high transaction rates. I've never seen a number greater than 0 result in performance improvement, although theoretically it could. If you want to experiment with values greater than 0, use the Performance Monitor counter I/O Trans. Per Log Record under the SQLServer object, which indicates whether this parameter change resulted in more transactions being picked up in one record by virtue of the sleep. Also measure your application's total throughput, and watch Performance Monitor by using the I/O Log Writes/Sec and I/O Transactions/Sec counters under the SQLServer object. If your total throughput is increased, log writes are reduced, and transactions per second are increased, it's a win. Again, this setting is much in the realm of fine-tuning to the nth degree. You shouldn't worry about this setting unless you've spent a lot of time tuning your system and are down to the last few tweaks.

tempdb in RAM   The **tempdb in RAM** configuration option allows *tempdb* to be made entirely memory resident—that is, *tempdb* will exist entirely in RAM and not on disk. (This is safe for *tempdb* since it is entirely re-created, not recovered, every time SQL Server is restarted.) Usually, enabling this option is undesirable. In most cases, that memory would be better used by SQL Server's cache. After all, if pages from the *tempdb* database are frequently used, they'll remain in cache automatically. By enabling this option, the memory used for *tempdb* is then not available for SQL Server's cache, and more times than not, performance actually decreases.

We included this option when we first moved SQL Server to Windows NT from OS/2. On OS/2 1.*x*, we were limited to just 16 MB of memory for the SQL Server process. (All processes were so limited.) Quite a few sites wanted to productively use more memory and took to using "RAM disks" (a vestige from the old MS-DOS days of 640-KB memory limits) for *tempdb*. When they moved to Windows NT, users at these sites were dismayed that Windows NT did not support RAM disks, which they had become accustomed to using. So we added this option to eliminate this barrier, although even then the sites demanding it probably would have been better off using the memory for a bigger data cache. Having said all of this, I *have* seen a few cases for which **tempdb in RAM** really did help. In these cases, data access was random and cache hits were poor, so using the memory for *tempdb* was more productive than using it for the data cache. So I don't rule out enabling this option—in a small number of cases, it can help. But I think enabling it is counterproductive in most cases.

Read Ahead settings   Recall that Read Ahead (RA) is a performance optimization whereby SQL Server detects that it is scanning and starts prefetching pages into the data cache. When (and if) the pages are subsequently needed, they are ready in the cache and the scan doesn't have to wait for a physical I/O to get them. If a page is prefetched and never needed, however, the read-ahead operation was wasted activity. I'll explain the several configurations related to RA here, but in general, I don't think most sites should change the default settings. The possible exception is the **RA worker threads** parameter: sites with SMP hardware might want to increase this parameter. Read Ahead is pretty sophisticated in terms of self-tuning when it should start and stop its activity. I'll describe the RA options below.

RA worker threads: This option specifies how many threads can be allocated to read-ahead operations. Each thread will manage a configurable number of structures (see the **RA slots per thread** option), where each of these structures (slots) represents an individual range scan. If the number of threads requesting RA scans exceeds the number of configured RA slots, a warning will be logged in the error log. Setting this value to 0 will disable read ahead, which is probably not something you want to do. If you have a fast I/O subsystem and an SMP machine, you might want to try configuring this value higher than the default of 3. That value is OK for a single-processor system, but it might be low for an SMP machine. You might try a value of three to five times the number of processors—that is, use 3–5 for a single-processor system, 6–10 for a dual processor, 12–20 for a quad processor, and so on. If your cache-hit ratio improves, increasing this value was a win.

RA cache miss limit: If SQL Server is scanning but it's finding the pages in cache already, even without starting an RA operation to prefetch, there is no reason to use read ahead. This setting configures how many pages must *not* be found in cache before read ahead will be initiated. The default is 3, and unless you have done a lot of empirical testing, you shouldn't tinker with it. If you change this setting, you'll almost surely want to increase it, not decrease it. If you set the **RA cache miss limit** to 1, it would cause an RA request to be made whenever a single data page was accessed from disk. That is overly aggressive and would likely result in wasted RA operations and hence a reduction, not an increase, in performance. But if you set this value too high, you might be waiting longer than is optimal to start the read ahead.

RA pre-fetches: This value determines how far ahead the RA Manager will read (on an extent basis) before the prefetch manager returns to idle. The default value of 3, an appropriate value, means that for each request posted, the RA Manager keeps three extents ahead of the current scan position, following the page chain.

RA cache hit limit: Read ahead will stop after this number of pages are found in the cache and will restart on the first miss after that. This value is used to keep read ahead from getting well beyond the range of pages that will need to be scanned and prefetching pages that will not be needed. The default value is 4, which is an appropriate value.

RA slots per thread: This value specifies the number of simultaneous requests that each RA service thread will manage. The number of threads multiplied by the number of slots equals the total number of concurrent RA scans that the system will support. The default value, 5, should be sufficient for most systems. If your system has an efficient I/O subsystem, you might be able to increase the number of scans that a single thread can handle. If you change this value, which most sites have no need to do, you'd probably increase it, not decrease it, and I doubt you'd want to go higher than about 10.

RA delay: When the querying thread calls for a read ahead, a slight delay might occur between that time and the time the operating system wakes up the RA thread. This option sets the amount of time the querying thread will sleep before resuming work, to ensure that the RA thread will have started. Setting this value to 0 will essentially disable read ahead because the querying thread will always be grabbing the next page before read ahead wakes up.

If you change any of the read-ahead parameters, be sure that you monitor the effectiveness of the change. A key measure is that of cache-hit ratio—if read ahead is effective, the pages are prefetched into the cache before they are needed and the cache-hit ratio improves. In addition, you can watch the performance of read ahead using the SQLServer object in Performance Monitor. It calls DBCC SQL-PERF(RASTATS), which returns four statistics. Sample output is shown below:

```
Statistic                    Value
-----------------------      -------
RA Pages Found in Cache      297.0
RA Pages Placed in Cache     12933.0
RA Physical IO               1644.0
Used Slots                   0.0
```

The following table gives the meaning of each of the four values returned:

Statistic	Definition
RA Pages Found in Cache	The number of pages the RA Manager found in the cache while trying to perform scans
RA Pages Placed in Cache	The number of pages brought into the cache by the RA Manager
RA Physical IO	The number of 16-KB reads done by the RA Manager
Used Slots	The number of RA slots being used by active queries; a single query can use multiple RA slots

affinity mask   The **affinity mask** setting can be used to bind threads to certain processors; by and large, this is something you probably don't want to do. By using this setting, you are restricting Windows NT from scheduling the thread to whatever processor is currently most available. You limit the automatic load balancing that happens when Windows NT is allowed to schedule a thread on any processor, and the threads tend to migrate from processor to processor.

This option was added in version 6.5 at the request of some major customers running SMP hardware with more than four processors. These sites were accustomed to options similar to this on UNIX or mainframe systems and insisted that they needed the option. Presumably, it is useful for them, but I don't see most sites needing this option. If you're interested in learning more, you can check out the description of the setting in the SQL Server documentation included on the CD-ROM. This setting is in the class of tweaking that simply won't pay dividends for most sites. In fact, most sites' performance would degrade, not improve, by your tinkering with this setting.

spin counter and time slice settings   I don't recommend that you change either of these settings from their defaults. The **spin counter** setting determines how long the internal SQL Server spinlock will spin before checking whether a resource is available. The **time slice** setting affects some internal points at which a given worker thread might voluntarily yield. These are exposed via **sp_configure** only because the developers working on the SQL Server engine didn't want to hard-code values to allow good values to be empirically determined. The default values are appropriate, and unless you've really spent considerable time empirically testing other values, you should not change them. The time spent tinkering with these values could be better applied in other areas of tuning your application.

Database Options

A couple of database-specific settings, **read only** and **single user**, affect performance because they eliminate locking in some cases. If your database is used only for decision support (for example, a data mart), it might make good sense to set your database to **read only**:

```
EXEC sp_dboption 'dbname', 'read only', TRUE
```

Once done, no locking is performed in the database; this greatly reduces overhead. This option is safe, since by definition no changes can be made in the database while this option is enabled. You can easily toggle off the **read only** option to perform tasks such as bulk loading of data. For an operation in which the data is changed via large batch jobs that can run in off-hours and the normal workload is query only, using **read only** is a good route to go.

Even if your database is not read only, you might want to perform off-hour maintenance tasks and bulk loading operations with the **single user** option enabled:

```
EXEC sp_dboption 'dbname', 'single user', TRUE
```

Operating in **single user** mode also eliminates the need for locking, since only one connection can use the database at a time. Locking, of course, is needed to make a multiple-user system behave like a single-user system. But, in this case, it *is* a single-user system, so locking is not required. If you need to do a big bulk load and index creation at night and no one else will use the system while that's going on, you can eliminate the need to take locks during the bulk load.

Insert Row-Level Locking

Chapter 13 discussed insert row-level locking (IRL). Under IRL, an additional lock hierarchy exists to allow multiple connections to perform insert activity on the same page, improving concurrency. We introduced this capability in version 6.5, and by default, the setting is off because of backward-compatibility concerns with applications developed before it existed and therefore is susceptible to some subtle behavior differences. However, if you are developing a new application and you expect multiple-user insert activity to the same table, I recommend enabling IRL. If you have an existing application that's experiencing contention for the last page on inserts, you can test your application with this option enabled. It's simple to enable (and equally simple to disable if necessary):

```
EXEC sp_tableoption 'authors', 'insert row lock', TRUE
```

Buffer Manager Options

In Chapter 3, I discussed in depth how the Buffer Manager (also known as the Cache Manager) uses a queue of "favored pages," which you can loosely think of as a least-recently-used (LRU) algorithm. You can use either of two options to directly influence the behavior of favoring pages: favoring index pages in cache or pinning a table in the data cache.

Favoring index pages in cache

If you enable trace flag 1081, index pages (root, intermediate, and leaf pages for nonclustered indexes) get one free trip through the queue of pages maintained by the Buffer Manager. (Set trace flag 1081 with **−t**, not **−T**.) That is, when the pages are accessed, they're marked as "favored," so they will get at least two trips in the queue. (A nonfavored page gets one trip unless it's accessed again.) If the page is accessed again, it is again favored and gets at least two more trips, and so on.

Deciding whether to enable this trace flag depends on your specific usage profile. If data access is random and cache-hit ratios for data pages are not very high, and if pages are located mostly via indexes, it might make sense to enable this trace flag. This flag keeps the index pages around longer by locating them closer to the top of the pyramid, and you might achieve a better cache-hit ratio. But the outcome is hard to predict, and if you think this option might improve performance, my best advice is to test both: monitor your cache-hit ratio with the trace flag enabled and also with it disabled. I think this option is seldom used (and not well known), but my hunch is that many sites could benefit from using it. In fact, I think that perhaps it *should* be the default behavior for the Buffer Manager.

Pinning a table in the data cache

You can permanently remove a table from the queue of pages such that once they are read into the data cache, they will never be forced from cache. (This favors them permanently, although it is really more than that: they are entirely exempted.) This option can be enabled either via DBCC PINTABLE or via the **sp_table-option pintable** stored procedure. This option is generally not appropriate for most sites. But if you get very random cache hits and you know that you have some relatively small tables that are relatively hot in comparison to other larger tables, this option might have some potential. If those small, hot tables keep getting forced out by the random access to larger tables and you have plenty of memory, you might want to pin those small, hot tables. By pinning, you are overriding the Buffer Manager. But keep in mind that when you pin a table, you take away the pages in cache used for that table, so you give the Buffer Manager less memory to work with. Pinning the table does not initially read it in; it just makes the table "sticky" so that once a page of the table is in the cache, it doesn't get forced out. If you want the table preloaded and sticky, you can enable the option and then do *SELECT * FROM table* to read all the pages into cache. If you use this option, be careful that you don't eat up your entire data cache if the table to be pinned is as big (or bigger) than the cache.

DBCC and Buffer Manager performance

Two good DBCC commands exist to watch the performance of the Buffer Manager: SQLPERF(WAITSTATS) and SQLPERF(LRUSTATS2). DBCC SQLPERF(WAITSTATS) gives you an overview of more than the Buffer Manager (although that's a key part of it): it helps you identify where a transaction is being delayed. It shows the total milliseconds of wait time and how much came from waiting for reads, waiting for different types of locks, waiting to add a log record to the buffer, or waiting for log buffers to be physically written. DBCC SQLPERF(LRUSTATS2) gives detailed information on the Lazywriter and the state of the cache, such as lazy-writes/sec, clean steals/sec, allocation page reads/sec, log page reads/sec, buffers examined/sec, and target and current free buffers and log buffers.

Startup Parameters on SQLSERVR.EXE

You can alter startup parameters to tune performance by disabling the performance statistics collection or specifying trace flags.

Disabling the performance collection

Normally, SQL Server keeps performance statistics such as CPU and I/O on a per-user basis. The values then get materialized in the *sysprocesses* table (really just memory) when queried. If you never query or monitor these values, the work to keep track of them is unnecessary. You can eliminate the calls that produce these performance statistics by passing the **–x** startup flag to SQLSERVR.EXE. Or you can add **–x** as an additional parameter from the Setup program via the Set Server Options dialog box.

Specifying trace flags

I have mentioned the use of trace flags several times, and I've shown examples that enable them using DBCC TRACEON. You can also specify a trace flag at server startup; some trace flags (like 1081) make the most sense if specified serverwide rather than on a per-user basis. To enable a trace flag serverwide, add the flag as a parameter when you start SQL Server from the command line (for example, *sqlservr.exe –c –t1081*). If you start SQL Server as a service (as most people do), you can use SQL Server's Setup program to enable the flag. From the Set Server Options dialog box in the Setup program, click the Parameters button and add a parameter of **–t1081**. Make sure you specify the hyphen, and click the Add button to move the parameter into the list of parameters. If you enable multiple trace flags, add each one as a separate parameter.

To support tracing on a per-user basis, a flag in the PSS (the Process Status Structure maintained for each user) must also be set to enable any of the trace flags that are tested with the original (non-user-specific) *TRACE* macro. Each place in the code that tests for these trace flags first determines whether the PSS flag is set before testing the trace-flag array. Many trace flags (such as 1081) don't make sense on a per-user basis. If you specify the lowercase *t,* SQL Server skips the per-user test to determine whether the trace flag is enabled. Using an uppercase *T* sets the PSS flag and requires per-user checking. A lowercase *t* flag will not be enabled unless at least one uppercase *T* is also set or until some connection executes a DBCC TRACEON with –1 (meaning it is set for all connections).

Maintain the System

SQL Server requires much less regular system maintenance than most comparable products. For example, because pages are automatically split, clustering characteristics of data is maintained. Most products that support data clustering make you do data reorganization to keep the data clustered. However, from a performance perspective, you should perform a couple of regular maintenance tasks.

You can easily schedule these maintenance tasks (such as updating statistics and rebuilding your clustered index) using SQL Executive or by using the Database Maintenance Wizard. In the earlier discussion of tuning queries, I explained the importance of index distribution statistics. You should update statistics frequently so that any significant changes in the volumes or distribution of data are reflected. Although it is not essential to dump and reload tables to keep clustering properties intact, it can be useful to rebuild tables to reestablish fill factors and avoid page splits. The simple way to do this is to rebuild the clustered index on the table, which also rebuilds the nonclustered indexes. Use the DBCC DBREINDEX command with the SORTED_DATA_REORG option, which also helps keep a table from becoming fragmented and makes read ahead more effective. You can use DBCC SHOWCONTIG to determine how contiguous a table is. Of course, you should also regularly do other tasks, such as performing backups and periodically checking the structural integrity of the database (for example, by using DBCC CHECKDB), but these are not performance-related tasks.

Monitor System Performance

Throughout this book, I've described various statements that are useful for monitoring some aspect of SQL Server's performance. These include procedures like **sp_who**, **sp_lock2**; *SET SHOWPLAN ON*, DBCC PERFMON, and DBCC SQLPERF; and various trace flags, such as 1204 for analyzing deadlock issues. SQL Enterprise Manager provides a graphical display that is kind of a combination of **sp_who** and **sp_lock2**, and you should make use of it. And SQL Trace makes it easy to watch the commands being issued to SQL Server.

All these utilities are useful, but the most important tool of all is Windows NT Performance Monitor; it's a great tool. One feature that makes it great is its extensibility, which allowed us to export SQL Server performance statistics so that you can monitor your entire system with the same tool. That's crucial, since such important statistics as CPU use must be monitored for the entire system, not just for SQL Server. In fact, many of the most important counters to watch while performance tuning SQL Server don't even belong to the SQLServer object. Performance Monitor is ubiquitous—it comes with Windows NT. Traditionally, in mainframe and minicomputer systems, you had to buy a separate system monitor—at considerable expense—or use a hodgepodge of utilities, some to monitor the operating system and others to monitor the database. Then, if you worked on some other system, it didn't have the same set of tools you were accustomed to using.

In the SQL Server program group, you click the icon labeled SQL Performance Monitor to start Performance Monitor with a saved .PMC file that instructs certain counters to be preloaded. So no actual SQL Performance Monitor exists; instead, you click on this shortcut to preload the .PMC file. You can also manually save your settings in a .PMC file and set up a shortcut in the same way.

Performance Monitor provides a huge set of counters—so many that it can seem daunting. I don't know of anybody who really understands all of them, so don't be intimidated. I urge you to peruse Performance Monitor and use the Explain button to gain a sense of its counters and capabilities.

> **NOTE** Volume 3 of the Windows NT Resource Kit, *Optimizing Windows NT*, by Russ Blake, is worthwhile reading that will help you to better understand Performance Monitor, and it has many good tips concerning general performance issues.

Performance Monitor Counters

In this section, I'll discuss several important counters that I find useful. I'll provide a brief explanation of how they can be useful and what actions you should consider based on the information they provide. Often, of course, the appropriate action is generic: for example, if CPU usage is high, you want to try to reduce it. The methods you can use to make such adjustments are varied and vast—from redesigning your application to reworking some queries, to adding indexes, to getting faster or additional processors.

Object: Processor
Counter: % Processor Time

This counter monitors CPU usage systemwide. If you use multiple processors, you can set up an instance for each processor. Each processor's CPU usage count should be similar. If not, you should examine other processes on the system that have only one thread and are executing on a given CPU. Ideally, you do not want your system to consistently run with CPU usage of 80 percent or more, although short spikes up to 100 percent are normal and expected, even for systems with plenty of spare CPU capacity. If your system is consistently above 80 percent usage or can be expected to grow to that level relatively soon, or if it frequently spikes above 90 percent and stays there for durations of 10 seconds or more, you should try to reduce CPU usage.

First, consider making your application more efficient. High CPU usage counts can often result from just one or two problematic queries. The queries might get high cache-hit ratios but still require large numbers of logical I/Os. Try to rework those queries or add indexes. If the CPU usage count continues to be high, you might consider getting a faster processor or adding processors to your system. If your system is running consistently with 100 percent CPU usage, look at specific processes to see which one or ones are consuming the CPU. It's likely that the offending process is doing some polling or is stuck in a tight loop; if so, the application needs some work, such as adding a sleep.

You also need to watch for excessively low CPU usage, which indicates that your system is stalled somewhere. If locking contention is occurring, your system might be running at close to 0 percent CPU usage and no productive work is happening! Very low CPU usage can be a bigger problem than very high CPU usage. If you have poor overall throughput but low CPU usage, your application has a bottleneck somewhere and you must find and clear it.

Note that the Task Manager (Ctrl-Alt-Delete) of Windows NT 4.0 also has a nice way to monitor CPU usage. For such CPU monitoring, the Task Manager is even easier to use than Performance Monitor.

Object: PhysicalDisk
Counter: Disk Transfers/sec

This counter shows physical I/O rates for all activity on the machine. You can set up an instance for each physical disk in the system or watch it for the total of all disks. SQL Server does most I/O in 2-KB chunks, although read-ahead I/O is essentially done with an I/O size of 16 KB. Watch this counter to be sure that you are not maxing out the I/O capacity of your system or of a particular disk. The I/O capacity of disk drives and controllers varies considerably depending on the hardware. But today's typical SCSI hard drive can do 80 to 90 random 2-KB I/Os per second, assuming the controller is able to drive it that hard. If you see I/O rates approaching these rates *per drive,* it is worthwhile to verify that your specific hardware can sustain more. If not, add more disks and controllers, add memory, or rework the database to try to get a higher cache-hit ratio and require less physical I/O (via better design, better indexes, possible denormalization, and so on).

Note that to see any of the counters from the PhysicalDisk object, you must reboot your computer with the Diskperf service started. Do this from the Devices applet in the Control Panel. Find Diskperf, and change its startup option to Boot; then reboot. When you're done monitoring, disable Diskperf.

Object: PhysicalDisk
Counter: Current Disk Queue Length

This counter indicates the number of I/Os that are currently outstanding for a disk. It is OK to experience occasional spikes, especially when such asynchronous I/O operations as checkpoint kick in. But for the most part, the disks should not have a lot of queued I/Os. Those I/Os, of course, must ultimately complete, so if consistently more than one I/O is queued, the disk is probably overworked. You need to either decrease physical I/O or add more I/O capacity.

Object: Memory
Counter: Pages/sec and Page Faults/sec

This counter watches the amount of paging on the system. As the system settles into a steady state, you want these values to be 0—that is, no paging going on in the system. If your system is experiencing regular paging, you must either reduce SQL Server's memory configuration or add more physical memory.

Object: Process
Counter: % Processor Time

Typically, you run this counter for the SQLServer process instance, but you might want to run the counter for other processes. The intention is to confirm that SQL Server (or some other process) is using a reasonable amount of CPU time. (It wouldn't make much sense to spend a lot of time reducing SQL Server's CPU usage if some other process on the machine is using the larger percentage of the CPU to drive the total CPU usage near capacity.)

Object: Process
Counter: Thread Count

This counter monitors the SQLServer instance to determine how many threads are currently active. Use this in conjunction with the **worker threads** configuration option as you try to achieve the best throughput in your application.

Object: Process
Counter: Virtual Bytes

Use this counter to see the total virtual memory being used by SQL Server. If your system is overcommitted on memory, you can use the counter to look at other processes' usages and take action in those processes, if necessary.

Object: Process
Counter: Working Set

The Working Set counter shows the amount of memory that has recently been used by a process. If this number is substantially below the amount of memory being configured for SQL Server, you might have SQL Server configured for more memory than it really needs. If that's not the case, fix the size of the working set using the **sp_configure set working set size** option so that Windows NT doesn't try to trim it.

Object: SQLServer
Counter: Cache Hit Ratio

There is no right value for the cache-hit ratio since it is application-specific. If your system has settled into a steady state, ideally you'd like to achieve rates of 90 percent or higher, but this is not always possible if the I/O is random. Keep adding (and configuring for) more physical memory as long as this value continues to rise or you run out of money. Test the use of trace flag 1081 to favor index pages in the cache.

Object: SQLServer-Procedure Cache
Counters: Procedure Cache Size
Procedure Cache Used %
Procedure Cache Active %

Refer to the discussion earlier in this chapter of configuring memory and procedure cache for an explanation of using these counters.

Object: SQLServer
Counter: Cache - Number of Free Buffers

This value should be close to the free buffers configuration value. If it drops below the free buffers value, try increasing the **sp_configure max lazywrite IO** option.

Object: SQLServer
Counter: I/O - Page Reads/sec

Watch this counter in combination with the counters from the PhysicalDisk object. If you are seeing rates approaching the capacity of your hardware's I/O rates (use 80 to 90 I/Os per disk per second as a guide), you need to try to reduce I/O rates by making your application more efficient (via better design, better indexes, possible denormalization, and so on). Or you can increase the hardware's I/O capacity. Remember that this statistic measures only read I/Os, not writes, and it does so only for SQL Server; you don't see the whole picture.

Object: SQLServer
Counter: I/O - Batch Writes/sec

Batch writes from SQL Server occur only during checkpoint, so you'll see a 0 count much of the time. During the checkpoint, you want to sustain as high an I/O rate as possible (perhaps hundreds per second) to get the checkpoint to complete as quickly as possible. If you have multiple disks and a fast controller, consider changing the **sp_configure max async IO** option to try to sustain higher rates and shorter durations for the checkpoint. You can also use the **recovery interval** parameter to affect the frequency of checkpointing.

Object: SQLServer
Counter: I/O - Single Page Writes/sec

This value monitors how often a single page was written. It does not include log writes, lazywrites, or data pages written out by checkpoint. Prior to version 6.5, a single page might have needed to be written if a free buffer were not found, but this is no longer true: the Lazywriter always writes out that page, so this value will never count pages that had to be written because a free buffer was not found. Some utility functions such as DUMP TRAN and CHECKPOINT need to do a few page writes of critical information (not the data pages themselves to be checkpointed) and cannot rely on write-ahead logging and the Lazywriter to be sure the data gets to disk. Prior to version 6.5, this was an important statistic to watch, but now it is far less important and you will usually see this count at 0.

Object: SQLServer
Counters: I/O - Outstanding Reads
I/O - Outstanding Writes

These counters are similar to Current Disk Queue Length under the Physical-Disk object. If multiple I/O requests are consistently outstanding, these counters indicate that the I/O system is being stretched to capacity. Occasional spikes are fine, but if you see outstanding I/Os, the system is probably stretched too thin. You need to reduce physical I/Os (add memory, add better indexes, change database design, or so on) and/or add I/O capacity to the hardware.

Object: SQLServer
Counter: I/O - Log Writes/sec

This value should be well below the capacity of the disk on which the transaction log resides. It is best to place the transaction log on a separate physical disk drive (or on a mirrored drive) so that the disk drive is always in place for the next write, since transaction log writes are sequential. If you have a separate drive (or mirror), log writes per second of less than 80 should be no problem. (Most drives could handle that figure pretty easily, especially given the nonrandom nature of log writes.) In a high OLTP usage, with log writes per second of perhaps 50 or more, you should consider increasing the **sp_configure logwrite sleep** parameter to achieve higher group commit activity. (Fifty can be handled OK, but you might be able to drive this value down and increase throughput.)

Object: SQLServer
Counter: I/O - Trans. per Log Record

This counter gives the number of transactions committed with one log write. Use this counter to see if changing **logwrite sleep** is worthwhile. If you are seeing high rates of log writes per second and values for transactions per log of only 1, consider increasing **logwrite sleep**. If log writes per second decreases and this counter increases, it's a worthwhile change.

Object: SQLServer
Counter: I/O - Transactions/sec

This counter actually measures batches per second, not transactions per second. (Otherwise, a query not in a transaction would not count.) Use this as a general indication as to your system's throughput. There is obviously no "correct" value— just the higher the better.

Other Considerations for Monitoring Performance

Anytime you monitor performance, you also slightly alter performance simply because of the overhead cost of monitoring. It can be helpful to run Performance Monitor on a separate machine from SQL Server to reduce the overhead related to the monitor. The SQL Server–specific counters are obtained by querying SQL Server, so they use connections to SQL Server. (Performance Monitor logs in as the *probe* or SA account, depending on the server's security mode.) It is best to monitor at any single time only the counters in which you are interested. Asking for everything but the kitchen sink adds to the overhead of performance monitoring, even though there is almost no limit to what you can monitor.

It is also possible to export your own counters to Performance Monitor, but the easiest way in most cases is to use the user-defined counters that SQL Server provides. If you want to monitor a particular value via Performance Monitor, you can write a stored procedure that will return a single integer value and replace one of the 10 available stubbed **sp_user_counter** procedures with yours. SQL Server provides 10 procedures, named **sp_user_counter1** through **sp_user-_counter10**. Make sure that you grant execute permission to the *probe* or SA account. Then you can simply monitor your value (although you must first understand what the returned values mean). Earlier, I listed a few DBCC commands, such as WAITSTATS, that can be useful, but these commands cannot currently export their values to Performance Monitor. You can write a simple procedure to invoke DBCC and get the value and then export it to Performance Monitor via one of these user-defined procedures.

SUMMARY

Configuration alone will rarely uncover a "magic bullet" that turns your slow, plodding application into a screamer. But performance improvements can be made, and more important, performance problems due to misconfiguration can be avoided. Some configuration options are important enough for everyone to take a look at, and others are less important but can still yield incremental gains if properly understood and fine-tuned. Still others should be avoided, as you're more likely to shoot yourself in the foot than help by adjusting them.

In this chapter, I described and categorized the configuration options available to you and I provided recommendations about each. As always, these are guidelines, and there is substantial variability possible based on your application, workload, and hardware.

As you fine-tune your configuration and as you make changes in your application and database design, it's important to carefully monitor the effects on your system's performance. Your main tool for doing this is the Windows NT Performance Monitor, to which SQL Server exports statistics. Using Performance Monitor lets you effectively approach performance using a scientific method of holding constant all but one variable; then you can measure the effect as you vary it. This chapter provided a highlight of what I consider the most important statistics to watch, and it included guidelines for desired values and some course of action to consider to achieve those values.

PART

FIVE

Appendix

Appendix

SQL Server Built-In Global Variables

The following information, referred to in Chapter 9, has been extracted from the SQL Server documentation. Global variables that maintain values specific to the connection are marked with an asterisk. Some of these global variables are used often, and others are rarely or infrequently used. I have marked in bold those variables that are used frequently.[1]

Global Variable	Description
@@CONNECTIONS	Specifies the number of logins or attempted logins since SQL Server was last started.
@@CPU_BUSY	Specifies the amount of time, in ticks (3.33 milliseconds), that the CPU has spent doing SQL Server work since the last time SQL Server was started.
@@CURSOR_ROWS*	Specifies the number of qualifying rows in the last-opened cursor. Returns -m if the cursor is being populated asynchronously (the value returned refers to the number of rows currently in the keyset); n if the cursor is fully populated (the value returned refers to the number of rows); and 0 if no cursors have been opened or the last-opened cursor has been closed or deallocated.
@@DATEFIRST*	Returns the current value of the SET DATEFIRST parameter. Indicates the first day of each week: 1 for Monday through 7 for Sunday.

---

1. This table has been adapted with permission from *Microsoft SQL Server Transact-SQL Reference*, which is available as part of the version 6.5 product documentation and on the CD with this book. Other excerpts from the documentation are also used with permission.

Global Variable	Description
@@DBTS	Specifies the value of the current *timestamp* datatype for the database. This *timestamp* is guaranteed to be unique for the database.
@@ERROR*	Specifies the last error number generated by the system for the user connection. This global variable is commonly used to check the error status of the most recently executed statement. Its value is 0 if the last statement succeeded.
@@FETCH_STATUS*	Contains the status of a cursor FETCH command. It is set to 0 if the fetch is successful, to -1 if the fetch failed or the row was beyond the result set, and to -2 if the row fetched is missing.
@@IDENTITY*	Saves the last-inserted @@IDENTITY value. This variable is updated specifically for each user when an INSERT or SELECT INTO statement or a bulk copy insert in a table occurs. If a statement changes the table without an identity column, @@IDENTITY is set to NULL. The @@IDENTITY value does not revert to a previous setting if the INSERT or SELECT INTO statement or a bulk copy fails or if the transaction is rolled back.
@@IDLE	Specifies the amount of time, in ticks, that SQL Server has been idle since it was last started.
@@IO_BUSY	Specifies the amount of time, in ticks, that SQL Server has spent doing input and output operations since it was last started.
@@LANGID*	Specifies the local language ID of the language currently in use (specified in *syslanguages.langid*).
@@LANGUAGE*	Specifies the language currently in use (specified in *syslanguages.name*).
@@MAX_CONNECTIONS	Specifies the maximum number of simultaneous connections that can be made with SQL Server in the current computer environment. The user can configure SQL Server for fewer connections by using the **sp_configure** system stored procedure.
@@MAX_PRECISION	Returns the level of precision used by *decimal* and *numeric* datatypes as currently set in the server. By default, the maximum precision is 28; however, a larger precision can be set when SQL Server starts by using the **/p** parameter with **sqlservr**.
@@MICROSOFTVERSION	A version used internally to track the current version of the server. If version checking is necessary, use @@VERSION or programmatically execute **xp_msver 'ProductVersion'**.

Global Variable	Description
@@NESTLEVEL*	Specifies the nesting level of the current execution (initially 0). Each time a stored procedure calls another stored procedure, the nesting level is incremented. If the maximum of 16 is exceeded, the transaction is terminated.
@@OPTIONS*	Provides information about the current values of SET options. The SET options can be modified as a whole by using the **sp_configure 'user options'** configuration option. Each user has an @@OPTIONS global variable that represents the user's environment. Values within @@OPTIONS are the same as the configuration values for **'user options'** in **sp_configure**.
@@PACK_RECEIVED	Specifies the number of input packets read by SQL Server since it was last started.
@@PACK_SENT	Specifies the number of output packets written by SQL Server since it was last started.
@@PACKET_ERRORS	Specifies the number of errors that have occurred while SQL Server was sending and receiving packets since the last time SQL Server was started.
@@PROCID*	Specifies the stored procedure ID of the currently executing procedure.
@@REMSERVER*	Returns the server name contained within a remote server's login record.
@@ROWCOUNT*	Specifies the number of rows affected by the last statement. This variable is set to 0 by any statement that does not return rows, such as an IF statement.
@@SERVERNAME	Specifies the name of the local SQL Server. You must define this name with the **sp_addserver** system stored procedure and then restart SQL Server. The Setup program sets this variable to the computer name during installation. Although you can change @@SERVERNAME by using **sp_addserver** and restarting SQL Server, this method is not usually required.
@@SERVICENAME	Specifies the name of a running service. Currently, @@SERVICENAME defaults to @@SERVERNAME.
@@spid*	Specifies the server process ID number of the current process (the *spid* column of the *sysprocesses* system table).
@@TEXTSIZE*	Specifies the current value of the TEXTSIZE option of the SET statement, which specifies the maximum length, in bytes, of *text* or *image* data that a SELECT statement returns. The default limit is 4 KB.

Global Variable	Description
@@TOTAL_ERRORS	Specifies the number of errors that have occurred while SQL Server was reading or writing since the last time SQL Server was started.
@@TOTAL_READ	Specifies the number of disk reads performed by SQL Server since it was last started (disk reads only, not cache reads).
@@TOTAL_WRITE	Specifies the number of disk writes performed by SQL Server since it was last started.
@@TRANCOUNT*	Specifies the number of currently active transactions for the current user.
@@VERSION	Specifies the date, version number, and processor type for the current version of SQL Server.

BIBLIOGRAPHY

American National Standard for Information Systems. *Database Language—SQL. ANSI.* American National Standards Institute, ANSI X3.135–1992, 1992.

Celko, Joe. *Joe Celko's SQL for Smarties: Advanced SQL Programming.* San Francisco: Morgan Kaufmann Publishers, 1995.

Date, C. J. *An Introduction to Database Systems,* 6th ed. Reading, MA: Addison-Wesley, 1995.

Date, C. J., with Hugh Darwen. *A Guide to the SQL Standard,* 3rd ed. Reading, MA: Addison-Wesley, 1993.

Gray, Jim, and Andreas Reuter. *Transaction Processing: Concepts and Techniques.* San Francisco: Morgan Kaufmann Publishers, 1993.

Massiglia, Paul. *The Raidbook: A Handbook of Storage Systems Technology,* 6th ed. San Jose, CA: Peer-to-Peer Communications, 1997.

Melton, Jim, and Alan R. Simon. *Understanding the New SQL: A Complete Guide.* San Francisco: Morgan Kaufmann Publishers, 1993.

Microsoft Developer Network (MSDN) Library (available via subscription from Microsoft).

Microsoft KnowledgeBase (available from http://www.microsoft.com).

Microsoft SQL Server version 6.5 documentation (*SQL Server Books Online,* available on the companion CD).

Pfister, Gregory F. *In Search of Clusters: The Coming Battle in Lowly Parallel Computing.* Englewood Cliffs, NJ: Prentice Hall, 1995.

"Performance Tuning and Optimization of Microsoft SQL Server 6.5," Microsoft Authorized Training Course #665.

SUGGESTED READING

Despite the considerable length of this book, it doesn't touch on all important areas, and it assumes that its readers have some knowledge of relational database management systems (RDBMS). I am often asked to recommend readings and resources, so I've included some in this section of the book. The most fundamental and important resource that I can recommend is to read, cover to cover, the SQL Server documentation. The companion CD contains the complete online documentation for SQL Server version 6.5 and also contains some worthwhile whitepapers. Start there. I recommend that you augment your reading with the following books and selections. I have listed the sources in order from introductory materials to detailed or specialized materials (rather than listing them alphabetically).

Using SQL   by James R. Groff and Paul N. Weinberg (Osborne McGraw-Hill, 1990). This book is an excellent primer (although a bit out of date) for those users new to SQL.

An Introduction to Database Systems   by C. J. Date (Addison-Wesley, 1995). A classic book, written by a giant in the field, that covers general relational database concepts. A must for anyone in the database industry.

Microsoft SQL Server Training   (Microsoft Press, 1996). Nice, self-paced training, including much about administration and security. Fairly introductory and suitable to those newer to SQL Server.

Handbook of Relational Database Design   by Candace C. Fleming and Barbara Von Halle (Addison-Wesley, 1989). A fine book discussing general logical database design and data modeling approaches and techniques.

DATABASE: Principles, Programming, Performance   by Patrick O'Neil (Morgan Kaufmann Publishers, 1994). This thorough textbook provides very good introductory materials, so I include it near the top of this list. It also covers a broad spectrum of information and contains great detail about many database topics, including explanations of issues such as buffer management and transaction semantics.

Understanding the New SQL: A Complete Guide   by Jim Melton and Alan R. Simon (Morgan Kaufmann Publishers, 1993). An excellent reference, and one that I consult frequently for issues regarding ANSI SQL-92 semantics and conformance issues. (Jim Melton is an active participant in the SQL standards work and was the editor of the ANSI SQL-92 standard.) Although you can get the ANSI SQL-92 specification directly from ANSI, this book translates the standard into understandable English.

A Guide to the SQL Standard   by C. J. Date with Hugh Darwen (Addison-Wesley, 1993). Similar in purpose and focus to the Melton and Simon book, this book's coverage is more compact, often provides additional insight into why something is the way it is, and provides more discussion of semantics. It is an especially good reference for issues about the use of NULL. I use this book hand in hand with the Melton and Simon book, and I find that the books' subtle differences in emphasis complement each other well.

Optimizing Transact-SQL—Advanced Programming Techniques   by David Rozen-shtein, Anatoly Abramovich, and Eugene Birger (SQL Forum Press, 1995). Lots of clever queries and solutions written with Transact-SQL. (Note, however, that the solutions here were authored before SQL Server had the CASE statement, and CASE sometimes would provide easier, more straightforward solutions.)

Joe Celko's SQL for Smarties: Advanced SQL Programming   by Joe Celko (Morgan Kaufmann Publishers, 1995). This is a very good book to consult for insight into subtle but powerful ways to write queries that are nonintuitive. In places, this one is truly the SQL book for the Mensa crowd—it has many mind-bending puzzles about how to write an SQL query to perform some nonobvious task. It has many examples—probably more than any other book on this list—and you can often find a solution to a problem very similar in scope to one you might face.

Inside ODBC   by Kyle Geiger (Microsoft Press, 1995). The finest book available on ODBC, period. Written by the "Father of ODBC." A must for C programmers working with ODBC and SQL Server. A fine discussion of cursors as well.

Client/Server Programming with Microsoft Visual Basic   by Kenneth L. Spencer and Ken Miller (Microsoft Press, 1996). A good book discussing programming aspects of Visual Basic, especially when accessing SQL Server.

Physical Database Design for Sybase SQL Server   by Rob Gillette, Dean Muench, and Jean Tabaka (Prentice Hall, 1995). Good pragmatic tips and techniques for deciding on actual database layout and making indexing decisions. Although the book was written about Sybase SQL Server, most of it is equally relevant to Microsoft SQL Server. If you're completely new to database design, use the Fleming and Von Halle book for the "logical" concepts and this one for the actual implementation.

Microsoft KnowledgeBase (various articles).   Available from http://www.micro-soft.com. Loads of good information, tips, and answers to common questions.

Frequently updated and of high quality. A must for any serious developer using any Microsoft development product, not just SQL Server.

Microsoft Developer Network (MSDN) Library   Various articles and resources are available from Microsoft. Like the Microsoft KnowledgeBase, MSDN contains information about all of Microsoft development products. A must for serious developers.

Optimizing Windows NT   by Russ Blake, Vol. 3 of *Microsoft Windows NT Resource Kit* (Microsoft Press, 1993). Great source of information for effectively using Performance Monitor, and a good discussion of general performance issues (not specific to SQL Server).

Configuration and Tuning of Microsoft SQL Server 6.5 for Windows NT on Compaq Servers   Compaq Computer Corporation Whitepaper, 3d ed., Document 415A-0696, June 1996. Available for download from http://www.compaq.com. Overall, high quality whitepaper discussing configuration and tuning options. It is obviously geared toward Compaq hardware, although the discussion is of general interest to all. (Note that in a few areas, the recommended configuration options are somewhat in conflict with the recommendations I've made in Chapter 15. The whitepaper recommends more tweaking with configuration than I do.)

Performance Tuning and Optimization of Microsoft SQL Server 6.5.   Microsoft Authorized Training Course #665. I'd recommend this fine course to people interested in becoming the SQL Server performance experts of their teams. Available from authorized training centers.

Transaction Processing: Concepts and Techniques   by Jim Gray and Andreas Reuter (Morgan Kaufman Publishers, 1993). Without a doubt, the best book ever written for in-depth explanation of such issues as locking, logging and recovery, and transactional semantics. Unusual (and terrific!) in that it is packed with detailed information yet still readable and understandable. Unlike many of the overly academic papers that seem more suitable for graduate school classes than for people trying to build actual solutions.

In Search of Clusters: The Coming Battle in Lowly Parallel Computing   by Gregory F. Pfister (Prentice Hall, 1995). A good source of information regarding scalability limits of SMP systems, such as Amdahl's law, the Von Neumann bottleneck, and other considerations for SMP systems. I especially recommend chapters 6 and 11.

Transaction Processing Council (TPC) Web site and full disclosure reports   at http://www.tpc.org. This is a good Web site to consult to help you stay abreast of current performance levels of competing hardware and software solutions. It also has plenty of information regarding the benchmarks. You also might want to order one of the full disclosure reports (FDRs) for a benchmark that uses Microsoft SQL Server to determine the exact and detailed hardware and software configuration used. If you will be running a very large system, such an FDR can be a very good template to use.

INDEX

Symbols and Numbers

+ (addition) operator, 416, 417, 421

− (subtraction) operator, 416, 421

- wildcard, 315

/ (division) operator, 416, 421

* (multiplication) operator, 416, 421

= (equal to) operator, 418

!= (not equal to) operator, 419

=* outer-join operator, 282

=> sargable operator, 706

= ANY in subqueries, 299–300

= NULL extension to ANSI SQL, 296–98

= sargable operator, 706

> (greater than) operator, 418

!> (not greater than) operator, 419

>= (greater than or equal to) operator, 418

> sargable operator, 706

< (less than) operator, 418

!< (not less than) operator, 419

< sargable operator, 706

<= (less than or equal to) operator, 418

<= sargable operator, 706

<> (not equal to) operator, 418

<> ALL, 300–301

<> ANY, 300, 301–2

(pound sign), private temporary stored procedure, 488

#, prefixing temporary private tables, 265

##, prefixing global temporary tables, 266

-- (double hyphen) before comments, 274, 411

% (modulo) operator, 416, 421

% wildcard, 315

& operator, 417, 421

*= outer join operator, 282

/* comment block */, 274, 411

@, designating local variables, 403

@@, designating global variables, 403

^ operator, 417, 421

[^] wildcard, 315

| operator, 417, 421

~ operator, 417, 421

[ ] wildcard, 315

32-bit Automation, 49

A

abort, 45

ABS function, 430, 431, 434

ABSOLUTE fetch type, 545, 555

Accent Insensitivity, 159–60

access methods, logical I/Os, 715–16

access privileges, granting, 43

accounts, changing, 144

ACID properties, 38–39

ACOS function, 431

active users, 105

ActiveX interface (Automation), 50

addition (+) operator, 416, 417, 421

adjust tables, 214

affinitized threads, 103

affinity mask, setting, 763

aggregate functions, 320–23, 421

    grouping, 321–23

    NULLs and, 324–26

    in queries, 309–10

alerts, providing, 52–53

alert stored procedures, 493

ALL, distinguishing from NULL, 333, 335

ALL value, 331

all licensed connections are in use message, 146

allocation pages, 75, 182

allocation units, 182, 377

ALLOW_DUP_ROW option in CREATE INDEX, 223

ALTER DATABASE command, 184–85

alternate keys, 34, 231

alternate result set, returning, 331

ALTER TABLE ADD CONSTRAINT, 233

ALTER TABLE command

    adding constraints, 245

    adding or dropping CHECK constraints, 253

    using defaults within, 254

ALTER TABLE DROP CONSTRAINT, 233

ALTER TABLE NOCHECK, 243

Amdahl's Law, 109

AND operator, 420, 421, 707

ANSI cursors, 537

ANSI format for dates, 527

ANSI null default database option, 188

ANSI_NULL_DFLT_OFF option, 525

ANSI_NULL_DFLT_ON option, 525

ANSI_NULLS option, 524

ANSI_PADDING option, 318, 319, 524

ANSI SQL-92 standard

    compliance with, 30, 522–23

    for scrollable cursors, 547, 552

ANSI_WARNINGS option, 524

API server cursors, 537–38

    guidelines for selecting, 545

    versus Transact-SQL cursors, 538, 540–42, 558

application design, enforcing solid, 662–67

applications

    optimistic concurrency control, 684–85

    designing efficient, 536

    impact on system performance, 116

    isolation levels required by, 683

    porting ISAM, 533

    scrolling, 544–45

application server in the three-tier client/server model, 402

APP_NAME function, 443

ARITHABORT option, 524

ARITHIGNORE option, 524

arithmetic operators, 416–17

arithmetic overflow error, 427

ASCII character set, 154

ASCII function, 435, 436

AS clause, specifying table aliases, 275, 276

Ashton-Tate/Microsoft SQL Server, 5–7

ASIN function, 431

assembly language, processor-specific, 641

asynchronous I/O, 96

asynchronous writes to data pages, 96

ATAN function, 431

ATN2 function, 431

atomicity, 38

atomic transactions, 75

attributes, 195

automatic variables, 403

Automation objects

    instantiating and executing, 635–37

    sp_ prefix with, 490

autostart procedures, 490–91

    preventing the execution of, 491

    setting *tempdb* privileges, 488

AVG function, 302, 320

B

backup domain controller, installing SQL Server, 142

backup

    needs, planning for, 141

    of the transaction log, 183

    strategy, choosing, 126

Banyan VINES Net-Library, 149, 150, 152

base datatypes, 201, 202–3

base table, 195

    modifying data in, through views, 367

batches, 68–69, 449–51

    compiling, 479–80

    executing, 451, 479–83

    monitoring, 771–72

BCP.EXE utility, 57, 229, 245, 358–59

    and FOREIGN KEY constraints, 374–75

bcp functions, 358

bcp libraries, specifics about, 360

BEGIN...END, 405

BEGIN TRAN blocks, counting the depth of, 474
BEGIN TRAN statement, 451
    incrementing the value of @@TRANCOUNT, 474
benchmarks, 109–10
    investing in, 117–18
    kit for SQL Server, 118, 671–72, 755
    test, 670
BETWEEN, 319–20, 706
binary (fixed-length) data, 203
binary (variable-length) data, 203
binary datatype, 203
binary large object (BLOB) support, 508
Binary sort, 160, 157
binary varying, 203
bind token, 649
bit datatype, 203
bit datatype columns, 418
bit masks, setting up, 417
bit operators, 417–18
blank spaces, 316–19
BLOB (binary large object), 203, 508
blocking, 683–84
    problems, 684–85, 693–97
blocks of comments, delineating, 411
Boolean data, 203
bootstrap problem, 244
bound connections, 649–50
branching constructs, 31
...BREAK, 406
breakpoints, setting, 505
B-Trees, 83
    indexes, 218–19
buffer, 211
buffer I/O, initiating, 89
Buffer Manager, 74, 88–93
    accessing pages via, 92–93
    DBCC commands for watching performance, 765
    function of, 89–90
    options in, 764–65
buffer pages, hashing, 94
Buffer section of DBCC PAGE output, 211
buffer slots, 747
buffer steals, 91
bulk copy (bcp) libraries, 358–60
bulk copy (BCP) utility, 57, 229
bulk loading of tables, utilities for, 358–60
burning set, 230

business rules
    in client/server models, 401
    encoding, 34
    placing in stored procedures, 32

C

C function, writing a wrapper around, 495
C source code, embedding SQL queries in, 59
C *sprintf* function, 495
cache
    favoring index pages in, 764–65
    keeping pages permanently in, 91–92
    processor's, 121
cache-hit ratio, 91, 713
    computing, 725
    improving by adding memory, 92
    monitoring, 122, 762
    watching, 743
Cache Hit Ratio counter, 743, 770
Cache - Number of Free Buffers counter, 771
cache space for the log, 758
candidate keys, 34, 231
Cartesian product, 274–75
CASCADE action, 248, 572
cascading delete, 248
cascading triggers, 503, 575–77
case-insensitive sorting, 156, 161
case-sensitive sorting, 160, 437
case sensitivity, 521–22
    of passwords, 164
CASE statements, 406–9
    in DEFAULT clause of CREATE TABLE command, 582
    comparing values to constants, 407–8
    derivatives of, 410–11
    in UPDATE statements, 365, 409
    in views, 409
CAST operator, 423
category column in the *sysdatabases* table, 187
CD-ROM databases, 188, 191–92
CD-ROM with this book
    install script, 168
    RUN_ISOLATION1.CMD file, 459
    SEMAPHORE.SQL script, 459
    SQLHDTST.EXE, 139
    SQL Server benchmark kit, 118, 671–72, 755
    triggers implementing referential actions, 575

CEILING function, 430, 431
character data
    fixed-length, 202
    functions for working with, 434–36
    generating randomly, 580–83
    variable-length, 202
characters
    deleting with UPDATETEXT, 517–18
    inserting with UPDATETEXT, 519–20
character sets, 153–56
    consequences of changing, 153
    conversions, 154
character strings
    concatenating with the addition operator, 417
    converting floating-point numbers to, 424
    inserting control characters into, 436–37
char datatype, 202
char entry, 160
CHAR function, 435, 436–37
CHARINDEX function, 435, 439
CHARSET.EXE program, 157
CHECK constraints, 35–36, 231, 250–53
    adding and dropping, 253
    default clashes with, 256
    global variables and, 253
    preventing NULL values, 253
    referring to more than one column in a row, 253
    regular expressions in, 253
    temporarily disabling, 253
CHECK CONSTRAINT statement, 245
checkpoints, 90
    performance issues and, 90
    processes, 755, 759
    purging transactions, 189
    records, adding to databases, 188
    write activities during, 90
client cursors, 538–39
clients, 403
    reducing intermediate processing of routines, 400
    supporting several simultaneously on different networks, 65
client/server applications
    developing efficient, 400
    three-tier model, 400–2
    two-tier model for, 401–2
client state at the server, minimizing, 536
Client Utilities, installing, 169
CLOSE/DEALLOC statement, 546

CLOSE syntax for cursors, 557
CLUSTERED attribute, 232, 240
clustered indexes, 219–20, 219
    choosing wisely, 675
    data pages on the leaf level, 84–86, 85
    directing inserts to specific pages, 377
    driving the scan, 714
    effect on space management, 376–77
    logical I/Os, 715, 716
    rebuilding, 83
    with sequential key values, 651, 652
    wasting on the primary key, 717
COALESCE function, 410, 443
code and internal structures, memory need for, 122
code pages, 154–55
code point, 154
coherent disk cache, 89
colid values for constraints, 259
collating sequences, 156
COL_LENGTH function, 443
COL_NAME function, 443, 445
column IDs, 207–8
column-level constraints, 233
    compared to table-level, 240
    explicitly naming, 240
    naming schemes for, 235
column names
    Hungarian-style notation for, 200
    matching in tables involved in FOREIGN KEY references, 240
columns, 195
    adding logically redundant, 666
    allowing NULL on, 204
    completely replacing the contents of, with UPDATETEXT, 517
    density of, 678–79
    explicitly naming in INSERT statements, 351
    naming, 197
    order in index keys, 678
    setting multiple, 363
    specifying the sorting of, 273–74
    stored computed, 620
    truncating with CONVERT, 424
    updating indexed, 677–78
Command Parser, 71
commands
    excessive, in ISAM-style code, 535
    issuing in batches, 681

comments, 411–12, 674
  adding in code, 243
  entering in queries, 274
  nesting, 274
COMMIT, 45
  closing cursors when issuing, 557
Committed Read isolation level, 77–78
  compared to Repeatable Read, 687
COMMIT TRAN statement, 451
  decrementing the value of @@TRANCOUNT, 474
  effect on nested transaction blocks, 473–74
comparison operators, 418–19
compatibility
  of page locks, 647, 648
  of table locks, 648
completion queue for worker threads, 105
COMPUTE BY operator
  compared to ROLLUP, 338–40
  similarity to CUBE and ROLLUP, 331
computed columns, selecting, 620
concurrency, 682
  trade-offs with consistency, 39, 682–83
  control with Transact-SQL cursors, 561–69
conditional logic in Transact-SQL, 405, 406
configuration block in the MASTER device, 177
configuration options
  for every site to examine, 743–47
  for fine-tuning, 750–63
  for adequate resources, 748–50
configuration settings
  changing, 163
  changing one at a time, 742
  in Windows NT, 740
Configuration tab of the Server Configuration Options dialog
    box, 165
connect events, 70
connection ID (spid), 698
connections, 649. *See also* user connections
  setting maximum allowable number as simultaneous, 748
  sharing lock space, 649–50
  versus users, 147
consistency, 682
  trade-offs with concurrency, 39, 682–83
  property, 38
constraints, 231
  adding after data, 245
  checking, 245, 375–76
  colid values for, 259

compared to triggers, 572–73
  creating, 233–44
  deferred option for, 244–45
  disabling, 243
  failures, effect on multirow data modification, 261–64
  names, system-generated, 258
  nullability of, 232
  Object IDs for, 258–59
  as objects, 259
  on temporary tables, 267
  reenabling, 374–76
  removing, 232
  specifying index attributes for, 232
  system functions with, 446
  triggers and, 243
context area per user, 106–7
CONTINUE, 406
control characters, inserting, 436–37
controllers, compared to channels, 125
control-of-flow tools, 405–6
conversion deadlocks, 512, 641, 642, 643
  example, 686–88
  preventing, 689
  UPDLOCK hint and, 688
conversion functions, 422–28
conversions of character sets, 154
CONVERT function, 341, 422–28
  adding trailing blanks, 319
  with arithmetic operations, 416
  formatting dates, 425
  with ISNUMERIC, 447
  joining two UDDTs, 225–26
correlated subqueries, 303–10
  compared to joins, 304–6
  compared to outer-join formulations, 306–7
  compared to self-joins, 308
  EXISTS statement in, 306
  UPDATE statements like, 364
COS() function, 431
cost-based optimizer, 31, 73
COT() function, 431
counters
  exporting to Performance Monitor, 773
  fields, 227
  in Performance Monitor, 768–72
COUNT function, 320
  alternative to using, 323

CPUs
    load balancing across multiple, 103
    monitoring systemwide, 768–69
    monitoring time for SQL Server, 770
    profiling, 122
crdate column in the *sysdatabases* table, 187
CREATE DATABASE command
    FOR LOAD option, 191
    issuing, 181, 182
    separating the transaction log from data space, 182–83
CREATE DEFAULT command, 254
CREATE INDEX command, 222–23
    ALLOW_DUP_ROW option, 223
    FILLFACTOR option, 222
    IGNORE_DUP_KEY option, 223
    IGNORE_DUP_ROW option, 223
    PAD_INDEX option, 222
    SORTED_DATA option, 223
    SORTED_DATA_REORG option, 223
CREATE PROCEDURE statement, 466–68
Create-Retrieve-Update-Delete. *See* CRUD chart
CREATE TABLE command, 196
    CASE statement in a DEFAULT clause, 582
    using defaults within, 254
create table privileges, establishing in *tempdb*, 266
critical transactions, evaluating, 664–66
CROSS JOIN operator, 274–75, 342–47
cross-tabs, 621–24
crows values, 728, 731, 732, 733
CRUD chart
    completing, 665
    identifying tasks running with critical transactions, 671
CUBE, 327–37
    always populating the full, 331
    filling out with placeholder rows, 346
current date, recording, 354
Current Disk Queue Length counter, 769
CURRENT_TIMESTAMP function, 448
CURRENT_USER function, 448
CURSOR_CLOSE_ON_COMMIT option, 524
@@CURSOR ROWS global variable, 554
cursors, 529
    abuse of, 532, 542
    appropriate use of, 542–52
    basics of, 530–32
    bridging set-based and record-based models, 529, 530
    choosing, 545–46
    closing, 531, 557
    compared to local variables, 553
    deallocating, 531, 558
    declaring, 530
    declaring as SCROLL, 553
    declaring with a given name, 552–53
    deleting, 557
    fetching a row from, 555–56
    fetching rows in, 531
    ISAMs and, 532–35
    judicious use of, 680
    keys, 550–52
    maintaining, 547
    membership of, 546
    models, 537–39, 547
    opening, 531, 554
    operations and network traffic, 535
    positioning, 530
    removing the definition of, 558
    in scrolling applications, 544–45
    for sequential operations, 593
    shared locks and, 564
    static, 547–48
    types, resulting from DECLARE statements, 559
    updating, 530
    updating a row in, 556
cursor threshold configuration option with sp_configure, 554
custom loader applications, 359
cycle deadlocks, 641, 642
    example, 685–86
    preventing, 689

D

data
    protecting modifications with exclusive locking, 397–98
    scrubbing, 223
    transforming into SQL Server format, 359–60
    and views, 350, 367–72
database
    backup strategy, nonlogged operations and, 510
    design, enforcing solid, 662–67
    objects, setting the maximum number of open, 750
    options, 187–90
    owner (DBO), 182, 197
    routines, encapsulating, 400
    size configuration option in sp_configure, 182

database devices, 174–75
    creating, 175–77
    default, 179
    dump (backup), loading immediately, 191
    errors related to creation and initialization, 179–80
    expanding, 175, 178
    fragments, 184
    mirroring, 180
    mounting and dismounting, 179
    relationship with databases, 179
    size preallocation, 175
database-logical addresses, mapping, 90
Database Manager, 75. *See also* OS/2 Database Manager
databases, 173–74, 185
    compared to schema, 191
    creating, 180–83
    expanding and shrinking, 184–85
    maximum size of, 184
    normalizing, 662–63
    setting the maximum number of open, 749
    special, 180, 192–94
database-specific settings, 763–64
data cache, 481
    increasing memory for, 122
    pinning tables in, 765
data definition language. *See* DDL
data integrity, 33–34
DATALENGTH function, 316, 440, 443, 444–45
    with ISNULL, 445
    with READTEXT, 514
data modifications, importance of indexes for, 677
data modification statements, 349
    affecting multiple rows, 264
    constraint errors in, 264
    triggers and, 501
data pages, 182, 208–10
    asynchronous writes to, 76, 89, 96
    components of, 208–10
    examining, 211–13
    flushing writes to disk, 90
    splitting, 87–88
data replication. *See* replication
data rows, 210
    structure of, 213–14
data scrubbing, 609–10
Data section of DBCC PAGE output, 212
data security. *See* security

DataServer, 4
datatypes, 35, 200–207
    explicitly converting, 341, 342
    functions for converting, 422–28
    matching in tables involved in FOREIGN KEY references, 240
    mixing in SQL, 423
    user-defined, 35, 224–27
    variable-length versus fixed-length datatypes, 201, 204–7
DATEADD function, 429
date and time data, 203
date and time functions, 428–30
DATEDIFF function, 429
DATEFIRST, setting, 527
DATEFORMAT, changing, 527
date formats, specifying with CONVERT, 425
DATENAME function, 429
DATEPART function, 429
dates
    ANSI format for, 527
    recording the current, 354
    style 102 ANSI for, 426
datetime data, inserting with only a date element, 426
datetime datatype, 203
datetime parameters, encodings for, 429
datetime values, operations on, 428–30
dBASE IV, SQL Server as a back-end for, 532
dBASE IV Server Edition, effect on scrollable cursors, 8
DBCC BUFCOUNT command, 754
DBCC DBREINDEX command
    rebuilding indexes, 222, 236
    with the SORTED_DATA_REORG option, 767
DBCC INPUTBUFFER command, 695–96
DBCC MEMUSAGE command, 746
DBCC OPENTRAN command, 100
DBCC PAGE command, 211–13
    displaying the page header, 701
    sections of output, 211–13
DBCC PERFMON command, executing directly, 743
DBCC PINTABLE command, 91–92, 765
DBCC PROCCACHE command, 746
DBCC SHOWCONTIG command, 75, 767
DBCC SHOW_STATISTICS command, 710
    viewing the steps on a distribution page, 712
DBCC SHRINKDB command, 184–85
DBCC SQLPERF(HASHSTATS) command, 94, 754
DBCC SQLPERF(LRUSTATS2) command, 758, 765

DBCC SQLPERF(RASTATS) command, sample output, 762

DBCC SQLPERF(WAITSTATS) command, 765

DBCC TRACEON command, 211, 212

DBCC UNPINTABLE command, 91

DBCC USER OPTIONS command, output, 525–26

DBCS encoding, 155

dbcursorclose cursor function, 546

dbcursor cursor function, 546

dbcursorfetchex cursor function, 546

dbcursorfetch function call, 538

dbcursoropen cursor function, 546

dbid, 92–93, 186

dbid column in the *sysdatabases* table, 187

DB_ID function, 443, 445

dbid-pageno values, uniformly distributing, 94

DB-Library
    API, 58–59
    cursor functions, 546
    executing batches from, 451
    future enhancement of, 59
    initial cursor specification for, 547
    ISQLW.EXE in, 426–27

DBMS-enforced data integrity, 33–34

DB_NAME function, 443, 445

dbo use only database option, 188

dbo username, 197

dbsqlexec, executing batches from DB-Library, 451

DBTABLE structure, 186

DCL (data control language), 349

DDL (data definition language), 349

DDL commands, keeping in a script, 196

DDL Manager, 480

deadlock handler, 690–92, 693

deadlocks, 512, 641
    trace flags for analyzing, 655, 702–4
    analyzing and resolving, 685–704
    detection, 642
    handling instead of preventing, 690–92, 693
    from page splits, 688–89
    preventing, 689
    protocols for avoiding, 644
    row-level locking and, 693
    types of, 641
    victim, volunteering, 692–93

deadly embrace, 641
    example, 685–86

DEALLOCATE command, 558
    undeclaring cursors, 531

deallocating pages, 397

debugging, 504–8

decimal datatype, 202

decision-support system (DSS), 676

declarative referential integrity (DRI), 34–35, 237

DECLARE/OPEN statement, 546

DECLARE statements, 552–53
    examples of, 559
    naming the cursor, 530

DECNet Sockets Net-Library, 149, 150, 152

deescalating locks, 651

DEFAULT and NULL precedence, INSERT statements and, 352

default behavior, overriding with hints, 734

default constraints, 254–58
    clashes with CHECK constraints, 256

default device pool, 179

default devices, 179

DEFAULT keyword, 36
    as a placeholder, 350, 479
    in the UPDATE statement, 364

default result set in a cursor, 540

defaults, 36, 254–58
    behavior with INSERT statements, 257–58

DEFAULT VALUES statement
    including random data in tables, 582–83
    with INSERT, 257

default values versus NULL, 256–57

deferred constraints, 244–45, 248

deferred updates, 80–81, 205, 378–79
    example, 389

DEGREES function, 431

delete/insert operations, 379

DELETE statements, 365–66
    effect of errors on single, 466
    executing against views, 367, 369
    syntax, 557
    triggers and, 501

"denormalized" databases, 663

density, 708
    of columns, 678–79
    of indexes, 709

derived tables, 31, 310, 312
    compared to views, 312
    finding rows with matching columns, 608–9
    treating views as, 584–85

DES, 74

descriptors, 191

design documents, 672–73

Developer Studio, debugging with, 505–7
development
    approach, nonprocedural, 735
    cycle, considering performance throughout, 659
    in a case-sensitive environment, 521
    interfaces for SQL Server, 58–60
    methodologies, 672–74
    process throughout, 670–74
    roles, evolvement of, 9–10
    team, developing expertise on, 660–62
devices
    fragments, 184
    mirroring, 175
    numbers, 177–78
    returning detailed information about, 177
DIFFERENCE function, 435, 441–43
direct-field-update strategy, 382
    examples, 386, 393
direct-mode update, 204–5
directories, 8.3-character names for, 175
direct updates, 80, 81–82, 379–82
dirty page, 92
dirty-read isolation level, falling back to, 683
dirty reads, 77, 457, 461
    example, 459–61
DISABLE_DEF_CNST_CHK option, 524
disappearing rows phenomenon, 373–74
disk controllers, guaranteeing completion of write operations, 136
disk device files, initiating on NTFS versus FAT, 176
disk drives
    backing up to, 141
    per SCSI channel, 125
    replacing failed, 136
DISK INIT command
    avoiding errors, 180
    creating database devices, 175–76
DISK INIT error message, 179–80
DISK MIRROR command, 180
disk pages, types of, 75
Diskperf service, 769
DISK REMIRROR command, 180
DISK RESIZE command, 178
Disk Transfers/sec counter, 769
DISK UNMIRROR command, 180
dismounting database devices, 179
DISTINCT clause, views and, 313
distributed data processing, 44–45

distributed join, getting the capabilities of a, 355
distributed keyword, 199
distributed partitioned insert, mimicking, 631–32
distribution column in the *sysindexes* table, 709
distribution pages, 72, 75, 708
    for indexes, 221
    viewing the values of, 711
division operator, 416, 421
DLLs (dynamic link libraries)
    dynamically loaded and executed, 495
    external, 33
DML (data manipulation language), 349, 480
DNOOP (Delete-No-Op) log record, 378, 379
documented stored procedures, 490
domain accounts, setting up SQL Server to run with, 143–44
domain integrity, enforcing, 231, 250
DONE_IN_PROC messages, suppressing, 681–82
double-byte character sets (DBCS), 155
double hyphen, 274, 411
double quotation marks, 198
double slash in C++, 411
drill-down report, 337
drives. *See* disk drives
DSS applications, segregating from OLTP, 704
DSS demands on the database, versus OLTP demands, 683
dummy rows, join operations with, 292–94
dummy update
    checking constraints with, 375–76
    issuing, 245
dummy values, drawbacks of, 294
DUMP DATABASE command, 189
dump devices, 174
DUMP TABLE statement, 361–62
DUMP TRANSACTION command, prohibiting, 189
dumptrdate column in the *sysdatabases* table, 187
duplicate rows, finding, 223
durability property, 39
dynamic cursors, 549–50, 551
Dynamic Index, 717, 718
dynamic link libraries. *See* DLLs

E

EDITBIN.EXE utility, reducing the stack size for threads, 744
EIDE drives, compared to SCSI drives, 124–25
e-mail
    automatically sending, 625
    integrating SQL Server with, 624–30
    processing incoming, 626–30

Embedded SQL precompiler, 59

encryption
>of network traffic, 42
>offered by the MultiProtocol interface, 151
>performance overhead of, 151
>of text stored in *syscomments*, 485

end-of-batch signal (GO), 451

environmental concerns in Transact-SQL programming, 521–27

equal to operator, 418

equijoins, 274, 275, 679
>specifying views as, 368
>writing as subqueries, 298

@@ERROR global variable, 263, 403
>compared to SET XACT_ABORT, 456
>RAISERROR and, 413
>selecting the value of, after each statement, 452, 454

errors
>checking in transactions, 452–57
>planning for fatal, 474–75
>in the Windows NT event log, 414
>state 127, 414

escalation points for table locks, calculating, 751, 752

event/alert subsystem, 52

event handlers, creating, 69

EVENT ID 17060, 414

exception handling, 106

exclusive extent (EX_EXT) lock, 647

exclusive locks, 397, 639, 645
>blocking with shared locks, 567
>releasing, 640
>serializing access to, 687

exclusive page (EX_PAGE) lock, 646, 648

exclusive table intent (EX_INT) lock, 646, 648

exclusive table (EX_TAB) lock, 646, 648

EXEC procedure with INSERT, 355–57

Execution Engine. *See* Executor

execution plan, 72, 73
>and FOREIGN KEY constraint, 241
>generating, 479–80
>recompiling, 482–83
>of stored procedures, storage of, 480
>for a trigger, 378

Executor, 73–74

exhaustive optimization, 72

EXISTS statement in correlated subqueries, 306

EXP function, 431

explicit conversions, 427–28

explicit JOIN syntax, 275, 275

explicit transactions, 451–52

expressions, unknown, 253

extended characters, 154

extended stored procedures, 33, 490, 495–500. *See also* stored procedures
>administration and monitoring, 500
>bound connections and, 650
>listing of, 500
>registering, 499
>stability issues, 498–99
>writing, 495

extents
>allocating, 377
>locking on, 647
>organizing, 75

F

−f minimal configuration parameter, 748

−f switch, preventing autostart procedures from executing, 491

factorial program
>iterative approach, 471–73
>writing with recursion, 469–70

factorial table, displaying, 470–71, 472–73

fallback server, 139–40

FALSE condition, 289

fast bcp, 360

FASTFIRSTROW optimizer hint, 669, 737–38

fatal errors, 414
>planning for, 474–75
>in transactions, 452

fat client, 401

fat cursor, specifying, 538

FAT file system, compared to NTFS, 142

favored pages, 91, 764

fetch, scrolling a cursor with, 529, 530

FETCH ABSOLUTE statement, 545, 549, 555
>dynamic cursors and, 550

FETCH NEXT statement, 550, 555

FETCH PRIOR statement, 555

FETCH RELATIVE statement, 555
>with dynamic cursors, 550

FETCH statement, 531, 546

@@FETCH_STATUS global variable, 531, 549, 555–56

FETCH syntax, 555–56

file compression, NTFS, 142

FILE_FLAG_WRITE_THROUGH flag, 143

file system, selecting, 142–43, 741

filler characters, adding, 440

FILLFACTOR option in CREATE INDEX, 222

FILLFACTOR parameter

creating space on pages, 688

re-creating clustered indexes, 88

firehose cursor, 540, 545

first normal form, 663

first row, returning quickly, 669

fixed-length columns, trailing blanks in, 318

fixed-length data, storage of, 213–14

fixed-length datatypes, versus variable-length, 201, 204–7

fixed-length rows, storage of, 214–15

float datatype, 202

floating-point data, 202

floating-point numbers, converting to character strings, 424

FLOOR function, 430, 431

flow of control, effect of ROLLBACK on, 474

FOREIGN KEY constraints, 35, 236–38

building indexes for, 241, 244

compared to update triggers, 249

compromising with BCP.EXE, 374–75

declaring, 238–39

enforcement of, 670

implementing NO ACTION, 572

list of actions not allowed by, 573

maximum per table, 241–42

NO CHECK with, 573

performance concerns about, 242–43, 244

practical considerations for, 243–44

protecting updates on views, 371–72

references, disabling checking of, 245

referencing UNIQUE constraints, 240

relationship, declaring for readability, 249

tables affected by, 573

variation in the creation of, 240

foreign keys, 35, 195, 390–91

FOR LOAD option in the CREATE DATABASE command, 191

FOR READ ONLY option compared to INSENSITIVE, 561

FOR UPDATE modifier, specifying with DECLARE, 553

FOR UPDATE OF modifier of the DECLARE statement, 569

forward-only cursors, 550, 560

fragments, 184

free buffers, 757

freeoff field in a page header, 209

free pages, fast access to, 94–95

free space, reserving in index leaf pages, 222

full-blown locks, 639–40

full delete/insert

examples, 389–91, 395–97

strategy, 383

update, 82–83

full outer join, 277, 278

functions

nesting, 422

user-defined, 422

fuzzy checkpoint technique, 90

G

GETANSINULL function, 443

GETDATE function, 429, 448

as the DEFAULT value, 364

values returned by, 600

global configuration options, changing, 169

global security choices, specifying, 169

global temporary stored procedures, 488

global temporary tables, 266

global variables, 403–4

CHECK constraints and, 253

user-declared, 403

watching the contents of, 505

GO end-of-batch signal in ISQL and ISQL/w, 451

GOTO label, 406

greater than operator, 418

greater than or equal to operator, 418

GROUP BY...COUNT, finding rows with matching columns, 607

group commit, 130, 759

GROUPING function, 333, 335

grouping NULL, 331

versus a NULL value, 335

grouping operators (parentheses), 419–21

H

Halloween problem, 81, 378

example, 395–96

hard-drive array, switching to a fallback server, 139

hardware

choosing appropriate, 679–80

overbuying, 117

selecting, 114–18

hardware RAID, 135–36
    controllers required for RAID-0&1, 129–30
hash buckets, 94
    configuration option, 753–54
hash function, 94
hashing, 94
HCL-approved system, 115
heap, 377
hexadecimal notation, specifying values in, 157–58
hierarchies, expanding, 611–17
hierarchy report, 337
high-severity errors, 414
hints, 734
    specifying for locking, 654–55
    types of, 734
HOLDLOCK hint, 513, 514, 564, 736
HOLDLOCK option, 640
horizontal partitions, replication in, 47
horizontal scan, 95
HOST_ID function, 443
HOST_NAME function, 443
hot pages, 92
hot pluggable drives, 136, 141
hot spots, 651, 652
hot-standby drives, 136
hot-standby server, 139–40
HPFS, 143
Hungarian-style notation, 200

I

IDE drives, compared to SCSI drives, 124–25
identifiers
    for Network Interface Cards (NICs), 147
    quoted, 198
    SQL Server rules for, 197
IDENT_INCR function, 228, 443
IDENTITYCOL keyword, 229
identity column
    creating a surrogate key, 678
    disabling the generation of values in, 228
@@IDENTITY global variable, 230
Identity property, 34, 227–30
    declaring on a column that uses a UDDT, 230
    DEFAULT keyword and, 257
    INSERT statements and, 352
    manufacturing surrogate keys, 232
IDENT_SEED function, 228, 443

IETF SNMP RDBMS-MIB (RFC 1697), 57
IF...ELSE, 406
IGNORE_DUP_KEY option, 609
    in CREATE INDEX, 223
IGNORE_DUP_ROW option in CREATE INDEX, 223
image datatype, 203, 508, 509
    functional drawbacks of, 509
    storage size of, 509
    storing data, 75
image of data in the buffer for dynamic cursors, 549–50
impedance mismatch, 529
impersonation feature of Windows NT, 42
implicit conversions, 427–28
implicit transactions, 451–52
IMPLICIT_TRANSACTIONS option, 524
IN clause, 296
incompatible locks, waiting for, 649
incremental backup, 183
increment values, 227–28
INDEX/, 735–36
INDEX_COL function, 443
indexes, 218–19
    attributes, specifying for constraints, 232
    checking the statistics of, 708
    clustered, nonunique, 377
    columns in joins, 678–79
    coverage, achieving in queries, 677
    creating, 222–23
    creating or dropping as needed, 679
    creating proper, 665
    determining usage of, 726
    distribution pages for, 221
    distribution statistics, updating, 767
    effect on data modifications, 86
    hints, combining with lock hints, 737
    intersection strategy, 718
    levels in, 218, 219
    nonclustered, 377
    rebuilding, 236
    selection, 708–18
    selectivity of, 708–9
    specifying for use to drive scans, 735–36
    statistics, checking, 708
    tailoring to critical transactions, 676–78
    trees, balancing, 83
    union, 717, 718
    uniqueness and, 221
    usefulness of, 674–79, 713–17

Index Manager, 80, 83–88
index pages, 75
    favoring in cache, 764–65
index selection rules
    for dynamic cursors, 551
    for keyset cursors, 552
indid field in a page header, 209
in-memory pages, fast access to, 94
INNER as an optional modifier, 275–76
inner join, 275–76
INOOP (Insert-No-Op) log record, 378, 379
IN operator, 420
IN predicate in subqueries, 299–300
INPUTBUFFER, 696
input buffers, 67
INSENSITIVE modifier with Transact-SQL cursors, 548
INSENSITIVE option
    compared to FOR READ ONLY, 561
    specifying with DECLARE, 553
INSERT command, DEFAULT VALUES clause, 257
INSERT...DEFAULT VALUES statement, 579
INSERT/EXEC statements, 355–57
insert page (IX_PAGE) locks, 646, 648, 653
insert row-level locking (IRL), 651–53, 764
INSERT/SELECT statements, 354–55
    effect of errors on single, 466
INSERT statements, 349–52
    behavior with defaults, 257–58
    effect of the failure of one, 351
    multiple-row, 354–58
    NULL and DEFAULT precedence, 352
    performing against views, 367–68
    simple examples of, 350–52
    triggers and, 501
    VALUES clause and, 353
INSIND (insert-indicator) log record, 379
install script, 167–69
int datatype, 202
integer data, 202, 213
integrated security
    related extended stored procedures, 500
    with Windows NT, 42, 150
integrity checks, 265, 402
integrity constraints, reenabling, 374–76
intent locks, 645, 513
intent-to-update locks, 645
interim violations, 80, 247–48, 378
intermediate index page, splitting, 87

intermediate level in indexes, 218
internal memory structures, 644
internal storage, 207–18
Internet
    client cursors and, 539
    licensing, 146–47
    publishing SQL Server data on, 53
Internet Information Server (IIS), 53–54
intervals, finding differences between, 599–604
INTO with INSERT, 349–50
I/O - Batch Writes/sec counter, 771
IOCompletion port, 105
I/O - Log Writes/sec counter, 760, 772
I/O - Outstanding Reads counter, 771–72
I/O - Outstanding Writes counter, 771–72
I/O - Page Reads/sec counter, 771
I/O rates for physical disks, 769
I/O - Single Page Writes/sec counter, 771
I/O throughput, 124
I/O - Transactions/sec counter, 760, 772
I/O - Trans. per Log Record counter, 772
IPC mechanisms, 65, 150
ISAM applications, porting, 533
ISAM processing, compared to SQL Server, 450
ISAMs, cursors and, 532–35
ISAM-style operations in SQL Server, problems with, 535–36
ISDATE() function, 444, 446
IS NOT NULL operator, 291
ISNULL() function, 295, 326, 410–11, 444
    with DATALENGTH, 440, 445
IS NULL operator, 291–92, 295
ISNUMERIC() function, 444, 446–47
ISO character set, 153–54
isolation, 38–39, 639
isolation levels, 76
    behaviors, 457
    expressing consistency in terms of, 682
    Lock Manager and, 640
    multiple degrees of, 39
    required by applications, 683
    of transactions, 457–65
ISQL character-based command-line utility, 56
ISQL end-of-batch signal, 451
ISQL.EXE 127, 414, 671
ISQL/w, 163, 164
ISQLW.EXE, 426–27
ISUD (Insert-Select-Update-Delete), 665

J

join clause, example of, 719–23
join condition, specifying, 274
join processing, compared to ISAM-like processing, 533–35
joins, 272–88
  alternatives to, 664
  compared to correlated subqueries, 304–6
  index columns used in, 678–79
  of more than four tables, 724
  and nested iterations, 679, 705
  reformatting strategy for, 723
  specifying the order of processing tables for, 735
  writing as subqueries, 298
join selection, 718–23

K

keys, keeping compact, 232, 666
keyset cursors, 548–49
  index selection rules for, 552
  missing rows applying to, 556
keywords, 197–99, 162
KILL command, issuing to clear a blocking problem, 694

L

language events, 70
languages, adding the text of messages in multiple, 413
latch, 641
Lazywriter, 94–95, 756–57, 765
leaf level in indexes, 218, 219
leaf pages
  of the clustered index, 676
  in index trees, 83
LEFT OUTER JOIN, 278
less than operator, 418
less than or equal to operator, 418
LE threshold maximum configuration setting, 751, 752
LE threshold minimum configuration setting, 751, 752
LE threshold percent configuration setting, 751, 752
level field in a page header, 209
licensing, 144–49
LIKE, 315
  as a sargable operator, 706
  compared to CHARINDEX, 439
linear scaling, 108
linked list, chaining to hash pages, 94

link page (LN_PAGE) lock, 646, 648, 653, 654
little endian format, 213
loader applications, custom, 359
loaders, writing your own, 359
LOAD TABLE, 360–62
  constraint checking and, 375
  DUMP DATABASE and, 362
LocalSystem account, 143
  running SQL Executive on, 144
local variables, 403, 404–5
  assigning to SELECT statements returning more than one row, 404–5
  compared to cursors, 553
  effect of ROLLBACK on, 474
  watching the contents of, 505
lock block, 644
lock contention, identifying areas of, 671
lock escalation, 654, 750–52
locking
  activity, watching, 655, 698–704
  cost of managing, 650
  data modifications and, 397–98
  hints, 654–55, 736
  introduced, 639
  mode, specifying a particular, 736
  monitoring, 694–95
  pileups, 695
  processing-intensive aspects of, 650
  recovery and, 98
Lock Manager, 79, 639
  coordinating with Transaction Manager, 76
  deadlock detection, 642
  isolation levels and, 640
lock owner block, 644
locks.
  acquiring, 79
  compatibility of, 647–49
  configuring, 654, 749
  deescalating, 651
  memory and, 644–45
  releasing, 79, 640
  setting the number of available, 749
  starvation, preventing, 649
  types of, 639–40, 645–46, 736–37
  viewing, 647
  waits, 641
log, cache space for, 758

logging
    disabling, 189
    TRUNCATE TABLE and, 366
logic, three-valued, 289
logical and grouping operators, 419–21
logical design, 663
logical I/Os, 713
    estimating, 706
    minimizing, 714
    summarized for different access methods, 715–16
logically redundant prepositions, 365
logical pages, 185
    mapping from, 186
Logical Reads, 724, 725, 726
LogLRU buffers configuration option, 757–58
LogLRU cache, 758
logon monitoring, 42–43
logptr column in the *sysdatabases* table, 187
log records
    displaying, 407–8
    produced for on-page delete/insert, 383
    produced for update-in-place, 381–82
log writes, monitoring, 772
logwrite sleep setting, 759–60, 772
loops in Transact-SQL, 405, 406
LOWER() function, 435, 437–38
LRU algorithm, 90, 91
LTRIM() function, 435, 438

M

mail integration features (SQLMail), 144
mail. *See* e-mail
maintenance tasks, scheduling in SQL Enterprise Manager, 49
master database, 177, 181, 192–93
    building and configuring, 162
    configuring with sorting options, 157
    rebuilding, 169
    reporting locks in, 693
    system stored procedures in, 490
    system tables in, 186
MASTER.DAT file, 177
MASTER device, 177
    removing from the default pool, 179
math functions, 430–34
max async IO configuration option, 755–56
MAX function, 320
max lazywrite IO configuration option, 756

Max Users Connected counter in Performance Monitor, 748
max worker threads, setting, 752–53
memory
    adding to improve the cache-hit ratio, 92
    addressing in 32-bit environments, 12
    autotuning, 745
    configuring, 123, 164–65, 742, 743–45
    estimating requirements, 745
    guidelines for, 122–24
    locks and, 644–45
    minimum requirements, 123
    overcommitted, 123
    overhead for license tracking, 149
    pages, maximum number for sorting per user, 752
    paging, avoiding, 743
    shared, 40
    showing the amount recently used by process, 770
    SIMMs, configuration of, 123–24
    use per SQL Server user, 106–7
    working with huge amounts of, 93–95
merge-join strategy, 723
messages
    logging to the Windows NT event service, 413
    in multiple languages, 413
    setting the severity level of, 413–14
metadata, 450, 538
Microsoft Developer Studio. *See* Developer Studio
Microsoft Distributed Transaction Coordinator. *See* MS DTC
Microsoft Internet Information Server (IIS), 53–54
Microsoft Open Data Services. *See* ODS
Microsoft SQL Enterprise Manager. *See* SQL Enterprise Manager
Microsoft SQL Server
    as a back-end for dBASE IV, 532
    accessing without a network card, 148
    benchmarking performance, 117–18, 671–72, 755
    changing the registered owner of, 170
    Client/Server Development Kit (CSDK), 19
    combining with other services, 121
    configuration settings, 66, 164–65, 742–65
    developing for Windows NT, 15–23
    development interfaces, 58–60
    engine, 28, 69, 70, 400
    family of components, 27–60
    general architecture of, 63–64
    integrated security features, 150–51
    integrating with e-mail, 624–30
    Internet capabilities of, 53–54

Microsoft SQL Server, *continued*
   licensing choices for, 144–49
   minimum memory requirements, 123
   multiprocessor scalability of, 102–4
   multiuser performance, 41
   Net-Library interface options, 150
   network card requirements, 140–41
   optimizer, 31, 72–73
   performance of, 107–10
   rebuilding Registry entries, 170
   removing, 169–70
   RISC version, 102
   running from the command line, 755
   running multiple instances of, 170
   running on raw partition, 143
   running under a user account, 507
   scalability of, 102
   Setup program, 56, 166
   system crashes and, 101
   system maintenance, 766–67
   utilities and extensions, 53
   Web Assistant, 53–58, 610
   Windows 95 and, 506
Microsoft SQL Server Distributed Management Objects. *See* SQL-DMO
Microsoft Visual Basic
   as a scripting environment, 50
   creating Automation objects, 635
   SDI availability for, 504
Microsoft Windows NT. *See* Windows NT
midnight internal time, 354
MIN function, 320
minlen field in a page header, 209
mirroring
   by SQL Server, 133
   database devices, 180
   of devices, 175
   RAID-1, 127–28
mode column in the *sysdatabases* table, 187
MODIFY log record, 380, 381–82, 394–95
modulo operator, 416, 421
monetary data, 202
money datatype, 202
Moore's Law, 20, 119
msdb database, 190, 194
MSDN viewer, 58
MS-DOS code pages, 154
MS DTC, 44–45, 76

multiple processors, benefits of, 106
multiple-row updates, 82, 391–92
multiple-row INSERT statements, 354–60
multiplication operator, 416, 421
multiprocessor scalability of SQL Server, 102–4
Multi-Protocol Net-Library, 42, 65, 66, 149, 150–51
multithreading, 40
mutual exclusion (mutex) functionality, providing with rlocks, 640

N

name column in the *sysdatabases* table, 187
named caches, 88
named columns join, 275
Named Pipes Net-Library, 69, 149, 150–51, 153
naming conventions, 198–99, 200
naming scheme for system-generated constraint names, 258
National Institute of Standards and Technology (NIST), 30
native thread-level multiprocessing, 103
native thread services of Windows NT, 103, 104
natural join operation, 276
negation operators in nonsargable clauses, 707
nested iterations for processing joins, 679, 705
nested stored procedures, 469
nested transaction blocks, 473–77
nested transaction sequences, 76
nesting
   checking for depth of, 696
   functions, 422
   levels of stored procedures, 469
   transaction blocks, 476–77
@@NESTLEVEL global variable, 469, 489
Net Command Queue Length counter, 753
Net-Libraries
   abstraction layer, 64–66
   interface options, 150
   pairing of, 67
   speed of, 66
network applications, 740–41
network buffer, 68–69
network cards, 140–41
network latency, minimizing, 31
Network Monitor, observing network traffic, 682
network packet size configuration option, 756
network protocols, 65
   choices, 149–53
   running essential, 742
   supporting many different, 64

network round-trips, minimizing, 681–82
network sniffer, securing data from, 151
network traffic
    effect of cursor operations on, 535
    encryption of, 42
network writes, effect of stalled, on page locks, 68
New Database dialog box in SQL Enterprise Manager, 181, 181
next extent (NX_EXT) lock, 647
NEXT fetch type, 555
nextpg field in a page header, 209
nextrno field in a page header, 209
niladic functions, 251, 447–48
    in CHECK constraints, 253
NO ACTION, 571, 572
    for FOREIGN KEY constraints, 248
NOCHECK CONSTRAINT statement, 245
nocheck keyword, 199
NOCHECK option, 374–75
no chkpt on recovery database option, 188
NOCOUNT option, 525
NOLOCK hint, 736
NONCLUSTERED attribute, 232, 240
nonclustered indexes, 220–22, 377
    column order in the keys of, 678
    compared to table scans, 675, 715
    driving the scan, 714
    leaf pages pointing to data pages, 83–84
    logical I/Os required for, 716
    making highly selective, 675–76
    on sequential key values, 652, 653
    using several on a table, 717
    versus scan-and-sort, 668–69
NONCLUSTERED keyword with the PRIMARY KEY constraint, 675
nonempty sets, checking for, 306
nonfatal errors in transactions, 452–56
nonfavored pages, 91
nonlogged mode with SELECT INTO, 357
nonlogged operations
    allowing, 189
    database backup strategy and, 510
non-null values, returning the number of, 320
nonorthogonal, 296
nonsargable clauses
    examples of, 707
    rewriting to sargable, 708

nonsyntax error messages, 71
NOOP warning message, 180
normalization, 662
normalized databases, 662–63
normalizing queries, 72
not equal to operators, 418–19
NOT EXISTS in queries, 308–9
not greater than operator, 419
NOT IN predicate in subqueries, 299–300
not less than operator, 419
NOT logical operations and three-valued logic, 290–92
NOT NULL
    explicitly declaring, 204
    returning the first, 410
NOT operator, 420, 421
NTFS
    compared to FAT, 142
    file compression, 142
    security features of, 142
NULL
    allowing on columns, 204
    dealing with, 288–92
    default, specifying, 188
    equality expression of, 295
    explicitly declaring, 204
    explicitly entering, 350
    implicitly entering, 350
    passing as a parameter, 479
    in the real world, 292–95
    text column, storage in *text* or *image* datatype, 509
    treating as less than zero with ISNULL, 585
nullability, 201
    of columns, 523
    of constraints, 232
nullable columns, 201
NULL and DEFAULT precedence, INSERT statements and, 352
NULLIF() function, 325–26, 410, 444
NULLs, aggregate functions and, 324
NULL values
    UNIQUE constraints and, 240
    versus default, 256–57
    versus GROUPING NULL values, 335
Number Of Free Buffers counter, 757
numbers, converting to character strings, 424
numeric datatype, 202
NWLink IPX/SPX Net-Library, 149, 150, 152
NX_EXT (next extent) lock, 647

O

object descriptor data structure (DES), 74

object_id, decoding with OBJECT_NAME(), 701

OBJECT_ID() function, 444, 445

object IDs for constraints, 258–59

OBJECT_NAME() function, 444, 445

    decoding *object_id*, 701

objects, 173

    constraints as, 259

objid field in a page header, 209

ODBC

    API, 58–59

    compared to DB-Library, 59

    cursor functions, 546

    executing batches from, 451

ODBC driver

    cursor functions in, 537–38

    development of, 547

    functions invoked directly by, 541

ODS, 33, 60, 66–71

ODS API, 495

ODS server applications, 67

offline database option, 188

offset tables, 214

Offset Table section of DBCC PAGE output, 213

old style JOIN SQL syntax, 275

old style outer-join syntax, limitations of, 282–88

OLE Transaction

    interfaces, implementation of, 44

    resource manager, 44

OLTP

    applications, selecting indexes for, 676

    demands on the database, versus DSS demands, 683

    and DSS, 704

online backup, dynamic, 43

on-page delete/insert strategy, 382–83

    examples, 387–88, 390–91

on-page delete/insert update, 82

OPEN cursor syntax, 554

Open Database Connectivity. *See* ODBC API

open databases configuration option, 749

Open Data Services. *See* ODS

open objects configuration option, 750

operating system, selecting, 141–42

operators, 416–21

    order of precedence of, 421

Optimistic Approach to ANSI compliance settings, 523

optimistic concurrency control (OPTCC), 561, 562–63

    choosing, 568

    scrollable cursors with, 684–85

    suitability of applications for, 563

    within a transaction, 564–65

optimistic concurrency mechanism, implementing, 685

optimizable clause, 706

optimization, exhaustive, 72

optimizer hints, 31, 73, 734

    for index selection, 551

optimizer. *See* query optimizer

optimizing queries, 72

@@OPTIONS global variable, 524

    decoding current connection settings from, 526–27

ORDER BY clause

    driving a scan using nonclustered index matching, 737–38

    with grouped aggregate functions, 323

    with UNION ALL, 342

ordered numbers, simple table of, 618

orderly shutdown

    checkpoints issued during, 90

    providing time for, 138

order of precedence for operators, 421

OR logical operations, evaluating with three-valued logic, 290–92

OR operator, 420, 421

    processing queries with, 717–18

    sargable clauses and, 707

orthogonal, 296

OS/2

    development for the 32-bit version of, 14, 15

    Database Manager in, 3–4, 75

    Extended Edition, 3

    limitations of, 11

    termination of joint development, 12

    version 1.3, 14

    version 2.0, 13, 15

OUTER, as an optional modifier, 281

OUTER JOIN operations

    join order in, 279–81

    parentheses and indentation in, 281

    with more than two tables, 278

OUTER JOIN operator (*=), 282–88

outer joins, 276–81

out-of-band data, 67

out-of-resource errors, 452

output buffer, 67

output parameter, passing to stored procedures, 467

outstanding reads and writes, monitoring, 771–72
overcommitted memory, 123
overflow pages, 86, 377

P

packed decimal data, 202
PAD_INDEX option, 222, 688
page faults, 106, 743
Page Faults/sec counter, 769
page file in Windows NT, 741
page header, 209–10
    displaying with DBCC PAGE, 701
page-level locking, versus row-level locking, 650–51
page locks
    compatibility of, 647, 648
    escalating, 654
    maximum and minimum values before escalation, 751
Page Manager, 75
pageno field in a page header, 209
page number (*pageno*), 92–93
page reads, monitoring, 771
pages
    accessing via Buffer Manager, 92–93
    allocating new, 377
    deallocating, 366, 397
    directing inserts to specific, 377
    fitting more rows on, 205–7
    initialization of, 182
    keeping permanently in the cache, 91–92
    locking two simultaneously, 86
    numbering of, 186
    pinning, 90
    reclaiming, 88
    splitting, 87
page splits
    deadlocks from, 688–89
    minimizing the frequency of, 88
    splicing in pages via, 83
Pages/sec counter, 769
page type, procedure for determining, 701–2
paging
    eliminating, 741
    monitoring, 123
    watching, 769
PAGLOCK hint, 737
parallel data scan, 95
parameters, passing to stored procedures, 297, 478–79

parentheses
    constant values in, 256
    grouping expressions with, 419–21
    in OUTER JOIN operations, 281
parent page, promoting rows after a split, 87
parity information, recording in RAID-5, 128
pass-by reference capability, 467
passwords, case-sensitivity of, 164
PATINDEX function, 435, 439–40
    with READTEXT, 514
PDC, installing SQL Server on, 142
peak usage, stating performance requirements for, 667–68
perceived response time for interactive systems, 668–69
performance, 107–10
    considering, 659
    guidelines for, 660–738
    impact of applications on, 116
    issues and checkpoints, 90
    monitoring, 767–73
    settings, 742
    stating requirements for peak usage, 667–68
    statistics, 55
performance collection, disabling, 766
Performance Monitor, 122, 767
    and cache-hit ratio, 122, 743–44
    counters in, 768–72
    exporting counters to, 773
    graph, 55
    integration with, 55
    I/O Log Writer/Sec counter, 760
    I/O Transaction/Sec counter, 760
    Max Users Connected counter, 748
    Number Of Free Buffers counter, 757
    running on a separate machine from SQL Server, 772
    Thread Count counter, 753
permanent tables, populating with SELECT INTO, 357–58
Per-Seat licensing, 145, 148
Per-Server count, changing, 148
Per-Server licensing, 145
    user count for, 147–48
phantoms, 78, 458, 640
physical disks
    I/O rates for, 769
    logical mapping to storage in, 174–75
physical I/Os, 122, 714
physical memory, adding, 122, 744
Physical Reads, 725
PI function, 431

pinning tables in the data cache, 765
pinning the page, 92
pipe, 68
pivot tables, 621–24
placeholder rows
    filling out the cube with, 346
    join operations with, 292–94
placeholder values, drawbacks of, 294
plurals, avoiding in searches, 439
PMC file, 767
pool of threads, 40, 104–7
positioned deletes, 531, 556, 557
positioned updates, 531, 535, 536, 556
POWER function, 431
power spikes, 137–38
predicates, multiple on a table, 717
preference = true directive, 158–59
prepositions, logically redundant, 365
previous extent (PR_EXT) lock, 647
prevpg field in a page header, 209
PR_EXT (previous extent) lock, 647
primary domain controller (PDC), installing SQL Server on,
    142
primary key, 34, 195, 231, 575-76, 666
PRIMARY KEY constraint
    creating for float or real columns, 232
    creating on a referenced table, 576–77
    declaring on every table, 231
    different ways to declare, 34, 233–35
    and FOREIGN KEY relationship, 237
    index for, 232
    introduced, 231
    seeing the names and order of columns in, 260
    violations, 262–63
primary server, 139–40
    backing up, 43–44
primary sort value, 159
prime numbers in hashing, 754
PRINT statements, 412–13
    handling the results of, 413
    triggers and, 503
PRIOR fetch type, 555
priority boost setting, 756–57
private temporary stored procedures, 488
private temporary tables, 265–66
probe, 772, 773
proc cache active DBCC value, 746, 747
Proc Cache Bufs, 747

proc cache size DBCC value, 746, 747
proc cache used DBCC value, 746, 747
procedure cache, 480, 481
    information on the current contents of, 746
    preloading, 481
    specifying the percentage of memory given to, 745
procedure cache configuration option, 745–47
procedures
    regular stored versus extended, 499
    monitoring the largest in the cache, 746
    sending as remote stored procedure events, 71
process ID versus server login ID, 698
processors
    adding, 122
    guidelines for, 119–22
    selecting, 115–16
processor-specific assembly language, 641
%Processor Time counter, 768–69, 770
Process Status Structure. *See* PSS (Process Status Structure)
process/thread model, 40–41
Proc Headers, 747
protocol-independent IPC mechanisms, 150
protyping, 670–74
pruning heuristics, 72
pseudocode, including with the design document, 672–73
pseudo–stored procedures, 541, 546
pseudo–system tables, 186, 693
PSS (Process Status Structure), 107, 506
    dumping for connections causing blockage, 696–97
    reserving memory for, 748
    setting trace flags in, 766
publication stored procedures, 494
publish and subscribe replication metaphor, 45
published database option, 188
pubs sample database, 29, 190, 193–94

Q

qualified retrieval, 74
qualpage routine, 74
queries
    achieving index coverage in, 677
    canceling, 684
    comments in, 274
    issuing interactively, 270
    limiting information returned to specified ranges, 271–72
    monitoring and tuning, 704–34
    nesting, 298–310

normalizing, 72
optimizing, 72
processing with OR, 717–18
testing with indexes, 677
query analysis, 706–8
query-intensive system, memory requirements of, 124
query operations, batching with cursors, 543–44
query optimization
    phases of, 706–23
    probability-based, 711
query optimizer, 705–6
    determining index usefulness without statistics, 716–17
    example strategies for, 720–23
    and trace flags, 727–34
    in Transact-SQL, 31
query tree, 71, 479
queued I/Os, showing, 769
quotation marks, enclosing keywords or reserved words, 198
QUOTED_IDENTIFIER option, 524
quoted identifiers, 198

R

RADIANS() function, 432
RAID
    acronym, 125
    Advisory Board, 135
    configurations for SQL Server, 130–35
    devices as data devices, 183
    solutions, 126, 130–35
RAID-0 (striping), 126–27
RAID-0&1 (striping and mirroring), 129–30
RAID-1 (mirroring), 127–28, 183
RAID-5 (striping with parity), 128–29
RAISERROR statement, 413–15
RAM disks, 760
RAND() function, 430, 432, 580
random I/O, 758
random number generator, 580
range partitioning, 128
range queries, clustered indexes for, 675
rankings
    cursor approaches to, 593–98
    getting, 587–98
    materializing time series and self-join, 603
ranks
    assigning to table rows, 584
    differences between adjacent, 599

RAS (Remote Access Services), 148
raw devices, use of, 174
raw partitions, 143
Read Ahead (RA) settings, 760–62
Read Ahead, 95
Read Ahead Manager, 725
Read Ahead Reads, 725
read buffers, 67
READ COMMITTED isolation level versus SERIALIZABLE,
    462–65
READ COMMITTED option, 457
read-only database option, 188
read-only setting, 763
read repeatability, using transactions to ensure, 513–14
READTEXT operations in chunks of 255, 632–33
READTEXT statement, 509, 513–16
READ UNCOMMITTED option, 457–58, 461
real datatype, 202
real time updates, 46
receive buffer, dumping, 682
RECONFIGURE command, 742
record-based approach, 529
recovery
    flags, 475-76
    interval configuration option, 759
    interval parameter, 771
    locking and, 98
    main phases of, 97–98
    processes governed by max async IO, 755
    timestamps and, 98–100
    transaction logging and, 96–98
recursion
    stack overflow with, 471
    in stored procedures, 469–73
redo recovery operations, 97–99
REFERENCES keyword, 237
REFERENCES permission, 244
referencing tables, 245-46, 573
referential actions, 248–49
    implementing with triggers, 571–78
    performed by triggers, 37
    for UPDATE and DELETE operations, 571–72
referential integrity, 34–35
    enforcing with constraints, 231, 237
    enforcing with triggers, 37
reformatting strategies
    for joins, 723
    showing, 726

Registry entries, rebuilding, 170
Relational-Divide query, 309
RELATIVE fetch type, 555
Remote Access Services. *See* RAS
remote procedure calls. *See* RPCs
remote setup option, 166, 167
Remote Stored Procedure Call Handler, 71
removable media databases, 188, 191–92
Repeatable Read isolation level, 76, 79, 565–66, 640
    changing to, in WRITETEXT, 512
    compared to Committed Read, 687
REPEATABLE READ option, 458
REPLICATE function, 435, 440
    generating filler, 580
replication, 45–47
replication stored procedures, 494
reserved words, 197–99
Reset button, effect on caching controllers, 138
resource errors, 452
resource locks, 80, 639, 644
resource manager in MS DTC, 44
response time, 533
    for interactive systems, 668–69
    versus throughput, 669
result sets
    behavior of the cursor in, 546
    extracting statistics and summary information from, 337
    fetching to an absolute position in, 549
    generated by SELECT statements, 450
    processing as quickly as possible, 684
    returning an alternate, 331
@retcode local variable, 455
retry logic
    for deadlock error 1205, 457, 458
    for handling deadlocks, 690
RETURN [*n*], 406
return status codes, 454–55
REVERSE() function, 435, 440
RIGHT() function, 435
right outer join, 278, 279–81
RISC platforms, 123
rlocks, 80, 86, 639, 640, 650
ROLLBACK
    effect on nested transaction blocks, 473–74
    executing from within a trigger, 502
    flow of control and, 474

rollback point, 478
Rollback record, marking a transaction, 97
ROLLBACK statements, naming transactions in, 475
rolling back triggers, 502–3
ROLLUP operator, 337–38
    extension to GROUP BY, 327
root level in indexes, 218, 219
root page
    in index trees, 83
    splitting, 87
ROUND() function, 430, 432
@@ROWCOUNT global variable, 354, 403
    checking for "no rows affected," 452
    with DELETE, 365
    restricting an update of a primary key, 575–76
    verifying the number of rows updated, 362
row counts of tables, getting, 619–20
row lengths, keeping compact, 666
row-level locking
    deadlocks and, 693
    for insert operations, 651–53
    versus page-level locking, 650–51
row offset table, 210
Row Operations Manager, 80–83
rows, 195
    adding to a table, 349–52
    changing existing, 362–65
    finding duplicate, 223
    finding with matching columns, 606–10
    fitting more on a page, 205–7
    generated by CUBE, 329
    generating with default values, 579
    identifying those containing duplication, 606–10
    operation on individual, 80–83
    placing in tables with no clustered index, 376
    preserving nonmatching in query output, 277–78
    preserving on the left-hand side of joins, 278–79
    purging all, 366
    refetching the current, 555
    removing existing, 365–66
    returning the number of, 320
    sampling every *n*, 606
    in the *sysdatabases* table, 187
    uniquely identifying, 34, 214
    updating, 204
rows column in the *sysindexes* table, 323

rows rank value, 584
RPC (remote procedure call), 45
    events, 696
    Handler, 71
    services of Windows NT, 65
RTRIM() function, 435, 438–39
    removing trailing blanks, 319
rule-based optimizer, 73
rules, 35–36, 250

S

safety buffer, 230
samples (steps), determining the number of, 712–13
sampling intervals, 606, 711
SA password, 164
SARG (search argument), 74, 706–7
sargable clause, 706
sargable expressions, rewriting nonsargable to, 708
sargable operators, 706
savepoints, 478
SAVE TRAN statement, 478
scalability
    limits of, 108
    of SQL Server and Windows NT, 102
scalar expressions in VALUES clauses, 353
scalar functions, 421–48
    combining inside aggregate functions, 434
    compared to stored procedures, 422
scan-and-sort, versus nonclustered index, 668–69
Scan Count, 725–26
scheduling engine, 52
scheduling stored procedures, 494
schema, 191
SCROLL, 53
scrollable cursors, 529, 530, 537
    with optimistic concurrency control (OPTCC), 684–85
scrolling applications, 544–45
    with large amounts of data, 545
SCSI controllers, advantages of, 125
SCSI drives, compared to IDE or EIDE drives, 124–25
search argument. See SARG
search expressions, wildcard characters in, 315
Search Manager, 74
secondary server, 139–40
secondary sort value, 159
security issues, 42–43, 169

Security Identifier (SID), testing, 42
seed values, 227–28
segments, 128
    as an alternative to RAID, 132
    data placement with, 132
select into/bulkcopy database option, 189, 357
SELECT INTO statements, 357–58
selectivity
    of indexes, 708–9
    of nonclustered indexes, 676
SELECT operations, effect of transactions on, 466
SELECT statements, 29, 269–72
    assigning values to local variables, 404
    identifying key values for keyset cursors, 548
    with INSERT, 354–55
    instead of iterating for every value, 617
    qualifying with WHERE clauses, 405
    result sets generated by, 450
    triggers and, 501, 503
self-describing data stream, 66
self-join
    compared to a correlated subquery, 308
    finding rows with matching columns, 607
self-referencing tables, 246–48
SEMAPHORE.SQL script, 459
sem_set procedure, 459–61
sem_wait procedure, 459–61
send-and-receive buffers, size of, 756
send buffer, dumping, 682
Sequencer, 72
sequence trees, 71, 479, 484
sequential key values
    clustered indexes with, 651
    nonclustered indexes on, 652, 653
sequential operations, cursor approach and, 593
serializability, 39, 640
Serializable isolation level, 78, 640, 682
    compared to READ COMMITTED, 462–65
SERIALIZABLE option, 458
server activity, displaying in real time, 54
Server dialog box, configuring server service software, 740, 741
server licenses, 145
@@SERVERNAME global variable, 630–31
server resources
    allocating in Windows NT, 740–41
    and ISAM-style operations, 536

servers
    and distributed queries, 630–31
    and searches, 437
session descriptor data structure (SDES), 74
SESSION_USER function, 448
SET ANSI_DEFAULTS ON statement, 523
SET ANSI_NULL_DFLT_ON statement, 204, 523
SET ANSI_NULLS ON statement, 522
SET ANSI_PADDING ON command, 201, 522
SET ANSI_PADDING option, 316–19
SET ANSI_WARNINGS ON statement, 319, 522
SET ARITHABORT ON statement, 523
SET CURSOR_CLOSE_ON_COMMIT ON statement, 523
SET DATEFIRST option, 527
SET DATEFORMAT option, 527
SET DEADLOCK_PRIORITY LOW | NORMAL statement, 643, 692
SET DEFAULT action, 248, 572
SET DISABLE_DEF_CNST_CHK ON statement, 248
SET FORCEPLAN ON statement, 735
set functions. *See* aggregate functions
SET IDENTITY_INSERT ON with INSERT statements, 352
SET IDENTITY_INSERT option, 228, 229
SET IGNORE_DUP_KEY option with UPDATE, 363
SET IMPLICIT_TRANSACTIONS ON statement, 452, 522
SET LANGUAGE setting, RAISERROR and, 415
SET NOCOUNT ON, suppressing DONE_IN_PROC messages, 681
SET NOEXEC ON, in conjunction with SHOWPLAN, 727
SET NULL action, 248, 572
SET options
    locale-specific, 527
    monitoring queries, 724
set-oriented approach, 529
SetProcessWorkingSetSize() Win32 API, 754
SET QUOTED_IDENTIFIER ON statement, 198, 523
SET ROWCOUNT 1 statement to limit SELECT, 578
SET ROWCOUNT extension, 585–86, 587
SET SHOWPLAN ON statement
    output of, 726–27
    update strategies and, 383
sets of data, processing in SQL Server, 450
SET statement for aborting transactions with errors, 263–64
SET STATISTICS IO, 722, 724–26
SET STATISTICS TIME ON, output, 726
SET TEXTSIZE, 515
SET TRANSACTION ISOLATION LEVEL, 466
SET TRANSACTION ISOLATION LEVEL READ UNCOMMITTED, 736

SET TRANSACTION ISOLATION LEVEL REPEATABLE READ, 736
SET TRANSACTION ISOLATION SERIALIZABLE, 640
Setup program, 56, 113, 162–66, 169–70
SET XACT_ABORT, 264, 455
@@SEVERITY global variable, 456
severity level
    of errors, 456
    of messages, 413–14
shadow processes, 39
shallow port, 533
shared-disk cluster hardware, 43
shared extent (SH_EXT) lock, 647
shared locks, 77, 397, 639, 645
    cursors and, 564
    holding, 564, 565–67, 568
    using update locks instead, 567–68
shared memory, 40
shared nothing clusters, 108
shared page (SH_PAGE) locks, 640, 646, 648
shared table intent (SH_INT) lock, 646, 648
shared table (SH_TAB) lock, 646, 648
SHOWPLAN, 31, 56
SHOWPLAN ON SET option for monitoring queries, 726–27
shrinking phase of two-phase locking, 640
SIGN() function, 432
Simple Network Management Protocol. *See* SNMP
SIN() function, 432
single page writes, monitoring, 771
single process architecture, 39–40, 103
single-processor system, versus multiprocessing, 119, 121
single-table views, data modifications in, 367
single user database option, 189, 764
smalldatetime datatype, 203
smallint datatype, 202
smallmoney datatype, 202
SMP concurrency setting, 757
SMP systems, 41, 107–8
SNMP, 57
software RAID, 135–36
SORTED_DATA option in CREATE INDEX, 223
SORTED_DATA_REORG option in CREATE INDEX, 223
sort order, 156–61
    consequences of changing, 153
    definition file, 160
    performance considerations, 161
    semantics of, 156–60
sort pages setting, 752

sort values, 159
SOUNDEX() function, 435, 441–43
SOUNDEX values
    comparing internally, 441–43
    trigger for maintaining, 620
source control products, 196
SPACE() function, 435, 440
    adding trailing blanks, 319
space management, clustered indexes and, 376–77
sp_addextendedproc stored procedure, 499
sp_addmessage stored procedure, 415
sp_bindefault stored procedure, 254
sp_bindsession stored procedure, 650
sp_certify_removable stored procedure, 192
sp_coalesce_fragments stored procedure, 184
sp_configuration 'nested triggers' stored procedure, 503
sp_configure free buffers stored procedure, 95
sp_configure hash buckets stored procedure, 94
sp_configure logwrite sleep parameter, 772
sp_configure max async IO option, 771
sp_configure 'procedure cache' setting, 481
sp_configure set working set size option, 770
sp_configure stored procedure
    changing user connections and memory settings, 165
    configuring locks, 654
    configuring user connections, 164
    cursor threshold configuration option with, 554
    enabling Show Advanced Options, 554
    fillfactor, setting the serverwide default for FILLFACTOR,
        222
    modifying system tables, 182
    setting configuration options, 742
    setting recovery flags to 1, 475–76
    storing results in a table, 356–57
sp_configure 'user options', 524–25
sp_create_removable stored procedure, 192
sp_cursorclose pseudo–stored procedure, 546
sp_cursorfetch pseudo–stored procedure, 546
sp_cursoropen pseudo–stored procedure, 546
sp_cursor pseudo–stored procedure, 546
sp_dbinstall stored procedure, 192
sp_dboption stored procedure, 188, 189–90, 192
sp_devoption stored procedure, 179
sp_diskdefault system stored procedure, 179
special databases, 180, 192–94
special system (LocalSystem) account, 143
specifications, purpose of, 672

SPECInt (integer) benchmark, 119
SPECInt92 ratings for various processors, 119, 120
sp_getbindtoken stored procedure, 650
sp_helpconstraint stored procedure, 233–36
sp_helpdb stored procedure, 190
sp_helpdevice stored procedure, 177
sp_helpdp stored procedure, 190
sp_helpindex stored procedure, 236, 260
sp_helptext, running against an encrypted procedure, 487
spid (connection ID), 698
@@spid global variable, 445
spin counter setting, 763
spinlocks, 641, 643, 650
sp_lock2 stored procedure, 694–95
sp_lock stored procedure, 640, 647, 695
sp_logdevice stored procedure, designating space for the log,
    184
sp_makestartup stored procedure, 491
sp_makewebtask stored procedure, 610
sp_password stored procedure, changing the SA password,
    164
sp_ prefix
    applying to extended stored procedures, 490
    on pseudo–system tables, 186
    for system stored procedures, 490
sp_recompile system stored procedure, 482
sp_repldone system stored procedure, 100
sp_sdidebug pseudo–extended stored procedure, 505–6
sp_sqlexec stored procedure, 630–31
sp_tableoption system stored procedure, 765
sp_tableoption system stored procedure, 653
spt_ prefix on pseudo–system tables, 186
sp_unmakestartup stored procedure, 491
sp_user_counter stored procedure, 773
sp_who stored procedure, 694–95
sp_who2 stored procedure, 695
SQL-92. See ANSI SQL-92 standard
SQL95, 24–25
SQL, 29, 269
    books about, 271
    mixing datatypes in, 423
    using as a programming language, 399
SQL approach to rankings, 588–89
SQL Client Configuration Utility, 56
SQL commands, compared to API functions, 538
SQL comments. See comments
SQLCTR60.DLL, 55
SQL Debugging Interface (SDI), 32

SQL-DMO, 49
   BulkCopy object, 359
   object model, 49–50, 51
   objects and methods, 50
   using for replication, 494
SQL/DS, 3–4
SQL Enterprise Manager, 47–49
   changing configuration settings, 163–64
   creating data devices, 176
   creating or expanding databases, 180–81
   interface of, 48–49
   issuing configuration tasks, 166
   monitoring locking, 694
   setting database options, 187
   table editor, 196
   using for replication, 494
   viewing the values of the distribution page, 711
SQLExecDirect cursor function, 546
SQLExecute, executing batches from ODBC, 451
SQL Executive, 52–53
   monitoring the state of SQL Server, 43
   running on a domain user account, 144
   stored procedures, complete listing of, 493–94
SQLExtendedFetch cursor function, 538, 540, 546
SQLFreeStmt cursor function, 546
SQLHDTST.EXE, 139
SQL language. *See* SQL
SQL NT. *See* Microsoft SQL Server for Windows NT
SQL_ODBC_CURSORS constant, 539
SQLPERF(LRUSTATS2), 765
SQLPERF(WAITSTATS), 765
SQL_PRESERVE_CURSORS option in the SQL Server driver, 557
SQL queries
   embedding in C source code, 59
   firing from a Web page, 53
SQLRowCount cursor function, 546
SQL-schema, 191
SQLSDI.DLL debug DLL for Visual C++, 506
SQL Security Manager, 55
SQL SELECT statement, 29
SQL Server. *See* Microsoft SQL Server
SQL Server database devices. *See* database devices
SQL Server databases. *See* databases
SQL Server Debugging, enabling in Developer Studio, 507
SQL Server Debug Interface (SDI), 504
SQL Server kernel, interaction with Windows NT, 100–110
SQL Server Management Information Block, 57

SQL Service Manager, 54, 163
SQLSERVR.EXE, startup parameters on, 766
SQLSetPos cursor function, 538, 546
SQLSetStmtOption cursor function, 546
SQL standard, enhancements to, 578–79
SQL statements
   issuing for configuration tasks, 166
   storing groups of compiled, 32
   writing batches of, 32
SQL Trace utility, 54
   seeing RPC events, 696
   watching network traffic, 682
SQL Web Assistant, licensing for accessing HTML files, 147
SQRT function, 432
stack, 40
   overflow with recursion, 471
   switching, 106
standard bcp, 360
standard MIB, 57
standby server, designating, 43–44
stateless management of data, 539
statement block, defining, 405
statements, for working with text data, 509–10
state parameter, 414
static cursors, 547–48
static structures, memory consumed by, 747
STATISTICS IO SET options for monitoring queries, 724–26
STATISTICS TIME ON SET option for monitoring queries, 726
STATS_DATE() function, 444
status codes, returning, 454–55
status column in the *sysdatabases* table, 187
status field
   in a page header, 210
   of *sysconstraints*, decoding, 260–61
status value, returning to a calling routine, 405, 406
steps, 708, 712–13
step width, 711
sticky threads, 103
stop light applet, 163
Stored Procedure Manager, 480
stored procedures, 32–33, 466. *See also* extended stored
   procedures; system stored procedures
   as an alternative to triggers for referential actions, 573
   breaking into multiple stored procedures, 484
   broad categories for grouping, 491–500
   catalog category, 493
   compared to scalar functions, 422
   creating, 466–68, 482–83

debugging, 504–7
encrypting text stored in *syscomments*, 485–87
executing against remote servers, 357
execution with and without, 481
extended category, 495–500
invoking subordinate, 469
issuing for configuration tasks, 166
marking as autostart, 490–91
nested, 469
parameters passed by, 467, 478–79
parameters passed to, 297
recursion in, 469–73
replication category, 494
security function of, 33
size limits for, 484
SQL Executive category, 493–94
starting automatically, 491
storage of, 484
subsequent executions of, 480
synchronous execution of, 491
system category, 491–92
temporary, 487–89
text limits for, 411, 412
using instead of dynamic SQL, 680
StreetTalk naming services, 152
stress test application for disk subsystems, 139
STR function, 422, 424, 436
string functions, 434–36
string manipulation functions, 439–40
strings, formulating and executing dynamically, 508
stripe size, adjusting in RAID-0, 127
striping
 (RAID-0), 126–27
 and mirroring (RAID-0&1), 129–30
 with parity (RAID-5), 128–29
strongly consistent data, 46
structured exception handling, 106
Structured Query Language. *See* SQL
STUFF function, 436
subordinate stored procedures, invoking, 469
subqueries, 298–310
subscribed database option, 189
subscription stored procedures, 494
SUBSTRING function, 436, 439
subtraction operator, 416, 421
suid column in the *sysdatabases* table, 187
SUM() function, 320
supported platforms, 141–42

surrogate keys
 creating using an identity column, 678
 manufacturing, 232
SUSER_ID() function, 444, 445
SUSER_NAME() function, 444, 445, 448
 as the DEFAULT value, 364
switch statement in C. *See* CASE statements
Sybase SQL Server, 5, 11, 12, 13–14
Sybase System 10, 16, 20–21
symmetric multiprocessing (SMP) systems. *See* SMP systems
Symmetric Server Architecture, 39, 103
synchronization mechanisms, 40
synchronous execution of stored procedures, 491
synchronous writes to the log, 96
syntax errors, 71, 452
syscolumns system catalogs, adding rows to, 207
syscolumns table, 207, 208
syscomments table, 412, 484, 485
sysconstraints table
 adding rows to, 207
 decoding the status field of, 260–61
 relationship to *sysobjects*, 259
syscurconfigs table, 186
sysdatabases table, 186–87
sysdevices system table, 177, 178
sysindexes system catalogs, adding rows to, 207
sysindexes table
 adding rows to, 207, 208
 distribution column, 709
 number of rows in a table, 619
 rows column in, 323
syslocks pseudo–system table, 186, 647, 693
 formatted and sorted listing of, 695
 reporting locks in, 693
syslogs table, 96
 decoding the op code field to the log record type, 407–8
sysobjects system catalogs, adding rows to, 207
sysobjects table, 484
 adding rows to, 207, 208
 incrementing the schema column of, 482
 setting the maximum number of open database objects, 750
 sysconstraints relationship to, 259
sysprocedures table, storing information about the sequence tree, 484
sysprocesses pseudo–system table, 186, 693, 698, 700
sysreferences system tables, adding rows to, 207
System 10. *See* Sybase System 10

System Administrator password, 164
system catalogs, 192
system catalog stored procedures, 417–18
system configuration, tuning, 739
system crashes, SQL Server and, 101
system data, 639
system data locks, 79
system functions, 443–47
    calling by table-level constraints, 253
    in CHECK constraints, 253
    in view definitions, 314
system-generated names for column-level constraints, 235
"system is hung," indication of a blocking problem, 693
system performance. *See* performance
systems
    ACID transactions among heterogeneous, 44
    maintaining, 766–67
    management, 47–53
system stored procedures, 489–90, 491–92. *See also* stored procedures
    complete listing of, 492
    monitoring locking, 694
system tables, 181–82
    in the *master* database, 186
    prohibition on direct modification of, 491–92
system tests, conducting, 671
system throughput, 116
SYSTEM_USER() function, 448

T

table aliases, 274, 275, 276
table-level constraint, 233
    calling system functions, 253
    compared to column-level, 240
table locks
    calculating escalation points for, 751, 752
    compatibility of, 648
tables, 195
    adding one row to, 349–52
    breaking into two, 667
    checking for the visibility of temporary, 489
    creating, 196, 207, 579
    cross-joining, 342–47
    determining if empty, 306
    emptying, 366
    enforcing logical relations between, 35
    joining, 272–88

joining via a virtual table, 272–73
joins of more than four, 724
loading a single, from an entire database, 361
loading multiple in parallel, 359
naming, 197
pinning in the data cache, 765
pivoting, 621–24
placing intent locks on, 645
populating with SELECT INTO, 357–58
publishing for replication, 188
referencing one another with FOREIGN KEY references, 244
reorganizing, 83
restrictions on dropping, 245–46
row counts of, 619–20
row placement with no clustered index, 376
self-referencing, 246–48
size of empty, 75
specifying the order of processing, for joins, 735
temporary, 265–67
uniquely identifying rows in, 34
updating or deleting rows at cursor, 531
table scans
    compared to nonclustered indexes, 675, 715
    forcing, 735
    logical I/Os required for, 716
    showing with SHOWPLAN, 726
TABLOCK hint, 737
TABLOCKX hint, 737
tabular data stream. *See* TDS
TAN() function, 432
Task Manager of Windows NT, 769
TCP/IP Sockets Net-Library, 66, 149, 150, 151–52
TDS (tabular data stream), 66–67
    protocol, 506
    traffic, minimizing, 681–82
tempdb database, 190, 193
    configuration option in RAM, 760
    creating procedures from direct use of, 488–89
    creating tables in, 265
    direct use of, 266
    listing of key values for keyset cursors, 548
    making entirely memory resident, 760
    memory allocated in RAM, 744
    placing in RAM, 193
    re-creation of, 487
    setting privileges in, 488
    system tables, 487

temporary database. *See tempdb* database
temporary stored procedures, 487–89
temporary table approach
    to finding rows with matching columns, 608
    to rankings, 589–93, 598
    to time series problems, 603
temporary tables, 265–67
    checking for the visibility of, 489
    constraints on, 267
    created by SQL Server, 190
    SELECT INTO with, 358
tertiary sort value, 159
test data, generating, 579–83, 599–601
testing throughout development, 670–74
text
    appending to a column with UPDATETEXT, 518–19
    copying to sequenced *varchar* columns, 632–35
text columns
    appending one to another with UPDATETEXT, 520–21
    chain of pages for each, 509
    working with chunks of, 509–10
text datatype, 75, 203, 508, 509
textimage data, chain of pages for, 509
text limits for stored procedures, views, and triggers, 412
Text Manager, 80
text pointers, 510
    initializing for *text* or *image* data, 510–11
    selecting valid, in WRITETEXT, 511–12
    using update locks on, 513
@@TEXTSIZE global variable, 515, 632–33
thin client, 401–2
third normal form, 662
thrashing, 753
Thread Count counter, 753, 770
threads, 40
    affinitized, 103
    binding to certain processors, 763
    managing in Windows NT, 740
    monitoring, 753
    number allowed to simultaneously access data, 757
    pool of, 40
    specifying for read-ahead operations, 761
    sticky, 103
    termination of, 106
three-tier model for client/server applications, 400–402
three-valued logic, 289
throughput, versus response time, 669

ties
    explicitly indicating, 592–93
    rules for dealing with, 593–94
time functions, 428–30
time series problems, 599–604
time slice setting, 763
timestamp column, 562, 685
timestamp datatype, 98
timestamp field in a page header, 209
timestamps, recovery and, 98–100
timing window, 136
tinyint datatype, 202
    maximum value of, 412
tokens, 66
top *n* values, getting, 584–87
totals
    in cross-tab tables, 622–23
    running, 604–5
TPC-B benchmarks, 118
TPC benchmarks, 117
    for SQL Server for Windows NT, 20
TPC-C benchmarks, 109–10
trace flags
    for analyzing deadlock activity, 702–4
    setting in the PSS, 766
    specifying at server startup, 766
trailing blanks, 316–19
@@TRANCOUNT global variable, 474
Transaction (TP) Monitor, external, 41
transactional resource managers, 44
transaction blocks, 473–77
TRANSACTION ISOLATION LEVEL, setting to REPEATABLE
    READ, 564
transaction levels, 640
transaction log, 43
    backing up, 183
    performing dumps of, 183
    RAID-1 mirroring for, 183
    recovery 96–98
    separating with CREATE DATABASE, 182–83
    synchronous writes to, 76
Transaction Manager, 75–77
transaction monitor, 105
transaction processing, 37–38
transaction protection for text pointers, 512
transactions, 37, 349, 451
    aborting, 45
    atomicity of, 38

transactions, *continued*
  committing, 45, 130
  demarcation of the beginning and ending of, 96–97
  effect of constraint failures on processing multiple, 261–64
  error checking in, 452–57
  evaluating critical, 664–66
  isolation levels of, 457–65
  keeping as short as possible, 684
  length of ISAM-style, 536
  locking, 640
  naming in ROLLBACK statements, 475
  optimistic concurrency control within, 564–65
  purging, 100, 189
  rolling back, 454–56
  running serially, 78
  savepoints in, 478
  separating concurrent, 38–39
  starting implicitly, 451–52
  syntactically nesting, 477
  tailoring indexes to critical, 676–78
  using to ensure read repeatability, 513–14
transactions per log record, monitoring, 772
Transact-SQL, 28–30, 399
  as a programming language, 400–403
  commands, 71, 74
  cost-based query optimizer, 31
  extensions, 30–31
  printing capability, 412–15
  programming constructs, 31–32, 403–48
  programming, environmental concerns, 521–27
  programming extensions, 399
  real debugging environment, 505
Transact-SQL cursors, 537
  behavior of, 558–59
  compared to API server cursors, 538, 558
  concurrency control with, 561–69
  forward-only, 560
  fully scrollable, 560–61
  INSENSITIVE modifier with, 548
  multiple batches and, 543
  in row-by-row operations, 542–43
  syntax, 552–58
  versus API server cursors, 540–42
triggers, 36–37, 500–502
  compared to constraints, 243, 572–73
  debugging, 504–7
  effect on underlying data modification, 466
  enforcing FOREIGN KEY constraints, 390–91

  enforcing referential integrity, 37
  execution plans for, 378
  firing, 501, 578
  implementing referential actions, 571–78
  limitation on the number of, 501
  maintaining aggregate summary data, 666
  maintaining SOUNDEX() values, 620
  overused cascading, 503
  rolling back, 502–3
  SELECT statements and, 501
  text limits for, 412
TRIM() functions, 438–39
TRUE condition, 289
TRUNCATE TABLE, 366
trunc. log on chkpt database option, 189
trusted connections, 42, 65. *See also* integrated login
    capability
truth tables, 290–92
T-SQL. *See* Transact-SQL
tuples. *See* rows
two-digit year, avoiding, 426
two-phase commit protocol, 45
two-phase locking (2PL) services, 640
two-tier model, 401–2
type of page, determining, 701–2

U

UDDTs, 35, 224–27
  checking for incompatible, 227
  declaring the Identity property on columns using, 230
  drawbacks of, 225
  joining, 225–26
unattended setup option, 166–69
Uncommitted Read isolation level, 77
unconditional branching in Transact-SQL, 405, 406
undo recovery operations, 97
  matching timestamps, 99–100
Unicode character set, 155
Uninterruptible Power Supply. *See* UPS
UNION, 341–47
  views and, 313
UNION ALL, 341, 342
UNIQUE constraint, 34, 231
  creating a table-level, 235–36
  creating on a referenced table, 576–77
  index for, 232
  NULL VALUES and, 240
unique database ID. *See* dbid

unique indexes, 677, 708–9
uniqueness, enforcing with Identity, 228–29
unique nonclustered indexes, logical I/Os required for, 716
unique numbers, generating efficiently, 34
unique numeric values, generating, 227
unit matrix table, 624
UNIX-based DBMS products, 39
UNIX file system, 143
Unknown condition, 289, 290
unknown expressions, 253
unnamed view, 584
unqualified update, 393
UPDATE/DELETE statement, 546
update/delete tables, 531
update extent (UP_EXT) lock, 647
update-in-place strategy, 82, 379, 380–82
    examples, 386–87, 388–89, 394–95
    with multirow updates, 391–92
update locks, 397, 639, 645
    choosing to hold, 568–69
    FOR UPDATE OF modifier and, 569
    guarantee of an exclusive lock, 644
    instead of shared locks, 567–68
    on text pointers, 513
update page (UP_PAGE) lock, 646, 648
updates
    analyzing, 727
    deferred, 378–79
    direct, 379–82
    processing, 204–7
    strategies for carrying out, 82
UPDATE statements, 362–65
    assigning values to variables in, 405
    CASE statements in, 409
    effect of errors on single, 466
    issuing against views, 367, 369–71
    triggers and, 501
UPDATE STATISTICS command
    executing, 709
    running to update indexes, 221–22, 708
update strategies, 378–85
    determining which to use, 383–85
    showing with trace flag 323, 384–97
UPDATE syntax, 556
UPDATETEXT statement, 509, 516–21
    compared to WRITETEXT, 517
    examples, 517–21
update triggers, compared to FOREIGN KEY constraints, 249

UPDLOCK hints, 569, 736
    conversion deadlocks and, 688
upgrading, 162
UPPER function, 436, 437–38
UPS, 137–38
    compared to battery backup, 138
Used Slots statistic, 762
user account for running SQL Server, 144, 507
user connections. *See also* connections
    configuration option, 748–49
    configuring the number of, 164
    estimating the number needed, 749
    memory consumed by, 122
    per megabyte of memory, 748
user context for SQL Server and SQL Executive, 143
user count for Per-Server licensing, 147–48
user data, lock types for, 645–46
user databases, 180, 181
user-declared global variables, 403
user-defined datatypes. *See* UDDTs
user-defined functions (UDFs), 422, 543
USER_ID function, 444, 445
user input, pausing transactions for, 684
user licenses, 145
User Mode of Windows NT, 101
USER_NAME function, 444, 445, 448
users
    active versus idle, 105
    allowing to stay connected, 106
    versus connections, 147
user threads, maintenance of, 41
utilities, 358–60
Utility Manager, 480

V

VALUES clause in INSERT statements, 353
varbinary datatype, 203
VARBINARY() function, 316
varchar columns, copying text to sequenced, 632–35
varchar datatype, 202
variable-length columns, 666
    retaining trailing blanks in, 318–19
    trimming trailing blanks for, 317
    updating, 204–5
variable-length data, storage of, 213–14
variable-length fields, updating, 386–87
variable-length rows, storage of, 215–18

variables, 403–5
  changing one at a time, 738
  naming in stored procedures, 468
varno values, 728, 729
VBA scripts, issuing for configuration tasks, 166
version column in the *sysdatabases* table, 187
vertical partitions, replication in, 47
viewing locks, 647
views, 195, 311
  CASE statements in, 409
  compared to derived tables, 311–12
  creating, 286–88
  data modifications in, 367
  deleting through, 365
  DISTINCT clause and, 313
  inserting data into, 350
  limitations on, 312
  modifying data through, 367–72
  protecting from updates with FOREIGN KEY constraints, 371–72
  specifying as equijoins, 368
  system functions and, 314
  system functions in, 445–46
  text limits for, 412
  UNION and, 313
  WITH CHECK OPTION, 313–14
Virtual Bytes counter, 770
virtual device numbers. *See* device numbers
virtual memory, 743
  monitoring the use of, 770
virtual page numbers, 178
virtual pages, mapping to, 186
virtual tables, 272, 311
visibility of temporary tables, 489
Visual Basic. *See* Microsoft Visual Basic
Visual C++
  debug DLL for, 506
  SDI availability for, 504

W

WAITFOR, 406
WaitForSingleObject, 759, 760
warnings in the Windows NT event log, 414
watch window, modifying the values of variables, 505
Web pages, putting data on, the fast way, 610–11

week, setting the first day of, 527
What If–type operations with a static cursor, 548
WHENEVER statement, 263–64
WHERE clause
  indexing on columns used in, 676
  old style outer-join syntax compared to the new, 288
  outer-join operators in, 282
WHILE loop, 406
  local variables for generated data inside, 581–82
wildcard characters in search expressions, 315
Win32-protected subsystem of Windows NT, 101
Windows Characters. *See* ISO character set
Windows Hardware Compatibility List (HCL), 114–15
Windows NT, 12
  configuration options in, 740
  crashes of, 101
  development, 12, 15–19
  disabling nonessential services, 741
  executable unit, 40
  impersonation feature of, 42
  integrated security with, 42
  interaction with the SQL kernel, 100–110
  optimization for, 102
  placing the page file on a different drive from SQL Server files, 741
  processes in, 645
  public interfaces to, 102
  RPC services of, 65
  scalability of, 102
  setting the SQL Server scheduling priority, 756–57
  stability of, 101
  trimming of the SQL Server working set, 755
  user accounts copied to SQL Server, 42
Windows NT event log
  errors written to from RAISERROR, 414
  writing error information regarding debugging to, 507
  writing logon attempts to, 43
Windows NT event viewer, logging messages to, 413
Windows NT–only strategy, 17
Windows NT Performance Monitor. *See* Performance Monitor
Windows NT Server, releases supported, 142
Windows NT Server License Manager, 148
Windows NT Workstation, support of, 141
WITH CHECK OPTION
  in CREATE VIEW, 313–14, 368
  for specifying views, 373–74

WITH ENCRYPTION to CREATE modifier, 485–86
WITH LOG clause in WRITETEXT, 510
WITH LOG option for errors of severity 19 or higher, 414
WITH NOCHECK option with ALTER TABLE, 245
WITH RECOMPILE options, creating stored procedures with, 482–83
worker threads
    maximum number of, 752–53
    pool of, 104–7
working set
    sizing, 754
    trimming, 755
Working Set counter, 770
worktables, created by SQL Server, 190
writable removable devices, 192
write-ahead logging, 76, 89
write-back caching controllers, 136–37

write buffer, 67
writes, guaranteeing completion of, 137
WRITETEXT statement, 509–13, 517

X

−x startup flag, passing to SQLSERVR.EXE, 766
XACT_ABORT option, 455
X/Open DTP XA-compliant interface, 44
xp_ prefix, 490, 499
xp_readmail capabilities of SQL Server, 626
xp_sprintf procedure, 495–98

Y

year 2000, 426
years, avoiding two-digit, 426

Ron Soukup is one of the original members of the SQL Server team at Microsoft. He joined Microsoft in 1989. Ron was general manager of the SQL Server group through the end of 1995, and he led the development and shipment of versions 1.1, 1.11, 4.2 (OS/2), 4.21 (Windows NT), 6.0, and 6.5 beta. After delivering version 6.5 to beta test, Ron stepped down from his duties as general manager and the years of "ship crunch" for a while to spend more time with his wife, Kay, and daughters, Kelly and Jamie. After a year away, Ron recently rejoined the SQL Server group, but in a more limited role that allows him to retain a personal life. He currently manages the group within the Microsoft SQL Server team working on the data replication capabilities to be delivered in future releases.

Ron has worked more than 16 years in computer and database systems, and he has experience with DB/2 (MVS), SQL/DS (VM), Oracle, Informix, Sybase, and Ingres systems. Prior to working at Microsoft, Ron held technical positions at United Airlines and AT&T. A longtime Chicagoan, Ron earned his B.S. and M.B.A. degrees from Northwestern University in Evanston, Illinois.

The manuscript for this book was submitted to Microsoft Press in electronic form. Galleys were prepared using Microsoft Word 97. Pages were composed by Microsoft Press using Adobe PageMaker 6.5 for Windows, with text type in Garamond and display type in Futura Medium. Composed pages were delivered to the printer as electronic prepress files.

Cover Graphic Designer
Tim Girvin Design

Cover Illustrator
Glenn Mitsui

Interior Graphic Designer
Kim Eggleston

Principal Artist
Travis Beaven

Principal Compositor
Dick Carter

Principal Proofreader
Devon Musgrave

Indexer
Richard Shrout

Get **ODBC** working for you!

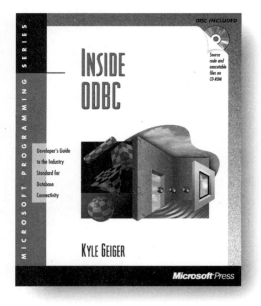

U.S.A.	**$39.95**
U.K.	£37.49 [V.A.T. included]
Canada	$53.95
ISBN 1-55615-815-7	

Open Database Connectivity (ODBC) is a standard API for accessing information from different data storage formats and programming interfaces. It is now an industry standard that nearly all DBMS vendors and major independent software vendors support, and it is a key ingredient of next-generation client/server computing. INSIDE ODBC, written by the architect of ODBC, Kyle Geiger, explains the design, the architecture, and some of the history of this technology. Important considerations for the next release of ODBC—version 3.0—are also covered. The companion CD includes 11 sample applications that use ODBC technology; source code in Visual Basic®, C, and C++ for sample applications and examples; the ODBC Driver Pack 2.0; and more.

The key to sharpening your database programming skills is INSIDE ODBC.

Microsoft Press

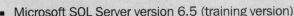

IMPORTANT—READ CAREFULLY BEFORE OPENING SOFTWARE PACKET(S). By opening the sealed packet(s) containing the software, you indicate your acceptance of the following Microsoft License Agreement.

MICROSOFT LICENSE AGREEMENT

(Book Companion CD)

This is a legal agreement between you (either an individual or an entity) and Microsoft Corporation. By opening the sealed software packet(s) you are agreeing to be bound by the terms of this agreement. If you do not agree to the terms of this agreement, promptly return the unopened software packet(s) and any accompanying written materials to the place you obtained them for a full refund.

MICROSOFT SOFTWARE LICENSE

1. GRANT OF LICENSE. Microsoft grants to you the right to use one copy of the Microsoft software program included with this book (the "SOFTWARE") on a single terminal connected to a single computer. The SOFTWARE is in "use" on a computer when it is loaded into the temporary memory (i.e., RAM) or installed into the permanent memory (e.g., hard disk, CD-ROM, or other storage device) of that computer. You may not network the SOFTWARE or otherwise use it on more than one computer or computer terminal at the same time.

2. COPYRIGHT. The SOFTWARE is owned by Microsoft or its suppliers and is protected by United States copyright laws and international treaty provisions. Therefore, you must treat the SOFTWARE like any other copyrighted material (e.g., a book or musical recording) except that you may either (a) make one copy of the SOFTWARE solely for backup or archival purposes, or (b) transfer the SOFTWARE to a single hard disk provided you keep the original solely for backup or archival purposes. You may not copy the written materials accompanying the SOFTWARE.

3. OTHER RESTRICTIONS. You may not rent or lease the SOFTWARE, but you may transfer the SOFTWARE and accompanying written materials on a permanent basis provided you retain no copies and the recipient agrees to the terms of this Agreement. You may not reverse engineer, decompile, or disassemble the SOFTWARE. If the SOFTWARE is an update or has been updated, any transfer must include the most recent update and all prior versions.

4. DUAL MEDIA SOFTWARE. If the SOFTWARE package contains more than one kind of disk (3.5", 5.25", and CD-ROM), then you may use only the disks appropriate for your single-user computer. You may not use the other disks on another computer or loan, rent, lease, or transfer them to another user except as part of the permanent transfer (as provided above) of all SOFTWARE and written materials.

5. SAMPLE CODE. If the SOFTWARE includes Sample Code, then Microsoft grants you a royalty-free right to reproduce and distribute the sample code of the SOFTWARE provided that you: (a) distribute the sample code only in conjunction with and as a part of your software product; (b) do not use Microsoft's or its authors' names, logos, or trademarks to market your software product; (c) include the copyright notice that appears on the SOFTWARE on your product label and as a part of the sign-on message for your software product; and (d) agree to indemnify, hold harmless, and defend Microsoft and its authors from and against any claims or lawsuits, including attorneys' fees, that arise or result from the use or distribution of your software product.

DISCLAIMER OF WARRANTY

The SOFTWARE (including instructions for its use) is provided "AS IS" WITHOUT WARRANTY OF ANY KIND. MICROSOFT FURTHER DISCLAIMS ALL IMPLIED WARRANTIES INCLUDING WITHOUT LIMITATION ANY IMPLIED WARRANTIES OF MERCHANTABILITY OR OF FITNESS FOR A PARTICULAR PURPOSE. THE ENTIRE RISK ARISING OUT OF THE USE OR PERFORMANCE OF THE SOFTWARE AND DOCUMENTATION REMAINS WITH YOU.

IN NO EVENT SHALL MICROSOFT, ITS AUTHORS, OR ANYONE ELSE INVOLVED IN THE CREATION, PRODUCTION, OR DELIVERY OF THE SOFTWARE BE LIABLE FOR ANY DAMAGES WHATSOEVER (INCLUDING, WITHOUT LIMITATION, DAMAGES FOR LOSS OF BUSINESS PROFITS, BUSINESS INTERRUPTION, LOSS OF BUSINESS INFORMATION, OR OTHER PECUNIARY LOSS) ARISING OUT OF THE USE OF OR INABILITY TO USE THE SOFTWARE OR DOCUMENTATION, EVEN IF MICROSOFT HAS BEEN ADVISED OF THE POSSIBILITY OF SUCH DAMAGES. BECAUSE SOME STATES/COUNTRIES DO NOT ALLOW THE EXCLUSION OR LIMITATION OF LIABILITY FOR CONSEQUENTIAL OR INCIDENTAL DAMAGES, THE ABOVE LIMITATION MAY NOT APPLY TO YOU.

U.S. GOVERNMENT RESTRICTED RIGHTS

The SOFTWARE and documentation are provided with RESTRICTED RIGHTS. Use, duplication, or disclosure by the Government is subject to restrictions as set forth in subparagraph (c)(1)(ii) of The Rights in Technical Data and Computer Software clause at DFARS 252.227-7013 or subparagraphs (c)(1) and (2) of the Commercial Computer Software — Restricted Rights 48 CFR 52.227-19, as applicable. Manufacturer is Microsoft Corporation, One Microsoft Way, Redmond, WA 98052-6399.

If you acquired this product in the United States, this Agreement is governed by the laws of the State of Washington.

Should you have any questions concerning this Agreement, or if you desire to contact Microsoft Press for any reason, please write: Microsoft Press, One Microsoft Way, Redmond, WA 98052-6399.